ALBERTA ON ICE

by Gary W. Zeman

Printed by Westweb Press
P.O. Box 5088, Station E, Edmonton, Alberta
Published and Distributed by GMS² Ventures Inc.
P.O. Box 8391, Station F, Edmonton, Alberta T6H 4W6

INTERNATIONAL STANDARD BOOK NUMBER (ISBN) 0-9692320-0-4
The text, pictures and text headings are set in English Times and Korinna type. This book is printed on a web offset press. Printed by Terry Clements, President, Westweb Press, Edmonton and published by Gary Zeman, President, GMS² Ventures Inc., P.O. Box 8391, Station F, Edmonton, Alberta T6H 4W6.
(Suggested retail price $19.95.)

Editors

GARY W. ZEMAN, Author and Editor in Chief
BRENDA ZEMAN, Chief Associate Editor
T.A. (TOMMY) GRAHAM, Managing and Associate Editor

Associate Editors

CLARE DRAKE
GEORGE S. HUGHES

Artist

JOAN HEALEY

Consultants

DAVID NORWOOD, Edmonton
RAY SPILLERS, Calgary
BOB ARKLEY, Calgary
COLIN KILBURN, Edmonton
JOSEPH ZEMAN, Saskatoon
CHUCK MOSER, Edmonton
J.S. (STU) PEPPARD, Calgary
OREST KORBUTT, Edmonton
JAMES A. HILL, Lloydminster
ART POTTER, Edmonton
DON STANLEY, Edmonton
JIM (DEAK) CASSIDY, Calgary
RAY KINASEWICH, Edmonton

Foreword

JUDGE J.J. KRYCZKA, Calgary

Archives and Photography Support

HELEN LA ROSE, JUNE HONEY, City of Edmonton Archives, Edmonton
GEORGINA KLASSEN, Glenbow Alberta Institute Archives, Calgary
MARLENA WITSCHL, Provincial Archives of Alberta, Edmonton
MICHAEL DAWE, Red Deer and District Archives, Red Deer

Manuscript Preparation and Computer Programming

JUDY HASLAM PEDDLE, Saskatoon
BARB MCEACHERN, Edmonton
CAROL REEDER, Edmonton
DIANNE DEVLIN SARARETTO, Saskatoon
MARILYN SHAND
WESTWEB PRESS, Edmonton
Typography: THERISE LUNDY AND DONNA DOYLE, YOUR TYPE, Edmonton

Patrons

RECREATION, PARKS AND WILDLIFE FOUNDATION
ALBERTA AMATEUR HOCKEY ASSOCIATION
ALBERTA CULTURE

Gary W. Zeman

GARY ZEMAN was born in Regina and grew up in Saskatoon, and is a graduate in Education from the University of Saskatchewan. He was an Athletic Director and District Recreation Coordinator for the City of Edmonton, Supervisor of Recreation and Physical Education at the Drumheller Federal Institution and a teacher.

In 1974 he co-authored *9 Innings of Baseball* for the Alberta Baseball Association and also served as the Alberta Baseball Coaches Clinic Coordinator. Other experience include co-chairman of the 1978 East Central Alberta Games in Drumheller and as a Director of the 1970 World Amateur Wrestling Championships in Edmonton. He has coached hockey at all levels including junior and is a Level 4 coach.

Brenda Zeman

BRENDA ZEMAN was born in Saskatoon. She received a Bachelor of Arts Degree from McMaster University, Education Degree from University of Toronto and Master of Arts Degree in Anthropology from California State University in Long Beach.

She has been a Foreign Students Advisor, and English as a Second Language teacher. Since moving back to Saskatchewan she has been a writer and a broadcaster for the CBC. She wrote *Hockey Heritage: 88 Years of Puck Chasing in Saskatchewan*, 1983. Although she has become a hockey historian she was a national level long jumper and hurdler (1967-1976) and a member of the McMaster University OWIAA Championship Figure Skating Team (1972).

Brenda now does photo-journalism, freelance writing and broadcasting.

Tommy Graham

Edmonton-born TOMMY GRAHAM has a wealth of experience and a well-recognized background in the sporting realm. He was a player, coach, manager and promoter of sport in the 1920's and 1930's. As a newspaper man in his younger years he was a reporter and columnist from coast to coast with a number of Canadian dailies including the Edmonton Bulletin and Journal, Windsor Daily Star, Vancouver Sun, Halifax Herald-Mail, Calgary Albertan, Toronto Telegram, and Ottawa Journal. During World War II, he was a Navy Public Relations Officer. Other experience includes sales and promotion in the oil industry, 16 years with the City of Edmonton and 11 terms as President of the Royal Canadian Legion, Edmonton Montgomery Branch Number 24. He and his wife Bernadette have six children, Andrea, Brenda, Melanie, Michelle, Shauna and son Tim.

Clare Drake   *Photo courtesy of Edmonton Journal*

CLARE DRAKE was born and raised in Yorkton, Saskatchewan. He graduated from the University of British Columbia with a Bachelor of Physical Education, the University of Alberta with a Bachelor of Education and from the University of Washington with a Master of Science. He has taught high school in Yorkton and Edmonton Strathcona Composite High School.

For the past 24 years he has been on the Physical Education staff at the University of Alberta where he is currently a Professor of Physical Education along with his responsibilities as head hockey coach.

He is the first Canadian university coach to win over 500 games including five Nationals and 15 Western Canadian Conference titles. He was head coach of the 1975-76 Edmonton Oilers in the WHA. In 1980 he was co-coach of the Canadian Olympic team. In 1967-68 Clare coached two Alberta Golden Bear National championship teams — one in football and the other in hockey. In 1984 Drake coached the Canadian team to the Spengler Cup gold medal in Davos, Switzerland.

He is now in the Alberta Sports Hall of Fame. Clare and his wife Dolly have two daughters, Deborah and Jami.

George Hughes

Photo courtesy of Edmonton Journal

GEORGE S. HUGHES was born in Vegreville, Alberta. He graduated in Agriculture from the University of Alberta. He then became a lecturer and recreation director at Olds College, City of Edmonton Assessor and Tax Collector, Commissioner of Public Affairs and Chief City Commissioner.

Hughes has been heavily involved in hockey and recreation for over 40 years. This includes being manager of the University of Alberta Golden Bears, coach of Vegreville Rangers (Provincial Intermediate B Champs 1955-56), President of Edmonton Federation of Community Leagues (1965-67), minor hockey coach in Ottewell Community League and Fasco Rental Bantams. He is a life member of Little League Baseball — Canada, the AAHA and is in Edmonton's Sports Hall of Fame.

As Commissioner of Public Affairs it was George Hughes who steered a major portion of the planning and development with the EMHA and Federation. This resulted in eight indoor arenas officially opening in Edmonton January 30, 1973.

He is now General Manager and Corporate Secretary of Edmonton Northlands. George and his wife Doreen have three children, Brent, Brian and Karen.

Joan Healey

Photo courtesy of Jim Cochrane, Edmonton Journal

JOAN HEALEY is a well known western Canadian artist who was born and lives in Edmonton. She is the mother of three, and the wife of an ex-professional hockey player.

Joan, basically self-taught, enjoys working with oils, watercolors and acrylics in expressing her love of children and nature on canvas.

In 1983, Joan joined the very limited group of Canadian Plate Artists through Rare Bird Limited in Ontario who produced her ''Canadian Dream'' series of collectible plates. Joan feels her success is due to striking a deep chord by portraying a very Canadian theme. ''Kids all over Canada begin to walk and then they skate. This is so much a part of our culture.'' The series is a story of children across Canada beginning with ''Going To The Rink,'' ''Lacing Up,'' ''Facing Off'' and ''The Winning Goal'' all outfitted in their hockey hero sweaters. The Canadian Dream has been selling in the U.S.A. as well as Canada, with some plates travelling as far as China, Japan and the United Kingdom.

''It's been a long time since we washed diapers in the Sudbury Wolves dressing room some 25 years ago and made headlines in their local newspaper.'' Joan is supported by her husband Rich, children Tim, Todd. Jody and son-in-law Wayne.

Contents

Chapter 6. University and College Hockey 228

Chapter 7. Native Hockey 247

Chapter 8. Ladies' Hockey Heritage 251

Chapter 9. Minor Hockey Highlights 261

Chapter 10.   The Hot Stove League 285

PREFACE

In this publication readers will find a historical account of the main features and accomplishments of people, teams and organizations in the formation of and development of hockey in Alberta. Photographs have been extensively used to portray the teams and individuals as they were.

Our principal objective is to interest as wide an audience as possible. We are presenting a comprehensive view of many aspects of hockey. It focuses attention on many individuals who were responsible for today's hockey program.

Alberta On Ice was the work of many minds. Each of the contributing writers has given generously of their time and effort to convey their knowledge and expertise. I also owe a deep appreciation to the hundreds of people who have contributed through letters, telephone calls, interviews, or photographs. Recreation, Parks and Wildlife Foundation made it possible to do the extensive research needed to complete the book.

Brenda Zeman, George Hughes, Clare Drake and Tommy Graham have read and edited material throughout the project. Their assistance in selecting topics and contributing writers is appreciated. Joan Healey's cover, Judge Joe Kryczka's foreword and all the consultants added greatly to this book.

I was fortunate to have a family with experience in hockey history. My sister Brenda was more than able to write articles, add and develop stories and finally pull the entire manuscript together. This was the most crucial period when decisions on what to publish were made.

My parents Joe and Jessie Zeman knew the problems I would encounter enroute to the final stages. My father-in-law and mother-in-law Casper and Hilly Ligtelyn gave moral support, as well as letting me spend many hours in their home composing material.

I must say the support given at home by my wife Marianne and children Suzanne and Spencer was most encouraging and definitely more than I or anyone could expect. Hockey was consistently on all our minds. "When would this be finished? Did you get the information or article you wanted?" I spent hours on the phone, in my study or away from home. The book could not have been done without their overwhelming support, assistance and patience.

To encompass the history of hockey in Alberta within this modest limit of pages was a difficult and awesome undertaking. We have to the best of our abilities done the job we set out to do — We seriously trust our readers agree.

GARY ZEMAN

FOREWORD

BY JUDGE J.J. KRYCZKA

Joe Kryczka *Photo courtesy of Gold Photo, Calgary*

If one were to be asked to write about his or her "first love," it would not be surprising if the reaction to such a request was either one of reluctance or trepidation or both. Not so in my case!

Ever since I was a small boy chasing hockey pucks (or facsimiles thereof) on the frozen sloughs of the Crowsnest Pass, or in the dimly-lit natural ice arenas in the same area and subsequently throughout the Province of Alberta, hockey became, and has since been, my "first love."

I am honoured and privileged to have been asked to write this introduction to *Alberta On Ice* — a task which I agreed to undertake with relish and without misgivings.

Like all those of us who were mesmerized by the voice of Foster Hewitt on *Hockey Night in Canada,* I dreamed of becoming a professional hockey player — that was not to be, although older brother Ted and younger brother Adam were both good enough and had those opportunities, which they rejected in favour of higher education.

My own involvement in hockey as a player, coach, referee and an administrator has given me some of the greatest moments of my life: A provincial midget championship in 1949-50; three consecutive WCIAU championship teams with the University of Alberta Golden Bears (1953-56); stints as the president of the A.A.H.A. (1967-69); of the CAHA (1971-73); and as Chief Negotiator of the Russia-Canada series in 1972. For all of those many opportunities, I am truly grateful to so many people that to try to list them by name would only mean to miss others.

This province has produced great teams and with great names: Edmonton Eskimos, Calgary Tigers, Lethbridge Maple Leafs, Coleman Grands, Blairmore Bearcats, Edmonton Superiors, Drumheller Miners, Calgary Stampeders, Turner Valley Oilers, Olds Elks, Edmonton Waterloo Mercurys, Edmonton Oil Kings — to be selective is to miss others — for those that I have unintentionally missed, I apologize.

In the 1920's and 1930's, it was Alberta and the Crowsnest Pass which supplied players such as "Tiny" Thompson and "Dutch" Gainor to fledgling teams of the National Hockey League, to be followed later by greats such as "Sweeney" Schriner, Lorne Carr, Herbie Lewis and Joe Fisher, and later still by the Gadsbys, the Barkleys, the Ullmans, the Bucyks and the Sutter brothers.

By good fortune, at some stage in my own limited hockey career, I was privileged to rub elbows with nearly all of those to whom I have referred.

Now you, as readers, will have a similar, albeit vicarious, opportunity by enjoying what follows in *Alberta On Ice* — a hockey history compiled by Gary Zeman, who must be commended for tackling a monumental task, well done. It is a fitting sequel to *88 Years of Puck Chasing in Saskatchewan,* authored and lovingly written by Gary's father Joseph and his sister Brenda.

I would be remiss if I did not acknowledge at least some of the people who have, through their individual efforts, let me enjoy my "first love" — Ray Spillers, Geo. "Shorty" Jenkins, Jimmy Evans, Dr. Don Smith, Clare Drake and J.S. "Stu" Peppard, great administrators such as Gordon Juckes, C. Jarvis Miller, Rose Kohn, Jimmy Condon, Dr. George Hardy, George Harvie, Lloyd Turner and Clarence Campbell.

I am certain that you will find what Gary Zeman and the contributing writers and researchers have compiled to be delightful and nostalgic reading — Read on!!

J.J. Kryczka
Justice
Court of Queen's Bench of Alberta

President (1967-69) Alberta Amateur Hockey Association — Life Member
President (1971-73) Canadian Amateur Hockey Association — Life Member
Amateur Sports Executive of Canada (1972)
Alberta Amateur Hockey Association Hall of Fame (1984)

Chapter 1
Alberta Hockey History —
Now 92 Years Old

On Saturday May 19, 1984, the Edmonton Oilers skated and shot their way past the New York Islanders to the Stanley Cup. Alberta closed up shop and rejoiced. It was the single greatest achievement in Alberta hockey; and, it took just 91 years to accomplish!

Edmonton could not have challenged for the first Stanley Cup in 1893. Alberta's first teams were just started. Calgary boasted three teams that first Stanley Cup year, the Tailors, the Northwest Mounted Police and the Calgary Town team. These original three "Alberta" (Alberta was not yet a province) clubs were playing on the Bow River while the top teams in Montreal had been playing in the comfort of Victoria Rink for twenty years.

The journey of the early Tailors to the modern Flames and Oilers has been as circuitous as the Bow River itself. There have been many memorable stops along the way at championship Alberta hockey towns such as Blairmore, Canmore, Coleman, High River, Lacombe, Luscar, Ponoka, Vegreville and Vermillion. Alberta's hockey success story, the Edmonton Oiler franchise, has been built on a kind of small-town Alberta enthusiasm for the game.

Alberta hockey success has come at all levels of competition. High-powered junior, intermediate and senior teams have won Western Canadian national titles. Alberta teams have won three world championships including the last Canadian Olympic hockey victory in 1952. University, college, minor, native and women's hockey also form a major part of our hockey tradition. In fact, the largest single expenditure for Alberta hockey is not the Flames or the Oilers; it is on the minor hockey program for the 44,000 young players registered with the Alberta Amateur Hockey Association. An estimated $75 million in matching grants from the province has gone to rink upgrading and construction since 1975.

Tradition is important in Alberta hockey. But on May 30, 1985 Wayne Douglas Gretzky and Company gladly broke with tradition. Instead of waiting another 91 years to reclaim the Stanley Cup they repossessed it in five games from the Philadelphia Flyers in 1985.

Albertans can hardly afford to be blaise about this second victory. There is the question of reputation in western Canada. As the record now stands Edmonton is only tied with Winnipeg for the most Stanley Cup wins in western Canada. Winnipeg won the Cup in 1896 and 1901.

Alberta On Ice portrays the Alberta rivalries and the players and towns that vied for hockey supremacy. Now, we turn the clock back to the origins as our hockey drama unfolds...

HOCKEY'S BIRTH IN CANADA

The word hockey has a French origin, and is derived from "hoquet", meaning "shepherd's crook." According to historical records the game had a comparatively late start in Canada's sport history. In 1942, W.A. Hewitt chaired a "Canadian Amateur Hockey Association" (CAHA) committee which declared that the first "official" hockey game in Canada was played in 1855 by the Royal Canadian Rifles, stationed in Halifax and Kingston.

A year later, Professor E.M. Orlick of McGill University stated that the first game of organized hockey was played at the Victoria Rink in Montreal in 1875. S.F. Wise and Douglas Fisher (*Canada's Sporting Heros,* 1974:44), "...the evidence bears out his (Orlick's) argument in every particular".

In 1885, the first hockey league in Canada was formed in Kingston, Ontario. The Canadian Hockey Association was formed in 1886 and in 1890 the Ontario Hockey Association was organized. Lord Stanley, the sixth Governor General of Canada donated the Stanley Cup for competitive play on February 23, 1893 to the Montreal Athletic Union. It was an amateur challenge cup.

In terms of professional hockey the National Hockey Association began in 1910 and led in 1917 to the formation of the National Hockey League. In professional hockey circles in the West, the Pacific Coast League started in 1911. All these professional leagues played off for the Stanley Cup; it had become the symbol of supremacy in professional hockey.

ALBERTA'S HOCKEY ORIGINS

In 1891 the area of Alberta had a population of 25,000. The census revealed that Edmonton and area numbered 3,875; 700 of the group resided in Edmonton. Calgary and area totaled 3,876. Edmonton's Northlands Coliseum or Calgary's Olympic Saddledome would hold almost three-quarters of that 1891 population.

In the beginning the established sports were curling, horseracing, skating, lacrosse, soccer and baseball. Curling was so popular that Calgary wanted to build its first indoor curling rink. This prompted the following comment from the "Calgary Herald" in 1888: "Athletics will certainly be provided for. Does it not appear about time that a reading room and library were started in Calgary?"

The established sports naturally had a much higher profile than hockey. They had been imported from other cultures but hockey was all-Canadian. It was destined to become our most popular game not only in Alberta but all of Canada.

In Alberta, the "Calgary Herald" reported the province's first hockey game. It reported on January 4, 1893 that the Town Boys defeated the Tailors by a score of 4-1. The game was played at Calgary's outdoor Star Skating Rink. On January 18, the North West Mounted Police and the Town Team faced off on the Bow River. The mounties got their men, 4-0. (Source: John Reid's Masters Paper, Univ. of Alberta.)

In a return engagement played at the Star Skating Rink, the Town Boys got their revenge by winning 3-0. No team rosters have yet been found for the NWMP or the Tailors. But, playing for the "Towns" in the 3-0 win were: T. Tarrant, T. Bruce, F. James, B. Goulin, F. Aitken, G. Henderson and A. Grierson. (L. Tarrant played in the previous match.) By the spring of 1893, Calgary had two more teams and a number of other groups were engaged in training.

Hockey came to Edmonton in 1894. An organizational meeting was held at the Thistle Rink on 102 Street, north of Jasper Avenue on the east side, on December 5th. Inspector Syd Synder headed a committee and was named team captain. J.A. Boyle became assistant captain and P, McNamara, I. Saunders and F. Robertson were called upon to select a team.

They decided to hold a practice every Friday afternoon in order to pick the team. They were slated to play teams from Strathcona and Fort Saskatchewan.

The first game took place on Christmas Day 1894, when the Thistle's team defeated Strathcona 3-2. Performing for the Thistles were, J.A. Boyle, W.T. Henry, Saunders, J.R. Fulton, F.M. Robertson, C.W.S. Bridges and Syd Snyder. Fort Saskatchewan included such players as Inspector Primrose, Constables Dyer, Baker, Lamb and Touche.

Although these early "hockey matches" were competitive, they were very sociable affairs. These early teams were elitist and based on the model of the English sport/social club. Teams such as the Thistles boasted some of Edmonton's most prominent residents. (Most of the early players were British Albertans; in fact, central and eastern names do not appear in hockey line-ups until much later.)

Two prominent Alberta family names appear in early Alberta hockey line ups.

The first name. "Brewster", shows up in a Banff lineup in the days when Brewster Bus Lines were wagon trains. On New Year's Day, 1898, Banff travelled to Canmore and won 3-0. Others on the Banff roster included Black, Frost, Brett, Douglas and Battington. The Canmore seven included Lowe, Cardell, Morand, Tedlock, Wallis, Hayward and Martell.

The second famous name occurs late in January 1898, when the Calgary Public School defeated Calgary College 8-4. Goal keeper for the college team was Clarence Lougheed, son of Senator James Lougheed and uncle of Alberta's Premier, Peter Lougheed.

The game itself was much different from today's brand of hockey. Teams were made up of seven players — goalie, point and cover-point (defence), three forwards and a rover — and there were no substitutes. For face-offs the three forwards lined up horizontally (left wing, centre, right wing). The rover, point and cover point lined up directly behind the centre in front of the goalie. It was a "T" formation.

In 1895, The Calgary Fire Brigade was a prominent club. The team rolled to a convincing 9-3 triumph over a team from Golden, B.C. Referee D.S. Lloyd made it clear from the outset that the "rough players" had to abide by the rules. He refused to tolerate players acting as "battering rams" as they made their charge down the ice. Referee Lloyd was not exaggerating the violence if one is to believe the following poem by A.B. Ankler ("Calgary Herald" January 3, 1896):

When I come home,
If home I come,
Escaped from all the "flies"
You may behold a broken nose
Likewise two sweet eyes.
Good night, Good night,
I go to strive for glory and for gore,
To chop the other fellows till
I can't chop anymore,
And if I fall upon the ice,
Then you shall share the pain,
Of him who lost his youthful life,
But won the hockey game.

CALGARY FIRE BRIGADE 1894-95
(Includes some of the original Alberta players from first recorded game)

Back (l to r): E.D. Marshall, S.L. Saunders, J.E. Wilson, R.S. Chipman, C.F. Comer. Front (l to r): H.R. Watson, T.W. Bruce, F.W. Atkins, G.W. Henderson.
Photo courtesy of Glenbow Archives

One of the first serious accidents recorded in Alberta hockey happened in January, 1898 in a game between Edmonton and the Calgary Fire Brigade. An Edmonton player shot the puck, raised his stick and hit Calgary's Marshall in the left eye. It did not appear serious; however, Calgary's Dr. Mackid later pronounced the eye severely damaged. After consulting with another doctor, Dr. Mackid removed Marshall's eye the same night. Even though

Les Francis of the Brigade received a broken nose and teammate Bruce a severe blow on the arm, there was not much on an outcry. The "Calgary Herald" simply reported that "Mr. Marshall was resting easily and no further trouble is anticipated". All three accidents were attributed to careless use of sticks.

Intense hockey rivalry between Edmonton and Calgary began in earnest in 1895. In March of that year a Calgary "All Star" squad came to Edmonton to play against the Edmonton Thistles and a NWMP contingent from Fort Saskatchewan.

The Calgarians easily defeated both teams and went on to victory against a Thistle/NWMP All Star team. Edmonton was determined to do much better next time 'round.

In February, 1896, Calgary travelled to Edmonton to play a three game series with the Edmonton Thistles, the NWMP from Fort Saskatchewan and the Edmonton Shamrocks. Lo and behold, the southern team repeated its victory from the year before and, as the "Calgary Herald" reported, "Gloried at their supremacy over Edmonton and district".

Medicine Hat became a new rival for Calgary. In 1896, in one of the fastest games of the year, Medicine Hat defeated Calgary 9-8. Early in the game Calgary had a 5-0 lead. The Calgarians became over-confident and over-generous. Calgary players decided to keep the score down so as not to embarrass their opponents. Medicine Hat then put on a spurt to win the game.

The winning goal was scored when the Calgary goalkeeper turned around and had his back to the puck. A reporter suggested he was either asking a boy how much time was left or, perhaps, what time of day it was!

Medicine Hat's lineup included J. Hargrave, Ben Niblock, D. McLoy, J. McClelland, T. Hardisty, A. Bassett, M. O'Hara. Calgary players included Johnston, Bruce, Henderson, Orr, Douglas, Chipman and Marshall. The referee was J.S. Smith.

EDMONTON HOCKEY CLUB 1897

Back (l to r): D. Harrison, missing, R. Hardisty. Front (l to r): Ralph Bellamy, Frank Hardisty, Aldridge, Cartier.

Photo courtesy of Provincial Archives, E. Brown Collection

Edmonton Thistles finally hit stride in 1899 with a 15-2 victory over the Calgary Fire Brigade. Calgary was dismayed. The "Herald" criticized the southern Fire Brigade for not bringing credit to itself or the town, for neglectful play and poor attendance at practice. Rumour had it that the "crafty and wiley" Edmonton supporters took Calgary players out for a "hot time on the old town" the night before the game.

Banff hockey supporters did not have to "resort" to such tactics against Canmore in March, 1899. All they had to do was sit back and let nature take its course.

The afternoon in question was a fine one, unseasonably warm. The fans enjoyed several muscial selections from a local band before the game. The game started. And then the flies came. Although the players were not prepared for the onslaught of flies, one gentleman in the crowd had come armed with a mosquito net. Despite the annoying distraction, Banff went on to win the game 11-1 and claim the Sifton Trophy. Obviously, the bugs had not been ironed out of Alberta hockey.

For example, a Calgary team was all set to play but they could not find a team to play against. A unique challenge appeared in the "Calgary Herald" February 16, 1899. Gin Sling challenged the Calgary hockey club to a game and offered a China Tea Cup as the prize. Perhaps the reason the Calgary team did not take up the challenge was because Gin Sling had written the offer in Chinese.

The number of challenges in the newspapers indicates there were no adult hockey leagues. In fact, the first league in Alberta was for school children in Edmonton. In March of 1898, the Edmonton Public School defeated a southside opponent and was presented a silver trophy inscribed "School Trophy for Edmonton District". Adult teams continued to play challenge games until 1900.

By that time hockey had become as popular as baseball and soccer. Alberta sports historian Cecil Blackburn wrote "every town and practically every village from Pincher Creek and Medicine Hat in the south to Edmonton in the north supported at least one senior team". Inter-town and district play with challenge matches and trophies had gained in popularity and number.

But the game was by no means standardized. Although Alberta hockey was played by rules laid down in Manitoba and the Northwest Territories, referees were not always well-informed of them. (Rules were quite different from today; for example, goalies could not go down on their knees to stop the puck. There was no forward pass; a player was "offside" if he was in front of the puck — there were no blue lines.)

There were great variations even in the size of the rinks. Some were big, some were small: some had lights, some did not. Edmonton's Strathcona Skating rink was opened in 1899, the Saturday before Christmas. The rink was 60' by 110' with a 20' skating course around the hockey arena. The ground was not very level so only the centre of the arena was used. A force pump was connected to the Town well reducing the level of the well by 10'. In the morning of the opening it was brought up to the proper level. After Christmas the rink was to get a dynamo from Jackson's Foundry to produce electric light with about 25 incandescant lamps.

Despite such variation and such innovation, one thing was certain; before Alberta had even become a province, hockey was here to stay.

THE TWENTIETH CENTURY

In 1900 T.G. Rothwell, a law clerk for the Dominion of Canada in Ottawa predicted greatness for Calgary and Edmonton on a western inspection trip to Alberta. He informed the media that

Calgary is now a very fine city and its main street is equal in appearance to any city in the East. The city is destined to be one of the greatest in the Dominion in years to come.

Of Edmonton he said,

It will be a metropolis one day. The energetic attitude of its people will abound and the pride in their city will instill an attitude of greatness which in time will see this city recognized the world over.

Rothwell was not slow in identifying the great rivalry between the two cities.

Calgary, (he added) will not at any level allow itself to play second fiddle to Edmonton and will endeavour to keep pace or even surpass the progress of their northern opponents in one of the greatest rivalries of modern time.

This rivalry continued in hockey in the two cities at the turn of the century. Whenever Calgary and Edmonton teams suited up against each other it turned into a fiercely competitive game. Hockey supremacy shifted back and forth north and south in the early years and has continued to do so until the present.

Although the rivalries were intense, the game was truly in its infancy in terms of facilities and organization.

Rinks continued to be built, often as much for pleasure skating as for hockey. In Calgary, for example, the promotional partnership of E. Fletcher and T. Smart built an open air rink 200' long by 100' at Reinach Avenue and First Street East. 200 skaters showed up for the opening on December 11, 1900. Admission was set at $.15

for men, $.10 for women and children and season passes were $3.50 for men, $2.00 for women and children. The new rink had dressing rooms and provisions were made for lights at a later date.

1900-1901 EDMONTON HOCKEY TEAM

Back, standing (l to r): Tom Houston, H. Campbell, Ed Sibbald, missing, missing. Sitting: Dr. Till, Rev. H.A. Gray. Front: A. McLeod, W. Ingles, Lennie Goodridge.

Photo courtesy of Provincial Archives

Electric lights were still a rarity in Alberta. The 1901 season ended in Edmonton when the local squad defeated Strathcona 5-4 after two overtime periods in the fourth game of a best-of-five series. The "Edmonton Bulletin" revealed that

> *the wickedness of the shooting made it particularly difficult for the goalkeepers to detect the puck by electric lights and, as a result, goals were let in by the defence and net minders of both teams, which, it is safe to say, would have been stopped in daylight.*

SECORD BUILDS EDMONTON'S THISTLE RINK IN 1902

(from *A Builder of the Northwest — The Life and Times of Richard Secord, 1860-1935* — researched and compiled by David Leonard, John E. McIssac, and Sheilagh Jameson)

While matters assumed for some time a doubtful aspect as to the possibility of being successful, Mr. Richard Secord had come to the rescue, by offering to build a rink suitable to the advanced and expanded requirements and that the rink would be ready for next season's curling. This most welcome announcement was received with great applause.

Shortly afterwards, Richard decided to combine this new curling rink with the largest indoor skating arena in the North West Territories. The site he chose was a corner of what is now 102 Street and 102 Avenue, on property owned by McDougall and Secord. Building on the complex began in the summer of 1902. The architect was H.B. Johnson, while the J.R. Manson Co. was employed to con-

struct the two buildings. When completed in December, they were purported to "rival the size and appearance of the largest city rinks and are a credit to the town as well as to the public spirit and enterprise of their proprietor.

The skating and hockey rink was two hundred and four feet by eighty five feet, standing eighty eight and one-half feet high. The walls and roof were arched in a semicircle supported by nine trestles to preclude the need for pillars. The ice surface was one hundred and eighty feet by sixty feet. It was surrounded by four-foot-high railings and four tiers of seats which could hold over 1,000 people. The entrance hall and waiting rooms partitioned from the ice by plate glass windows above the boards, were to the south and incompassed an area eighty five feet by ten feet. All of them were two rooms to be used as band stands or simply for viewing hockey matches. The total cost of the rink was $13,000. Other signs on the building included Massey Harris Bicycles and Capital Bicycle Company. As well, the large sign depicting the rink said Thistle Roller and Ice Rink.

INSIDE EDMONTON'S THISTLE RINK 1902

* * *

Junior hockey at the turn of the century illustrates the problems created because of poor or little organization. The earliest known junior competition was played in 1902 and was called the Jackson Cup Challenge. The only stipulation was that the game be played in Calgary. In the first challenge Calgary defeated Banff 5-2.

There were problems, however, when Edmonton challenged for the Cup in 1904. Since no provincial body governed the teams, no one checked the ages of the players; they went on trust. Edmonton lost the first game but found out that Calgary had three overage junior players (more than 18 years old). Edmonton refused to play a second game unless the seniors were dropped. The Edmonton manager stated they were "deliberately deceived before the trip and were treated in an unsportsmanlike manner" by Calgary. To add insult to the injury Edmonton had used "the most expensive practice times and expense money ever spent by the club". Calgary received similar treatment in Medicine Hat later that same year. "The Hat" shut out Calgary 6-0; then it was discovered that the winning team had used four senior age players. Like Edmonton had done, Calgary refused to play another game and took the next train out of town. These incidents continued until junior hockey became an official category in 1914.

In senior hockey Edmonton and Calgary still dominated, but by 1902 the game was on the rise throughout Alberta. Teams from Lethbridge, Taber, Medicine Hat, Pincher Creek and Drumheller in the south and Ponoka, Lacombe, Red Deer, Wetaskiwin and St. Albert in the north, played each other in their districts.

St. Albert had improved steadily and by 1903 the team was ready to challenge the highly regarded Edmonton Nationals. To the surprise of everyone, St. Albert romped to a 12-1 victory. Coloncleough was sensational in net while point player J. Beauchamp was the leading scorer. Edmonton protested that these players were professionals, but, in fact, they were not. Coloncleough had only been on skates three times and had to hold on to the goalposts to stand up!

Challenges came from the most unusual places in the days when hockey was not organized. In 1903, in Calgary, the boarders at Mrs. McLaughlin's boarding house challenged Mrs. Bowden's boarders to a hockey game. Heady from success, Mrs. McLaughlin's boarders then challenged Mrs. McKinnon's boarders.

This second match proved more serious. A Calgary physician, Dr. Sullivan, agreed to referee while Harry Binion and Billy Reilly consented to be goal judges. The match was tied 4-4 after regulation time. Reilly refused to go into overtime because some of his calls had been questioned during the game. Nevertheless, the game went on. After two overtime periods of five minutes each the game was still tied. Three minutes into sudden death overtime Mrs. McKinnon's team scored. Dr. Sullivan, the referee, called it a goal. Mrs. McLaughlin's team protested vigorously. Reilly throught it a joke that boarding houses would take this hockey so seriously. But it was no joke to the players.

FIRST HOCKEY TEAM IN OLDS 1903

Back (l to r): George Cloakey, Zeigler, Fred Webster, Fred Shackleton, Bob Hainstock. Centre: W.J. Brumpton, C. McCutcheon, S.R. Scott, Eddie King, Bob Logan. Sitting: Dick Robertson, Ernie Scott. *Photo courtesy of Provincial Archives*

Referees such as Dr. Sullivan were prominent citizens and were sometimes not very well-versed in the rules of hockey. This caused problems. A February 25, 1903 game between Strathcona (now southside Edmonton) and Medicine Hat is a case in point. Medicine Hat went down to defeat 8-6 and protested that the referee, the Strathcona Postmaster, favoured his home team. The teams could not agree on a new referees so Strathcona went home.

None of these referees had any special training. It would be over fifty years before any concentrated effort was made to train referees. Most of the referees in the early days were simply doing their civic duty. But, even from the earliest days of hockey in Alberta, referees had to put up with a certain amount of "spit and abuse".

Early adult hockey leagues were beginning as early as 1901, the year the Calgary Senior Hockey League was formed. It had four teams. Usually, team members worked at the same type of business. The bankers had two clubs, one made up of members from the Bank of Montreal, the Bank of Commerce and the Bank of Nova Scotia and the other one comprised of Molsen's Union and the Imperial Bank employees. Other entries included the Calgary City Team and the Canadian Pacific Railway.

Railway routes often determined which teams joined a league. In the first Central Alberta Hockey League of 1903 Didsbury, Olds, Lacombe, Red Deer, Wetaskiwin and Leduc were all members because they were on the same line. For the same reason Medicine Hat, Pincher Creek, McLeod, Frank (Alberta teams) and Fernie, British Columbia all played in the Crowsnest League at that time.

The Hobbema Hawks of the present day AJHL are not the first native team to play top-notch hockey. That honour goes to the High River Industrial School Hockey Team otherwise known as the "Dunbows". On February 4, 1898 the Dunbows played the Dewdney Hockey Club on a fenced rink on the river near the school. The native team stormed to a 6-1 victory (there was a blizzard in the last two periods).

DUNBOW SCHOOL HOCKEY CLUB OF HIGH RIVER 1899

Top left: Father Naessens. (Other identifications unknown.)

Photo courtesy of Provincial Archives

A few weeks later Reverend Father Naessens, the "Father of Native Hockey in Alberta", took the Dunbows to Calgary to play the highly-rated Calgary Fire Brigade team. Dressed in attractive yellow and black jerseys the Dunbows lost 5-4. Despite several inspired rushes by Mooney, a school instructor, he was unable to put the puck past Brigade goalie Charlie Comer.

In keeping with the social tradition of early hockey the native team visited the Brigade rooms after the game. Rev. Father Naessens delivered a speech which was followed by group singing. Playing and singing for High River; in goal George Vielle, point John English, cover point W. Mooney, forwards Beauchamp, D. Callihoo, S. Dakota and Red Crow.

The Dunbows challenged and defeated many of the top senior teams in Alberta before there were senior leagues. One of the most talented native players on the team in this era was Francis Eagle. After 1905 there is no mention of this team in provincial play. (For more on native hockey see J. Wilton Littlechilds' articles in Native Hockey.)

As the calibre of hockey improved; so did the quality and variety of equipment. By 1906 there were four main types of hockey boots and skates. Although no brand name was advertised, the most popular pair of skates and boots was constructed of genuine mule hide with double uppers. No ankle support was required. A pair cost $3.50. Box calf hockey boots of top grade leather went for the same price. They appealed to the buyer because of their ''close fit and durability''. A kangaroo green tan boot, soft and pliable as well as waterproof, was considered impossible to scuff or tear and was available at the same price. The cheapest boot was a men's oil grain hockey boot at $2.50 made of a good quality leather and rated as strong, convertible and serviceable. No mention was made of the type of blades. (Today the best hockey skates retail at $250.00)

OLDS — CENTRAL ALBERTA HOCKEY LEAGUE CHAMPIONS 1906-07

Photo courtesy of Provincial Archives

One of the most competitive aspects of early hockey happened off the ice. It was the fight to attract top imports to play for local clubs. Such competition was keen in the Central Alberta League. In 1907, in the final between Olds, and Lacombe, both teams used imports from Calgary. When the final game ended in a tie a title encounter was scheduled on neutral ice at the Auditorium in Calgary. Rules and regulations of the league were rather lax as to who could play for what team. In this case both teams needed more players so substitutes were permitted. The Calgary seniors objected when some of their players were involved but the Calgary coach relented and allowed some of his team to play. Olds added goalkeeper Anderson and defenceman Hemsworth. Lacombe used two Calgary players, Flummerfelt and McHugh.

Graham played his first game in goal for Lacombe and was declared the game's outstanding player. Chalk, King, Sherman and Flummerfelt also played well for Lacombe. Olds' stars were Cutten, Hemsworth, Cook and Davey. Olds won the closely fought match and became the initial winners of the Edmonton Brewing Company Trophy.

In 1907, more emphasis was placed on interprovincial play. Regina boasted one of the most promising teams in the West and travelled to Alberta in the spring for competition. The Edmonton club won two games including the final 6-1 to capture the Alberta-Saskatchewan championship. After the setback, Regina journeyed to Calgary where it won 3-1. (Edmonton's victory sparked enough hockey interest that in 1908 the club challenged for the Stanley Cup.)

Gambling played a big part in early hockey. In 1907 Calgary had a unique hockey league, the Hotel Association, where regular roomers and hotel staff formed teams. Two of the leading hotels were the Royal and the Grand Union and whenever they faced off in a hockey game there was big betting.

In order to avenge a loss Grand Union supporters challenged the Royals to a rematch. Backing themselves with a certified cheque for $200 they placed it in the custody of city Alderman Moody. Moody, who was also manager of the Calgary Hotelman's Association, requested the Royal supporters to match the bet. They not only matched it; they collected $300 because the Grand Union followers had upped the bet. Naturally, the fans anticipated an exciting game with the purse finally set at $600, not to mention side bets.

A week before the game a young man by the name of "Allan" registered for a room at the Grand Union Hotel. Immediately, Royal supporters questioned Allan's eligibility; he was an unknown quantity and they were afraid of him. Deep dark whisperings of previous Stanley Cup participation surrounded his arrival. Nevertheless, the bet was placed with the official stake holder less than an hour before the game. Grand Union had won the roll permitting Allan to play.

Midway through the game the teams were tied 2-2 and, at the end of regulation time it was 5-5. The game went into a ten-minute overtime period. Grand Union scored two goals in the extra sessions to win 7-5. Allan, the disputed player, did not figure in any of the scoring.

BEGINNING OF THE ALBERTA AMATEUR HOCKEY ASSOCIATION

By 1907 hockey had expanded to most of the well-populated areas of Alberta and senior leagues were springing up in larger centres. The time was ripe for a provincial association to orchestrate Alberta hockey. Although Manitoba hockey enthusiasts tried to organize a provincial body that same year, they failed while the Alberta Amateur Hockey Association (AAHA) officials succeeded. (Saskatchewan (SAHA) organized in 1912, Manitoba (MAHA) in 1914 and British Columbia (BCAHA) in 1919 in the West.)

The AAHA was born on November 29, 1907 in Red Deer. Representatives came from Edmonton, Wetaskiwin, Olds, Lacombe, Didsbury, Crossfield, Medicine Hat, Calgary and Red Deer. R.N. Brown of Red Deer became the first president and his executive included Vice President R. Rhinestock of Olds, secretary C.H. Bristow of Edmonton and treasurer Norman Carruthers of Lacombe. J.A. Brand, J. Taylor and J.H. Borsch made up the executive committee.

The main purpose of the association was to foster and develop amateur hockey in Alberta. It was hoped that more towns and cities would become interested and would join the association. The AAHA hoped to maintain control of the game and keep out of professional hockey. Teams were admitted into the association at a general meeting of the AAHA in December 1907. Schedules, a constitution and rules and regulations were determined.

It was decided that there would be two classes of senior hockey. Edmonton and Strathcona would be entered in Class 'A' leagues and could include Battleford, Saskatchewan, provided they were agreeable and would abide by the amateur rules of the association. (Battleford was on the railway line to Edmonton and was more likely to "hook up" with Alberta teams rather than teams in southern-based Saskatchewan hockey.) Class 'B' would have teams from Red Deer, Lacombe, Stettler, Didsbury, Olds, Crossfield and another team from Edmonton.

The AAHA would be divided into two districts, north and south, with Edmonton, Lacombe and Stettler competing in the north and Olds, Red Deer, Didsbury and Crossfield in the south. Calgary decided not to send a delegation to the second organizational meeting held in Red Deer, and was omitted from the schedule.

Calgary decided not to join the association or the league because the team claimed that travelling expenses were prohibitive. (It is possible there was more to it than that. Edmonton was a "powerhouse" and perhaps Calgary did not want to compete in the same league.) Calgary teams played locally for the time being.

The reason Edmonton and Strathcona were put in the 'A' category is unknown. Alberta sport historian, Cecil Blackburn speculates that, "by categorizing these two teams by themselves the fledgling provincial association probably averted a major amateur-professional scandal."

The Alberta Amateur Athletic Union (AAAU) was organized in May, 1908 to govern most sports activity in the province. The association, along with the Canadian Amateur Athletic Union, took the definite stand that amateurs and professionals would not be allowed to compete against each other. Professional regulations were so tough that if one was paid for one sport, he could not compete in another sport as an amateur. Amateur sport advocates perceived professionals as "tainted", unfit company.

The AAHA became one of the organizations under the AAAU. It had teams registered in the 1907-1908 season. Two years later sixteen teams played in four separate districts. Didsbury, Airdrie, Crossfield, and Olds competed against one another. Red Deer, Lacombe, Stettler, and Castor comprised another division. Lloydminister, Vermilion, Kitscoty and Lashburn, Saskatchewan, made up another one while Strathcona, Vegreville, the Edmonton YMCA and Edmonton Wanderers were in the fourth division. During the first three years of the Alberta Amateur Hockey Association's existence there were no member teams south of Airdrie, 20 kilometers north of Calgary.

By the 1910-11 season, however, the AAHA had become a province-wide organization. Teams from Taber, Lethbridge, MacLeod and Pincher Creek competed in a new division. Calgary St. Mary's and the Calgary Athletic Club joined teams from Lacombe, Stettler and Didsbury in another. In the early days the AAHA concentrated on forming leagues for adults. As time progressed, all ages became part of the association.

At a meeting of the AAHA on November 14, 1910, it was announced that J.H. Woods of the Calgary Herald, had donated a trophy to be awarded to the champion of the league and that H.W. Laird and Company would supply medals to all players and officials on the winning team. The Treasurer's report revealed a $40 surplus 'in the kitty'. A committee was formed to revise the constitution. A semi-pro league was discussed at length, but it was decided that such a loop would not be feasible and Calgary delegates indicated they preferred to remain amateur.

Edmonton representatives agreed to support amateur hockey as in the past but also indicated support for the semi-pros as they felt there was sufficient talent in their domain to sponsor both. The delegates to the meeting agreed unanimously that their organization was the largest and the best in the West and suggested that a north and south division would enhance their position.

A four team southern league, featuring Fort MacLeod, Pincher Creek, Lethbridge and High River was formed. Teams from Red Deer, Lacombe, Olds, and Ponoka competed in a central division. Edmonton and district had five teams while Calgary St. Mary's and the Calgary City team plus teams from Okotoks and High River, formed the Calgary division. The AAHA would be ready to start the next season with seventeen senior teams under its jurisdiction.

Like any fledgling organization the AAHA had not anticipated certain problems. One of these was the constant flow of imports or "ringers" from town to town. This movement often caused bad feelings between teams and communities and was disruptive to long-term planning. The problem was that the eligibility rule was too weak. All a player had to do was show up ten days before his new team's first game in order to establish residency.

The AAHA changed the rules for the 1910-11 season. AAHA president Dr. Gibson and his executive decreed that any player who started with one team could not transfer to another. The ten day residency requirement stayed the same. This so-called "tough-stand" did not solve the problem and, in fact, residency problems still occur.

From this beginning the AAHA has evolved into an organization of over 2600 teams in 1984-85.

As senior hockey grew in stature it was only natural that youngsters should want to play the game too. Backyard hockey is almost a thing of the past, but here is the way it was in 1907:

Railwayman Alf Fiddler and his eldest son built a rink in their backyard in Calgary. One day in early January, Fiddler was returning from work when he noticed a group of boys fighting in his yard. Alarmed, he ran as fast as he could only to discover that "the youngsters were engaged in a hockey tussle". The scrub team named the Athletics defeated the Wanderers 4-1.

Hockey was really catching on in Calgary on wood as well as ice. In 1908 a new sport, roller hockey, made its appearance at the Sherman Rink. The game was similar to hockey in some respects. But players on roller skates passing a ball while music played in the background was hardly competition for ice hockey.

EDMONTON HOCKEY TEAM IN STANLEY CUP

Hockey fever was so high in Edmonton that on Christmas Day, 1907 more than 3,000 people turned out to watch a slugfest between Edmonton and Strathcona. Fred Whitcroft starred for Edmonton in the 9-7 victory.

A year later Whitcroft was instrumental in Edmonton's bid for the Stanley Cup. It was the first Alberta team to take up the challenge. Whitcroft spared no expenses in recruiting players from across Canada. He also recruited Mrs. Mary Deeton, wife of centre Harold Deeton. Mrs. Helen McCleary of Camrose, daughter of the Deetons, recalls that ''my mother made the trip with the team and ended up as security custodian of the equipment which was stored in her hotel room in Montreal''.

In preparation for the trip to Montreal the team practised on an open air rink on McDougall Avenue near McDougall United Church and at the indoor Thistle Rink a few blocks away on 102nd Street northeast of Jasper Avenue.

On December 14, 1908 the Edmonton club signed Tom Phillips and Lester Patrick, two of Canada's top players. (Later, Lester and his brother Frank Patrick formed the highly successful Pacific Coast League.) Phillips hailed from Vancouver and Patrick from Nelson, British Columbia.

EDMONTON HOCKEY TEAM
(Alberta's First Try for Stanley Cup)

Top (l to r): Oscar Hetu, Jack Miller, Bill Crowley, Ernie Chauvin, Hugh Ross. Front: Fred Whitcroft, Mary Deeton, Harold Deeton. Missing: Lester Patrick, Tom Phillips. (Photo taken January 1909.) *Photo courtesy of Edmonton Archives*

Photo courtesy of Edmonton Archives

PLAY BY PLAY TELEGRAM OF 1908 STANLEY CUP

Face Deeton gets it . Gardner takes it gives to Glass shoots and misses. Glass crosschecked Miller and is put off .Deeton passes to Vair to Miller who loses to Gardner passes to Smith who scores eighth game for Wanderers, in 2 mins by Smith. Edmonton 4 Wanderers 4. Face Smith gets the draw Deeton takes it from him passes to Whitcroft to Smaill now Vair rushes down and shoots wild. Miller is put over with body check face Deeton gets draw passes to Vair who shoots wild Ross rushes loses to Pitre who loses to Smaill . Miller gets it rushes to Deeton who runs down and scores.

Photo courtesy of Edmonton Archives

Every other player on the team except Edmonton's Harold Deeton was imported. Bert Lindsay (father of future Detroit Red Wing Ted Lindsay) came from Renfrew, Ontario. Jack Miller was from Peterborough, Harold McNamara from the Montreal Shamrocks, Hugh Ross from Portage La Prairie and D.T. Petrie from Montreal Shamrocks and Nationals.

The ten players, team officials A.M. Stuart (President), Ernest Chauvin (Secretary), Bill Crowley (Trainer) and Mary Deeton made the trip to Montreal in a private CNR car called Glencairn. It was decorated in the team colours of black and orange.

EDMONTON HOCKEY TEAM
Champions of Western Canada 1908-09

Back (l to r): W. Field, O. Hetu, E.E. Chauvin, D. Cameron (donator of trophy), W.F. Crowley (trainer), H. Ross. Front: J. Miller, H. Deeton, F. Whitcroft (manager and captain), B. Boulton, W.C. Nicholson. *Photo courtesy of Helen Deeton McCleary*

Edmonton faced the Montreal Wanderers. In the first game of the two game total-goal series Edmonton lost 7-4. In the second game Coach Whitcroft replaced Phillips and McNamara with Deeton and Miller. Edmonton won 7-6. Whitcroft claimed that the 13-11 total point loss might have been different if he had made the line-up changes sooner. In the second game Deeton scored three times, Miller twice.

Reports in the Ottawa Citizen stated that penalties played a big part in the outcome and that "the Edmonton squad suffered seriously from the rugged play with a number of their players requiring medical attention". Steve Vair was cut on the head, Petrie had a laceration across his mouth and nose, McNamara suffered a knee injury and Tom Phillips' ankle was broken. Phillips had played 45 minutes with the injury. He informed his trainer and team officials that he was alright, that it was "only a slight sprain". The Ottawa Citizen reported that Lester Patrick was "by far the outstanding player in the series, although the westerners lost, they gave a good account of themselves and were worthy opponents for the new champs".

ALBERTA'S SECOND STANLEY CUP ATTEMPT

In December, 1909 Edmonton Hockey Club challenged for the Stanley Cup a second time. The team set to play a two-game total-goal series against the Ottawa Senators in Ottawa on January 18th and 20th, 1910.

Playing Coach Whitcroft reported that Lester Patrick would play for the Renfrew Ontario Millionares instead of Edmonton. He added, however, that he would field a strong competitive team with goalie Jack Winchester, Harold Deeton, Jack Miller, Burt Boulton, H. Ross and W. Field.

On January 18, 1910 more than 5,000 spectators watched Edmonton and Ottawa face off at the Ottawa Arena. At 8:33 p.m., Earl Grey, Govenor General of Canada (donor of the Grey Cup for football supremacy in Canada) dropped the puck.

EDMONTON HOCKEY TEAM
Second Try at Stanley Cup

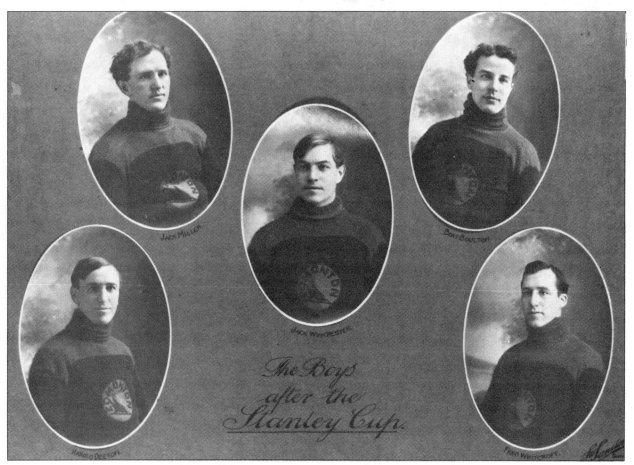

Jack Miller, Jack Winchester, Bert Boulton, Harold Deeton, Fred Whitcroft. *Photo courtesy of Sanderson Photo*

The game was stopped after Fred Whitcroft scored Edmonton's third goal to give them a 3-2 lead. One of the Edmonton players "lost his trousers" — and had to go to the dressing room. Later, cigarette and cigar smoke polluted the rink, and the players had to go to the dressing room with ten minutes left to play in the first half. Ottawa was in the lead. After the smoke was eliminated, the teams resumed play. Edmonton was no match for the easteners and lost 8-4.

In between games a few of the Edmonton players gained the attention of eastern team managers. Fred Whitcroft was offered $2,500 to play for Renfrew for the next season but he refused. Other Edmonton players preferred to stay together and play for Edmonton.

The second game on January 20th was more like a battle than a hockey game. Ottawa won the slugfest 13-7 and took the Stanley Cup by a two-game-total-goal margin of 21-11. Despite its loss to Ottawa, Edmonton finished off a successful season in the West. The team won the Fit-Reform Cup series by defeating Prince Albert, Saskatchewan 3-1 to retain its Western Hockey Championship.

16

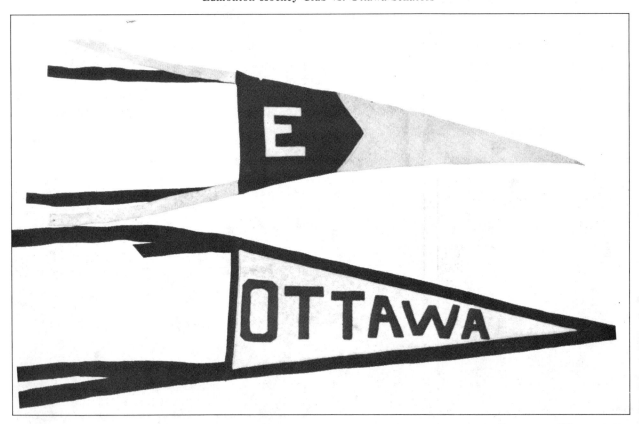

Photo courtesy of Edmonton Archives

This sparked talk of a western professional league early in 1909. Calgary, Edmonton and Nelson, B.C. were all interested. Edmonton had the Thistle Rink but Calgary needed a new facility and was not prepared to build one. There were objections to professional hockey in Calgary. Player and cigar store operator, Dan McLeod stated that, "I never received a cent playing hockey and never intend to. I am only a professional when it comes to selling cigars. I am an amateur in sports." McLeod's philosophy was common to many athletes and fans in his era.

Meanwhile, Whitcroft and his Edmonton team accepted a challenge from a select Calgary team to be played at the Sherman Rink in Calgary. Edmonton won the encounter 5-0. The *Calgary Herald* reported, "The Edmonton Eskimos could have easily piled up a big score, but they didn't bother. They seldom extended themselves but when they did, showed to be far superior to the locals." (The team had always been called the Edmonton Hockey Team. The term "Eskimo" was used here. Later it became the name for Edmonton's next two professional teams.)

In 1910-11, amateur hockey regained its prominence in Alberta. The Edmonton Hockey Team had no aspirations for the Stanley Cup. The team was broke. Edmonton started to develop other senior clubs.

Two newspapers, the "Calgary Herald" and "Edmonton Journal" agreed to co-sponsor a trophy for the Alberta Amateur Hockey Championship. The initial winner in 1910-11 was Calgary St. Mary's who defeated the Edmonton Deacons 5-1 and lost 7-5 to win the round 10-8.

The Allan Cup had been donated in 1908 by Sir Montague Allan to be a challenge trophy for amateurs. St. Mary's was now eligible to challenge Winnipeg Victorias. The team did not go because one of their players had an appendectomy operation and it were unable to find a replacement.

As the hockey season of 1911 was drawing to a close, Calgary's Lloyd Turner assumed duties as manager of that city's Sherman Rink. Turner had previously looked after several of Calgary's outdoor rinks. It was the start of a long management for Turner.

Many Alberta teams continued outdoors. In Pincher Creek electric lighting was provided at the rate of $12 per month, provided that all school children under 15 years of age be allowed free skating for three hours every

Saturday afternoon. Rink managers Hodson and Allison agreed to the terms. Other teams in the league included Coleman, Frank, Lundbreck and Blairmore.

ST. MARY'S OF CALGARY
Champions of Alberta 1910-11

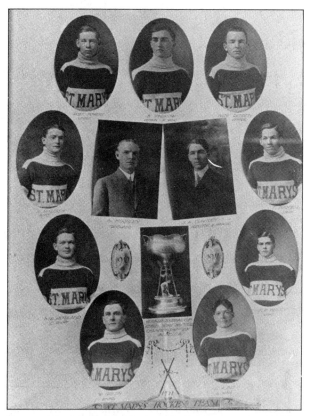

Top row (l to r): Robert Powers, B. Sparrow, Ivan Reddon. Third row: E. Maluish, A. McKinley (treasurer), J.A. Clancy (president and manager), J. Purcell. Second row: A.W. Rowland, J.P. Bell. Bottom: W. Green, E. King.

Photo courtesy of Calgary Exhibition and Stampede

In 1912 the Taber Chefs were one of the top senior teams in Alberta. The team was not known for its culinary expertise; it was called the Chefs because it had four Cook brothers — A.B., Lloyd, Wilbur, Leo plus A.G. Cook and J. Ernie Cook. The only non-Cooks on the team were Alf Barbour, G. Baird and A. Glendening.

The team was very popular. In January 1912, 250 Taber hockey fans chartered a hockey train special to Pincher Creek. The Taber band played lively music on the train and at the game.

On this particular trip A.B. Cook had purchased all the tickets. But A.B. forgot to bring the tickets. As the train neared Barnwell (10 km. west of Taber) the conductor asked people for their tickets, and, of course, nobody had them. The train had to backtrack to Taber to pick up the tickets. Then, when the train arrived at Pincher Creek the Taber crowd had to get off and pile into large wagon box bobsleighs for the two mile ride from the station to the rink. The trip ended on a happy note as Taber won the game.

In 1912, the Taber Chefs won the AAHA championship when they defeated the Edmonton Eskimos 2-0. It was called one of the "biggest upsets" in Alberta hockey history. Even though Taber won the 1912 and 1913 finals they never did represent Alberta in Allan Cup playoffs.

The previous year (1911) champion St. Mary's of Calgary did not go to the Allan Cup because one player had an operation. The AAHA decided that this club deserved a second chance in 1912 and ordered Taber to play them. On February 28, 1912, Calgary defeated Taber 5-3 in a sudden death game.

On March 5, the Winnipeg Victories easily defeated Calgary 11-0. The Alberta team did better in the second game but lost 8-6.

The Taber Chefs under Fred Douglas did go to Manitoba for two scheduled exhibition games. On March 17, the Winnipeg Monarchs and the Chefs tied 8-8. A second game was not played due to illness of several Taber players.

Once again in 1913, the Taber Chefs played the Edmonton Eskimos in a sudden death game. The winner thought they would go to Winnipeg in quest of the Allan Cup. Taber defeated the Eskimos 6-3 and once again should have gone. Events unfolded in such a way that the 1913 Alberta championship was done over again.

Professionalism was the problem. The Board of directors of the Alberta Amateur Athletic Union suspended the amateur card of Taber's Leo Cook for the season. Another player named Piette of the Calgary Shermans then forfeited his amateur card and confessed that he had played professional hockey in Galt, Ontario under a different name.

In 1913 the Alberta championship started again. The Chefs were ordered to play the Calgary Shermans. Taber lost the only game 3-2. The previous turmoil caused Taber to go home and not play a second match. It now seemed that the Shermans would play the Edmonton Eskimos.

This time, Lloyd Turner, manager of the Shermans, refused to play the Eskimos. Turner felt it would be an injustice since Taber had already defeated Edmonton.

AAHA president Robert Pearson, decided that since the Shermans would not play; the Edmonton Eskimos were the 1913 Alberta champions. Turner then contacted "Deacon" White, manager of the Eskimos, to try and play the Eskimos in Winnipeg to determine a real champion. The Eskimos refused and on March 13, 1913, the club met the Winnipeg Winnipegs. The Eskimos lost their Allan Cup bid 18-8 in a two game total-goal series.

Taber had won the championship twice on the ice and had lost both times in the board room.

EDMONTON ARENA OPENS CHRISTMAS DAY — 1913

In his book *Edmonton Exhibition, The First One Hundred Years,* Tony Cashman wrote the following:

On Christmas Day 1913, some 2,000 fans, equivalent of 20,000 today, rode street cars to the east end for their bestever Yuletide treat. They were to see hockey on the biggest ice surface in Canada — 220' long, 40' more than the Thistle. Their view was unobstructed by the wire-mesh screen which protected the players from the fans. Fans in box seats looked down on the action from a "lordly" elevation of 6'.

Around 2:00 P.M. Harold Deeton dropped the puck for the first faceoff on the big ice, the ice that would be an operating theatre for men of heroic stature like Shore, Keats, Gagne, Colville, Reardon, Clovechuk, Hall, Ullman, Bucyk and others whose names are legend. One of the greats was on the ice for the opening faceoff. Barney Stanley was a defenceman for the Dominion Furriers, and in goal behind him was Court May, brother of famous-Flyer-to-be, Wop May. The Dominions were opposed by the Eskimos, owned by Deacon White and Shorty Campbell.

The Eskimos took a 1-0 lead into the dressing room but the Dominions came out rushing in the second half — that's correct, the second half — and won 4-2. And the fans went home to their turkey dinners taking with them the very first memories of a hockey game at the Arena.

The Edmonton Arena later became called the Edmonton Gardens.

* * *

Lloyd Turner arranged for the first professional hockey to come to Calgary in March 1913. It was an exhibition match between New Westminister and Vancouver of the Pacific Coast League. Six man hockey was played for the first time in Alberta.

New Westminster defeated Vancouver 10-8. The winners' line up included Dutch Lehman in goal, Rochon and Ernie Johnson on defence, Jimmy Gardner at centre, McDonald and Ken Maliam on the wings. Vancouver's goalie was Parr, Si Griffis and Fred "Cyclone" Taylor on defence, Frank Patrick centre, and Kendall and McDonald on the wings. Alberta teams continued to play seven man hockey until the 1920's.

Teams in 1913-14 were still not organized anywhere close to today's standards. Lineups were small and sometimes there was no coach. On January 6, 1914, the "Calgary Herald" reported that Mount Royal defeated the Calgary College 7-3.

(Douglas) Lougheed in goal for the University played the star game of the afternoon and his performance was worthy of an experienced net guardian. It looked at one stage of the last period that his play might have saved the day, but with clear ice before them the Mount Royal forwards found their way in.

It was said the University played enough combinations but at the wrong time. "This will no doubt improve under a coach." (Lougheed was the uncle of Premier Peter Lougheed. Calgary referred to Calgary College as the University. Calgary College applied to become a university but never succeeded.)

Hockey playoffs in this era were also difficult to organize. Transportation off of rail routes was difficult, but the lack of artificial ice remained a major problem. In January 1914, W.B. Sherman, owner of Calgary's Sherman Rink, indicated he intended to install artificial ice. The ice would be for skating and hockey in winter. In the summer it would provide ice for those with ice boxes. Although plans went ahead, no artificial ice was installed in Alberta for more than twenty years.

The number of teams in Alberta had increased enough to expand. The AAHA formed the intermediate level in 1913 and junior in 1914. The book is now divided into three separate sections to reflect these organizational changes. Cross-references are necessary in some years when intermediate would play senior to represent the province. Similarily, in the 1960's the Central Alberta League had teams from intermediate, senior and junior in the same league. Professional hockey is combined with senior.

CHAPTER 2
PROFESSIONAL AND SENIOR HOCKEY

Professional and senior hockey go together in this section because when one was strong the other was weak. Alberta did not always support them both at the same time.

Alberta has had five periods of professional hockey; in the twenties, the thirties, the fifties to the sixties and from the World Hockey Association in 1972 to the NHL in 1979. Teams in the first and last professional period competed for the Stanley Cup.

One of the reasons professional hockey died in the first two eras was that there was no artificial ice in Alberta. Had there been, the course of professional hockey in Calgary and Edmonton might have been very different. But, during the depression there was little enough money for pucks, let alone artifical ice and professional hockey.

The major achievement in Alberta hockey was the Edmonton Oiler Stanley Cup victory in 1984; the team repeated in 1985 and appears to be well on its way to a dynasty.

Senior hockey was the "original brand" in Alberta. Teams ranged from communities such as Olds, Turner Valley, Luscar, Drumheller, Lloydminster, Coleman, Lethbridge, High River and, of course, Calgary and Edmonton. Senior hockey teams competed for the Allan Cup. It was a most prestigious cup and became a truly community challenge. The best senior teams from each province played off; then, as the excitement mounted in each elimination round, all provincial champions played off to determine the best amateur club in Canada. The Calgary Stampeders, Edmonton Flyers and Drumheller Miners have each won the Allan Cup.

Senior hockey is dead in Alberta. The high cost of maintaining a senior club and the popularity of the professional game made it virtually impossible for it to stay alive. Although the name of today's game is youth and professionalism, senior hockey has had a colourful past in Alberta.

This part of the senior-professional hockey story begins in 1913-14 season because intermediate and junior hockey became official categories. Each part is done separately.

On February 23, 1914, the Edmonton Dominions played Medicine Hat in the Alberta Senior championship. At the end of the first thirty minute half the Dominion team was leading 7-1. Edmonton ran away with the Cup by winning the game 11-5. The Dominion lineup consisted of just seven players: Court May in goal, point McGovern, cover Lloyd Cook. rover Russell "Barney" Stanley (later Hall of Famer), centre Leo Cook, left wing Baird and right wing Manners.

Edmonton won the senior crown in the 1914-15 season as the Eskimos defeated the Calgary Vics 9-4 in the provincial final. The next round of Allan Cup playoffs was scheduled for Calgary; however, the Sherman Rink burned to the ground and caused the series to be moved to Regina.

The Eskimos played a sudden-death game against the Vancouver Black Brothers in Regina. The first half was played under B.C. rules and the second under the Alberta constitution. The Eskimos won a 12-11 shoot-out to earn the right to play the Winnipeg Monarchs.

Standouts for Winnipeg were Dick Irvin, Alex Irvin and Clem Loughlin. The Monarchs easily won the first game in Regina 9-3. Ice conditions were soft and slushy and the second game was moved to Moose Jaw where the Monarchs won the game 8-5 and the series 17-8.

FIRE DESTROYS CALGARY'S SHERMAN RINK

The Sherman Rink was built in 1904 and had a cement addition in 1907. It started out as a roller skating rink before it became a hockey rink and hosted events from prize fights to public forums. During the eleven years of use the Sherman was Calgary's main covered centre. But on February 24, 1915 all that remained on 17th Avenue and Centre Street was charred timbers, red hot iron and shattered concrete blocks.

The Sherman Rink fire was discovered by several members of the Crescent Ladies Hockey Club who were practising that fateful day. As soon as they smelled the smoke they rushed for the exits.

Photo courtesy of W.J. Oliver

Soon Lloyd Turner, manager of the rink, and his wife Hazel, learned of the fire. They occupied an apartment in the newer concrete portion of the Sherman. The Turners lost all of their personal belongings, including many hockey photographs, and a considerable amount of hockey equipment. Calgary's Monarch hockey team also lost $200 worth of equipment.

Total loss was estimated at $50,000. W.B. Sherman, owner of the rink, never reconstructed it. The Horseshoe Building became Calgary's next arena (Victoria Arena).

* * *

On December 31, 1915, James T. Sutherland, the new President of the Canadian Amateur Hockey Association, stressed that Canada had to concentrate on the war effort.

> *There can be no future security for our homes and loved ones until this is accomplished, and this gigantic task cannot be accomplished until every available man fits himself for the great and glorious effort. It takes nerve and gameness to play the game of hockey. The same qualities are necessary in the greater game now being played in France and on the other fighting fronts.*
>
> *The thousands of hockey players throughout the Dominion have all the necessary qualifications. Therefore, I earnestly urge all such to rally around the flag. With every man doing his bit, Canada will raise an army of brains and brawn from our hockey enthusiasts, the like of which the world has never seen. The whistle has sounded. Let every man play the greatest game of his life.*

Hockey continued in local leagues and few teams had aspirations of interprovincial playoffs. In the spring of 1916, Leroy Chown, President of the AAHA, awarded the Alberta Senior championship to the Edmonton Borden Bearcats by default. The Calgary Vics were the southern champs. The Vics had already spent more than $50.00 on a previous trip to Medicine Hat. To go to Edmonton, the Vics wanted a guarantee. The Bearcats said they offered $125.00 but the Vics claimed it was $80.00. The Vics ended up refusing, thus the Edmonton Bearcats were provincial winners.

Hockey was played in the armed forces. The 63rd Battalion defeated the 89th Battalion of Calgary for the Military Championship of Alberta.

No senior championship was held in 1917, but in 1918 a club called the Calgary All-Stars represented Alberta in interprovincial playoffs. It played against the Saskatoon Quakers in a three game total series. Calgary lost two games and still won the series 13-12 on a total point basis.

EDMONTON BORDEN BEARCATS 1915-16

Top row (l to r): W. Letson, P. Talbot, Frank H. Drayton (manager), George Bissett, Ira J. Stuart, H. Geddes. Bottom (l to r): D. Lynn, R. Davidson, Frank Drayton Jr. (mascot), Lou Grant, Joe Drussault. *Photo courtesy of Edmonton Archives*

In the first game, Herb Gardiner, Howard Dea and A.B. Cook led the All-Stars to an easy 7-2 win. Saskatoon avenged their loss when they outscored Calgary 6-3 and 4-3. Prominent in goal for Saskatoon was 16-year-old Charlie Hay, much later the President of Hockey Canada.

The All-Stars advanced to the Western Canada final against Winnipeg. In the concluding game of the three game total point series, Calgary won 4-3 and took the series 13-8. This was as far as Calgary could go that year. Nevertheless, no Calgary team had done so well in interprovincial play.

On November 11, 1918, World War I ended. On November 12, the "Calgary Herald" listed the war statistics. Up to and including October 31, 1918, the casualties totaled 34,877 dead from wounds and disease, 15,477 wounded, 152,799 presumed dead, 8,245 missing or prisoners of war; for a total of 211,358. Many of those were hockey players.

The flu epidemic of 1918 also proved to be disastrous in Alberta. From December 20th to December 30th, 1918 there were 10 deaths and 24 new cases reported in Calgary. It was also reported that some 45,000 cases of influenza had affected the citizens of Alberta. In Mundare, Alberta, it was believed that 95% of the citizens had been confined to bed because of flu.

Despite the effects of war and sickness, hockey revived quickly in Canada and Alberta.

The Armistice signalled the return of many hockey players to Canada from Europe. Dick Irvin, who had played for the Winnipeg Monarchs and would later play for the Calgary Canadians and Regina Capitals, and then coach the Toronto Maple Leafs and the Montreal Canadiens, wrote from Europe before the end of the war. Part of the letter from the November 18, 1918 "Calgary Herald" said,

> *At present, I am sitting writing on an old empty wine keg in a little French village. We are out in the morning at 5:30, feeding and watering our horses, then a breakfast of bacon, mush and tea. Then we drill or have some maneuvers of some kind, that is when we are not in action. Our meals are all very good and we get lots of cheese, jam and bread. I have no complaint to make and have never been real tired since I have been in the army. I don't know what some of the other fellows want. I think I could go out and play three 20 minute periods anytime.*

(After Dick Irvin's signature there was a post-script.)

> *I hear they are going to reinstate professionals who have gone overseas. Is it true? I hope it is as this boy would like another chance at the old Allan Cup.*

In November 1918, military authorities told the Exhibition Board in Calgary that the Horseshoe Building would no longer be required as a military base. The board decided to turn it into a rink and turned over management to Lloyd Turner. All proceeds were to be turned back to the Exhibition. The ice surface was a large 220' by 100'. It became the Victoria Arena.

VICTORIA ARENA (CALGARY ICE PALACE)

Photo courtesy of Calgary Exhibition and Stampede

Skating was popular at the Victoria Arena. On New Year's Eve, 1919, what was termed the largest skating crowd in the history of Calgary celebrated. It was said "the rafters even bulged".

At 9 p.m. a horde of people skated to a live band. After every six pieces of music Lloyd Turner's score of workers rescraped the ice with the assistance of a team of horses. At 11:59, two buglers from the troops stationed at the barracks blew the last post in honour of the men and women who had died. At the stroke of 12, the band played 'Reveille' and then 'Auld Lang Sang'. Cheers broke out and in the absence of something stronger, people toasted each other in the New Year over Aaron's hot coffee. The Victoria Arena, also known as 'Lloyd Turner's Ice Palace', was a popular place.

In 1919 the NHL Montreal Canadiens played in the Victoria arena in mid-March after their regular season. The Canadiens played against selected players from Calgary. The goalkeeper for Montreal was Georges Vezina. (This is the same Georges Vezina who had so much stamina he played 307 consecutive league and playoff games and fathered 22 children before his death in 1926. The Vezina Trophy is named for him.) The 4,000 spectators also saw Newsy Lalonde score five goals as the Calgary squad were defeated 12-1. The "Calgary Herald" reported that:

> They saw Newsy Lalonde in action at his best. With bursts of speed and superb stickhandling and cool, calculated attacks, Lalonde thrilled the fans.

In the 1920's Lalonde came out west to play in Saskatoon who competed against the Calgary Tigers and Edmonton Eskimos and Regina Capitals in professional hockey.

LETHBRIDGE VETS 1920-21

(The 1919-20 senior champions shown the following year.) Top (l to r): P.V. Lewis, G.V. Roger, W.S. Henderson, H. Paul, P.W. Henderson, G.R. Dixon. Bottom: F. Grant, Frank Boucher, G.E. Reber, J.H.C. McPhee. *Photo courtesy of Provincial Archives*

Hall of Famer, Frank Boucher, played for the Lethbridge Vets in 1919-20 while he was a mounted policeman. The Vets defeated the Edmonton South Siders to win the Alberta Senior championship. On February 28, 1920, the "Calgary Albertan" commented:

> When it is considered that they (Lethbridge) have had only seven workouts this season, have been off the ice for fully three weeks, and have had to play on a sheet of ice half the size of the Horseshoe Arena (Victoria Arena), their performance was indeed a surprise.

The star player of the game was Frank Boucher who went down the ice twice, pulled the goalie on each occasion and placed the puck in the net. The Lethbridge Vets were not members of Alberta's Big Four league, the forerunner of the Western Canada Professional league. Although Big Four teams were not officially professional, they did not enter Allan Cup playoffs. Instead, the Vets became Alberta's representative in the 1919-20 season.

The Vets travelled to Winnipeg where Fort William trounced them.

The following article on Frank Boucher was written by Jim Coleman in the "Calgary Herald" on March 8, 1951. Coleman is now retired from writing daily sports columns for Southam News across Canada and is doing public relations for Stampede Park and writes in the *Calgary Sun*. Coleman was inducted into the Canadian Sports Hall of Fame in 1985 as a builder.

THE STORY OF FRANK BOUCHER

BY JIM COLEMAN

All but his closest friends have forgotten that it was in Lethbridge that fearless Frankie Boucher, the manager of the New York Rangers, served his hitch with the Royal Canadian Mounted Police.

In the days when he could still see his own shoes over the edge of his stomach, fearless Frankie was inspired by the stories which he had read in Chums, the Boys Own Paper and the volumes of James Oliver Curwood.

Bolstering himself with a cup of coffee at Bowles Lunch, he strolled up the hill to the offices of the Royal Canadian Mounted Police and presented himself to the Commissioner.

"Sir," said Frankie, standing up so straight that the buttons popped off his jacket and struck the opposite wall like tracer bullets, "I wish to volunteer for service in your most dangerous outpost".

"Well, son", said the Commissioner kindly, "We're fresh out of dangerous outposts at the minute but I'll do the best I can for you".

So armed to the teeth, Boucher was sent to Lethbridge to bring the law to this uninhibited section of the country. On the train journey to the West, he kept his eyes open, searching for card sharks and other miscreants.

The porter parted the curtains at Boucher's berth to tell him to be ready to make his train connection at Medicine Hat and found himself staring down the barrel of a 45. The porter took off across the stubble and hasn't been seen again to this day.

Fearless Frankie was much surprised that no one shot a hole through his hat when he detrained at Lethbridge. But, swallowing his disappointment, he reported for duty at the local headquarters of the RCMP.

"Boucher of the Mounted, reporting for duty," he said, saluting smartly as he paraded before the detachment commander. "Where are the evil-doers? Let me at them."

"Gad, Boucher", said the officer, "but we're glad you arrived. You're just the man for us. There's a frightful situation here and you're just the man to clean it up."

With which, the detachment commander gave Frankie a curry comb, a pitchfork and a small wheelbarrow and escorted him to a building behind the office. In the building were 12 horses which nickered affectionately at Boucher.

"Horses", yelped Boucher in astonishment. "I thought they were things that hauled milk wagons."

"Yes, horses," said the officer gently. "We ride horses in the Mounted Police, you know."

Well a year later, Boucher of the Mounted still hadn't fired a single shot but he had learned all about the duties of a personal maid for 12 horses. He had worn out 3 curry combs, 4 pitchforks, and 2 wheel barrows. Over in the stable yard, there was a pile 20' high, which today, stands as a monument to Boucher's industry.

One morning he walked into the office, put his curry comb on the desk and said, "I'll have to resign Sir. My nerves can't stand this constant excitement. I think that I'm going to have a nervous breakdown."

And that, kiddies, is how fearless Frank Boucher became a great professional hockey player.

* * *

The Big Four of 1919-20 included the Calgary Canadians, Calgary Tigers, Edmonton Dominions and Edmonton Eskimos. The Eskimos won the league championship and then played the Moose Jaw Maple Leafs, the equivalent title holder in Saskatchewan. In the series' opener against Moose Jaw, a crowd of 5,000 watched Edmonton win 4-3 at home. Games two and three were played in Moose Jaw where the Eskimos won a pair 3-1 and 8-5.

Duke Keats and Barney Stanley played major roles for the Eskimos while Hal Winkler was outstanding in goal for Moose Jaw.

In the 1920-21 season the Big Four League consisted of the Calgary Canadians and Tigers and the Edmonton Eskimos and Dominions. None of these teams entered Allan Cup playoffs. In fact, Alberta's Allan Cup plans were dropped after Frank Patrick, President of the Pacific Coast League, charged that at least ten of the Big Four players were professional. Patrick put up $1,000 and dared anyone to prove him wrong.

Patrick had an agreement with the NHL. All players west of the Lakehead belonged to the PCHL. If Patrick could prove that Big Four players were professional, he could have them.

The Big Four was content to play in "no man's land". The league did not declare itself amateur or professional. Instead, it became an independent league. No one had any need or desire to challenge Patrick's claim and he kept his $1,000.

On December 29, 1920, the Big Four season started quietly enough. But it ended on one of the most controversial notes in Alberta hockey.

On February 11, 1921, the Edmonton Eskimos introduced Bill Tobin (later General Manager of the Chicago Black Hawks), in goal. Calgary protested. The Canadians and Tigers said that Tobin was not eligible because he had not fulfilled the residence requirements.

Big Four President Allan McCaw, Vice President Eddie Morris and J.A. Ross, a Supreme Court clerk in Edmonton, heard the evidence. Tobin had lived in Edmonton up until November 15, 1920, the eligibility date. After that day he had gone to Ottawa to work for the Soldier's Settlement Board. Calgary claimed Tobin had played some hockey while in Ottawa.

The protest was turned down. Calgary was not appeased and discussions continued. Edmonton agreed to replace Tobin with University of Alberta goalie Slim Morris; however, Morris declined because he wanted to retain his amateur status. Calgary refused Edmonton another goalie. President McCaw threw his hands in the air and ruled that the Big Four would terminate and that there would be no league champion.

The fans wanted a championship anyway. Tobin returned to the net for the "unofficial" championship of the Big Four. True to form the first game ended in a rhubarb when Duke Keats rammed Calgary's John Mitchell into the boards. The final score was 2-0 for Calgary.

The clubs were still fired up in the second game. Edmonton edged Calgary 2-1 to force a third game. Calgary became "unofficial champions" with a 3-2 victory.

ALBERTA PACIFIC GRAIN 1920-21

Top (l to r): D. MacKenzie, M. Pruden, H.G. McLeod, C. Thompson, J.F. Fraser, R.G. Gould. Middle: A.J. McTeer, Leo O'Grady, J.I. McFarland, R.G. LeBeau, L.J. O'Grady. Bottom: C. Reid (coach), C.M. Hall (vice-president), J.G. Capstick (president), H. Black (secretary treasurer).

Photo courtesy of Chris Cowman

The senior amateur championship of that 1920-21 season pitted the Calgary Alberta Pacific Grain team against the University of Alberta. Calgary high school student Cecil "Tiny" Thompson led the Grainmen to a 6-5 win in Edmonton, a 2-2 tie in Calgary and a 5-4 decision on neutral ice in Lacombe. The Calgary team did not compete in inter-provincial play.

PROFESSIONAL HOCKEY IN ALBERTA

The Big Four controversy in the 1920-21 season set the scene for the first professional circuit on the prairies. The Big Four boasted some of the most respected names in hockey. The Edmonton lineup included Bill Tobin, Joe "Bullet" Simpson, Howard Dea, "Duke" Keats, Art Gagne, "Red" Bridon, Anderson and Bob Muirhead. Calgary Tigers had Charlie Reid, Herb Gardiner, Gordon Fraser, Barney Stanley, Jocko Anderson, Hammie Baker, A.B. Cook and John Mitchell. Mervyn "Red" Dutton and Dick Irvin played for the Calgary Canadians. Many of these players jumped into the professional ranks the next year.

A secret meeting was held in Calgary on August 9, 1921. The Big Four was disbanded and the Western Canada Professional Hockey League was born. In late August, E.L. Richardson, manager of the Calgary Exhibition Board and President of the new league, announced that the league champion would play off against PCHL and NHL league winners. The WCPHL would play six man hockey and have an eight player roster (later that year lineups had nine players).

The original teams did not all start. The Edmonton Dominions and the Calgary Rovers dropped out before the season. The Calgary entry name was changed back to the Tigers. The Edmonton Eskimos joined as planned and the new entries were the Saskatoon Crescents (later called the Sheiks) and the Regina Capitals. Later that season the Saskatoon franchise moved to Moose Jaw and became the Orphans. The next season the team returned to Saskatoon.

The first regular 24 game schedule ended in a tie at 29 points each for Edmonton and Regina. An extra game was played before 6,000 fans in Edmonton. The Eskimos easily won 11-2 to win the 1921-22 pennant. The Capitals then played against the third place Calgary Tigers to determine a playoff finalist. Hockey in this era usually tended to have low scores. Regina continued this trend when they defeated Calgary 1-0 and tied the second game 1-1 to win the series 2-1 and reach the final.

It was thought that Edmonton would have no problem in the final. However, the Regina Capitals tied the Eskimos 1-1 in Regina. Dick Irvin scored for Regina and Joe Simpson replied for Edmonton. The final in Edmonton surprised the critics. The Edmonton Eskimos lost 2-1. George Hay and Amby Moran scored for the Capitals while Bob Trapp replied for the Eskimos.

The Regina Capitals became the first prairie league representatives in Stanley Cup playoffs. The Caps won their first semi-final match against the PCHL Vancouver Millionaires 2-1 in Vancouver. Hockey fever was high in Regina. However, the 6,000 fans in Regina saw the Caps lose their chance for the Stanley Cup final when they lost 4-0.

In 1922-23, the Moose Jaw Orphans went back to Saskatoon and became the Crescents. The Crescents also were known as the Sheiks because a popular song of the day was "The Sheik of Araby". Saskatoon owner, Bob Pinder, signed Newsy Lalonde from Montreal Canadiens for a reported $4,500 which was estimated to be twice as much as the NHL club paid.

Some rule changes were made to have the PCHL and WCPHL uniform. Some of the modifications were no team was to have more than eight players dressed for a game, sudden-death overtime was limited to twenty minutes, substitution during a game was only to be permitted after a whistle, kicking the puck was permitted however the puck could not be kicked into the goal. A penalty shot had to be taken from the point of the foul. The player shooting had to actually shoot and was not allowed to carry the puck. In a later announcement $500 was offered to any person who could give any information on any player under contract who agreed or conspired to lose a game.

Season tickets for Edmonton Eskimo hockey games were available at Joe Simpson's Sporting Goods Store, 10043 Jasper Avenue for a box of six at $125 and for four at $84. All other seats were $1.25, $1.00 and $.75 per night.

The Edmonton Eskimos before 7,000 fans at the Edmonton Arena, defeated the Regina Capitals 4-3 to win the WCPHL championship of 1922-23. The winning goal was scored on a penalty shot after 30 minutes and 25 seconds of overtime. Edmonton's Ty Arbour headed towards Regina goalie Laird. Laird rushed at Arbour and prevented him from getting a shot.

The referee, Eddie Poulin from Calgary promptly awarded a penalty shot. Duke Keats took the shot and scored Edmonton's fourth goal. This goal gave Edmonton the Western Canada Professional League championship. It is hard to imagine a penalty shot being called today in an NHL playoff game in overtime, at such a crucial time. The call in 1923 eliminated the Capitals.

The Eskimos departed for the Stanley Cup final in Vancouver. The Ottawa Senators from the NHL and Vancouver Maroons from the PCHL played first. The Senators won 5-1, giving them the right to play the Eskimos for the crown.

In game one, 6,000 spectators watched Cy Denenney of Ottawa breeze down left wing, side step Joe Simpson and score on Hal Winkler for a 2-1 Senator victory. Ottawa, in this contest, played a defensive game. It was said that the Eskimos skated rings around all Ottawa players except Frank "King" Clancy.

EDMONTON ESKIMOS — STANLEY CUP FINALISTS 1922-23

Top (l to r): **Bob Trapp, Art Gagne, Joe Simpson, "Duke" Keats, Ty Arbour, Hal Winkler. Middle: Bill Tobin, Johnny Sheppard, "Crutchy" Morrison, Reuben Brandow. Bottom: Abby Newell, Helgy Bostrum, Kenny McKenzie (manager), "Spiff" Campbell, "Kid" Scaler (trainer). (Missing from photo — Howard Dea.)** *Photo courtesy of Provincial Archives*

Edmonton scored the first goal when Ike Morrison took a pass from Joe Simpson and scored on Ottawa's Clint Benedict. At the 15 minute mark in the third period Hitchman intercepted a Duke Keat's pass and tied the game. Denenney then got the winner.

The second game ended 1-0 for Ottawa. Harry 'Punch' Broadbent shot from 40' out and beat Winkler in the first period for Ottawa's margin of victory. From this point on Ottawa played defensive hockey and won the Stanley Cup.

'King' Clancy did what no player has ever done in the Stanley Cup final. In the second period, of game two, Ottawa goalie Clint Benedict received a two minute penalty. Clancy played goal during the penalty.

Clancy recalled later, "As Benedict was skating to the penalty box, he tossed me his big goal stick, and said 'Take care of this place until I get back'." Clancy did not allow a goal.

Clancy played all six positions for the Senators in the Stanley Cup final. The Senator line-up had eight players plus a goalie. It is unlikely any one will ever duplicate this record.

The Ottawa Senators had other stars such as George Boucher and Eddie Gerard on defence and Frank Nighbour at centre. They not only won the Stanley Cup, but got a record "cleanup" for themselves. It was announced by Frank Patrick that Ottawa players would get $700 for participating in 6 games, Vancouver $310, and Edmonton $116. It didn't matter that Edmonton had reached the final. They got less because they only played twice.

Gordon 'Duke' Keats of the Eskimos was one of Canada's super stars. Deacon White, coach, organizer and promoter of Edmonton hockey and football wrote special articles for the Edmonton Bulletin. On February 27, 1924, he said of Keats:

> *At stickhandling and shooting, Keats is in a class by himself. He beats anything in the business with his accuracy and powerful shooting. He does not have to look up for the nets. He seems to sense the exact location of the goal and can shoot from any angle in which the puck may happen to catch him. To delay in shooting is fatal unless there is no opposition player near and well the Duke knows this. He smacks them in on the fly, backhand, or with his back to the goal, and he shoots for some open spot in the nets, not for the goal tender. Duke has no peer at passing and taking a pass and he has the uncanny sense of knowing exactly where and when to pass.*
>
> *Can you ever recall his doing the wrong thing, pulling a boner so to speak, such as shooting when the proper thing to do was to pass, or passing when he should shoot? He sure can size up situations, and he can turn on some speed too, when he sees an opening. He has the weight to bore in and to go through a defence. In short, the Duke from North Bay, Ontario, is a hockey wizard.*

The WCPHL of 1923-24 was incredibly close. Deacon White felt that the Edmonton Eskimos and the Regina Capitals were the best clubs but thought the Saskatoon Crescents or Calgary Tigers could win the league at any time. In the case of Calgary, White said:

> *They have a nice hockey team this year. They may not even get into the playoffs, but they should, because they have the class... it's hard to tell where their regulars end and subs begin.*

The Regina Capitals ended the season for Edmonton when they edged the Eskimos 3-1. This qualified Regina to meet the Calgary Tigers in the league final. The Tigers won the WCPHL crown when they shut-out the Capitals 2-0. They now advanced to play the Vancouver Maroons champions of the PCHL. The winner of this inter league series was to meet in the Stanley Cup final. The Calgary Tigers won the series but did not totally eliminate the Maroons.

These two teams ended up not playing to eliminate each other but to make more money. Both Vancouver and Calgary ended up in Montreal ready for the Stanley Cup final. Calgary earned a bye to play the Montreal Canadiens.

CALGARY TIGERS — STANLEY CUP FINALIST — 1923-24

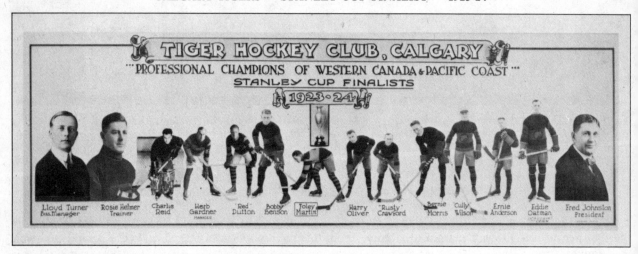

Left to right: Lloyd Turner (business manager), Rosie Helmer (trainer), Charlie Reid, Herb Gardiner (manager), Mervyn "Red" Dutton, Bobby Benson, Foley Martin, Harry Oliver, "Rusty" Crawford, Bernie Morris, "Cully" Wilson, Ernie Anderson, Eddie Oatman (captain), Fred Johnson (president).

Photo courtesy of Glenbow Museum

The Western final opened in Vancouver and the Maroons won 3-1. On March 12, 1924, in Calgary the Tigers thrilled 5,000 fans when they defeated Vancouver 5-3 to tie up the series. The final was moved to Winnipeg where the Tigers won 3-1 to win the series and apparently go to the Stanley Cup final. They went, but to their surprise, Vancouver also boarded a train for Montreal. Merv Dutton, in a 1984 interview said, ''We were amazed that Vancouver was to be included by the owners of the teams after we had beaten them.''

Montreal Canadiens defeated Vancouver two straight to meet the Calgary Tigers. The Tigers had only earned a bye when they defeated Vancouver. The Canadiens won 6-1 and in the second game it was 3-0, to give Montreal the Stanley Cup.

The first game was described as,

> *almost vicious, being played at blinding speed with the fans having very few dull moments from the time that Prime Minister Arthur Mieghan dropped the ceremonial puck to start the game until the conclusion.*

Numerous penalties were handed out by referee Art Ross. (Ross was later manager of the Boston Bruins and developer of the Art Ross goal nets.)

Ice conditions in Montreal, due to warm weather, were not considered satisfactory so the 3-0 second game was moved to Ottawa. After the series, Lloyd Turner, part owner and manager of the Tigers paid tribute to the Canadiens:

> *We are pleased beyond words at the treatment we have received during our stay in the east. I won't forget it. Leo Dandurand (owner of Montreal Canadiens) is a fine fellow and he has welcomed us and looked after us in fine style. We are naturally disappointed in losing out, but we have no complaints to make.*

It was typical of Lloyd Turner.

The complications for Calgary in earning a bye have to be recorded as one of the strangest professional playoffs.

EDMONTON ESKIMOS 1925-26

Back row: Leroy Goldsworthy, Barney Stanley, Duke Keats, Kenny McKenzie (manager), Ernie Anderson, Bobby Benson, Lloyd McIntyre. Front: Bob Boucher, Spunk Sparrow, Stuart, Art Gagne, Eddie Shore, Johnny Sheppard.

Photo courtesy of McDermid Studios, Edmonton

In the spring of 1925, the Calgary Tigers were defeated in the Western finals by the Victoria Cougars. Lester Patrick was in charge of the Victoria club. The Cougars went on to defeat the Montreal Canadiens and win the 1924-25 Stanley Cup. They were the last Western Canadian team to win the Stanley Cup until the Edmonton Oilers in 1983-84 and 1984-85.

The Calgary lineup for the Victoria series included Hal Winkler, Merv Dutton, Herb Gardiner, Reg Mackie, Rusty Grawford, Ernie Anderson, Emory 'Spunk' Sparrow, Harry Oliver, Eddie Oatman, Cully Wilson and Greg McFarland. Victoria had Clem Loughlin (later retired in Viking, Alberta) and super-star Frank Fredrickson in their lineup.

Representing the WCPHL in 1925-26, the Edmonton Eskimos entered into a two-game-total-goal series against the Victoria Cougars in Vancouver. The first game was won by Victoria 3-1 and the second ended 2-2 to give Victoria the series 5-3.

The second match in front of 5,000 fans was exciting. It appeared that Edmonton might win the series when Johnny Sheppard and Art Gagne scored to tie the series. Legendary Eddie Shore was at his best on defence for Edmonton but Victoria came on strong to win the game and series. Edmonton's lineup included Stuart, Barney Stanley, Eddie Shore, Art Gagne, Duke Keats, Johnny Sheppard, Spunk Sparrow, Ernie Anderson, Bob Benson and Lloyd McIntyre.

After this season the Western Canada Professional League folded. Many players from every team ended up in the National Hockey League. Finances were a problem as was the lack of artificial ice. But while the WCPL lasted it boasted some of the most exciting players in professional hockey (see Lloyd McIntyre's interview in the Hot Stove League).

Another pro circuit was started in 1926-27 called the Prairie Hockey League. It was not eligible to compete for the Stanley Cup like the previous WCPHL. The league included the Edmonton Eskimos, Calgary Tigers, Saskatoon Sheiks, Moose Jaw Maroons and Regina Capitals.

In the 1927 final the Sheiks won the opener of the final 2-1 over the Calgary Tigers. Calgary replied in the second game on two goals by "Spunk" Sparrow to win 2-1 in Calgary. Saskatoon was not pleased with the referee Harry Scott, so it went home even though another official, Carl Battell, was offered. The Tigers were declared league champions and a $1,500 fine was imposed on Saskatoon.

CALGARY TIGERS — WESTERN CANADA CHAMPIONS 1926-27

Top row (l to r): Norman "Dutch" Gainor, Irvine Frew, Gordon Savage, "Sad" Sam Timmins, Ronnie Martin, Pete Mitchell, "Buster" Huffman. **Bottom:** George Steward (president), Ferne Headley, "Spunk" Sparrow (captain), Ernie Anderson, Rosie Helmer (manager).

Photo courtesy of Calgary Exhibition and Stampede.

One more series against the Winnipeg Maroons was left for Rosie Helmer's Tigers. In play for the Merchants Casuality Trophy for the new Western Canada Professional Hockey title, Calgary Tiger's Norman "Dutch" Gainor and Ernie Anderson scored and they won 2-1. This turned out to be the final game as the Maroons of the American Hockey Association were ordered to finish off their own league. The last two series played by Calgary did not conclude. Every score was 2-1.

This officially ended pro hockey in Alberta until the 30's. On October 11, 1927 it was announced by the "Edmonton Fans Hockey Limited" at a meeting at Mikes' News, that difficulties during the 1926-27 season had caused the fans to try to assist the team. This group would not assist for the following year.

Pro hockey concluded in Calgary as well. A deal was made between E.L. Richardson, Manager of the Calgary Exhibition, S.G. Steward and Rosie Helmer. Helmer and Steward held Calgary's franchise and would now just operate the Victoria Arena in place of Lloyd Turner. Turner went to Minneapolis but would return to the Arena in a couple of years. Pro hockey would also return to Alberta in 1932-33.

SENIOR HOCKEY 1921-22...1932

During the time of professional hockey in the 20's, the seniors continued their quest for the Allan Cup. The Calgary Fourex became the senior champions of Alberta in 1921-22. The Fourex tied the Edmonton Hudson Bay Beavers at Edmonton Southside Rink. In Calgary, the Fourex and Beavers tied at 3-3 and overtime was necessary. Each club scored in the first overtime. Edmonton's principal hopes were lost when Sirr scored for Calgary in the second overtime for a 5-4 win and a total score of 9-8 after 140 total minutes of play.

Calgary Fourex gained 3-2 and 2-0 wins over the Vancouver Towers to win the B.C. — Alberta playoff 5-2. In the next round, the Regina Victorias secured an early lead and defeated the Fourex 6-2 in Regina. In the final game Regina won 10-3 for a total of 16-5.

In the fall of 1922, the AAHA decided not to enter Allan Cup playoffs. They felt that the clubs in Alberta were not competitive enough but probably the main reason was that the AAHA could not afford to guarantee the necessary fees for senior play. However, a change of mind took place and Alberta did compete. Blairmore Bearcats won the senior category when they defeated the Edmonton Southsiders 7-1 and 12-7 to win the round 19-8.

After winning the seniors, Blairmore then played the intermediate champion Calgary Hustlers for the right to go on in Allan Cup playoffs. The Bearcats experienced few problems as they defeated Calgary 8-3 in game one. The second game made it official that Blairmore went to Vancouver. The Crowsnest Pass club scored a 2-1 victory for a 10-4 series win.

Blairmore's crack team of amateurs defeated the Vancouver Young Liberals, the B.C. Senior Amateur champions, 4-3 in the first game. The Young Liberals came back to edge the Bearcats 3-1 and win the series 6-5. Starring for the Blairmore in the final game were Levasseur and Rennicka. The Bearcats were behind 3-0 when Rennicka scored in the third period but they could not tie up the series.

When Cecil "Tiny" Thompson played in goal in 1920-21 for Calgary's Alberta Pacific Grain, the team won the province but did not compete in interprovincial playoffs. Thompson got his chance in 1923-24 to play in the Allan Cup eliminations for the Bellevue Bulldogs. The Bellevue Bulldogs also had Norman "Dutch" Gainor who later joined the NHL.

The Bellevue Bulldogs qualified for the Western Allan Cup final when they defeated Melville Millionaires, the Saskatchewan champions, 3-0 and tied 3-3 to win the round 6-3. In the next round against the Selkirk Manitoba Fishermen. Bellevue proved to be strong on defence but did not show the necessary finish around the opposition's goal. The Fisherman won both games 3-1 and 4-0.

Cecil "Tiny" Thompson was a wizard in goal and kept Bellevue in contention. Mackie made many dangerous rushes while Jim Hanson was a strong back checker for Bellevue. Norman "Dutch" Gainor had the Selkirk defence "dizzy" as they tried to stop him. Merv Dutton recalled a radio interview where Clem Loughlin described Gainor in the NHL. "I don't know where Gainor is going and I sometimes wonder if Dutch does." Dutton spoke highly of Gainor's ability and said "Tiny Thompson was the best goalie who ever lived." People in the Crowsnest Pass still speak of Gainor and Thompson.

In 1924-25 the senior category title remained in the Crowsnest Pass region when the Coleman Tigers defeated the Edmonton Vics. The Tigers travelled to Vancouver and completely overwhelmed Rossland 13-5 in a two-game-total-goal series. Just like Bellevue the year before, the Tigers now reached the Western Allan Cup final.

Once again Alberta's champions travelled for a playoff. No artificial ice in Alberta was the reason. The Port Arthur Bearcats, Manitoba champions provided the opposition. Coleman grabbed a 4-2 victory in the first game. Speed, a set of forwards who could travel up and down the ice and a sound defensive system gave the Tigers the first win. The Albertans were then forced to take one player out of their lineup as he had been declared ineligible. In the second game, the Tigers were unable to cope and Port Arthur won 5-1 to take the series 7-5.

The 1925-26 Canmore Miners became senior champions when they defeated the Blairmore Coal Diggers in a two-game-total-goal series. The series appeared to be easy for Canmore as they won the opener 8-2. However, back in Blairmore, the Diggers replied 7-2 but lost the series 10-9 on total goals.

The season ended for the Miners in Vancouver. Canmore lost the series when they dropped the first game 4-2 and only tied the second 3-3.

Teams from outside of Edmonton and Calgary continued to dominate the provincial senior playoffs. Teams from Canmore, Blairmore, Coleman and Bellevue had good development programs for players. Other players were recruited to work in coal mine related jobs and fan support was intense.

The population of the following cities and towns in Alberta from the 1931 Canadian Almanac may help give a better idea about hockey interest and level of play in the smaller centers compared to the two major cities. The figures come from the 1926 census.

The six cities populations were as follows. Calgary 65,291, Edmonton 65,163, Lethbridge 10,735, Medicine Hat 9,536, Red Deer 2,2021 and Wetaskiwin 1,884. The towns of over 1,000 were Blairmore 1,609, Camrose 2,002, Coleman 2,044, Drumheller 2,578, High River 1,377, Lacombe 1,151, Olds 1,003, Ponoka 1,931, Taber 1,342, Vegreville 1,721 and Vermillion 1,203. Canmore was not listed.

Alberta and Canada had estimated populations of 660,000 and 9,934,500 in 1930. In High River in the 1928-29 provincial final, 1,300 fans attended. This would also include the many from the immediate farming area who also considered hockey as their best form of entertainment.

Canmore repeated as champions in 1927-28 when they defeated the Edmonton Superior Aristos 3-1 in each game of a two game series. Canmore had an edge in both games because of their back checking and tireless skating. The Canmore squad then defeated the intermediate champions from Lacombe to represent Alberta. In Vancouver for the second year, to represent Alberta, Canmore suffered defeats of 6-0 and 9-4. The shining lights in this final series for the Miners were the Jerwa brothers.

(It was not important at the time but the Edmonton Superior Aristos became the nucleus of the Edmonton Superiors, one of the top senior clubs in Alberta in the thirties.)

Canmore made it three senior titles in a row when they defeated Edmonton Maple Leafs 7-0 in game one and lost 2-0 in the second. Canmore were challenged by Lacombe the intermediate victors. Against Lacombe it appeared the intermediate division would finally represent Alberta. Goalkeeper Watt of Lacombe stopped 43 shots

Top row (l to r): Joe Jerwa, Frank Jerwa, Vic Riva, K. Oughton, Art Sihvon, John Bleskan. Middle: Joe Bleskan, R. Hawke (manager), Ron Mackie (captain), C.C. Scott (secretary treasurer), A. Jerwa. Bottom: Norman Wright.

Photo courtesy of Provincial Archives

and Riva of Canmore handled 45. However, the game ended as a 2-2 draw. In Canmore, the Miners won the second match 4-1 and went on to play Trail Smokeaters.

Trail won the first game 9-3 to take a six goal lead. The second game was more competitive. At the end of the first period, Trail led 3-2 and by the end of the second, it was 4-4. Trail got one more in the third to eliminate Canmore. For Canmore Riva, Wright and Sihvon played well against Trail.

The new B.C.-Alberta champions then played the Delisle Bulldogs. The Saskatchewan Allan Cup representatives lost 2-0 and 9-0 to the Smokeaters. In the future, five of the Bentleys from Delisle would play for the Drumheller Miners and the Trail Smokeaters became the World Champions.

A doctor in High River, Alberta, Dr. York Blayney played goal for the Flyers in 1928-29. Blayney was outstanding in helping the Flyers win the senior championship. High River defeated the Edmonton Maple Leafs 3-1 and 1-0 to win the series 4-1. (Dr. Blayney's son, Bruce practices medicine in High River today.)

High River then played the intermediate champion, Blairmore Bearcats. If the playoff had been a two-game-total-goal series as in the past, Blairmore would have been the first intermediate team to defeat the senior champions. Before 1,300 fans in High River, the teams played on a watery surface but the home team won 3-1. In the second game on better ice, Blairmore outhustled High River 9-1. This was a best-of-three and the third game was scheduled for neutral ice at Nanton before 1,500 fans.

The ice was covered with water ("Nanton Water") and it was difficult for the players. Both teams still played well, however, High River edged the Bearcats 4-3. The winning goal was scored by Arnold twenty seconds into the third period. Near the end of the game Blairmore fired shots from all angles at Blayney, however, the 'Doc' did not allow any more goals.

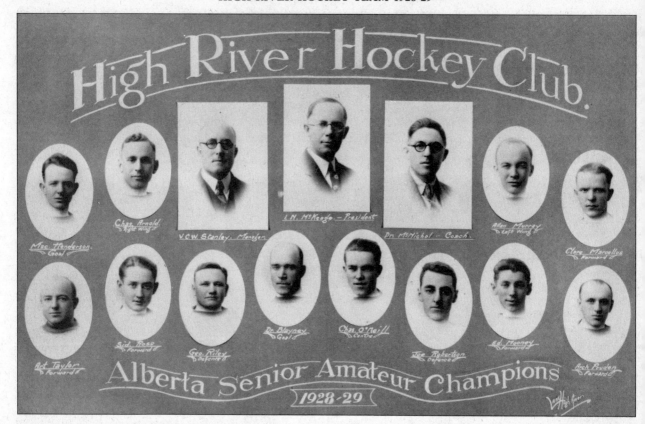

Top row (l to r): Mac Henderson, Chas. Arnold, V.C.W. Stanley (manager), L.N. McKeagle (president), D.R. McNichol (coach), Allan Murray, Clare Marcelles. Bottom row: Art Taylor, Sid Ross, George Riley, Dr. York Blayney, Chas. O'Neill, Joe Robertson, Ed Mooney, Archie Pruden.

Photo courtesy of Glenbow Archives

Over 2,500 fans attended the Victoria Arena in Calgary for the B.C.-Alberta final. Once again ice conditions were poor as a complete sheet of water made passing plays almost impossible. High River's fortune on poor ice ran out as the Trail Smokeaters defeated the Flyers 4-0 and 4-2 to win the round 8-2.

The Blairmore Bearcats continued southern Alberta's domination of senior hockey when they won the Alberta Senior championship in 1929-30. To reach the southern finals, Blairmore tied "Doc" Blayney and the High River Flyers 2-2 and won the second game 3-2.

In another southern round the Calgary Broncs won two straight, 2-0 and 2-1 over the Drumheller Miners. The Miners had an outstanding team which included Duke Wainman, Connie King and Tommy Anderson (an NHL Hart Trophy winner in the 1940's.) The Broncs then defeated Banff, the champion of the Rocky Mountain League 2-1 and 7-1 to finally play Blairmore in the southern final.

Blairmore completely surprised the Broncs when they scored an 8-1 win in the first game in Calgary. The Broncs returned to their playing form and won the second game 3-1, but lost the round.

In the north the Edmonton Superiors won a three game series over the Edmonton Imperials and then met the Lloydminster Elks. Jack and Roy Bentley were not enough for the Elks and they lost 2-1 and 3-1. The Edmonton Superiors and Blairmore then met in the provincial final.

The provincial final of 1929-30 was an outstanding series. In Blairmore, Jimmy Graham scored for the Superiors in the first minute of the game and it looked like it might be a rout. However, McKay from Tony Vejprava tied it up at one each and the score remained 1-1. Immediately after the game both teams took the same CPR train back to Edmonton. The second game went three overtime periods and stayed at 4-4. The third match was moved to Calgary where 4,468 fans from all over Alberta viewed a thrilling game. The Bearcats' Jimmy Kemp, scored at the eight minute mark of the third period to give Blairmore the 1929-30 senior title.

The Bearcats were eliminated in the next round of Allan Cup action by the Trail Smokeaters by two identical scores of 3-1. In the second game Blairmore got back in the series when Jimmy McVey scored first, but Trail replied three times to win the game and series.

Back row (l to r): J.V. McDougall (secretary treasurer), Alex McVey (trainer), Gordon McPhail (substitute goal), Robert Gray (president), W.W. Scott (manager-coach). **Middle row (l to r):** J. Dicken (centre), A. Vangotsinoven (defence), H.A. "Hughie" Manson (left defence), W. "Bill" Johnston (right defence), F.H. "Fred" McKay (right wing), J. "Puffy," Kemp (right wing). **Front row (l to r):** Tony Vejprava (left wing), Jack Oakes (centre), Dave Kemp (goal), Idris Evans (right wing), James McVey (left wing).

Photo courtesy of Gushel Studio, Blairmore

A city finally won the senior crown again in 1930-31. The Edmonton Superiors won the right to enter the provincial final when it edged the Drumheller Miners 1-1 and 3-0 in a total goal series.

Fans from every section of the Red Deer River Valley jammed the Drumheller Arena to witness the first match. Bob Crossland scored for the Superiors while Jack Bentley scored Drumheller's only goal. Other individual stars for Drumheller were Roy Bentley, Pete Lemiski and Norman Wright, while Jimmy Graham and Don Stuart (goalie) were outstanding for Edmonton.

The second game attracted 5,000 fans in Edmonton. The defensive unit of Duke Wainman and Tommy Anderson played well for the Miners, however Jimmy Graham scored twice and Buster Brown once in a 3-0 win. This allowed the 'Soops' to play Canmore Briquetters. Edmonton won both games over Canmore 5-1 and 3-0. In the last game Rollie Hills and Cam Smith paired up on the blueline to stop Canmore rushes for the shut-out while captain Jimmy Graham scored two of the three goals and assisted on the other.

The Trail Smokeaters finally met their match in the Edmonton Superiors. In game one, the Soops tied Trail 3-3. Kelly Walker celebrated St. Patricks Day scoring one while Bob Crossland and Bob McMillan got the others.

Edmonton hockey fans had the opportunity to hear a broadcast of the second game, but not in the usual manner we are used to today. John Michaels of Mikes' News had a line put in his business from the rink in Trail and play by play descriptions were given on loud speakers in front of the store. The broadcast was exciting as the Superiors won 3-2 as Jimmy Graham scored the first three goals of the game. Trail scored their second goal at 15:02 of the third period but Don Stuart stopped the rest of the shots. Clarence Campbell refereed the series.

Top row (l to r): Buster Brown, H. Dyer (secretary), O. Muckelston (vice-president), Ira Stuart (manager and coach), C. Gainer (president), Kelly Walker. **Middle row (l to r):** D.A. Gilles, Jimmy Graham (captain). **Bottom row:** Bob MacMillan, Cameron Smith, Pat O'Hunter (trainer), Don Stuart, Rollie Hills, Bob Crossland.

Photo courtesy of A. Blythe

The Western Allan Cup final was played in Winnipeg. Kelly Walker scored for the Superiors while Vic Linquist replied for the Winnipeg Winnipegs for a 1-1 tie. Ira Stuarts' Superiors were outmatched in the second game when Winnipeg shut them out 3-0. (The Winnipeg team name is not an error. There have been other teams called the Toronto Torontos, Regina Reginas and Fort William Forts.)

The Calgary Bronks became the Alberta Senior champions of 1931-32 when it defeated the Edmonton Superiors 2-0 before 2,500 fans in Calgary and 2-1 in front of 4,500 in Edmonton. The second game had its moments. Two minutes remained in the second period when the Soops Jimmy Graham fired a shot at Calgary's D.P. McDonald that seemed to go into the cage. The goal judge signalled a goal and the crowd roared their disapproval.

Calgary players claimed the goal did not go in. Referee Ken Paul, of Calgary, listened and agreed. Judge of play (today called a linesman) Edmonton's Clarence Campbell questioned the decision but could not overrule it. Despite the controversy, the Calgary Broncs won the Alberta crown.

Rosie Helmer's Broncs then defeated the Trail Smokeaters. The first game in Calgary ended 0-0 as both clubs relied on defensive ability. Over 5,000 fans watched a brilliant display of goalkeeping by D.P. McDonald as the Broncs eliminated the Smokeaters 2-0 in the second game. Dave 'Sweeney' Scriner and Harry Walshaw scored for the Broncs.

The Weyburn Beavers were outclassed by the Broncs 5-0 in the first game of the next round. In Weyburn the Broncs won the second game 6-1 to advance to the Western Allan Cup final.

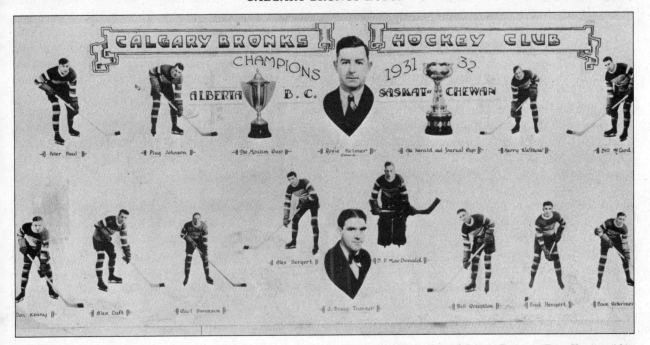

Top (l to r): Peter Paul, Plug Johnson, Rosie Helmer (coach), Harry Walshaw, Bill McLeod. Bottom: Don Kenny, Alex Cuft, Carl Sorenson, Alex Hergert, J. Bruce (treasurer), D.P. MacDonald, Bill Creighton, Fred Creighton, Dave Schriner.

The Fort William Forts defeated the Broncs 3-0 in the opener of a two-game-total-goal series. The Forts were favorites from the start as they had just defeated the Winnipeg Winnipegs, the 1932 World and Olympic Champions. In the second match the Forts continued to win as it shut-out the Broncs 2-0 to reach the Allan Cup final.

In the fall of 1932-33 the Edmonton Gainers' Superiors were Canada's representatives at the International Championship in St. Moritz, Switzerland and the Paris Cup in Paris, France. Edmonton's J.R. "Buster" Brown was a member of the team. Buster also represented Canada at the 1932 Summer Olympics in Los Angeles and ran on the same sprint relay team as Percy Williams. His brother, Joe, was a member of the Superiors and later played in England and for the Kirkland Lake Blue Devils, Allan Cup champions. Buster retired in 1972 after 42 years at Gainers. The Superiors were the first Alberta team to play international hockey. Seventy-five year old "Buster" describes this European hockey adventure in the following article:

EDMONTONS' GAINERS' SUPERIORS

BY J.R. "BUSTER" BROWN

We left Edmonton, November 13, 1932, from the old CP railway station on 109th Street and Jasper Avenue. The "Soops" as we were called were to visit Great Britain, France, Belgium, Poland, Czechoslovakia, Germany, Switzerland, Norway and Italy. Very few of us had ever been outside of Alberta. We started on our three month hockey tour. At the station about 200 people (friends, relatives and a few fans) gathered to wish us good luck. The Alberta Amateur Hockey Association was represented by its President, Dr. W.G. Hardy and Secretary George Lynch. The Edmonton Hockey Association was represented by George Mackintosh and Secretary Clarence Campbell.

We sailed from Montreal on the Duchess of Athol and landed in Glasgow on November 27, 1932. None of us had ever been on a ship this size before. The first day on the boat we intended to keep in shape by running, skipping and exercising. The rough waters cancelled any such notion as nearly everyone was seasick and a few spent the entire trip in bed. Captain Jimmy Graham, Harry Brown (no relation) and my brother Joe Brown hardly ate a meal for several days. When we got half way to England we really found out the vessel's nickname was the "Rocking Duchess". No one had to tell us about how it got its "monicker".

All of us on the Superior team worked. Six of us were employed at Gainer's at 96th Street and 80th Avenue (Bob Crossland, Jimmy Graham, Joe Brown, Buster Brown, Harry Brown and John Lammie). Pal Power and Don Stuart worked at Imperial Oil, Bill Montgomery was a school teacher from Strathcona Commercial, Ira

Stuart from Stuarts' Mens' Wear, on Jasper between 101st and 102nd Street, Kelly Walker a travelling shoe salesman and Bob McMillan was an auto mechanic.

We were happy to have a few months off and take the trip of a life time. If I remember correctly, the firms everyone worked for helped with the wages. Gainers made up any difference plus the cost of the trip with the CAHA. Cliff Gainer, President of our team and Pat O'Hunter, our trainer who worked for CNR, also accompanied the team. This was indeed a small group compared to teams now going to Europe. Two forward lines, two defencemen, one extra forward, one extra defenceman and a goalie comprised our roster.

The trip was awarded to us because of the Superiors record as an established team. Two seasons before we had beaten the Trail Smokeaters in Trail with Clarence Campbell as referee. The crowds in Trail were very hostile causing Clarence to have to be escorted off the ice between my dad (Bill Brown) and John McIntyre. McIntyre, sho used to be a boxer, used some of his skills on a couple of fans. Needless to say, Clarence got safely to the dressing room. In 1931-32 the "Soops" reached the Alberta Senior final.

Our first games overseas were in Glasgow, Scotland. We got off the ship about 12:00 noon and played at about 8:00 p.m. the same day. "Dazzle, stickhandling, amazing speed, and wonderful team work by the ice hockey masters from Canada" were some of the compliments given the Gainers Superiors in the "Glasgow Daily Record" of November 28, 1932. Bob Crossland, who was our best stickhandler and goal scorer, was recognized immediately by the media for his skills. Another paper, the "Glasgow Bulletin" of November 28, 1932, described Bobby as a "slim slip of a boy, can only be described as a crazy stickhandler. He gets the puck on the end of his stick, weaves the stick in and about when surrounded by opponents. They simply can not get him." He used a short stick in both length and blade. He was one of the few players I ever remember at that time, who tailor-made the manufactured stick to his own liking. Crossland resembled Gretzky as I think back of his style and slim appearance. Whenever someone hit him he was always able to get up and get going again.

SUPERIORS IN ST. MORITZ, SWITZERLAND 1933

**Back (l to r): Pat O'Hunter (trainer), Jimmy Graham, Joe Brown, Bob Crossland, Harry Brown, Don Stuart, Kelly Walker.
Front row: Pal Powers, Bob McMillan, John Lammie, Cliff Gainer (president), Ira Stuart (coach), Buster Brown, Bill Montgomery.**

Photo courtesy of Edmonton Archives

Compared to most of the teams in Europe, we had better puck handling skills and seemed able to recognize open spots on the ice to move to and to pass the puck to. Passing at this time had to be horizontal (across the ice) on the whole rink. Our team had good morale with Don Stuart, Harry Brown, and John Lammie leading the way. In Great Britain the rinks were smaller in ice surface size than Canadas' which suited our stickhandling style of play. In Europe, most of the rinks had a larger ice surface than Canada or Great Britain. The line I played on — 'The Three Browns' — were quite able to adjust to the larger rink size as were the rest of my fellow players.

I remember the Palais des Sports in Paris where 14,000 saw us split two games against the French team. The ''French'' team consisted mainly of French Canadians brought over by Jeff Dickson, the owner of the Palais. In the second game, which was our only loss on the whole tour, we were defeated 3-0. The second game was rough by European standards and to the European writers and fans. Chairs, hats and boots littered the ice during one point of the game. The European edition of the Chicago Sunday Tribune of December 18, 1932, said Pal Power was ''out to kill, ramming all and sundry into the boards. He tried to smash Moussette but the little Ottawa star dodged and sent him spinning with a neat leg trip.'' Some fans had to be escorted out of the rink. Both teams were mainly Canadians and it wasn't much more than a normal game. We won the Paris Cup when we defeated the Massachusetts Rangers 2-0.

We played one game in Prague, Czechoslavkia, before an outdoor crowd of at least 10,000 people. Bob Crossland, Harry Brown and I scored in a 3-0 victory. Very high bleachers surrounded the rink. The Czechs were good skaters and had good size. In all places we played, the crowd cheered for both sides.

We got to the International Championship in St. Moritz. It was beautiful, the sun was out, and yet it wasn't melting. It was perfect for outdoor sports. Throughout most of the European tour, Sonja Henie, Olympic Ladies' Figure Skating Champion dropped the puck at centre ice to start many of the games. Sonja and her mother joined our team for many special events and meals.

The Gainers' Superiors were the favorite team in St, Moritz. We stayed at the Carlton Hotel. It was a real posh place. We had to wear a ''tux'' for supper every night at this hotel. We were lucky as the CCM people in Winnipeg who outfitted our team, advised us to have a tuxedo, otherwise we would miss out on various functions. In Great Britain, France and Switzerland we had to war our tuxedos at various times.

The games at the 1933 St. Moritz Tournament were easier than most of the exhibition games. Our final game was against the Czechs who did not lose a game until they played us. Our hockey team played 38 games in Great Britain and Europe, winning 34, tying 3, and losing 1. The team was kept busy playing to crowds of up to 16,000.

All of us were really proud to have Ira Stuart for a coach. We were glad Cliff Gainer came. Besides playing hockey and winning most of our games, we went to a few night clubs like the Follies or the Lido. A few times we would order food and refreshments and send the tab over to the fellow sitting at the next table with some of our players. That fellow was Cliff Gainer.

PRO HOCKEY RETURNS BRIEFLY

Professional hockey returned to Alberta at the start of the 1932-33 season. The Edmonton Eskimos, Calgary Tigers, Saskatoon Crescents and Regina Capitals formed the Western Canada Hockey League. The league did not compete for the Stanley Cup like the previous pro circuit of the 1920's. The Caps folded during the season and became the Vancouver Maroons.

EDMONTON ESKIMOS 1932-33

Left to right: Ernie Kenny, Chubby Scott, Cam Smith, Ollie Redpath, Hoot Gibson, Duke Keats, Ade Johnson, Earl Robertson, Art Gagne, Joe Thorsteinson, Buster Huffman.

Photo courtesy of Provincial Archives

The final of 1932-33 took six games to settle. The Edmonton Eskimos won three, tied two and lost one against the Calgary Tigers. League president E.L. Richardson ordered the series to terminate in the sixth game even if a double-header was necessary. No artifical ice was in Alberta and weather conditions were spring-like. It was determined that three wins would be enough. Only one more game was required, as Art Gagne scored one goal in regulation time and another after four minutes of overtime from "Duke" Keats to give the Eskimos the championship of the WCHL.

The 1932-33 professional hockey attendance and gate receipts in Edmonton and Calgary amounted to peanuts when compared to the NHL. In 21 games in Edmonton, including playoffs, 67,755 fans paid $33,110.00 while in Calgary attendance for 15 games was 34,050 who payed $17,947.00. Of the total revenues, 10% went to the provincial government while the rink in Edmonton took 25% and Calgary's arena got 20%.

In the final playoff game on March 25, 1933, the Edmonton Eskimos drew their largest crowd; 6,061 who payed $2,977.00. Calgary's largest crowd of the season was on December 26, 1932 when 4,107 fans payed a total of $2,143.00. Today the Edmonton Oilers and Calgary Flames sell out their rinks for every game. No official figures are ever released but it is estimated each team, in gate receipts alone, grosses $300,000.00 per game or 100 times a professional game in 1932-33. Radio, television, novelties and advertising are additional revenue.

In 1933-34, the professional circuit was called the North Western Professional League. The Tigers and Eskimos from Alberta, played against the other league members who were the Seattle Sea Hawks, Vancouver Lions and Portland Buckeroos.

The Calgary Tigers won the league in regular season play. In playoffs the Edmonton Eskimos lost two straight to the Vancouver Lions and were eliminated. Calgary Tigers won the best-of-five final against the Vancouver Lions in the fifth game when they defeated the coast city 6-1 in Vancouver. All games were played in Seattle and Vancouver because they had artificial ice.

CALGARY TIGERS 1933-34

Top (l to r): Leo Coupez, Ralph Blyth, Red McCusker, Smokey Harris, Hurd. Bottom (l to r): Max Sutherland, Bill Hutton, Dutch Gainor, Ernie Anderson, Gordon Savage, Johnny Houbregs. *Photo courtesy of Calgary Exhibition and Stampede*

The following season in late February 1935, the Edmonton Eskimo hockey team disbanded as a result of internal difficulties in the NWPL. President Gordon D. Leetch of Portland announced that Portland and Vancouver would not make their last scheduled trip to Alberta. This caused Edmonton to fold first and the Calgary Tigers right after.

The reasons given for cancelling the trip were that Calgary could not meet its guarantees to visiting teams from the coast and Edmonton was unwilling to give any extra to take care of any deficits. Another major reason was still that Alberta did not have artificial ice. This caused the coast teams concern over coming so far and maybe not being able to play. The depression itself could also be listed as a reason for the end of pro hockey in Alberta. Professional hockey did not return to Alberta until the 1950's when the team names became the Calgary Stampeders and Edmonton Flyers.

SENIOR HOCKEY 1933...1949-50

While professional hockey was being played in Alberta, the senior category continued. In the spring of 1933, the Edmonton Superiors returned from Europe and won the Alberta Senior championship over the Calgary Broncs. The final game appeared to be over as the Superiors were ahead 3-1 and only 20 seconds remained. Some of the players were headed for the dressing rooms when Calgary's Dave Schriner scored. Bill Creighton then scored for the Broncs five seconds before the end of the game. The 3-3 tie was broken when A. Palister "Pal" Power scored for the Superiors to give Edmonton the Alberta Senior title in 1932-33.

EDMONTON SUPERIORS 1932-33

Photo courtesy of Alf Blyth Studio, Edmonton

In the next round, before 5,500 in Edmonton and 4,000 in Saskatoon, the Superiors were eliminated from Allan Cup play by the Saskatoon Quakers. Cooney Wood, the Quaker goal tender, proved to be a stumbling block as the Superiors lost 3-0 in the final game in Saskatoon. (The Quakers went on and lost the Allan Cup final to Moncton Hawks. Including this 3-0 game, Wood earned 6 successive shutouts, including three scoreless games. Total shutout time was 418 minutes.) The 'Soops' pressed only to have Elmer Piper break away late in the third period and slide the puck past Don Stuart to cinch the series. The only altercation for referee Clarence Campbell to handle were penalties given to Edmonton's Joe Brown and Saskatoon's Hobb Wilson for cross-checking and slashing in the second period.

The Luscar Indians became the 1933-34 senior champions when they eliminated the Edmonton Superiors and Drumheller Miners. The Indians carried Alberta's colors in Allan Cup playoffs when they defeated Jimmy Rodger's Miners two straight, 4-3 and 6-2 in the best-of-three. Bob Kennedy scored four goals for Luscar in the deciding game.

In almost all the playoff games, Luscar played away from home. Transportation to Luscar was available but it was considered out of the way and too far for the usual home-and-home series. The B.C./Alberta playoff in 1933-34 was played in Calgary.

Luscar and the Kimberly Dynamiters wore similar red sweaters and arrangements had to be made to borrow sweaters from a Calgary commercial club. This confusion caused a recommendation to be made that teams competing in future Allan Cup play have a home and away set of sweaters. The B.C. champions blanked the Luscar Indians 3-0 before 2,500 fans in the first game. Art Mackie scored all the Kimberly goals. In game two, the Indians edged the Dynamiters 4-3, but lost the two-game-total-goal series 6-4.

The Edmonton Superiors came back in 1934-35 to win another Alberta Senior championship. Edmonton then played the North Battleford Beavers, a team considered to be one of the best in Western Canada at the time. The Beaver roster, which included Elmer Piper, Vic Myles, Eddie O'Keefe, Les Schwab, won two of three games from the Superiors.

EDMONTON SUPERIORS 1934-35

Top row (l to r): O. Muckleston, C.E. Gainer, J. Anderson, J. Lammie, Robert (Bob) Crossland, W. Montgomery, Ira Stuart (manager), Joe Brown, L. Grove, Gordie Watt, Jimmy Graham, Lloyd McIntyre (coach), P. O'Hunter. Bottom: A. McNab, P. Faulder, Buster Brown, Buz Jones, A. Purcell, Don Stuart.

Photo courtesy of Edmonton Archives

LUSCAR INDIANS 1935-36

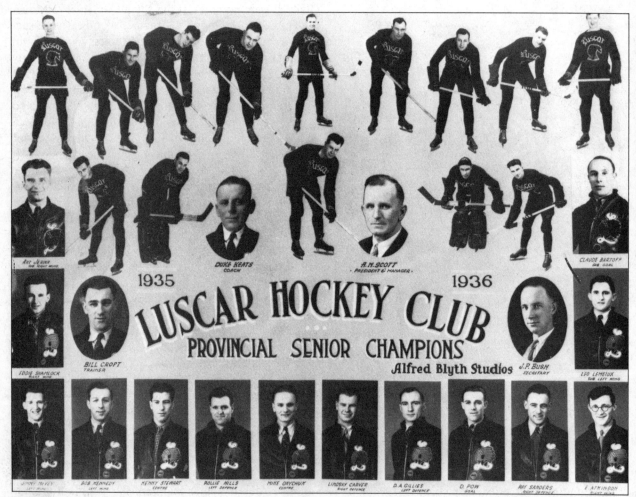

Top row: Art Jerwa, Duke Keats (coach), A.N. Scott (president and manager), Claude Bartoff. Middle row: Eddie Shamlock, Bill Croft (trainer), J.P. Bush (secretary), Leo Lemieux. Bottom: Jimmy McVey, Bob Kennedy, Kenny Stewart, Rollie Hills, Mike Onychuk, Lindsay Carver, D.A. Gilles, Dave Pow, Ray Saunders, E. Atkinson.

Photo courtesy of Blythe Studios

In 1935-36, Luscar Indians and Edmonton Superiors continued their battle to represent the north. This time A.N. Scotts' Indians took the north and in the provincial final defeated Coleman. The coach of Luscar was Frank Coulson who took over after "Duke" Keats went east to assist the Boston Bruin organization.

Calgary was originally slated to hold the next playoff round between Luscar and Prince Albert Mintos. (Calgary now had artificial ice.) However, Prince Albert raised an exceptionally large $1,400.00 guarantee to hold the first game. The largest crowd in the history of Prince Albert to this time, 3,500, watched the Mintos down the Indians 6-3. Officials Ike Morrison of Mossbank, Saskatchewan and Clarence Campbell of Edmonton called only four penalties.

A crowd of 4,000 in Calgary watched the Mintos defeat the Indians 6-5. The Indians were crippled by illness and injuries to players. Mike Onychuk was sent to hospital and Lindsay Carver was moved to centre. This left Rollie Hills and D.A. Gilles on defence. Hills was also injured in the second period of the second game and could not finish the match. Jack Dundas of Prince Albert broke a 5-5 deadlock when he shot the puck past Dave Pow to give the Mintos the series.

After the series, Bill Lewis of the "Edmonton Bulletin" said:

Lacking competition in their own sector all season, Luscar still was able to come down out of the mountains and whip the Superiors and Coleman Canadians in turn, thus clinching the provincial championship...This is an achievement of which manager A.N. Scott and all his boys may well be proud, for it shows that the club must be better than the opposition they met by quite a good percentage.

Edmonton still did not have artificial ice which caused Lewis to write:

Hampered by the lack of artifical ice here in Edmonton, fans are forced to go to Calgary to see any of the outstanding playdown games they care to witness and there will be scores of them on every train, bus and car that is southward bound tonight and tommorrow. Lloyd Turner has certainly showed the way to other hockey promoters in the west with his artificial plant in the 'City of the Foothills'.

LAUREL AND DALE HARNEY

Photo courtesy of Edmonton Archives

LAUREL HARNEY THE MAGICIAN

In the Laurel and Hardy movie "Going Bye Bye" (1934) Ollie (the fat pompous one) says to Stan (the skinny dumb one), "Another fine mess you've gotten me into! Why don't you do something to help me?"

That is exactly what goaltender Laurel Harney should have said to his teammates on the 1936-37 Drumheller Miner team when the Edmonton Superiors peppered Harney with 105 shots in a regular league game on January 17th, 1937.

Laurel Harney's son Dale is one of Canada's most talented magicians. But on that night in the Drumheller arena the elder Harney was pure magic. He stopped all but four shots. Since his teammates scored five times, the Miners won the game and regained sole possession of third place in the Alberta Hockey League.

Laurel Harney is 77 today. Although he remembers the game, he claims that he had so many shots he did not have time to count them.

* * *

When Calgary got artificial ice for 1935-36 it solved a big problem in "chinook country". It meant that Calgary could attract championship hockey and big revenue late in the season. The artificial ice did not come soon enough to save the professional league in the 30's, but it certainly was a boost to amateur hockey.

Top row (l to r): Albert "Scotty" Munro, Walter Hunter (manager), Lefty Grove (playing coach), Lloyd McIntyre (assistant coach), Sandy Robertson (secretary treasurer), Fred Layetzke. Third row: Harold Sutton, Pat O'Hunter (trainer), D. "Casey" Jones (assistant trainer), Stan Moher. Second row: Bill Gauf, Doug Hargraves, Lefty Grove, Lorne Robertson (mascot), Peter Rule, Tom Brant. Bottom: Albert Darkes, Jerry Brown, Danny McLeod, Bob Haxby, Jimmie Anderson, Andy "Shorts" Purcell.

Photo courtesy of Edmonton Archives

On February 20, 1937, Jack Kelly of the "Edmonton Bulletin" reported that,
for the first time in history, the Allan Cup Hockey Finals would come to Alberta. Dr. W.G. Hardy, Senior Vice President of the CAHA announced that Calgary would be the "lucky" city and the dates would be April 6th, 8th, 10th, 12th, and 14th, 1937. In addition to making history by bringing the Dominion Finals to this province, the CAHA decided the series would be a three of five games, instead of the previous two of three. Not only does Calgary get the Allan Cup games, but also has the Western Finals of March 26th, 27th and 29th.
This choice plum comes to Calgary simply because it is the only city in the Prairies with enough enterprise to put in an artificial ice plant. Saskatoon is now assured, however, of having a modern artifical arena by next winter, and it will be in time to get some mighty attractive playoff hockey.
Lloyd Turner and the Calgary group were considered to be the leaders in hockey at this time. Calgary's artificial ice was admired by everyone associated with the game.

The Edmonton Dominions advanced to the provincial senior final of 1936-37 when they defeated the Drumheller Miners 3-2 in the third and deciding game of the playoff series for the Alberta Senior Six championship, before 5,000 fans at the Edmonton Arena. The teams played on a watery surface which caused Andy 'Shorts'

Purcell, of the Dominions, to think his club "should also claim the water polo title". In the provincial final the Dominions defeated the Coleman Canadians from the Crowsnest Pass League 4-0 in the third and deciding game played in Calgary. The Dominions then fought the Nelson Maple Leafs in a series that included 119 minutes of scoreless hockey.

The fans in Nelson got top play for their money. After three overtime periods of ten minutes each, 14 penalties, and a lot of hard checking, the first match eneded 0-0. For goal tenders Albert 'Scotty' Munro of the Dominions (no relation to Roderick "Scotty" Munro) and McKay of Nelson, it was a long night. It was one breakaway and power play after another. The teams then went to Edmonton to finish the series.

The goal keepers were in terrific form. No goals were scored for 119 minutes (including 90 minutes in the first game). Culley of Nelson finally scored to give Nelson the lead. So far the Dominions had not scored; however at 12:44 of the third period, Jimmy Anderson tied the game. It had taken Edmonton 142 minutes and 44 seconds to set up their first goal to tie the series. 'Shorts' Purcell then scored the winner for the Dominions for a 2-1 win. A Nelson win in game three would have called for a fourth game because of the first scoreless draw. However, the Dominions came through and defeated Nelson 5-4 to advance against the North Battleford Beavers. After the long demanding series with Nelson the Dominions were outscored 4-2 and 15-3 by the Beavers.

The Calgary Rangers became the 1937-38 Champions of the Alberta Senior Six Hockey League when they defeated the Drumheller Miners 6-2 and 5-2 after being held to a 1-1 draw in game one. The final for the province took place at Mountain Park, Alberta, where the Calgary Rangers met the Luscar Indians in the first game. This was the first provincial playoff game in the Coal Branch area of Alberta.

Bob Mamini, sports editor of the "Calgary Herald" described the first game of the Luscar-Ranger series in Mountain Park in the March 9, 1938, Herald:

> The Rangers didn't take kindly to the idea of being ordered to the Coal Branch to open the series. 'King' Kelly, who handled the team from the bench, believed that it would be the last time the Provincial finalists would have to make the long trip. Monday's game was the first important contest, citizens of Mountain Park, Luscar and Cadomin have seen (this particular year). The Indians have had few games this season. Their last was on January 21, 1938 but they managed to keep in fighting fettle to be the team that has provided some of the toughest league competition ever offered in Alberta's senior rinks.
>
> The travelling takes a lot out of a team for a championship contest. There is the trip to Edmonton, a 3 hour sprint westward...and then to Edson and then Luscar...It's a steady uphill grind to Mountain Park. The last 9 miles takes you up 1,000' and the players just have time to dress for the game which starts at 8:00 p.m. Built by the Miners on volunteer labor, the Mountain Park Rink on the valley bed, is 6,000' above sea level. A series of steps leads to the hotel at 6,200', where around the corner and up another grade is Joe's Lunch, 6,300'. That was as high as any of the Rangers went. Coal Branchers live highly and don't mind working deep down. They like their hockey too. John Gerlitz, who played baseball and football for Calgary teams, volunteered the information that it took $5.00 (including transportation) to see the game, going from Cadomin. Admission was $1.25 and there were about 800 fans. There is no motor road in, but Coal Branchers own 150 cars to run over their 18 miles of road. Like their rink, most of the road was built by the miners. It would take another 16 miles to connect the sector with the highway leading to Jasper. They are also proud of their coal, which they say is the best in Canada. Their hockey team is also pretty fair.

Back in Calgary, the Rangers defeated the Luscar Indians in the final game 5-1 to win the 1938 Alberta Senior Hockey championship.

The season took a quick and dramatic turn as the Trail Smokeaters, coached by Elmer Piper, defeated the Rangers 7-0 in game two. The Rangers lost game one 5-0 at Trail. This placed the B.C. team in the Western Canada semi-finals. Duilo "Duke" Scodellaro, in goal for Trail, performed flawlessly and earned his fifth shutout in seven playoff games.

ALBERTA SENIOR SIX HOCKEY STATISTICS 1937-38

LEGUE STANDINGS

	Points
Calgary Rangers	41
Edmonton Dominions	34
Drumheller Miners	32
Olds Elks	28
Edmonton Superiors	13
Calgary Broncs	8

FIVE BENTLEY BROTHERS

Left to right: Roy, Scoop, Reg, Doug and Max.

Centre Max Bentley, the "Dipsy Doodle Dandy" of Delisle, Saskatchewan, played for Drumheller Miners in the 1937-38 season. He scored 28 goals and 15 assists for 43 points to lead the league. Teammate Bob Kennedy (formerly of Luscar Indians) had 40 points. 'Shorts' Purcell and Lefty Grove of the Edmonton Dominions had 38 and 36 points respecicely. Wilby Lennox of the Rangers had 34 points to finish in the top five for individual scoring. Max Bentley was also voted MVP among the four southern teams of the Alberta Senior Six Hockey League. On the eve of his 18th birthday, Bentley received the Gordon Efficiency Medal.

In late March, 1938, it was announced that five Bentley brothers would join the Drumheller Miners for the 1938-39 season. Drumheller had already acquired Roy, Scoop and Max from Saskatchewan. The new recruits were Doug and Reg. Drumheller could have had a full team of Bentleys; unfortunately, the oldest brother Jack retired and went farming in Delisle.

The Bentleys also had seven sisters. Four of them were older than the boys and all of them were talented hockey players.

In *Hockey Heritage: 88 Years of Puck Chasing In Saskatchewan* (1983), co-authors Brenda Zeman and Joe Zeman include the following by writer Stan Fischler (p. 337):

>...the Bentley brothers would play regularly against the Bentley sisters by NHL rules. Poppa Bentley, who loved his sons as much as any father, refereed those games. 'My girls' hockey teams,' says Poppa Bill, 'could beat the blisters off the boys nine times out of ten.'

When the Drumheller Miners played, the opposition always had trouble checking the Bentleys. However, Don McKay CJCJ (later CKXL) of Calgary and Gordon Williamson CFRN Edmonton had the chore of broadcasting. The odd time they would slip and say "Bentley to Bentley to Bentley", but it was first names only on the air. To add color McKay, later a Mayor of Calgary, used the phrase, "tisket, a tasket, Bentleys in the basket", when one scored.

DRUMHELLER MINERS 1938-39

Photo courtesy of Vogue Studio

The Alberta Senior final of 1938-39 featured Lethbridge Maple Leafs and the Drumheller "Bentley" Miners. Drumheller defeated Turner Valley Oilers and the Olds Elks, to reach the final.

The Miners were down two games in the best-of-five against the Leafs; however, they won 5-1 before 2,000 fans in Drumheller. The Miners displayed speed, poise and total co-ordination in their win. During the game E.A. Toshach, President of the Miners, presented Doug Bentley with the MVP award as chosen by the fans. Bentley got a radio. Lethbridge regained their previous form and defeated the Miners 7-1 before another capacity crowd in Drumheller. This win allowed the Maple Leafs to play the Kimberley Dynamiters in the B.C.-Alberta Allan Cup round.

The Kimberley Dynamiters defeated the Freddy Metcalf's Maple Leafs in Calgary in three straight games. In the final game before 5,000 fans, the Leafs lost 4-2 on an empty net goai.

Top row (l to r): H. Hill, S. Chakowski, D. Cairns, W.L. "Pete" Atkinson, A. Chakowski, L. Doling, E. Martinson, P. Davis, Sid Craddock, S. Krizan. Third row: R. Brown (director), Elmer Piper (coach), D. Young, R. Roche, W. Currie (trainer), W. McKay, T. Dawson, E. McKay (manager), F. Cameron (director). Second row: G. Boller (director), R.E. Trammell (president), R. Will (director). Bottom: W.S. Herron (director), M. Newell (director), W.S. Herron Jr. (vice-president), T. Beaver (director), S. Heard (director), L. Maggs (director). *Photo courtesy of Lane Photo, High River*

When the 1938-39 Alberta Senior League came to an end every team, except Calgary, had lost money. Edmonton suffered a deficit of nearly $8,000.00. The Coleman Canadians lost $1,600 and Lethbridge was just slightly into the red. Olds, Drumheller, and Turner Valley all lost at the gate. Calgary drew 66,000 fans that year and were the only team to break even.

During that year there had been many community projects to raise money for local teams. One such reported project involved Wong Pond (family name goes first in Chinese tradition), owner of the Public Lunch in Olds. Wong dropped a puck to start one of the games in Olds. To get the puck back he agreed to make a $100.00 donation to the Olds Elks Senior Hockey Club. It was a very generous amount since coffee was only $.05 and pie $.10 at the Public Lunch.

In the summer of 1984, Frank Wong, the 85 year old son of Wong Pond, said that his father donated so much money because "he was part of the community and hockey was important".

(Wong Pond passed away in the 50's and Frank Wong just this year. The $100.00 helped, no doubt, but the rest of the story is: the Public Lunch started in 1902, months before the formation of the Central Hockey League, and 83 years later, after the death of senior hockey, Stewart Wong, grandson of Wong Pond and son of Frank Wong still owns the Public Lunch in Olds.)

In 1939-40 the Calgary Stampeders moved from last place the year before to first. The Turner Valley Oilers defeated the 1938-39 champion Lethbridge Maple Leafs to play Calgary in the final. The Oilers were a formidable crew. The team included Syd Craddock, Pete Ettinger, Doug Cairns, Pete Atkinson, Jake Milford, Percy Davis and Richard 'Toad' Klein. The Stampeders continued their fine season and defeated Turner Valley.

The Stampeder's lineup included Dave Duchak, former member of the North Battleford Beavers. The year before he had played with the World Champion Trail Smokeaters. But in the spring of 1940 he was playing against Trail.

CALGARY STAMPEDERS 1939-40

Top (l to r): W. Pearson, Cam Burke, J. Bruce, J.B. Cross, Marty Burke, Les Thurwell. Second row: Pat Hill, Art Rice-Jones, Chuck Millman, Tony Demarais, Dave Duchak, Tommy Dewar, J. McNamara, A. McFadyen. Bottom: Howie Hill, Mike Patrick, Syd Fenn, Joe Shannon, Jimmy Jempson.

Art Rice-Jones was outstanding in goal for Calgary as the Stampeders defeated Trail three in a row. The Stampeders won the second game 5-2. Ab Cronie of Trail scored on Rice-Jones. This goal broke a shut-out streak started in the Turner Valley series that lasted for 225 minutes and 26 seconds. Rice-Jones already had three shut-outs in a row. In the third Trail game, Cronie scored again for the Smokeaters 17:50 in the third period.

In the 1939-40 season, the Calgary Stampeder club became the first Alberta team to reach the Allan Cup final when it defeated the Port Arthur Bearcats. Rice-Jones was sensational in the nets in the final 4-3 victory in the series. The bumping of 'Big' Chuck Millman, Tommy Dewar and Pat Hill during the early stages of the game had a great deal to do with the victory. The Dave Duchak, Joe Shannon and Cam Burke line showed good offence and backchecked relentlessly. Scorers Tony Demarais, Jimmy Jempson and Les Thurlwell were effective. Mike Patrick filled in where necessary for coach Marty Burke. The Stampeders used only eleven players to reach the final. (Syd Fenn had a sore throat and flu and Howie Hill injured his knee before the game.)

The Stampeders moved to Toronto's Maple Leaf Gardens to play the Kirkland Lake Blue Devils in a best-of-five Canadian final. Attendance for the opener was 13,359 and by the third game it fell to 3,836 as Kirkland Lake easily won the Allan Cup. Joe Brown, former member of the 1932-33 Edmonton Superiors, and goalkeeper Bill Durnan, later with the Montreal Canadiens, played for the Blue Devils.

In the 1940-41 season it appeared the Calgary Stampeders would represent Alberta. They had defeated the Edmonton Flyers 9-1 to win a place in the Alberta Senior League final against the Lethbridge Maple Leafs. The Maple Leafs had a fine season however, and edged out Calgary by one point. This game gave Lethbridge the extra home game in the best-of-five final.

Marsh Darling, Alex "Seabiscuit" Kaleta and Mel Lunde scored for Lethbridge in an opening 3-1 win. The home club won the first four games which sent the fifth game back to Lethbridge. Manager Herman Tholes and coach Kenny Stewart's Leafs racked up a 4-0 win to eliminate the defending Western champions three games to two.

After the B.C.-Alberta win, the Maple Leafs played the Regina Rangers in the Western Allan Cup final. No games were played in Lethbridge as the rink was considered to be too small.

LETHBRIDGE MAPLE LEAFS 1940-41

Photo courtesy of Edmonton Archives

In the first game, the Rangers won 1-0 when Frank Mario, right winger of Regina coach Fred Metcalf's 'Kid Line', flipped a puck towards Lethbridge goalie Andy Young. It was considered a fluke goal but it turned out to be the only one. (Grant Warwick and Scotty Cameron were line mates of Mario.) Lethbridge's Andy Young and "Sugar" Jim Henry for Regina were spectacular in goal for each club.

Walter 'Whitey' Rimstad scored at 17:50 in the third period of game two in Regina to give Lethbridge a 2-1 lead. Alex Kaleta scored later while Regina was pressing for a tie to give the Leafs a 3-1 win and tie up the series. Game three moved to Moose Jaw where the Rangers assumed a 2-1 lead in games when they edged the Leafs 4-3.

The series ended up in Calgary at the Victoria Arena. A major reason for this change in site was because the CAHA Annual Meeting for 1940-41 was in Calgary. In the 27 year history of the national association this was the first in Calgary.

Over 5,000 fans plus CAHA officials watched Regina defeat Lethbridge 3-2. To win the final game, the Rangers had to come from behind twice and then goalie 'Sugar' Jim Henry was outstanding. Regina later defeated the Sydney Millionaires to win the 1940-41 Allan Cup.

The meeting of CAHA included discussions on how hockey would continue during World War II. It was recognized the teams and lineups would change because of enlistments. Attending the meeting were Dr. W.G. Hardy, President of the International Ice Hockey Association, and George Mackintosh, Secretary, both of Edmonton.

In 1941-42 Eastern British Columbia and Alberta senior hockey clubs combined to form the Alberta-British Columbia Senior Hockey League or the ABC League. The Calgary Stampeders met the Trail Smokeaters and Lethbridge Maple Leafs the Kimberley Dynamiters in the league semi-finals in best-of-five rounds.

The Stampeders defeated Trail in three straight games while the Leafs took a two-game lead against Kimberley. Because only 1,200 fans watched the second game in Lethbridge, Dr. Hardy, Past-President of the CAHA called off the series. Kimberly and Lethbridge agreed to this because the attendance was not sufficient enough to pay the bills and they wanted the next round to start.

(In the Trail-Calgary series one of the players for Trail was former Calgarian Larry Kwong. At the time he was known as the "China Clipper". According to Vic Mah of Edmonton, Larry was the first and Normie, later player on the Edmonton Eskimo football club, the "Second China Clipper." Normie's son Randy went to China in November, 1984, to play for the AAHA Midget All-Stars in a three week series of exhibition games.)

The Stampeder-Maple Leaf final was a surprise. Calgary had finished 13 points ahead of Lethbridge in regular season play but lost the league playoffs. Goals by Hector Negrello, Alex Pringle and Walter 'Whitey' Rimstad in the final game eliminated the Stampeders 3-1.

The success of the Lethbridge Maple Leafs came to a halt when the Port Arthur Bearcats defeated them 4-3 in the fifth and deciding game of the series in Lethbridge. Over 3,000 fans watched Edgar LaPrade get the fourth goal for the Bearcats to eliminate the Leafs from the Western Allan Cup final.

The All-Star team for the 1941-42 ABC League was tabulated by Doug Smith, sports announcer at CFCN Calgary, Art Rice-Jones of Calgary was in goal, the defence pair was Pete Slobodian of Lethbridge and Frank Warshawski of Red Deer and forwards were Ab Cronie and Mike Buckna of Trail (Buckna is still known as the "Father of Hockey" in Czechoslovakia) and Dunc Grant of Calgary.

Alberta hockey the following year (1942-43) was restricted, due to World War II. The top level became was military hockey. There was no professional hockey in Alberta. Some players from the NHL and others who could not become professional due to being enlisted, performed in Alberta.

Tiny Thompson made his return to Calgary for the RCAF Mustangs on March 13, 1943, and shut-out the Lethbridge Bombers for 60 minutes. Few people at this game remembered that Tiny's last appearance for Calgary had been in his last year of high school when he played for Alberta Pacific Grain, the Alberta Senior champions. Since then he played for Canmore, Bellevue, Duluth and Minneapolis, and finally in the NHL for the Boston Bruins where he won four Vezina Trophies.

Another player, Tommy 'Cowboy' Anderson, from Drumheller and later a member of "Red" Dutton's Brooklyn Americans also played military hockey in Alberta. On March 13, 1943, Anderson, the playing coach of Calgary's Currie Barracks officially received the Dr. David Hart Trophy he had won the previous year in the NHL. The Hart Trophy was first presented in 1924. Herb Gardiner of Calgary was the first westerner to win it in 1927. Former Eskimo, Eddie Shore won it four times and Edmonton Oiler Wayne Gretzky six years in a row.

The All-Star team in the Alberta Service's Senior Hockey League selected in the spring of 1943 was impressive. On the first team was goalie Frank McCool, Garth Boesch and Pete Slobodian on defence. Don Deacon was the centre, Alex Kaleta right wing and Don Culley left wing. The second team featured Ed MacAnaley in goal, Wilf Field and 'Cowboy' Anderson defence, Walter "Whitey" Rimstad centre, Johnny Chad right wing and Jack Adams left wing.

President D.P. McDonald of the Armed Services League released the statistics for the 1942-43 season. Alex Kaleta of Currie had 23 goals and 35 assists for 58 points while teammates Tony Desmarais and Don Deacon tied with 52 points each. Pete Slobodian of the Lethbridge Bombers was the 'Bad Man' as he spent 83 minutes in the penalty box.

Currie Army took the Alberta Senior Hockey championship in 1942-43 when it defeated Calgary RCAF Mustangs 3-1 in the deciding game of the best-of-five before 5,099 fans at Victoria Arena. The Canmore developed players on the Army squad were Art Michaluk and Pete Stasiuk on defence and Alex Kaleta, Andy Chakowski and Scotty McPherson. Only Saskatoon, Calgary and Edmonton came close to supplying the number Canmore players on the provincial title holders and they only had three each.

The British Columbia senior champion Victoria Army eliminated Currie Army three games to two to oppose Winnipeg RCAF Bombers in the Western Allan Cup final. Goalie Art Rice-Jones and Nick Metz played for Victoria in the final match.

Victoria Army met the Ottawa Commandos in the 1943 Allan Cup final. Games in the final were played in Winnipeg, Regina and Calgary. The Commandos were led by Edmonton products Neil and Mac Colville and Ken Reardon as they won the Allan Cup.

In 1943-44 the military final in Alberta, Currie Barracks met the Red Deer Army Wheelers in a best-of-three. Alex Kaleta and Max Bentley scored for Currie while Larry Kwong replied for Red Deer in the 2-1 game. The Currie club made it two straight when they defeated Mac Colville and the Red Deer squad 9-6 before 5,121 spectators in Calgary. The line of Max Bentley, Bob Carse and Alex Kaleta scored a total of 14 points (goals and assists) out of the 35 scoring points in the match.

Doug Smith of CFCN Calgary announced the All-Star team of 1943-44 for the armed services. The players were outstanding and many were certainly good enough for the NHL. Max Bentley, who won the Lady Byng Trophy in the NHL the previous season, and Tommy Anderson, former Hart winner, were on the second team.

The first team had 'Sugar' Jim Henry in goal, Mac Colville and Pete Slobodian on defence, Doug Cairns centre, Alex Kaleta right wing and Dave 'Sweeney' Schriner on right wing. On the second squad Russ Dertell was in goal, Eddie Wares and Tommy Anderson on defence, Max Bentley centre, Ray Sawyer right wing and Bob Carse at left wing. Other players in the noteable category included Riley Mullen, Ed McAnaley, Doug Lane, Ken Stewart, Bill Dertell, Eddie O'Keefe, Jack Forsey, Don Emery, Johnny Chad, Dunc Grant and Eddie Slowin-

RED DEER A20 WHEELERS 1943-44

Left to right: Sugar Jim Henry, Riley Mullen, Eddie Slowinski, Jim Colquhoun, Warren Stewart, Jack Forsey, Billy Van Deelen, George Pargeter, Mac Colville (coach), Eddie O'Keefe, Johnny Lyons, Bill Ratke. *Photo courtesy of Red Deer Archives*

A16 CURRIE SENIOR HOCKEY TEAM 1944-45

Photo courtesy of Edmonton Archives

ski. These two teams and list of other players gives a good indication of the calibre of players and play. (Smith of CFCN, then went to Montreal to become the English language broadcaster for the Montreal Canadiens.)

Due to military travel restrictions, Currie Army did not represent Alberta in the 1943-44 Allan Cup. The Edmonton Vics made up of many former pros did the honors. The Vics played the New Westminster Lodestars in Calgary and were defeated in three straight games. Members of the Edmonton squad included Earl Robertson, Alex Molyneaux, Paul Runge, Jimmy Anderson, Bruce McKay, Don Culley, Bill Ingram, Al Emory, Louis Holmes and Joe Brown.

The 1944-45 Allan Cup was not up for competition because of World War II. The only two requests, one team from the west coast and the other from Quebec caused the CAHA to decide the eventual winner could not be a true champion so no playoffs were held.

The Alberta Service Senior Hockey League continued in 1944-45 and Currie Army defeated RCAF Mustangs 4-3 in overtime to win the championship. Max Bentley scored on an assist from his brother Reg at 9:06 of overtime.

In league statistics, Ken 'Red' Hunter of Calgary RCAF Mustangs won the scoring championship, 29 to 28 points over Max Bentley of Currie. Navy's Ed Slowinski had 26 points while Alex Kaleta of Currie was fourth at 25 points. The Jack Gordon Efficiency Medal for the player judged most efficient to this team was won by Hunter. Once again the calibre of hockey in Alberta, as can be judged by the type of players, would have matched the NHL. They never played each other to find out.

At 12:01 a.m., European time on May 8, 1945, Victory in Europe or VE Day was declared. Shortly after Prime Minister Mackenzie King announced that Canada would participate more fully on the Pacific front.

The book *The Canadian Army 1939-1945* by Colonel C.P. Stacey gives the total enlistments as 1,086,771 or 9.65% of the 11.26 million 1939 population of Canada. It was further estimated that 40.6% of the male population between 18 and 45 served in one of the three armed forces. In all three forces the total fatalities known by July 1947 totalled 41,992 or 3.86% of the total enlistment. For six years Canada had been occupied with the war. Sports was used primarily as a vehicle to keep morale high and provide recreation. Now, troops were coming home to rebuild the country and sports such as hockey could resume more normal conditions. Many of the players now turned their talents towards the NHL, minor pro, senior, intermediate or junior hockey levels.

In 1945-46 the Western Canada Senior Hockey League was formed. It was comprised of the Saskatoon Elks, Regina Caps, Calgary Stampeders and the Edmonton Flyers.

At the conclusion of the regular season, President D.P. MacDonald released the scoring statistics which showed Bob Carse in first place with 17 goals, 22 assists, for 39 points. He was followed closely by Red Hunter of Calgary with 38 points, Dunc Grant of Calgary 35 points, Stan Devicq of the Edmonton Flyers with 26, and Bob Brownridge of Calgary with 25 points. Other players with 20 or more points included Don Stanley of Edmonton and Tony Demarais of Calgary.

The Edmonton Flyers under the direction of coach Riley Mullen defeated the Saskatoon Elks 4-3 in overtime to advance to the Western Canada Senior Hockey League final against the Calgary Stampeders. The first two games were won by the Stampeders in Calgary, while the third game in Edmonton saw Calgary take a three game lead with a 3-2 victory in front of 6,500 fans. The third game featured brilliant goal tending by Russ Dertell of Calgary and Ken McAuley of the Flyers.

In game four, the Flyers came back with a thrilling 3-2 triumph against the Stampeders. In the fifth game of the series, the Stampeders prevailed with a 5-0 shut-out victory to win the Western Canada Senior Hockey League Championship four games to one.

The Calgary Stampeders went on to win Alberta's first Allan Cup. Dave Duchak, Manager of the Stampeders recalls in the following account how Calgary won it all.

THE CALGARY STAMPEDERS — ALBERTA'S FIRST ALLAN CUP CHAMPIONS

BY DAVE DUCHAK

The Allan Cup, emblematic of the Senior Amateur Hockey Championship for Canada, was to become the target set by the Calgary Stampeders hockey club during its 1945-46 season.

It all started with an announcement by the secretary of the Calgary Buffalo Athletic Association at their general meeting held at the Calgary Brewery on the night of August 2, 1945. As secretary of the Buffalo Association sponsors I advised the meeting of the executives of the decision to sponsor a senior franchise in the next Alberta Senior Hockey League. This team was to be known as the Stampeders.

J.B. Cross, President of the Calgary Brewing and Malting Company, was the sponsor of the Buffalo Association. The hockey program of this Association, beginning in 1943, included a six team Pee Wee League, a four team Midget League, a four team Juvenile League and the Calgary Buffalo Junior Hockey team. A senior team seemed a natural development to inspire future player graduates. The Stampeder name would continue from the pre-war years starting in 1939 when the Stampeder name was first used.

Not long after the August 23rd meeting, I was called to a meeting at the Palliser Hotel, presided over by Cross, J. Charles Yule (Calgary Exhibition Stampede), and Lloyd Turner (Victoria Arena). I was appointed manager of the Calgary Stampeder Hockey Club, and we were to use the offices of the Calgary Exhibition and Stampede for our Club administration. I was to represent the team in the meeting, to be held in early September, of hockey officials from Calgary, Edmonton, Saskatoon and Regina. This meeting subsequently formed the Western Canada Senior Amateur League with D.P. McDonald as its first President.

Jack Arbour became our first WCSHL coach. This was an easy choice as Jack had been our most successful coach in the Buffalo Hockey Association program. He also had a wealth of playing and coaching experience in the professional ranks with the Detroit Olympics, Toronto Maple Leafs, Windsor Bulldogs plus experience in Seattle, Portland and Spokane.

CALGARY STAMPEDERS 1945-46

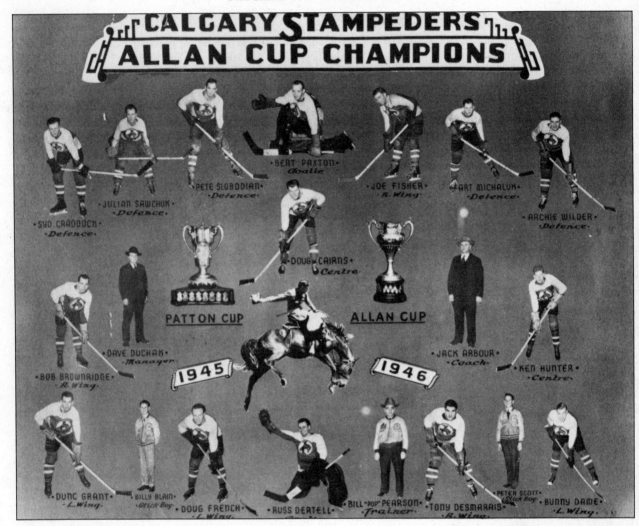

Photo courtesy of E.W. Cadman, Oliver Studio, Calgary

Shortly after VJ Day on September 2, Ken 'Red' Hunter became the first signed player. This opened the door to the successive signatures of Bob Brownridge, Dunc Grant, Bert Paxton, Les Christiansen, Doug Cairns, Art Michaluk, Doug French, Tony Desmarais, Bunny Dame, Ab McDonald, Russ Dertell, Johnnie McIntyre, Pete Atkinson, Archie Wilder and Syd 'Tiny' Craddock. These were the sixteen players who opened the team's season on November 7, 1945 in Edmonton. Trainer, Jim Bruce and equipment manager, Bill 'Pop' Pearson, rounded out the team roster. Joe Fisher, Pete Slobodian and Julian Sawchuk were added later.

The season started and eventually developed into a three team race. The Stampeders held a slight edge over Saskatoon and Edmonton who were neck and neck for second place going into the new year. Slowly, but surely, Calgary pulled ahead and finished the schedule with a 7 point lead over Edmonton for first place with 57 points, made up of 28 wins, 7 losses and a tie.

The Stampeders created many new records. The team scored 219 goals in 36 games for an average of 6.1 goals per game. There were many individual record achievements for senior hockey as 'Red' Hunter scored 81 points and Dunc Grant had 45 goals for the season. Tony Desmarais scored 3 goals in 1 minute and 43 seconds, which at the time was one of the fastest ever registered in senior hockey. Dunc Grant's 5 goals in one period in a game against Regina, and Russ Dertell's season of allowing 95 goals against in 36 games, gave him a 2.6 goals against average and shattered previous records.

After defeating the Edmonton Flyers to win the League championship we then met and defeated the Winnipeg Orioles in three straight. The Western Canada final against the Trail Smokeaters was a close and hectic series, ending in Calgary's favor with 2 ties and 3 wins. Without question, the continuous support and encouragement the players, coach and manager received from the team president, the executive and all the Calgary fans, helped sustain our aim to win the Allan Cup. The Calgary Stampeders became the first Alberta team to win the Canadian Amateur Hockey Championship on Saturday, April 28, 1946.

* * *

The Calgary Stampeders defeated the Hamilton Tigers 1-0 to win the series and the Allan Cup at the Edmonton Arena. Goalkeeper Russ Dertell, earned the shut-out and Archie Wilder scored the winner. Bob Mamini of the "Calgary Herald" wrote:

A lot of credit for the success of the Stampeders this year goes to the manager-coach combination (Duchak and Arbour) of the Calgary Club, for they have kept team harmony throughout, and it was the team play of the Calgary club that was the real forte in the Championship drive.

In 1947, Ken Hunter of the Calgary Stampeders, won the scoring race in the WCSHL, with 29 goals, 48 assists for 77 points. Dunc Grant of Calgary, was second with 37 goals, 33 assists, for 70 points. The two bad men in the league were Bob Solinger (Solinger is credited by Alberta players as the "originater" of the slapshot) with 72 minutes in penalties, followed by Tony Desmarais of Calgary with 70 minutes in penalties.

The Lethbridge Maple Leafs won a berth in the final round of the WCSHL playoffs with a clean cut 6-3 victory over the Edmonton Flyers before 3,000 fans in Lethbridge. Sweeney Schriner's Leafs, which finished third in the regular schedule, eliminated the second place Flyers in four games of the best-of-five series for the right to meet the Calgary Stampeders, the defending Allan Cup Champions of 1946. The Stampeders advanced past the Leafs and then defeated the Kimberley Dynamiters 4-3 in Calgary to take the six game series four games to two.

Stampeders continued on to defeat the Winnipeg Flyers 4-3 in the final game of the Western Canada Allan Cup championship. In the final win Dunc Grant scored 2 goals and singles went to Bob Brownridge and Tony Desmarais. For the Flyers it was Don 'Bones' Raleigh with 2, plus a single by Bud Craig.

On April 22, 1947, the Stampeders were given a rousing send off by hundreds of Calgary fans who had gathered at the CPR station. Stamps were rated by their supporters as at least an even money bet to win the national final against the east.

While the Calgary Stampeders were on their way east, the Montreal Canadiens and the National Hockey League All-Stars dished up some entertaining hockey at the Victoria Arena in Calgary. Close to 4,000 fans watched Maurice "The Rocket" Richard score 2 of his "masterpiece goals", Kenny Reardon with his end to end rushes and Max Bentley and Bob Carse play superb hockey. Bill Durnan was a tower of strength in the nets for the Canadiens and Turk Broda played well for the All-Stars. In this first of four exhibition games held in Alberta (two in Edmonton and two in Calgary), the Montreal Canadiens demolished the National league All-Stars 8-3.

Other great players for the Canadiens were Billy Reay and Hector 'Toe' Blake. The All-Stars included Doug Bentley, Bill Mosienko, Syd Abel, Grant Warwick, and Ted Lindsay. For the hockey fans in Edmonton and Calgary, it was an excellent way to end the home season.

Even though the Stanley Cup champions and the NHL All-Stars were in Alberta, and the Calgary Stampeders were on their way east, some Calgary youngsters had more on their minds than hockey. Bobby Gillstrom 12, Frank Vercammen 15, Ronald Millon 13, Don McArthur 15, Buddy Fulton 6, Jimmy Takaoka 14 and Ernest Fulton of Calgary made placards protesting the increase in the price of chocolate bars. The six McDougal School youngsters picketed stores carrying $.08 candy bars on 7th, 8th, and 9th Avenue in Calgary. They wanted the $.05 bar back again.

On the Allan Cup scoreboard, the Calgary Stampeders were having as difficult a time against the Montreal Royals as the kids in Calgary were having in trying to get back the nickel candy bar. After the fourth game of the series, the Stampeders were behind 3-1 in the Allan Cup final. The series continued on to the seventh game, where, before 11,200 people in Montreal, the Royals won Montreal's first Allan Cup in 17 years (The last winners for Montreal were the Montreal Winged Wheelers in 1930).

The weather was 70 degrees F outside, and fans sat in short sleeved shirts. The Royals opened the final game quickly with four goals in the first period. They got three more in the second before the hardpressed Stampeders got one past Gerry McNeil in the Montreal net. Cliff Malone, Jerry Plamondon, Doug Harvey, Jimmy Galbraith, Ernie LaForce, and Floyd Currie were the scorers for the Montreal Royals. Bob Brownridge and Doug Cairns connected for Calgary. Russ Dertell, in the Calgary net, had a busy night stopping 46 shots to McNeil's 21.

Alberta still had a lot to cheer about in May of 1947, as the Leduc Oil Field was being drilled and the oil boom was hitting Alberta. The Calgary Stampeders, however, could only be cheered for being good sports and taking the Montreal Royals to the seventh game of the Allan Cup final.

The 1946-47 All Star team in the Western Canada Senior Hockey League included Al Rollins of Edmonton in goal, Gordie Watt (Edmonton) and Gus Kyle (Regina) on defence, Morey Rimstad (Edmonton) centre, Ab McDougal (Regina) and Dunc Grant (Calgary) as wingers. Joe Fisher (Regina) was selected as coach.

The individual scoring race in the WCSHL for 1946-47

	Total Goals	Assists	Points
Morey Rimstad (Edm)	35	45	80
Ab McDougall (Reg)	36	39	75
Steve Latonski (Leth)	21	54	75
Bill Kyle (Reg)	20	43	72
Roy Heximer (Leth)	33	38	71

Don "Buckets" Fleming describes the Edmonton Flyers of 1947-48. Fleming made road trips on the train, knew the players and wrote the stories for the Edmonton Journal on the Flyers. He covered hockey for over 30 years and now works at Northlands for one of his loves — the races.

EDMONTON'S ALLAN CUP — 1948

BY DON "BUCKETS" FLEMING

The second Great War brought Alberta into the 1940s and still the rich agricultural province had not won the Allan Cup, the prized bauble of amateur hockey. The Regina Victorias had won the nation's senior hockey crown in 1914 and until the mid-30s the Allan Cup had not travelled farther west. Even then, it did not stop in Alberta but hopped into the mountains to the lair of the Kimberley Dynamiters in 1935-36, then two years later to the smelter stronghold of the Trail Smokeaters.

At long last Jack Arbour's Calgary Stampeders brought the Cup to Alberta in 1946 as the nation strove to put the pieces together following cessation of the world hostilites. Nearly 200 miles to the north, the Edmonton Exhibition Association was always building toward an Allan Cup. A former professional defenceman, Riley Mullen had gathered together the makings of a great senior team, but he went to the Saskatoon Quakers and wasn't around to see his efforts reach fruition.

Frank Currie had come west from Montreal to lead the Edmonton Flyers in the 1947-48 season, and plugged a few holes here and there. The affable Currie succeeded in having it all come together. A major coup was achieved when Currie acquired Al Rollins to mind the nets, with Jack Manson the backup goalie. Rollins, of course, was to go on to win the Vezina Trophy with Toronto as the National league's top goal tender and the Hart Trophy as the league's Most Valuable Player with the Chicago Black Hawks in 1954.

On defence was the captain of the Flyers, Gordie Watt, with Pug Young, Bud MacPherson, Doug Lane and Bill Pettinger. The first forward line was centered by Morey Rimstad, with Johnny Black and Bill Maher on his flanks. Doug Anderson was the pivot of another line with Andy Clovechok and Bing Merluk. The other forward line was cutely called the "Receding Hairline", for the obvious reasons of being "hailed out" on top. They were Elmer Kreller, Alex Pringle and Freddy Smitten. Utility players included former professional Louis Holmes and Gordon Buttrey, with Doug Hardy trainer, Ira Stuart equipment manager, Bill Morrissey stickboy and Gordon McDonald Exhibition Director.

They set out on the Allan Cup Trail after emerging from last place in the Western Canada Hockey League with playoff victories over Calgary Stampeders and the Regina Caps. They headed into the Kootenays to blast the Trail Smokeaters in games at Nelson and Trail, then came home to wrap up the series in four straight, 2-1 and then with the "coup de grace" 10-0. That sent them on to Winnipeg to take on the Winnipeg Reo Flyers for the Western title. It was a sometimes-tempestuous series in which Winnipeg writers described 'Pug' Young as "one of the worst hoodlums in hockey today". Edmonton lost the first game in Winnipeg, but evened the best-of-seven series before leaving Manitoba, took the lead in Saskatoon and then swept the fourth and fifth games in Edmonton 11-0 and 3-2. By this time, hockey fever had caught the Edmonton citizenry up in a frenzy. Scores of businessmen donated prizes that would be awarded to members of the Flyers, from wrist watches to lingerie for the wives and sweethearts of the players.

The Flyers won the opening game of the Allan Cup final in Regina 6-2 over the Ottawa Senators, Champions of the East and bearers of the same name that won the Stanley Cup over the Edmonton Eskimos 1-0 and 2-1 in 1923 at Vancouver. But the Senators came back to even the series in the Edmonton Arena 3-2 with Frank Mathers scoring the winning goal. However, before going to Calgary to resume the series, the Flyers regained the lead by trouncing Ottawa 7-0 with Johnny Black and Freddy Smitten each scoring twice.

EDMONTON FLYERS 1947-48

Photo courtesy of A. Blyth Studios

Victoria Park Arena in Calgary was the scene for a 5-3 Edmonton victory and a 3-1 lead in the series before 5,500 fans who caused a bitter reaction in the Edmonton media for throwing their support behind the Senators. But another sellout crowd in Calgary two nights later saw Andy Clovechok fashion a hat trick for another 5-3 Edmonton triumph and the Allan Cup. The Flyers had come from behind a 3-1 deficit. It was bedlam in the Flyer's dressing room, and the voice of the Flyers on CKUA, Art Ward, watched in dismay as his longtime trademark, a buffalo coat, was ripped into shreds by the jubilant Allan Cup Champions.

Back in Edmonton the Flyers were given the keys to the city and a parade down Jasper Avenue witnessed by more than 60,000 wild-eyed fans. The crowning touch came when Mayor Harry D. Ainlay told Police Chief Reg Jennings to make room for the Flyer's famed badman, defenceman Pug Young, to serve as the city's honorary police chief for the next two weeks. "It was the Wild West all over again."

* * *

In 1948 the Edmonton Flyer's Allan Cup had similarities to the 1984 Oiler's Stanley Cup parade. The biggest crowd of its kind in the City's history, estimated at 60,000, jammed Jasper Avenue street intersections. In New York news reel fashion, the yelling thousands lined the streets and showered the champions with snow storms of confetti. Right from 109th street and Jasper, the start of the procession, solid lines were along the route.

High a top every building were thousands more, waving banners, flags and throwing showers of paper on the heads of the winning team. Crowding, pushing, shreaking fans, of the younger variety delayed the parade, wrecked a public address system and threatened to overturn the float. Nobody cared. This was on May 10, 1948.

The reason — the Edmonton Flyers were being welcomed as the Edmonton hockey team that went down the entire senior play off trail and brought home the famed Allan Cup, emblematic of Canadian Supremacy in Amateur Hockey.

Defenceman Gordon Watt and his wife Gretta had more on their minds than winning the Allan Cup. On May 1, 1948, a son was born. He was 6 lbs. 4 oz. (2,84 kilos). Thus, the public relations director today of the Edmonton Eskimo Football Club is Allan James Watt. On May 9, 1948, the Edmonton Flyers with Gordon Watt playing defence celebrated the birth by winning the Allan Cup.

The season after the Flyer Allan Cup victory, sports editor, Stan Moher of the Edmonton Bulletin selected the players he felt should be on the WCSHL All-Star team. In goal, Bev Bentley (Regina), Bud McPherson (Edmonton) and Vic Myles (Regina) on defence, Ken Hunter (Calgary) centre, Ab McDougall (Regina) right wing and Dunc Scott (Calgary) left wing.

The second team was equally as impressive. Russ Dertell (Calgary) goal, 'Black Jack' Evans (Lethbridge) and Harvey Barnes (Regina) defence, Elmer "The Shadow" Kreller (Edmonton) centre, Andy Clovechok (Edmonton) right wing and Stan Maxwell (Lethbridge) right wing. Stan's selection for MVP was Dunc Grant, while for Rookie of the Year it was Colin Kilburn of Edmonton. (Kilburn and teammate Doug Anderson were nicknamed "The Gold Dust Twins".)

The Regina Capitals finished first in the regular 1948-49 WCSHL schedule and won the playoffs when they defeated the Edmonton Flyers four games to one. Regina went on to defeat Trail B.C. and Fort Francis, Ontario and became the fourth WCSHL team in a row to reach the Allan Cup final. The Caps lost the national championship to the Ottawa Senators.

1949 was not the best year for the WCSHL Flyers and Stampeders, but for Harry Ornest it was a great year. Ornest, the present owner of the St. Louis Blues of the NHL grew up in Edmonton and was a hockey referee. In 1948-49 Ornest came back to Edmonton after refereeing in the United States. During the season he also got the chance to be a linesman for three NHL games. Ornest told the "Edmonton Bulletin" that working in the NHL was "a great thrill, a wonderful experience". Although he was undecided about his future plans, Harry said, "about all I know is I expect to be around for the next three weeks, at least".

In 1949, Ornest was an acquaintance of Bill Hunter. It would be more than three decades later that Ornest would lead his group of investors while Hunter spearheaded a Saskatoon group to purchase the NHL St. Louis Blues. Ornest succeeded in getting back in the NHL. Hunter is still trying in Saskatoon.

Calgary in the spring of 1949 was in need of a new rink. The city still had the same manager, Lloyd Turner, but the Victoria Arena needed to be replaced. On March 31, 1949, plans were released for one of the most modern fire proof arenas in Western Canada. The Directors of the Calgary Stampede and Exhibition Board hoped the building would be completed by August 31, 1950. J. Charles Yule announced the Calgary Corral would be made of concrete and steel, seat 6,050 and have additional room for 2,200 to stand. The hockey ice surface would be 200' x 85' while the building outside would have dimensions of 400' x 210'. Calgary's Corral was considered large; however, budgets in 1948-49 were small compared to today.

The Edmonton Flyer's budget in 1948-49 would have trouble paying an average NHL salary for one player in 1985. The Flyers showed a profit of $1,031.19. Total expenditures were $79,283.66. Of this, salaries were $50,822.00 and additional bonus cheques were $3,500.00. Some other liabilities were $293.00 for a banquet, $350.00 for executive expenses, fees to associations $2,420.00, stationary, postage and telephone $460.00, medical $541.00, ice rental $657.00, advertising $1,289.00, insurance $165.00 plus Christmas gifts and sundry expenses for $612.00. The ice rental total of $657.00 would hardly cover 10 hours of extra ice-time for a minor hockey team in Edmonton in 1985.

The Calgary Stampeders won the WCSHL championship in 1949-50. The Stamps eliminated Bill Hunter's Saskatoon Quakers four games to one to reach the final against the Edmonton Flyers. Stampeder Mitch Pechet scored winners at 16:45 of the third period in a 3-1 win to capture the series four games to two.

The Stamps success continued when they eliminated the Kamloops Elks four games to one to reach the Western Allan Cup final. Against Fort Francis, Calgary won the opener 11-0. This second game in Edmonton still attracted 6,000 fans. Some discussions were held to have the series reduced to a best-of-five because of the one sided opener. However, in game two the Canadians rejected the odds and won 3-2. The series resumed as originally planned. It ended in five games as Calgary won 9-1, 5-2 and 4-3.

Stan Devicq scored the winner for Calgary against Fort Francis at 19:52 of the third period to allow the Stamps to meet Harold Ballard's Toronto Marlboros in the 1949-50 Allan Cup final. The final games were split between Edmonton and Calgary. This was to promote hockey in a region rather than one city plus it gave the visiting team a fairer opportunity.

CALGARY STAMPEDERS — 1949-50

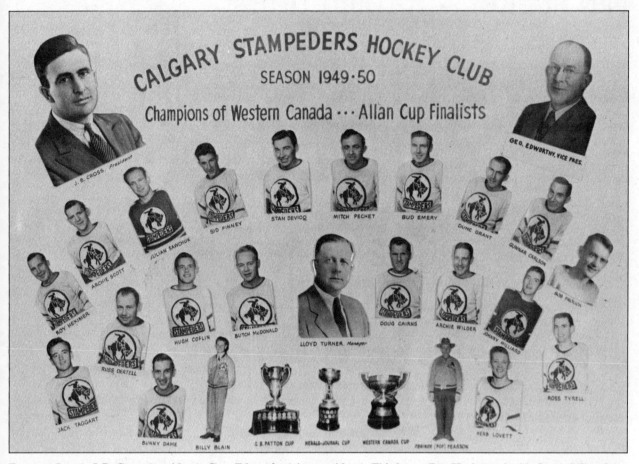

Top row (l to r): J.B. Cross (president), Geo. Edworthy (vice-president). Third row: Roy Heximer, Archie Scott, Julian Sawchuk, Sid Finney, Stan Devicq, Mitch Pechet, Bud Emery, Dunc Grant, Gunner Carlson, Bob Frolick. Second row: Jack Taggart, Russ Dertell, Hugh Coflin, Butch McDonald, Lloyd Turner (manager), Doug Cairns, Archie Wilder, Johnny Milliard, Ross Tyrell. Front: Bunny Dame, Billy Blain, "Pop" Pearson.

The Marlboros won the first game 6-5. After the game coach Joe Primeau went back to Toronto to attend the funeral of his father. Ballard coached the club and the Stamps tied the series at one game each when they won 5-4. Primeau returned and Toronto moved ahead in the series two games to one.

The Edmonton Arena later renamed the Edmonton Gardens, was the site for the fourth game. Tickets were difficult to obtain for fans in Edmonton and Calgary. The Garden's prices were scaled to what was termed "CAHA prices" at $2.00, $1.75, $1.50, and $1.00 per seat. In Edmonton before 7,200 fans the Marlboros won the 1949-50 Allan Cup as they defeated the Stampeders 9-5 to win the series in five games.

Dunc Grant opened the scoring for Calgary after 44 seconds of play. It was said "this caused Harold Ballard to check the railway schedules". Supposedly Ballard and the Marlboros had their bags packed before the game. George Armstrong, then 19 years old, tied up the match for Toronto just over a minute later. Ballard must have felt more secure about being able to leave as his team scored at 7:14, 7:53, 9:01 and 9:34 of the first period for a 5-1 lead.

Armstrong finished the game with three goals. Al Buchanan, Bill Johnson, Scotty Mair, Chuck Blair, Danny Lewicki and Johnny McLellan had singles. Dunc Grant for the Stamps tallied three goals and Stan Devicq and

Herb Lovett scored once. (Alberta had two hockey playing Dunc Grants — the other played in the same era on the Ponoka Stampeders in intermediate hockey.)

The following season (1950-51) the WCSHL became the Western Major Hockey League and played for the Alexander Trophy.

The next portion will be on the return to professional hockey in Alberta, which ends again after the 1962-63 season. Allan Cup hockey in Alberta will start again from 1950-51 after the professional section.

PRO HOCKEY — A THIRD TIME

In 1950-51 the WCSHL became the Western Major Hockey League and competed for the Alexander Trophy. This was considered a step up from the Allan Cup. The old WCSHL had represented Western Canada in the Allan Cup final every year since it started in 1945-46. The new category allowed the league to be more open about the degree of professionalism it had reached.

The WSCHL champions from 1949-50, the Calgary Stampeders, did not play up to their form of the previous year in the new Calgary Corral although Sid Finney was the top scorer with 44 goals in the season.

The Quakers won the WMHL when they defeated the Edmonton Flyers 6-1 in the final game of a round robin playoff. The Quakers had six wins and two losses, Edmonton was at four and four while Calgary had only two wins in eight games. The Quakers then lost against Toronto St. Michael's Majors in a best-of-seven series for the Alexander Trophy, emblematic of major senior hockey supremacy.

In 1951-52 professional hockey officially arrived for the third time in Alberta. In 1951-52, Saskatoon, Edmonton and Calgary joined the Pacific Coast Hockey League. (Regina did not join.) Once again, the Saskatoon Quakers eliminated the Edmonton Flyers in a 3-2 overtime win after 31 extra minutes. Before 6,556 fans at the Edmonton Gardens, playing coach Doug Bentley scored the winner from Alex Kaleta and Johnny Chad. Bentley had two goals in the game and Bob Manson the other. Gus McLeod and Colin Kilburn replied for Edmonton. Lorne 'Gump' Worsley of the Quakers stopped 22 shots and Bill Brennan who was overworked for Edmonton had 45. The Quakers won the PCHL finals over the Victoria Cougars four games to two to win the President's Cup.

In 1952-53, Edmonton Flyers and Calgary Stampeders met in the fifth and deciding game to determine who could advance to the league semi-final. (This season the PCHL changed its name to Western Hockey League because of the prairie entries.) Tension was high at the Calgary Corral as Edmonton was behind 5-2 after 12 minutes in the third period. Then the Flyers came to life.

8,000 fans watched Len "Comet" Haley score from Frank O'Grady at 12:01. Jimmy Anderson scored 31 seconds later from rookie Al Arbour. Flyer goalie Glen Hall was removed from the game for a sixth attacker. Larry Zeidel picked up a rebound and passed it to Bill Hughes who scored at 19:52 to cause overtime. At 5:58 Ray Hannigan scored from Frank O'Grady to eliminate the Stampeders. The Flyers went on to defeat the Vancouver Canucks four games to one and enter the WHL finals against the Saskatoon Quakers.

Norman Couch, manager of the Saskatoon Arena, said that if he had 9,000 seasts, "they could all be sold" but only 5,300 fans could be accommodated.

Don Fleming of the Journal wrote, "You know there is only one guy some people don't pay much attention to, and I'm afraid he could do us much damage in the series. That's Jackie McLeod". McLeod scored the first two goals in game one and the Quakers won 6-2. The Flyers came back and assumed a 3-2 lead in games. Unexpectedly, the hero for Edmonton in game six was Leon Bouchard. Bouchard was a replacement when Hugh Coflin was injured and Rags Raglan was called up to the Chicago Black Hawks. Bouchard connected and scored three goals. Ray Hannigan got two while Larry Wilson, Jimmy Uniac, Earl "Dutch" Reibel and Jimmy Anderson had singles in the final 9-4 win before 8,000 at the Edmonton Gardens. Glen Hall had 25 shots while Bev Bentley for the Quakers had 52.

It had been an uphill climb for the Flyers to win the President's Cup. Hal Pawson, sports editor of the Edmonton Journal summarized the season:

Courage and hustle did it for Bud Poile's Flyers. They entered all three playoffs as underdogs, after an up and down season that saw them finish fourth. But, when the chips were down, they kept coming with the kind of hockey that made them champions last night when they worked Saskatoon into the ice.

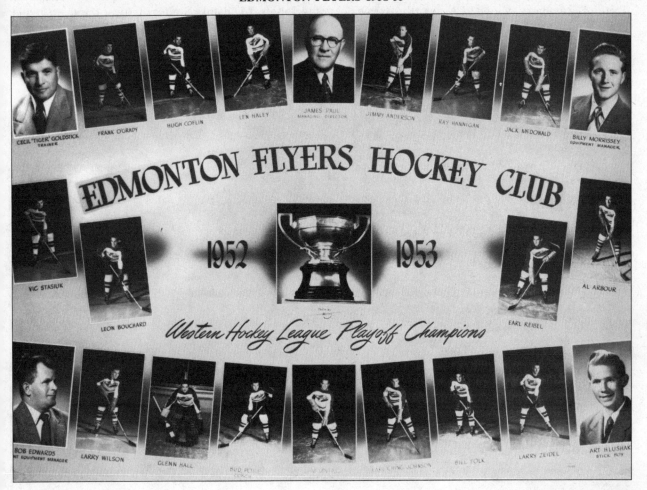

Gorde Hunter was sports editor of the "Calgary Herald" when the Calgary Stampeders won the WHL and finally the Edinburgh Cup. Hunter, who now works at the *Victoria Times Columnist* recalls 1953-54.

'54 STAMPS — WHAT A TEAM!

BY GORDE HUNTER

It was 1954 and the Calgary Stampeders had one helluva hockey team. And Calgary was just the best franchise in all minor professional hockey. The Stampeders deserved the fans, the fans deserved the Stampeders. It was a championship year winning the WHL title and winning the Edinburgh Cup, emblematic of supremacy of the whole minor pro world. They were heady days as Frank Currie took the team to win "all the marbles". It was a team that would finish in the playoffs of any NHL division you care to name today.

They packed 8,575 fans into the old Corral for the final Stampeder, Vancouver Canuck clash — the fourth game of a best-of-seven and it was 3-1 for the Cowboys as slick Sid Finney led the way with 2 of the prettiest goals you'd ever want to see. But hell, all of Finney's goals had the unmistakeable touch of class and genius to them. If Sid played in today's NHL he would score a bushel, or, as his one-time teammate Ed Dorohoy said of him, "Sid would kick in 20 a season in the NHL today."

Winning the WHL crown was only a stepping stone in '54 because there was the Edinburgh Cup for the battle between the WHL and the American Hockey League. And the Stamps were up against George 'Punch' Imlack's Quebec Aces in that one. Naturally, Calgary won because Calgary was the best. They did it in six games in the best-of-nine, the final one at the Corral before 6,500 happy home folk. That total, incidentally, boosted the season home attendance to an unheard of 302,396. For the record Steve Black, George Pargeter with two and Finney were the Calgary scorers in the 4-2 triumph.

And what a rollicking group they were. Bill Brennan in goal and a rock-hard defence of Art Michaluk (may be the hardest bodychecker in all of hockey) the wild and wooley Gus Kyle, Max Quakenbush, Pat Coburn and

Bill Shvetz. Up front, the superb Finney along with the speed demon, Jimmy McFadden, Steve Witiuk, Walt Trentini, Ray Barry, 'Gopher' Ashworth, Archie Scott and Johnny Michaluk. Stu Hendry was the spare goalie. Frank Currie had coached championship teams before, but never, according to him, anything like the 1954 Stampeders. He said it was the best-balanced team he'd ever seen in minor pro hockey and indeed, it is doubtful there has been one as good ever since.

CALGARY STAMPEDER HOCKEY CLUB 1953-54

Back row (l to r): D. Kricken (stick boy), W. Trentini, A. Scott, R. Barry, J. Michaluk, P. Lundy, M. Kricken (stick boy). **Middle row (l to r):** Frank Currie (coach and manager), S. Finney, M. Quackenbush, P. Coburn, B. Shvetz, S. Black, A. Michaluk, Dr. B.W. Black (team doctor), F. Porteous (trainer). **Front row (l to r):** S. Hendry, F. Ashworth, S. Witiuk, M. Hartnett, G. Kyle (captain), Crawford Frost, J. McFadden, G. Pargeter, B. Brennan. *Photo courtesy of Glenbow*

This was hardly the day of big buck hockey. The word was that Sid Finney was the highest paid player on the squad at $8,000, but those Stampeders played harder for their money than many of the pros in today's NHL — pros drawing a quarter of a million bucks and more for the same 80 game season. The season crowd total of over 300,000 was also a magnificent mark when you consider Calgary's population in those days was 150,000. Yet another factor was the fact Calgary also did a pretty handsome job of supporting the Stampeder pro football team at the same time.

The word "halcyon" is overworked these days, but truly, in terms of the Western Hockey League of the 50's, those were indeed the "halcyon days", quiet and peaceful days, and we're not likely to see them repeated.

* * *

TOGETHER AGAIN

During Len 'Comet' Haley's time with the Edmonton Flyer pro hockey team he feuded with manager/coach Norman "Bud" Poile. In the 1953-54 season the Comet was in Poile's bad books too. Haley was known to keep a good supply of home brew wine in his basement. It was a popular place for the Flyers to gather to celebrate a win or drown a loss.

When Poile found out about the home brew he moved Comet to the bench. The Comet accepted his benching calmly. At a crucial point in the game Poile looked down the bench and there was Haley reading a comic book.

The 'Comet' was on the next train to Saskatoon. But time healed all, and eventually Haley was traded back to the Flyers where he performed well, but the feud continued. Poile shipped him off to San Francisco.

In later years Detroit and Bud Poile parted company. Poile became coach and general manager of, you guessed it, the San Francisco Seals of the WHL. Once again, the "Comet" and Poile were reunited.

* * *

In 1954-55, 6,997 fans at the Edmonton Gardens watched the Flyers edge out the Calgary Stampeders 4-2 in the first game of the WHL final. Blond wingman Lorne Davis scored to tie the game and then provided the winner against Calgary goalie Doug Stevenson. The Flyers then went on to defeat the Stamps in four straight to win the President's Cup in the WHL. In the regular season, the Flyers finished first. They became the first club in the history of the WHL to win the Director's Cup for league games and then the President's Cup for the playoffs.

The Flyer's final victory was 5-2 in Calgary. Bronco Horvath, who scored 110 points during the regular season, and Norm Ullman scored two each while Jerry Melnyk scored a single. For the Stampeders, Ray Barry and Gerry "Doc" Couture had singles.

Calgary's John Michaluk spoke about Edmonton netminder Glen Hall:

I used to think Hall was just lucky... but he's not. He's just too good, that's all. Too good for this league. He's unbalanced it. We have to get him out of it. We're pulling for him to get a shot at the NHL.

At this time the NHL had only six teams and most teams depended upon one main goalie. (Hall did get his chance at the NHL and is now listed as one of the greatest goalies of all time.)

1954-55 EDMONTON FLYERS

Photo courtesy of Edmonton Archives

The Flyers now played the Shawinigan Falls Cataracts for the Edinburgh Cup. The Flyers were heavy favorites to win the up in the best-of-nine. They left by CP Rail on April 17, 1955 after a two week layoff.

The first game was a squeaker. After 60 minutes of regular play and one 20 minute overtime, the score remained three all. Finally at 19:49 Edmonton's Bronco Horvath scored from Ed Stankiewics. It had taken almost 100 minutes and was over at 1:15 in the morning.

The Cataracts assumed a 3-2 lead in games after a 2-1 win at the Montreal Forum. Ken Reardon, general manager of Shawinigan Falls felt Edmonton still had a chance. The Flyers changed to their other set of sweaters in an effort to win but the Cataracts won again.

For the last game Glen Hall was in goal suffering from injuries, and defenseman Ed Zeniuk was sidelined due to a shoulder separation. The Flyers dug deeper as coach "Bud" Poile suited up on defence. Poile had not played since January 14. It was not enough as the eastern squad won 3-1 before 6,150 fans back in Shawinigan Falls. Playing coach Roger Leger scored two for the Quebec team while Connie Broden had a single. Edmonton's lone goal came from Bud's younger brother, Don 'Beaver' Poile.

The series was considered an outstanding financial success. A gross gate of $70,000.00 was paid by 52,000 fans. The winners got $10,000 and Edmonton $7,500.00 plus expenses. Don Fleming wrote:

> The Duke of Edinburgh Trophy playoff boasted their playoff earnings to $25,500 which is being cut
> up fifteen ways, which gives each player about $1,650.00... a tidy sum to add to their average salary
> of a little over $4,000.00.

(When Glen Hall made the NHL there were times he had problems in getting the contract he wanted. It was always reported that Glen needed the increases to paint his barn. Salaries in those days were comparibly low compared to a 1985 NHL contract. As of this writing, Glen is still in hockey assisting the goal tenders on the Calgary Flames and still has his barn in Stony Plain, just west of Edmonton.)

The WHL All-Star team of 1954-55 had Glen Hall in goal, Lloyd Durham (Victoria) and Larry Zeidel (Edmonton) on defence. Bronco Horvath (Edmonton) centre, Andy Hebenton (Victoria) and Gerry Couture (Calgary) were wingers. The second team had Johnny Bower (Vancouver) goal, Art Michaluk (Calgary) and Keith Allen (Edmonton) defence, Max McNab (New Westminster) centre and Johnny Bucyk (Edmonton) and Jackie McLeod (Vancouver) were wingers.

The closest balloting was for goalie as Hall edged out Bower by six votes. The first team received $100.00 and $50.00 went to the second. Johnny Bucyk was voted Rookie of the Year ahead of Norm Ullman (Edmonton) and got an extra $100.00. Many of the players on the 1954-55 All-Stars became prominent in the NHL as players and later in team management.

In 1955-56 the Calgary Stampeders got the furthest from Alberta when they reached the final of the prairie section of the WHL. The Stamps were defeated 4-3 and lost the series to Winnipeg Warriors four games to one. Paul Masnick scored the three Winnipeg goals and Mike Nykoluk had a single. For Calgary in the final game, Steve Witiuk, Dave Duke and Bud Syverson shared the scoring.

During 1955-56 attendance figures slipped in Edmonton to 108,993. This was a drop of 12,214 from the previous low in 1954-55. It was 1951-52 that the Flyers had the league high when they drew 165,895 fans. Winnipeg was the attendance leader in 1955-56 at 166,290 followed by Calgary 157,803, Edmonton, Vancouver 107,911, Victoria 99,107, New Westminster 79,915, Seattle 77,570, Saskatoon 64,710, Brandon 58,700. (Brandon's attendance included 14 games in Regina that drew only 11,430.)

The Edmonton Flyers and Calgary Stampeders met in the semi- final of the Praire Division of the WHL in 1956-57. The best-of-three went to a third game after Calgary won 4-2 and lost 4-2. In the third contest the Flyer's Cummy Burton scored twice, and Tom McCarthy and Jerry Melnyk once each for a 4-1 win. The only shot that eluded Flyer goalie Dennis Riggin was a slapshot by Vic Dzurko.

Calgary coach Lee Fogolin (father of present Oiler Lee Fogolin) congratulated Flyer coach Bud Poile. Poiles' veterans Tony Leswick, Don Poile, Jerry Melnyk and Chuck Holmes all had an effective series. Stampeder ace Sid Finney was held pointless in all three games.

Edmonton had finished the year 10 points behind the prairie leaders, the Brandon Regals who had 92 points. Mammoth Lucien Duchene in net for Brandon proved to be a major obstacle for the Flyers in the prairie final. The Flyers won the opening game 5-4 and then Brandon won four straight including a final 3-0 win to eliminate Edmonton. Former Lethbridge Native Son, Bill Voss got two of the three goals.

For Alberta, the highlight of the 1957-58 season was the constant rise of the Calgary Stampeders in the standings to gain a playoff position and finally reach the WHL final. The Stamps slid past the Edmonton Flyers and Seattle Americans to meet the Vancouver Canucks in the final. The Canucks defeated the Stampeders 6-5 in overtime to win the series in four straight games and win the President's Cup. In the final game, all six Vancouver goals were scored by ex-prairie hockey players, Bill Dobbyn (Manitoba) had two goals, including the winner and singles went to Jackie McLeod (Saskatchewan), Orland Kurtenbach (Saskatchewan), Ron Hutchinson (Manitoba) and Brent McNab (Alberta). For Calgary Sid Finney the WHL scoring leader had two while Sandy Hucul, Chuck Blair, and Murray Wilkie had singles.

Ever since the prairie teams joined the coast group in 1951-52, one of them always won the championship. Saskatoon Quakers, Edmonton Flyers twice, Calgary Stampeders, Winnipeg Warriors and Brandon Regals. Vancouver's win in 1957-58 was the first for a coast team in that period.

The Calgary Stampeders continued to win in 1958-59 when they defeated the Winnipeg Warriors 5-2 for their fourth straight win in the Prairie Division of the WHL final. The Stamps had won previous games 3-2, 5-2 and 5-4. They were so confident in Winnipeg that they packed their bags before the fourth game.

Once again in the WHL final, the Coast Division winners defeated the Stampeders four straight. Victories of 4-0, 4-2, 5-1 and 5-1 by the Seattle Totems sent the President's Cup to the coast city. For Seattle, this was their first playoff championship since the Seattle Sea Hawks won the old PCHL in 1936.

The Calgary Stampeders failed to reach the WHL playoffs in 1959-60. The Edmonton Flyers finished in third place and met the highly favored first place Vancouver Canucks. Vancouver finished the year tied with the most wins of any WHL club. They had 44 wins which duplicated Brandon in 1956-57 and the Canucks of 1957-58.

Former Edmonton Flyer Colin Kilburn scored the winner after 34 minutes of overtime and Flyer Lou Marcon was fined $10.00 in the first game of the Edmonton-Vancouver series. The teams were tied at 3-3 when Hal Pawson of the "Edmonton Journal" wrote:

> that referee Scotty Morrison (present NHL referee in chief) watched Lou Marcon and some Flyers involved in a tussel. Morrison did not blow his whistle for at least 45 seconds.

EDMONTON FLYERS 1960-61

Top left: Rich Healey, Hugh Coflin, Roger DeJordy, Bruce MacGregor, Lou Marcon, Dennis Rathwell. Second row (l to r): Dr. W. Eadie, Eddy Joyal, Bob Solinger, Lloyd Haddon, Eddie Diachuk, Gordon Labossier, Edward Yuzda. Front row (l to r): Len Haley, Don Poile, Bud MacPherson, Dennis Riggin, Bud Poile, Chuck Holmes, Gene Achtymichuk.

Photo courtesy of Leo Keats

During this time three Vancouver players kept playing. Ray Cyr passed to Danny Belisle who spotted Kilburn who scored from close in on Dennis Riggin. Marcon was so incensed at Morrison that he was assessed a 10 minute misconduct which called for an automatic $10.00 fine. The Canucks then won the next three games of the series to eliminate the Flyers.

Lou Jankowski, Norm Johnson and Ron ''Squeak'' Leopold of the Calgary Stampeders were the top forward line in the WHL 0f 1960-61. Jankowski had a league goal record of 57 plus 47 assists for 99 points, Leopold had 51 goals, 41 assists for 92 points while Johnson had 23 goals and 64 assists for 87 points. Jankowski was edged out for the league scoring title by Art Jones of Portland Buckeroos who got an assist in his final game for 100 points. Calgary coach Gus Kyle rested his number one line in the final league game. The perennial scoring leader, Guyle Fielder, had won the title five times which included four straight. Fielder finished with 95 points including 71 assists.

The Edmonton Flyers had a difficult season and finished out of the playoffs. The Stampeders appeared to be ready for a long playoff drive, but in semi-final action, the Seattle Totems won four games and lost one. Seattle's defensive play was effective against the high scoring Stampeders who had scored 300 goals in the regular season. In the final 2-1 win, the Stamps were able to get only 14 shots on Seattle net minder Bev Bentley.

One of the great physical rivalries of the time (1961-62) was between Howie Young of the Flyers and his Calgary Stampeder counterpart George McAvoy. Fans in both cities were enthused whenever the two tangled on the ice. Young later went to the Detroit Red Wings where he became one of the leagues most ''famed'' badmen.

The Edmonton Flyers ended up winning the league championship in 1961-62. They won an all Alberta Northern Division final over Alf Pike's Calgary Stampeders in three straight including a final 9-2 win. In this final match 5,560 in Edmonton watched Doug Messier (father of Paul and Mark Messier) score twice and Bill McNeill, Don Poile, Ed Joyal, Knobby Walsh, Len Lunde, Chuck Holmes and Howie Young get singles. It was Poiles' 200th goal in professional hockey. Replying for the Stampeders were Lou Jankowski and Doug Barkley.

EDMONTON FLYERS 1961-62

Back row: Don Chiz, Billy McNeill, Lionel Dewis (trainer), Eddie Joyal, Keith Walsh. Second row: Robert Merkle, Howie Young (#15), Doug Messier, John Miszuk, Len Lundy, Lloyd Hadden, Roger Dejordy, Bob Edwards. Front row: Warren Hynes, Lou Marcon, Ed Yuzda, Gilles Boivert, Bud Poile, Chuck Holmes, Don Poile. *Photo courtesy of Edmonton Archives*

The Flyers moved into the WHL finals and won the Lester Patrick Trophy when they defeated Colin Kilburn's Spokane Comets 4-2 in the seventh game of the series. The roof of the Gardens just about flew off when Flyer captain, Chuck Holmes, checked Spokane's Gord Stratten behind the Comet net and passed to Don Poile who scored to break a 2-2 tie. This goal occurred while Howie Young was in the penalty box. Len Lunde scored the extra goal into an empty net to give Edmonton its third WHL championship.

About a week later, Bud Poile, manager-coach of the Flyers resigned. Poile had coached the club to a full season on top of the WHL standings and the playoff victory over Spokane. It appeared at the time he was to be the replacement for ''Jolly'' Jack Adams, the GM of the Detroit Red Wings. However, Bruce Norris, Wing's owner, announced that Syd Abel would take over from Adams. This series of events caused Poile to resign. His long tenure in Edmonton had been well accepted by Edmonton fans.

1962-63 was the last season of pro hockey during this professional era in Alberta. The Edmonton Flyers defeated the Stampeders 4-1 in their final league game and eliminated Calgary from the playoffs. Edmonton had 58 points and gained the third and last playoff spot.

In the playoff round Keith Allen's Seattle Totems defeated the Flyers in the first round. In the final game Bob Barlow received a Guyle Fielder pass at 1:44 of sudden death overtime to give the Totems a 3-2 win. Goalie Gilles Boivert in the Flyer net continued his outstanding play for the year, but it was not enough to keep Edmonton alive. The last two goals ever scored for an Alberta team in the WHL were by Doug Messier and Bo Elik. The Totems outshot the Charlie Rayner's Flyers 39-14 in the concluding game.

In May 1963, the Calgary Stampeders announced their disenchantment towards their affiliation with the Chicago Black Hawks. The Calgary Exhibition and Stampede Board voted unanimously for voluntary suspension from the WHL for 1963-64. Gordon Love, Chairman of the Stampede Board said,

> We have been treated so shabbily by Chicago, that we have no alternative... Ivan (referring to Tommy Ivan of Chicago) simply wasn't interested in the future of hockey in Calgary, and that's all there is to it.

This announcement came after a disappointing season. The Stamps lost 45 games and $90,000.00. Edmonton followed suit and pulled out as well.

Both the Flyers and Stampeders did not rejoin the league in 1964-65. Rising team costs plus the lack of buildings suitable for pro hockey were the major reasons. The Edmonton Gardens was considered the poorest facility when compared to the Corral.

The WHL itself was in turmoil as the Los Angeles Blades and San Francisco Seals were trying to get into the NHL and Denver and Vancouver were losing money. The only successful franchise was the Portland Buckeroos. The Edmonton Exhibition and Calgary Exhibition and Stampede Boards were the owners of Alberta's last WHL teams. Al Anderson, the Edmonton Exhibition manager, and his counterpart in Calgary, Maurice Hartnett, said the major drawback was the rink situation in Edmonton. WHL teams were now costing $250,000.00 to $300,000.00 a year and the Edmonton Gardens could not command the gate receipts. Calgary could have done it for a short while in the Corral, but could not go alone into the league. Professional hockey was now officially dead in Alberta. It would be some ten years later, that professionals would come back in the form of the World Hockey Association.

The rink situation in Edmonton became positive as Northlands Coliseum was built, however, Calgary would not get the Saddledome until the 1980's. The exit of pro hockey left an opening for senior, junior, intermediate and university levels to be the prime focus during the interval.

ALBERTA SENIOR ALLAN CUP FROM 1950-51...1980-81

When the Western Canada Senior Hockey League played for the Alexander Trophy in 1950-51, other Alberta teams competed for the Allan Cup. This left an opening for the top intermediate level teams to move up one category to senior. Alberta senior hockey had only one more Allan Cup championship team, the Drumheller Miners in 1965-66.

In 1950-51, Edmonton Mercurys (1950 World Champions — see Intermediate Hockey) entered Allan Cup playoffs. They won the Alberta crown when they defeated the Calgary Hillhurst Hustlers 13-1 and 13-3. The Mercs then eliminated the Yorkton Legionnaires three games to one. The season came to an end when the talented Nanaimo Clippers won the next series three games to one.

The following season (1951-52) while the Mercurys (See Intermediate Hockey) were winning the Olympic Gold at the Olympics, the Edmonton Pats represented Alberta in senior playdowns. The Pats took their name from Cal Pickles, whose son was named Pat, and because Jimmy Graham was their coach. To win the Alberta senior playoffs the Pats easily eliminated the Canmore Legionnaires in two games. The final game before 2,000 fans in Edmonton ended 13-2.

The Pats surprised their fans when they defeated the Trail Smokeaters in the B.C./Alberta round. Goals by Billy Maher and Freddie Smitten past Smokie goalie Johnny Sofiak in the first period gave the Pats a final game 2-1 victory. Wilbur Delainey was sensational in goal as he only allowed Bob Weist to score at 19:03 in the third period. Players known to Albertans for Trail, included Bill Ramsden, Terry Cavanagh (later Edmonton Mayor) and Bobby Kromm.

The Western Allan Cup final against the St. Francis Canadians went six games before the Pats were eliminated. In the final game, the Canadians scored twice in a ten minute overtime to win 5-3. Scoring for Edmonton were Johnny Black, Harry Allen and Alex Pringle.

In the game rugged Pat forward, Billy "Dutchy" Van Deelan received a two minute cross checking penalty and argued with referee Paul Bozak. Van Deelan pushed Bozak and was also accessed a ten minute misconduct. ("Dutchy" later became one of Alberta's most prominent referees and today is an NHL supervisor of officials.)

The Pats still had a good year. They started the season as a "fun" team and did not have the same type of sponsorship as earlier teams. A group of Edmonton businessmen, plus gate receipts, and some players funding the rest, supported the Pats. Despite the fact that photographer Al Ernst of Goertz Studios was team manager, no team photo was taken. The lineup for the Pats included Wilbur Delainey, Eddie Cutts, Frankie Morris (later Canadian Football League Hall of Famer), Gordon Watt, Jim Kilburn, E. Zukiwisky, J. Zukiwisky, Bill Gostick, Bill Maher, Fred Smitten, Alex Pringle, Elmer Kreller, Billy "Dutchy" Van Deelan, Johnny Black, Harry Allen, Bill Hodgson and Doug Campbell.

After the 1951-52 Edmonton Pats, Alberta stayed out of Allan Cup playoffs until 1957-58. Senior hockey could not be supported financially because of the appeal professional hockey had in the WHL. At the AAHA November 1957 meeting in Lethbridge it was recommended that the Central Alberta Hockey League winner be the Alberta representative in the Allan Cup and the runner up go on the intermediate trail.

The Red Deer Rustlers represented Alberta in the 1957-58 Allan Cup playoffs. The Rustlers almost failed to get out of their own league after winning the regular season schedule. Their first opposition, the fourth place Lacombe Rockets made the Rustlers go seven games in the first round of the CAHL playoffs. Red Deer was behind three games to one before they won three straight which included a final 7-3 win. The Rustlers won the Vold-Dittberner Trophy for the CAHL when they defeated Olds Elks 6-5 to win the series four games to one.

Red Deer defeated the Regina Caps, three games to one and advanced one step further in Allan Cup playoffs against the Winnipeg Maroons. Billy Reichart scored two goals and Ray Barry one to give Red Deer a 3-1 win in the opening game before 2,400 fans at home. After splitting two games, the series moved to Winnipeg. The Maroons won the next two to eliminate Red Deer. In the final game a sparse crowd of 593 viewed a 9-2 Maroon victory.

For the next three seasons (1958-59, 1959-60, and 1960-61) Alberta had no representation in senior or Allan Cup playdowns. The CAHL winners decided to just enter intermediate. The CAHL won the provincial intermediate 'A' and represented Alberta (See Intermediate Hockey).

In 1961-62, the Calgary Adderson Builders represented Alberta in Allan Cup playoffs. The Builders played the season in the Big Six League which included Coleman Grands, Calgary Buffaloes, Great Falls Americans and Taber Chefs. In the league final the first place Builders fell behind two games to one against Coleman. They came back to win two and win the Bill William's Memorial Trophy for the Big Six. Calgary then moved into Allan Cup play.

Their first and only opposition was the 1961 World Champion Trail Smokeaters. Coach Al Rollins was absent for the Trail series as he was called up to the WHL Portland Buckeroos to play goal.

For manager Joe Carbury and new coach Neil Winchester the first game in Trail is one they probably would like to forget. It finished 15-1 for Trail. A better performance by Calgary kept the second game at 8-4. The series moved to Calgary for the third and final game.

Originally tickets were to be priced at the Corral from $1.25 to $2.00 which was the same price for playoffs in the WHL. Tickets were reduced to $1.25 for adults and $.50 for children. The difference in score was reduced as well to 7-6 for Trail. Warren Hicks scored two and Rock Crawford, Ken Gardner, Bruce Lea and Mick Gilday got one each for Calgary. Adam Kryczka for the Builders and Seth Martin for Trail each stopped 39 shots.

Senior hockey in Alberta was weak as clubs played in intermediate calibre leagues. In 1962-63 the CAHL tried senior again. The Lacombe Rockets represented the province against the Saskatoon Quakers. Herb Jeffery of Saskatoon scored in the third period to give the Quakers a 3-2 win and eliminate the Rockets three games to one in the Western Allan Cup semi-final. George Seniuk scored the other two Quaker goals while Al LaPlante and Jimmy Brown replied for Lacombe.

One of the major problems of all teams in junior, intermediate and senior hockey during playoffs was the inability of all players to get sufficient time away from regular jobs to play away games. This gave the home team a distinct advantage in many of the playoff series held. In 1963-64 the Lacombe Rockets went to the fifth and deciding game against the Kimberley Dynamiters. Lacombe won the first two games of the series at home 7-5 and 4-3, but when they went to Kimberley, they lost three in a row by scores of 7-2, 8-5 and 7-4.

In the final 7-4 win the "Nitro Line" for Kimberley of Les Lilley, Ken McTeer and Walt Peacosh accounted for five goals. Dick Vincent and Don White scored the other two. For Lacombe, Tony Kollman, Dick Dunnigan, Ron Tookey and Dave Carlyle replied.

The Lacombe Rockets went overseas in late 1964 to play in the invitational Ahearn Cup in Stockhom, Sweden. Don Hay, a former Rocket of the 50's, served as one of the executive on the team. Don describes the arrangements made in Lacombe and the trip.

LACOMBE ROCKETS GO OVERSEAS

BY DON HAY

In July 1964 the Lacombe Rockets Hockey Club was notified by the Canadian Amateur Hockey Association, that the team had been selected to represent Canada on a 25 day, 14 game exhibition tour of Europe. At a subsequent well attended hockey meeting in Lacombe, a nine member Board of Directors was elected headed by President, Garth Wagner. The Board rehired Art Park, as the team coach and appointed Marv Leiske the team manager. Park and Leiske were to begin immediately putting a team together for the coming season. At the same meeting a 20 member Rocket Booster Club was formed, headed by Chairman Vic Popow. The Booster Club was to organize and implement fund raising projects as money was required to provide the team with new uniforms, equipment bags, team blazers, souvenirs and pins, plus many other incidental expenses.

ROCKETS LEAVE FOR EUROPE NEXT WEEK

Here's the 1964-65 edition of the Lacombe Rockets hockey club, which represented Canada on a European hockey tour of Germany, Switzerland, Sweden and Czechoslovakia. From left to right top row: Marv Leiske, manager; Ed Zemrau, Ron Tookey, Al LaPlante, Vic Dzurko, Bill McCulley, Vince Downey, Wayne Gee, Butch Tomlinson, Harvey Linnell, Clare Drake (assistant coach); front row: Rich Healey, Dick Dunnigan, Tony Kollman, Russ Gillow, Art Park (coach), Dale Gaume, Dave Carlyle, Remi Brisson, Bob Solinger, Austin Smith.

Photo courtesy of Kanata Studios

In mid-September the Rockets opened their training camp in Edmonton, as ice was not available in Lacombe until mid-October. Thirty to forty players turned out three times a week, trying for positions on the team. Also, at that time, Clare Drake, coach at the University of Alberta, was appointed assistant coach, to aid coach Park in the selection of the team.

In Lacombe the Booster Club members were busy. Booster buttons reading "I'm a Rocket Booster" were now available and the first one was sold to Mayor Wes Jackson for a dollar. Five thousand buttons were sold through the Community and district. Local businesses were canvassed for donations and letters written to major Alberta suppliers. The support received was outstanding. The Lacombe Board of Trade announced that they would contribute $700, to the cost of purchasing souvenirs. These souvenirs included 8,000 autographed team picture postcards, 50 dozen pins, with crossed hockey sticks, 50 dozen Lacombe lapel pins, 100 dozen ballpoint pens, plus gifts to be presented to opposing players and officials of towns and cities, where the club would play. The Government of Alberta announced that they would provide the team members with sport jackets of the Alberta Tartan.

In late October the Rockets played their first exhibition game at home. Prior to the game the Booster Club organized a turkey dinner and catered to a crowd in excess of 500 people. At the dinner, a group of high school girls sang the Rocket Booster song, composed by Booster member Marg Whyte. It really caught on and was played regularly every morning over CKRD Radio for many weeks following.

In early November an Auction Sale organized by executive members, Ken Kocher, contributed $875, to the club coffers. Donations were picked up throughout the district and 180 pieces were sold by the four volunteer auctioneers. One goat was sold several times to add to the sales.

On December 19 a 23 man contingent, resplendent in their tartan blazers and brown slacks, departed from the Edmonton Airport heading for Ft. William and the start of their exhibiton tour. Members of the team included goal tenders Dale Gaume and Russ Gillow, defencemen Vic Dzurko, Rich Healey, Harvey Linnell and Ed Zemrau, forwards Rimi Brisson, Dave Carlyle, Vince Downey, Dick Dunnigan, Wayne Gee, Tony Kollman, Al LaPlante, Bill McCulley, Lloyd Orris, Austin Smith, Bob Solinger and Ron Tookey. The coach was Art Park, assistant coach Clare Drake and club manager Marv Leiske. Also accompanying the team were club President, Garth Wagner and AAHA Representative Jim Brown from Camrose.

The Rockets were impressive in their tour opener. In Ft. William they defeated an All-Star team made up of players from the Thunder Bay Senior League 6-2.

Leaving Ft. William, the Rockets then flew to Geneva, Switzerland. In the Pamoloi Ice Stadium the Rockets defeated the home town Sevets 5-2 in a crowd pleasing game before 5,000 fans. Bob Solinger celebrated his 40th birthday on this day. Prior to the game Swiss officials presented him with a cake bearing 40 candles.

Lacombe's next appearance was in Stockholm, Sweden, where they participated in a six team invitational tournament, for the Ahearne Cup. Although the team didn't win the tournament, they did receive lavish praise from the critical European press. Newspapers in Stockholm complimented the Rockets for their outstanding play, their hard but clean checking and good sportsmanship. One sports editor wrote,

> this is Canadian hockey at its best. It has already been determined that Lacombe Rockets are much better than expected and in my opinion, I can't remember a better Canadian team since the Whitby Dunlops were here in 1958.

Apparently, before the tournament started the Rockets were reported to be poor representaives of Canada and one early headline read: "Shame that the Lacombe Rockets should represent the motherland of hockey".

After winning their first two games, the Rockets were favoured to win the tournament. However, they proceeded to lose their next three and ended up in third place. Their toughest game was against the Russian National Junior team, who beat them 3-2. The Rockets outplayed and out-shot the juniors 31-17, but were unable to capitalize on their scoring chances. The Russians tied for first place, with the Swedish champions from Brynaes; but Brynaes were awarded the Ahearne Cup on the basis of best goals for and against.

From Sweden the Rockets then flew on to Prague, Czechoslovakia. In Czechoslovakia they played six exhibition games. Two games were against top senior teams and four games against the National Junior team. The games were played in six different cities and the Rockets won two games and tied four. This was an impressive record considering the team had to play six games in a nine day period against excellent opposition. Two of the games in Banska-Bistrica and Litvinov were played in outdoor arenas, which was quite a change to our usual type of ice accomodation. By contrast the arena in Ostrova was the finest they had seen in Europe. It had seating for 10,000 people and the dressing rooms were ultra modern and the complex even included a swimming pool.

The Rockets wound up their European tour on a triumphant note with a 4-3 win over the East German National team, in a thrill packed game before 10,000 wildly cheering fans in Weiswasser, East Germany. The win gave the Rookies an enviable record. Of fourteen games played — they won seven, tied four and lost three. All three losses came in succession during the Ahearne Cup tournament in Stockholm.

The Rockets were nothing but a success in the eyes of the CAHA. They surprised a lot of so-called experts by their record of only three losses in fourteen games and they pleased everyone with the way they did it. They were truly ambassadors for Canadian hockey and left good impressions wherever they visited, both on and off the ice.

* * *

In the 1964-65 final of the CAHL, the Drumheller Miners defeated the Red Deer Rustlers and represented the province in senior playoffs. The Miners had previously reached their highest plateau during the thirties. In those days players such as Tommy Anderson, "Duke" Wainman, the Wrights and later the Bentley brothers, made the Miners a top draw in rinks all over Alberta. However, the Miners never won the provincial senior title until 1964-65.

DRUMHELLER MINERS 1964-65

The British Columbia champion Nelson Maple Leafs, proved too powerful and eliminated the Miners three games to one. Drumheller suffered two losses in Nelson and then won 3-1 in Drumheller to make the series interesting. Ron Loughlin, John Ivanitz and Jack Wilson (from Calgary Spurs) scored for the Miners while Howie Hornby scored the lone goal for Nelson. Seth Martin of Nelson and Ron Mathers of Drumheller were outstanding in goal.

Nelson ended the series when they shut-out Roy Kelly's Miners 3-0. Martin had to earn his shut-out as he made 46 saves. This ended the Miner's Allan Cup bid but it made the club more determined than ever for the next season.

The 1965-66 Miners were an outstanding club. Jim Fisher was the manager. His duties as manager had to be fitted in as he was also the play-by-play broadcaster for the Miners on then CJDV, Drumheller. The highly skilled broadcaster for the Miners went to Salt Lake City, Utah to become the 'Voice of the Golden Eagles' on 50,000 watt "clear channel" KSL. Fisher is now back in Drumheller supporting hockey, broadcasting on Q91 and is manager of the Big Country Tourist Association. Here is his account of the Allan Cup champions of 1965-66.

DRUMHELLER MINERS — 1966 ALLAN CUP CHAMPIONS

BY JIM FISHER

Many said it couldn't happen — others were surprised. But in twenty years since, no Alberta hockey team has been able to duplicate the feat of the Drumheller Miners. In analyzing the Miners of 1966, we had a club that would be competitive among many professional teams of today, yes, even in the company of NHL teams.

Numerous obstacles stood in the way of the Miners. Only three years before this club was whipped 17-0 at the hands of the mighty Lacombe Rockets, a club based on University of Alberta and former pro talent. On that night Drumheller coach, Roy Kelly, vowed he'd see the day the Miners got even and would "kick the pants off everybody". By 1966 the rugged Central Alberta Intermediate 'A' League had been renamed the Alberta Hockey League, purposely not adopting any category. One of Canada's premiere Junior 'A' Clubs was also a member in the Edmonton Oil Kings, a team in those days supported by the Detroit.Red Wings. In fact, as Edmonton Oil Kings went, so went Western Canada. They were in a class of Junior 'A' hockey by themselves.

The 1965-66 season began with a tumultuous situation. The AAHA, Calgary and Drumheller became embroiled over player rights. By the rules, the Miners held the rights to certain players. But, the AAHA decided which one could stay or which one could go to Calgary. Then, just as the Miners were to start training camp, an arsonist set the old building ablaze and, suddenly, no home. Even the "Edmonton Journal" had a favorite pastime of writing about the "old barn" (Drumheller Arena) and maintained fans who couldn't find their way out in the spring were still there when the hockey season started in the fall.

A quick decision had to be made in the fall of 1965 — fold the team or, struggle against high odds? A team representative was dispatched to Hanna — 50 miles to the east — and that community adopted the club with open arms, cancelling all regular programs to give the team a new home. Having accomplished this, again the question, how could this work? After all, every player, with the exception of four, resided in Calgary. That meant a 300 mile round trip every time. Many had played professional — won awards in the NHL. Afterall, Al Rollin the Vezina and Hart Trophy winner in the National Hockey League had better things to do or, then again, did he? Added to this was the fact Calgary fans tried to tell anyone who would listen that they had a far superior club in the Western Canada Senior Hockey League. Of course, Drumheller couldn't see that line of thinking and proved it.

That season the Edmonton Oil Kings were touted to have a club as big as any team in the National Hockey League. (They went on to win the Memorial cup, eliminating Bobby Orr and company in the Canadian final.) When Detroit sent their budding stars to Hanna, fans hung from the rafters, sometimes 20' above the ice. Drumheller and Edmonton finished the regular season tied for first place but "Wild" Bill Hunter and coach Ray Kinasewich of the Kings agreed the Miners would be awarded top spot because of a better record between the two teams. Inevitably, the clubs would collide for the league title.

How many times have you heard a discussion — is Senior 'A' or Junior 'A' the best? We can't tell you. After sudden death overtime in game seven including even a 45 minute riot, — team management got together with the score still deadlocked 1-1. It was decided this was nonsense because, despite their bitter rivalry, Edmonton and Drumheller were "sticking" together. After all, in two nights, Edmonton opened against Calgary in the Memorial Cup playdowns while Drumheller opened with Calgary in senior competition in just three days. Bill Hunter and I, the respective managers, decided to call off the series since both teams appeared to have excellent chances at a Canadian title.

The reasoning was — why beat each other around any more? The Alberta Hockey League Governors didn't see it that way and immediately placed us under suspension. The night Edmonton and Calgary opened in Memorial Cup play, a League vote reinstated us and the CAHA welcomed the teams into competition.

Drumheller went on to eliminate Calgary Spurs in straight games, pointing clearly to where the power actually was. Following the sweep, the CAHA stepped in and decreed the Hanna rink was too small. One thousand, two hundred maximum wasn't good enough. So, again, the hunt was on to find another home. Despite protests from the Calgary club (they were already eliminated) they didn't want Drumheller playing in the Stampede Corral.

Mervyn "Red" Dutton stepped in. He not only sympathized with a hockey club without a home but expressed a love for the City of Drumheller and the Valley. He strongly suggested that should the Miners continue to win, every possible date at the Corral be made available. As it later turned out, the ice was in and out a number of times as the Miners played their games at the Corral and when that wasn't available, used another home at the University of Calgary.

What many still claim to have been the largest crowd to ever witness a hockey game at the Stampede Corral occured on Good Friday evening, 1966. The Kimberley Dynamiters charged into the cowtown with a flair. They even promoted a downtown parade. On good authority, the building (seating 6,666 at that time) was said to have had over 9,300 fans with "another 3,500 turned away." Those who got into the Corral won't forget that night for a long time. The power-laden Dynamiters struck quickly — a 3-0 first period lead. They hit 3 goalposts too, or it could have been 6-0. The Cranbrook broadcast team, at the first intermission, chided Alberta for sending such a weak opponent into Allan Cup play. Period two — Kimberley was in trouble.

The Miners were known as a rough hockey club — not dirty — not chippy but, a good, rough, grinding club that played the game hard — the way the game should be played. Very infrequently, we see a current National Hockey League game played in that style. By the end of regulation time the game was tied 3-3. Into overtime, no scoring.

Now, along comes the second sudden death overtime stanza. Another 20 minutes almost over — it was midnight. Ron 'Squeak' Leopold showed in professional company he could score goals in a more precise manner than most NHL performers today. But, of all his great goals, nothing was like this. Tired, Leopold struggled to centre ice, flipped the puck into the Kimberley zone, wide of the net. 'Squeak' slumped on the bench and couldn't figure why the roof of the Corral seemed like it was coming down. He had scored — no, he hadn't seen it. The puck hit the back boards and bounced back, hit the goalie and it went into the net.

'Slippery' Sid Finney, one of the smoothest of them all, was said by a Chicago Black Hawk scout to be playing well enough for Drumheller, that he could have been the number one centreman for the Hawks in the old six team league. With the teams embroiled in another tough one, the score was tied at 2-2 in game two. Seth Martin had just returned from a hero's welcome, having performed as an All-Star in the World Hockey Championships. Being applauded as a national sports figure with a standing ovation, the teams prepared to faceoff (Seth had replaced the injured, starting goal tender). Later, the official was to say that the puck hadn't touched the ice. When he dropped it, to the right of Martin, Finney connected in mid-air, whipping the puck between Martin's pads.

In that series Kimberley used the intimidation approach, but that could never work with the lineup Drumheller boasted. Huge defencemen who could stop you cold in mid-ice — defencemen who "owned" every corner of the rink such as Rudichuk, Sawka, the Braithwaites and the smooth former Toronto Maple Leaf, Bobby Solinger. And, up front, the three policemen — Rock Crawford — Patty Halas and big Bill McCulley. Bill who tipped the scales at 220-230 lbs. — could skate with anyone and he didn't tolerate the opposition getting out of line. He was also quite a boxer on skates and, while he never went looking for trouble. He was there.

The Miners went on to win that series in straight games, then eliminated Saskatchewan and Manitoba.

The Canadian title was to be decided in Calgary — a-best-of-seven. Serge Aubrey backstopped the solid Quebec Club — the Sherbrooke Beavers. Nine players had been or were in the process of being offered pro contracts, according to the stories received prior to the series. The Miners took the first game but the Flying Frenchmen were just too fast in games two and three. In fact, they had a player they toted as faster than the great "Montreal Roadrunner", Yvan Cournoyer. Whether this was true, or not, there wasn't much to choose. The goal tending was hot. Coach Roy Kelly was one of the finest tacticians in hockey, be it pro or amateur. He was forever assessing exactly what the opposition did from period to period.

Game four, and the Miners trailed two games to one. Quebec was pressing. Early in that fourth game on Corral ice, Drumheller found themselves two men short in the early going. A fellow who both amateurs and pros will readily admit was one of the finest puck-control artists to play the game — Tony Kollman — spearheaded the Miners. He ragged the puck 20-30 seconds at a time. Even Al Rollins (Chicago Black Hawk and Toronto Maple Leaf goal tender) played "defence" skating from one corner to the other as the Miners set up a box formation. Whenever Kollman was in trouble, back came the puck to the defencemen or to Rollins.

Kollman was a tremendous instigator — the type of player you hated but, also the very player you would select as your first choice if you started a club. By this time, Tony was really coming into his own. The Quebec squad figured enough was enough. Three men charged Kollman in unison. Kollman knew he was going to "get it" and, in the manner of a great competitior, took the hammering. He held the puck until the last second — manouevered the Quebec club into the position he wanted and, when a teammate stepped out of the penalty box — fed him with a break away pass. Kollman got decked, but the Miners took a 1-0 lead. That seemed to be the turning point of the series.

DRUMHELLER MINERS — ALLAN CUP CHAMPIONS 1965-66

Front row (l to r): Ron Mather, Lorne Braithwaite, Ernie Braithwaite, Ray Sawka (captain), Pat Halas, Jack Hudichuck, Bob Solinger, Al Rollins. **Middle row (l to r):** Ken Flager (promotion), Roy Kelly (coach), Glen Whittaker (vice-president), Rock Crawford, Bill Voss, Bruce Vickers (president), Gene Lambert, Sid Finney, Jim Fisher (manager), Doug Wilton (equipment man), Jack Bond (promotion). **Third row (l to r):** Ken Noonan, Owen Mailey, Harvey Linnell, Ron Leopold, Ron Loughlin, Tony Kollman, Al McDonald.

Vancouver Canuck trainer and former Drumhellerite, Kenny Fleger can point to the fact he was probably the only fan ejected from that Allan Cup series. He got into a verbal disagreement with Aubrey as the series returned to the University Rink. The long arm of the law escorted him out but Fleger eventually won the argument, pointing out if he went, so did the Quebec goalie. The Miners won the series in six games. On May 18, 1966, two nights previously, Edmonton had won the Memorial Cup at Maple Leaf Gardens.

The Canadian Senior and Junior 'A' Champions playing out of the same league is probably a first and probably the only time it will happen. In the early 1960s Drumheller wanted to join the league, embracing Edmonton. But, the northerners didn't want this. Finally, the Miners garnered enough votes and soon, Edmonton became our biggest supporters and, vice-versa. After all, how else would Edmonton be required by the Fire Department to lock their rink 20 minutes before game time, thanks a lot to train after train-load of fans Drumheller would send into Edmonton.

No doubt fellows like former Oil King, Glen Sather, look back on the 1960s and the league as good hockey, and with a few chuckles. Many Edmonton players who went into the NHL say the roughest and toughest hockey they got into was against the Drumheller Miners. Some would kid about the "Munson Flu". Munson is a small village 7 miles north of Drumheller. When their team approached Drumheller players would be kidding they had come down with the flu, not looking to challenging the Miners in the corners. Jack Rudichuk at 6'3" had a habit of raising players off the ice and into the screen. Some say we will never see those days again. We may, but the only problem if that happens few of us will realize how good the hockey of that time period really was.

* * *

The following season (1966-67), the Drumheller Miners were selected to represent Canada on a European tour. Jim Fisher reports that the Miners were good ambassadorsina "difficult situation compounded by the lack of support of hockey officials involved in the series in Sweden." It was the Bunny Ahearne Tournament. The Miners started out well but the politics of international hockey "soured everyone". The Miners, as did most Canadian clubs, played to sellouts. Even the Canadian Embassy had problems getting tickets. Fisher notes that "the Russians in this tournament always played to small crowds."

MINERS IN EUROPE, OUTSIDE THE NEW ICE STADIUM IN STOCKHOLM, SWEDEN...1967

Back row (l to r): Jim Fisher, Jim Baird, E. Braithwaite, Bill Voss, Glen Lambert, Don Rehill, B. Wilton, Glen Wittaker, Bud Syverson, J. Kosiahsic, Bruce Vickers, Ray Sawka, Roy Kelly, J. Rudichuck, Art Potter. Front row (l to r): J. Yucytus, Sid Finney, Ron Leopold, H. Flemming, Pat Hahas, P. Crawford, Tony Kohlman, R. Mathews, M. Dodd.

The Calgary Spurs became the 1966-67 Alberta representatives in Allan Cup play. They were league members in the Western Canada Senior League. The WCSHL replaced the old CAHL. The Spurs started as a club in 1964-65 and played exhibition games. In 1965-66 they finished the WCSHL in first place only to lose to the Allan Cup bound Drumheller Miners from the AHL.

Other clubs in the WCSHL of 1966-67 included the Red Deer Rustlers, Saskatoon Quakers, Yorkton Terriers, Edmonton Nuggets, Moose Jaw Play-Mors and Regina Caps. The main factor in the birth of the league was that pro hockey did not exist in Alberta or Saskatchewan. Sufficient ex-pros were able to make teams competitive.

Calgary businessman Ron Butlin was the general manager of the Spurs and former professional Tony Schneider was the coach. The Spurs ended up in first place in 1966-67 and in their first 17 playoff games, won 13. The line of Marty Demarais, Warren Hicks and Dave Parenteau accounted for 68 points in playoffs while John Ivanitz, Jimmy Brown and Doug Cairns produced 57 points in the first 17 games. The last and only Calgary team to win the Allan Cup were the Stampeders of 1945-46. Demarais's father, Tony, and Cairn's father, Doug, both played then.

In the spring of 1967, the Spurs eliminated Red Deer Rustlers and then in the WCSHL finals defeated the Saskatoon Quakers. The Nelson Maple Leafs lost in three straight and the Spurs were in the Allan Cup final.

The Allan Cup final was played in Drummondville, Quebec, against the hometown Eagles. No western team had won the Allan Cup in the east since the Trail Smokeaters defeated the Kirkland Lake Blue Devils in 1938. This season proved to be the same. The Drummondville Eagles blanked the Spurs 4-0 in the first game and then won three more in a row.

In 1967-68 the Drumheller Miners advanced further than the other clubs in Alberta in Allan Cup playoffs. Drumheller played in a revamped Alberta Senior Hockey League and played the Spokane Jets, Saskatoon Quakers and St. Boniface Mohawks before being eliminated.

The Edmonton Monarchs, members of the rival WCSHL, lost to the Saskatoon Quakers four games to three. This allowed the Quakers to represent their league in further playoffs against the Drumheller Miners. Drumheller were ahead two games to one. In the fourth game Ted Demchuk, recruited from Red Deer for the playoffs, scored at 5:06 of the third overtime period to advance the Miners to the Western Allan Cup final. The final match before 2,300 fans in Drumheller took four hours and 45 minutes of actual time to play. Jim Shaw of the Quakers had 31 shots in the 35 minutes of overtime for a game total of 61 while Al Rollins had 41 saves for the Miners.

The Miners lost the Western Allan Cup in three straight 4-3, 4-2 and 6-0. St. Boniface Mohawk playing coach, Gary Aldcorn scored two goals and singles went to Leo Duguay, Lorne Boransky and a young Butch Goring. Jim Fisher recalls that,

> a young hustling junior came out in that first game in Drumheller and showed the fans why he was to become an NHL star. He probably had the same helmit in that Drumheller series as he wore when the New York Islanders started their domination. Butch Goring — what a tremendous, hardworking checker. He was probably the key to the series win for St. Boniface.

Goring is now the 1985-86 coach of the Boston Bruins.

The name Calgary Stampeders returned to senior ranks in 1968-69. The Stamps advanced to the Western Allan Cup final when they defeated the Spokane Jets 4-2 to win the series three games to two. Ted Demchuk scored twice while Sid Finney and Pat Halas had singles. Don Scherza and Alan "Buddy" Bodman replied for Spokane. The Stamps won the west when they defeated the Port Arthur Bearcats three games to one. In the final game, Jack Owchar scored for the Cats but Calgary came back as Warren Hicks, Jack Yucytus, Ted Demchuk, Pete Wesson, George Hill, Ken Cairns, and Paul Chachka each replied in a 7-1 win.

The Allan Cup final of 1968-69 proved equally as disasterous for the Stamps as it had been for the Spurs in 1966-67. Business commitments kept ten Calgary players away for the first two games against the Galt Hornets in Galt. This left eight forwards and three defencemen for the opening games. The Hornets completed their four game sweep when they downed the Stamps 7-2. In the series, Calgary was outscored 27-8. The major problem for the Stamps was to have players able to get time off of work. The longer seasons and playoff series made it almost impossible to ice a constant team.

The Edmonton Monarchs appeared to be the 1969-70 Alberta Allan Cup team when they had a three to one lead in games over the Calgary Stampeders. The Stamps came back to win two in a row and force a seventh match at their home Corral. Some 7,945 fans attended plus an estimated 2,000 were turned away for this game. The fans were ecstatic when Stampeder Don Haley opened the scoring. His goal turned out to be his second straight game winner as the Stamps carried on to a 3-0 victory. Outstanding goal tending by Gary Simmons and other goals by Pete Wesson and Tom Burger sent Calgary to play the Spokane Jets.

Al Rollins had played for Roy Kelly in Drumheller and now they coached against each other. Rollin's Jets showed their superiority when they won the first two games in Calgary 4-1 and 4-0. Veteran goalie Seth Martin was almost unbeatable. In the third game in Spokane, the Jets turned it on to win 5-2 and the series in three straight.

George Hill was the Alberta Hockey League's leading scorer. According to George Bilych of the "Calgary Herald," Hill was "the best Stampeder on the ice Saturday but it took a lot of doing. Attending a convention in Mexico City last week, George cut short his trip and spent 14 hours on various planes and at airports, arriving in Spokane just a couple of hours before game time."

Senior Hockey in Alberta did not have the pro variety for competition and still lost money. The 1969-70 Stamps drew almost 8,000 for the seventh playoff game against Edmonton and over 3,000 to each of the home games against Spokane. They expected to lose close to $20,000.00 for the season. Bilych reported that for Stamp owner Nado Gallelli "this has got to be good news considering the red ink last year was in the vicinity of $42,000.00." Gallelli was looking forward to the following season; however, he died in November, 1970. The Stampeder name carried on in seniors for only two more years.

To reduce costs, cut down on the length of each series, and to allow players less time away from work, the Allan Cup playoffs in Western Canada played a tournament to determine a finalist in 1970-71. The Stamps defeated the Nelson Maple Leafs 4-2 in a final sudden-death game in Yorkton, Saskatchewan. Brian Dickie, Carl Forester, George Hill and "Spike" Houston accounted for the Calgary goals and sent them to the Allan Cup final in Galt, Ontario.

The Galt Hornets continued the eastern mastery and won the series in four straight games. This was the third Allan Cup in four straight games. On this occasion it was much closer as the Hornets only outscored the Stamps 18-13 in the series.

CALGARY STAMPEDERS 1970-71
Western Finalists Senior Allan Cup

Front row (l to r): Carl Forster, Mike Orman, Bob Peers, Gary Simmons, Nado Gallelli, Jim Brady, George Hill, Carl Chawaka, Larry Dobson. Middle row (l to r): Frank Ashworth, Ted Demchuk, Tom Burgess, Pete Weston, Dave Haley, Pat Halas, Rick Hextall, Rod Collins, Roy Kelly (coach). Back row (l to r): Deak Cassidy, Gordon Worsley, Randy Ward, Scott Watson, Jim Kryway, Ed Worsley, Harvey Jameson.

After an opening 4-2 loss, the Stampeder's Scott Watson tied the second game 5-5 at 19:48 of the third period. Unfortunately for the Stampeders it was not sudden-death overtime. Len Haley scored first but Galt came back to equal the score at six. Cec Hoekstra scored for Galt at 6:28 of the second overtime to give the Hornets a two game lead. The third game was won by Galt 3-2 when they scored at 14:32 of overtime. A final 4-3 Galt win before 2,533 fans ended the Stampeder's hopes.

The Edmonton Monarchs of 1971-72 were the first Edmonton senior team in twenty years to represent Alberta. The last Edmonton team to do so had been the Edmonton Pats in 1952. Dr. Neil Cuthbertson, long time hockey supporter, was President and Gene Achtymichuk was the coach. The Monarchs won the Prairie Hockey League and went on to play the Spokane Jets. The Jets won the first two games 6-1 and 5-2 in Spokane.

Slightly over a thousand turned out in Edmonton to see the Monarchs drop the third game 6-4. The fourth and final loss of 5-0 at the University Rink ended the season and an era in provincial senior hockey ended.

The Calgary Stampeder's name in senior hockey folded and many of the players played intermediate for teams such as the Banff Bisons. The Edmonton Monarchs were the last senior club to represent the province, who had Allan Cup intentions from the start of the year. Future Allan Cup contenders from Alberta were intermediate clubs. The other factor in Edmonton was the birth of the Edmonton Oilers of the WHA in the fall of 1972. Compared to professional the senior variety could not compete.

The players for the Monarchs at the end were Jim Knox, Mike Ballash, Jim Seutter, Ross Barros, Ray Sawka, Dale Conrad, Ron Tookey, Art Hart, coach Gene Achtymichuk, Grant Evans, Milt Hohol, Len 'Comet' Haley, Dave Rochefort, Mel Gushattey, Oliver Morris, Ivan Andrews, Art Scott, Lou Halat, Brian Bennett, Terry Ewasiuk, Ray McLeod, manager John Gattens and assistant coach Roger Gelinas. Gary Simmons, Gary McQuaid, Randy Murray and Wally Kozak were picked up from the Stampeders for the series against Spokane.

In the 1977-78 provincial Allan Cup playoffs the Drumheller Miners and Edmonton Bruins were the only teams entered. Both teams were classified as intermediate. Alberta had not had an Allan Cup representative since the 1971-72 season. The WHA , NHL expansion and the growth of minor hockey had almost forced senior hockey out. It was even hard to keep an intermediate team going in Alberta.

Bill La Forge was the Edmonton Bruin coach. (For a short time in the 1984-85 NHL season he coached the Vancouver Canucks at the tender age of 33.) La Forge was determined to keep his intermediate club alive.

EDMONTON MONARCHS 1971-72

Front (l to r): Bob Johnson, Ray Sawka, Ron Tookey, Milt Hohol, Jim Knox, Wally Serediak (equipment manager). **Second row (l to r)**: John Mandryk (executive), Lou Halat, Mel Gushatey, Jim Seutter, Dale Conrad, Mike Ballash, Ivan Andrews, Dave Rochefort, Gene Achtymichuk (playing coach). **Back row (l to r)**: Len Haley, Art Hart, Grant Evans, Oliver Morris, Art Scott, Hank Labercane (trainer).

Photo courtesy of Rick Ervin

The Bruins started in November 1973, as an intermediate team in the Yellowhead Hockey League. La Forge was coach and Ross Tyson manager. The team could not find a suitable rink in Edmonton because minor hockey had most of the ice. They played in Onoway, 50 kilometers northwest of Edmonton for home games. In the mid-seventies the Bruins played one year in Gibbons, 40 kilometers north of Edmonton.

The next step for the Bruins was the Edmonton Central League. La Forge wanted to see the league have a higher profile. The league changed its name to the Alberta Intermediate Major Hockey League. By this time he had negotiated for ice time in Edmonton's Jasper Place Arena. Peter Skrabyk, a Bruin player, recalls that the team "issued regular press releases, player profiles and had the best equipment available". The players sold Grey Cup tickets and La Forge did all the other organizing. The Bruins even put on free hockey schools for minor players in the Jasper Place area of Edmonton to build up fan interest and to become part of the community.

In December 1977, the Edmonton Bruins played the Drumheller Miners in Alberta Allan Cup playoffs. They lost four games to one. Their only victory was a 3-2 win in double overtime.

The Edmonton Bruins folded in early January 1978. In one of the team's last games, 28 paying fans watched them play the Stony Plain Eagles. La Forge regrouped and formed a team on the Enoch Indian Reservation called the Enoch Tomahawks. He then became coach of the Regina Pats, Oshawa Generals, Kamloops Oilers and Vancouver Canucks. After the Canucks he went to the Hamilton Steel Hawks of the OHA.

Most NHL coaches have played some professional hockey. Few, if any, have had the grassroots experience of William John Patrick La Forge. (Bill La Forge, the most streetwise coach to hit the NHL, is the nephew of Tommy Graham, Managing and Associate Editor of *Alberta on Ice*.)

EDMONTON BRUINS 1977-78

Back (l to r): Gerry Isbister, Greg Olsen, Willy Babcock, Lance Guse, Gord Gamble, Gord Lang, Gord Stewart, Gary Busch. **Middle (l to r):** Stan Osylko, Peter Skrabyk, Claude Warwick, Rick Phipps, Paul Jones, Ron Anderson, Grant Quist, Willie Moolyk, Wayne Reidford, Bob Soskolowski. **Front (l to r):** Gord McDermit, Al Olsen, Al Otto, Bill LaForge (coach), Ross Tyson, Mark Wollen, Wade Williamson, Rod Carlson.

Photo courtesy of Edmonton Archives

DRUMHELLER MINERS 1977-78

BY RICK TREMBECKY

(Drumheller's Rick Trembecky was a former junior with the Calgary Centennials. This was Drumheller's final provincial senior victory and last try at the Allan Cup.)

The 1977-78 edition of the Drumheller Senior Miners temporarily ended one of the most exciting eras of Senior Hockey on the Canadian Prairies. That year Jim Fisher, General Manager of the Miners and Coach Rick Trembecky combed all over the province in search of suitable talent to rebuild an Allan Cup contender — it wasn't to be. Operating costs began to skyrocket, player availability diminished, competition from Junior Hockey, cable T.V. and video systems began to take fans and players elsewhere.

Allan Cup fever in the mid-60s was an incurable disease amongst hockey fans in Drumheller. There were sell-out crowds and bizarre fan antics — you had to be there! It was a proven fact across Canada that in order to challenge for the Allan Cup, players with professional and semi-pro experience were a must. Jobs in the late 70s were no longer available to players wanting to move and play for the Miners, the economy was taking a fast and abrupt turn for the worse.

The Miners managed to get only three players with any pro or semi-pro experience in 1977-78. The Richardson brothers, Frank and Steve, along with Wayne Morin, made up the nucleous of the team. They only had brief stints with the defunct World Hockey Association. Most other players were just over aged juniors who wanted to keep playing for the sake of playing.

In the Alberta Senior final, we managed to fill the arena for three games and defeat Bill La Forge and the Edmonton Bruins. Spokane Jets then took the Miners in four games in the Western Canada Final. The talent just couldn't match that of the "Squeak" Leopolds, Sid Finneys and Al Rollins which had brought the Allan Cup to Drumheller. Unofficially, the hunt for the Cup was over for the "Mighty Miners".

In late January of '82, the Drumheller Oldtimers played the Montreal Canadien's Old Timers. Everyone who had been a Miner fan was there — a 2,200 sell-out. December of '84 saw a touring Midget team from Sweden play the local Midget 'B' Dinos, 1,600 fans attended, temperatures were over 30 degrees below zero. Perhaps in the near future engineers will start mapping out a new Allan Cup Trail for Drumheller hockey fans. History

Back row (l to r): Wayne Morin, Lynn McDonald, Frank Richardson, Milo deBernardo, Brent Taylor, Rich Pozzo, Ryan Wecker, Doug Hunter (president), Sandy McLean, Steve Richardson, Robert Cook, "Chupe" Colbourn, Stan Smith and Rick Trembecky (coach). Front row: Brian Reynolds, Doug McKenzie (Alberta Amateur Hockey Association), Dave Colbourn, Brian Smith, Kevin Carr, Wayne Colbourn, Brian Hannigan, Rod Gillespie. Missing from photo: Mike Sweet and Don Simitiuk. *Photo courtesy of Edmonton Archives*

has a habit of repeating itself. Any Miner fan will tell you that it was the "Drumheller Miners" who put Drumheller on the map, not the Dinosaurs.

THE CAMROSE MAROONS OF 1978-79 AND 1979-80

BY JACK HELLER, Manager

CAMROSE MAROONS — ALBERTA CHAMPIONS 1978-79

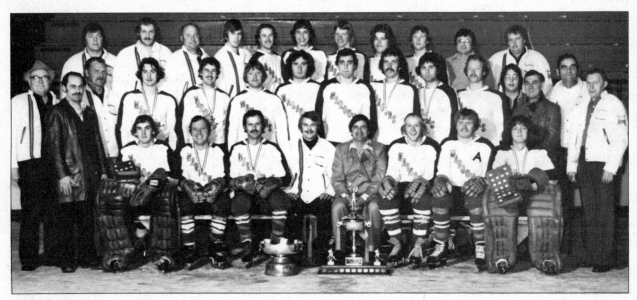

Back row (l to r): Glenn Smith (executive), George Mudry (executive), Svend Green, Len Gumpinger, Ellard Dillworth, Jack Heller (manager), Darcy McGahn (coach), Bill Andreassen, Jim Ofrim, Doug Sheets (goalie). Second row (l to r): Brian Smoole, Andy Crenshaw, Brian Stolley, Rick Kelewiky, Rick Van Slyke, Peter Brullin, Jim Grant, Kevin Lyseng, Mark Henderson (stick boy), Bill Grant (executive), Norm Henderson (executive), Fred Heck (executive). Front row: Doug Galenza (executive), Ernie Brandt (executive), Dan Zietarsky (executive), Robbie Daums, Bob Large, Joe Miller, Dale Jackson, Bob McGowan, Rick Vanance, Dennis Burrell, Clarence Trembley.

The 1978-79 hockey season for the Camrose Maroons, started off on a pretty good note. The club had a fine nucleus of veterans and rookies. We played well for most of the year, but it looked as though the club was going to tail off at the end. We finished second in the league only to lose in the first round of the playoffs to the Stony Plain Eagles. But the Provincial Playoffs were to be a different story. The first series was against Red Deer, which I believe was the reason for us not only winning that series, but not losing until we hit the Western Allan Cup semi-final.

Red Deer pulled tactics such as running off penalty time between periods and starting the clock when play was stopped. We fell behind 4-2 in the first game. Most of the players were so upset that they knew revenge would be theirs in the second game. The second game started quickly. Within one minute, Andy Crenshaw and Jim Ofrim, combined to score three goals. From then on the series was over.

In the next round, the Maroons easily eliminated the Stettler Sabres. It was then on to Stony Plain. Again the Maroons played amazing hockey. This setup an Alberta final against Didsbury. The first game in Didsbury was an easy win for Camrose. The final game in Camrose was a bit closer but the goals for and against were too much for the Didsbury club to overcome.

It was on to the Western Allan Cup in Manitoba. The Maroons were registered as an Intermediate 'A' team not a Senior 'A'. But the AAHA had decided that the winner of Alberta would go to the Allan Cup and the loser of the final game would represent Alberta in the Intermediate 'A' category. The Maroons were very much rated as the underdogs.

In the first game the Steinbach Huskies posted a 5-3 victory. The final goal was scored into an empty net. Game two was quite different when the Maroons posted a 6-5 double overtime win. This was to be their only win of the series as injuries took their toll. Peter Brown (defence) badly bruised ankle, Bob McGowan (defence) measles, Len Gumpinger (defence) had a sprained back. This left us with only three defencemen. We kept pace with the Huskies; only to lose the next two games by small margins.

The 1979-80 season proved successful. The Maroons entered this season as a registered Senior 'A' team. They finished their league season in first place, went on to win the league championship and post the provincial championship with a final 5-0 victory over the Fort McMurray Oilers in the Senior 'A' category.

Things seemed to be in our favour until we ran into the Spokane Flyers. The Flyers, in the previous season, were the Edmonton Oilers farm club. Then Edmonton stopped their support. A majority of the players stayed with the Flyers and Spokane went to go on to win the Allan Cup. They compiled an undefeated record right across Canada.

The 1979-80 season was to be the final year for the Camrose Maroons. Due to lack of executive and financial help the Maroons folded. Thus, an era of hockey supremacy by one of the oldest and finest amateur hockey teams in Alberta ended.

THE INNISFAIL EAGLES

BY HAP CLARKE

(A.H. 'Hap' Clarke, now retired, is a former owner and publisher of the Drumheller Mail and Innisfail Provincial Weekly and was a feature columnist for the *Edmonton Journal*.)

Alberta's representative in Allan Cup playoffs was the Innisfail Eagles in 1980-81. The club played the season in the intermediate category. As a result of defeating Bonnyville in the final, the club then became senior and the Pontiacs went intermediate.

The playoff season started against High River. The Eagles were forced to the limit when each team won 4-3 which caused overtime in the second game. Kim Weinkauf flipped a shot that seemed harmless but it was the winner for the Eagles. The Eagles then played the Bonnyville Pontiacs. By virtue of a 14-9 two game-total-goal victory the Eagles became the senior representatives. (See Intermediate for the Pontiacs) The team then played the British Columbia champions.

Three former members of the Medicine Hat Junior Tigers, the Gassoff Brothers played for the Quesnal B.C. Kangeroos. The combination of the Gassoffs and a few more ex-pros proved to be too physical and the Eagles lost three in a row, 2-0, 6-1, and 4-1. Al Ladd scored both our goals in the series.

John Waugh of the Eagles recalled the pressures of intermediates playing against senior and ex-pros:

Bob Galloway our goalie kept the scores at a respectable level but stopped over 45 shots a game. The Gassoffs let you know they were going to hit you. They could be classified as old fashioned compared to today's lack of bodychecking. Some of us really paid the price when we were hit by those brothers.

A highlight of the 1980-81 season for the Eagles was a 7-4 home ice win over the Japanese Nationals who were on a Canadian tour. The game attracted 1,300 fans and caused concern for Innisfail Fire Chief Del Fehr. After the game, it was decided that future games in the 1947 War Memorial Arena (now Memorial Arena) would have a capacity of 940.

The Eagles in 1981-82 won their sixth straight Alberta title. This included all categories of intermediate hockey. It was their third straight Intermediate 'A' final and for the second time in a row they represented the province in the senior category.

Victories were obtained over the Banff Mountaineers, High River Flyers and Taber Buccaneers to garner the south. The two game series against Taber became one game due to a Central Alberta blizzard. Taber got to Innisfail a few hours before the game but only eight local players could get to the rink. Game officials from Red Deer had to stay at home and it was agreed to play one game in Taber. The Eagles won 5-3 and then played the Bonnyville Pontiacs.

INNISFAIL EAGLES — CHINOOK HOCKEY LEAGUE 1981-82
Alberta Senior "A" Champions

Back row (l to r): Ron Jarvis (director), Dan Kinsella, Dwayne Howell, Rob Jacobson, Ray Bennett, Jim Shanahan (manager), Cam Beaton (director). Middle row (l to r): John Waugh (coach), Frank Layden (director), Jack MacDonald, Russ Hall, Rich Hileman, Dale Chatwood, Dean Edgar, Bob Mullen, Rick Wannamaker, Randy Glasgow (director), Don Fellows (vice-president), Joe Bacque (president). Front row (l to r): Tim Wilf (secretary treasurer), Bob Galloway (goalie), Greg Scott, Phil Jensen, Kim Weinkauf, Al Ladd, John McPhee, Ken Purcell, Ralph Rigel (director), Bill Wright (director). Missing: Grant Pushie, Rick Odegard, Al Churchill (executive).

The Eagles won the provincial final 11-7 in two games and then continued in senior. (See Intermediate for Bonnyville.) Team manager Jim Shanahan of the Eagles remembered some controversy over sending intermediates into senior, however, the Eagles played the Cranbrook Royals.

Cranbrook compared to Innisfail had experience. One of their lines, Bob Murdock, Danny Springs, and Bernie Lukowich had at least 15 years of pro experience. The Royals completely dominated the Eagles in three straight 12-3, 7-2 and 13-4 and averaged over 60 shots a game.

* * *

The 1981-82 Innisfail-Cranbrooke series turned out to be the last time Alberta had Allan Cup representation. It had been proven on the ice that Alberta's top intermediate club could not compete or afford to play clubs who had senior and ex-pro players.

In 1984-85 no Alberta team entered senior for the province. Revamping of the structure to have Allan Cup playoffs in each province is a priority of the CAHA. The once proud category of senior hockey, when Alberta teams such as the Stampeders, Flyers, Miners, Bearcats, Superiors, Indians played, is but a shadow. In Alberta, the NHL Flames and Oilers have more than filled the gap for the fans.

* * *

Back (l to r): Lester Patrick, Ab Demarco, Jack Dempsey, George Herman "Babe" Ruth, Ott Heller, Oscar Obershok. Front: John Mahaffey, Ken McAuley, Frank Boucher, Ferdanand Gauthier.

Photo courtesy of Edmonton Archives

CHAPTER 3
WORLD HOCKEY ASSOCIATION AND NATIONAL HOCKEY LEAGUE IN ALBERTA

Alberta had not seen professional hockey since the WHL left in the early sixties. Previous to that pro hockey had been here in the 30's and 20's. On these occasions it failed because of costs, a lack of artificial ice (20's and 30's), or because of small facilities. Now in 1972, the World Hockey Association was coming to Edmonton. Bill Hunter was at the helm and promosed to bring a good product to the city even though the Edmonton Gardens was inadequate but Northlands Coliseum was to come.

In Calgary a franchise would not come until later in the WHA and it would play in the Corral. Before the decade ended, Calgary had lost pro hockey again; however, the winning of the 1988 Winter Olympics helped to change everything.

Edmonton Oilers and Calgary Flames are now in the National Hockey League and hockey support has never been stronger. It helps when the clubs are competitive in the league and against each other. However, when the Edmonton Oilers reached the Stanley Cup final in 1982-83 and won the Stanley Cup in 1983-84 and again in 1984-85, the province officially became hockey mad.

The purchase of a young player Wayne Gretzky from the Indianapolis Racers negotiated between Nelson Skalbania and Peter Pocklington, has had unbelieveable consequences on Alberta hockey. No player in hockey history has dominated the game like Gretzky.

Before the 1983-84 Stanley Cup and the Oilers, Flames in the NHL, the Oilers and Cowboys in the World Hockey Association, were regarded by many as teams in a ''watered down'' professional league. Some of those fans remembered the teams in the WHL of the 50's such as the 1953-54 Stampeders and the 1954-55 Flyers. Former Edmonton Flyer coach and general manager Norman Poile recalled after 1983-84's Stanley Cup victory that:

> the present Oilers have some great players, but when you stop and think of the players that played in Edmonton during the 50's you suddenly realize that the calibre was very high. When you mention players like Hall, Bucyk, Ullman, Stasiuk, Reibel, MacGregor, Hyrmnak, Holmes, Coflin, D. Poile, Zeidel, Kilburn, Arbour, Melnyk, you know what I mean...Yes, the Flyers of the 50's produced some great players...I realize it is just a pipe dream but wouldn't you like to see a game between the '55 Flyers and the '84 Oilers?

Some fans in 1972 remembered the previous professional days and did not give the WHA any chance of success. The Oilers began anyway but had to compete for publicity against the most famous hockey series of all — 'The 1972 Canada-Russia Series'. Older readers well might recall where they were when the Penticton V's won the World Championship in 1955 and many today know where they watched the eighth game of the '72 series.

Canadians became extremely excited about the September '72 showdown between Team Canada (NHL) and the Soviets. The opponents were unknown to each other but some former NHL players such as Bobby Hull, Gerry Cheevers, J.C. Trembley and Derek Sanderson had left for the WHA and predictions were more uncertain. Columnist, Jim Coleman was definate and predicted Canada would win seven of eight. The Russian team shocked Canadians and the NHL.

In game six, Canada scored three goals in a 90 second span in the second period to win 3-2. The Soviets were now ahead three games to two and had one tie. Coleman was still positive and said, ''Don't forget what I've been telling you since that awful night in Vancouver. Team Canada is still going to win the series.'' In game seven Paul Henderson scored on Vladislav Tretiak as the clock ran down to nearly two minutes for a win and the series was tied.

Wednesday, September 27, 1972...Almost everyone old enough remembers watching this game on television...Paul Henderson scored for Canada. There were only 32 seconds left in the game and it gave Canada a 6-5 win. This triumph by Team Canada did much to improve the image of pro hockey in North America. Had the NHL lost the series, it would have ruined the image of their league and the new WHA.

On September 29, 1972, Coleman wrote from Moscow:

> *I don't know what the heck you are worrying about. I kept telling you that Canada would make a clean sweep of this series on Moscow ice. I can hardly wait to get home to have a few words with those weisenheimers who've been sending me all that charming mail. Never has there been another hockey show which has matched this one with sustained excitement.*

Bill Hunter remained positive about the opening of the WHA. They announced various plans to capture fan interest including the possibility of experimenting with an orange puck. Ken Brown, Oiler goalie commented, "I like it, I can see it without any problem." The other goalie Jack Norris said he had trouble finding it behind the net.

Hunter said, "We promised a league with a difference and feel these are some innovations which make good sense and provide more excitement for the fans."

Jim Matheson, hockey writer for the *Edmonton Journal,* the Sporting News and color commentator on CFRN road games looked at the Oilers' first years in a 1983 Journal article.

THE OILERS' FIRST YEARS

BY JIM MATHESON

For 10 years the Oilers have been entertaining the fans of Edmonton from their humble beginnings as a WHA franchise playing at the Edmonton Gardens to their magnificent reign as one of the NHL's premier franchises. The team that Gretzky made famous will go down in history as one of the most exciting ever.

BILL HUNTER PROMOTES THE ALBERTA OILERS

Photo courtesy of Provincial Archives

To most people, the Edmonton Oilers didn't really come alive until a cold night in November, 1978, when Wayne Douglas Gretzky arrived in town on a charter Lear jet from Indianapolis. It cost owner Peter Pocklinton $225,000 to buy the long-haired kid from Nelson Skalbania and another $7,900 for the hurried up ride in style at 30,000 feet. It was the best money the franchise ever spent. For the first time people knew and even cared that the team existed. Before Gretzky, there was little for Oiler fans to go "bonkers" about.

ALBERTA OILERS HOCKEY CLUB 1972-73

Front row (l to r): Ken Brown, Jim Harrison, Al Hamilton, Bill Hunter (general manager, coach), Zane Feldman (president), Ray Kinasewich (assistant general manager), Val Fonteyne, Doug Barrie, Jack Norris. Second row (l to r): Ron Walters Sr. (trainer), Bob Wall, John Fisher, Ken Baird, Ron Walters, Bernie Blanchette, Ron Anderson, Bob Falkenberg, Steve Carlyle, Ed Joyal, Ross Perkins, John Blackwell (equipment manager). Third row (l to r): Roger Cote, Rusty Patenaude, Bob McAneeley, Hank Barrie, stickboy, Bill Hicke, Brian Carlin, Dennis Kassian.

From the time the Oilers (first called Alberta Oilers) were officially born in the fall of 1972, until Gretzy showed up six years later, it was a slow gestation period. There were many nights of frustration with a few foilies and chuckles thrown in to break the monotony of the losses. There was Hall of Famer, Norm Ullman, scoring his 500th career goal as an Oiler; one of the game's greatest goalies, Jacques Plante, turning back the clock for a couple of months in 1974; centre Jim Harrison racking up 10 points in a game in '73; defenceman Al Hamilton carrying the team on his back, overcoming two shattered knees to keep playing.

On the whole though, the Oilers struggled to survive their own mediocrity. They went through five coaches (Ray Kinasewich, Brian Shaw, Clare Drake, Bep Guidolin and Bill Hunter (three times), before current coach Glen Sather restored some stability to the post in the spring of 1977. He's been there ever since.

They went through an army of no-names. There was Ice Fortunato, Wayne Zuk, Gary Doyle — kids who weren't ready for prime time. And Derek Harker, who when last heard of was serving time of another kind for armed robbery. Some of the Oilers were legends in their own minds, almost none were legends on the ice, save for Ullman and Plante, who were in their 40s when they signed with the team.

It made for history, though. Not always colorful; but history nonetheless. The Oilers are 10 years old today and that says something. Somehow they persevered — outliving a rink that was an eyesore, a run of forgettable teams (New York Golden Blades, who played in white skates) and a league that almost decided to play with orange pucks.

It all started in February, 1972, when GM Bill Hunter drafted 97 players in a special lottery in Anaheim where 1,037 names were selected in 121 rounds. The list of selections included the Governor of Minnesota and former U.S. Olympian Wendell Anderson. Everybody except Oliver, the kid in "Love Story". The Oilers went for 33 NHLers of varying stature and a Soviet mountain named Alexander Ragulin. "We took Ragulin because he's a great player and you have to be prepared for the possibility that one day the entire Soviet team might defect," said Hunter. When Ragulin decided not to defect, the Oilers made do with a crew of more able but slightly less Everest-like defencemen.

JIM HARRISON WITH DOLLARS

Photo courtesy of Edmonton Journal

The first seven signees, announced to much trumpeting were Al Hamilton (Buffalo), Doug Barrie (LA), Bob Wall (Detroit), Eddie Joyal (LA), Brian Carlin (Springfield), Ross Perkins (Fort Worth) and Roger Cote (Cleveland). "We have more than $2 million of hockey talent," said Hunter. Only Hamilton survived the depression days until the Oilers arrival in the NHL in 1979. Barrie, Wall and Joyal were good journeymen, Cote's claims to fame were playing with a toothpick wedged between his teeth — a forerunner of U.L. Washington, the Kansas City Royals shortstop — and a keen sense of humor.

I remember one night he (Hunter) whispered down the bench that we should all stand up at the next whistle, recalled an ex-Oiler. When we did, the bench mysteriously rose up and fell on Hunter's instep. I can still see him hopping around in pain, trying to make the next line change. Us? We were trying not to laugh.

On a more serious note, the Oilers made a strong pitch for Ullman, one of the game's heralded stars in '72 but found their centre in Jim Harrison, instead. It cost them $75,000 — a small fortune in those days. He was pictured in a daily newspaper with a shopping cart full of dollar bills. If the money wasn't enough enticement to jump from the Toronto Maple Leafs, the Oilers gave him a new car and promised to transport his wife's horse from Eastern Canada to Edmonton.

Ray Kinasewich, who worked with Hunter as the coach of the junior Oil Kings — one of Canada's powerhouse teams — was the team's first coach. He took a leave of absence from a prosperous laundry business in town to go behind the bench. The way the team played, he must have felt like waving a towel of surrender some nights. There were more hijinks than highlights.

The Oilers opened with a win; ex-Montreal Canadien's winger Billy Hicke scoring on penalty shot in a 7-4 verdict over the Ottawa Nationals. A few months later, Harrison set a major hockey record (since equalled by Darryl Sittler) with 10 points (3 goals, 7 assists) against the New York Raiders on January 30, 1973. For the team there were more valleys than peaks. The only promising aspects were the play of goalies Ken Brown and Jack Norris and the attendance at the dank, dissipated Edmonton Gardens, where 4,900 fans were watching nightly in an antiquated 5,200 seat building.

Kinasewich was the convenient scapegoat when fired February 13th, by Hunter, with the Oilers in fifth place in the six team division. Good defence. No offence. Hunter took over and the Oilers almost made the playoffs. They tied with the Minnesota Fighting Saints for the last spot and lost a winner-takes-fourth game in Calgary. It was a not-too-famous ending for the team owned partially (30%) by Famous Players Theatre chain. They lost a coach, the playoffs and about $400,000 in revenue because they had to play in a bandbox rink.

The next year, Brian Shaw took over as coach — another ex-Oil King boss. The Oilers started with a bang, 2-1 at one point, prompting Shaw to playfully boast, "We may never lose again". They made the playoffs, but not without some ups and downs. One of the big up-and-down incidents occurred on a charter flight, the plane hit some clear-air turbulence and plummeted thousands of feet. Players were tossed around the cabin like ragdolls, eventually moaning about sore necks and plates of food they were wearing. A stewardess was knocked cold. The plane was knocked out of commission with a large crack along the wing.

In 1974, goal tender Jacques Plante accepted a two year $150,000 a season contract — turning his back on a smaller pact as GM of the Quebec Nordiques. He was several years older than Jack Benny (six), but he was heralded as a "messiah". For a time he was daring, roaming into the corners, stopping breakaways. (He was 8-1 and a 2.54 average at one point, but after colliding with an errant elbow in practice with the junior Oil Kings, he had trouble with his balance and his stats.) He finished 15-14-1 playing almost exclusively at home which rankled the other goalies — Brown and Chris Worthy, "I think he played two... maybe three road games," said Brown, who was making considerable less money and playing more often than not in a rink other than the new $15 million, then 15,300 seat Edmonton Coliseum. (Note: Plante played the first Oiler game in goal at the Coliseum.)

The Coliseum was a palace compared to the facility called the Gardens. They didn't tear down the doors the first year the building was open, but they drew more people (418,150) than any other WHA team. They could see a little light at the end of the tunnel. The Gardens had been smalltime — and very costly; the Oilers lost more than $1 million in gate revenues while playing there.

Plante's contract was terminated just prior to the 1975-76 season — about seven months after Shaw was fired as coach. Shaw, the current GM of Portland Winterhawks Junior 'A' team, was a vision of sartorial splendour. One day in Chicago, the team bus was held up while Shaw made it back with a wardrobe of suits from a clothing store. If he looked like something out of Gentlemen's Quarterly behind the bench, he didn't coach well enough to please Hunter, who made a second coming as coach in early March of the 1974-75 season. The Oilers missed the playoffs for the second time in three years.

With Plante gone — still collecting a salary on the second year of his contract — the Oilers made do with two new faces in 1975-76. There was another new coach (U of A's Clare Drake); and a new centre (Norm Ullman). Drake lasted until January, replaced even though owner Dr. Charles Allard said "it wasn't his fault". Ullman was signed after the Oilers made a strong attempt to get free-agent Marcel Dionne, and lasted two years. He had 87 points his first season, fine numbers considering he was 40. His 499th and 500th career goals came on December 11, 1975, against the Nordiques. He beat Peter Donnelly with a 20-footer, for number 500. "I wish it could have come in the National Hockey League," admitted Ullman, "but I guess it just wasn't meant to be".

Bill Hunter was stripped of his authority after a survey of fans showed 60% blamed him for Oiler troubles. After the "super salesman" got the Oilers off the ground and pushed for a new building — his two greatest feats — he resigned as GM, opening a 73 paragraph speech with a verbal volley on the "critics, rumor mongers and sadists who have a field day expounding on their views". He stayed on as a part-owner, but only until Chairman of the Board, Dr. Charles Allard sold half the team to Nelson Skalbania prior to the 1976-77 season.

EDMONTON OILERS HOCKEY CLUB 1974-75

Back row: Jack Gibson, Ken Baird, Tom Gilmore, Bill Morris, Ken Brown, Steve Carlyle, Blair MacDonald, Gary Cunningham, Bill Laing. Centre row: Ray McKay, Barry Long, Ross Perkins, Mike Rogers, Rusty Patenaude, Barry Debenham (trainer), Jim McKay (stick boy), Dick Bielous (trainer), Bobby Sheehan, Don Herriman, Ron Climie, Ed Joyal, Jim McCrimmon. Front row: Jacques Plante, Bruce MacGregor, Jim Harrison, Bob Freeman (chief scout), W.D. (Bill) Hunter (vice-president, general manager), Brian Shaw (coach), Al Hamilton (captain), Doug Barrie, Chris Worthy.

Skalbania, a real estate wheeler-dealer from Vancouver, eventually bought out Allard and brought in Peter Pocklington as an equal partner. They allegedly found $600,000 in unpaid bills, $900,000 owed to players who couldn't make the team and a $1.6 million loan to a bank. "The team was terrible. Management had been dreadful. It just wasn't a businesslike operation. The contracts were crazy," said Skalbania. "There was one guy on

Top row: Joe Micheletti, Ace Bailey, Steve Carlson, Dave Semenko, Dennis Sobchuk, Ken Barry, Dave Hunter, Clare Alexander, John Blackwell, Jim Neilson, Dave Langevin. Second row: Bruce MacGregor, Peter Millar, Glen Sather, Bill Flett, Brett Callighen, Peter Driscoll, B.J. McDonald, Wayne Gretzky, Ron Chipperfield, Peter Pocklington, Larry Gordon. Bottom row: Stan Weir, Ed Walsh, Paul Shmyr, Dave Dryden, Al Hamilton, Ed Mio.

the club with a contract that said if he went to another club we had to pay his wife $14,000 because she would have to change jobs.''

Amidst the turmoil, Bep Guidolin was hired as coach and GM; Sather was recruited from the Minnesota North Stars as captain. In truth, Sather ran the team in practices; Guidolin behind the bench in game situations. Guidolin stepped aside in early March. ''I'm not bailing out on the club'' said the ex-Boston coach. Sather told a different story. ''He said if I didn't take the job I'd sit in the stands,'' recalls Sather. Sather got the team into the playoffs with a stirring charge, playing and coaching at the same time.

Before the 1977-78 season, Guidolin was gone as GM, replaced by Brian Conacher. Skalbania left too — at least in person. He bought 51% of the Indianapolis Racers for $1, retaining his half-share in the Oilers. Eventually, he sold it to Pocklington with a rider that he would retain an option to repurchase his share should the Oilers enter the NHL. It was never exercised. After an uneventful 1977-78 season — the Oilers made the playoffs but exited in a hurry, as usual — Pocklington paid Skalbania $500,000 to wipe out the ''option to purchase'' clause and another $325,000 for the contracts of Gretzky, New York Ranger goalie Eddie Mio and winger Peter Driscoll in November, 1978.

Five months after Gretzky had flown into Edmonton in Skalbania's private jet to tell the world he's signed a $1.75 million contract with the Indy owner, the 17-year-old centre became an Oiler. ''In Nelson's eyes, he felt he was doing us a favor'', said Gretzky, who ironically scored his first 2 pro goals against the Edmonton Oilers prior to the trade. He said, ''Edmonton was the best city in North America.'' If it's not the best town, it's the most grateful. (Wayne Gretzky article by Terry Jones in the Hot Stove League.)

The Oilers were the only WHA survivors — Quebec, Winnipeg, Hartford — that didn't win an Avco Cup in their seven years there. With the Boy Wonder, and a strong supporting cast, they may be the first to win a Stanley Cup.

* * *

Calgary did not enter the WHA at the beginning. The city got its taste of the WHA for two years (1975-76 and 1976-77). Daryl Slade, sports writer for the *Calgary Herald* turns the clock back.

THE COWBOYS LACKED APPEAL FOR CALGARY

BY DARYL SLADE

The World Hockey Association never allowed an opportunity to catch more than a glimpse of aging superstars like Gordie Howe and Bobby Hull when teams played in the southern city. The Cowboys, who flunked out as

CALGARY COWBOYS HOCKEY TEAM 1976-77

Back row (l to r): G. Morrison, J. Mayer, J. Miszuk, D. Krysko, Butch Deadmarsh, J. Arbour, W. Morrin. Centre row (l to r): L. Lillman, Dr. G. Stewart, A. Micheletti, V. Ketola, L. Powis, D. Tannahill, Jim "Bearcat" Murray, Allan Murray, Joe Crozier. Front row (l to r): Smokey McLeod, P. Turbenche, J. Locas, W. Miller, P. Driscoll, R. Chipperfield, R. Ward, C. Evans, G. Bromley.

Photo courtesy of Calgary Exhibition and Stampede Board

the Blazers of Philadelphia and Vancouver, were perceived by the paying public as a minor-league team playing out of a minor-league arena.

Seldom had the aging 6,500 seat Stampede Corral attracted more than a half-full house to watch coach Joe Crozier's Cowboys. Before the team finally died a slow, agonizing death on August 18, 1977, after only two years in the Stampede City, owner Jim Pattison and team officials clung to the hope they would be part of an eventual NHL expansion. The problem was that only slightly more than 2,000 people shelled out for season tickets in a last-ditch attempt by Pattison to keep the team afloat. The "missing link" was a suitable arena required to persuade NHL governors, who wanted no part of the Corral.

Ironically, only three years later, after hope was given up on the city ever achieving major-league status, the NHL permitted the Flames to play out of the Corral for three years. They were allowed to move here only on the promise that a new 15,000 plus facility be built. It's doubtful that the Cowboys, having played in Calgary ever made any difference in whether the NHL took a chance on the southern Alberta City's market. The same fans who had turned their backs on the Cowboys clamored for Flames' tickets.

Aside from the Hulls and Howes, both only a shadow of their former selves, there was no legitimate drawing power, particularly on the part of the hometown Cowboys. The biggest name was Danny Lawson, a man who scored just 28 goals in 219 NHL games, yet managed 223 in 392 WHA contests. The first year the team had a respectable 41-35-4 record. Lawson was the most prolific Cowboy scorer, with 44 goals and 96 points. They beat Quebec in the quarter-finals and lost in the semi-finals to the Winnipeg Jets. Lawson was shipped off to the Jets late in 1976-77 as the Cowboys floundered and missed the playoffs at 31-43-7. Ron Chipperfield, another former junior star who never could cut it in the NHL, led the Cowboys with a mere 27 goals and 54 points.

Don "Smokey" McLeod also was a popular figure in Calgary, but he too never made the grade in the NHL. His best NHL days were in Houston and Vancouver. Others who toiled in the Cowboy uniform who will be lucky to be remembered in obscure trivia questions, include Butch Deadmarsh, Peter Driscoll, Bobby Leiter, John Miszuk and Don Tanahill.

If people didn't care about what happened to their former pro heroes before the Flames arrived, there is even less reason for them to care now.

The Calgary Flames officially became a part of the NHL on October 9, 1980. Steve Simmons, sports columnist, *Calgary Herald,* describes the beginnings and the positive future of the franchise.

THE FLAMES OF CALGARY

BY STEVE SIMMONS

Nelson Skalbania, the same whirl-wind entrepreneur who signed a teenaged Wayne Gretzky to his first professional contract, was the man who will be remembered for bringing a NHL team to Calgary.

It was a move so typical of the bold and unpredictable Skalbania. The Flames nearing the end of their financial life in Atlanta, were up for sale. A group in Atlanta, headed by actor Glenn Ford; attempted to keep the franchise in the south. A group of prominent Calgary businessmen, headed by Daryl and Byron Seaman of Bow Valley Industries, appeared to be the favorites to purchase the club and move them north.

Skalbania, using the same business tactics that have made him both wealthy and in debt during his lifetime of financial infamies, virtually came out of nowhere to outbid the Seaman brothers and purchase the Flames from Atlanta businessman Tom Cousins for $16 million U.S. And before the announcement was even officially made, Skalbania had wheeled and dealed again; selling 50% of the franchise to the two Seaman brothers and four other Calgarians, Ralph Scurfield, Norm Green, Harley Hotchkiss, and Normie Kwong. On May 21, 1980, the official announcement was made. Calgary had become part of the NHL.

In Skalbania-like fashion, sixteen months later he had totally divested himself of any shares in the Flames. The six Calgarians he had originally outbid for the franchise became the new owners. Skalbania had made a buck quickly, and got out just as quickly.

The Calgary Flames, keeping the red, white and gold colors of their Atlanta days, moved from the Modern Omni (capacity 15,141) to the dark and dingy Stampede Corral (capacity 7,242) where they would play for three seasons. They opened at the Corral on October 9, 1980, and played to a 5-5 tie with Quebec Nordiques. That first game was a sell out, so was the last Flame's game at the Corral and every game inbetween.

CALGARY FLAMES HOCKEY CLUB 1980-81

Front row (l to r): Dan Bouchard, Eric Vail, Al MacNeil (coach), Cliff Fletcher (general manager), Nelson Skalbania (team owner), David Poile (assistant general manager), Pierre Page (assistant coach), Brad Marsh, Pat Riggin. Second row (l to r): Bobby Stewart (equipment manager), Pekka Rautakallio, Bob Murdoch, Guy Chouinard, Kevin LaVallee, Randy Holt, Don Lever, Paul Reinhart, Bob MacMillan, Bearcat Murray (trainer). Third row (l to r): Earl Ingarfield, Kent Nilsson, Brad Smith, Bill Clement, Willi Plett, Jim Peplinski, Alex McKendry, Phil Russell, Ken Houston, Bert Wilson.

Photo courtesy of Calgary Flames

CALGARY FLAMES 1981-82

Front row (l to r): Rejean Lemelin, Al MacNeil (coach), David Poile (assistant general manager), Norman Kwong, Daryl Seaman (owners), Cliff Fletcher (president and general manager); Harley Hotchkiss, Ralph Scurfield, Norman Green (owners), Pierre Page (assistant coach), Pat Riggin. Second row: Jim Murray (trainer), Kevin LaVallee, Gary McAdam, Guy Chouinard, Bill Clement, Phil Russell (captain), Bob Murdoch (assistant coach), Pekka Rautakallio, Jamie Hislop, Denis Cyr, Kent Nilsson, Bobby Stewart (assistant trainer). Third row: Paul Reinhart, Mel Bridgman, Steve Konroyd, Pat Ribble, Ken Houston, Willi Plett, Jim Peplinski, Charlie Bourgeois, Ed Beers, Lanny McDonald, Dan Labraaten. Absent: Byron Seaman (owner).

Photo courtesy Calgary Flames

CALGARY FLAMES HOCKEY CLUB 1983-84

First row (l to r): Rejean Lemelin, Doug Risebrough (co-captain), Bob Murdoch (assistant coach), Al Coates (assistant to president), Cliff Fletcher (president and general manager), Bob Johnson (coach), Lanny McDonald (co-captain), Don Edwards. Second row: Al Murray (equipment manager), Mike Eaves, Hakan Loob, Byron Seaman, Harley Hotchkiss, Norman Green, Daryl Seaman, Ralph Scurfield, Norman Kwong (owners), Dave Hindmarch, Jim Jackson, Peter Marchuk (fitness consultant). Third row: Jim Murray (trainer), Paul Baxter, Allan MacInnis, Steve Konroyd, Eddy Beers, Charles Bourgeois, Jim Peplinski, Tim Hunter, Jamie Macoun, Bobby Stewart (assistant trainer). Fourth row: Steve Bozek, Steve Tambellini, Paul Reinhart, Carey Wilson, Colin Patterson, Kent Nilsson, Dan Quinn, Richard Kromm, Kari Eloranta. Missing: Al MacNeil (assistant general manager), Jamie Hislop.

Photo courtesy of Calgary Flames

Calgary, which failed as a World Hockey Association city, seemed well on its way to success in its first NHL season. The Flames had little difficulty selling out more than 10,000 season tickets at $21 per seat (which included half-season packages). The team caught fire and had its most successful season. After eight seasons in Atlanta in which the team never won a playoff round, the Flames advanced all the way to the Stanley Cup semi-final that first season, losing out to Minnesota North Stars. Calgarians became hockey crazy, and that love affair has not since dampened.

The club moved into the state-of-the-art $99 million Olympic Saddledome in October, 1983, and on that night lost to the eventual Stanley Cup Champion, Edmonton Oilers.

When the Flames moved from Atlanta to Calgary, with them moved many of their front office personnel. Cliff Fletcher, the only general manager the Flames had in Atlanta, became general manager in Calgary. Later, he took on a more significant role, as Governor and President of the club. David Poile, Fletcher's assistant in Atlanta, became his assistant in Calgary before taking the general manager's job with Washington Capitals. Al MacNeil, the coach in Atlanta remained for two seasons as coach in Calgary, before being replaced. MacNeil took Poile's spot when he left for Washington, Bob Johnson, the first American to ever coach a Canadian NHL franchise, took over as coach.

The Flames are now as secure financially as any NHL team, with a major league building, strong ownership, and loyal fans. Hockey has become the No. 1 sport in Calgary — and that hasn't always been the case.

* * *

CALGARY FLAMES HOCKEY CLUB 1984-85

First row (l to r): Rejean Lemelin, Lanny McDonald (co-captain), Bob Murdoch (assistant coach), Al Coates (assistant to president and director of marketing), Cliff Fletcher (president and general manager), Al MacNeil (assistant general manager), Bob Johnson (coach), Doug Risebrough (co-captain), Don Edwards. Second row: Jamie Hislop (assistant coach), Paul Reinhart, Mike Eaves, Norman Kwong, Ralph Scurfield, Norman Green, Harley Hotchkiss, Daryl Seaman, Byron Seaman (owners), Jim Jackson, Hakan Loob, Bobby Stewart (equipment manager), Al Murray (assistant trainer). Third row: Peter Marchuk (fitness consultant), Colin Patterson, Carey Wilson, Tim Hunter, Eddy Beers, Charles Bourgeois, Jim Peplinski (co-captain), Jamie Macoun, Al MacInnis, Steve Konroyd, Jim ''Bearcat'' Murray (trainer). Fourth row: Paul Baxter, Steve Bozek, Yves Courteau, Kari Eloranta, Dave Hindmarch, Steve Tambellini, Richard Kromm, Dan Quinn, Kent Nilsson. Missing: Joel Otto, Gino Cavallini, Perry Berezan, Glen Hall (goalie consultant), Rick Skaggs (public relations director)

Photo courtesy of Calgary Flames

CALGARY'S OLYMPIC SADDLEDOME

BY STEVE SIMMONS

In time, few will remember that Calgary's Olympic Saddledome was built $11 million over budget and completed ten months later than originally scheduled.

Photo courtesy of Calgary's Olympic Saddledome

In time, the Saddledome will be remembered for what it is — one of the World's leading all-purpose sporting facilities. The home of the National Hockey League's Calgary Flames. The home of the Canadian Hockey Research Centre. The home of the 1988 Winter Olympic Games. Canada's finest hockey building.

"They say if we could leave town for three years, people would want to hold a parade to welcome us back," said chief architect, Barry Graham on October 15, 1982. The day the building officially opened, Graham was speaking about the cloud of speculation that surrounded the building's eventual cost of $99 million, $11 million more than was originally budgeted for in the project, which was jointly paid for by all three levels of government.

The Saddledome was built not just to give the Flames a home, but to enhance Calgary's bid for the 1988 games it eventually won. The building which seats 16,673 for NHL hockey and slightly less than that for the International Games, sits on the grounds of the Calgary Exhibition and Stampede, adjacent to the Stampede Corral, ironically considered to be something of a palace when it was first built.

The building is unique, not merely in its outward design with its "Saddle" shaped roof, but also inside. The ice surface is interchangeable in a matter of hours from the smaller NHL size surface to the larger International surface. Dressing room facilities, restaurant, concessions and bar facilities are second to none.

The Saddledome is young, and there are still some kinks to be worked out. In time, it will be thought of for what it is — a state of the art facility that Western Canada can be proud of.

EDMONTON'S NORTHLAND'S COLISEUM

BY GEORGE HUGHES, General Manager, and CAROL McKNIGHT, Public Affairs — Edmonton Northlands

When the first WHA Edmonton Oiler fan passed through the turnstiles of Northlands Coliseum on November 10, 1974, little evidence remained of the hectic, last-minute effort to ensure every seat was bolted in its rightful place.

It was opening night for both the Edmonton Oilers squad of 1974 and their new home — Northlands Coliseum. Previously, the team in the orange and blue colors had been toughing out their matches in the ailing, 4,500-seat

Edmonton Gardens. Over a decade later, the Edmonton Oilers, NHL Stanley Cup Champions of '84 and '85, remain the most frequent — and most famous — occupants of Edmonton's versatile superstructure.

In 1972, some 60 years after the construction of the Edmonton Arena, (later called Gardens), the Edmonton Exhibition Association (now known as Edmonton Northlands) ended the debate over whether or not Edmonton should have a new modern facility for sporting, entertainment and business venues by building just such a structure.

For some 10-15 years previously, various proposals to build a downtown Coliseum, an Omniplex and others had come forward with no results. In 1971 the Edmonton Exhibition Association hired Woods Gordon Co. to do a development study which recommended as one component of the redevelopment the building of a Coliseum on the site. The conclusions of this study coupled with the formation of the World Hockey Association and the Edmonton (Alberta) Oilers by Dr. Charles Allard, Bill Hunter and Zane Feldman led to a June 1972 approval by the Board of Directors to proceed.

EDMONTON'S NORTHLANDS COLISEUM

Photo courtesy of Northlands

From its inception, the project was spearheaded by three long term volunteers, Edmonton Exhibition President Jack Bailey, First Vice President Harry Hole and Second Vice President Ted Mildon, and General Manager Al Anderson. These men with the suport of the Board carried the project through to completion and twenty months and $17 million later, Northlands Coliseum was ready for use.

Designed by the Vancouver architectural firm of Phillips, Barrett, Hillier, Jones and Partners, who designed the Pacific Coliseum, in association with the Edmonton firm of Wynn, Forbes, Lord, Feldberg, Schmidt, the project was managed by a local firm, Batoni Bowlen Enterprises. Original funding was provided by a $3.7 million construction grant from the province of Alberta, a matching grant from the City of Edmonton for land acquisition over 10 years, and a $10 million loan from the Federal Government. Subsequently in 1978 an additional $3.7 million in lottery funds were provided to assist in reducing the loan, which will expire in 1999.

The site chosen was the north side of 118 Avenue, at the junction of the Capilano Freeway and was conected to the rest of Edmonton Northlands by a million-dollar pedway over 118 Avenue.

Inside, Northlands Coliseum is a tri-level facility with seating capacity of 17,498. When the Edmonton Oilers are playing one of their 40 regular season home games, there's little chance of obtaining a ticket, despite the addition of 1,300 expansion seats in 1980.

As northern Alberta's largest entertainment facility, Northlands Coliseum is rented by outside organizations who bring in concerts with international appeal and stars, Ice Capades, sporting events like wrestling, boxing, basketball's Harlem Globetrotters, tennis matches and the circus. These events fill Northlands Coliseum 90 per cent of the time, with Edmonton Northlands' sponsored activities like Northlands Superodeo, Canadian Finals Rodeo and Edmonton's Klondike Days Exposition using the remaining 10 per cent of a yearly schedule. a yearly schedule.

Athletes who have been honored by the City of Edmonton have a permanent place in Northlands Coliseum Hall of Fame. Established on the north concourse level, the showcases are filled with the names and accomplishments of those individuals from all fields of sport, who have been chosen by the City of Edmonton to be inducted into the Hall of Fame. On the south concourse level, another showcase holds tributes to those in the Alberta Amateur Hockey Association Hall of Fame.

Built by the spirit and determination of volunteers, Northlands Coliseum is a fitting palace for winners. Winners who saw the vision of a new coliseum, winners who took Northlands Coliseum from ground-breaking to completion in record time some 10 years ahead of the Saddledome in Calgary.

Knowledgeable hockey people credit the building of the Coliseum for the presence of Edmonton in the NHL; for without the Coliseum, at the breakup of the WHA, it is unlikely that Edmonton Oilers would have made it. What they did is history — and the Stanley Cup acquired in '84 and '85 have put Edmonton and Alberta on the world hockey map.

OILERS...TO THE CUP

Negotiations between the WHA and NHL produced an agreement that merged the two leagues. The WHA cities of Edmonton, Winnipeg, Hartford and Quebec City joined the 1979-80 NHL. The four new teams were only able to protect two goalkeepers and two other players. Any other player who was on a previous negotiation list on an NHL team became the property of that club. Coach Glen Sather now started what amounted to a new team.

OILERS 1979-80

Top row: Brett Callighen, Kari Makkonen, Dave Lumley, Barry Ashby, Bob Freeman, Lee Fogolin, Dave Hunter, Colin Campbell. **Second row:** Bruce MacGregor, Peter Millar, Lyle Kulchisky, Risto Siltanen, Don Murdoch, Mark Messier, Pat Price, Dave Semenko, Kevin Lowe, Doug Hicks, Al Hamilton, Peter Driscoll, John Blackwell, Rick Elaschuk, Dave Dryden (assistant coach). **Bottom row:** Ron Low, Wayne Gretzky, Glen Sather, Peter Pocklington (owner), Bryan Watson (assistant coach), B.J. McDonald, Ed Mio.

Photo courtesy of Edmonton Oilers

The Oiler's first choice in the NHL draft of 1979-80 was forward Cam Connor from the Montreal Canadiens. The two goalies kept were Dave Dryden and Eddie Mio. Wayne Gretzky and Bengt-Ale Gustafson were the two players the Oilers protected. (It was later ruled by NHL President, John Ziegler that Washington Capitals could get Gustafson.) Defenseman Kevin Lowe from the Quebec Ramparts was the Oiler's first round junior draft selection. Dave Lumley, Dave Semenko, Risto Siltanen and Dave Hunter were on the Oilers through negotiations by Sather. In the draft itself, after Connor, the Oilers selected Lee Fogolin, Pat Price, Colin Campbell, Larry Brown, goalie Pete La Presti, Ron Areshenkoff, Inge Hammerstrom, John Gould, Doug Hicks and Tom Edur. Another junior selection was 18-year-old Mark Messier.

The Oilers played their first league NHL game on October 10, 1979, against the Black Hawks in Chicago Stadium. Kevin Lowe scored the first goal and Wayne Gretzky and Brett Callighen drew assists at 9:49 of the first period on Tony Esposito. Even though Gretzky would receive the Lady Byng Trophy for the season, he drew the Oiler's first penalty at 5:19 for slashing.

Victory number one for the Oilers in the NHL was on October 19, 1979, when Blair MacDonald scored three goals in a 6-3 win over the Quebec Nordiques. The Oilers won enough games to finish their first season in fourth place in the Smythe Division. They played the Philadelphia Flyers in their only playoff series. Led by Bobby Clarke, the Flyers eliminated the Oiler in three straight, however two games went into overtime.

Signs of good things to come were on the horizon as Gretzky tied Marcel Dionne for the scoring title. Each had 137 points but Dionne was awarded the Art Ross Trophy because he had two more goals. Gretzky was declared ineligible for the Rookie of the Year Calder Trophy because he had played professional in the WHA the previous season. To add to the collection, Gretzky won the Hart Trophy as MVP and the Lady Byng.

In 1980-81, the Oilers were starting to show championship form. They had a young team which included Mark Messier, Glen Anderson, Dave Hunter, Jari Kurri, Paul Coffey, Wayne Gretzky and Andy Moog. (Moog spent most of this season in Wichita in the Central Hockey League.) Bryan Watson was appointed coach and Glen Sather became General Manager. The player's response to Watson was negative so Sather fired his long time friend and became coach. Once again the Oilers finished fourth in the Symthe Division, tied for 13th overall in the NHL.

Gretzky scored at a rate never seen before. At the end of the season he had 164 points from 56 goals and 109 assists and won the Art Ross Trophy. For the second time he won the Hart Trophy as the MVP.

In the 1980-81 playoffs the Oilers won their first post season playoff in the NHL. This series against the Montreal Canadiens was probably the most significant. Andy Moog was called up from Wichita. He was marvelous in goal in 6-3 and 2-1 wins in Montreal. Edmonton fans could not believe the ex-WHA team was ahead of the Canadiens. In the third game at home, Guy LaFleur of the Canadiens was held scoreless by Dave Hunter. Gretzky got three assists in the first period to tie an NHL record and Andy Moog allowed only two goals while Edmonton scored six. It was almost like a Stanley Cup win.

The Oilers played the New York Islanders and lost four games to two. The team had gone further in the playoffs than expected and support for the next year grew.

Grant Fuhr joined the Oilers in goal for the 1981-82 season. Sather had to decide between Moog, Ron Low and Eddie Mio. Even though Moog had been brilliant at the end of the previous season, he had a poor training camp and was sent to Wichita. Fuhr lost his opening game on October 14, 1982 and then won 23 in a row. In his 48 games played, Fuhr finished with a goals against average of 3.31 and had only three losses.

Gretzky scored an astonishing 212 points on 92 goals and 120 assists. Mike Bossy, of the Islanders, was 65 points behind in second place. Maurice 'Rocket' Richard had the league mark of 50 goals in 50 games from 1944. Gretzky broke this record in the 39th game. It was obvious the Rocket's record would be broken, but the ability of Gretzky to do what he wanted was never more evident.

In the previous game, Gretzky scored four goals on the Los Angeles Kings which left him at 45 goals after 38 games. On December 30, 1981, he scored four goals against the Philadelphia Flyers. Pete Peeters was pulled from the Flyer net. Three seconds remained and only Bill Barber stood between Gretzky and the record. Gretzky scored. Number 99 established another record when he scored 76 goals in 63 games. Phil Esposito had the previous high of 76 goals in 78 games.

The Oilers basked in awards. Gretzky and Mark Messier were on the first All-Star team. Grant Fuhr and Paul Coffey were on the second unit. The Hart and Art Ross Trophies went to Gretzky. Based on their previous year, the Oilers were expected to go far in the playoffs.

The Los Angeles Kings, coached by Don Perry had finished the 1981-82 season 48 points behind the Smythe Division winning Edmonton Oilers. The Oilers also won five of the six league contests. In game one, the Oilers lost 10-8 even though they once had a 4-1 lead. The next game produced an Edmonton 3-2 win. No problems were anticipated.

In the Los Angeles Forum, the Oilers, in game three, took a five nothing lead. In the third period the Kings scored five goals to tie the game. Daryl Evans then scored for the Kings in overtime. The Oilers replied to win

3-2 again and tie up the series. Everyone except Don Perry (a former Edmonton junior) and his Kings thought the Oilers would win. The Kings defeated the Oilers 7-4 to eliminate a team favored to reach the final. This was the historical low point for the Edmonton Oilers until their first Stanley Cup win, two seasons in the future.

Few player changes were made to start the 1982-83 season. Jaroslav Pouzar was acquired from Czechoslovakia and Ken Linseman in a deal which involved Boston and Hartford. The Oilers reached the Stanley Cup final. The last time Edmonton was in the final was sixty years ago. At that time players for the Eskimos included Duke Keats, Joe 'Bullet' Simpson and Mark Messier's great uncle, Howard Dea. This was the first time a Stanley Cup final playoff game was ever played in Edmonton.

Tickets were at a premimum. Gary Poignant of the "Edmonton Sun" found one scalper who grossed $760.00 on eight tickets originally priced at $22.00 each. Others got as much as $250.00 for a pair of the best seats in the gold section.

Billy Smith, New York Islander goalie, immediately stopped the Oilers when he shut them out 2-0. Duane Sutter and Ken Morrow scored for the Islanders. Billy Smith became a thorn in the side of Edmonton fans and players when he used his goal stick on Glen Anderson.

In game two, Smith continued to torment the Oilers when he slashed Wayne Gretzky and received a five minute penalty. The Islanders won their second straight by 6-3. Near the end of the game, Dave Lumley tried his own brand of retaliation on Smith and drew a spearing penalty. Terry Jones wrote:

GRANT FUHR

Photo courtesy of Bob Mummery

And while I can't condone for a second the stick work of Smith, that's part of it. He's getting to them and he knows it. All Billy Smith cares about is winning. He's winning.

The Islanders continued their mastery over the Oilers when the series went to Nassau County Coliseum in New York for games three and four. Only Jari Kurri beat Smith when the Islanders won their third straight 5-1. The Sutters (Duane and Brent) each scored for the Islanders.

On May 17, 1983, the Islanders ended the final playoff in four straight when they doubled the Oilers 4-2. Mike Bossy, Bryan Trottier, John Tonnelli and Ken Morrow scored for New York while Jari Kurri and Mark Messier replied for Edmonton.

The Islanders dominated the 1982-83 finals as Wayne Gretzky was held scoreless in four games. The Oilers failed to capitalize on scoring opportunities as they had all year. Bill Smith was at his best and won a 1983 Pontiac Trans Am and $1,500.00 for the Conn Smythe Award as the MVP in the playoffs.

The 1983-84 Stanley Cup final featured the Oilers and Islanders. The Oilers moved ahead 1-0 in the series when they shut-out the Islanders 1-0.

Predictions and thoughts of a possible Edmonton victory in the series were more evident. Gordie Howe said, "I really like that big kid (Messier) and, of course, that other kid (Gretzky)". Jim Matheson wrote of Grant Fuhr who struggled the previous year.

> *Fuhr was too good to leave his career on a greasy plate, though. The grown-up, rather grown-out Fuhr has served up a diet of superb games this year, and none better than the Stanley Cup opener this May.*

The Oilers finally made it in 1983-84. Their first round was easy as they defeated John Ferguson's Winnipeg Jets in three straight games. The Calgary Flames proved to be difficult and took the Oilers to a full seven games. In the seventh game, the Oiler were down 4-3 at one point and came back to win 7-4. It was close as the Flames played extremely well.

1982-83 EDMONTON OILERS

Top row (l to r): Garry Unger, Tom Roulston, Don Jackson, Dave Semenko, Randy Gregg, Todd Strueby. Third row: Ken Linseman, Laurie Boschman, Jaroslav Pouzar, Dave Hunter, Paul Coffey, Kevin Lowe, Charlie Huddy, Garry Lariviere, Marc Habschied. Second row: Barrie Stafford (trainer), Pat Hughes, Ted Green (assistant coach), Glen Sather (coach), Peter Pocklington (owner), Bruce MacGregor (assistant general manager), John Muckler (assistant coach), Mark Messier, Dave Lumley, Peter Millar (physiotherapy). Bottom row: Lindsey Middlebrook, Glenn Anderson, Lee Fogolin, Andy Moog, Wayne Gretzky, Jari Kurri, Grant Fuhr.   *Photo courtesy of Edmonton Oilers*

To reach the final of 1983-84, the Oilers had four straight wins over the Minnesota North Stars, including a final 3-1 win. Only once in the series did the Stars challenge. They scored four times while Dave Lumley served a major penalty in game three. The Oilers then scored six straight to win 8-5. Now the Oilers were in the Stanley Cup final for the second straight year.

Al Arbour's Islanders came back to win a convincing 6-1 verdict in the second game. Clarke Gilles scored three, Bryan Trottier two and Greg Gilbert one for New York. Randy Gregg got Edmonton's lone goal. Islander's

Brent Sutter, Butch Goring and Trottier kept Gretzky and Kurri in check. Arbour said, "we won the little battles in the pits."

Some Edmonton fans had changes in opinion. Callers to *Edmonton Journal*'s Marc Horton such as Wally Stankey of Buck Lake said, "How can you and John Short (*Journal* columnist) have such tunnel vision? Do you really think the Oilers can win the Cup with a coach like Glen Sather?"

Teddy Lawrence of Sherwood Park said, "The Oilers showed their true colors tonight and were soundly beaten. They're going to be annihilated in the rest of the series."

Billy Smith finally took his medicine in game three. The Oilers scored six goals on Smith in 46 minutes to cause his removal. The final score was 7-2. The Oilers were now were ahead three games to one. The Stanley Cup was close.

Fans continued to phone Fan Feedback at the Journal. Herb Mueller of Beaumont exclaimed, "The Oilers are making the Islanders look like the New Jersey Devils."

Early on May 19, 1984, Glen Sather said, "I don't think anybody is over confident. We're scared to death. We're playing for our lives so we can prevent going back to New York." Only the Islanders did go back to New York. The Edmonton Oilers after five seasons, as owner Peter Pocklington had told Dick Beddoes at one time...became Stanley Cup Champions...the very best.

Rod Phillips has been and still is the 'Voice of the Oilers' on CFRN-126 throughout the entire history of the Oilers in the WHA and NHL. He has done every broadcast except part of one home league game when he lost his voice — Cory Elliot took the mike. On September 25, 1981, his daughter Quinn was born. Phillips was replaced during the game by Al Coates. The CFRN broadcast crew for the game that won the Stanley Cup included Phillips, Ken Brown, John Short, Greg Pilling and Engineer, Walt Buehler. In the following story, Phillips recalls the Oiler's first Stanley Cup victory.

STANLEY CUP GAME
BY ROD PHILLIPS

EDMONTON OILERS — STANLEY CUP CHAMPIONS 1984

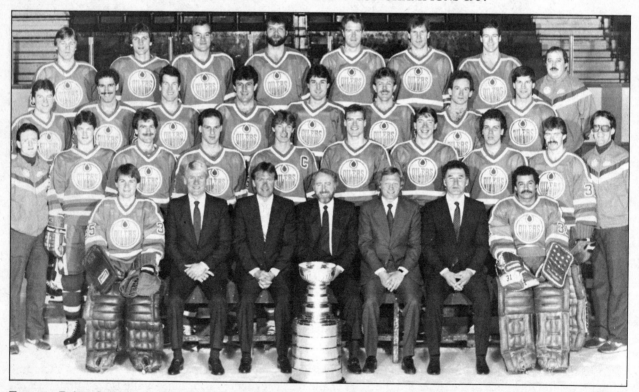

Top row: Raimo Summanen, Kevin McClelland, Rick Chartraw, Dave Semenko, Randy Gregg, Don Jackson, Kevin Lowe, Lyle Kulchisky. **Second row:** Pat Conacher, Charlie Huddy, Dave Hunter, Jaroslav Pouzar, Paul Coffey, Willy Lindstrom, Ken Linseman, Larry Melnyk. **Third row:** Barrie Stafford, Pat Hughes, Glenn Anderson, Lee Fogolin, Wayne Gretzky, Mark Messier, Jari Kurri, Dave Lumley, Mike Zanier, Peter Millar. **Bottom row:** Andy Moog, John Muckler, Glen Sather, Peter Pocklington, Bruce MacGregor, Ted Green, Grant Fuhr.

Photo courtesy of Edmonton Oilers

I remember waking up on the morning of May 19, 1984, and saying to my wife, Debby, "I hope we don't have to go to New York tomorrow morning." There was nothing special about that day. It started for me like any other game day. Coffee at home and breakfast at the Sportex Cafeteria. Practice that morning wasn't any different from the hundreds of practice sessions the Oilers had every day of the season. You could sense the Oilers wanted it to be over. From practice it was out to the television station to put together a feature for our "Eyewitness Sports", then lunch at home, put together my afternoon radio show, tape it, and then prepare for the game broadcast.

I met Glen Sather in his office, and we did the pre-game show for our 109th Oiler's broadcast of the season. Glen and I chatted for a while, and as I left, I said to him, "I don't think there is a team in the world that can beat you tonight."

Glen said, "I hope you're right."

Our broadcast began, and we ran our taped interview with coach Sather. Ken Brown interviewed a rather somber Al Arbour. Jim Matheson of the "Journal" joined us for the last half of the pre game show, and we spent a lot of time talking about how tough the Islanders would be this night. But we concluded the pre game show by saying it would be a tough task to beat these young Oilers. We were right.

The game began at a torrid pace. The 17,498 fans made more noise than I ever heard Edmonton fans make. Wayne Gretzky scored on a break away, and it was a mad house. Moments later, a three on one, with Jarri Kurri, Dave Semenko and Wayne. Kurri took it in across the Islander blue line. Semenko broke for the net. Kurri dropped it back to Gretzky. He took a couple of strikes and ripped a "howitzer" between the legs of Billy Smith (the Edmonton fan's villain). It was 2-0 and crazy. In the second period, Ken Linesman scored to make it 3-0 and then Kurri made it 4-0. Now the entire building sensed what was happening. The Edmonton Oilers were about to make history.

Pat Lafointaine of the Islanders tried very hard to spoil Edmonton's biggest ever party. He scored twice early in the third period. But the Oilers tightened up and with only 13 seconds remaining Dave Lumley fired the puck into an empty Islander net. It was 5-2 and all over. Northlands was a sea of emotion.

My own emotions were running high. When Lumley scored we knew it was over. The feeling was like nothing I ever experienced at any sporting event I have covered. Two people I admired and respected very much came to mind seconds after Lumley scored. Hal Pawson, the former Sports Editor of the "Edmonton Journal", and Henry Singer, the greatest sports fan Edmonton has ever had. I mentioned that I wished they could have been there that night. It was a proud evening for our city. I will always have the feeling that they were watching from up above.

Our post game show from the Oilers dressing room was a very emotional scene. For those of us who watched the team from the beginning, it was more than special. When we signed off the air, I spent a few moments sipping champagne with Lee Fogolin. I admire him as a man and a player. We both enjoyed a good cry. It was the same with Kevin Lowe, Wayne Gretzky, Barry Fraser and just about everyone in the room.

After that we had a party at the Agricom. Debby left for home at about 1:00 a.m. I stayed and celebrated with assistant coach, John Muckler. At 3:00 a.m. we were standing on Jasper Avenue watching thousands of people whoop it up. It was incredible. After John drove me home I spent the rest of the night watching the replay of the game on my video cassette recorder. Sleep came after 6:00 a.m., on May 20, 1984.

It was "ENORMOUS"!

* * *

OILERS REPEAT THE FEAT

BY TERRY JONES, EDMONTON SUN SPORTS COLUMNIST

The theme of the dream was to repeat the feat.

The Edmonton Oilers had won their first Stanley Cup in 1984 but there were still some to be convinced that they were true champions capable of winning ti more than once.

"It's only a one-year dynasty for Gretzky and Team Arrogance. If there is such a thing as a one-year dynasty, the Oilers are it," wrote Stan Fischler in the Inside Sports hockey preview.

Champions? Or one year wonders?

When it was over the Stanley Cup was still in Edmonton.

The year before the Oilers got their names engraved on a Cup. In 1985 the Oilers got them etched on an era. The names Gretzky, Coffey, Kurri, Messier, Fuhr, Lowe, Sather, etc., are now welded together forever. Like Clarke, Parent, MacLeish, Barber, Leach, Scultz and Shero. Or Orr, Esposito, Bucyk, Cashman, Cheevers, Westfall, Sanderson and Sinden.

The Edmonton Era.

With their second straight Stanley Cup victory in their third straight trip to the final, it was not yet a dynasty but it definitely became the Edmonton Oilers Era. And of all the eras in Stanley Cup history, there'd never been one quite like this one.

Six years after the Oilers had joined the National Hockey League, they'd won back-to-back Stanley Cups. And they'd rewritten half the record book.

The 1984-85 season started with an undefeated 15-game undefeated bolt from the gate, rainy-day golf date with former U.S. President Gerald Ford, the end of a 20-game winning streak over the Winnipeg Jets and an end of year slump that had everybody nervous heading into the playoffs.

The Oilers bounced Los Angeles and Winnipeg in straight games and won the first two from Chicago as they challenged the all-time Stanley Cup playoff winning streak. But the Black Hawks took six games to shake. Losing the first game of the final, the Oilers won the next one and headed home to sweep the three in Edmonton and win the Cup on home ice for the second straight season.

When it was over the players were left to contemplate how they should be rated on the sands of time.

"We've got to be rated as good as any team that ever won two in a row," bubbled Wayne Gretzky as people poured champagne on his head in the Oilers dressing room.

"All I know is that 15 years from now I'm going to say 'Gawd, I played on a great hockey team!'"

Gretzky said it wasn't as exciting to win the Cup again, but it was more satisfying.

"In terms of emotion and excitement the first was bigger. But to do what we had to do to win it twice...well, we proved a lot of things by winning it twice. And it's going to take a darn good team to take it away from us."

As usual, Gretzky won the scoring race with 208 points. As usual, Gretzky won the Hart Trophy as the MVP. But for the first time, he was named winner of the Conn Smythe Trophy as the most valuable player in the playoffs.

Defenceman Paul Coffey, for the first time, won the Norris Trophy as the top defenceman in the NHL. Coffey had his own thoughts on what it all meant.

EDMONTON OILERS — STANLEY CUP CHAMPIONS 1985

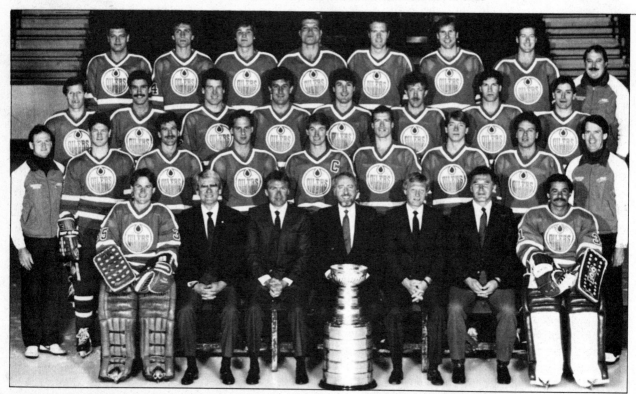

Top row: Esa Tikkanen, Kevin McClelland, Mike Krushelnyski, Dave Semenko, Randy Gregg, Don Jackson, Kevin Lowe, Lyle Kulchisky (assistant trainer). Second row: Mark Napier, Charlie Huddy, Dave Hunter, Jaroslav Pouzar, Paul Coffey, Willy Lindstrom, Larry Melnyk, Billy Carroll. Third row: Barrie Stafford (trainer), Pat Hughes, Glenn Anderson, Lee Fogolin, Wayne Gretzky, Mark Messier, Jari Kurri, Dave Lumley, Peter Millar (athletic therapist). Bottom row: Andy Moog, John Muckler (assistant coach), Glen Sather (general manager, coach), Peter Pocklington (owner/governor), Bruce MacGregor (assistant general manager), Ted Green (assistant coach), Grant Fuhr. Missing: Bill Tuele (public relations director).

Photo courtesy of Edmonton Oilers

We haven't won four in a row or five in a row, but I would think we have the start of a dynasty. If we continue to be dedicated, with the players and the organization we have here, there is no reason we can't be a dynasty.

It's better the second time around. The first one is a funny feeling. You don't know what to expect. And this year, with the length of the season because of the Canada Cup camp in August and tournament in September and because so many people doubted us in the last five weeks, it's a better feeling. To win the Stanley Cup and not really know what it's about is one thing, but to win it and to know...to go into every city in the league with everybody trying to beat you because you are the Stanley Cup champions...well, we proved we have a lot of character.

When we won the Canada Cup, I said it felt better than winning the Stanley Cup the first time. But right now I feel that with how much work and effort went into winning the Stanley Cup again, this has to be bigger.

The Oilers, playing the game the way it is supposed to be played with perhaps the greatest player in the history of the game and one of the greatest defencemen ever, gave the game a classic club. What athlete would you want your son to idolize and hero worship more than Wayne Gretzky? And what team would you want your son's coach to copy more than the Edmonton Oilers?

Once a cocky, immature team which would boo on the bench, the Oilers matured into a championship team with character and charisma.

There was some question after the first one how the Oilers would carry themselves as champions. For the most part, they carried themselves with class.

They also set themselves above so many other teams which had earned an era. They put their names in so many places in the NHL and Stanley Cup record books that it almost looked like they authored it.

The Boston Bruins of Orr and Esposito won two Stanley Cups in their era. But they didn't win them back-to-back like this team did. And they were every bit as much a team for all time as those Philadelphia Flyers of Clarke and Parent.

Those two eras in Stanley Cup history weren't that long ago. But they were a million miles away from Edmonton back then. That was a long time before Edmonton was in the NHL. The Stanley Cup? Edmonton? In the same breath much less married like they are now.

Repeating the feat. What a theme for that dream.

* * *

PROFESSIONAL AND SENIOR EPILOGUE

Senior hockey was strong in the thirties, waned during World War II and peaked in the late forties in Alberta. The Calgary Stampeders' Allan Cup victory in 1946 and the Edmonton Flyers' win in 1948 illustrate the strength of Alberta senior hockey in that era. Several players from both teams (and other from other senior teams in Alberta) could have performed superbly in the NHL had it been a ten-team rather than a six-team league.

Senior hockey died in Alberta the minute the WCSHL became a minor professional league. Although senior players had often been making "under the table money" as amateurs, the new professional league in the 50's enticed seniors to turn professional.

Senior hockey revived briefly in 1966 when the Drumheller Miners won the Allan Cup for the last time in Alberta. Although it was a splendid win and generated much enthusiasm, the Allan Cup had lost some of its lustre from a national perspective. There was no place for senior hockey in the new hockey structure; minor professional expansion and, later, WHA and NHL expansion made junior the preferred brand of hockey. The Innisfail Eagles was the last Alberta team to compete for the Allan Cup in 1981-82. The team may be the last because there is no economic reason for senior hockey to continue.

Professional hockey is the "biggest show in town" in Alberta. Wayne Gretzky has become an obsession for big kids as well as little kids. There is at least one ten year old boy (and maybe thousands of other boys and girls) in Edmonton who checked passing cars for two years hoping for a glimpse of "The Great One". The thrilling moment came in 1984 when Gretzky actually pulled up beside my son six blocks from our house!

Gretzky is the most prolific scorer professional hockey has ever seen. "Records are made to be broken" but in Gretzky's case it appears the NHL schedule will have to be lengthened for other players to break his. He dominates his sport more than any other professional in any other sport; he is in the same league as those in the Golden Age of Sport in the 20's — baseball's George Herman "Babe" Ruth, boxings' Jack "The Manassa Mauler" Dempsey, track and field's Paavo "The Flying Finn" Nurmi, golf's Robert T. "Bobby" Jones, tennis'

"Big" Bill Tilden, football's Harold "Red" Grange and figure skating's Sonja "The Norwegian Doll" Henie. Gretzky is "the name" in professional sport in the 80's.

Gretzky is only 24 years old. His future is as bright and promising as professional hockey in Alberta.

(See Wayne Greztky by Terry Jones in Hot Stove League.)

CHAPTER 4
INTERMEDIATE HOCKEY

Intermediate hockey was officially formed in Alberta on November 14, 1913 at an Alberta Amateur Hockey Association meeting at the Calgary YMCA. Up until this meeting the AAHA had consisted of senior teams only. As hockey improved in Alberta the best senior teams were not prepared to compete against weaker senior teams. Rather than have weaker teams drop out of hockey, the AAHA hoped to keep good players in the game by introducing the intermediate level. Hockey officials wanted to keep developing enough players to fill rosters for championship amateur teams; and, in case the professional Pacific Coast League decided to expand into Alberta they wanted to be ready. Another practical reason for the intermediate level was that it would be an advantage to have two categories to shorten playoffs in an era of natural ice.

The 1913 meeting was one of the most heated of the entire period. Some teams objected to losing their senior status. They felt they were being "demoted to intermediate" and that they would lose the right to challenge for the Allan Cup, the most prestigious award in amateur hockey.

In order to appease them, five teams designated "intermediate" were listed as senior and intermediate. This move allowed these "two level" teams to play off with the winner of the senior level teams in a challenge game or series for the Allan Cup. This compromise carried on well into the 1920's. By the 30's intermediate teams could not challenge senior teams and vied only for the Western Canadian title. But, surprisingly, three Alberta intermediate teams won three successive World Hockey championships beginning in 1950. It was not until the 1970's that intermediate teams could challenge for a truly national intermediate title. This national trophy was named after Dr. George Hardy, former President of the AAHA, CAHA and the World International Ice Federation, and is called the Hardy Cup.

Today intermediate hockey is still played in Alberta; senior hockey has died. All non-professional adult contact hockey is intermediate. Even though there are several categories of intermediate hockey the focus will be on Intermediate A, the highest level.

EDMONTON JOURNAL HUSTLERS — 1914-15 INTERMEDIATE CHAMPIONS

Back (l to r): George Bisset, Pete Talbot, Curly Shea (manager), Ira Stuart. Front: Roy Davidson, Dunny Dunlop, Buck Grant, Joe Dussault.

Photo courtesy of George Stuart

In 1913-14 the first Alberta intermediate champions were the Calgary Victorias. The Vics defeated Lacombe, the northern winners, 2-1 and tied the second game 1-1. Both games were played in "chinook conditions" at the natural-ice Sherman Rink in Calgary. Lloyd Turner, the rink manager, had the task of preparing the surface. (Almost twenty five years in the future Turner brought the first artificial ice to Alberta.)

The Intermediate championship moved north in 1914-15 when Edmonton Journal Hustlers tied Lacombe 3-3 and won the second game 3-1. The Edmonton team was much younger than most intermediate teams: the average age was only eighteen.

Transportation in the Peace River Country of northern Alberta has always been a problem. The 1915 teams in this region were often restricted because of distances. Peace River Crossing (since 1919 called Peace River) travelled to Lake Saskatoon (east of Grand Prairie) to play a best-of-three final series.

The ''Edmonton Bulletin'' reported that:

This will be the first sporting expedition to involve Grande Prairie and marks another step in the advancement of civilization, as the Crossing was unable to support such a venture. The trip by horse and wagon consists of 140 miles (one way) and would require 3½ days each way. An elaborate program has been made up for the party both enroute and at the Prairie.

Lake Saskatoon won the series and the Peace River Hockey championship. Perhaps this is one of the first examples of a team that lost a series due to ''horse lag''.

CAIRSTAIRS — 1919-20

Left to right: ''Dad'' Beaucock, MacDonald, Stuart Hall, Charlie Yule, Wes Shantz. Centre: Harper Miller, Jack Beaucock, Jack Pearson, Art McCoy, King Kelly, George Pearson, Gilman. Front: Raymond Gilman, Roy Sheriff, Glen Durant, Lloyd Liesemer.

Photo courtesy of Glenbow Archives

Intermediate level playoffs resumed after WWI in the 1919-20 season. On March 13, Carstairs defeated the University of Alberta Intermediates. The University won the opener 3-2 but lost the second match 3-1 in overtime in the two game total-goal series. Leisemer scored the winner for Carstairs after four and one-half minutes of overtime. Roland Michener, later Govenor General of Canada, was a member of the University team.

In a letter written on June 19, 1984, Michener recalled some of his hockey days.

I attended the University of Alberta from September 1917 to April 1920, and played on the University hockey team for the last two years. Except for the last four months of 1918 when I was absent in the Air Force, our university team played seven man hockey. As a left-hander I usually played left wing.

UNIVERSITY OF ALBERTA INTERMEDIATES 1919-20

Roland Michener is second from left in front row. *Photo courtesy of Maski-Pitoon Historical Society, Lacombe*

I continued playing hockey in the following years for Oxford University where I was attending as a Rhodes Scholar from Alberta. We played for two winters from 1921 to 1923, spending six weeks in Switzerland playing against Cambridge and all-comers. Other games were against the Belgium Olympic team in Brussels, the French Olympic team in Paris, one German team as well as several Swiss teams. One season we went undefeated.

Michener played with the Right Honorable Lester B. Pearson, later Prime Minister of Canada, Edward Pitblado and Richard Bonnycastle of Winnipeg and Ronnie McCaul and John Farthing of Montreal during his hockey career.

THE CALGARY MILLERS

A unique game took place in Calgary at the open air Crystal Rink on January 31, 1920. It was the second game of an exhibition series between a team of Calgary law students and the Calgary Millers. After a previous 4-3 win the Millers tied the students 4-4.

At least one fan sat up proudly and cheered whenever the Millers scored. He cared little about the score or who won. His desire was to see a well-played game. The proud fan and father watched his sons, Westley in goal, Lorne and Clinton on defence, Clifford as a rover, Harper at centre, Vance on'left and Stanley on right wing.

Records of four years before indicate the Millers were a prominent sports family as at least four of them played football as well.

* * *

DAYSLAND HOCKEY TEAM 1920
CHAMPIONS OF HIGHWAY 13 LEAGUE

Top row (l to r): K.J. Anderson, Kenneth Roddick, Jim Roddick, Doug Machon, C.W. Barnes. Centre: Stan McLaughlin, Lawrence Dumont. Bottom: Allan P. DEForest, Carl Carmichael, Percy DEForest.

Canmore has been a hockey stronghold in Alberta. The centre won its first Alberta Intermediate championship in 1920-21 when they defeated Blairmore 5-0. In all four playoff games, Canmore did not use a substitute for any of their six regulars. They won all fifteen league, playoff and exhibition matches played.

W.H. Evans, Canmore manager, challenged the senior champion Alberta Pacific Grain from Calgary. The challenge was not accepted. Earlier in the year Canmore had defeated A.P.G. 8-4 in an exhibition game. Canmore fans were disappointed as they felt they had the best team in Alberta. Canmore teams continued to be prominent over many of the next thirty years.

The first Colonel W.C. Craig Trophy was awarded twice in 1922 to the champion of the Big Six Hockey League in eastern Alberta. Vermilion Farmers won the east division while the Vegreville Hustlers the western side. In the two game total goal final the Hustlers won the series 5-2. Fans who watched the final game in Vermilion stood on five feet of snow and nearly froze during the hour and one-half allotted for the game.

After the series a message was received from C.D. Battrum of Calgary, secretary of the Alberta Amateur Athletic Union, that stated a sudden-death game was necessary. One player from Vegreville and two from Vermilion were ineligible.

Neutral ice at Mannville was selected. On March 10, 1922, Vermilion Farmers took back the Craig Trophy and represented the league when they edged the Hustlers 2-1. This allowed Vermilion to play Okotoks in the 1921-22 provincial final. Okotoks shut out Vermilion 4-0 to win the provincial championship and the Black Trophy.

Lacombe had lost the intermediate finals in the first two years of Alberta intermediate hockey. In 1922-23 Red Deer brought 250 fans by train to Lacombe for the final. Another 600 Lacombe fans, the largest crowd in the centre to this time, watched their team skate to a 6-2 win. Lacombe then challenged the senior champions in the Allan Cup playoffs. (See Professional and Senior.)

CANMORE HOCKEY TEAM 1920-21

Top row (l to r): Cyril Powers, J. Shellion, Victor Riva, Orton Evans, Oliver Reinikka, G. Mackie. Middle: John Mackie, E.A. Colebrook (secretary treasurer), W. Dodd (mascot), John Bleskans. Bottom: W.H. Evans (manager).

Photo courtesy of A.L. Hess Photo

In those days hockey seasons started later. In 1924 for example, Okotoks did not open its season until January 2, at the new Vulcan Rink. Playing manager A.B. King (later AAHA executive) and three Overand brothers (Robert A., Laverne and Earl) were feature players. On the train trip to Vulcan, Okotok's player "Goosey" McRae forgot his boots and skates. Manager King proceeded to lecture him on his carelessness. While looking for McRaes' skates, King suddenly found that he had forgotten his own. The "Okotoks Review" refused to publish what the team said to King. King's skates were brought to the rink in time by other fans from Okotoks.

Okotoks proceeded to win eight straight and the right to be called champions of their area. In provincials, Okotoks defeated King Kelly's Carstair's club in a two-game-total-goal series 9-7. After the game it was learned that Kelly played the last game with broken ribs.

Okotoks then defeated Red Deer of the Big Five League 4-1 and 3-1. In the first game in Red Deer, ice conditions were so soft that the game had to start at 10 p.m., when the temperature was colder.

Some problems occured in selecting an intermediate finalist in 1923-24 to play Okotoks. Medicine Hat Monarchs and Bassano Bearcats played two games. After two games, Medicine Hat claimed victory over Bassano. Natural ice conditions in Bassano were so bad that Medicine Hat refused to play. Since the crowd was large, the Monarchs finally played and won. Bassano stated that the second game was only an exhibition match while Medicine Hat thought the game should count.

The AAHA listened to the protest and scheduled a sudden-death game at the Second Street Rink in Medicine Hat. The Bearcats won 3-2. Due to the lateness of the season, a single game was played for the provincial crown. Okotoks defeated Bassano 10-3.

Intermediate hockey was also competitive in Central Alberta. Red Deer and Lacombe had 17 points while Ponoka and Wetaskiwin were tied at 15. Leduc was in last place and had 12 points. Wetaskiwin won the league playoffs by a goal over Red Deer in a two-game series.

The intense rivalry between the teams in central Alberta continued. This is an account by Gordon MacLeod of Ponoka, whose father was manager of the Ponoka Intermediates, the 1924-25 provincial champions.

PONOKAS' MIGHTY EIGHT

BY GORDON MACLEOD

Whenever we wanted to get my father (Mac) talking about old times we would ask him about the Ponoka Intermediates who won the Black Cup in 1924-25.

It wasn't so much the telling of the winning that stirred your blood as it was the pride in his voice when he would say,

"we had only eight players in those days, you know; six on the ice and two substitutes in the box. There were the Longmans, Vern the secretary treasurer and his borther Shorty. There were the Sayers, Bill and Barry. There was Milt and Bruce Stephens-Milt played goal you know. And don't forget the two telephone linesmen, Al Strahan and Gus Hayes, who the storm had brought in".

PONOKA HOCKEY TEAM
INTERMEDIATE CHAMPIONS OF ALBERTA 1924-25

Top row (l to r): B.E. Kyler (president), D.R. Morgan (vice president), B. Stephens (left wing), V. Longman (secretary treasurer), A.A. MacLeod (manager). Middle: W. Sayers (right defence), G. Hayes (left wing), M. Stephens (goal), A. Strahan (ring wing), H. James (left defence). Bottom: H. Sayers (centre), O. Longman (right wing).

Dad would count them on his fingers and when the eighth finger fell he would pause; these eight were an extension of his family.

The Ponoka Intermediates played eight home and eight away from home games in the Big Five League against Red Deer, Wetaskiwin, Lacombe, and Leduc. (Lacombe being the envy of the league because they had the only covered rink.) All travel was done by train and usually entailed an overnight stay in a hotel and a return trip the next morning. At the end of the year Ponoka was leading the league with a total of 18 points but Lacombe had made a great surge to come from last place and finish second with 16 points. This show of strength by Lacombe was going to make the playoffs interesting.

On Saturday, February 13th, with the crowd standing three deep around the Ponoka rink, Lacombe took a 3-1 lead in the home-and-home league playoff series. Monday night 150 Ponoka fans boarded a special train for Lacombe to see their boys come back and win the Driard Shield. However, it just was not to be. Lacombe humiliated Ponoka 7-1, scoring 4 goals in the last period to win the Big Five League that year. This series was never mentioned in our home.

The battle cry was now to be, "shake off the loss boys, Provincials are starting." The first draw saw Stettler at Ponoka for a Friday encounter. Snow fell steadily throughout the game and after having to stop and scrape the ice twice during the game, the score was 4-3 for Stettler. Well it was a long quiet ride to Stettler on Monday. However, Bill Desilde had faith in the team, for just before the game he jumped on the ice in front of the crowd and soon had $100 covered. Ponoka led 4-1 after the first period and finished up 8-5.

"Bring on Carstairs", the fans hollered as the town filled for the Saturday game. The Ponoka Herald reports that it was a lightening fast game with Harry Sayers scoring twice for Ponoka in the 2-2 tie.

Sunday, after service at the Union Church, Angus called Harry James to the creamery and for two hours they talked about what they would have to do on Monday night to stop Ted "King" Kelly and the Carstairs team. "You know Harry," dad said, "they haven't been beat at home in two years". Harry continued to listen patiently but when finally allowed to leave he was seen kicking a horse dropping down the street muttering, "does that man ever get tired of talking hockey?"

A whole book could be written about the game in Carstairs. It is enough here to say that in the second period two goals for Ponoka were scored by James and Stephens. Ponoka then held on through a climatic finish which did not end with the final bell. After the game, while the team was eating in a Chinese restaurant, an RCMP constable came in and said:

We have got a nasty crowd outside boys. Just finish eating quietly like nothing is happening and when you are done follow me out the back door. We've got your bags from the hotel in two cutters and we will escort you to Didsbury where we have booked hotel rooms for you.

The next morning they took the train home to the safety of Ponoka.

The series with Okotoks could be titled the 'Tale of Two Rinks'. During the first game on March 7th, Okotoks was lost on Ponoka's large ice surface and ended up being down 2 goals. But then Ponoka's luck changed. It was bad enough that Ponoka's train hit snow drifts and was late getting to Okotoks Monday night, but one look at the small ice surface and they knew they were in trouble. "You see," Al Strachan told me, "you had to be on-side at both blue lines in those days". The puck had to be carried over each blue line. The forward pass, as we know it today, was not allowed until 1933 in amateur hockey. "It was really Milt Stephens who held us in that game until we learned to get the puck out of our own end." Okotoks scored two goals in the first period and the series was tied up. Infact, it stayed tied until Harry Sayers scored the winning goal at the six minute mark of the third ten minute period. That night Okotoks hosted a late banquet for both teams and at 3:00 a.m. they got to bed.

* * *

Red Deer won its first Intermediate title in 1925-26. A new rink was built in Red Deer. One of the team's toughest battles was against arch-rival Lacombe.

Competition between Lacombe and Red Deer had always been strong. In the second game of the playoff round in Lacombe, two hundred and fifty fans and the Elk's Boys' Band went by special train to Lacombe. The Red Deer fans sang ditties such as:

'Wherever we may roam,
We can always beat Lacombe.'

The group returned home even happier because Red Deer won 3-2. This gave Red Deer a 5-4 total goal victory for the two games.

Top (l to r): H.C. Munn (manager), O. Asmundson, C. Hewson (coach), R. Carpenter, H. Lavender (president). Middle: J.C. Martin (captain), L. Steers, P. Weber, H. McMahan. Bottom: K. Dell, H.J. Malcolm. *Photo courtesy of Fleming Photo*

On March 17, 1926, in Red Deer, High River was defeated 3-1 in a sudden-death final. Only one game was played in the provincial final due to the lateness of the season and because High River, southern champions had no ice remaining. Red Deer played a total of thirty-one games; this was considered a lengthy season.

The twenties was a colorful era for nicknames. In 1926-27 Lacombe, the Intermediate champions, had this line up: Earl "Toughy" Calkins, Louis "Cours" Calkins, "Cyclone" Burke, "Pop" Steele, "King" Day plus Van Wassenove and Edmans. The provincial final against the Calgary Wheat Kernels was close when the southern team won the first game 2-1. In the final game at Lacombe the series became tied 3-3 after regulation time. Near the end of the second ten minute overtime period, "Toughy" Calkins broke the tie and gave Lacombe the provincial championship.

Hockey prices for 1928 were extremely low compared to today. However, in the January 26, 1928, "Red Deer Advocate," mention was made of the increases for the provincial rounds.

> The price of admission is 50 cents for adults, and 25 cents for children. These prices are set by the Alberta Amateur Hockey Association, and the local hockey Executive has to make these changes.
> But with the class of hockey we are getting, every fan will get a big run for his money.

Increases were required to assist in travelling expenses throughout the province.

Again Lacombe was the provincial power of Intermediate in 1928. They advanced through the playoffs to enter the finals against High River. A 2-1 win in High River plus a 2-2 tie at home before 1,300 fans gave Lacombe the title.

Top row (l to r): York Blayney, V.C.W. Stanley (manager), I.N. McKeage (president), W.C. McNichol (coach), G. Riley. Middle: C. Arnold, E. Overand, J. Kwasney, G. Mattson. Bottom: A. Taylor, J.M. Henderson, J. Robertson, C. McCorquadale.

Photo courtesy of Lane Photo, High River.

Lacombe then had the opportunity to play the senior Canmore Miners for the right to go to the Allan Cup playoffs. The Miners tied Lacombe 2-2 in the first game. Lacombe's season ended on Canmore ice when the Miners won 4-1 to win the round 6-3.

The Northern Intermediate Championship for 1929 was exciting as Red Deer edged out Lacombe 4-2 in goals after two games. A goal by Scotty Reid in the second period in Red Deer of game two turned out to be the winner.
Red Deer, however, was no match for the Blairmore Bearcats as it lost both games in the provincial final 9-0 in the south and 8-4 at home. Blairmore was heralded as a great team. Players such as Tony Vejprava, Jim Dicken, Jimmy McVey, Jimmy Evans and Albert Vangotsinoven combined to give the Bearcats the 1929 crown.

In 1930 Lacombe and Red Deer continued their hockey battles. This time Lacombe defeated Red Deer 4-2 and then tied 2-2 to win the Northern Intermediate championship.

In the south the Coleman Canadians and Medicine Hat Monarchs clashed in a series that took three games. In these games a total of only nine goals were socred. The first two games ended in stalemates of 2-2 and 1-1. In the third period of the final, Quail scored the winner for the Monarchs to win the south.

MEDICINE HAT MONARCHS 1929-30

Top row (l to r): Wilf Knight, Alex Thompson, Ed Holly, Ross Mc. Middle: Maurice Stonehon (secretary treasurer), Harold Scott, Bob Lauder (trainer), Ned O'Connor (manager and captain). Bottom: Bill Clarke, Mickey Carven, Tommy Charles, Fred Lait, Bus McDougall, Jack Quaill.
Photo courtesy of Smith Family, Medicine Hat

Medicine Hat continued to participate in tight games. The first game of the provincial finals in Medicine Hat against Lacombe ended 2-2. Led by the sensational goalkeeping of Charles for Medicine Hat in the second game, the Monarchs were able to win the first Alberta Intermediate 'A' crown for their city. The Monarchs then had an opportunity to play against the senior champions; however, because of the number of games the team declined.

Charles Graham's Lacombe Rangers had a record of twenty-six wins, one tie and one loss before entering the 1931 provincial intermediate finals. Blairmore Bearcats offered little opposition in the finals as it lost by a total goal score of 13-1 in two games.

Lacombe then played the senior category, but was defeated 4-0 by the Canmore Briquetteers. Canmore's defence was superior, which caused most of Lacombe's shots to be directed from outside the blue line. The second game of this Alberta Allan Cup semi-final the Briquetteers won 7-2. This set up the provincial senior finals between Canmore and the Edmonton Superiors. (See Senior Hockey)

For most years, intermediate finalists had been teams from outside of Edmonton and Calgary. In 1932, however, Edmonton's McDonnell Miners and the Gleichen Gunners met. Both games were evenly matched. The Gunners tied the first game 1-1 and won the second 2-0 to play the senior champion Calgary Bronks.

The senior champion Bronks took command over the Gunners 4-0 and 3-1 to win the round 7-1. Rosie Helmer's Bronks had an impressive lineup including Sweeney Schriner, Fred Hergert and Peter Paul. This gave the Bronks the right to play Trail Smokeaters in further Allan Cup play. (See Senior Hockey)

To this point, intermediate hockey champions in their challenges to represent the province had never beaten the senior champion. In the fall of 1932 more recognition was given to the intermediate level when Dr. W.G. Hardy, President of the AAHA, reported that $1000.00 from the CAHA had been voted to organizing Western Intermediate playoffs. It was understood that any deficit would be shared equally by each branch entering the playdowns. This amount of money from the CAHA was quite significant in 1932 as it was during the depression. One lunch item at Woodwards included chicken creole soup, roast leg of pork stuffing with sweet potatoes, apple sauce plus choice of potato and vegatable, choice of desserts which included apple, lemon or strawberry cream pies and tea, coffee or milk for $.25. Still, getting hold of a quarter was a problem.

Powerful teams in intermediate and senior hockey in Alberta came from coal mining areas. Three such areas producing teams were the Coal Branch, the Crowsnest Pass and Drumheller. The major attraction in these areas was the availability of work. In 1933, Luscar, a coal mining town, near Hinton, produced the top intermediate club in Alberta. The Indians also got the honor of being the first Alberta intermediate club to be in interprovincial playoffs. Today, only a coal mine exists at Luscar.

CADOMIN COLTS 1934-35
INTERMEDIATE "B"

Back (l to r): Nick Melynk, Art Garside, Bill "Wal" Stene, Trevor Jones, Art Solley, Ken Stewart, Tony "Bolt" Stene. Middle: Walter "Ducky" Duckworth, Howard Dea (coach), J.H. McMillan (manager), Alex "Unk" Matheson. Front: Eddie "Doc" Purcell, Stan Amos, Courtney Patrick.

Photo courtesy of Provincial Archives

The Alberta championship was won against the 1932 champion Gleichen Gunners. The first match went 55 minutes before a goal was scored, and the penalty free game ended 1-1. In the second game the total score was tied 1-1. 2-2 and then 3-3 at full time. Bob Kennedy's goal at the start of the second overtime period and D.A. Gillies insurance marker were enough to win the Alberta crown. The Indians travelled to North Battleford, Saskatchewan to play Unity in the first Intermediate Championship of Western Canada. Unity became the first Western winners defeating Luscar 2-1 and 4-3.

In the following years, the Luscar Indians played and won at the senior level but did win the provincial intermediate level again in 1940 and 1942. Few provincial games were held at Luscar, Cadomin, or Mountain Park who all had teams. The area was considered remote in relationship to the rest of the province. These clubs learned how to travel and did very well in provincials.

In 1934 Olds and Vegreville reached the northern final for the first time. Before a record crowd of 725 in Vegreville, the Rangers tied Olds at two and then in the second game in Olds, before 1,000 fans, it ended at 1-1. In overtime Bob Gooder scored two goals to end the season for Vegreville.

A victory over Gleichen Gunners gave the Coleman Canadians the Southern Alberta Intermediate crown.

COLEMAN CANADIANS 1933-34

Back row (l to r): F.G. Creegan, C.J. Devine, R.F. Barnes, Jack Kwasney, Dr. K. McLean, Rev. Roy C. Taylor, J.A. McLeod. **Second row (l to r):** R. Pattinson, Ivor Bolt, H. Gardner, V. Lilya, J. Joyce, J. Oliva, John Kapalka, J. Atkinson. **Front row (l to r):** F. Brown, R. Johnson, V. Cologrosso, W. Fraser, C. Kanik, R. Kwasney, George Jenkins.

Photo courtesy of Gushel Studio, Blairmore.

Coleman continued its winning ways over Olds, then met the Swift Current Indians of Saskatchewan for the Western Intermediate Championship of 1934. The first game remained tied at four after three ten-minute overtime periods. It took overtime again, but Coleman won the second game 4-2. The third game was all Coleman. Brown scored three, Joyce two and singles by Lilya and Fraser were enough for a 7-2 win. This gave the Canadians the first Western Canada Intermediate Championship for an Alberta team.

After 1934, Vegreville Rangers, still under coach Jack Moss, improved their record in 1935 and again in 1936. The 35' Rangers won Northern Alberta when they edged Red Deer 2-1 and 4-3. In the next step for the provincial final against the Lethbridge Maple Leafs, the Rangers overwhelmed the Leafs 7-1 in the first game of the best-of-three. Lethbridge came back with a 3-1 victory only to see Vegreville win the championship in the third game 3-2.

Coach Moss tried everything he could do to get and keep his club ready for Lethbridge. He wanted to keep his players from going out between games so one shoe was removed from everyone. Some of the team found other footware and went out anyway. The team still won.

Arrangements were made for the final two games in Lethbridge to be broadcast on the Calgary Albertan's station, CJCJ. At first the station decided to broadcast regardless of whether it was sponsored. Sponsorship was quickly obtained for the last period in the last game of the series. The Vegreville Chamber of Commerce succeeded in getting $90.00 to pay for the first two periods.

The Rangers entered the Western Canadian Final against the Kerrobert Saskatchewan Tigers. All merchants on Main Street in Vegreville agreed to shut their doors at 8:00 p.m. to allow their staff to see the game. Customers were asked to get their orders in early so the game could be seen. On Saturday night more than 1,100 fans packed the Vegreville rink and saw the teams tied at the end of regulation time. In overtime, the Rangers lost 3-1. In Kerrobert, the Tigers again took the Rangers to overtime and won 5-3.

A few days later, on March 23, 1935, the Rangers completed their regular Big Five League playoffs for the Craig Trophy. Vegreville won the first game 3-2 but lost the second match against its league rivals, the Lloydminster Prolites, 4-2 in overtime. These two losses at the end of the 1935 season made the Rangers more determined to succeed in 1936.

VEGREVILLE RANGERS 1935-36
Western Canada Intermediate Champions

Back row (l to r): R. McKinnon, W. Mozel, S. Waldenburg, Laurel Harney, W. Gauf, W. Onufreychuk, P. Leminski (captain), M. Barr, H. Trace, Pete Kolmatycki. Front: P. Scrimbitz (mascot), Jack Moss (coach), K. McIntyre (trainer).

The Rangers of 1936 advanced over its northern rivals and met the Strathmore Red Wings in the provincial final. A 5-2 win and 2-2 tie gave Vegreville the Alberta championship.

In 1935, the Lloydminster Prolites had won the local league against the Rangers. Now in 1936 the same two teams met. However, Lloydminster represented Saskatchewan in the Western Canada Intermediate final. The final 4-2 win gave the Rangers the series in two straight and concluded three successful years in a row. Their 1936 record was twenty-two wins, three losses and five ties.

The Lethbridge Maple Leafs of 1936-37 became Western Canada Intermediate champions. The club avenged its 1935 loss to Vegreville when it won three straight to win the Morgan Cup. (This trophy was awarded for the second or 'B' level of intermediate hockey in Alberta.) The Leafs then played Wetaskiwin Colonels for the top 'A' provincial honors. Previously, the Colonels defeated the Canmore Briquetters.

Leaf's defenceman Ken Stewart scored after five minutes of overtime to give Lethbridge a one game lead. A 6-5 win gave Duke Wainman's Leafs the 1937 Black Trophy and the right to play the Rosetown Red Wings of Saskatchewan in intermediate play.

Youthful Max Bentley and the Red Wings were decisively beaten 6-1 in the opener. The Red Wings did not quit as Bentley scored all his team's goals for a 4-2 win in the second game. The first Western crown came to Lethbridge when the leafs shut-out the Red Wings 3-0 on two goals by "Slim" Anderson and one by Christenson in the final.

The season for Lethbridge continued as it still had to play their local playoffs in the Crowsnest Pass League. Lethbridge opened this series winning 2-1 but lost the second game to the Coleman Canadians 3-1. The Canadians, who were the 1936-37 Alberta Senior finalists, won the Wright Cup. (The Lethbridge Maple Leafs now became a power in both senior and intermeditae hockey, which would include their 1951 World Amateur Hockey Championship.)

In 1937-38, Vin Stanley a long-time AAHA executive, presented a trophy for presentation to the 'A' intermediate champions of Alberta. The 'B' winners would continue to play for the Morgan Cup; the 'A' for the Stanley Cup and the two would play off for the Black Trophy as the overall champion. (Trophys change through the years. In later years the Vin Stanley award ends up as the Northern Alberta Trophy.)

The Edmonton Capitals became the first winners of this Stanley Trophy when they defeated Calgary Jenkins Green Bombers in a total goal series in Calgary. After an initial 4-2 loss, playing coach Jimmy Graham led the Capitals to a 6-0 win.

CANMORE BRIQUETTEERS 1937-38
Western Canada Champions

Top row (l to r): Albert Grainger, Alex "Goosie" Anderson, George "Fergie" MacPherson, Jim Antoniak, Buck Kaleta, Nick Kazimer, Steve Jerwa, Mike Golowski, Louis Sandelli. Bottom row: Joe Golowski, Vic Riva, Andy Chakowski.

The Canmore Briquetters won the Morgan Cup for the 'B' level in the provincial final, Canmore defeated the Capitals 4-1 and lost 4-2 but won the round 6-5. The Briquetteers went on to capture the 1938 Western Canada Intermediate title over the Saskatchewan champion Rostern Wheat Kings 10-5. The series was intended to be a two-game-total-goal affair, but poor attendance and the supremacy shown by Canmore made officials decide one game was enough. In the final game Andy Chakowksi tallied five goals and Steve Jarwa got five assists. The Briquetters won the Edmonton Journal Trophy.

The 1938-39 Edmonton Capitals captured the Western Canadian Intermediate title. To win the championship, the last three rounds were played away from home. The Capitals defeated the Gleichen Gunners 4-1 in Gleichen and 3-2 at the Victoria Arena in Calgary for the Alberta crown.

GAINERS CAPITALS 1938-39

Back Row: J. PHILLIPS Stick Boy, H. WISMER Defense, R. LEMIEUX Forward, H. CALVERT Forward, W. PHILLIPS Manager, J. LAMMIE Defense, T. BRANT, Defense, E. PELANT Trainer, H. DYER Sec. Treas.
Front Row: H. WALKER Forward, J. GRAHAM Playing Coach, T. MOTTERSHEAD Goal, R. GRAHAM Forward, H. HORNE Forward, P. YANEW Forward

Photo courtesy of Ted Mottershead

Intermediate hockey in Western Canada became a four province final in 1938-39. The Bralorne Gold Diggers represented British Columbia. The Capitals outscored the Diggers 4-1 and 3-1 in a series played in Vernon. The Carman Beavers won the Manitoba Saskatchewan playoff.

The Capitals lost their first game against Carman 4-3 in the second overtime period but Bobby Graham scored three goals and had two assists to lift the Capitals to a 5-3 win in game two. The last game was scoreless for 55 minutes until the Capitals errupted. Bob Graham, Harold Wismer and Tommy Brant scored quick goals to give Ted Mottershead a 3-0 shut-out and the Western Canada championship for the Edmonton Capitals.

Teams often changed categories. Luscar in the early 30's was intermediate, then went senior. But in 1939-40 the Indians won the Alberta Intermediate championship. Over 1,300 fans watched the final at Camrose. Fans came from Canmore and the Coal Branch to witness a 1-0 win for Luscar. A 3-3 final game gave the Indians the Alberta title by a 4-3 total score.

The Indians went to Vernon, B.C. where they lost the opener to the Vernon Blue and Whites 3-2. They came back with a 4-1 win to qualify against the Swift Current Indians. The series against the Saskatchewan champions was also played in Vernon. After overtime, the Saskatchewan club won the first game 5-4. The second game was just as close but Luscar went down to a 4-3 defeat in the final 25 seconds.

The 1941 Alberta Intermediate champion was the Canmore Briquetteers who took three games to eliminate Luscar's rival team, the Mountain Park Provincials. Canmore won the first game on home ice 7-3. In the second game, the Provincials put up a fierce battle and even after overtime the score remained at 1-1. The Briquetteers won the provincial crown when they defeated the Provincials 6-3 in the final played on neutral ice at Camrose. Don Stanley registered a hat-trick, Andy Chakowski got two and Barney Antoniuk one to account for Canmore.

Canmore then played the Naniamo Clippers. Playing at home, the Clippers won the opening match 5-4. Canmore came back to win 4-2 but lost the final 2-1.

During World War II hockey used to improve morale. As the 1941-42 season opened the country's concern continued to be World War II. The Royal Bank of Canada's October Newsletter showed that 490,000 Canadian soldiers, sailors and airmen were enlisted and 100,000 were overseas. Teams had changes in rosters but interest remained high.

REFERENCE LETTER FOR HARRY WALKER IN 1942

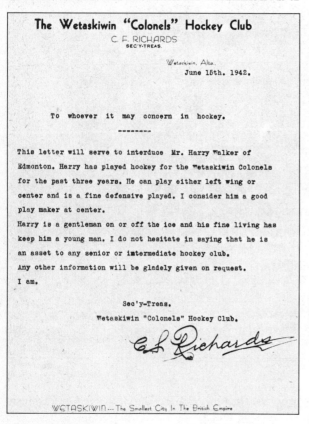

The Wetaskiwin "Colonels" Hockey Club

C. F. RICHARDS
SEC'Y-TREAS.

Wetaskiwin, Alta.
June 15th. 1942.

To whoever it may concern in hockey.
————————

This letter will serve to interduce Mr. Harry Walker of Edmonton. Harry has played hockey for the Wetaskiwin Colonels for the past three years. He can play either left wing or center and is a fine defensive played. I consider him a good play maker at center.

Harry is a gentleman on or off the ice and his fine living has keep him a young man. I do not hesitate in saying that he is an asset to any senior or imtermediate hockey club.

Any other information will be gladely given on request.

I am.

Sec'y-Treas.
Wetaskiwin "Colonels" Hockey Club.

C. F. Richards

WETASKIWIN - The Smallest City In The British Empire

Photo courtesy of Edmonton Archives

Hockey during World War II also provided major entertainment for Canadians. Hockey also assisted in fund raising efforts. The 1942-43 Calgary Buffaloes, in addition to their playoffs played an exhibition game in Calgary in front of 6,180 fans. It netted $2,026.60 to be used for Milk to Britain Sea and Army Cadets and Benevolent Funds.

The provincial final of 1942 featured the Luscar Indians and Medicine Hat Tigers. Warm weather conditions in Medicine Hat caused the March 11th game to be played on wet stickey ice. Luscar edged out Medicine Hat 3-2. Discussion followed about moving the series to Lethbridge because of poor ice. A telegram from V.C.W. (Vin) Stanley, vice-president of the AAHA, decided the 1942 championship. It said:

> *Impossible to get ice. Do hereby declare Luscar winners on their one-game victory. The ice in Medicine Hat was in such poor shape that both teams did not want to play in order to prevent serious injury.*

Both teams had wanted artificial ice at Lethbridge and were willing to play an abbreviated two-game-total-goal series but it could not be arranged.

Luscar's season ended in Naniamo when the Clippers won the best-of-three B.C.-Alberta series in two straight games. Two Albertans, Dave McKay and Don Stanley led the Clippers in their wins.

The Calgary Buffaloes of 1943 went to Vernon, B.C. for the Western Canada Intermediate 'A' championship after they defeated the Edmonton Manning No. 3 Pool 9-8 and 11-2.

The highlight of the March 4, 1943, 11-2 win was the scoring feat of Calgary's Pete Atkinson. Atkinson scored a total of five goals. Three of them came in the third period at 10:29, 10:36 and 10:46 in a total time of seventeen (17) seconds.

The Buffaloes then won the Western Canada Intermediate Championship and the Edmonton Journal Trophy. Calgary had a collection of seasoned senior veterans playing at the intermediate level. Besides Atkinson, the linup included Doug Cairns, Joe McGoldrick, Dave Duckak, Jack Arbour and "Sad" Sam Timmins.

The opening game saw Calgary edge the Vernon Military All-Stars 4-3 on three second period goals by Dan Sprout on goalkeeper Johnny Kiszkan. (Kiszkan later changed his name to Johnny Bower, a later well-known NHL star.) A 4-4 tie in the second game provoked the Buffaloes as they wanted to play overtime. After the game, Calgary protested and it was agreed that if the third game was tied, Calgary would win the series on the basis of their opening victory.

The strategy failed and Vernon won the third game 6-2 to force a fourth match. The Buffaloes finally scored the way they had most of the year and drubbed the All-Stars 9-2 to capture the Western Canada crown for 1943.

Back (l to r): Art Jerwa (playing coach), Clyde Newsome, George Ross, Mike Onychuck, Bill Stene, Walter Holden, Protti, Jim McVey. Front: Sandy Dominchelli, Elliot Bellow, Dave Hamilton (trainer), Claude Bartoff (goalie), Goerge Bonner, Bill Kulyk.

Photo courtesy of Provincial Archives

At the conclusion of the season, the Buffaloes and their wives were dinner guest of J.B. Cross, their sponsor. Each player was presented with a coffee table with the club crest on it engraved in silver. Included on the Buffaloes of 1943 were players and management who would form and play for the Senior Allan Cup, Calgary Stampeders in 1946.

In 1943-44 the Canmore Briquetteers won the Black Cup, for intermediate hockey in Alberta. Canmore trounced Edmonton Aircraft Repair 7-0 as Andy "Cyclone" Chakowski scored three goals. A 6-4 score in the second game gave Canmore the championship.

Prince Albert M. and C. Warhawks won the 1944 Western title when they defeated Canmore 3-2 and 4-1 in Prince Albert. Johnny Bower, after losing with Vernon the year before, played goal for his home town, Prince Albert.

Canmore Briquetteers in 1945 eliminated the Calgary Burns Shamrocks 10-5 and 8-4 to win the Alberta Intermediate Championship 18-9.

John Arichuk, Mike and Joe Gilowski, Stan and Andy Chakowski took Canmore to the fifth game against the Laura Beavers in the Western Canada Intermediate hockey finals played in Saskatoon. Laura, a small town near Delisle, featured Johnny Bower, Squee Allan, Marshall Bentley and Doug Bentley. Canmore won the first and third games 9-5 and 8-2 while Laura won 7-5 and 5-2.

The largest crowd of the series, 3,300 in Saskatoon saw the Laura Beavers win a runaway 11-3 victory over the Canmore Briquetteers. An injury to John Arichuk reduced Canmore's lineup to nine players and was a factor in the Saskatchewan club's domination plus Doug Bentley had already played in the NHL and would return the following season.

Intermediate hockey's hold in Alberta moved to Edmonton and area for the next few years. Edmonton and Camrose had the powerful clubs from which two World champion teams were molded.

Edmonton Intermediate hockey of this era comprised a local league made up of teams from Swifts, Burns, New Method Laundry and Edmonton Transit. A team from this group of clubs called the Edmonton Independent All-Stars won the Northern Alberta Championship over the Wetaskiwin Colonels.

The south was represented by the Calgary #13 District Depot, otherwise known as Calgary Army. The Army defeated the Okotoks Legionnaires. The Edmonton squad then defeated Calgary Army 15-6 in a two-game-total-goal series to win the 1945-46 Alberta Intermediate championship.

The All-Stars advanced in the final intermediate round against the Winnipeg Jack Kings. Even though the All-Stars lost their opening match 3-2 before 2,600 fans in Edmonton, they came back to defeat the Kings 7-3 and 5-4. A former Chicago Black Hawk, Louis Holmes scored twice and picked up three assists in the final win.

A protest by the Edmonton Independent All-Stars assisted them in winning the Western title against the Vernon Legionnaires. Vernon scored a 3-2 win in the opening game that took four periods of overtime to decide. It was claimed Vernon used four imports instead of the regulation three. Al Pickard, of Regina, Vice-President of the CAHA upheld the protest and disallowed the first encounter.

The series was originally to be a best-of-five but with the first game already declared void it was reduced to a best-of-three. Victories of 4-3 and 4-2 gave Edmonton the 1945-46 Western Intermediate title in two straight games. In the final match it was Louis Holmes who scored three goals to pace Edmonton. Russ Klesko got the winning goal after one minute of the third period.

EDMONTON INDEPENDENT ALL STARS 1945-46

Photo courtesy of Kensit Studios

Coach of the All-Stars was Jimmy Graham who became coach of the 1950 World Champion Edmonton Mercurys. Player Louis Holmes would become coach of the 1952 Olympic Champion Mercurys while Billy Dawe would be the captain. Colin Kilburn was a sixteen-year-old on the All-Stars. His career lead to junior hockey and later as a star in the Western Hockey League.

New Method Laundry in 1947, defeated Coleman Grands 6-3 and 8-7 to win the Alberta Intermediate championship in two straight. The second match was won in overtime after scoring sprees by both clubs. Coleman scored five straight to take a 6-3 lead only to have New Method score three goals in the last six minutes and force the overtime.

Overtime was not sudden death as sixteen-year-old Alex Kovacik combined with Ted Kryczka for Coleman. George Stuart on an assist from Billy Dawe tied up the game. The eighth and winner came from Dawe from Louis Holmes to give New Method the title.

New Method were now scheduled to play in Vernon but the players felt they could not be away from their jobs for up to two weeks. They wanted some of the series to be in Edmonton. As well a guarantee of $2,000 a game was requested and seemed to be accepted. The Vernon Arena then insisted on getting the games and New Method Laundry did not represent Alberta. Thus, Coleman Grands represented Alberta in a tournament type series against the Trail All-Stars of British Columbia and the Notre Dame Hounds of Wilcox, Saskatchewan.

NEW METHOD LAUNDRY HOCKEY TEAM 1946-47

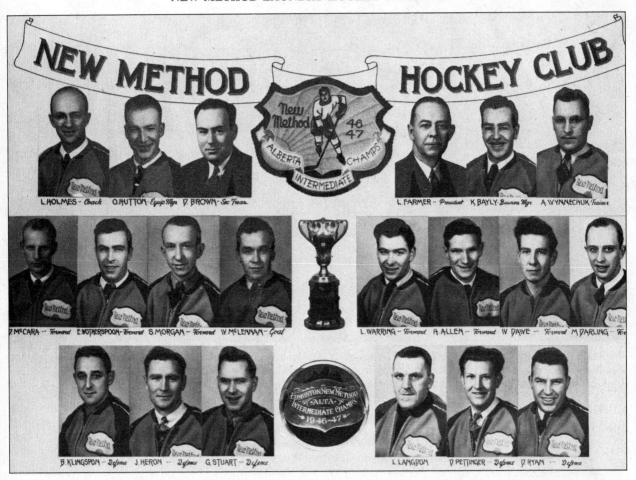

After defeating Trail, the Coleman Grands lost two to the Hounds and fought back to edge Notre Dame 2-1 before 2,600 fans in game three. All the scoring took place in the second period on goals by Alex Kovacik and Jimmy Joyce for Coleman and Jackie McLeod for Notre Dame.

The series went the full five games. Coleman won the Edmonton Jounral Trophy for Western Canada by virtue of a 5-2 win. Three goals by Bill Fraser along with singles by Joe Beguin and Kovacik eliminated Frank Germann's Hounds.

The 1947-48 edition of the Camrose Maroons won the Alberta Intermediate crown. To win, the Maroons defeated some of the soon to be best known names in Alberta intermediate hockey, the Ponoka Stampeders, Calgary Arena Dukes, Edmonton Waterloo Mercurys and Lethbridge Maple Leafs.

Top: Bill Fraser (captain). **Third row (l to r):** Don Atkinson, Rudolph "Duke" Kwasnie, Richard Antonenko, Ron Collings, Joe Biegun. **Second row:** Fan, Joe Paulus, Jimmy Joyce, Ted Kryczka, Edmonton Journal Trophy, Alex Kovacik, Bill Gate (coach), Bill Mozell, Dave Pow and a piper. **Front:** Barry Fraser (mascot).

The competition was tough and so were the roads for Camrose. John Protti, former Camrose player, now in Richmond, B.C., said that:

> *In 1948 roads were not paved and highway maintenance was difficult. The snow drifted badly so we often had to shovel to get cars moving to Stettler, Ponoka or Wetaskiwin. When we had a home game and roads were plugged, farmers would drive to the main highway on their tractor to help clear the way.*

The Maroons advanced to play the Melville Millionaires, and won three straight, 6-3, 13-2 and 11-2.

The Western Intermediate final against Paul Thompson's New Westminster Cubs was a best-of-seven. All the games were played in New Westminster which led hockey fans in Camrose to wonder why. They felt games in Alberta would do much better than attract 700 fans a game. The Maroons were ahead in the series three games to two. Hockey enthusiasm was high in Camrose and Byers Flour Mills sponsored a broadcast of the remaining games over CJCA Edmonton. It was unusual for a station to broadcast a game involving "outside" teams.

The series went the full seven games before the Cubs edged the Maroons 4-3. Injuries to Maroon players did not keep them out of the series. Goalie Wilbur Delainey had a broken nose while Tony Hauck played with a broken hand. Joe Voytechek, Tom McCready, Walter Dutchak, Pete McGregor and Max McLean all suffered from injuries or sickness but they all played.

The Camrose Maroons issued a financial statement in August 1948, for the previous 47-48 season. Receipts totalled $16,337.26 and expenditures were $16,013.95. Even though they were over $300.00 in the black the club took until the fall to get organized.

CAMROSE MAROONS 1947-48

Top row (l to r): Max McLean, Dunc Grant (coach), Wilbur Delainey, "Bim" Barker, Walter Dutchak. Third row: Tom McCready, Rudy Magneson (secretary), James Dabbs (president), Nathan Warden (equipment manager), Tony Hauk. Second row: C. Marshall, Joe Voytechek. Bottom: Bill Gostick, Fred Kirstien, E. Bello, Pete Gregor, Jim Malin, John Protti.

Photo courtesy of Langbell Studio

In 1948-49 the Maroon played in the Northern Alberta Intermediate League against Ponoka, Wetaskiwin and the Edmonton Waterloo Mercurys. Camrose was the toughest opposition the Mercs had during the 1948-49 in the Alberta northern playoffs.

The Mercurys were able to win the Alberta Intermediate title and dispose of the Naniamo Clippers from British Columbia. The finals for Western Canada were played in Kelowna, B.C. where the Mercurys met the Melville Millionaires. Harry Allen fired three goals in the fourth game for Edmonton to give the Mercs a commanding 3-1 lead in games in a 7-2 win. Five goals in the third period of the next game were enough for a 9-6 win and the Western Intermediate championship for the Waterloo team.

This victory allowed the Mercurys to represent Canada in the 1950 World Hockey Championships in London, England. The Mercurys had a team of players who had played in interprovincial playoffs with the Independent All-Stars and New Method of Edmonton, Camrose Maroons of intermediate plus some with senior experience.

Some of the players may have been good enough for professional hockey but World War II curtailed this type of ambition.

EDMONTON WATERLOO MERCURYS 1948-49

Dr. W.G. Hardy of Edmonton at the time was President of the International Ice Federation, must have recognized the talent as he assisted in getting the Mercurys approved by the CAHA for the Worlds. The other key person behind the scenes was James Christiansen, then owner of Waterloo Motors and the team sponsor. The arrangement of Edmonton Waterloo Mercurys representing Canada led the Lethbridge Maple Leafs going in 1951 and the Mercurys returning in the Olympic year of 1952.

Not everyone thought the Mercurys were good enough for the 1950 championship. In December, 1949, Jack Park of the London Ontario "Free Press" commented that, "now despite the criticism given last year's pick up team, Sudbury Wolves, who does the Canadian Amateur Hockey Association send this year? An Edmonton Intermediate team!?"

The Mercurys left for St. John's, New Brunswick by air on December 28, 1949. On December 30th, they boarded the Empress of Canada on the voyage to Grennock, Scotland. The championships were scheduled for March 13th to 22nd, 1950. During this time they played thirty-three exhibition games in six countries. The team name as announced by owner Jim Christiansen simply became the Edmonton Mercurys.

The opening of the World Hockey Championship was officiated by Dr. Hardy who besides being the President was also Professor of Classics at the University of Alberta. One of the easier wins for the Mercs was a 33-0 drubbing administered to Belgium on March 15th. Every member of the club except goalie Wilbur Delainey figured in the scoring. Statistics reveal that Belgium netminder Jacques Heylen handled 114 shots compared to 14 for Delainey. The first Mercury goal came after fifteen seconds for a total of 14 in the first, 10 in the second and 9 in the third period.

EDMONTON MERCURYS WIN WORLDS OF 1950

BY MARSHALL DARLING

(Marshall Darling, team captain of 1950, formally played with the Edmonton Athletic Club of 1939, Olds Elks, Lethbridge Maple Leafs and New Method Laundry recalled the team and the tournament.)

Mr. James Christianson, known to his players as the "Chief", owner of Waterloo Motors and Waterloo Industries, took over sponsorship of the Mercurys in the fall of 1947. They became Western Intermediate 'A' Champions of 1948-49, World Champions in London, England 1950 and Olympic Champions in 1952.

The "Chief" was very generous and also very patriotic. He made it clear that to represent Canada in Europe was an honour and there would be no misbehavior or poor conduct by any member of the team during the trip. Anyone caught for any violation would be sent home immediately. The Mercs even held practices lining up along the blue line, with sticks placed at an exact angle during the playing of the National Anthem and no one was to move until the anthem was over.

Team members who had to take leaves of absence from their jobs without pay were taken care of by the Chief. Everyone's wife received the usual monthly cheque while the players were away for the three and a half months. The Chief also paid for skates, pads, pants, sticks, etc. as well as the transportation to Saint John's, N.B. Some other expenses such as sweaters and socks were handled by the CAHA.

The players had a choice at a team meeting as to whether they wished to fly all the way or take a ship. We chose the ship. We boarded the ship in Saint John's after an exhibition game. Although the ship never left the dock until the next morning, a few of the players failed to report for breakfast due to "sea" sickness.

EDMONTON WATERLOO MERCURYS — WORLD CHAMPIONS 1950

Back (l to r): Jimmy Kilburn, Jack Manson, Wilbur Delainey, Doug MacAuley. Second row: Ab Newsome, Marsh Darling (captain), Pete Wright, Hassey Young, Don Stanley, Al Purvis, Harry Allen, Don Gauf. Bottom: Bob David, Jack Davies, Joe Hanley (manager), James Christiensen (sponsor and owner), Jimmy Graham (coach), Monty Ford (trainer), Bill Dawe.

Photo courtesy of Edmonton Archives

The team rookie, nineteen-year-old Doug MacCauley had never been further from home than Wetaskiwin, and the rest of us were about to embark on the tour of our lives. We spent New Year's Eve, 1950, somewhere on the Atlantic. Most had a great time while others suffered from sea sickness. Jack Manson and Jimmy Kilburn provided "unexpected" New Year's entertainment.

The team was not considered to be in the best of condition on departure due to the difficulty of obtaining ice for practice. However, after about a month of practices and games, the team reached excellent form and played fast, clean hockey which the fans enjoyed. Some reporters who travelled with the team reported that the Mercurys were the best team for Canada since the Trail Smokeaters of the 30's.

At this time the Russians did not compete at the world level of hockey. The Czechs, Swiss and Swedes were the powers of Europe. During our tour of France, Italy, Switzerland and Sweden, we were told that the Czechs were scouting our club. The day prior to the championships, the Czechs withdrew. Countries competing in 1950 were Great Britain, Norway, France, Canada, Switzerland, Belgium, Sweden, United States and Holland.

The hustling, hard checking Edmonton Mercurys became the 1950 World Hockey Champions. It won all eight games in the round robin and outscored its opposition 88 to 5. Messages of congratulations were sent to the Mercurys by Edmonton Mayor Sid Parsons, Alberta Premier Ernest Manning and Harold Brandeth, President of the AAHA. Mr. Brandeth said:

> *"The fact our Association had a hand in sending the Mercurys over makes us happy about the whole thing. I know all hockey followers in Alberta will be proud of a team from this province brought back the world title back to Canada.*

* * *

When the Mercurys returned to Edmonton, Dick Beddoes then of the "Edmonton Bulletin" retouched the 'Easter Parade' into the 'Mercury Parade' on April 16, 1950.

> ### THE MERCURY PARADE
> *Put on your Easter bonnet with*
> *"Mercurys" written on it*
> *And the greatest fellows in the*
> *Mercury Parade;*
> *And as you look them over,*
> *You'll know their back*
> *From Dover,*
> *Where they won this town.*
> *A title without Marshall aid*
> CHORUS
> *Down the Avenue, Jasper Avenue,*
> *all the people will shout out,*
> *As they jam the long rout;*
> *Oh, we will write a sonnet with*
> *the Mercury history on it,*
> *All about the guys were cheering*
> *in the Mercury parade*
> *So doff your Easter bonnet to*
> *The float with Mercurys on it,*
> *For their the grandest fellows*
> *in the Mercury parade.*

LETHBRIDGE — WORLD CHAMPIONS 1951

While the Edmonton Mercurys were overseas the Lethbridge Maple Leafs were fashioning their own story. It won the 1949-50 Western Canada Intermediate Championship against the Melville Millionares in the eighth game of a best-of-seven (there had been a tie game.) Hector Negrello's sharp shooting led Lethbridge to the western win and to the 1951 World Championship. Negrellos scored three times in the seventh game of the Melville series to give the Leafs a 6-3 win. In the extra game, Negrello scored the deciding goal at 18:04 of the third period in a 3-2 win. Guyle Fielder of the junior Lethbridge Native Sons was allowed as a replacement for the final game.

Alberta teams had won the World Championship two years in a row. Bob Mamini, sports editor of the "Calgary Herald" said:

> *Coach Dick Gray and his players only gave up on one point. They finally quit trying to convince the opposition in Europe that there are many teams in Canada that could take their measure in hock-*

ey combat. Throughout the European tour the opposition looked upon the Leafs as Canadian Champions, and the Leafs were certainly all of that by coming through with the honors in the manner they did during the World Tournament. The Maple Leafs were a credit to the game as played in Canada. They made thousands of friends — better than 400,000 took in their games. The hockey supporters, while not always admiring the manner of Canadian play, had to praise the way the Canadian pucksters went to work on the ice lanes.

Stan Obodiac was a member of the 1951 Lethbridge Maple Leafs. He was one of the leaders of the club as he scored at least one point in 62 straight games. During the trip, Obodiac completed notes every day and wrote a book called *No Substitute for Victory*. Obodiac stayed in hockey and was Public Relations Director of Maple Leaf Gardens before his death in 1984. The following excerpts are from his book:

LETHBRIDGE MAPLE LEAFS 1949-50

Front row (l to r): Shorty Malacho, Don McLean, Karl Sorokoski, Mallie Hughes, Bert Knibbs, Nap Milroy. Middle row: Hec Negrello, Tom Woods, Stan Obodiack, Dick Gray (coach), Bill Gibson, Whitey Rimstad, Lou Siray. Back row: Ken Branch, Don Vogan, Bill Chandler, Bob MacGregor, Jack Sumner. *Photo courtesy of Sir Alexander Galt Museum, Lethbridge.*

These are the fellows that are going to represent 14 million Canadian people. It is like war when they went to fight for them — now they go to play for them. Mallie Hughes, Carl Sorokosi, Dick Gray (coach), Don Vogan, Shortie Malacko, Whitey Rimstad, Rob McGregor, Billy Gibson, Hector Negrello, Don McLean, Tom Wood, Bill Chandler, Stan Obodiac, Lou Siray, Napper Milroy, Bert Knibbs, Jack Sumner, and Ken Branch. (Roth, Flannigan and Flick were added by the CAHA.)

Doctor W.G. Hardy, President of the International Hockey Association, mused over the possibilities of sending the Lethbridge team to Europe to represent Canada. At first, Dr. Hardy thought Dick Gray (age 30) was too young a man to lead a team to Europe, what with all the diplomacy and embassadorial knowledge needed to voice satisfactorily Canada abroad. But now Dr. Hardy suffers no queasiness in regard to Dick...Dick is a determined young man. He is extremely conscientious. He not only wants to win but he is cocksure that he is going to win. Gray is a task master.

Seventeen thousand packed the Palais des Sports. The Swedes hung back in their defensive zone all evening. They could beat the Swiss on goal average, for the title, that was their strategy. Soon Don McLean picked up a Bigson pass and scored the first goal. Hec. Negrello added another from Gibson. Mickey Roth scored our third from Bill Flick to put us three up. Sweden then scored one. McLean scored his second goal on a pass from Negrello, and the crowd seemed to be admiring us more now, and turning our attention away from the underdogs, Sweden. Mickey Roth ended the scoring on a play with Flannigan and Flick.

All of a sudden the game was over...we were World Champions. This was our fortieth straight game without defeat. Then they played 'Oh Canada', and raised our flag for the victory. We all faced it as it rose to the top. Bill Gibson said there was a tear in his eye. Tommy Wood said it was the happiest day of his life... We skated in a victory circle around the rink carrying our trophy. Movie cameras ground...the crowd applauded.

LETHBRIDGE MAPLE LEAFS
1951 WORLD CHAMPIONS

Back (l to r): Denny Flannigan, Don McLean, Dick Gray (coach), Whitey Rimstad, Bill Gibson, Stan Obodiac, Tom Wood, **Hector Negrello (captain), Bill Flick. Middle row:** Mickey Roth, Jim "Shorty" Malacko, Mallie Hughes, Bill Chandler, Don **Vogan. Bottom row:** Nap Milroy, Carl Sorokoski, Lou Siray, Bert Knibbs. **Missing:** Jack Sumner, Ken Branch, Bob McGregor.

In the six tournament games Lethbridge scored 62 goals and had 6 scored against them. For Lethbridge: Bill Flick, Denny Flannigan, and Mickey Roth. Obodiac had 12 goals, Gibson had 8, McLean had 5, Roth 5, Flannigan 8, Flick 5, Chandler 5, Negrello 4, Whitey Rimstad 3, Gray 2, Vogan 2, Wood 1, Knibbs 1, Milroy 1, Seray 0, Malacko 0.

One of the letters from home said that the Lethbridge Radio Station was announcing "CJOC Lethbridge...the home of the World Champions".

We liked that.

So ended one of the greatest days in our lives...World Champions, and as General McArthur once said — 'there is no substitute for victory.'

* * *

Intermediate playoffs continued in Alberta while the Lethbridge Maple Leafs were in Europe. The High River Flyers of 1950-51 season became Alberta's representative in interprovincial playoffs.

THE HIGH RIVER FLYERS
BY FRANK McTIGHE, High River Times

The High River Flyers, a team of senior hockey mercenaries from Calgary defeated Edmonton Sparling-Davis 2-0 March 23, 1951 to win the D.E. Black Trophy, emblematic of Intermediate Amateur hockey supremacy in Alberta. The Flyers were based in High River but players who lived and worked in Calgary, won the provincial title in an unusual sequel to the best-of-three final in Edmonton.

Edmonton defeated High River 9-1 in the opening game of the series. The Flyers staved off elimination the next night with a 4-4 tie to set the stage for a hockey marathon the following evening. The teams entered the third game knowing if High River won the game and tied the series, a fourth match consisting of three 10 minute periods would be played the same evening to decide the winners.

HIGH RIVER FLYERS 1950-51

New champions of the Big Six hockey league winning the Hudson's Bay trophy, after beating Universal Meteors 7-4. Back row (l to r): Paddy McCuster, Bob Ross, Ralph Jackson, Bob Broadfield, Neil Winchester, Jimmy Kirkwood, Bill Rogers, Jimmy Stevens, Don Stevens, Stu Kinnibrough (coach). Front row (l to r): Pete Pickersgil, Jim Tupkal, Pete Snell, Hank Howie, Bill Fraser, Bil Kilroe. Kneeling in front is "Rusty" the stickboy. Missing is Lorne Thurston. *Photo courtesy of Dick Curtis, Calgary*

High River skated to a 5-2 victory in the game to force the tie-breaker, which began at 12:40 a.m. Friday. The teams battled scoreless through the final period, but Pete Snell of the Flyers scored the eventual winner at the two minute mark of the second period. Ken Brown added an insurance marker with the Edmonton net empty with less than a minute to go.

The Flyers, who played only five games in High River during regular season play in the Big Six League (based in Calgary), accepted the Black Trophy from AAHA official Harold Brandeth after playing 225 minutes of hockey in three nights. They had reached the provincial final with come from behind victories in the Southern Alberta Intermediate 'A' semi-final and final.

Coleman Grands posted a 7-4 win in the first game of the best-of-three series, but High River rallied to win the second game 7-4 a week later, and clinched the series with an 8-4 win March 10th in Coleman. The win allowed the Flyers to advance against the Army squad in Calgary, who defeated Canmore Legionaires in the other semi-final.

The Flyers dug themselves into an early hole in the series, losing 2-1 in the opening game of the best-of-three. High River tied the series with a 5-2 win before 4,000 fans in Calgary to force the deciding game. High River took a 5-2 lead before going into a defensive shell that almost cost them the series. Army scored 3 times in the final period to send the game into a 10 minute overtime. The Currie Barracks club scored first, but Brown tied the game at 6-6 and Rogers added the winner moments later. With goalie Stu Hendry pulled in favour of the extra attacker Army applied heavy pressure late in the game but were unable to beat Hank Howie in the High River net.

The Flyers continued their winning ways with a two-game sweep of Melfort, Saskatchewan in the Western Canada final, defeating the Athletics 5-3 and 8-6 in their own arena. The season came to an end for the Flyers on March 31, 1951 in Trail, B.C. when they lost 9-3 and 6-5 in the Western Intermediate 'A' final.

It was the second season in the blue and gold High River sweaters for most of the players, but despite their success the people of High River never got behind the team because there were no local players on the team.

* * *

In 1951 the Western Canada Senior League became minor professional; therefore, teams in that league could not enter Allan Cup playoffs. Although the World Championship Edmonton Mercurys was an intermediate team, it entered Allan Cup playoffs to fill the senior void in Alberta (See Senior Hockey)

MERCURYS WIN CANADA'S LAST OLYMPIC GOLD

In 1952 the Mercurys represented Canada at the Winter Olympics in Oslo, Norway. James A. Christiansen, owner of the Waterloo Motors, had sponsored the team in the 1950 World Championship. He also sponsored the Mercurys on its road to the Olympics.

There was no problem with professionalism. Doug Grimston, President of the CAHA, agreed that players who received five pounds a week spending money (in Europe) could "hardly pay their laundry and postage stamps". The players took their own extra money and did not expect to be reimbursed.

Christiansen said he would report to the CAHA on the advisability of further Canadian participation unless "a proper pre-paid guarantee" could be made to cover player expenses. It was estimated that the cost to Christiansen for the championships of 1950 and 1952 was about $30,000.00 each time. Later the CAHA did become more involved in the financial aspects of sending a team to the Worlds, but in these years, the team itself was responsible to a large extent. Once again, it was Dr. W.G. Hardy who recommended the Mercurys represent Canada.

The Mercurys went to Europe months ahead of the Olympic Games. The tour consisted of fifty games in four months (including Olympic Games).

In Olympic competition at Jordal Stadium, the Mercurys faced off against the American team in the eighth and final game. The Canadian team had already won seven games and, as coach Louis Holmes commented, "We figured right from the start the U.S.A. was the team to beat in this tournament".

Bill Dawe and Lou Secco gave Canada a 2-0 lead only to see the Americans retaliate with goals by Johnny Mulhern and Rubem Ejorkman. Don Gauf put Canada ahead with ninety seconds left in the second period. American Jimmy Sedin poked home a goal mouth scramble in the third period to tie the game.

The tie was enough to clinch the Olympic gold medal for Canada. The Canadian team ended with 15 points and the United States with 13. Czechoslovakia was third, Sweden fourth, Switzerland fifth and Finland sixth.

Back row (l to r): Monty Ford (trainer), Jack Davies, Bob Meyers, Tom Pollick, George Abel, Don Gauf, Lou Secco, Eric Paterson, Bob Watt, Louis Holmes (coach). Bottom: Al Purvis, Sully Sullivan, Gord Robertson, Bruce Dickson, Jim Christiansen (owner), Bill Dawe (captain), Ralph Hansch, Dave Miller, Bill Gibson. *Photo courtesy of Provincial Archives*

The Mercurys won forty-five of their fifty games. On their return from Europe, the team was given a motor car parade through Edmonton. Official dignitaries were Edmonton Mayor William Hawrelak and Art Potter, Vice President of the CAHA.

At the time the Mercury's victory did not seem historically significant as Canada had won Olympic gold medals on a regular basis. Canada has won World Championships since 1952 but, to this date, no more Olympic gold medals. The Waterloo players told Canadians about the future strength of European hockey. The players we spoke to now find it hard to believe that they won Canada's last Olympic gold medal.

Jim Christiansen passed away in early 1953 and the Edmonton Waterloo Mercurys ceased to exist. Players ended up playing for various teams in the Edmonton area including the Ponoka Stampeders. The Stampeders became the top team in Alberta during the early fifties. The President and owner of Waterloo Motors, Al Purvis, was a member of the Olympic champions. Some of the players still work at Waterloo. (Dave King, present Olympic coach, writes on Canada's 1988 plans in the Hot Stove League.)

* * *

Ponoka has had a long hockey tradition including the 1924-25 Intermediates (See article by Gordon MacLeod). Gordon was a member of the Stampeders before they won provincial intermediate titles in the fifties. The team became well known in the province for their sweaters as much as their winning record. Ponoka had a "99" before Wayne Gretzky was born.

The Government of the Province of Alberta
The City of Edmonton
The Edmonton Chamber of Commerce

request the pleasure of the company of

_____

to a

Complimentary Dinner

tendered to

The Olympic and World Champion Mercury Hockey Team

THE SALONS
MACDONALD HOTEL

TUESDAY, APRIL FIRST
6:15 P.M.

R.S.V.P. MERCURY RECEPTION COMMITTEE
C/O 301 CIVIC BLK.

DRESS INFORMAL

Photo courtesy of Edmonton Archives

BIG NUMBERS COME TO PONOKA

BY DUNC GRANT, Ponoka Stampeders

(Dunc Grant, hockey coach and player on the Stampeders writes about how and when Ponoka got these numbers. This Dunc Grant played for Ponoka while another Dunc Grant was well known as a member of the Calgary Stampeders.)

The town of Ponoka can claim the honour of introducing "big numbers" on hockey sweaters. The Ponoka Stampeders were in need of new uniforms including pants as everyone was dressed slightly different. As a result Harry Dittberner the team's finance manager (who ran a garage), Harry Vold (Auctioneer and Rodeo Promoter), the Ladies Auxiliary of the team and others put together enough money. The Ponoka Stampeders were to get a new set of uniforms including sweaters. This was the summer of 1951.

In those years, teams from Southern Alberta would go down to Great Falls, Montana to play exhibition games. We were contacted by a promoter to go in the fall. Conversations with this man sold us on getting fottball sweaters to serve our purpose. We then learned of an American set of sweaters that a football team had not picked up. They were heavy and thus ideal for the many unheated arenas of the day. We went to Great Falls on the third weekend in November for the game. Socks and pants were to be included plus our black and red sweaters with a bucking horse on the front and Stampeders on the back across the numbers, but the sweaters weren't ready.

Our lineup in Great Falls included Pete Melnechuk and Fred Hickmore in goal. Defence was Dunc Grant, Jim Malin, John Johnson and Ken Clapp, along with forwards Dave Shantz, Idris "Shorty" Jones, Al Shantz, Don Kramer, George "Shorty" Gordon, Jack Fuller, Jim Smith, Bill Novak, Gordon MacLeod and Ron Raugust and coach Don Stewart.

We won both games 12-4 and 10-7.

Later in the hockey season the sweaters finally arrived with the big numbers. The goalies had 00, Dunc Grant

44, Al Shantz 22, Jim Smith 77 to name a few. Large numbers at that time known as the "Crazy Numbers" by the fans were a novelty. Many of the fans of the 50s still recall when "Big Numbers" came to Ponoka. They must have helped us in our playing success. Our winning record improved as the records relate.

* * *

We would like to report the Stampeders had a number 99. He was George "Shorty" Gordon. Grant still has his #44. The Stampeders are the first team known in Alberta and possibly first in hockey where all the players wore 'Big Numbers' on their sweaters.

The Big Six Leagues in Calgary and area represented the top intermediate league in Southern Alberta. In 1951-52, the league had five members, the Canmore Legionnaires, Strathmore Red Wings, High River Flyers, Universal Meteors and the Hillhurst Hustlers. This level of competition was popular. In Calgary on Sunday, February 24, 1952, close to 5,000 fans watched the Canmore Legionnaires tie Universal Meteors at the Corral in a regular league game. Calgary also had the professional hockey Stampeders so fans had other alternatives.

Canmore had the best team in the league in 1952. Andy Chakowski of Canmore led the Big Six in scoring. He had 28 goals and 44 assists for 72 points. Seventeen points behind in second was teammate Johnny Hrushka and three other Canmore players; Vince Bannon, Spud Whitehead and Andy Knowchuk. Sixty-four minutes in penalties gave Canmore's Archie Kaleta the bad-man honors.

The Legionnaires played provincial and interprovincial playoffs at the same time as their league. On April 6, 1953, the Legionnaires won a sudden-death final, 8-5, against Universal Meteors to win the Bill Williams Memorial Trophy for the Big Six. The one game final was because the Legionnaires had just won the British Columbia — Alberta Intermediate in Kamloops and were on the way to Brandon, Manitoba to start the Western final.

Canmore won the provincial title in 1952 when they defeated the Ponoka Stampeders in two straight games, 6-1 and 6-2. The Legionnaires advanced to Kamloops. Fred Herget scored the winner in Canmore's opening match against the Kamloops Bessett Loggers. This series went the full five games before Canmore doubled the Loggers 8-4 to win the series.

The type of playoffs arrangement for the Western Intermediate final changed in 1952. The first three games for Canmore against the Dauphin Kings were played in Brandon and the next four in Calgary. Usually games were played in one centre but it was decided attendance back in Calgary could warrant such a change. By the sixth game, Canmore was ahead three games to two. It looked as if the Legionnaires could win the championship, but Roy Bentley's Kings forced a seventh game.

In the final game at the Corral, Bill Mosienko, back from the Chicago Black Hawks, scored the winner for Dauphin late in the second period for a 3-1 victory.

Canmore's history in hockey goes back to the late 1890's. The town produced players at the junior, intermediate and senior levels. Through the Briquetteers and Legionnaires, Canmore made a name for itself in hockey circles. The Legionnaires were the last Canmore team to win a major championship in Alberta. The present system of young players moving to major centers to continue a hockey career or seek other job opportunities almost makes it impossible to develop an adult system in a place as small as Canmore. The Britquetteers and Legionnaires at intermediate and senior hockey are now part of history, but they had their days as the best.

The next years in intermediate hockey were filled with glory for the Ponoka Stampeders. The Stampeders won the Alberta Intermediate 'A' Championship four years in a row from 1952-53 through 1955-56. Home talent, players brought in from Edmonton and good local organization were successful ingredients for the Stampeders.

In 1952-53 the Stampeders played in the competitive Central Alberta Hockey League. Other team members included the Red Deer Monarchs, Olds Elks, Lacombe Rockets, Didsbury Ramblers, Stettler Imperials, Alix Maple Leafs and Camrose Maroons. The Red Deer Monarchs under coach Sandy Sandalack finished the 1952-53 season in first place tied with the Olds Elks. Red Deer, however, had a superior goals for and against record. The Ponoka Stampeders finished third.

After initial rounds Ponoka met Red Deer in the Northern Alberta final. Goalkeeper Eric Paterson of Ponoka shut out the Monarchs 3-0 and 4-0 to move the Stampeders into the provincial final. Johnny Hopkins, then sports editor of the Red Deer Advocate wrote, "to the closer observers it was evident that Ponoka big wigs had come up with a sweet little team balanced with plenty of hustle."

Sportscaster Ned Corrigal picked Stamps to take it all.

Ponoka also moved wisely in getting players for provincial action. They plucked off a net mending sharpie named Eric Paterson, one department in which they weren't too strong. They then plugged a hole on defence with Al Purvis.

The Stampeders won their first of four Alberta titles in a row by eliminating the Calgary CPR Beavers 4-2 and 6-2. The following series against the Trail Smokeaters was originally to be a best-of-five. Ponoka won the first game 6-2 in Edmonton and the series was reduced to a best-of-three. This would allow the next series to start on time and not have any team waiting and it cut expenses. The second game went to Trail 8-1. It was also decided that overtime would decide the series in the third game, but only ten minutes would be played. Trail and Ponoka fought to a 4-4 draw to force a fourth game.

Ken Head scored the winner and Shorty Jones the extra goal to earn Ponoka goalie Eric Paterson a 2-0 shutout. Ponoka now moved to the Western Intermediate final against the Kenora Thistles.

The Kenora Thistles won the Western Intermediate Championship of 1953. In the sixth game of the series, Kenora defeated Ponoka 5-1. The Stampeders were beaten in the final game by Kenora's four Robertson brothers. "Sugar" Robertson scored two, Murray got one while the other brothers Sam and "Spike" got assists on the other two goals.

When the Stampeders returned to Ponoka they were greeted by four thousand people and a tractor parade. Each tractor carried the name of the player perched on top. Stampeder player Bill Novak had just become a new father. As the parade route went past the hospital Novak leaped from the moving tractor and ran to see his wife and baby daughter who were watching from their hospital room. Later the Stamps were honored at a banquet. Team President Angus MacLeod presented engraved watches to the players. MacLeod had seen a lot of hockey as he was manager when Ponoka won its last provincial championship in 1925.

PONOKA STAMPEDERS 1952-53

Front row (l to r): Harry Dittberner, Dave Schantz, George Gordon, Al Purvis, Eric Paterson, Jim Malin, Bing Merluk, George Gage. Back row: Angus MacLeod, Dunc Grant, Nestor Charuk, Al Schantz, Bill Novak, Ralph Vold, Jim Smith, Bobby Watt, Quinn Fate, Idris Jones.

Photo courtesy of Red Deer Archives

In 1953-54 Camrose left the Central Alberta Hockey League. The Red Deer Monarchs and Ponoka Stampeders were in the same position as the previous year as they were to meet in the CAHL finals and in provincial playoffs. Ponoka won the third game of the provincials to enter the Alberta final for the third time in three years.

The Stampeders continued their provincial successes when they defeated Olds Elks 3-0 in the fifth and deciding game of the Alberta final. An attendance record for the time of 3,417 viewed the game in Red Deer.

The British Columbia-Alberta final had the first three games in Trail and the rest of the series in Alberta. The Smokeaters ended the Stampeder's playoffs in the sixth game of the series. In game five it appeared Ponoka was on the way to a series win as they whipped Trail 8-2. The final 8-5 win for Trail gave the Smokeaters the series four games to two.

The regular league playoffs in the CAHA resumed. Doug Lane and his Ponoka Stampeders suffered their second setback of the year as the Red Deer Monarchs won the CAHL playoffs. A final 9-5 win gave the Monarchs the series three games to two and possession of the CAHL Red Deer Motor Trophy for 1953-54.

The 1954-55 Ponoka Stampeders won the Central Alberta Hockey League Championship by outclassing the Lacombe Rockets 12-2 to win the crown in four straight games. The league was now a five team circuit. Ponoka in the thirty-two game schedule won 29, lost 2 and tied 1 for 59 points. The Olds Elks were far behind with 35, followed by the Red Deer Shamrocks at 25, Lacombe Rockets 23 and Didsbury Ramblers 20. Bing Merluk of Ponoka led the league in scoring with 92 points followed by teammate Ken Head at 77.

The Stampeders won Alberta's Black Trophy over Canmore in a 5-2 win over the best-of-seven in five games. Almost every team Ponoka played went down to defeat in 1954-55. Ponoka had lost to Trail the previous year but this season was different. The "Big Number" team put the Trail All-Stars to the sidelines in three straight games. The final game in Ponoka saw 2,200 spectators more than fill the 1,500 capacity rink.

PONOKA STAMPEDERS 1954-55

Front row (l to r): Frank Mickey, Remi Brisson, Jack Moore, Rod Fonteyne, Eric Paterson, Bing Merluk, Ken Head, George Gordon. **Back row:** August Cerveny, Ray Vylett, David Schantz, Idris Jones, Frank Joyal, Dunc Grant, Jim Malin, Bruce Lea, Ken Clapp, Don Clark, Al Schantz, Art Barnes, Angus MacLeod.   *Photo courtesy of Red Deer Archives*

But Ponoka ended the season on a loss. In the Western Canada Intermediate finals the Brandon Wheat Kings defeated the Stampeders 3-1 to win the series four games to two. The Stampeders, "The Pride of Ponoka," would have to be patient until next year.

The next year, 1955-56 Ponoka continued to dominate the Intermediate 'A' category when it eliminated the Medicine Hat Cantalinis in the provincial final. The first game was played in Medicine Hat. The report of March 27, 1956 in the *"Ponoka Herald"* gives some details on the Medicine Hat Arena as seen by an outsider:

The Ponoka crowd felt that "Arena Gardens" might be somewhat of a misnomer since there appeared to be nothing "Garden like" in the more than 30-year-old, rather out-moded, poorly lighted building, perhaps a bit smaller than our own arena (Ponoka). The crowd of 1,200 very well filled it. There were no ushers, and after several vain attempts to locate our reserved seats, we finally gave up and squeezed in with a good natured group of Ponoka fans.

The "Gardens" definitely had one thing which was superior to our own, and that was the accomodation for radio broadcasting. There were two cubicles for the convenience of sports announcers and their equipment — these being at opposite ends of the arena and strategically placed at points above the red centre line, which afforded a very good, as well as safe, view of the entire arena. This must have been a treat for sports commentator, Stan Sparling (CKRD Red Deer) in comparison with the inadequate set up which we provided for him at Ponoka.

Jackie Moore combined two goals with Ron Tookey to give goalie Eric Paterson a 2-0 shut-out. This game on April 7, 1956 before an unbelievable crowd of 2,649 in Ponoka, moved the Stampeders into the now familiar position of playing in the Western final.

If you keep trying hard enough people say you have to succeed. The Ponoka Stampeders of 1955-56 once again got to the Western final. This year was different. Percy Wolfe scored the winner before 3,361 fans in Red Deer when the Ponoka Stampeders won their first and only Western Canada Intermediate championship over the Edgar La Prade coached Port Arthur Bearcats 5-2. Bruce Lea's Stampeders won the series four games to two. The victory ended four years of effort by the Ponoka Stampeders.

Goalie Eric Paterson credits the success of the Stamps because it was:

basically a community club with a good minor system and only a few imports — individuals such as Angus MacLeod, trainer Frank Mickey and players who helped organize as well such as Dunc Grant and Shorty Jones. They were instrumental in shaping the Stampeders.

After winning the championship of 1956, the Stampeders were hosted to a banquet by the Ladies' Auxiliary of the Ponoka Stampeder's hockey club. Dr. Winston Backus revealed that a lot of medical attention was used to keep the boys in shape. He did say "he was going to write some of his old professors who thought that one should rest a severe 'Charlie Horse'." Bruce Lea proved that if you refused advice and persisted in giving an injured leg plenty of exercise, it would get better anyway.

PONOKA STAMPEDERS 1955-56
Western Canadian Champions

Front row (l to r): Percy Wolfe, Larry Hodgson, Idris Jones, Eric Paterson, Bill Thomas, Jack Moore, Rex Turple. Back row: Frank Mickey, Norman MacLeod, Bobby Manson, Ron Tookey, Bruce Lea, Dunc Grant, Cy Whiteside, Jerry Kernaghan, Ray Uylett. Top inserts: Ralph Vold, Maurice Wolfe, George Gordon.

Photo courtesy of Red Deer Archives

Allan James read a poem written by himself in honor of the Stampeders. The poem was entitled 'Ponoka Hits the Jackpot,' from the *"Ponoka Herald,"* May 1, 1956.

Ponoka won the silverware;
Enough to claim great fame
They have cups and shields, etc.
that put the Red Deer Club to shame.
They played terrific hockey and were worthy of the wins
To play with such determined force,
We'll overlook their sins.
This isn't the first time Ponoka reached the top;
But this year the Club boiled over and never thought to stop!
They polished off old Red Deer, and played a while with Olds,
And paused to play with Medicine Hat to clear the odd head colds.
They next took on Nanaimo and the play was rough indeed.
Ponoka had the edge on them with the pressure and the speed.
Port Arthur sure was different with their clean and fast attack;
They were certainly "Picture Players" and we'd like to see them back.
...Good luck to our Stampeders! It was a worthy win.
We are proud you won the honors and took it on the chin.
The town will celebrate tonight.
We hope you love it all;
And don't forget we'll have some ice again — about next fall!

One of the highlights of the year was credited to Hobemma's Larry Hodgson. On January 28, 1956 in a game for the Ponoka Stampeders in Ponoka, Hodgson scored 3 goals in 20 seconds. The Stampeders went on to defeat Red Deer Indians 5-2 in that game.

MEDICINE HAT CANTALINIS
1956-57 Provincial Champions

(Photo taken before provincial final.) Back row (l to r): D. Smith, L. Ramstead, J. Crawford, B. McCully, G. Hall, R. Craven, B. Chachlias, R. Moch, J. Irving, D. Vogan. Second row: V. Link, L. Pudwell, A. Bestplug, J. Baird, P. Stach, B. Korneilson, L. Brumbach, J. Smith (manager). Front row: F. King (trainer), B. Starling (coach), A. Cantalini (president), J. Smith Jr. (stickboy), J. Cantalini (vice-president). Missing: Don Moog.

Photo courtesy of J. Smith

In 1956-57 Johnny Young of the Lacombe Rockets racked up 103 points in thirty-two games to set a new league record. In the Big Six League of southern Alberta, Bill McCulley of the Medicine Hat Catalinis broke Young's record with 105 points in a forty game schedule.

That same season, the junior Edmonton Oil Kings joined the Central Alberta Hockey League. The Lacombe Rockets eliminated the Kings from the CAHL playoffs when they defeated the Kings 5-3 before 3,000 fans in the new Lacombe Arena. This match featured Oil Kings coach Pug Young and Rocket playing-coach Bill Ramsdeon. Ramsden hit Young with his stick. The slightly bleeding Young pulled Ramsden into the Oil King box where most of the Kings took part. The Kings then waited seventeen days for the Saskatchewan representative in junior playoffs. (See Junior Hockey.)

Then Ponoka reached the CAHL finals defeating Red Deer 4-1 in the fifth and deciding game.

Once again, Ponoka Stampeders became the CAHL intermediate winners when they defeated Lacombe 11-1 in the sixth game to win the series four games to two. Ron Tookey paced the Stamps to victory as he scored five goals and had three assists.

Ponoka ran out of steam in the 1956-57 championship when the Medicine Hat Cantalinis became provincial champions. This ended the Stampeders streak that had started in 1953. For Medicine Hat it was only the city's second Intermediate 'A' championship. (The Medicine Hat Monarchs won in 1930. Monarch teams before this had won a lower Intermediate level, the November 15 Group.)

Besides McCulley, the Medicine Hat lineup included goalie Don Moog, the father of present Edmonton Oiler goalie, Andy Moog. This was not enough as the Kimberley Dynamiters defeated the Cantalinis 6-3 to win the best-of-seven, four games to one in Kimberley.

In 1957-58, Medicine Hat Cantalinis again reached the Alberta final but their northern opposition, the Olds Elks, won. Olds represented the CAHL as the second best team. The league champion Red Deer Rustlers decided to represent the province in senior or Allan Cup while Olds continued in intermediate. (See Red Deer in Senior and Professional Hockey.)

Olds easily advanced into the Western Canada Intermediate final when they drubbed the Naniamo Clippers, the B.C. representatives 7-1, 9-4 and 10-2.

OLDS ELKS 1957-58

Front (l to r): Ken Phillips (president), Murray Dodd, Archie Scott, Steve Gaber (coach), G. Carlson, Bob Schmied, Bill Burns, Everett Ulry (manager). Second row: Joe Clark, Jack Yucytus, Art Driver, Howie Lacombe, Bob Pitts, Mick Gilday, Frank Ashworth. Third row (executives): Oscar Urkuhart, Clarence DeGear, Gordon "Red" Knecht, Merl Goddard, Gordon Habkirk, Dr. George Burland, Stewart Wong, Sam McMillan. Missing: Ken Raymond. *Photo courtesy of Edmonton Archives*

Charlie Rayner's Kenora Thistles were eliminated in the western final when Frank Ashworth scored after four minutes of overtime for a 7-5 Olds win. The big scorer in the final game was Gunner Carlson who got three goals. Singles were added by Steve Gaber, Ken Raymond and Jack Yucytus. The Olds Elks were a well-known name in hockey for years but the 1957-58 championship was their first major championship victory.

Ray Hannigan in 1958-59 coached the Red Deer Rustlers to victory in the CAHL and over the Okotoks Oilers to win the provincial title. Against the Vancouver Carlings, the Rustlers fired 70 shots at netman Al Weisner in an easy 14-3 win. The result of this first game was so one-sided that Edmonton's Art Potter, convenor of the series, threatened to stop the series if Vancouver did not put up a better game. Vancouver coach Mike Shabaga claimed the ten day layoff, the overnight train ride and the strange ice did not help his team.

The Carlings improved but Red Deer won the series three games to one. The final game was considered rough and tempers were high, but (today NHL referee supervisor) Bill "Dutchy" Van Deelan and "Fuzzy" Solowan handled all the problems.

Red Deer had decided to go intermediate because senior was too costly. They took on the Fort Francis Canadians in the western final. The series site was split between the two teams. In Red Deer, the Rustlers assumed a 2-1 lead in games when they defeated the Fort 6-2.

RED DEER RUSTLERS, WESTERN CANADA INTERMEDIATE "A" CHAMPIONS 1958-59

Back row: App. Dorohoy, Rod Fontayne, Ron Walters, Henry Sanderson, Monk Burton, Clair Smith, Rich Healey, Ray Hannigan, Spud Whitehead, Ron Moch, Don Rehill, Fred Neilson. Front and kneeling: Rex Turple, Jim Grant, Ron Menard, Art Lariviere, Remi Brisson, Chas. Curr. Missing from picture: Ron Tookey, Bob Watt, H. Wilson, B. McCulley.

Red Deer repeated the Old's win of the year before when they downed the Canadians 7-4. This win gave the Rustlers the 1958-59 Western Intermediate 'A' championship. Ron Tookey and Ron Menard scored twice each and singles were scored by Remi Brisson, Rex Turple and Don Rehill in the final victory.

The Central Alberta League continued its domination of hockey in Alberta when the Lacombe Rockets became the 1959-60 Intermediate champions of Alberta. Lacombe became a powerhouse for the next six years representing Alberta in either intermediate or senior categories. Many of the imports became known as the "University Boys." These were students, graduates or instructors who drove from Edmonton to play in Lacombe. Some of these players included Austin Smith, Doug Messier, Lorne and Ernie Braithwaite, Vic Dzurko, Al La Plante, Clare Drake, Ed Zemrau, Dick Dunnigan and Murray Dea. Lacombe also had its compliment of regular CAHL stars such as Johnny Young, Guy Menage and Murray Dodd who helped keep the Rocket's lineup consistent.

The Calgary Adderson Builders and the Rockets played the 1959-60 provincial final. The Builders took the first two games 5-3 and 6-5. Home ice was advantageous to Lacombe when they came back to win 5-1 and 3-1.

For the first time since the 1920's, Lacombe won an Alberta Intermediate 'A' championship. Before 1,598 fans the Rockets ousted the Calgary Adderson Builders of the Big Six league 3-1 at Jubilee Stadium in Lacombe. The Rockets had been in the cellar of the CAHL before Christmas.

It was now off to Naniamo to play the Labatts. The Rockets were weakened when Vic Dzurko, Doug Messier, Bill Voss, Murray Dea and Gord Flaman stayed home to write exams at the University of Alberta. The playoffs could have been in Lacombe except the $1000.00 guarantee per game was secured by Naniamo and could not be assured by Lacombe.

Doug Messier was flown out for the fifth game and Gord Flaman for the fourth. Despite the addition of these two players the Rockets lost the final game in the best of five.

Three straight victories, including a final 6-0 score over Olds Elks, gave the Lacombe Rockets the CAHL championship in 1960-61. The Rockets won the provincial title again from the Big Six Champion Lethbridge Maple Leafs. Four straight wins of 7-4, 5-3, 9-2 and 8-0 powered the Rockets to their second straight provincial title. Arrangements were made to play the Trail Hotelmen in Lacombe. Three straight wins put the Rockets in the Western final against the Terrace Bay Ontario Superiors.

The Rockets opened the Western final quickly when George "Dick" Dunnigan fired three goals to lead Lacombe to an 8-3 win before 1,783 fans in Lacombe. Remi Brisson scored two and singles came from Ed Young, Al La Plante and Ed Zemrau. Lacombe won the west as they won three out of four in the best-of-five including 7-3 in the final match. Jimmy Brown, President of the AAHA, presented the Edmonton Journal Trophy to team captain Johnny Young.

LACOMBE ROCKETS 1960-61

Back row (l to r): Murray Dea, Ernie Braithwaite, Doug Messier, Vic Dzurko, Al LaPlante, Ed Young, Austin Smith, Bill Voss, Percy Thompson (president), Marv Leiske (manager), Scotty Armstrong (trainer). Front row: Murray Dodd, Art Park (coach), Remi Brisson, Johnny Young (captain), Dick Dunnigan, Russ Gillow, Ed Zemrau, Leigh McMillan, Clare Drake. Missing: Jack McManus. *Photo courtesy of P.A.A. and Advance Studio, Lacombe*

The Lacombe regulars and the "University Boys" continued to dominate in the 1961-62 season. The All-Star team for the CAHL announced by CAHL's secretary-manager Fred Rowett of Red Deer had Adam Kryczka of Olds in goal, Ed Zemrau and Vic Dzurko of Lacombe on defence, along with forwards Bruce Lea and Ted Demchuk of Ponoka and Johnny Young of Lacombe as forwards.

The Rockets won the CAHL as they won a thrilling 3-0 victory over the Drumheller Miners in the seventh and deciding game before 3,015 fans at Jubilee Stadium in Lacombe. Dick Dunnigan scored two and Austin Smith a single for the championship. The Rockets were declared provincial champions when the Coleman Grands of the Big Six League defaulted.

The British Columbia champions, the Tri-City Macs, was a combination of Kelowna-Penticton and Summerland. The weather in Penticton was a balmy 70 F; however, the season was quickly brought to a conclusion when the Macs sidelined the Rockets 9-6 and 6-2.

Rockets success continued in 1962-63 but the team entered senior playdowns and the Olds Elks represented the CAHL in intermediate. The Elks defeated Medicine Hat Cantilinis in the provincial finals. Other CAHL

Back row: Ack McDonald, Red Knecht, Dave Ehrardt, Oscar Urquhart, Murray Alm, Chas Rosehill (president), Dr. George Burland. Second row: Wayne Yoos, Otto Knecht, Everett Ulry, Jack Chesney, Adolph Rosehill, Stewart Wong (secretary). Third row: Chas. O'Shaughnessy, Cliff Wylie, Clayton Thompson, Gerry Kernaghan, Murray Dea, Jack Yucytus, Bob Pitts, Andy Jackson. Fourth row: Dick Higgenson (trainer), Dave Jones, Mick Gilday, Frank Novosel, Rock Crawford, Con Collie. Front row: Ken Phillips (manager), Tony Kollman, Ron Loughlin, Adam Kryczka, Ron Mathers (sub-goal), Jack Samuels, Archie Scott (captain), Bob Schmied (coach). Missing: Murray Massier and Fred Churla.

players, Jack Samuels, Tony Kollman and Ron Loughlin from the Drumheller Miners joined Olds for the playoffs as allowable imports.

The Elks continued to win by slowing the Kamloops Chiefs 5-0 to capture the B.C.-Alberta round three games to one. Adam Kryczka recorded the shut-out. Loughlin scored two and Kollman, Murray Massier and Mick Gilday netted one each for Olds.

The Western final of 1963 was against the Warroad Minnesota Lakers who were the Thunder Bay-Manitoba-Saskatchewan champions. The best of the Warroad players were Ed Kryzanowski, formerly a member of the Boston Bruins, and Bill and Roger Christiansen, former members of the famed 1960 United States Olympic hockey championship team.

Olds won their second western title when they defeated the Lakers 4-2 before 1,148 fans in Olds. This gave them the series in three straight.

The Central Alberta League of 1963-64 once again had the first place team enter senior and the runner up be in intermediate playoffs. The Rockets edged out the Red Deer Rustlers 3-2 before 1,783 fans at home to win the CAHL.

The second place Red Deer Rustlers defeated Medicine Hat Cantilinis in two straight games to win the Black Trophy for intermediate hockey in Alberta. Wayne Hanna led Red Deer by scoring three goals, Ted Demchuk got two while singles were notched by Bernie Haley, Harvey Fleming and Don Rehill to give the Rustlers a 7-5 win in game two. Replying for Medicine Hat were Vic Link, Bill Chacalias, Ken Schmautz, Bill Thieman and Ted Hall.

The Kamloops Chiefs then outplayed the Rustlers to win the B.C.-Alberta round three games to one by posting a 6-3 win in game four. For Red Deer, Ted Demchuk scored his seventh goal of the series and Rex Turple got two but it was not enough.

In 1965 the Red Deer Rustleres won all four games on Lacombe ice to win a best-of-seven. Ted Demchuk scored at 9:07 or overtime for a 1-0 win in the seventh game before 2,223 fans in Lacombe. The Rockets had a fine season and even toured Europe (see story in Senior Hockey) but for the first time since the 1959-60 season failed to make the playoffs. Lacombe's population in 1961 was 3,029 and in 1964 was 3,140. The small community certainly made its mark on Alberta hockey.

The Rustlers and Drumheller Miners met in the 1965 Central Alberta Hockey League final. Drumheller won its first CAHL crown as the team defeated the Rustlers 6-4 to win the series four games to one. Drumheller continued to play senior while Red Deer went into intermediate playoffs.

The Rustlers first opposition was the Vernon Luckies. Three victories in a row including a final 5-1 win gave the Rustlers the British Columbia-Alberta round. Alf Cadman led Red Deer in the final game when he scored two goals in the third period in a span of six seconds. Bill McCully, Ron Moch and Wayne Hanna scored the other goals for the winners.

RED DEER RUSTLERS 1964-65

Back row (l to r): Ray Marsh (secretary-treasurer), Russ Gillow, Harvey Fleming, Bill McCulley, Hank Sanderson (trainer), Don Pasutto, Del Thompson (practice goal keeper), Les Bunch (assistant trainer), John Price. **Middle row (l to r):** Ted Demchuk, Bob Solinger, Alf Cadman, Wayne Hanna, Don Rehill, Clayton Thompson, Dick Dunnigan, Ron Baryluk. **Front row (l to r):** Jack Clowes (league representative), Jim Read, Dr. Bill Carter (club doctor), Owen Mailey, Dale Gaume, Harold Badrock (president), Ron Moch, Ron Yanosik (playing coach), Jimmy Brown (AAHA representative).

Photo courtesy of Red Deer Archives

Red Deer captured the Canadian Intermediate Hockey Championship (Eastern Canada did not compete) at home when they defeated the Flin Flon Warriors 7-1 to win the series three games to one. "Ancient" Bob Solinger (see article by Don Hay in Senior and Professional Hockey), a former American and Western player, was borrowed from the Lacombe Rockets. Solinger and Ted Demchuk scored twice and Bill McCully, Jim Reid and Clayton Thompson got singles in the victory.

By the end of the 1964-65 season, the Central Alberta Hockey League had nearly run its course as the premiere league in Alberta. The following year the Edmonton Oil Kings won the Memorial Cup and Drumheller Miners took the Allan Cup. However, the cost of operating this type of hockey was beginning to show.

In the case of Lacombe, the players from the University who drove to every game from Edmonton had started to pursue their own personal careers and others on the roster were starting to look elsewhere for a place to play. As their interest waned, fan support tapered off in Lacombe in the following year.

The CAHL showed amazing adaptability since its inception in 1903. In 1956-57, for example, it permitted the junior Edmonton Oil Kings to join the league after the WCJHL had folded. Although teams in this league were really intermediate, both junior and senior teams went on to become national champions (see 1965-66 Oil Kings in Junior Hockey and 1965-66 Drumheller Miners in Senior Hockey).

By the 1965-66 season the CAHL was called the Alberta Senior Hockey League. The name change occurred for at least two reasons. It permitted basically intermediate teams to enter Allan Cup competition with other teams from the new Western Canada Senior Hockey League; in addition, the new name carried more prestige.

The success of the Drumheller Miners (and the junior Oil Kings the same year) illustrates the strength of this league. But it also serves to show the trend in senior hockey in Canada. It was not that intermediate hockey had become so strong that a basically intermediate team could defeat the best seniors; it was that the calibre of senior hockey had diminished. In the 1930's and 40's no team calling itself "senior" would have emerged league co-champions with a junior team as happened in the 1965-66 season.

Central Alberta supported senior hockey for two more years. But after that it could not compete with teams in the WCSHL. Many local players turned junior with AJHL teams and never returned. Other older local players went to cities for jobs and school. The cost of imports to fill depleted rosters was prohibitive. Support dwindled and top level hockey in central Alberta died out. The league could no longer adapt to stay alive.

Intermediate leagues such as the Chinook Hockey League and strong minor hockey programs keep hockey going in central Alberta. But many still remember the Olds Elks, Drumheller Miners, Lacombe Rockets, Didsbury Ramblers, Red Deer Indians, Monarchs and Rustlers and the Edmonton Oil Kings as some of the best teams in Alberta hockey history.

The Eastern Alberta Hockey League became the power in 1965-66. However, the possibility of the EAHL becoming as forceful was already evident two or three years earlier. Lloydminister built a new rink for the 1963-64 season so citizens such as Jim Hill, Kay Strate, Bill Foster, Al Dornstauder and Alex Robertson were asked to produce a team of Intermediate 'A' level.

Eastern Alberta had produced teams of provincial level years before such as the Lloydminster Elks and later the Prolites and Huskies. Vegreville had the powerful Rangers of the thirties. Now in 1963-64, Max Bentley was brought in to be Lloydminster's playing coach along with his son Lynn as a player. This type of development started to create a trend of blending imports and local players.

The Eastern Alberta Hockey League teams at the start of the 1965-66 season included the Lloydminster Border Kings, Vermilion Tigers, Vegreville Rangers, Bonnyville Pontiacs, St. Paul Darts and a Saskatchewan entry called the Maidstone Jets. The Darts pulled out during the season. The Border King's captain Glen Armstrong received the Craig Cup for Lloydminster when they defeated the regular league first place club, the Vegreville Rangers in the playoffs. The Craig Cup was first donated in 1922 and Lloydminster had not won it for eight years.

Byron McCrimmon coached the Kings to the Alberta Intermediate 'A' title of Alberta's 1965-66 over the Okotoks Oilers. This was Lloydminster's first 'A' championship in Alberta. The Vin Stanley "Rosebowl" Trophy for Northern Alberta and the D.E. Black Trophy for Alberta were presented by Jim Brown of Camrose, Past President of the AAHA.

The Border Kings then defeated the Quesnel Kangaroos in the B.C.-Alberta round. Bill Moore and John Belcourt, two pickups from the Vermilion Tigers scored six points each in the series to lead the Kings to three wins while suffering one loss in the best-of-five.

Travel was one of the toughest chores for Lloyd. As soon as they got back from the B.C. win, they almost immediately left for the Western Intermediate final in Flin Flon, Manitoba. The Flin Flon Warriors dropped the Kings in three straight by 6-1, 2-1 and 5-2 scores. Goalkeeper Gerry "Spike" Schultz kept the Kings in the series as he stopped in excess of forty shots a game.

The building of more covered rinks in the province from this period of time and during the seventies added room and better facilities for minor hockey in Alberta. On February 11, 1967, the Archie Miller Arena opened in Lloydminster. Miller was one of the area's best hockey supporters. He took an active part in all sports which even included playing with Lester and Frank Patrick in Victoria in 1915. On the occasion of the official opening, Archie was appreciative of the honor and for once in his life, without words.

In 1966-67 the Border Kings once again became the top team in Alberta. They won the provincial crown when the Medicine Hat Catalinis failed to ice a team for a sudden-death contest. As a result the now Alberta champs advanced to a best-of-five series against the Powell River Regals from British Columbia.

This season, the Kings would have the opportunity to play the remaining playoff games at home at the Centennial Civic Centre. Home ice proved to be an advantage, as the Kings won the best-of-five in four games. Bob House, a pickup from Bonnyville Pontiacs, was instrumental in wins as he hit everything that moved and fired bullets at the Regal net. Centreman Vic Smith scored five times for the Kings in the series.

After the B.C.-Alberta victory the Kings became the Canadian Intermediate 'A' champion and Edmonton Journal Trophy winners when they defeated the Kindersley Clippers 5-0. They won the first two games 7-2 and 4-2 and then were trounced 10-4 by the Clippers before their shut-out. A crowd of 2,140 plus 600 children cheered as Gord Hubbard, Sam Belcourt, Vic Smith, Frank Mapletoft and Glen Anderson shared the five goals.

LLOYDMINSTER BORDER KINGS 1966-67

Back (l to r): Gordon Hubbard, Bob Napper, Gordie Smith, Gary Clements, Cliff Galloway, Jerry Mills. Middle: Larry Nordquist, Owen Rogers, Frank Mapletoft, Vic Smith, Norman Thorpe, Chuck Umphrey. Front: Dave Boyer, Bryon McCrimmon (playing coach), Glen Armstrong, Bobby Hull (team guest), Jim Hill (manager), Keith "Kaye" Strate. Missing: "Spike" Shultz, Frank Roggeveen, Billy Moore, Bill Armstrong.

Photo courtesy of Provincial Archives

Team manager Jim Hall recalls that, "We had our own fan leader in Cece Bellward who blew the trumpet. The fans would yell "charge" similar to the wave situation of today. It was inspiring."

Lloydminster fans thought they were possibly going to see more hockey. After the Border King Centennial Championship, manager Hill was contacted from Ontario about the chances of a challenge. Nothing resulted but the interest for a Canada wide competition was in the works.

Everything did not work out well on the ice for the Lloydminster Border Kings of 1966-67. The Vermilion Tigers became the EAHL champions and holders of the Craig Trophy when they defeated the Kings 6-2. Playing coach Henry Wasylik and former Border King George Severin led the Tigers by scoring twice and singles were netted by Reg Fleming and Bob Tidsbury.

The competition between Lloydminster and Vermilion continued in the 1967-68 season. However, the Kings and Tigers would have to wait until provincial playoffs as the EAHL folded. Both clubs had problems getting games. Nick Kulbisky, hockey columnist for the Vermilion Standard gives his account of the Vermilion Tigers, the 1967-68 Alberta Intermediate champions.

VERMILION TIGERS
BY NICK KULBISKY

The 1967-68 version of the Vermilion Tigers, who played Intermediate "C" hockey in the EAHL, was a combination of rookies, seasoned veterans, and several experienced imports from Edmonton.

Locally the players were Jim Fleming (Captain), Lou Jarock, Barry Gregory, Bill Wilson, Stan Hartwell, Blake Tidsbury, playing coach Henry Wasylik, and 17 year goal tender Ken Brown. From Elk Point came Dave Zarowny, from Edmonton were other seasoned veterans of hockey wars, Henry Hodgson, Frank Joyal, George Severyn, and former pro Rich Healey.

VERMILION TIGERS 1967-68

First row (l to r): Jim Fleming, Henry Hodgson, Lou Jarock, Ken Brown, Frank Joyal, Barry Gregory. Second row: Bill Wilson, Bill Pettigrew (manager), Henry Wasylik (playing coach), George Severyn, Stan Hartwell, Dave Zarowney, Rich Healey, Nick Poburan (trainer), Paul Mistal (manager). Back row: Bob Hartwell, Peter Trach (equipment manager), Dave Gabelhouse, Gerry Schmidt, Ken Woywitka, Blake Tidsbury.

Photo courtesy of Nick Kulbisky

Other members of the club and executive: Paul Mistal and Bill Pettigrew, managers; Peter Trach, Equipment Manager; Nick Poburan, Trainer; Vic Dowhaniuk, President; Gordon Ell, Secretary-Treasurer; Arnold Usenik, Vice-President; Jim Green, Ernie Mayowski, Alex Sieben, Irvin Gordon, Fred Brimacombe, Frank Donald, Tom Smith, Bill Sutherland, Scotty LaRocque, and Don Maggs.

Wainwright, Provost, and Hardisty were the other teams with the Tigers in the EAHL which had to suspend operations during 1967-68 season because the Vermilion team became too powerful. The Tigers were then forced to play exhibition games for many weeks prior to playoffs but they still managed to tangle with superior clubs such as Edmonton Maple Leafs and Edmonton Movers (both teams of the AJHL), and Weyburn Flyers. In post-season play, the Tigers captured the Craig Cup, which was emblematic of Senior Hockey in the area. Wainwright Commandos beat the St. Paul Rockets and our club took out Wainwright.

The Vermilion Tigers, playing now with great exuberance and confidence entered the Intermediate 'A' playdowns.

Their next encounter was a best-of-seven series against their next-door rivals, the Lloydminster Border Kings. In a hard-fought series the Tigers were triumphant four games to two. In the deciding game played in Vermilion, the score was 2-1 for the Tigers with Jim Fleming and Frank Joyal the goal scorers. Replacing starry Ken Brown in the nets who was sidelined with a knee injury for this deciding game was Lyn Bardon who was acquired from Edmonton Junior Maple Leafs. In this series, a record crowd of 2,487 packed the Vermilion Agriplex to witness the hockey action in the 4th game.

Next, the Tigers won the Alberta Intermediate 'A' Championship in a two-game-total-goal series against the Red Deer Imperials. The first game was a 6-6 deadlock; the Tigers winning the second game 6-3. Scoring for the Tigers in the deciding game were Jim Fleming and Frank Joyal with 2 goals each and George Severyn and Henry Hodgson with singles.

It was on to Quesnel, B.C. to meet the B.C. Champions, the Quesnel Kangaroos. The Tigers bolstered their club by picking up Frank Mapletoft from Lloydminster and Dave Joyal from Edmonton.

The toughest team the Tigers ever met, the Kangaroos were big, rough, and very adept at body-busting. The Tigers again surprised everyone by defeating their opponent three games to one to capture the Alberta-B.C. Intermediate 'A' Championship in a best-of-five series.

The Tigers, after winning the first two games 7-6 in overtime and 5-4, dropping a 5-2 decision to the Kangaroos setting up the deciding game which went as follows: (from the Quesnel Cariboo Observer, April 4, 1968).

Monday was another "do or die" game for the Roos. And after the Tigers scored with the game only 15 seconds underway it looked pretty grim. But 2 minutes later Dick Cusson skated the Roos back into the game, only to have Vermilion go ahead 2-1 to end the first period.

Hopes were still running high for Quesnel and the full house was waiting for the hometown squad to break loose. The second period was underway and George Severin broke free to increase the Tigers' lead 3-1. George Redl brought the Roos one goal closer as the crowd brought the 'Go Roos Go' chant to a roar. When Herb Greyeye's slapshot tied the game the Quesnel Civic Arena nearly burst its seams. During the next eight minutes Vermilion native son, Ken Brown, was fired at from every angle under an unending barrage of shots. No matter how close they came, the Roos just couldn't put it in the net. Plagued by frustration and desperation, spectators and players alike waited for the red light to go on after every scramble. Then with 2 minutes and 48 seconds to play in the game, Vermilion playing coach Henry Wasylik scored the series' winning goal. A great end to a great series.

The Tigers now advanced to the Western Canada Intermediate 'A' final against the Saskatchewan-Manitoba winner, Meadow Lake Stampeders. Their climb to immortality came to an end when the Stampeders swept the Tigers three straight games with all played in Vermilion before hockey crowds of 1,500, 1,600 and 2,000. The three games were close, 4-3, 6-3, 6-4 and it was heads-up hockey all the way, but for the Tigers they had given it all in the previous series against Quesnel.

What made the Vermilion Tigers go so far? They did not possess the best hockey talent in the world. They had a workhorse goal tender in Ken Brown and the rest of the skaters played a tough, courageous brand of hockey. If there was one word to describe the 1967-68 Vermilion Tigers, it was Desire.

* * *

In the 1968-69 season the Lloydminster Border Kings joined the Western Saskatchewan Intermediate League. Other teams were the Rosetown Red Wings, Kindersley Clippers, Biggar Nationals, Swift Current Indians and Unity Canucks. Bryon McCrimmon left for Rosetown to coach the Red Wings and Owen Rogers became the new coach. Jerry Mills became the co-manager with Jim Hill. The Kings won the pennant and playoffs in the

WSIL but competed in Alberta for provincial playoffs. The Kings also got the chance to compete on a fully national basis.

The Peace River Country supplied their opposition for Alberta provincials. Intermediate hockey clubs in the 'A' category for playoffs had only three entries. The High Prairie Regals emerged from the Peace River area but were defeated 5-2 and 10-3 by Lloydminster. History from two years before repeated as the Powell River Regals now played the Alberta champion Border Kings.

The Kings were confident and sidelined the Regals 4-2 in the final game to win the series in three straight. In the final victory before 2,100 fans, Owen Rogers, Gary Checknita, Cliff Galloway and Frank Roggoveen tallied for Lloydminster.

It was now the Fort Francis Canadians who provided an extremely tough series for Lloydminster. The Kings were down two games to one at one time but two straight wins gave the Border Kings the Edmonton Journal Trophy as Western champions. The scoring in the final 3-1 win was equally divided between veterans Cliff Galloway, Owen Rogers and Vic Smith. The Border Kings were now in the Canadian final.

A strike by machinists of Air Canada caused concern for the Border Kings for their 1969 Canadian Intermediate final in La Tuque, Quebec. The club was booked on a flight from Calgary to Montreal and then would go the remaining 160 miles to La Tugue by bus. The Kings caught the last flight out of Calgary before the strike.

Playing in La Tuque was a unique experience for the Border Kings. They had never heard of the small city. The team name was "Les Loups" which in English means Wolves. The population of La Tuque at 16,000 was twice as large as Lloydminster and Canadian International Paper was the main industry. Their rink, the La Tuque Colosseum, had five rows of seats along both sides and in one end zone and the ice surface was around 90' by 200'. The seating capacity was 1,530 but it was never filled for any of the games.

Team manager Jim Hill remembers that the Wolves were a very good hockey team. "Most of them seemed to be farm hands of the Montreal Canadiens." The Kings had a three week wait to play this Canadian final. The Wolve's defeated Lloydminster in three straight games by scores of 8-3, 8-5, and 7-3 and won the Dr. W.G. Hardy Trophy for winning the Canadian championship. This was the second awarding of this national trophy. In 1967-68 Meadow Lake, Saskatchewan ended up against Sept-Iles, Quebec. The Quebec team won the initial series.

On the trip home the Border Kings watched an NHL game at the Forum in Montreal. Hill says, "today we take it for granted when we see the Oilers or Flames. But in 1969, most of us were seeing our first live NHL game".

The Border King's success in Alberta provincials continued in 1969-70 but in Western Saskatchewan Intermediate 'A' League they were defeated in the playoffs. The Rosetown Red Wings won the league.

In Alberta provincial playoffs the Kings defeated their Alberta rival, the Vermilion Tigers, three games to one. Some concern was expressed about the apathy of the fans in Lloydminster and it was hoped the crowds would increase for the provincial final.

The first game was held in Peace River where the Border Kings won 7-2 and took a five goal lead. It was announced that Bob Bourassa would bring his organ to the Civic Centre in Lloydminster to help stir up excitement at the game. Two thousand fans came out to see the Kings win the Black Trophy by defeating the Stampeders 6-3 and the round by eight goals. Once again the Kings met the Powell River Regals to determine the B.C.-Alberta winner.

The Kings were defeated in Powell River three games to one. The Regals then became the first western team to win the Dr. W. G. Hardy Trophy when they defeated Val D'Or, Quebec Olympics in the Canadian final.

Dave Boyer became the new coach of the Border Kings and Jerry Mills remained as manager for 1970-71, The majority of the team were Lloydminster products. In the Western Saskatchewan league the Kings were defeated by the Kindersley Clippers. Once again the Kings entered Alberta intermediate playoffs.

Lloydminster won the provincial crown and then defeated the Prince George Mohawks to annex the B.C.-Alberta section. Their season ended when Byron McCrimmon coached his Rosetown Red Wings to victory over the Kings in the western final.

1971-72 was the last provincial winning year for Lloydminster in intermediate 'A' hockey. The "older" players under playing coach Al Butt decided to give it one more try. In the Western Saskatchewan Intermediate Hockey League the Kings defeated the North Battleford Bohs in three straight and the Rosetown Red Wings four in a row to win the Sick's Bohemian Trophy.

A new playoff arrangement was made for the Alberta final of 1971-72. The Grande Prairie Athletics played the Border Kings in a four game total goal series. The main reason for the four games was to make the series a financial success because of the travel distance between the two centers.

The Border Kings were surprised when Grande Prairie shut them out 2-0 in the first game. Goalkeeper Doug Everett stopped 31 shots for the A's. Al Moan for Lloydminster earned a shut-out in the second game as the Kings bounced back 3-0. Back in Grande Prairie the Kings earned victories of 4-1 and 8-2 to win the four game total goal series 15-5.

The British Columbia representatives were the New Westminster "Shmyr" Flyers. They were sometimes just called the Shmyr Flyers. Three Shmyr brothers played and another coached the club. The Kings showed the will to comeback as they won games four and five to win the best-of-five three games to two. In the final 3-2 win Al Popoff, Owen Rogers and Gary Checknita scored for the Kings.

Now the Kings would face their Saskatchewan rival the Rosetown Red Wings. Mel Swyryda scored for Rosetown at 6:50 of sudden-death overtime to beat the Kings 3-2. Near the middle of the third period Swyryda also scored the tying goal. Terry Simpson (present coach of Prince Albert Raiders, 1985 Memorial Cup Champions) scored the other Red Wing goal while Al Popoff and Gary Checknita replied for Lloydminster. This victory gave Rosetown the Western Intermediate 'A' championship. The first coach of a championship squad for Lloydminster in the sixties, Bryon McCrimmon was coach of the Red Wings who won in 1972.

The Border Kings domination of Alberta Intermediate hockey ended in an early round in 1972-73. The Fort Saskatchewan Barons overcame a five goal deficit to tie the Kings in total goals after two games. At 8:10 of the second overtime period, Richard Thorne picked up a rebound off a shot by Jim Seutter to eliminate the Lloydminster Border Kings. The Border Kings had won the Alberta Provincial 'A' six times in seven years.

Intermediate hockey in southern Alberta had almost become extinct at the 'A' level. Times changed and in 1972 the Banff Bisons won the province.

The Bisons, Calgary Canadian Colts and Canmore Flyers were members of the Big Six Hockey League in September. 1972. The league also included the Calgary Tigers, Campbell Jets, Gas Company, Calgary Police and the Calgary Fire Department.

BANFF BISONS 1972-73

Pictured standing (l to r) are: Joe Owchar (manager), David Christou (stick boy), Bob Peers, Tim Gourlay, Howie Colborne, Wallay Kozak, Pete Weston, Grant Baudais, Mike Orman, Scotty Watson, Pat Halas, Jim Van Tassell, Dan Calles, Howie McHenry (trainer), and Norm Murray. Front row (l to r) are: Howie Goon, George Hill, Carl Chwachka, Phil Kotchonoski (coach), Brian Randall, Bernie Gould, and Don Vosburg.

Photo courtesy of Jack R. Wilson

The uniforms of the Bisons were orange and white, the same colors as the NHL Philadelphia Flyers. The key players came from Calgary and had played for the defunct Calgary Stampeders or the earlier Spurs. The eight were George Hill, Pat Halas, Wally Kozak. Mike Orman, Scott Watson, Bob Peers, Pete Wesson and Carl Chwachka. Coaches were Phil Kotchonoski and Joe Owchar. The team executive consisted of President Bill Kitsul, Vice-President V.P. Van Christou and Secretary-Treasurer Elwyn Smith.

Banff was one of the first communities in Alberta to play hockey. From the Brewsters in the late 19th and early 20th century through the Banff Winter Carnivals, this community supported hockey. In 1972-73, Banff won their first and only provincial intermediate 'A' championship. They defeated the Grande Prairie Athletics 4-2 and 7-2 to win the Black Trophy.

In the final match at the Banff Recreation Centre Paddocks before 674 fans, the Bisons outshot the Athletics 47-25 to win 7-2. Pete Wesson and Wally Kozak scored twice while Brian Randall, Bob Peers and Pat Halas got singles. Chuck Gesse scored both Grande Prairie goals.

The Bisons forfeited their right to carry on in the playoffs against Prince George, B.C. Coach Kotchonoski said that the team had averaged 800 fans a game and still lost money.

In playoffs the Bisons did not lose a game. They defeated the Nanton Palaminos, Okotoks Oilers, Canmore Flyers, Stettler Sabres, St. Albert Comets and Grande Prairie.

After this the Calgary Trojans became the team to beat. The failure of the Calgary Stampeders Senior club to continue in operation made players available who now played intermediate hockey.

THE CALGARY TROJANS' FOUR INTERMEDIATE CHAMPIONSHIPS

BY WALLY KOZAK AND BILL FRASER

PROVINCIAL CHAMPIONS

STANS

Calgary TROJANS

Calgary Trojans Hockey Magazine

Seventy-Five Cents

(The Calgary Trojans won the intermediate title in Alberta four straight years (1973-74, 1974-75, 1975-76, 1976-77). The Trojan story was written by Bill Fraser and Wally Kozak. Kozak's playing background includes University of Saskatchewan Huskies, Saskatoon Quakers, Calgary Stampeders, Banff Bisons and Calgary Trojans. He coached the Calgary Canucks to one AJHL title and in 1984 took the Alberta Amateur Hockey Association Midgets to China. Fraser also contributed to the Trojans in coaching and organizational capacities.)

'Stans' Tire Trojans' as the players called themselves won the provincial Intermediate Championship four consecutive years. The team of young Senior players, ex-pros and vibrant youth provided Calgary and Alberta with some exciting hockey. Under the benevolent sponsorship of Stan Will — owner of a Calgary Tire shop — the team hung together through many rivalries along the playoff trail. In its initial success as a member of the Big Six League the Trojans upset the higher ranked Calgary Fire Department team before packed houses at Foothills Arena.

The Big Six League was one of the oldest and longest running adult leagues in Calgary and its popularity reached a "modern era" peak with this series. In the next few years the most vicious rivalry was with the Okotoks Oileres. It seemed like everyone was a brother on the Okotoks team. Snodgrasses and Wedderburns provided half of their team. Ex-Centennial Jim Hunt provided additional muscle for the Oilers while former pro Randy Murray, Wayne Magnusson (brother of Chicago's Keith) and "Terrible Teddy" Olsen (MPP — most penalized player) in the Western Canada Junior League proved the equalizers. The older Trojans were often inspired by their "over-the-hill" reference of the Okotoks fans as they sucked it up for three more provincial championships. The games were rough and tough — "old time hockey" as Eric Bishop referred to it and the fans more than got their money's worth.

Those were the days of the Calgary Cowboys of the World Hockey Association who provided the professional show in town. In contrast Big Six League players toiled for the pleasure of a beverage after and the in between period laughs while recalling humorous happenings from the past. Players played for the love of the game as they moved along the playoff trail; the crowds grew as did the appreciation. Unfortunately, as the team advanced in provincial play the level of play became more difficult to maintain.

The fact that most players held full time jobs proved a strain on extended playoff efforts. The sacrifice of going to the National for the "love of the game" would seem too costly in terms of job commitments, finances and family life. The team lost out in Western playoffs and a sense of relief was evident for continued success meant missing work and a larger financial risk for owner, Stan Will. Without the support of Stan and his friends who pitched in to oversee and manage the team a real void would have occurred for excellent hockey in Alberta.

The teams' rosters carried numerous ex-Centennial stars — Carlin, Weinich, Molvic, MacNeil returned from pro in their prime to lead the team and carry some of the older more experienced players. Ex-pros like Randy Murray and Tim Gould from the University of Denver Pioneers and senior players like Peers, Kozak, Tuff, Wiseman, Pozzo, Norwdon, Bilings, Fraser, Sloan, Magnusson and Sawatsky. The brother acts included Howie, Dave, Doug, Donnie and Wayne Colborne, while both Ted and Dick Olsen contributed toughness and skill. The Trojan teams will be remembered for being able to play any way you wanted. Finesse or physical they seemed to be able to do it all.

TROJANS RECEIVING 1976-77 TROPHY

Left to right: Larry Smith (AAHA), Doug MacKenzie (AAHA), Nick Spacinski (Sherwood Park Barons), Wally Kozak (receiving trophy), Gordon Mills (AAHA).

Tough teams found them equally tough and fast teams equally fast. Although Les Gathercole coached the team — like all coaches of good teams the players really coached themselves and Les knew how to handle their humor and emotions and he listened well to their feedback. It proved to be four great years of hockey.

The one year stint of a Calgary Senior team in the B.C. Senior League proved fruitless and spelled the demise of the Trojans. It was a costly experiment. With the expansion of professional hockey in the 70's and 80's and the dilution of top calibre play, the Intermediate game proved its worth. Players loved to play — they came to play for nothing while they established themselves in chosen vocations and professions. Their high quality performance proved that the best motivation for playing the game is the love of the game.

It was an era of hockey for fun — played with intensity. That fun may not be realized by future upstarts in the game — hopefully it will be remembered as an important part of Hockey's History in Alberta.

* * *

SHERWOOD PARK BARONS

BY BOB McGILL, coach 1975-76 to 1977-78

The Sherwood Park Barons won the Alberta Intermediate 'A' title in 1977-78. This was the highlight of the team's development. However, as one looks at our beginnings, it is difficult to imagine being Alberta champions.

Our team started the same way as clubs did since the beginning of hockey. It was outdoors in the mid-sixties where a group played in a Sunday evening house league. By 1966-67, they became formalized and joined their first league called the Highway 16 East League. Three years in succession, the Barons won the championship. Included on the roster were Herb Holland, Cy Smith and Wayne Sarginson who became instrumental in organizational or coaching roles for the Barons in future years.

In 1970-71 the Barons joined the Edmonton Central League. This league was a higher calibre, but its team membership changed so often, it ran out of Edmonton clubs. In 1975-76 the name changed to the Alberta Major Intermediate League. Besides the Barons, other teams were Stony Plains Eagles, St. Albert Comets, Leduc Oilers, Enoch Tomahawks, Westlock Eagles. Fort Saskatchewan Huskies, Camrose Maroons and Wetaskiwin Colonels.

A brief review of the Baron's record from 1973-74 through 77-78 shows a team that won four northern and one provincial title. In 1973-74 the Calgary Trojans defeated the Barons in Intermediate 'A'. Okotoks were victorious in the 'B's in 1974-75 and Calgary Trojans won the 'A' section over the Barons for two more seasons. Finally in 1977-78 the Barons won the Alberta Intermediate 'A' when it defeated the Calgary Trojans.

The first game of the championship year was played in Calgary and ended in a 4-4 draw. The return match was played at the Sherwood Park Recreation Center before 1,100 fans. The Barons doubled the Trojans 6-3 to win the round 10-7.

The team represented Alberta in Prince George, B.C. The format was a six team tournament for the Western Canadian championship. In our round robin division of three teams, the Barons won one game and lost against Prince George Mohawks. Because the Mohawks won both their games in the round robin, we were eliminated.

In succeeding years the Sherwood Park Barons changed names to become the Strathcona Barons and played in the County of Strathcona out of the Fultonvale Arena.

Over the years, the Barons were made up of players of limited experience up to those who had played professional. Others associated with the club as coaches and managers included Bud Fields, Milt Hohol, Jim Seutter, John Griffin, John Robinson and Doug Barrie. The efforts of the Barons and other teams in intermediate hockey to survive and keep going is commendable. We learned a lot from our one major Alberta championship and probably a lot more by trying. I still have a difficult time today thinking of the original Barons who started playing outdoors.

OLDS-DIDSBURY RAMBLERS

1978-79 Alberta Intermediate 'A' Champions

BY LYNN McDONALD, Olds College

(McDonald is a brother of Calgary Flame's Lanny McDonald. In this 1978-79 season Lynn scored 28 goals and had 43 assists for 71 points.)

The Olds Didsbury Ramblers won the Chinook League and the Alberta Intermediate championship of 1978-79. Olds and Didsbury combined to form a team since the Olds Arena burned in November, 1978. The team was coached by Norm Haynes who did a good job of blending players from two rival towns into a winning team.

The team had a good combination of size, speed, experience and youth. Former WHA players were Brent Taylor, Steve Richardson, Larry Israelson and Rick Wannamaker while Frank Richardson had played in the

American Hockey League. The youth and speed came from Mike Jackson, Doug Miller, Wayne Krebs and Larry Richardson plus fine goal tending from Mike Holub and Kevin Carr.

During the season Frank Richardson had 30 goals and 46 assists for 76 points. The key to the team probably rested with the "big four" on defence consisting of Brent Taylor, Steve Richardson, John Price and Rick Wannamaker.

The Ramblers lost the provincial final to the Camrose Maroons. However, Camrose went into Senior or Allan Cup and Olds Didsbury continued in Intermediate. The interprovincials were played in Prince George, B.C. We defeated the Prince George Mohawks 5-3. During this game "Crazy George" was cheering against our club. Since we won, Crazy George then switched sides and cheered for us. Our squad responded by tying the Vancouver Hurry Kings. In the final we lost out to the Warroad Minnesota Lakers who then respresented Western Canada in the national final.

OLDS-DIDSBURY RAMBLERS 1978-79

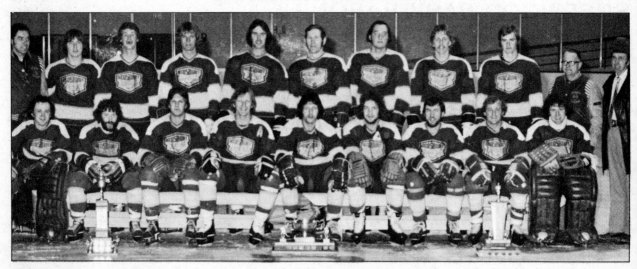

Back row (l to r): Norm Haynes (coach), Mike Jackson, Brian Kimmel, Larry Richardson, Cal Brassard, Lynn McDonald, Doug Miller, Frank Richardson, Larry Israelson, Al Rutherford (trainer), Art Jackson (equipment manager). Front row (l to r): Kevin Carr, "Mop" Miller, Tom Murphy, Steve Richardson, Wayne Krebs, Rick Wannamaker, Miller McCoy, Randy Bartley, Mike Holub. Missing from picture: Brent Taylor, John Price.

INNISFAIL EAGLES 1979-80

BY A.H. "HAP" CLARKE

The Innisfail Eagles had a fine record in intermediate hockey as they had won the 'B', 'C' and 'D' levels. In 1979-80 the team won the 'A' category when they defeated their traditional rivals from the Chinook League, the Didsbury Ramblers by a total score of 10-7 in two games. The squad then went on to defeat the Strathcona Barons 11-8 in a home and home total-goal series representing Alberta.

The Eagle's flight in interprovincial action was short as the Burnaby Lakers won the best-of-five in four games at Langley, B.C. The series was voted by Eagle players as the roughest and hardest in team history. Two of the games were lost in overtime in the penalty-filled series.

The following two years (1980-82 and 81-82) the Eagles defeated the Bonnyville Pontics in the Provincial Intermediate Championships. On each occasion the winner was declared the senior champion and represented Alberta in that group while the loser became the Intermediate 'A' champion (See Senior hockey.)

The Eagle success story can be attributed to a skilled and hard working executive. Some of these people include Elmer Messards, Tim Wolfe, Jim Shanahan, Ron Jarvis and Joe Bacque. The squad itself was made up of players developed in the Innisfail Minor Hockey Association along with supplements from neighboring Red Deer. (See Senior Hockey for the Eagles of the 80's.)

BONNEYVILLE PONTIACS WIN PROVINCIAL — 1980-81 AND 1981-82

BY DANIEL JOHNS, editor Bonnyville Nouvelle Newspaper

The most recent peak of Pontiac power occurred between 1980 and 1983 when Bonnyville was competitive in exhibition games with the colleges and universities. They had astrong record in National playoffs, played three

Back row (l to r): Len Hopkins, John Leslie, Dale McMullen, Al Ladd, Dwayne Howell, Dean Edgar. Middle: Richard Millie, Jim Wolf, Joe Bacque, Randy Glasgow, Don Fellows, Ron Jarvis, Fred Hucal, Jack McDonald, Frank Layden, Bob Mullen, Jim Hurelbut, Dave Bristow, Chris Golem, John Waugh, Jim Shanahan, Elmer Messaros. Front: Bob Galloway, Del Northcott, Dan Kinsella, Greg Scott, John McPhee, Rick Holt.

International matches and earned trips to Fairbanks, Alaska to play the Gold Kings, the United States Amateur Champions.

Winning was nothing new to Bonnyville. The town had a team called the Bruins prior to World War II. They adopted the Pontiac moniker in 1949 because their goal tender, Walter Lochansky the sponsor, ran the Pontiac dealership. The club played on outdoor rinks with any team that could be enticed to town.

By 1956 the Pontiacs joined the Eastern Hockey League with teams from Alberta and Saskatchewan. The team in 1960 was in high gear winning their first of four Craig Cups, the League Championship. They didn't surrender the cup easily in 1964 as the series against Vermilion was decided in the second overtime period in the seventh game. The Eastern League folded in the late 60's and out of the ashes sprang the Norlake League. Bonnyville was in the League final seven years in a row before it finally won in 1977, the year when the signs of another dynasty were becoming visible. The St. Paul Rockets were the league power.

That year Bonnyville lost to the Innisfail Eagles in the Provincial 'D' Playoffs by one goal in a two-game-total-goal series. The Pontiacs were down 4 goals late in the final match, but set a world record for quick goals, 3 in 12 seconds (2 by Mitch Sylvestre and 1 by Randy Yavis), but lost the game. The record stood until an American team bettered the mark in 1983. (See Hot Stove League.)

Bonnyville cruised through the Norlake League with 22 wins, 2 losses and 1 tie to finally win the 1977-78 Norlake League Championship.

In 1979 Bonnyville won the Intermediate 'C' Provincials over Medicine Hat, but was not as dominant in the Norlake League, losing to Wainwright in the final after a 19 win, 9 loss, 2 tie record.

The Pontiacs regained momentum in 1979-80 with the addition of twelve rookies, all town residents.

Bonnyville finished the Norlake season with a 20 win, 3 loss, 1 tie record and played Lloydminster in the final. This series was never completed due to a dispute of game dates.

The team was not frustrated by the lack of a Norlake title, as it had won the Intermediate 'B' final against Stettler, setting the stage for the most recent peak of Pontiac might beginning in 1980-81.

That year Bonnyville had a 17 win, 1 tie record in Norlake before the League fell apart due to the tremendous superiority of Bonnyville. After beating Strathcona, the Bonnyville Pontiacs became the Alberta Intermediate 'A' Champions of 1980-81. The Pontiacs lost to the Innisfail Eagles who went Senior. Bonnyville then hosted Victoria in the first round of the Hardy Cup and became the first Alberta team in several years to beat the British

Columbia representatives. They went on to Winnipeg to face the rough Northend Flyers, and lost three games to one.

Among the highlights of the season was a 6-0 win over the Japanese National Olympics, Bonneyville's first International match.

The following year, 1981-82, Bonnyville played a series of exhibition games against colleges and universities as it no longer had a league to play in. A few players from the recently defunct Norlake League, particularly from Grand Center, strengthened the roster. Bonnyville once again earned a berth in the Hardy Cup Playoffs by beating the Stony Plain Eagles. They travelled to Quesnel, B.C. losing the first round three games to one.

BONNYVILLE PONTIACS 1980-81

Front (l to r): Wilfred Robinson (trainer), Phil Kossowan, Glen Dutertie, John Matichuk (manager), Denis Sagnan, Rene Beaudoin (coach), Gordon Kissel, Grant Ferbey, Warner Crawford. Second row: Rollie Germain (trainer), Mitch Sylvestre, Gino Levesques, Bob Foley, Kevin Dancy, Bernie Morin, Gilles Choquet, Abby Hebert, Laurent Vallee (secretary), Ivan Chatel (treasurer). Back: Maurice Sylvestre, Rosaire Robinson, Garth Campbell, Micky Sagnan, Doug Ewanowich.

Photo courtesy of Provincial Archives

In 1982-83 the Pontiacs once again made do with an exhibition season, travelling twice to Fairbanks, Alaska and beating the Japanese again 7-2. In the second year of their own invitation tournament they finally won it by defeating the Leduc Bruins in the final.

However, in the provincial playoffs, the Pontiacs lost the Northern Alberta title to the Stony Plain Eagles, two games to one, marking the end of the current dynasty. Bonneyville joined the Centennial League for the 1984-85 season and hopes to continue its winning tradition.

Competition now comes from Goodfish Lake and the CFB Cold Lake Packers, the national Military Champions. When will the next dynasty evolve in Bonnyville? It is difficult to say but the Pontiacs rise to the top every few years and are sure to do it again.

* * *

THE STONY PLAIN EAGLES 1982-83 and 1983-84

BY RICHARD GEORGE, President of Stony Plain Eagles

Senior hockey began in Stony Plain in the early 30s. The name 'Eagles' was incorporated by coach, Ernie Johnston, in the late 50's. For years, Stony Plain was in leagues consisting of teams from the Highway 16 West area.

The Eagles entered 'A' competitions in 1966. Coaches of the teams, since that time, have been Henry Singer, Herb Brown, Clarence Berndt, Cece Armstrong, George Matsuba, Sam Belcourt, Mickey Checknita, Hugh Berry, Richard George, Rene Beaudin, and Gary Bredin. Players on the team had been basically local. The additions of top players from Spruce Grove, Onoway, Wabamun, Darwell, and Edmonton, has added spice to the team, from year to year. The addition of the Stony Plain Flyers, Junior 'B' team, in 1971, has strengthened the system.

The 1982-83 season for Stony Plain was the most successful in the Eagle's history. The Eagles captured the "Zyg's Jewellery Award" have league winners for the third time. Stony Plain defeated the Bonnyville Pontiacs to capture the Vin Stanley Trophy, for the second time since 1974-75. This trophy was the Northern Alberta Intermediate 'A' Championship, started in 1938 and presented by the AAHA.

The Eagles defeated the Lethbridge Maple Leafs to have their name engraved, for the first time, on the George Harvie Memorial Trophy. This trophy started in 1974 and was for the winners of Intermediate 'A' competition in the Province of Alberta. This trophy replaced the original championship trophy called the D.E. Black Trophy.

STONY PLAIN EAGLES 1982-83

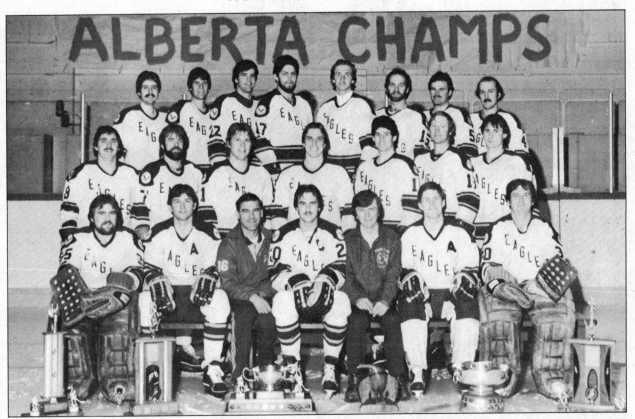

1982-83 trophies (l to r): league trophy, league top scorer, Alberta Intermediate "A" championship trophy, team mascot, Northern Alberta Intermediate "A" championship trophy, league top goaltender. Players — bottom row (l to r): Darrell Furmanek, Ron Reeve (manager, assistant coach), Richard George (president), Mike Williams (trainer), Blair Bristow, Dan Doyle, Randy Zutz. Middle row: Denis Moullierat, Dan O'Connell, Keith Sarich, Vince Tworek, Robbie Wagner (coach), Gary Bredin, Brad Schultz. Top row: Pat Hall, Rick Rouleau, Elmer Ray, Doug Berg, Brian Rimmer, Grant Truckey, Barry Shepherd, John George.
Photo courtesy of Provincial Archives

The next stop toward the Hardy Cup final was the West Coast interprovincial competition. The Eagles defeated the Quesnel Kangaroos in a best-of-five-series. Winnipeg was the site of the Western Canada final for the Edmonton Journal Cup. The Winnipeg Northend Flyers defeated the Eagles in a best-of-seven series four straight.

The 1982-83 campaign paved the way for an exciting 1983-84 season. Stony Plain defeated the Lacombe Merchants in two games to win the Northern Alberta title. Stony Plain then went on to defeat the Innisfail Eagles, 2-0 to capture the Alberta Provincial 'A' Championships. They then travelled to Quesnel, B.C. to play the Kangaroos and lost the best-of-five series three games to one.

The final highlight of the 1984 season, other than the Provincial, was the trip made by the Eagles to Fairbanks, Alaska, to play the Gold Kings, the U.S. Intermediate National Champions. We split the two-game series. The team also went to Tokyo, and the Japanese province of Hokkaido to play the six "NHL" teams of their country. We won five and lost one, while representing Alberta and Canada.

* * *

LEDUC BRUINS WIN 1984-85 TITLE

BY BILL INGLEE, Leduc Representative

Leduc Bruins won the Alberta men's intermediate 'AA' hockey championship Sunday, March 24, 1985, beating Lacombe Merchants two games straight.

The saga of the Bruins trip to the championship began in the Stony Plain Centennial Arena as Leduc faced traditional rival Stony Plain Eagles, led by player-coach Gary Bredin.

A checking line of Stan Lubchynski, Pete Snaterse and Bruce Jacobsen held down the high-scoring Bredin, stopping the Eagles offence.

"The checking line helped shut down Stony Plain's scoring. Lubchynski checked Gary Bredin and he was the main scorer for Stony Plain in the first two games. Our line has speed so they won't be manipulated. When we took out Bredin, it showed," said Bruins coach John Belcourt.

In the series' final game, March 16, rookie Randy Mein on loan from the Leduc Riggers Junior "B" team played on a line with veterans Alex Belcourt and Pat McGill.

Belcourt played professional hockey with Muskeegon in the International Hockey League while McGill was a veteran of the junior hockey ranks, who played with New Westminster Bruins.

On the way to the final win in Leduc's Black Gold Arena the Bruins exhausted both regulation time and the first overtime period, finally moving to sudden-death.

In a repeat of the first game, Leduc scored three minutes into sudden-death as Mein picked up a pass from Belcourt to score.

Coming back from the emotional high of beating Stony Plain proved difficult as Leduc narrowly won a close contest against Lacombe.

LEDUC BRUINS 1984-85

Back row (l to r): Larry LeBid (trainer), John Belcourt (coach), Bud Langstrom, Jim Van Derlee, Jeff Crawford, Peter Snaterse, Bruce Jacobson, Doug Korpleinsky (assistant coach). Front row: Stan Lubchyski, Alex Belcourt, Carey Winquist, Pat McGill (playing manager), Bruce Young. Missing: Richard Rivard, Scott McLeod, Barry Willows, Randy Mein, Darryl Kramchynski, Randy Parker, Rory Rost, Warren Sanregret, Terry Bakken, Steve Shuchuk, Darcy Rasmussen, Reynold Johnson, Bill McLeod (assistant coach).

Photo courtesy of Bill Inglee, Leduc Representative

"We were really too much for them. The guys were playing well," said Belcourt.

Bruins goalie Carey Winquist had his last shutout spoiled as Russ Graham scored the lone Lacombe goal. Leduc went on to win the provincial final 8-1.

"He played well. The goaltender is so important at the start of the game and after that it becomes a support system with everybody doing their jobs," said Belcourt, describing the 32-year-old netminder. Winquist started playing intermediate hockey with the Stony Plain Eagles before moving to Leduc in 1983.

The Bruins went on to lose a close series to Quesnel 3-2 in the first round of Hardy Cup playoffs. Along the way the team attracted the biggest hockey crowd in Leduc's history, packing 1,500 people into the Black Gold Arena.

* * *

HOCKEY IN THE MIGHTY PEACE RIVER COUNTRY — NORTH AND SOUTH

BY FRED WINDJACK

(Fred Windjack was a player, sports writer for 12 years in the Peace Country. He continues with minor hockey in a coaching and executive capacity. Before he moved "south" to Edson in 1980 he was honored with a special night in Peace River. In 1982, he coached the Edson Bantam 'B' club to the Alberta championship.)

This is just a capsule of intermediate hockey highlights in the 50s, 60s and 70s. Hockey in the Peace Country when competing with other areas of Alberta has done so at the intermediate level. In the north it has often been referred as senior.

The North Peace Hockey League operated as a league in the 1953-54 season. The early 50s saw the Fairview Outlaws (later changed to the Elks) have some great clubs with players such as Tony Doll, Johnny Smart, Vic Chelivk and goal tender Joe Hemstock playing super hockey. The Fairview entry had a great rivalry with the Peace River Stampeders who in the 50s had some great guns in the likes of goal tender Ron Campbell, players like Tommy Tucker (later in the 60s, a bantam tournament was named after Tommy Tucker and today may be the oldest existing Bantam tournament in the province) and other players such as Glen Murphy, Johnny Mac-Millan, the Martineau Brothers, Shiny Buchmeir, Dal Bradner and many others.

The team that won a lot in the 50s was the McLennan Red Wings. They had the Johnson brothers, the Pelland brothers, Johnny Listhaeghe (later moved to Spirit River), Roger Maisonneauve and were led to victory after victory by their outstanding defenceman playing coach Bo Carlson, from Prince Albert, Saskatchewan.

Near the tail end of the 50s High Prairie constructed a new arena and immediately applied for a North Peace League franchise. They didn't do real well in their first two seasons, but in the 1959-60 season they captured the North Peace Hockey League title. John and Pete Cuzy of North Battleford provided tremendous offensive spark for the Regals. Prior to the Czuy brothers arriving the High Prairie team got some service out of guys like Laurie Saville, Joe LeBeauf, and Elmer Guse. Gentlemen who worked hard behind the scene for senior hockey and other levels in High Prairie for years were George Bishop, Ike Lawrence, Bill Smith and Larry Shaben, to name a few.

In the 1959-60 season, the Regals beat out the Grimshaw Huskies to win the North Peace Hockey championship. They then went on to challenge the South Peace winners (that league consisted of Grande Prairie Athletics, Dawson Creek Canucks, Fort St. John Flyers and Hythe Mustangs) for the All Peace Hockey Championship. This series featured the Regals from High Prairie and the Canucks from Dawson Creek.

Dawson Creek with no less than three Joyal brothers (Pete, Frank and Dave) in their lineup edged the Regals and the Czuy brothers by a single goal before complete sellouts in a series which many claim was one of the best ever played for the Coachways Cup, emblematic of senior hockey supremacy in the Mighty Peace River Country.

The Regals added a few more titles to their records as they added some new outstanding players to their lineup such as Bill Dyck and Ralph Walker from the Estevan Bruins, Don Passuto of the Edmonton Oil Kings, Danny Muloin from Quebec senior circles and local players like Jimmy McLean and Jim Kozie. McLean probably was the longest playing member of anybody in the North or South Peace Leagues, having played well over twenty years with the same High Prairie club. Kozie joined the Regals as a real young star, and then left to play a number of years with Scotty Munro and the Estevan Bruins.

The Regals drew packed crowds at home games and added a great hockey name to their lineup, Reg Bentley, one of the famous Bentley brothers from Delisle, Saskatchewan. Although Reg was well in his 40s he played very good hockey in an almost all import league.

The Falher Pirates were not big winners in the 50s, but they did have some great stars in the likes of Mike Martel, Pete Serbu, Gilbert Lauze, Rene and Rollie Turcotte and some young players in the likes of Bob Rooks (later went to Fort St. John), Don Veins and Roger Bellerive who later played Junior 'A' hockey with Moose Jaw Canucks.

In the early 60s, the Peace River Stampeders were drawing great crowds even with a losing team. If they ever had a chance to win a championship, it should have been in the 1957-58 season when they lost in the playoffs to McLennan. That particular team had the famous non related Smith line (Don, Clare and Bob) who really thrilled the cowboy fans. The Smiths got work in the north with oil companies.

However, in the 1961-62 season, the Stampeders got a big lift when the Czuy brothers of High Prairie Regals transferred to Peace River with their jobs. Although the Stampeders came close to winning that year, they won it all the next season (1962-63) including the Alberta Intermediate 'B' Championship. From that year on, the Stamps won nine consecutive North Peace Hockey League titles, three provincial titles, and two All Peace Championships, when they defeated the best in the South Peace League for the Coachways Cup.

Some of the big names who wore Stampeder colors for a number of years were John and Pete Cuzy, Bill Dyck, Ralph Walker, Moe Provencal, Fred Windjack, Cecil Swanson who was a playing coach, Don Weaver, Glenn Moren, Vern Galzier, Dan Lovsin, Fred Weise, Cliff Mein, Clare Smith, Dave Clelland, Art Clearwater, Roy Blais and Norm Cassault.

Many of these players were on the team which won the Alberta 'B' title in 1963-64 and lost to Kindersley Clippers for the Western Canadian Intermediate 'B' championship.

PEACE RIVER STAMPEDERS 1964-65

Front row (l to r): Pete Czuy, Fred Windjack, Dave Clelland, Don Weaver, Cecil Swanson (playing coach), Bill Dyck. Middle row: John Czuy, Glen Moren, Vern Glazier, Roy Blais, Fred Weise, Cliff Mein, Dan Lousin, Ralph Walker, Clare Smith. Back row (l to r): John Bernath (trainer), Bill Szaroz (trainer), Ted Van Dyck (trainer), Ken Wright (manager). Missing: Ron Campbell.

Photo courtesy of Edmonton Archives

The stiffest opposition for the Stamps came from the Grimshaw Huskies who were early winners (just prior to the Stamps winning streak) and they had some great players in the likes of Norm Skrudland, Tommy Greig,

Buddy Houlder and Mel Drolet, just to name a few. The Huskies and Stampeders of Grimshaw and Peace River were only 15 miles apart but the rivalry was fantastic as both arenas were packed when these two teams met.

One big reason why hockey started to draw great crowds was because Al ''Boomer'' Adair was broadcasting numerous league and all playoff games on CKYL. In addition to broadcasting Al was the league statistician for a number of years and overall did a great selling job for senior hockey before going into politics in the early 70s.

Some people who worked tremendously hard behind the scenes in Grimshaw were Paul Mercier, Al Fordyce, Mel Drolet and Bud Houlder. In Peace River, Bev Luther, Ron Campbell, John Bernath, Cecil Swanson and of course others were instrumental in making that town a great hockey hot bed.

In the early 70s, the Grimshaw Huskies dominated, with the Paul brothers, the local star Bill McFadden who was a junior star with Swift Current and then drafted third overall by the young Vancouver Canucks. McFadden returned to play with his home town and they were tough to beat. The Huskies got some good coaching from Chuck Curr and later from Bud Houlder with a fairly young team. One young player Wade Campbell played with the Alberta U of A Golden Bears and then signed with the Winnipeg Jets of the NHL.

PEACE HOCKEY MEETING

Back row (l to r): Ted Umback (Peace River), Ron McKenzie (Manning), Bill Smith (High Prairie), Mel Drolet (Grimshaw), Al ''Boomer'' Adair (Radio CKYL — Peace River and league statistician), Al Fordyce (Grimshaw), Ron Campbell (Peace River).

Manning Comets became a new entry in the league in the late 60s and they drew great crowds with gentlemen like Jack McAvoy, Joe Hesse and Melvin Grimm. Frank Heese did most of the organizing.

Fairview Elks were always good competitiors with Fraser Robertson their playing coach. Falher Pirates had some great skating teams in the 70s with the DeSaulnier brothers playing great hockey.

IN THE SOUTH PEACH HOCKEY LEAGUE

While the Peace River Stampeders were winning in the 1960 era in the North Peace Hockey League, the Fort St. John Flyers were big winners in the South Peach League. They had some great stars in the likes of Rod Fonteyne, Gordon Strate of the Detroit Red Wings, Bob Brooks, Don Veins, Floyd Sikorski, Jimmy Anderson, Dale Lock and many others. Executive members who did great jobs with the Flyers were Bill Spicer, Jim Tompkins and a great team manager in Joe Wasylyk.

The Dawson Creek Canucks were also big performers in the 50s and 60s. In addition to the Joyal brothers, they had one of the best defencemen in either the north or south league in Lloyd Hadden, another player with NHL experience.

Another team that performed well in the South Peach League was the Grande Prairie Athletics with all-star defencemen Pete Wright leading the way. John Benson, Ken Head, Cliff Riggler and Max Henning were great players, and possibly one of the most entertaining players to watch was Charlie Turner, a fellow that played for over 25 years. Roy Borstad was one of the key persons behind the scene with the A's. He was their team manager. Other players who played well for Grande Prairie were Gary and Merney Nellis, Chuck Hessex, Dale Guame and Fred Zasadny.

As mentioned, the Dawson Creek Canucks got great scoring from the Joyal trio but they also were sparked by goalie Dave Leopkey and former professional Ed Diachuk.

The Spirit River Rangers joined the league in the late 60s and drew record crowds. Some players who were great with the Rangers were Fred Hilts (Detroit Red Wings), Johnny Listahge, Fred Zasadny, George Watts and Danny Muloin.

The Hythe Mustangs got tremdous scoring from the Berg brothers, Alton and Rod. Rod joined the High Prairie Regals in the late 60s while Alton stayed to play with the Mustangs alongside Art Patterson, one of the finest centres in either league. Harold "Flukey" and Norm Kjemhous were other excellent scorers.

Fairview Elks joined the South Peace Hockey League for two seasons, late in the 60s, but later rejoined the North Peach Hockey League.

The history of intermediate hockey in the North and South Peace is something greater than just mentioned here. I have covered the highlights.

* * *

INTERMEDIATE HOCKEY EPILOGUE

Intermediate hockey has always been hockey for the masses — with a few exceptions. A few very talented intermediate teams challenged top senior teams in Allan Cup competition before the Edmonton Journal Trophy became the symbol of intermediate supremacy in western Canada. At that point, senior and intermediate teams ceased to compete against each other. Therefore, since the two categories are distinct, it is inaccurate to say that intermediate hockey replaced senior hockey. In its day senior hockey was the elite brand of amateur hockey in Alberta.

However, intermediate hockey keeps the chase for a national title alive in small Alberta communities. The introduction of the Hardy Cup in 1967-68 ensured that. In recent years it has become an expensive proposition (in all intermediate categories). As the number of intermediate teams entering playoffs declines, the number of commercial, recreational and old-timer clubs continues to rise. Despite this trend, no one is predicting the death of intermediate hockey. Anyone who has visited a cold rink in a small Alberta town with an intermediate hockey club knows that the game is alive and well and remains an exciting brand of hockey.

CHAPTER 5
JUNIOR HOCKEY

By the start of World War I it was time to form a junior category of hockey. Until then, hockey had been very much an adult game. Many of the players had come from eastern Canada where the game had an earlier start than in the west. But by 1914 Alberta had a new generation of home grown hockey players.

Junior hockey started officially in Alberta on November 7, 1914 at the AAHA annual meeting at Edmonton's YMCA. Only a few new teams were formed that year, but it provided an opportunity for younger players not quite good enough to play for intermediate or senior teams. It also ensured that hockey would not die in Alberta when men volunteered for duty in World War I.

Junior hockey had a low profile in Alberta until the mid 1920's. Then, in 1926 the Calgary Canadians won that city's first and only Memorial Cup, the highest award in junior hockey in Canada. It was the first national championship in the history of Alberta hockey.

In the Depression junior hockey was anything but depressed. Junior hockey had been mostly a southern Alberta pastime. But in the 30's Edmonton teams came on strong and helped make junior hockey a truly provincial category. The status of junior hockey improved consistently; even though it was the Depression fans turned out to support junior teams. Fans realized that some day their favourite junior players just might be starring in the NHL.

Junior hockey had its major breakthrough during World War II when NHL teams began direct sponsorship of junior clubs. Sponsorship bred excellence. The Edmonton Oil Kings under the sponsorship of the Detroit Red Wing organization became synonymous with junior hockey in western Canada for over two decades beginning in the 50's. Alberta has only won the Memorial Cup three times and the Oil Kings have won it twice.

But NHL sponsorship did not help to broaden the base of junior hockey in Alberta. On the contrary, the Edmonton Oil Kings so dominated junior hockey that Alberta became a one team province in that category. For half of their reign the Oil Kings did not have a junior league to play in. In order to extend the junior base the Alberta Junior Hockey League was formed in the 1960's.

The formation of the Alberta Junior Hockey League led ultimately to the division of junior hockey in the province. Top-ranked teams such as the Oil Kings and the Calgary Centennials played in Tier 1 and shot for the Memorial Cup. Teams in the AJHL became Tier 2 and competed for the right to represent Alberta in Centennial Cup playoffs. The Red Deer Rustlers have won the Centennial Cup twice and the Spruce Grove Mets once.

Junior age limits have been hotly debated over the years. Maximums have ranged from 19 to 21 years of age. Many believe that the changes have usually benefitted professional leagues more than junior hockey leagues.

Today it is in the interest of the NHL to draft more junior players than ever and at a younger age. With 21 team rosters to fill it is no surprise that the draft age keeps dropping. Now the draft age is 18.

Eddie Poulin, Jimmy Condon, Leo Le Clerc, Ed Bruchet, Scotty Munro, Bill Hunter, Ed Chynoweth. These are a few of the names to watch for in any history of Alberta junior hockey.

The Edmonton Beavers became the first Alberta junior champions in the spring of 1915. They played in what was called the Junior Alberta Amateur Hockey Association League with Edmonton clubs. Games were played at Diamond Park and the South Side Rinks. Besides the Beavers the league included the Journal, Crescents, Rink Rats from the South Side and the News Boys Band. The Beavers won their league and were declared the first Alberta Junior Provincial champions.

Interest in junior hockey at the beginning and throughout World War I was low as players of age were also old enough to serve in the armed forces. As a result no champion was declared for 1916.

In 1917, the junior title was won by the Calgary Crystals (also known as the Crystal Juniors). They defeated Medicine Hat in a two-game-total-goal series, 13-4. Despite an 8-0 loss in Calgary, Medicine Hat made a strong showing in the second match but lost 5-4 before a packed rink of enthusiastic spectators at home.

The next two years of junior hockey were won by default as no challenge from other teams was made. In 1918 the St. Mary's Club of Calgary and in 1919, the Calgary Crystals were declared champions. Andy Baxter's Crystals did win the Intermediate Championship of Calgary after a season of undefeated play.

Finally by 1920 the first Alberta junior winner played outside the province in search of the Abbott Cup for Western Canada. The Calgary Monarchs defeated the Vancouver Blue Birds 8-0 and 1-0 to win the first junior championship series between Alberta and British Columbia by 9-0. The Monarchs advanced only to lose to the Selkirk Fishermen 8-2 and tie 3-3. Especially outstanding for Calgary in the second game was future Hall of Famer Cecil 'Tiny' Thompson who stopped 41 shots.

Calgary continued to be the center for junior hockey in 1921 as the Calgary Beavers challenged for the Abbott Cup. They were known as the Canadian Pacific Railway Beavers but when they played the Regina Vics a name change to Calgary Beavers was made as they felt they represented all of Calgary. The Regina Vics proved superior with 5-3 and 6-3 wins at home to eliminate the Beavers.

The following year Medicine Hat became the victims of the Calgary Hustlers. The Hustlers won the first game 7-2 and then demolished the Hat 22-0 to advance against the Regina Pats. In a close playoff the Hustlers lost 7-6 in the two-game-total-goal series.

Compared to junior clubs of the future the money needed for operations was relatively low. No record of the total budget was found, but the Hustlers did receive a cheque for $150.00 for expenses to play in Regina. A cheque in the fall to clear up the account for $34.00 was received as well. The Hustler club was very pleased with both transactions. (By comparison, the Wainwright Junior 'B' Bisons of the 1983-84 operated on a budget of over $54,000.00 a year while Junior 'A' clubs from the AJHL budget an average of $125,000 and the WHL teams can go up to $500,000.)

CALGARY CANADIANS 1922-23

Top row (l to r): Johnny Loucks, Johnny Gleason, Art Howard. Fourth row: Stewart Adams, Berg Irving. Third row: Leo Murphy, Jack McKay. Second row: Vic Ripley, Herbie Lewis, Pete Mitchell. Bottom: George Lynch (secretary), Eddie Poulin (manager), Lou Doll (chairman).

Photo courtesy of A. Lottess

CALGARY — A HOT BED OF JUNIOR HOCKEY

The 1922-23 season was a turning point for the development of junior hockey. Calgary continued to be a hotbed of growth when Gene "Musty" McGill, Lloyd Turner, Eddie Poulin and Jimmy Condon (owner of the Palace of Eats — 8th Avenue and 1st Street West) of Calgary promoted junior hockey in the southern city. McGill was responsible for the 1922-23 formation of a three team Calgary Junior League which comprised the Maple Leafs, Hustlers and Canadians. (Stu Peppard, uncle of actor George Peppard, later President of the AAHA, played for the Maple Leafs.)

The Calgary Canadians under Eddie Poulin won the Alberta crown and finally defeated the Regina Pats in the next round leading to the Abbott Cup. After losing the first game 3-1, the Canadians regrouped and won the second game 6-2 for a 7-5 total score victory. This was the first team from Alberta to be in the Abbott Cup final.

The Canadians lost their bid to play in the Memorial Cup final as the University of Manitoba Juniors won the two-game-total-goal series 10-7. To this point, this was the furthest any junior team from Alberta had advanced.

It got better in 1923-24 for the Calgary Canadians as they advanced one step further to the Memorial Cup final. In the Alberta round, the Coleman Canadians lost to the Canadians 7-5 and 10-3. Herbie Lewis and Vic Ripley scored three goals each in the series for the Canadians.

In the Abbott Cup final the Canadians became Alberta's first team to reach the Memorial Cup with a 7-6 two-game-total-goal win in overtime over the Regina Pats. This victory allowed them to play in the Canadian final against the Owen Sound Greyhounds. Two losses to the Greyhounds ended the Memorial Cup hopes of the Canadians.

CALGARY CANADIANS 1923-24

Photo courtesy of Glenbow Archives

Defenceman Johnny Loucks of the 1923-24 Canadians in a 1984 letter recalled the thrills of playing in the final and noted a major difference from teams of today:

Almost every team today is supplied with everything. We were supplied with a full uniform, skates and sticks. Before I played for Eddie Poulins' juniors, you bought your own.

The Canadians were the Alberta representatives in 1924-25. To get to the Abbott Cup playoffs the Calgary club won 16 games in a row. The Saskatchewan representatives, the Regina Pats, ended the streak with wins of 2-1 and 4-3. These games were played in Winnipeg as there was no artificial ice in Saskatchewan or Alberta. Believe it or not, Ripley (as in Vic) scored all four goals in the series for Calgary.

CALGARY CANADIANS WIN MEMORIAL CUP

BY AL MAKI, sports writer
(Excerpts from the April 8, 1984 Calgary Herald)

Calgary is today justly proud of a clean cut combination of young athletes all products of local hockey, whose record is one that will go down in sporting history.

So read the lead story on the sports page of the Calgary "Daily Herald", Saturday, March 27, 1926, when Calgary Canadians fought back to defeat Kingston Juniors in their best-of-three Dominion Championship. It marked the one and only time this City has ever won the Memorial Cup. (Scores were 2-4, 3-2, and 3-2.)

In 1926, silent movies at the Palace Theatre cost $.40. The average income was $100 a month. And Calgary, for all its 65,000 people, had only one covered rink.

Their reputation (the Canadians) was enhanced further when the majority of the team went on to play in the National Hockey League. Some, like Paul Thompson — who played on three Stanley Cup winners and was the Chicago Black Hawks leading scorer for six consecutive seasons — went on to stardom. Today only five members of the Canadians are still alive. Three in Calgary, one in Vancouver and another in Florida. All agree their team was unique in more ways than just the Memorial Cup precedent.

We had talent, we had guts, we had determination, recalls 76 year old Irvine Frew. We all wanted to win something awful. I watch hockey today and it's a different style, everything is happening but nothing is happening.

We were a unit, says forward Joe McGoldrick, We worked hard, we had to come from behind to beat Saskatoon, the Tammamy Tigers (from Winnipeg) and Kingston. Stu Peppard (one of Alberta's greatest hockey organizers) played against the Canadians and remembered the key to the team's success. Coach Ed Poulin picked his players in October and didn't change one all winter. They played together game in and game out. Oddly enough they were all local boys.

Don MacFadyen, 77, living in Pompano Beach, Florida says the Canadians were "a hell bent for leather group," bouyed by goalie Sam Timmins. "He was the basis on which we operated. You have to be crazy to be a good goalie and Sam was a real scrapper. With Frew and Gordon Savage on defence, Chuck Dunn and Thompson we had every element."

Four days after their Memorial Cup win, the Canadians were honored with a Civic reception. More than 9,000 people attended and each team member was presented with a gold watch.

I haven't forgotten that day, says Thompson. I was just a kid but I was thrilled. I'd rank it right up there with playing in my first Stanley Cup. Looking back on it all, I don't know how any of us could have imagined how important winning the Memorial Cup really was.

CALGARY CANADIANS 1924-25

Top row: Lou Doll, Johnny Gleason, Eddie Poulin, Vic Ripley, Pete Egan. Middle row: Ralph Manarey, Stewart Adams, Berg Irving, Pete Mitchell, George McTeer. Bottom: Donnie McFadyen, Ernie Lewis, Joe McGoldrick, Paul Thompson, Bert Taylor.

Photo courtesy of Glenbow Archives

In the 1926-27 season the Blairmore Tuxis Juniors won the 'B' Class Alberta Junior Championship. In overtime they defeated the Edmonton Navy in Blairmore 4-3. Under coach Rev. W. Young, the Crowsnest Pass squad challenged the Calgary Canadians, the 'A' champions of Alberta, for the right to represent the province in interprovincial playoffs.

Young's team then surprised the 1926 Memorial Cup champions Canadians 3-1. They lost the second game 1-0 but won the total-goal-series. It was a significant victory as the Tuxis became the first junior team outside of Calgary or Edmonton to leave the province to try for the Abbott Cup. The Regina Pats dropped the Tuxis 6-2 and 8-3 to win the round 14-5. The only championship won by the Canadians during the year was the Men's Hockey Championship at the Banff Winter Carnival when they defeated General Supplies of Calgary 4-1.

Now under sponsorship of the Blairmore Legion (formally Tuxis), Rev. Young repeated as coach of the 1927-28 Alberta Junior champions. This time they won the first interprovincial round against the Vernon Rotarians and then lost 13-1 in two games to the Regina Monarchs. Junior hockey continued in the Crowsnest Pass region but no champions appear until the 1940's when the Lethbridge Native Sons represent Alberta.

In March of 1929 "the roaring twenties" ended in Junior hockey as the Calgary Candians regained their previ-ous form to win the Alberta crown. The southern part of the province was captured over Bellevue. The Canadi-ans then scored two straight wins over the Edmonton Eskimo Juniors to represent the province. They met the Nelson Cubs.

CALGARY CANADIANS 1925-26

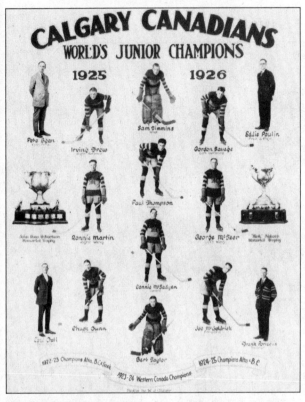

Top row (l to r): Pete Egan (vice president), Irving Frew, Sam Timmins, Gordon Savage, Eddie Poulin (manager and president). Third row: Ronnie Martin, Paul Thompson, Ge-orge McTeer. Second row: Lou Doll (business manager), Chuck Quinn, Donnie McFadyen, Joe McGoldrick, Frank Porteous (trainer). Bottom: Bert Taylor.

Photo courtesy of W.J. Oliver and Glenbow Archives

In the *Calgary Herald* seats were advertized at $1.00 for box seats and 50 cents for general admission. Lorne Carr, later Toronto Maple Leaf, scored 3 goals in the fi-nal 7-3 win over Nelson to advance against the Regina Pats. The Pats became the next victims after a 2-2 tie and 5-0 win for Calgary.

In the Abbott Cup final against Elmwood Millionaires, the Canadians seemed safely ahead by 2 goals with only 8 minutes of play left. However, in 3 minutes and 30 se-conds, the Canadians gave up 3 markers and the series. Calgary was favorite as it had won 16 straight games be-fore the Elmwood series.

In 1930, the junior hockey championship for Alberta stayed in Calgary. Bill Lewis, sports editor of the *Edmon-ton Bulletin,* described the power of the Canadians on March 5, 1930:

> *Playing championship hockey throughout the three periods, Eddie Poulin's Calgary Cana-dians annexed the Provincial Junior title and earned the right to represent Alberta in the Memorial Cup playdowns here last night when they skated to their second successive triumph over Barney Stanley's Edmonton-Poolers — In handing the Poolers their second straight defeat of the series last night, the Cal-garians proved themselves a worthy represen-tative of the Province in the hunt for the Dominion Junior Hockey laurels, and effec-tively quashed any doubt that may have ex-isted in the minds of hockey followers as to their real class. (Scores were 6-1 and 10-1)*

Dave "Sweeney" Schriner, another future Toronto Maple Leaf, played alongside Carr and it seemed to be a team that could defeat all opponents. In the next round the Canadians edged out the Vancouver Ex-King Ge-orges 2-1 in each game to win the round 4-2. Saskatchewan's "Silver Fox", Al Ritchie then, coached the Regina Pats to 2-0 and 4-0 games to end the 1930 Memorial Cup hopes of the Calgary Canadians.

Eddie Poulins' Canadians continued in 1930-31 to win their eighth provincial crown in ten years as it defeated Edmonton Southsiders. The Canadians saw history start to repeat from the previous year as they took two straight games from the Vancouver Ex-King Georges to win the series 6-2. Again, against the Regina Pats the Canadians were shutout 4-0 and 1-0.

In the 4-0 Pat win, Poulin noticed the Regina goalkeeper's pads. A measurement was done causing the pads to be reduced from 11" to 10". Even this tactic failed as Canadian stars like Schriner, Hube Gooder and Peter Paul were unable to score.

Edmonton's chances for the Provincial Junior Hockey Championship of 1931-32 were spoiled when Jimmy Condons' Calgary Jimmies defeated the NADP (Northern Alberta Dairy Pool) Poolers 4-1. The Poolers were coached by Barney Stanley (former Chicago Black Hawk coach and player with Edmonton Eskimos, Calgary Tigers, Vancouver Millionaires) and managed by Art Potter (later President of AAHA and CAHA). Even players Neil Colville, Louis Trudle, Art Wiebe and Andy Maloney for the Poolers could only beat Jimmy goalkeeper Bert Marshall once in the final game.

The Jimmies met their match in Charlie McCool's Saskatoon Wesleys who won 2-1 and 4-1. "Peg" O'Neil, left winger of the Wesleys (now living in Edmonton) stole the show. John "Lefty" Ducey, then of the Edmonton Bulletin described O'Neil as the answer to a hockey manager's prayer. He wrote O'Neil was "solid of frame and a strong, powerful skater, with a bullet shot, the Irishman was a treat to watch."

BLAIRMORE TUXIS 1926-27

Back row (l to r): Jock McAndrew (trainer), Eric Hornquist (defence and spare goalie), Jolette Houbregs (defence), Alfred "Gusty" Vangotsinoven (defence), Walter Scott (manager). Front row (l to r): Jimmie McVey (left wing), Jack Oakes (centre), Dave Kemp (goalie), Idris Evans (right wing), Norman Anderson (left wing and defence).

Photo courtesy of Gushel Studios, Blairmore and Coleman

In 1933 it appeared the Edmonton Canadians would win the province for the north. Fred Layetzke in goal, Alex Stevenson, Louis and Morey Rimstad, Bill Carse, "Bunny" Dame and Oscar Purrin were enough to win the first game 5-3 but the Calgary Jimmies tied up the series by virtue of a 4-3 win. The provincial final was dramatic as the Jimmie's Jerry Thompson took Howey Hill's pass in the third overtime period of the third game to give Calgary the 1933 junior championship.

In interprovincial playoffs the Jimmies found the Trail Smokeaters easy when they scored a 12-2 two-game-total-goal victory. Once again, the Regina Pats won the Abbott Cup for Western Canada when the Jimmies lost the round 4-3 in overtime. Les Cunningham, a former Jimmy, scored on a pass from Murray Armstrong (later Regina Pat and University of Denver coach) to send the Jimmys back to Calgary.

Except for the first year of junior hockey when the Edmonton Beavers won the province and in the 1927 and 1928 playoffs with Blairmore, Calgary junior teams proved their superiority. In the 30's hockey organizations such as the Edmonton Athletic Club, Canadians, Maple Leafs, and the Southside started an Edmonton domination in junior hockey for most of four decades. Stu Peppard recalls that Calgary junior hockey was basically operated by one owner and in the long run "an organization can usually do better".

In Edmonton the EAC's were led by Art Potter, Ken and Eric Duggan, Ken Montgomery and Clarence Campbell. The Canadians had Jim McAdie, Fred Lupul, Smythe Flemming and Ken Henry. The Southside prominent organizers were Tom Green, Monty Ford, Pep Moon and Red Turner while the Maple Leafs had Henry White, Ted Allard and Jimmy and Bert Crockett in their early years.

BLAIRMORE CANADIAN LEGION 1927-28

Back row (l to r): Jack McAndrew (trainer), Charlie Joyce (utility), Jolette Houbregs (defence), Norman Anderson (defence), Walter Scott (coach). Front row (l to r): Idris Evans (right wing), Jimmy McVey (left wing), Dave Kemp (goal), James "Puffy" Kemp (right wing), Jack Oakes (centre).
Photo courtesy of Gushul Studios, Blairmore and Coleman

In Calgary the Buffaloes were formed later and were the main organization for years. The high degree of competition in Edmonton because of more groups of individuals working together was a successful formula for junior hockey in Edmonton.

The Edmonton Athletic Club (EAC's) came into prominence in 1933-34. They advanced out of Alberta and toppled the Trail Smokeaters 12-0 and 7-0. The family combinations of Morey and Walter "Fats" Rimstad and Neil and Mac Colville were prime factors in the overwhelming victory. The EAC's then soundly defeated the Sasktoon Wesleys 6-0 and lost 5-4 but won theround 10-5. The Wesleys were led by Doug Bentley and Jack Leswick.

Walter "Babe" Pratt and the Port Arthur West Ends constituted the opposition for Edmonton in the Abbot Cup final. Fred Layetzke was unbeatable in the 4-0 second game shut out. He stopped 47 shots to earn Edmonton its first western trophy and its first try for the Memorial Cup.

Toronto's St. Michael's College and the EAC's played in Winnipeg because Alberta still had no artificial ice. Edmonton was shut out 5-0 and then 6-4 in overtime and St. Michael's College won the 1934 championship.

CALGARY CANADIANS 1929-30

Top row (l to r): Mickey McConnell, Frank Porteous (trainer), Pat Hill, Eddie Poulin (president, manager, coach), Peter Paul, Tom McKenna (secretary treasurer), Dave "Sweeney Schriner. Bottom: Hank Dyck, Sing Johnson, Bill McKay, Pat Aitken, Les Moss, Lorne Carr.

Photo courtesy of Calgary Exhibition and Stampede

CALGARY JIMMIES 1932-33

Standing (l to r): A. Laven, C. Sorenson, R. Ferguson, J. Thomson, A.J. McTeer (manager), J. Spencer, M. Snowdon, A. Cronie, G. Langley, G. Gardiner. Sitting (l to r): L. Wade, E. Wares, V. Bibby (trainer), Pat Aitken (coach), J. Condon (president), C. Palfrey (secretary), H. Hill, J. Forsey.

Photo courtesy of W.J. Oliver and Glenbow Archives

EDMONTON ATHLETIC CLUB 1933-34

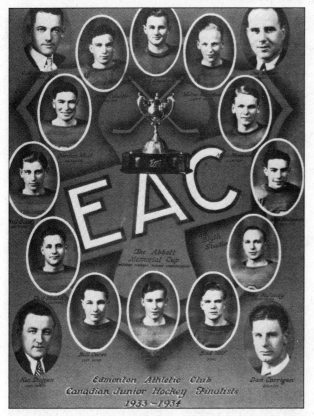

Top row (l to r): Colin Martindale (manager), Neil Colville, Fred Layetzki, Walter Rimstad, Joe Baker (secretary treasurer). Fourth row: Gordon Watt, Morey Rimstad. Third row: Bill Gauf, Alex McSporran. Second row: Ted Heath, Andy Maloney. Front row: Ken Duggan (assistant coach), Bill Carse, Mac Colville, Bud Wolf, Dan Carrigan (coach).

Photo courtesy of Edmonton Archives

In 1934-35 another Edmonton junior team, known as the Edmonton Safeway Canadians had a titanic struggle against the Edmonton Southside Athletics. Of all the series covered in *Alberta on Ice* this is one of the most incredible. Lefty Grove's Canadians almost failed to make it out of the Edmonton city playoffs.

After game three of the best of three the two clubs played 275 minutes and failed to break the deadlock. In game four it took the Southside just 47 seconds in the third period to score two goals to tie the game at 2-2. Three more overtime periods of ten minutes were played but to no avail as the score remained at two apiece. In the fifth game, Pep Moon's A's won 2-1 on a goal by Doug Hargrave. This tied the series at a win and a loss for each club and three ties. By this time interest was great as 5,000 fans watched the sixth game. The Edmonton Canadians won 4-2.

To eliminate the Southside the series took 470 minutes or the equal of almost eight games (including overtimes) to decide the best of three. For the series the referees were either Clarence Campbell, later President of the National Hockey League or Johnny Melynk, uncle of Jerry Melynk, later a Detroit Red Wing player and now a Philadelphia Flyer scout.

The Edmonton Canadians then won the Alberta championship and played the Saskatoon Westleys in action leading to the Abbott Cup. Fan interest remained high. Five thousand fans watched the Canadians lose 6-2 and 4-0 to the Westleys. This ended the 1934-35 season for Edmonton.

The junior championship moved south in 1935-36. In the southern final the Calgary Rangers defeated the Medicine Hat New Club Tigers 4-2 in Calgary after a 1-1 tie in Medicine Hat. The final game had an oddity as both goal judges were replaced. The second goal judge was removed for frantically waving signals to the referee and holding up play.

The Rangers won the province over the Edmonton Canadians 3-2 and then 2-1 in two overtime periods. The Trail Tigers of British Columbia eliminated the Rangers even though Calgary won the first game 6-0. Losses of 5-3 and 2-1 in the next two games sent the Rangers to the side lines. Calgary did not win a provincial 'A' junior championship until 1949.

Bill Ruff's 1936-37 Edmonton Gas Rangers started their Edmonton final poorly as the EAC's humiliated them 5-0. A 3-2 comeback win for the Rangers forced a third game. In the final game with three minutes left, the Rangers Pete Yanew scored from Don Stanley when two EAC's were in the penalty box to advance the Edmonton club.

Before 2,200 fans in Medicine Hat, the Rangers defeated the Tigers 3-1 in the third and deciding game to win the Alberta title. Next, against the Saskatoon Wesley's forward Sid Abel and goalie Charlie Rayner proved too much as the Gas Rangers lost 4-0 and 5-1. In game one Abel scored all four goals.

To win the 1937-38 Alberta championship the Edmonton Athletic Club won two straight over the Calgary Knights of Columbus. K of C Goalkeeper, Frank McCool (later Toronto Maple Leaf) kept Calgary in the first game and lost 4-3 in overtime. Calgary was no match in the second game as they lost 10-2. Then a decisive 8-0 win over the Trail Tigers advanced the EAC's against the Saskatoon Chiefs. A 6-3 win in game three gave Edmonton the right to play the St. Boniface Seals for the Abbott Cup. It turned out that the EAC's would have to look forward to the following year as the Seals won the third game 6-5.

Cecil "Tiger" Goldstick, an Edmonton sportsman of many years, felt the EAC's were ready to go past the Seals into the Memorial Cup final. After the opening win by Edmonton, Tiger (now of CFRN Edmonton) bet

Top (l to r, in circle): W. Batchelor, O. Sollayich, E. Donald, L. Lemieux, E. Shamlock, T. Allard, E. Munroe, R. Haxby, H. Robertson, A. Lemieux, M. Flett, E. Ward. Team management: W. (Bill) Ruff (manager), Sandy Robertson (secretary), E. Franks (trainer), Lefty Grove (coach).

Photo courtesy of A. Blyth Studio and Provincial Archives

Clarence "Shrimp" Moher, brother of EAC coach Stan, that the EAC would win the second game. The 8-3 loss in the second game resulted in Tiger having to push a peanut about 150 yards along Edmonton's main street, Jasper Avenue. History shows Tiger should have placed his bet the following year.

In 1938-39, the EAC's who had players from the previous year advanced out of Alberta when they scored a 1-0 win over the Calgary Jimmies. It became more obvious Edmonton was a powerful team as they shellacked the Trail Tigers 16-3 and 14-1. Edmonton then breezed past the Moose Jaw Canucks in three straight to play the Brandon Elks who featured future Boston Bruin "Sugar" Jim Henry in goal.

Dr. George Hardy, of Edmonton (see story in Hot Stove League), the President of the Canadian Amateur Hockey Association wrote some personal notes during the Brandon series. From the University of Alberta Archives and courtesy of his daughter, Mrs. Margaret Simpson, Dr. Hardy described the suspension he gave to George Agar of the EAC's in game two of the Brandon series.

Suddenly right in front of me an Edmonton player (Edmonton's George Agar) *flashed across the ice and brought his stick down so hard on the head of a Brandon player* (Chuck Taylor) *that the stick shivered. The Brandon player fell to the ice. Play was stopped. The Brandon player was carried off and the Edmonton player penalized. The game went on. Then my work* (President of the CAHA) *commenced with considerable excitement. The CAHA doesn't mind if players use fists occasionally, it's good clean fun. But it frowns on sticks as the method of offence. Normally, the Edmonton player would have been suspended for six games. But, this was a important playoff series. Edmonton claimed*

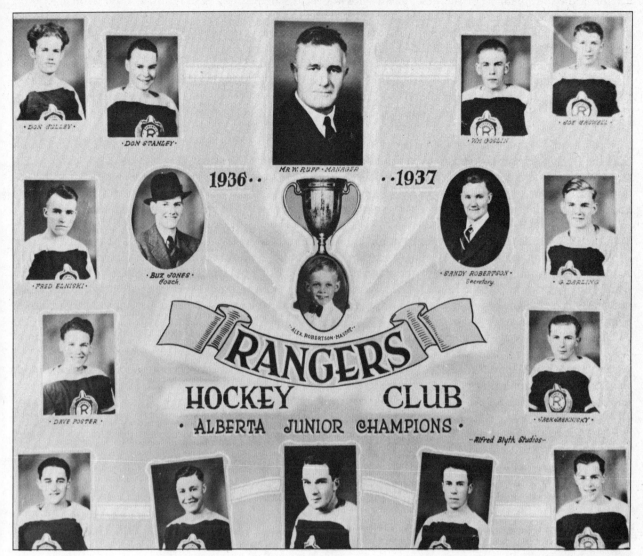

Top row (l to r): Don Cully, Don Stanley, Bill Ruff (manager), Bill Goslin, Joe Caswell. **Third row:** Fred Elniski, Buz Jones (coach), Alex Robertson (mascot), Sandy Robertson (secretary), G. Darling. **Second row:** Dave Foster, Jack Jacknisky. **Bottom:** B. Klingspoon, B. Maguire, Art Quinn, Pete Yanew, Allan McDonald.

Photo courtesy of A. Blyth and Provincial Archives

one game was equal to six in a regular season. Further, we all know that the Edmonton player had been "butt ended" before he made his assault...However, I set the penalty at a two game suspension. ...Edmonton without the suspended player lost by 5-0. All Edmonton must have been hanging over the radio. At any rate as soon as the game was over my phone began to ring. My errant anonymous fellow citizens called me every name they could lay their tongues on...It was demanded that I lift the remaining one game suspension. Fortunately for me, the Edmonton team, still without the suspended player, won the fourth game and ended the series.

The suspension terminated after the two games, and Agar was allowed to play in the Memorial Cup final.

After the victory over Brandon, Coach Lefty Grove and manager Charlie Smith took the EAC's east to play the Oshawa Generals. High humidity in Toronto and Billy "The Kid" Taylor of the Generals proved too much for Edmonton. The EAC's, also known as the Roamers by newspapers outside of Edmonton because of their affiliation with the New York Rangers, lost 9-4 in the first game. Billy Taylor (On March 9, 1947 Taylor of the New York Rangers and Don Gellinger of the Boston Bruins were suspended for life by the NHL for alleged gambling activities. The suspensions were lifted in 1970) ran riot through the Edmonton ranks as he scored five goals. In the second game, Taylor scored four goals and had five assists to give Oshawa a two game lead in the best of five series. A huge crowd of 11,698 in Maple Leaf Gardens watched Edmonton's Elmer Kreller shadow

Taylor in the third game. For the first time Taylor was held scoreless and as a result of Edmonton's 4-1 win, Kreller became known as "The Shadow".

Edmonton could not extend the series. Before 11,000 fans, Oshawa won the 1939 Memorial Cup as the McAtee brothers, Norm and Judd led the Generals to a 4-2 win and the cup.

The EAC's were the second Edmonton team to reach the Memorial Cup final. On the EAC's were Bobby Carse, Bruce MacKay, Ken "Beans" Reardon. Jack McGill, Cliff Kiburn, Dave Farmer, Bob Pentland, George "Sonny" Agar, Johnny Chad, Paul Steffes, Elmer "The Shadow" Kreller, Bud Foley, Harry Patrick, Harry Pardie, Harvey "Pug" Young and Marshall Darling.

Victories of 5-0 and 8-1 over the Calgary Hustlers gave the 1939-40 Alberta title to the EAC's. A 6-2 win over the Regina Abbott-Generals moved the EAC's into the Abbott Cup final. Regina was led by defenceman Grant Warwick (later playing-coach of the 1955 Penticton V's, World Hockey Champions) but still lost the series 3-1. The magic of the previous year was gone when the Kenora Thistles led by Charlie Rayner, Bill Juzda and Vic Lofvendahl tied Edmonton 2-2 to gain 6 points in the best of five series and eliminate the EAC's.

In the 1940-41 the EAC's continued to dominate Alberta junior hockey. Bud Foley, a 22 year old University of Alberta student and former EAC player coached the squad to its fourth straight Alberta championship. The Athletic Club, in interprovincial play, got off to a quick start with a 5-2 win over the Saskatoon Quakers. Forward Tony Leswick and goalie Russ Dertell led Saskatoon to a 3-1 win to tie the series even though Harold Laycoe, the Quaker's high scoring defenseman was out with tonsilitis. The next two wins of 6-5 and 2-1 for Saskatoon eliminated the EAC's.

The EAC's continued as a junior club until the late 40's but never again won the Alberta Junior championship.

The Edmonton Maple Leafs of 1941-42 continued Edmonton's domination in junior hockey. In Edmonton, the Leafs won a convincing 11-4 game over Calgary and then Johnny Black scored three goals for an 8-6 win and the right to represent Alberta. Steve Orlander then coached the Leafs past the Regina Abbotts 4-0 in the fifth game. Edmonton had two wins and two ties and one loss against Regina's Bill Warwick (later player for the 1955 Penticton V's and later President of the Sherwood Park Crusaders of the Alberta Junior Hockey League) who played for Regina.

In Winnipeg, the Portage La Prairie Terriers captured the Abbott Cup in three straight with a 7-6 win. For the Terriers it was their 22nd victory in a row. A major factor in the series loss was an injury to Edmonton's Ollie Dorohoy who had provided much of the Maple Leaf scoring thrust.

In 1943 the Edmonton Canadians defeated the Calgary Royals to win the provincial title. Hal Dean, sports editor of the "Edmonton Bulletin" wrote the following on the Canadians:

> Junior hockey has always been well supported in this city and making due allowance for the handicap under which it has had to be played, on account of the loss of the Arena, there is no reason to suppose that there should be any great difference this season...(Edmonton Arena became Manning #3 Depot for World War II).
> The youngest team to participate in the playdowns in the history of Edmonton hockey with the possible exception of the famous Colville, Carse and Rimstad combination, the Canadians are a strong club from the goal out.
> Bill Lancaster, 18 years old, is rated as the finest goalie Edmonton junior representatives ever possessed. Bob Causgrove and Glenn Gray, both eligible for juvenile competition, constitute a formidable defence and Earl Chisholm and Frank Popovich are two very capable performers.
> Of the forwards Ken Cox and Jim Fleming are also eligible for juvenile hockey and Frank Baer and Hassey Young are both only 18 years of age. This will be the last year in junior for Vic Kuzyk, Fred Smitten, Jock Tennant and Don Dewar.

The young squad then eliminated Trail 5-2 and 4-3 in a best-of-three series. The Canadians had high expectations but a 19 day wait to play the Saskatoon Quakers did not help them. Saskatoon's Gerry "Doc" Couture scored each winning goal to give the Quakers 3-2 and 4-3 wins and advance them against the Winnipeg Rangers.

The provincial champions of 1943-44 did not represent Alberta in the next round. World War II caused the southern winner, the Calgary Royals, to withdraw due to players enlisting. The two Edmonton teams, the Canadians and HMCS Nonsuch played in the final. In the fourth game of the best-of-five, Gerry Dea scored three goals to give HMCS Nonsuch the crown. Due to military travel restrictions the Navy did not advance. Jack Moss

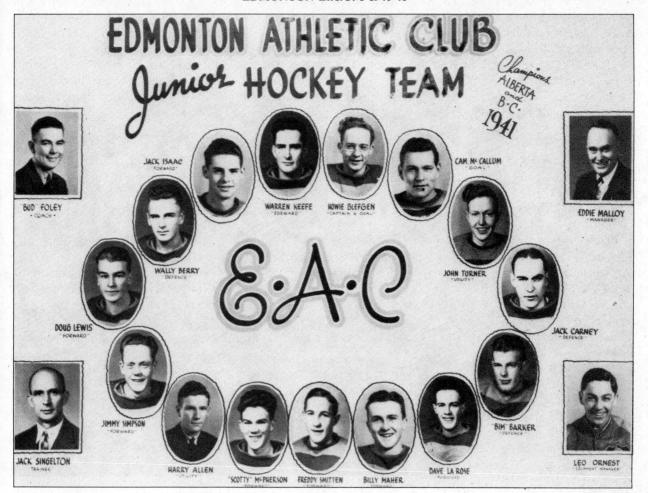

EDMONTON ATHLETIC CLUB
Junior HOCKEY TEAM

Champions
ALBERTA
and
B.C.
1941

E·A·C

BUD FOLEY
- COACH -

JACK ISAAC
- FORWARD -

WARREN KEEFE
FORWARD

HOWIE BLEFGEN
"CAPTAIN & GOAL"

CAM. McCALLUM
- GOAL -

EDDIE MALLOY
- MANAGER -

WALLY BERRY
DEFENCE

JOHN TURNER
- UTILITY -

DOUG LEWIS
- FORWARD -

JACK CARNEY
DEFENCE

JACK SINGELTON
TRAINER

JIMMY SIMPSON
"FORWARD"

HARRY ALLEN
- UTILITY -

"SCOTTY" McPHERSON
FORWARD

FREDDY SMITTEN
FORWARD

BILLY MAHER
FORWARD

DAVE LA ROSE
FORWARD

"BIM" BARKER
DEFENCE

LEO ORNEST
EQUIPMENT MANAGER

Photo courtesy of Edmonton Archives

of Vegreville, President of the AAHA announced that Joe Brown's CAC's would play Trail. Trail took out the Canadians in two straight games 6-3 and 6-1.

Bill Gadsby (later NHL Hall of Famer) who had played previously for Harold Brandreth's Tuxedo Park Midgets and Avenue Grill Juveniles of Calgary came to Edmonton in 1944-45 to help lead the Edmonton Canadians to victory over the Calgary Avenue Grill Juniors. The Canadians then met an obstacle in the Moose Jaw Canucks. The Canuck's Bert Olmstead and Metro Prystai helped defeat the Canadians in four straight of the best-of-seven.

In 1945-46 teams played a more defensive game a shorter schedule than today. The individual scoring title in the Edmonton Junior Hockey League was won by John Rypien who scored 18 goals and had 16 assists for 34 points. Bill Black also a Canadian had 29 points. Bud MacPherson, then a left winger and future Montreal Canadian defenseman led the league in goals with 22 and was third in points. Bill Gadsby was fourth with 14 goals and 12 assists for 26 points.

The Canadians advanced further in the 1945-46 season when John "The Milkman" Rypien and Gadsby helped to defeat the Naniamo Clippers. The Canadians evened up their loss of the previous season by edging the Moose Jaw Canucks and goalkeeper Emile "The Cat" Francis 4-3 before 6,672 fans in the final in Regina. Edmonton thought it was Memorial Cup bound. In the Abbott Cup final they won the first game at home against the Winnipeg Monarchs. The Monarchs then won the remainder of the games to win the western title.

Lethbridge for its first time became the provincial champions in junior hockey in 1946-47. The Native Sons dropped the first two games of a best-of-five against the Edmonton Canadians but then won three straight. A

Top row (l to r): P.O. Crockett (trainer), S.Lt. A. Lorriman (sports officer), Lt. Cmdr. J.A. Dawson (commanding officer), S.Lt. T. Davies (coach), S.Lt. Stevenson (manager), Ldg. S.B.A. Hurl. Bottom row: P. Shirvell (right wing), A. Boyco (centre), J. Slattery (left wing), K. Younger (captain, centre), B. Hanarhan (right wing), J. Frew (defence), J. Ingram (defence), G. Dea (left wing), B. Lancaster (goal). Missing: Sammy Samson, Frank Quigley.   *Photo courtesy of Edmonton Archives*

crowd of 3,140 in Lethbridge watched their stars Vic Stasiuk, Eddie "the Pistol" Dorohoy, Bill Ramsden and Louis Holmes (nephew of Edmonton's Louis Holmes) win the final 4-2.

The Native Sons won their first interprovincial round over the Trail Smokeaters three games to one. However, Metro Prystai, who assisted on all 5 Moose Jaw Canuck goals, ended the season for Lethbridge in a 5-1 win. Even though the Sons lost three straight to the Canucks considerable interest was built up in Lethbridge for 1948.

SCOTTY MUNRO'S SONS OF 1947-48

BY DON PILLING, former editor, Lethbridge Herald

The season 1947-48 will always be remembered as the year Lethbridge came so near, yet so far, in capturing its first National Junior championship and possession of the Memorial Cup. That was the year, for the first time in history that the Western Champion was determined on an Eastern Canadian ice surface. Ed Bruchet's Lethbrige Native Sons, with Scotty Munro at the coaching helm, was a powerhourse in Western Canada junior circles. So were the Port Arthur Bruins, and it was only fitting that they would eventually meet for the Western Championship.

The Native Sons, let by their high-scoring line of Eddie Dorohoy, Freddie Brown and Bill Ramsden, completely dominated the Southern Alberta Junior League and eliminated the Calgary Buffaloes in four straight games in the southern final. Wetaskiwin Canadians,transplanted that year from Edmonton, were also no match for the team that Bruchet built. They too, fell four straight 4-2, 5-1, 8-3, and 6-1. The Native Sons were half way home, and Lethbridge hockey fans were beginning to taste their first Memorial Cup conquest in history.

Moose Jaw's stubborn Canucks, sparked by Jackie McLeod, Jim Bedard, Hugh Coflin and Larry Popein, pushed the Native Sons to six games before succumbing. Sports editor Dave Dryburgh of the Regina "Leader

EDMONTON CANADIANS 1944-45

Top row: L. McLachlin (secretary), Val Berg (second vice-president), K.F. Blackmer (president), Ken Henry (first vice-president), Gordon Campbell (treasurer). **Sixth row:** Bob Murdock (director), F. Hinchberger (director), Smythe Fleming (director), Bill Gray (director), Herb Shires (director). **Fifth row:** Clarence Motter (coach), John McIntyre (trainer). **Fourth row:** Don Murray, S. Hergert. **Third row:** W. (Bill) Gadsby, Jim Fleming, Bernie O'Connor, Ken Anderson, Leo Sorsa. **Second row:** Don Campbell, Ray Spencer, Julian Sawchuck, A. Kaleta, Leo LeClair, Eddy Thomas. **Bottom:** Cy Thomas, Doug Anderson, Jim Slugg, Vince Bannon, Johnny Rypien.   *Photo courtesy of Edmonton Archives*

Post'' called the Sons one of the most polished junior squads he'd ever seen. The Sons ended the series in a flourish, trimming the Saskatchewan Champions 7-3 in overtime, before 5,200 fans at Calgary's Victoria Arena, the largest crowd of the era to ever see a junior game in Calgary.

A special train was chartered for the Calgary game, and 600 Native Son supporters paid $5.00 (hockey ticket included) to journey to Calgary to see the Sons take another giant step forward in their Memorial Cup bid. A year long plan was coming into place with the Sons now pitted against Port Arthur in the Western final.

The Native Sons won the first two games at home and Lethbridge had never seen such a demand for tickets for a sporting event, or anything else, for that matter. The Lethbridge Arena (which burned to the ground in 1971) held 3,100 and it was jammed to the rafters for both games. Ed Bruchet felt he could have sold 15,000 tickets for the two games.

The third and fourth games, and fifth, if necessary, were scheduled for Port Arthur, and the remaining two, if needed, in Winnipeg. Hockey fever was also running rampant in Port Arthur. Like Lethbridge, the Lakeland city had never laid claim to a Memorial Cup.

Bruins won the third game 7-4, and Native Sons went ahead 3-1 in the series when they won game four 5-4. Port Arthur took the next one 4-2, and that's when trouble flared.

The sixth and seventh games were originally scheduled for Winnipeg, but due to a mixup in dates, the Winnipeg Arena had been booked for an ice show. No ice, at least for hockey purposes, was available. The CAHA ordered the final two games to be played in Port Arthur. Ed Bruchet rebelled and said he would pull his club out of the series unless the series was shifted to neutral ice.

Bruchet was not bluffing. The Native Sons were packed and train reservations made for the return trip to Lethbridge. The CAHA had a dilemma on its hands. After an all night bargaining session, Bruchet agreed to play the sixth game in Port Arthur provided the seventh game, if necessary was moved out of Port Arthur. The CAHA agreed and booked Maple Leaf Gardens in Toronto for the seventh game.

The Bruins sent the series into a seventh and deciding game by winning 6-4 on 2 late goals by Rudy Migay and Bart Bradley. Toronto was the final stop for the showdown.

Native Sons were on the limp. Ace centre Eddie Dorohoy, one of the real sparks in the Native Sons success story of the year, was sent spinning to the sidelines with a knee injury. Captain Slim Lavell was hobbled by a creaky ankle, and the wear and tear of the bitterly-fought first six games of the series had taken its toll in other areas. With 1,200 fans on hand in Maple Leaf Gardens, the Lethbridge Memorial Cup dream was shattered.

Port Arthur with Danny Lewicki leading the way, destroyed the Native Sons 11-1. And they went on to win their first Memorial Cup by bouncing Barrie Flyers four straight in the National final.

Despite the shellacking the Native Sons suffered in the final game of the Western final, it was still a year that has a special place in Lethbridge hockey history. They played 63 league, playoff and exhibition games, winning 50, losing 10 and tying 3. Six of their defeats came along the Memorial Cup playoff trail. The Dorohoy-Brown-Ramsden line administered many sunburns on rival goal tenders during that season, collecting 418 points in the 63 games played. Ramsden scored an unbelievable 107 goals. Dorohoy collected 86 assists.

Top (l to r): Lloyd McLaughlin (assistant manager), Ron Mathews, John Rypien, Bill Pettinger, Ken Henry (general manager), Don Robinson, Vince Bannon, Bill Gadsby, Earl Robertson (coach). Second row (l to r): Harry Groves, Leo Lucchini, Doug Anderson, Dick Sissons, Leo Sorsa. Bottom (l to r): Don Slater, Cy Thomas, Johnny Sofiak, Don Murray, Eddie Thomas, Billy Black, stickboy, Ken Campbell. Missing: Leo LeClair, Stu Hart (trainer). *Photo courtesy of Glenbow Archives*

As far as Ed Bruchet was concerned, 1948 was a year that ended in frustration and diappointment. He never did realize the dream of a Memorial Cup for Lethbridge.

In 1948 he was so near, yet so far.

* * *

RHUBARB IN WETASKIWIN

"We never had a minute of trouble with other teams but against Edmonton it went all wrong", says 81 year old Roy Bentley of the famous hockey family of Delisle, Saskatchewan.

Bentley is referring to the 1948-49 season when he coached the Wetaskiwin Canadians to the northern Alberta final against the Edmonton Athletic Club. "Larger cities don't like to lose to smaller centres," Bentley explains.

Wetaskiwin may have been a small city but the team was mostly imported and was sponsored by the Chicago Black Hawks of the NHL. Bentley claims that Wetaskiwin's "Brent McNabb and Fred Hucul were the best juniors by a country mile."

Edmonton had won the first two games in the best of five series. In the third game the Wetaskiwin team decided to use their home ice to full advantage. At the start of the first and second periods the Canadians sat in their dressing room until the last possible moment in order to let 1,200 Wetaskiwin fans "boo" the Edmonton club.

Earlier, both teams had used this form of intimidation. But the tactic backfired on both teams at the start of the third period of the third game. Both teams sat in their respective dressing rooms waiting for the other to make its move.

Top row (l to r): Jack Evans, J. Rodinyak, G. Rodinyak, B. Wood. Third row: Bill Ramsden, O. Lavell, "Babe" Phaelen (trainer), Ed Bruchet (manager), Scotty Munro (coach), Howie Milford, Bob Manson. Second row: Eddie Dorohoy, J. LeClair. Bottom: F. Brown, D. Berry, R. Richardson, M. Maglio, T. McLean, L. Holmes, G. Murphy.

Photo courtesy of A.E. Cross Studio, Lethbridge

The dressing rooms were directly across from each other. When Bentley peeked out he could see Edmonton coach Clarence Moher peering back at him. The Canadians had waited eight minutes to appear at the start of the second period but in the third period it was several minutes after that and neither team was heading for the ice. Finally, the referee called the game and the fans went home.

Bentley and Moher were suspended. Ernie Smalian filled in for Moher and Herb Shires for Bentley at the next game in Edmonton. The Athletics won the game 6-3 to take the northern title and move into the provincial playoffs against the Calgary Buffaloes.

EAC Director Leo "The Lip" LeClerc announced the team would fly "first class" to Calgary, a rarity in those days. Despite Edmonton's first class travel the Buffaloes won the provincial crown in the fifth game with a 5-2 win.

From game two of the Buffalo series, Roderick "Scotty" Munro replaced Smalian as the EAC coach. This is pure speculation; but what if the EAC had hired Munro the next season? Bill Hunter and Scotty Munro may have ended up in the same town.

The line up for the Wetaskiwin Canadians included Brent McNabb, Fred Hucul, Don Appleton, Bob Henderson, Pat Hayworth, Ray Hamilton, "Moose" McNaughton, Elwood Shell, Walt Abbott, Bob Leask, Don Haley, Len "Comet" Haley and Bill MacPherson.

Lorne Carr's 1949 Calgary Buffaloes then won their way into the Western Canada Junior Hockey final when they defeated the Moose Jaw Canucks 5-2 to win the best-of-seven series 4-2. The Buffaloes won their games 5-1, 5-0, 6-2, and 5-2 and lost to the Canucks 3-2 and 7-2. In the final game, Calgary's goals were scored by Bob Gilhooly, Al Tyrell, Sid Finney, Jack Steele and Bo Carlson.

Top row (l to r): Don Perry, Duke Edmundson, Jimmy Crate (trainer), Ernie Smalian (manager), Eddie Cutts (coach), Lawrence Cantera (stickboy), Dave Little, Doug Kilburn. Third row: Dale McKee, Leo Dupuis, Jack Schofield, Eldor Thomas. Second row: George McAvoy, Stu Robertson, Wally Laubman, Bruce Dickson, Ken Head. Bottom: Bob Losie, Jerry Ball.

Photo courtesy of Edmonton Archives

The Brandon Wheat Kings, however, won the berth in the 1949 Memorial Cup final for the first time in their city's history. A 4-1 victory over the Buffaloes allowed them to win the best-of-seven Western Abbott Cup final series 4-1 in games to advance against the Eastern champion Montreal Royals. Sid Finney scored Calgary's lone marker in the final period which saw Calgary put on a brilliant offensive display only to be thwarted by Ray Frederick in the Brandon goal.

In 1949-50 Guyle Fielder, centre for the Lethbridge Native Sons was voted the Western Canada Junior League's Most Valuable Player. He became the first holder of the Bruchet Trophy donated by Lethbridge's Ed Bruchet.

The format of junior hockey in Alberta changed when Alberta and Saskatchewan clubs formed the Western Junior Hockey League. The league champion would be the representative in Memorial Cup playoffs rather than having a provincial champion. Edmonton was not in the original league.

The Regina Pats captured the 1949-50 WCJL title when they edged the Lethbridge Native Sons 2-1 in the fifth and deciding game. With three minutes left to play, manager Ed Bruchet, substituting for regular coach Pete Slobodian, pulled goalie "Boomer" Rodzinyak for a sixth attacker. Lethbridge who had finished 16 points ahead of Regina failed to score.

CALGARY BUFFALOES 1948-49

First row (l to r): Bill Sherriff, Bob Bartlett, Bruce McDonald, Barry Milton, Bob Carlson, Bob Schmied, Sid Finney, Jim Ray, F. Porteous. Second row: Bob Gilhooly, Stew Cruikshank, John Michaluk, Bob Hunt, Al Purvis, Jack Steele, Cal Oughton, Eldon Willock. Back row: Art Rice-Jones, Ross Tyrell, Bob Rutter, Ray Robson, Jack Smith, Lorne Carr, Walter Bruce.

The strength of junior hockey in 1950-51 continued in the far south of Alberta. A 4-1 victory by the Crowsnest Pass over the Lethbridge Native Sons moved the Lions into the final against the Regina Pats. Scotty Munro's Lions won the first game 3-2 but the Pats came back in the seventh game with a similar 3-2 win to take the series.

Edmonton Oil Kings were formed in 1950-51 under coach Morey Rimstad, manager Ernie Smalian and sponsored by James A. Christiansen. The Kings did not play in the Western Canada Junior League and completed in a separate series against the Trail Smokeaters. The winner was to play the Regina Pats. After defeating Trail, the Kings were eliminated in four straight by the Regina Pats.

It was announced in April 1951, that the Edmonton Oil Kings would join the Western Canada Junior Hockey League for 1951-52. The WCJHL would now have seven entries. (Edmonton, Lethbridge, Calgary, Crowsnest Pass, Medicine Hat, Moose Jaw and Regina.) Edmonton and area players could now stay at home rather than moving to further their careers.

In semi-final action in the spring of 1952, the Regina Pats defeated the Calgary Buffaloes 3-1 to win the best-of-five in three straight. The only goal registered in this game for Calgary was by Ray Kinasewich. The Pats then defeated the Oil Kings three games to two to win the WCJHL.

On the Oil Kings during their first season in the WCJHL players such as John and Bill Bucyk, Billy McNeill, Jerry Melnyk and Norm Ullman stood out under manager Leo LeClerc and coach Ken McAuley.

Even though Edmonton had a powerful lineup in 1952-53, the Lethbridge Native Sons eliminated the Kings and the Flin Flon Bombers to advance against the St. Boniface Canadiens in the Western Canadian final. Lethbridge featured a high calibre team led by goalie Seth Martin plus Ed Zemrau, Larry La Plante, Harold Jones, Steve Arisman, Billy Dea, Clarence Jaster, Earl Ingarfield and Les Colwill.

Against St. Boniface in the sixth game, the Sons battled back to a 6-1 win before 5,000 fans in Winnipeg. The series was now 3-2 with one tie in favor of the Canadiens. In the seventh game the Canadiens overwhelmed the Sons 12-1 to win the Abbott Cup and advance to the Memorial Cup final.

BELLEVUE LIONS 1948-49

Top (l to r): A. Kovacik, A. Salus, P. Kotchonoski, Roderick "Scotty" Munro (coach), L. Hyssop, V. Pachal, M. Wakaluk. Third row: Ralph Nunn, John Kubasek. Second row: D. Antonenko, J. Sinneave, R. Greer (goalie), B. Shuetz, D. Pontorolla. Bottom: I. Petrovich, F. Kubasek, M. Scodellaro. *Photo courtesy of A.E. Cross and Glenbow Archives*

OIL KINGS TO MEMORIAL CUP FINAL (1953-54)

The 1953-54 Edmonton Oil Kings became WCJHL champions and eventually entered the Memorial Cup final against the St. Catharines' Tee Pees. The Kings were a highly regarded team. On April 4, 1954, the Kings entered the Western Canada Abbott Cup final by trouncing the Flin Flon Bombers 7-2. For Ken McAuley's Oil Kings this stretched their winning streak to thirty four straight games. They had not lost since their third contest of the year on December 7, 1953. Edmonton advanced past the Ft. William Canadians and to the Memorial Cup final. Edmonton's team was considered to be the strongest ever to represent Western Canada.

The lineup included: Al Jacobson, Frank Roggeveen (P), Lionel Repka (P), Bob Cowan, Gord Strate (P), Chuck Holmes (P), Ray Kinascwich (P), Jerry Melnyk (P), Norman Ullman (P), Billy McNeill (P), Johnny Bucyk (P), George Congrave , Ron Tookey, Jack Moores, Ed Diachuk (P), Jack Lamb, Harry Smith (P), Dave Joyal and Len Lunde (P).* The manager of the Kings was Leo LeClerc, assistant manager Fred Windwick, trainer Ian McLean, equipment manager Walter Serediak and team physician was Dr. Neil Cuthbertson. (*(P) Players who became professional hockey players. Jack Lamb became a professional football player with the Edmonton Eskimos and Calgary Stampeders.)

(The Edmonton Oil Kings began in the early 1950's. They were formed to take the best players from the four team Edmonton Junior Hockey League to be competitive with the rest of Canada. At this time some of the

CROWSNEST PASS LIONS 1950-51

Left to right: Scotty Munro (coach), George Zwolinski (left wing), Gordie Vejprava (centre), Leonard Allen (left wing), Walter Trentini (right wing), Clarence Jaster (left wing), Allan Bucholz (goalie), Mike Vrabec (defence), Gene Achtymichuk (centre), Jack Muir (defence), Vern Pachal (centre), Ted Lebioda (defence), Ralph Vold (defence), Gordon Andre (defence), Bruce Lea (left wing, not in uniform). Manager Raymond Blake is missing. *Photo courtesy of Tony Vejprava of Blairmore and Glenbow Archives*

Back row (l to r): Carl Trentini, George Zwolinski, Leonard "Len" Allen, Clarence Jaster, Mike Vrabec, Jack Muir, Glen Nelson, Ralph Vold. Front row (l to r): "Mufty" Wakaluk, Gordie Vejprava, Walt Trentini, Allan Bucholz, Gene "Ack Ack" Achtymichuk, Vern Pachal, Ted Lebioda, Gordon Andre. Missing: Bruce Lea, Scotty Munro (coach, deceased), Raymond Blake (manager, deceased).

Photo courtesy of Cunningham Photos, Edmonton

Edmonton and area players played elsewhere while other equally as good had to play locally. The local league could not develop players compared to the Western Canada Junior League. At the time no one really thought the Kings would begin a domination of junior hockey in Alberta. The 1953-54 Kings trip to the Memorial Cup final started their rise in junior hockey in Alberta. Leo LeClerc until the mid 60's and Bill Hunter into the 70's, managed strong organizations. Both eras had Clarence Moher who scouted players so effectively that Alberta almost became a one team junior province.)

In the Memorial Cup final, the bubble burst for Edmonton. After an 18 day layoff waiting for the Eastern final to be completed, the Oil Kings, playing in Toronto, lost 8-1, 5-3, 4-1 and in the fourth game tied the St. Catharine's club 3-3 in overtime. In game five the Eastern Champions defeated the Kings 6-2 to win the Canadian Junior Hockey final and the Memorial Cup.

Coach Rudy Pilous of the Tee Pees had Barry and Brian Cullen, Hugh Barlow, Elmer "Moose" Vasko and Ed Hoekstra as his star players. Historically, the Kings of 1954 were a great hockey team. The long layoff waiting for the Eastern finalists to be declared, was a contributing factor in the King's loss in the Memorial Cup final.

LEOS' "PAY" DAYS

BY NORM ULLMAN

I recall my days with the Oil Kings in the early 1950s with a great deal of pleasure. Under the most capable coaching of Ken McCauley and the direction of Leo LeClerc our team played for the Memorial Cup. It was also at that time I realized that I could have a future as a professional hockey player.

I had a unique experience in hockey because I had the opportunity to play under Leo LeClerc's influence. As a manager he was well respected — a man of understanding, with a great sense of humour and drama. I remember that when I finished my rookie year (a good one) I had to negotiate another contract for a second season with the team. Leo invited me to his home presumably for discussions in a relaxed atmosphere. As events unfolded it was anything but that.

Top row (l to r): Ed Zeniuk, George Townsend, Norm Ullman, Jack Moore. Second row: Ray Kinasewich, Ken McAuley, Bill Bucyk, John Bucyk, Gerry Karpinka, Gord Strate, Art "Babe" McAvoy, Chuck Holmes. Front row: Bob Cowan, Billy McNeill, Bob Sangster, Dino Maniago, Walt Serediak. Missing: Gerry Prince, Jerry Melnyk, Al Jacobsen.

In those years the renumeration on the Oil King team was preset — $100 a month for the first year, $125 a month the second, etc. I felt justified in asking for more than the average after having led the league in scoring my first year. All of us who know Leo understand that he is rather "excitable" but I believe I brought him very close to cardiac arrest. On hearing my demand he leapt from his chair. "So you don't want to play for the Oil Kings!" He ran and fumbled for the telephone exclaiming, "What team do you want to play for? I'll make the trade!"...All this over a $25 monthly increase? Needless to say, I played my second year for the standard fee.

I remained very apprehensive of contract negotiations from that day on realizing that not only were we dealing in finances but with personalities as well. Never again in my hockey career, however, was I to meet anyone quite like Leo Louis LeClerc.

In the years that followed I grew to value Leo's friendship and I regard Leo as one of the most positive influences in my hockey life. I will always appreciate the encouragement and guidance he offered me through the years.

Returning "home" to such friends and to family in the mid- 70s to play with the Oilers seemed a fitting climax to a most rewarding career. I thank all Albertans and the fans in Edmonton particularly, for their unwavering support.

FOOTNOTE:

Ullman became an NHL Super Star. LeClerc helped Johnny Bucyk and Ullman to negotiate their contracts before "paid" agents. Before the careers of these two fine products were over in the NHL both had 16 seasons of 20 or more goals. The durable Gordie Howe had 22 seasons of 20 or more goals for the record. Tied in second place with the two Edmonton players is Phil Esposito. Frank Mahovlich had 15 years of 20 goals for third spot.

* * *

LETHBRIDGE NATIVE SONS
Abbott Cup Finalists — 1952-53

Front row (l to r): Butch McDonald (coach), Billy Dea (captain), Larry Winder, Seth Martin, Jerry Koehle, Les Colwill, Clarence Jaster, Ed Bruchet (manager). Second row, standing: E.S. Niels (president), Roger LaPlante, Steve Arisman, Harold Jones, Ed Ferenz, Dave Magee, Earl Ingarfield, Dick Ward (assistant trainer), Babe Phalen (trainer). Back row: Bud Laidler, Ed Zemrau, Don Smith, Howie Yanosik, Bill Sinclair, Jerry Sorenson, Dick Lamoureaux.

EDMONTON OIL KINGS 1953-54

Standing at back: Jack Moore, George Congrave. Left to right: Dr. Neil Cuthbertson in white hat, Wilf McMullen, Ron Tookey, Mike Melynk (wearing hat), Dave Joyal, Reno Zanier, Norm Ullman, Bill McNeill, Bob Cowan, Ray Kinasewich, Ken McAuley (coach). Next row: Frank Roggeveen (brush cut), Neil Moher (glasses), Lionel Repka, Gord Strate, Al Jacobsen, Harry Smith, John Bucyk. Leaning on car: Jerry Melnyk, Charlie Holmes. In car: Jack Lamb, Len Lunde, Ed Diachuk (behind wheel).

Photo courtesy of Edmonton Archives

In the WCJHL of 1954-55, the Oil Kings who had strolled through the west so easily the previous year, were defeated by the Lethbridge Native Sons in five games. In the final game Bill Voss scored two goals including the winner. Voss scored winners against the Kings three times during regular league play plus a hat trick in the fourth game of the playoffs.

LETHBRIDGE NATIVE SONS 1954-55

Front row (l to r): E.S. Neils (president), Rock Crawford, Dick McGhee, Gus Adams, Bill Ramsden (coach), Don LeRose, Bill Haslam, Aut Erickson, Ron Morgan, Jack Lakie (secretary treasurer). Second row (l to r): Ed Bruchet (manager), Alan Dipasquale, Andy Drobat, Lawrence Ruptach, Larry "Chief" Mead, Norm Usselman, John MacMillan, Al Schaefer, Babe Phalen (trainer). Third row (l to r): Earl Ingarfield, Jim Powers, Bill Voss, Les Colwill.

The Regina Pats won four and lost only two to eliminate the Native Sons in the WCJHL final.

The most powerful junior squad in Alberta in 1955-56 continued to be Ed Bruchet's Lethbridge Native Sons. The Sons moved into the WCJHL final by defeating the Edmonton Oil Kings 3-2 to win the best-of-seven in five games. Lethbridge came from behind to win. Centre Len Lunde gave the Kings the lead after 15 seconds but Larry Ruptash, Andy Drobot and Bill Voss replied for the Sons. Pierre Joyal scored the King's second goal which allowed King's coach Ray Hannigan to pull goalie George Kirkwood for the final 90 seconds. The strategy failed and Lethbridge went on again to face the Regina Pats.

Regina (under the coaching of Murray Armstrong) continued to dominate Lethbridge. Over 2,500 watched in Lethbridge as the Sons lost 6-5 in overtime to lose the series four games to one. Overtime was not sudden death as Lethbridge scored first only to have Regina tie the match. Joe Lunghamer scored the winner at 9:18 to eliminate Lethbridge.

After the 1955-56 season the WCJHL format was changed. Due to financial pressure caused by lengthy travel the Saskatchewan centres plus Flin Flon formed the Saskatchewan Junior Hockey League and left Edmonton as the sole Junior 'A' team in Alberta interested in going on for the Memorial Cup. The Oil Kings joined the Central Alberta Hockey League. This experience against ex-pros, senior and intermediate calibre players turned out to be excellent competition for juniors.

In the 1956-57 Pug Young coached Edmonton Oil Kings advanced to the Western Canada Abbott Cup playoffs against the Flin Flon Bombers. The King's lineup included George Kirkwood, Ed Babiuk, Tom Kalis, Warren Back, Mike Lashuk, Rick Healey, Darryl Havrelock, Ed Diachuk, Doug Messier, Fred Gardiner, Wes Dakus,

LETHBRIDGE NATIVE SONS 1955-56

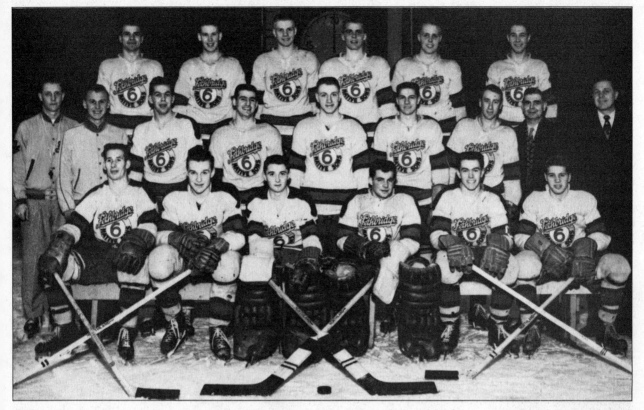

Front row (l to r): A. McLuskey, J. Nicholl, C. Grisak, G. Wood, J. MacMillan, D. Caunt. Second row (l to r): Bill Ramsden (coach), Paul Rusznak (trainer), L. Travis, N. Usselman, J. Kosiancic, A. Tambellini, A. Drobot, Ed Bruchet (manager), E.S. Neils (president). Third row (l to r): L. Ruptash, J. Powers, B. Voss, L. McLaren, A. Erickson, A. Dipasquale.

Austin Smith, Ron "Squeak" Leopold, John Utendale, Eddie Johnson and Terry Lomnes. Flin Flon had a lineup with George Wood, George Konik, Mike Kardash, Duanne Rupp, Ted Hampson, Mel Pearson and Patty Ginnell.

The Bombers displayed their mastery in the final game by winning 6-1 to take the series four games to two. The Bombers overall play was the best the Kings had seen all season.

In the spring of 1958, the Calgary Reps became the first Calgary Junior 'A' club since the 1953 Calgary Buffaloes to compete in provincial play leading on to the Memorial Cup. The Reps competed in the Big Six Intermediate League and finished the season in fifth place. President of the Reps was Dave "Sweeney" Schriner while Gerry Bissell was manager and Roy Kelly the coach. All the players except Fred Gardiner and goalie Dave Watson had come through local Junior 'B' ranks and were considered the best Calgary had to offer. Ken McAuley's Edmonton Oil Kings were heavy favorites and advanced past the Reps in straight games to meet the Regina Pats.

Billy Hicke (later an Edmonton Oiler) celebrated his 20th birthday and scored both goals for Regina in a 2-0 win over the Kings. Victories of 6-2 and 9-7 on Edmonton ice and a third game 3-1 win gave the Pats the series.

The Edmonton Oil Kings repesented Alberta in the 1958-59 junior playoffs. The Flin Flon Bombers who played in the Saskatchewan Junior Hockey League eliminated the Kings four straight. It was reported that flu hampered players like Bruce MacGregor and Bill Lawson, slowing them down considerably. Players such as Don Chiz and Tom Burgess were confined to bed. However, the Bombers possessed a powerful lineup including Cliff Pennington and Gordon "Red" Berenson.

The series had its controversy. Regina's "Red" Berenson had played at the University of Michigan during the season but the Bombers picked him up for the playoffs. For the final two games in Edmonton, the fans booed Berenson because they thought the CAHA should not have allowed him to play. With Berenson's help the Bombers won 6-3, 8-3, 10-1 and 11-6.

In regular season of the Central Alberta League (intermediate) the Oil Kings finished last in 1959-60 but this had no effect in junior playoffs. In the Western Canada Junior 'A' semi-final series Harry Allen's Edmonton

Oil Kings finally defeated the Flin Flon Bombers. Edmonton won three games 8-5, 8-3, and 5-3. Flin Flon came back with two wins. In the sixth match in Flin Flon Don Chiz and Bobby Goebel fired three goals each with singles from Bruce MacGregor and Tom Burgess for an 8-1 win. After three years the Kings had finally beaten Bobby Kirk's Bombers and advanced to the Abbott Cup final.

EDMONTON OIL KINGS 1959-60

Back row (l to r): John A. "Fats" McDonald, Wayne Parker, Dunc McCallum, Edgar Ehranverth, Bob Cox, Dave Creeland, Cliff Pennington, Bill Lougheed, Emery Samson, Jim Mitchell (trainer). **Middle row:** Larry "Peaches" Lund, Tom Burgess, Lorne Braithwaite, Sonny Roberge, Bruce MacGregor, Bob Goebel, "Fiery" Phil Dutton, Ted Demchuk, Don Pasutto. **Front row:** Wally Serediak (equipment manager), Bob Marik, Russ "Light Bulb" Gillow, Don Chiz, Harry Allen (coach), Wayne "Gert" Muloin, Dale Guame, Ed "The Mayor of St. Albert" Joyal, Jimmy "Humphrey" Brown.

In the Abbott Cup final coach John Caverly "Jake" Milford and the Brandon Wheat Kings took a two game lead in the series. The Oil Kings came back however, in the third match in the Edmonton Gardens 3-2. After this game, Hal Pawson, sports editor of the "Edmonton Journal" wrote:

> By getting off the floor, after spotting the Brandon Wheat Kings two goals, to win 3-2 in an emotion-charged final seven minutes in the Gardens, the current Kings joined the junior greats of the past, the EAC's of 1934 and 1939 and the Oil King machine of 1954. Those others, for the most part, did it on talent. These Kings did it on heart — the kind of heart that has carried them from nowhere to the Western Memorial Cup Final, a strange stirring kind of courage which thrives on adversity.

By the sixth game, the Wheat Kings came back to defeat the Oil Kings 6-3. Milford told his club to "grab a sandwich if you want, then hit the sack. It's the game of your lives coming up and I won't accept any excuses". The advice failed as Edmonton became the fourth Edmonton team in history to reach the Memorial Cup Final by winning 6-1.

Writing from Toronto, the site of the 1960 Memorial Cup, Ron Glover of the "Edmonton Journal" wrote:

> The Edmonton Oil King manager was at his snarling best Sunday afternoon. When the team took a fearful 9-1 trouncing from St. Catherines Tee Pees, Leo lowered the boom. In an effort to shake the Western Champs out of the fog that has surrounded them on recent days, LeClerc has slapped on a tight curfew, laid down new eating regulations and ordered road work twice daily.

A disciplined Oil King team won the fourth game 9-3 to tie the playoffs at two games each. Eddie Joyal, the "Mayor of St. Albert", had four goals while Cliff Pennington (picked up from Flin Flon) and Bruce MacGregor scored two each and Bob Marik one. Eight thousand fans in Toronto cheered the St. Catharines Tee Pees winning of the 1960 Memorial Cup 7-3 in game six.

EDMONTON OIL KINGS 1960-61

Back row (l to r): John A. McDonald, Larry Lund, Dennis Kassian, Butch Barber, Vince Downey, Jim Eagle, John Leshyshyn, Phil Dutton, Tom Burgess, Lorne Braithwaite, Earl Gray, Larry Hale, Jim Mitchell. Second row: Wayne Muloin, Owen Mailley, Don Chiz, Dale Guame, Leo Le Clerc, Walter Serediak, Buster Brayshaw, Paul Sexsmith, Roger Bourbonnais, Bob Cox, Bob Marik. Front row: Tom "Swede" Knox (stick boy), Jimmy Brown (stick boy).

Coach Russell Ambrose "Buster" Brayshaw rejoined the Kings for the 1960-61 season. The previous year, due to poor health, he was replaced by Harry Allen. The Oil Kings defeated the Regina Pats 3-1 to win the best-of-seven and once again be in the Abbot Cup final. A 7-5 win over the Winnipeg Rangers gave the Kings their second straight berth in the Memorial Cup.

Edmonton finally hosted the Canadian final but Father David Bauer's Toronto St. Michaels' College Majors won three straight (4-0, 4-2, 4-1). Edmonton rebounded 5-4 and 4-2 only to lose the sixth match 4-2.

The Kings needed to recruit good young players. Glen Sather,presently the President, Coach and General Manager of the Edmonton Oilers, joined the Oil Kings for the 1961-62 season. A profile of young Sather on April 22, 1962 in the "Edmonton Journal" said:

Glen Sather — *juvenile star from Wainwright* (also Viking), *plays left side on Oilers celebrated 'kid line' with Butch Paul and Max Mestinsek. Sather, 5'10", 160 lbs., attends Eastglen Composite High School. A hard skater, he likes to bump. Plans to become a Recreation Director. Eighteen years old, with two seasons left as a junior.*

In 1962 the Kings swept into the Abbott Cup final for the third straight year when they eliminated the Calgary Buffaloes, Kamloops Rockets, and Moose Jaw Canucks. The Abbott Cup took seven games against the Brandon Wheat Kings. In the 5-3 seventh game win over Brandon, Roger Bourbonnais scored two goals and Phil Dutton, John Lesyshen and Max Mestinsek got singles.

Bourbonnais, now a British Columbia lawyer, had a lengthy trip before the seventh game. After game six, he flew back to Edmonton for a University of Alberta examination and back in time for the final game. It was said Roger had less than six hours sleep in three days. The King's private volunteer pilot, Wilf McMullen had even less.

The Hamilton Red Wings eliminated the Oil Kings 7-4 in the fifth game of the best-of-seven Memorial Cup final before 7,071 fans in Kitchener's Auditorium. The Oil Kings came from a 2-0 deficit in the final game and went ahead 3-2 after two periods. However, the Wings deadlocked the game by firing three goals in 1 minute and 23 seconds to end the Oil King's hopes for that year.

Back (l to r): Lou Halat, Gregg Pilling, Vince Downey, Ron Sarnowski, John Lesychyn, Jim Eagle, Reg. Taschuk, Larry Hale, Willie Moffatt. Second row: Dr. Tullock, Ian "Butch" Barber, Harold Fleming, Doug Fox, Glen Sather, Stewart "Butch" Paul, "Marvellous" Max Mestinsek, Cliff Coolidge, Jim Mitchell (trainer). Front: "Swede" Knox, Russ Kirk, Phil Dutton, Leo LeClerc (manager), Wayne Muloine, Buster Brayshaw (coach), Roger Bourbonnais, Harrison Gray, Walter Serediak (equipment manager).

Photo courtesy of McDermid Studios, Edmonton

Notable for the Red Wings in the final game were Wayne Rivers who scored two goals while Paul Henderson (hero of Canada-Russia series of 1972), Lowell McDonald, Pat Martin, Bob Wall and Howie Menard had singles. Replying for the Oil Kings were Mark Dufour, Butch Paul, Vince Downey and Roger Bourbonnais.

After the series, Ron Glover summarized the season in his Journal column called 'Sport Gleamings':

Hamilton may have the Memorial Cup, but Edmonton has something they can be equally proud of — a gang of kids who came streaming out of nowhere to make a futile but nervy grab at the highest honor in amateur hockey.

Glover also gave praise to Clarence Moher, Leo LeClerc and Buster Brayshaw.

A goodly measure of the credit for the Oil King's success has to go to scout Clarence Moher, the pint-sized sharpy with the knack of digging up potential stars in the weirdest places. Some must go to manager Leo LeClerc, who knows every trick in the book and invents more whenever the need arises, in his tireless effort to build winners. Most deserving I suppose is coach Buster Brayshaw, a student of the game, a stickler for the fundamentals and a thinker who eats, sleeps and breathes hockey twelve months a year.

EDMONTON'S FIRST MEMORIAL CUP

The three men continued to guide the Oil Kings for the 1962-63 season. The highlight of the playoff route occurred when the Oil Kings met Scotty Munro's Estevan Bruins. Munro was never at a loss for words. On this occasion, Scotty said:

We can outskate the Oil Kings on any given date. And on the large (Edmonton) Garden's ice it will be even better. Their goal tending is terrible and their defence is slow afoot...their club would be pressed to finish fourth in our league (Saskatchewan) and I'm serious.

Munro's words were tough but the Bruins lost the round four games to two even though they won the first two games of the series.

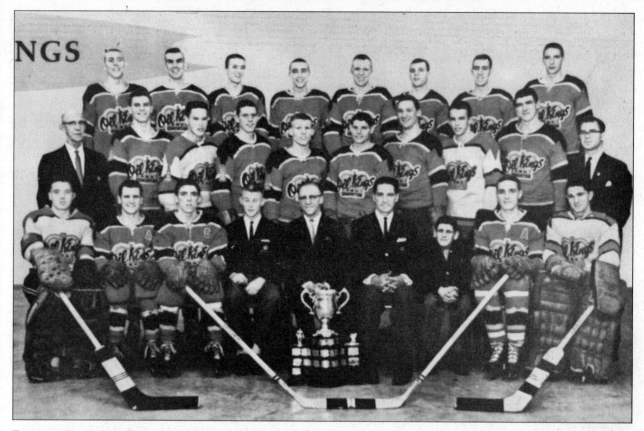

Front row (l to r): Russ Kirk, Harold Fleming, Roger Bourbonnais (captain), S. Knox, Leo LeClerc (manager), Buster Brayshaw (coach), Walter Serediak (equipment manager), Jim Eagle, Tom Bend. Second row (l to r): Jim Mitchell (trainer), Bert Marshall, Jim Chase, Ron Anderson, Gregg Pilling, Rich Bulloch, Dave Rochefort, Jim Brown, Pat Quinn, Dr. Tullock. Third row (l to r): Bob Falkenberg, Vince Downey, Max Mestinsek, Butch Paul, Glen Sather, Butch Barber, Doug Fox, Reg Taschuk.

Saskatchewan radio broadcasters Ken Newans of CHAB Moose Jaw and Linus Westberg of CJGX Yorkton entered the verbal battle too. The two broadcasters had their hockey radio rights suspended by Edmonton's Art Potter, President of the CAHA, for "continually and severely criticising officials and thereby giving an erroneous picture of the game as played".

In Moose Jaw, Newans said, "I believe that the series as handled by the CAHA, has severely hampered both clubs in playing the high calibre hockey they are capable of". The comments that paritcularly irked Potter were the references to the Oil Kings as "being a bunch of butchers". (Newans is now sports director at CFCN Calgary.)

The Abbott Cup final of 1962-63 against the Brandon Wheat Kings went five games inlcuding three overtime games before the Oil Kings won.

The Memorial Cup final was held at the Edmonton Gardens. Words flew before the series when manager Hap Emms of the Niagara Falls Flyers "bad mouthed" Buster Brayshaw and Leo LeClerc of the Oil Kings. Emms claimed that the nets at the Gardens were fifteen feet from the end boards and that this was a violation of the CAHA hockey rule book. Brayshaw refused to allow the Flyers or anyone else to view his practises. However, on at least one occasion the Flyers found a southside door open. Brayshaw immediately stopped his workout and asked Emms to leave the premises.

In the first game Niagara Falls annihilated the Kings 8-0. Wayne Maxner scored two goals while Gary Dornhoefer, Gary Harmer, Ron Hergott and Bill Goldsworthy got one goal apiece. Niagara Falls also won the second game.

In game three, Dornhoefer (later Boston Bruin player and now CBC colorman) probably had the longest night of his junior hockey career. Pat Quinn (Philadelphia Flyer and now Los Angeles Kings coach) known as the "Enforcer" at 214 lbs., sized up Dornhoefer and gave him a crushing check. (In the game Dornhoefer had 4 minors and a misconduct and was not the favorite of the Edmonton fans.) 6,424 fans saw the Flyer forward carried off the ice with a broken leg. The broken leg also broke the spirit of Niagara Falls.

The casualty list for Niagara Falls included Dornhoefer and Gary Harmer with fractured tibias, Rick Morin a head cut, Bill Goldsworthy a torn solar plexus, Terry Crisp a charley horse, Ron Hergott face lacerations, Don Awrey a concussion and two black eyes, George Gardiner (goalie) a concussion and Wayne Maxner stretched rib muscles. Pat Quinn had the only injury for the Oil Kings, face laceration requiring four stitches.

Game five was played on May 11, 1963. Edmonton claimed the Memorial Cup with a 4-3 victory. An Alberta team had not won since 1926 when the Calgary Canadians defeated Kingston.

This is how it happened: After the Kings initial 8-0 loss, the team managed 7-3, 5-2 and 3-2 victories. The fourth game ended in a 5-2 loss.

At 9:01 of the third period in game five Edmonton was ahead 4-0 on goals by Doug Fox, Glen Sather, Butch Paul and Gregg Pilling. Niagara Falls came back with three goals. The third one by Terry Crisp slid past Oil King goalie Russ Kirk at 18:21 in the final period. Emms pulled his goalie but the Kings held on to win the Memorial Cup. While other games in the series were violent, the final match had only one penalty assessed to Oil King Max Mestinsek.

From the 1962-63 Kings, Glen Sather, Bert Marshall and Pat Quinn became NHL head coaches.

The Edmonton Oil Kings represented Alberta in the 1963-64 season. The Kings had no difficulty against the Kamloops Rockets. They won 10-1 and 7-2 to advance to the Memorial Cup quarter-final against the Brandon Wheat Kings. The Wheat Kings lost in five games. The Oil Kings faced the Estevan Bruins and defeated the team in five games to qualify for the Memorial Cup for the fifth straight year.

When Hal Pawson, then sports editor of the "Edmonton Journal" left for the final in Toronto he made a few comments:

"I forgot to deliver a bottle of tranquilizers to Leo. (LeClerc did not make the trip) He's not going and will need them. Can someone take these over to him? Also, I forgot to mention that Bryan Hall (now CJCA) who is coming home to CHED after the Cup, has been appointed Oil King's Easter Divisional Manager. That'll confuse the Marlies."

Before the Oil Kings left they took part in a booster club rally at the Sales Pavillon led by CJCA disk jockey Barry Boyd, Wes Dakus (former Oil King) and the Rebels and a folksinging group. The Edmonton Eskimo Football Club's coach Neil Armstrong presented the Oil Kings with Eski Mascots. Edmonton's three national champions, the junior football Huskies and the Varsity Bears of football and hockey all made presentations. It was a fitting send off the the Kings.

The broadcaster in 1964 for the Oil Kings was Wes Montgomery of CHED. Harold Ballard and Maple Leaf Gardens refused to allow CHED to broadcast the game to Edmonton unless the station paid $500 a game. CHED refused (Montgomery is now at CISN).

A "Fair Play for Edmonton Committee" was chaired by Jim Bateman. This committee sent telegrams to Prime Minister Lester Pearson, Opposition Leader John Diefenbaker, Minister of Agriculture Harry Hays, the President of Ford Canada and Conn Smythe of Maple Leaf Gardens. A telegram containing more than 1,000 names was sent to Garden's Vice President Ballard.

CHED's production manager Jerry Forbes said, "there was nothing his company could do but wait for the results". Wes Montgomery advised CHED the case was hopeless. Al Anderson, manager of the Edmonton Exhibition Association said, "we are surprised at the attitude adopted by the Maple Leaf Garden management and will register a protest with them today".

CAHA President Art Potter of Edmonton stated that:

The action of Maple Leaf Gardens is unfair, unwarranted and a display of the poorest type of sportsmanship on the part of the organization which is purported to be interested in the promotion of sport.

Ballard's reply was:

Temper will get the west nowhere. This is business - Maple Leaf Garden business...I'm here to make money for my directors, so I have to know what I am doing, even if they (CHED and CAHA) don't.

Hal Pawson reported that Ballard left for New York with a deluge of telegrams of protest. Ballard also said, "I wouldn't mind the fuss but why do people like the Prime Minister have to call about it? It's just business."

In the 1963-64 Memorial Cup final the Oil Kings lost the first two games to the Toronto Marlboros and their fans in Edmonton became more restless. Four hockey fans in Edmonton even picketed the Devonian Building at 111th Street and Jasper Avenue, then the offices of Imperial Oil, to try and get the "Hockey Night in Canada" sponsors to do something.

By the fourth game of the series, the Marlies went ahead 3-0 in games. Leo LeClerc went to Toronto. At a press conference at the Westbury Hotel, bilingual LeClerc attempted to get his Kings going by blasting the organizational abilities of Maple Leaf Gardens.

...the dictatorial actions, the doubled seat prices, the denial of game broadcasting in Edmonton - these things have held Maple Leaf Gardens crowds down to two thousand persons per game. That is like drawing two hundred and fifty people to a Memorial Game in Edmonton or Regina.

Art Potter then announced that should the series go to a sixth game or more they would be played in Kitchener and CHED would have full broadcast rights.

What actually happened on the ice in the 1964 Memorial Cup final was anticlimatic. The Marlboros defeated the Oil Kings 7-2 to win in four straight games. In the final game "Marvelous" Max Mesinsek got both Edmonton goals while for Toronto, Mike Walton, Pete Stemkowski, Gary Dineen, Rod Seiling, Andre Champagne, Grant Moore and Mike Harboruk scored. Other players for Toronto included Ron Ellis and goalkeeper Gary Smith.

It was the "Silent Series" for Edmonton fans. For Jim Bateman, chairman of the Fair Play for Edmonton Committee (later an Edmonton Alderman) for the Junior Chamber of Commerce, it was a frustrating time. However, on the ice the Toronto Marlboros, under coach Jim Gregory, were a superb team.

In 1964-65, junior hockey in Alberta added a new league. The Alberta Junior Hockey League was formed. At first this league was rather insignificant, but its importance grew. (See Alberta Junior Hockey League.) The Edmonton Oil Kings still played in the Central Alberta Senior League. The year is also remembered because of the Derek Sanderson incident.

The Oil Kings got to the Abbott Cup final by defeating the Calgary Buffaloes of the AJHL and the Regina Pats. Helmets were not common at that time, but Regina's Fran Huck wore a golden one and was known as the "Golden Hawk". In the seventh game the Kings defeated the Pats 6-2 to enter the Abbott Cup final. After being ahead 2-0 in games the Kings lost twice in succession to Winnipeg Braves, but won two more to once again move on to the Memorial Cup final in Edmonton, against the Niagara Falls Flyers.

Western teams were allowed "pickups" from other teams for Memorial Cup . For this final the Kings added Fran Huck from Regina, Joe Carter from Weyburn and goalie Wayne Stephensen from Winnipeg. In the first game the Flyers defeated the Kings 3-2 as Bernie Parent handled 21 shots for the Flyers compared to 18 for Stephenson. A 5-1 loss in the second game did not please manager Leo LeClerc. Bud Debrody scored two goals for Niagara Falls, while Bill Goldsworthy, Derek Sanderson and John Arbour registered singles. Huck scored Edmonton's lone goal.

Game three became the Derek Sanderson incident. Three and one-half minutes remained to be played and the Oil Kings were ahead 5-1. It then took 25 Edmonton City Police to subdue the Edmonton crowd.

It happened this way according to the "Edmonton Journal":

Just after the Oil King's fifth goal, Flyer Rosaire Paiement highsticked King defence ace Al Hamilton, whose heavy but clean bodychecking had been a game highlight and they fought. Hamilton went to the bench with a bloody nose. Flyer defenceman John Arbour reached around a peacekeeping official and punched King rookie, Ace Bailey, then Ted Rogers and Flyer Dave Woodley tangled, with the referee trying to break that one up. While Bob Falkenburg watched, Derek Sanderson came along side and floored him with a sucker punch to the temple. He then jumped on the unconscious Falkenburg and punched him five more times before an official grabbed him (Oil King Bob Falkenberg was taken to the hospital with a concussion.)

At this point Flyer Guy Allen pulled down Regina Pat star Fran Huck — an Oil King replacement and began pummelling Huck. The referee then called the police out on the ice.

The Journal went on to report that by this time all the Flyers but one were on the ice. No Oil King came out on the ice, leaving only three players and a goalie after Hamilton and Falkenburg were injured.

Controlling the Oil King's bench at the time were coach Harry Allen and trainer Jim Mitchell. During the course of the battle, with each manning a gate, they somehow were able to keep their players on the bench.

Gordon Jukes, secretary manager of the CAHA, gave Sanderson an indefinite suspension while Flyer's Rick Ley and Oil King Ron Anderson were given one-game suspensions for stick swinging prior to the major outbreak.

In game four, 5,326 fans expected to see the Kings repeat with a victory but were disappointed as Niagara Falls won 8-3. The Oil Kings were eliminated in the fifth game 8-1.

Bernie Parent was outstanding in goal for the Flyers. During the year he had a 2.56 goals against average per game, while in playoffs he was even better at 1.5.

After the 1965 season Leo LeClerc retired as manager of the Edmonton Oil Kings. To be successful a team requires organization and continuity. During his tenure, LeClerc was probably one of the most creative organizers of hockey in Alberta's history. (A story of LeClerc by Lorne Braithwaite is in the Hot Stove League)

EDMONTON'S SECOND MEMORIAL CUP

The 1965-66 season in junior hockey began the Bill Hunter era in Edmonton. Hunter had managed hockey clubs in Regina, Saskatoon and Medicine Hat. Hunter , also known as ''Wild Bill'', hired Billy Warwick as his first coach of the Oil Kings. Warwick stayed until November and was followed by Ray Kinasewich.

The Oil King's regular season was still played in the Alberta Hockey League (some called it the Central Alberta Hockey League). The Kings and the Drumheller Miners could not determine the league championship. After splitting six games and failing to break a tie in the seventh game played on neutral ice in Calgary, it was decided the teams would become co-holders of the championship. Drumheller went on to win the Allan Cup and the Oil Kings the Memorial Cup. (See Jim Fisher's story on the 1966 Miners in Senior Hockey.)

The King's route to the Memorial Cup included straight game victories over the AJHL Calgary Buffaloes and the New Westminster Royals. It was then Hunter's Kings against Scotty Munro's Estevan Bruins. At or before games Bill and Scotty carried on dialogues with the press that made fans want to go to the rink. Away from the rink they were best friends. Hockey was business.

In the hockey ''match-up'' the Estevan Bruins easily defeated the Kings 5-2 in the opener. The Kings then got back on the winning track by defeating the Bruins 3-1 in front of 3,200 fans in the tiny Estevan Agriculture Auditorium. Kinasewich and Hunter couldn't wait to return to Edmonton to play in the larger Edmonton Gardens.

The big news of the day was Douglas Leiterman, Executive Producer of the CBC's ''This Hour Has Seven Days''. His show and hosts Patrick Watson and Laurier La Pierre, along with singer Dinah Christie was taken off the air. Seven Days was considered too controversial. Bill Hunter and Scotty Munro also managed to use controversy to their advantage.

EDMONTON OIL KINGS 1965-66

Front row (l to r): Don McLeod (goal), Dr. Neil Cuthbertson (club physician), Al Hamilton (defence), Ray Kinasewich (coach), Bob Falkenberg (defence), W.D. (Bill) Hunter (president and general manager), Dave Rochefort (centre), Jim Mitchell (trainer), Ross Perkins (centre), Jim Knox (sub goal), Murray Pierce (stick boy, kneeling). Middle row (l to r): Swede Knox (assistant equipment manager), Red Simpson (left wing), Doug Barrie (defence), Ross Lonsberry (left wing), Garnet Bailey (left wing), Ron Walters (centre), Ted Hodgson (right wing), Galen Head (right wing), Jim Harrison (left wing), Ted Rogers (centre), Borden Lapowy Junior (manager and coach), Waldo Serdiak (equipment manager). Back row (l to r): Don Caley (spare goal), Jim Schraefel (left wing), Kerry Ketter (defence), Brian Bennett (left wing), Ron Anderson (right wing), Craig Cameron (right wing), Eugene Peacosh (left wing), Harold Myers (defence), Brian Hague (defence). *Photo courtesy of Wells Studio, Edmonton*

When Estevan came to Edmonton for the third game, controversy arose as to the physical condition of the Edmonton Gardens. Jim Graham, Edmonton's Fire Chief, (not the same Jimmy Graham of the 1932 Edmonton Gainers Superiors) said he would condemn the building if he had the authority because of its rundown and hazardous condition. The Edmonton Journal ran the story with full coverage. A diagram of the Gardens was drawn showing all the exits plus a listed seating capacity of 6,729. The "Journal" noted that "it's recommended that arena patrons make careful note of them". This added danger gave excitement to the game as well. Precisely 6,740 fans paid their way to watch the Oil Kings defeat the Bruins 6-4.

Commented Clare Drake, University of Alberta hockey coach, "It was an exceedingly heavy crowd, but it didn't surprise me. I expected the crowd to be heavy because every second fan was carrying his own fire bucket filled with water."

"Sheer bravery," marvelled Bill Hunter. "That's real fan fortitude and loyalty to the most exciting game in the world, junior playoff hockey, when you consider the amount of adverse publicity on the condition of the Gardens."

Scotty Munro was not to be outdone. "I have to think that the drawing power of the Estevan Bruins exceeds the power of the press, which has condemned the rink into which we put 6,740 fans."

Hunter and Munro obviously knew how to draw people into Alberta arenas.

The Estevan-Edmonton series went six games when the Kings edged the Bruins 5-3 back in Estevan. This was the seventh time in a row, the Oil Kings won the Abbott Cup. Now they flew to Toronto to meet the Oshawa Generals, featuring young Bobby Orr, for the Memorial Cup.

Jim Coleman, sports columnist for *Southam News,* felt the Memorial Cup had lost much of its lustre and was being played in "semi-secrecy" in Maple Leaf Gardens. Coleman, with tongue in cheek, commented on Edmonton's sports writers and broadcasters. Referring to Hal Pawson, Gordon Fisher, Ernie Afaganis, Al McCann and Wes Montgomery, he said "the truth is, though, that these gentlemen have become sober and dignified as the years have added furrows to their noble brows..." In Coleman's opinion the Memorial Cup was not the event it once was when hundreds of westerners followed their teams annually to Toronto.

Once behind two games to one, the Oil Kings came back and won 5-3, 7-4, and 2-1 to win the Memorial Cup on May 15, 1966.

Jim Harrison (from the Estevan Bruins) and Ted Hodgson scored for Edmonton while Bill Heindl replied for Oshawa. Starring for the Kings were defensemen Al Hamilton and Bob Falkenburg. For Kinasewich, the victory over Bep Guidolin's Generals brought back memories of his playing for the Oil Kings in the 1954 final when the team that should have won failed.

Guidolin said that he did not want to make excuses but playing without the injured Bobby Orr at the end of the series gave the Generals little hope of winning.

Hal Pawson noted the importance of the scouting of Clarence Moher and then said:

> Hunter is fiery, excitable, at times even momentarily inclined to stinging outbursts. But at all times he treated this club as made up of men — adults. Kinasewich, in contrast is calm at all times, always understanding. He too, treated the club as adults. And the Oil Kings responded, by playing like champions and men.

The Drumheller Miners, also from the Alberta Senior League, won the Allan Cup when they defeated Sherbrooke Beavers 5-0. Don Fleming of the "Journal" wrote:

> Whose for tying up tag ends? — like I mean, letting the Alberta Senior League playoffs wither on the vine, still comes under the heading of unfinished business...Besides it's too bad in a way these two fine aggregations (Kings and Miners) don't have a showdown.

They never did.

Later in 1966, the top junior teams in Canada formed a league called the Canadian Major Junior Hockey league (CMJHL). The western group included teams from Winnipeg, Brandon, Flin Flon, Moose Jaw, Swift Current, Regina, Estevan, Weyburn, Sasktoon, Edmonton and Calgary and was called the Central Major Junior Hockey League. Conflict between the CAHA and the CMJHL resulted as the CMJHL raised the junior age limit to twenty-one from twenty and the CAHA lowered its junior age to nineteen.

The age change resulted in the CMJHL losing its right to participate for the Memorial Cup. Owners of franchises in the CMJHL wanted players on their teams for the extra year in order to increase revenue and have a more consistent lineup from year to year. Thus, the CMJHL operated as an independent league, and in Alberta, teams from the Alberta Junior Hockey League entered Memorial Cup playoffs without any Alberta playoff outside their league required. (See section on AJHL)

In the regular CMJHL schedule the Edmonton Oil Kings finished first and met the fourth place Moose Jaw Canucks. It was decided to have a nine game series. The Canucks, coached by Brian Shaw, previous coach of the Jasper Place Juveniles, and other Edmontonians Ken Brown and Don Walker, eliminated the Oil Kings.

EDMONTON OIL KINGS 1967-68

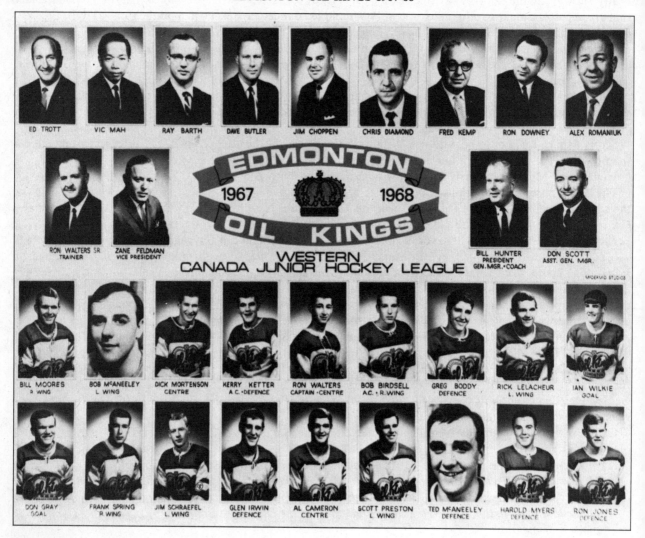

Photo courtesy of Edmonton Archives

The Moose Jaw-Edmonton series included three ties including the final game. After the series, Oil King coach Bill Gadsby said, "I'm going to be dreaming about tie hockey games for the rest of the summer".

During the 1967 summer the CAHA and the CMJHL came to an agreement. The major junior league would not compete for the Memorial Cup. They would operate as a separate group as tier 1 while leagues such as the AJHL would be tier 2. (Tier 2 leagues got their own national trophy (Centennial Cup) in 1970-71 and tier 1 again played for the Memorial Cup.)

The Estevan Bruins won 45 of 60 games in 1967-68. Players such as Greg Sheppard and future Edmonton Oiler Jim Harrison led the Bruins to this western crown.

The rivalry between the Calgary Centennials and Edmonton Oil Kings took shape in the 1968-69 season. In the Western Division the Centennials thrashed the Kings 6-0 to take a two point lead in the best-of-seven series. One game had been tied. (two points for a win and one for a tie) The first team to get eight points would win the series.

Bill Hunter said after the shutout, "that was the worst playoff performance by one of my clubs in twenty-three years in the business".

A fan remarked, "they should have cut the intermissions in half because there was no need to refinish the ice in the Calgary half of the rink".

However, Billy Moores scored two goals for the Oil Kings as they defeated the Centennials 5-1 before 6,500 fans in Edmonton. In what Scotty Munro of the Centennials described as a "near perfect game", the Oil Kings defeated Calgary 3-2 and advanced against the Flin Flon Bombers for the Western Canadian title and the right to play in the Canadian Hockey Association national final. The Calgary-Edmonton series attracted nearly 40,000 fans in seven games. The number likely would have been higher had the Oil Kings not been forced to play the fifth game at the 3,000 seat University of Alberta Rink because of previous bookings at the Gardens.

Before the Flin Flon series, Hunter announced he was going to quit coaching and continue as general manager after the season because doctors told him he could not stand the strain of both. A two game lead by the Kings surprised the powerful Bombers; however, Flin Flon won the series.

The Canadian Hockey Association final for 1969 between the Bombers and St. Thomas Barons was a disaster. The Bombers were ahead 3-0 in games. In the fourth game St. Thomas took its team off the ice. St. Thomas complained about the roughness of the series. CHA President, Ron Butlin of Calgary, awarded the championship to Flin Flon and suspended St. Thomas.

In 1969-70 junior hockey in Alberta continued in the limelight as professional hockey still had not returned. The Centennials defeated the Saskatoon Blades and the Oil Kings eliminated the Swift Current Broncos to meet again in the Western Division final of the Western Canada Hockey League for 1969-70.

Once again Scotty Munro, known at times as the "Rotund Rascal" and Bill Hunter the "Firey Leader" would meet. The King's style was tough checking while the Centennials were high scoring and speedy.

The series event seemed to go on forever as the clubs reached the seventh game of the best-of-nine. Hal Walker, sports editor of the "Calgary Herald" said:

> I think it is time for the Western Canada Hockey league to look at itself in a large mirror...The entertainment dollar can only be stretched so far and when the electricity in it is lost some people get hurt".

EDMONTON OIL KINGS 1969-70

Front row (l to r): Ray Barth (treasurer), Jim Pelehos (executive assistant), Ted McAneeley (assistant captain), Bill Hunter (general manager, coach), Bill Moores (captain), Zane Feldman (president), Ron Jones (assistant captain), Ron Walters (trainer), Jerry Blackwell (equipment assistant). Second row (l to r): Ron Williams, Randy Wyrozub, Derek Harker, Jim Schraefel, Doug Kerslake, Dan Spring, Larry Bignell, Ian Wilkie. Third row (l to r): Henry Van Drunen, Don Murray, Jack Cummings, Grant Evans, Bob McAneeley, Ron Malin, Doug Bentley Jr., Dave Glasgow. *Photo courtesy of McDermid Studios and Edmonton Archives*

In game seven, the Centennials defeated the Kings 4-2 to move ahead 3-2 in games plus two tied games. Munro said after the game, "that should teach Hunter and his hatchet men we are not going to take that forever. We kicked the stuffing out of them, didn't we?" Fans in Edmonton and Calgary continued to flock to the rink for game eight. More than 6,500 watched the Oil Kings edge out the Centennials 3-2 at the Corral in Calgary, to tie up the series. WCHL President Ron Butlin announced that the ninth game would be played to a finish rather than having a tenth match in case of a tie. Besides more games the series cost more dollars.

Munro raised ticket prices in Calgary from $1.75 to $2.00 for adults; however, Hunter in Edmonton raised childrens' from 50 cents to $1.00 and adults at $2.50 and $3.00. It was inflation.

Finally on April 29, 1970, Hunter's Oil Kings edged Munro's Centennials 1-0 before 6,149 fans in Calgary. Randy Wyrozub scored on Calgary goalie Ed Dyck at 7:05 of the first period. Ian Wilkie, the Edmonton goalie, had twenty-seven shots for the shutout.

For the second straight year the Kings played the Flin Flon Bombers for the Father Athol Murray Trophy in a best-of-seven. The Bombers defeated the Kings 4-3 on a goal by Reg Leach at 8:57 in the third period before 4,574 fans in Edmonton. This concluded the season for the Bombers as well. The problems caused by the withdrawal and suspension of St. Thomas the year before had not been resolved and no Canadian playoff was held for 1970 for major junior hockey.

In 1971 the Calgary Centennials and the Edmonton Oil Kings met for the Western Canada Hockey League Western Division Championship. The "Cents" defeated the Swift Current Broncos 4-3 to win their semi-final playoff series 3-0 with two games tied. The Kings won their berth by eliminating the Sasktoon Blades 4-1 in games.

It was the third straight year Edmonton and Calgary met for the Divisional title. There were problems in booking ice April 1st. Hunter was told the Gardens would not be available until April 13th because of the Rodeo and Boat Show. Hunter indicated that the series may not resume until the 13th and gave no indication of when tickets would go on sale.

Wayne Overland, in his column on April 2, 1971 in the "Edmonton Journal", poked fun at the Oil Kings and Centennials. He made up a crystal ball of sports events to come in the future in Edmonton for 1971.

July 15th, Edmonton Oil Kings and Calgary Centennials to play their seventh straight tie playoff game
July 18th, Oil Kings and Centennials tie
August 27th, Oil Kings and Centennials tie
August 28th, Scotty Munro says he is opposed to overtime in playoff games
September 15th, Oil Kings and Centennials tie

In other words, Overland expected a long, long season again. The press criticized this type of series. but the fans still came to watch. This was the best hockey in Alberta as there still was no professional.

After losing the first two games and going down to Calgary for the third game, Bill Hunter took over officially as coach from Harvey Roy. Before a crowd of 7,945 fans at the Corral, Don Kozak scored 2 goals as the Oil Kings downed the Centennials 3-2. Jack Cummings was outstanding in the Edmonton net. Part of this victory was also psychological, as Munro had never defeated Hunter in a playoff series.

Hunter used Doug Bentley Jr. against Calgary's Bob Nystrom and tried to have Danny Spring take faceoffs against Jim Masters and Allan Rycroft. The Kings also played without defenceman Tom Bladon, who was out with a knee injury.

In game four, the Kings trailed the Centennials 3-1. Oil King goalie, Jack Cummings, was replaced in goal by Larry Hendricks. Ed Dyck in the Calgary goal started to waiver and when the game was over the Kings had rallied for a 7-4 victory to tie the series 2-2.

The Kings took a 3-2 lead in the series, defeating the Centennials 7-3 before 5,200 fans at the Edmonton Gardens. Danny Spring scored 3 goals. Others came from Don Kozak, Darcy Rota, Dave Kryskow and Bert Scott. John Davidson, up from the Lethbridge Sugar Kings of the Alberta Junior Hockey League, played in goal for Calgary.

For the third successive year, the Oil King's jinx continued over the Centennials as Hunter's team beat Munro's. The Kings won their fourth straight game with Hunter coaching them to a 2-1 victory in the Calgary Corral. Goals by Darcy Rota and Danny Spring held up as 15-year-old goalkeeper Larry Hendricks stopped everything except one shot by Calgary defenceman Wayne Gibbs.

After dropping the first two games in this series, the Oil Kings came back to win four straight over the Centennials.

It would now be the fourth consecutive year Hunter and Flin Flon's Patty Ginnell would meet in a playoff showdown. Ginnell had players such as Bobby Clark and Reg Leach and predicted the Bombers team would win in four straight games.

The first two games were split in Edmonton and the third game was a 5-5 tie. After four games, the series stood at two games to one for the Edmontonians with one game tied.

Edmonton was finally successful in Flin Flon as the Oil Kings became Western Canada Hockey League champions with a 7-6 victory over the Bombers. This was a first victory for a Bill Hunter team in playoffs over Flin Flon in four consecutive tries.

In the 1970-71 season, the Oil Kings were the winners of the Western Division and the club with the best win-loss record in the ten team league. After the Kings had won the Western Canada Hockey League championship, there was uncertainty about whether or not there would be a Canadian final under the supervision of the CAHA. Negotiations were finally completed between the Edmonton Oil Kings, Earl Dawson of the CAHA and the Quebec Ramparts, winners of Eastern Canada. The problems created when St. Thomas withdrew in the 1969 final in Flin Flon were resolved. This now caused Tier 2 teams from leagues such as the AJHL to play for another trophy. The Centennial Cup became their trophy.

EDMONTON OIL KINGS 1970-71

Front row (l to r): Ron Walters (trainer), Jim Pelehos (executive assistant), Ron Jones (captain), Bill Hunter (general manager), Zane Feldman (president), Harvey Roy (coach), Derek Harker (assistant captain), Dan Spring (assistant captain), Bob Freeman (chief scout). Second row (l to r): Phil Russell, Tom Bladon, Rick Worozub, Brian Duquette, Jerry Blackwell (equipment), Larry Hendricks, Wayne Meier (director of player personnel), Bert Scott, Randy Smith. Third row (l to r): Darcy Rota, John Rogers, Don Kozak, Dale Bowler, Hugh Perron, Jack Cummings, Doug Bentley Jr., Glenn Kosak, Henry Van Drunen, Dave Kryskow.   *Photo courtesy of McDermid Studios and Edmonton Archives*

It was decided to have a junior final against the Ramparts, a best-of-three national series in Quebec City for the Memorial Cup. The Remparts had become champions of Eastern Canada because the St. Catharine's Blackhawks had refused to appear in Quebec City for the sixth game of the Eastern final. St. Catharines apparently felt that its team would not get adequate protection from fans in Quebec City.

Hunter said his team had nothing to fear from fans in Quebec city,

"I think that it is a disgrace that St. Catharines should pick up their ball and bat and go home...Quebec City has a great tradition of hockey. It has produced stars such as Jean Beliveau and Guy LaFleur.

Due to lack of ice in Edmonton at the time, the Oil Kings practiced at the Royal Glenora Figure Skating Club.

The Oil Kings lost to the Ramparts in game one, 5-1 in Quebec City. In the game, Guy LaFleur scored one goal and assisted on three others and proved that he was indeed the best junior hockey player in Canada at that time. If the Kings were going to go any further they would have to find a way to prevent LaFleur from doing the same things he had done in the first game.

In game two, the Oil Kings had a 2-2 tie after the first period, but were unable to stay with the Quebec squad which scored three unanswered goals to win 5-2 and sweep the best-of-three Memorial Cup final in two straight games. LaFleur, however, was held to one point by checker Dave Kryskow. Jean Landry and forward Jacques Richard scored two goals each with Andre Savard getting a single. Derek Harker and Bert Scott replied for Edmonton.

Ron Butlin, President of the WCHL said at the time, "You have to see LaFleur to believe it". The crowd support for these two games in Quebec City was outstanding. More than 10,000 fans stood, clapped, sang and danced.

Edmonton's last trip to the Memorial Cup was in 1971-72. In the 1972 Western Canada Hockey League Western Division Semi-Final series the Edmonton Oil Kings were defeated 4-2 in the third game by New Westminster Bruins. The Oil Kings won the best-of-seven series 4-1. The Brian Shaw coached team was much better defensively with Tom Bladon and Phil Russell as stalwarts on defence.

The Calgary Centennials made the finals through the efforts of goalkeeper John Davidson. The Centennials took on the Medicine hat Tigers, coached by Jack Shupe in the other division semi-final. The Tigers defeated the Centennials 4-1 to take a 2-0 lead in games. Defenceman, Jim Watson, of the Centennials pulled the Calgary squad into a 3-3 tie with Medicine Hat, deadlocking the series 2-2.

EDMONTON OIL KINGS 1971-72

Front row (bottom, l to r): Wayne Meier (director of player personnel), Larry Hendrick, Darcy Rota, Phil Russell, W.D. Hunter (general manager), Zane Feldman (president), Brian Shaw (coach), Tom Bladon, John Rogers, Doug Soetaert, Bob Freeman (chief scout). Second row (l to r): Terry McDonald, Curtis Shokoples, Don Kozak, Ron Walters (trainer), Fred Comrie, Henry Van Drunen, Terry Smith, Fleuri Perron. Third row (l to r): Jim Pelehos (executive assistant), Marcel Comeau, Randy Smith, John Davidson, Dave Inkpen, Brian Ogilvie, Jerry Blackwell (equipment manager). *Photo courtesy of McDermid Studios*

Due to the efforts of Davidson, the Calgary squad finally reached the final against the Oil Kings. Shupe, of the Tigers, felt his team would have beaten the Centennials in four straight games if it was not for Davidson. Calgary coach Chuck Holdaway, claimed that Davidson was the best junior goalkeeper he had ever seen.

In the Western Division final, the Edmonton Oil Kings under Brian Shaw, defeated the Calgary Centennials 4-2 and won the best-of-seven series four games to two. With Doug Soetaert playing brilliantly in the Edmonton goal, Darcy Rota scored two goals. Singles were scored by Brian Ogilvie and Don Kozak. The Kings advanced to the Memorial Cup final.

The King's string of wins ran out in the Memorial Cup final in Ottawa. In this three team tournament the Cornwall Royals and the Peterborough Petes both defeated the Edmonton Oil Kings. (The Royals were coached by Orval Tessier and the Petes by Roger Neilson.) In the final before 10,155 fans in Ottawa, the Royals beat the Petes 2-1 in sudden death, to win the Memorial Cup.

These losses by the Oil Kings ended their almost total domination of junior hockey in Alberta and Western Canada. Professional hockey came to Alberta. Fans in Edmonton supported the new Alberta Oilers (renamed the Edmonton Oilers in their second season) and the Oil Kings declined.

The Medicine Hat Tigers had their best year in 1972-73. Ed Willes, sports writer of the Medicine Hat News, describes that season and other Tiger highlights.

MEDICINE HAT TIGERS

BY ED WILLES

The list of Memorial Cup champions reads like a time schedule for CP rail...Hull, Cornwall, Owen Sound, Barrie, Kitchener, Sudbury, Portage La Prairie, Flin Flon, New Westminster...It is these places where one discovers hockey is truly Canada's game. The junior game flourishes as an essential, grassroot level in small centres that is foreign to city slickers.

There is nothing pretentious or manufactured about the love of the game here. The sport stamps the city with a sense of identity. The teams become a source of community pride, fiercely defended in defeat and cherished in victory. Moreover, hockey also provides the locals with a much needed source of entertainment in dreary winter months. Have you ever tried to kill a winter in Flin Flon? And, every now and then a team comes along in these places that becomes the stuff of legends. The players are revered, the team is a much-discussed item in ad hoc hot stove leagues all over town...''How many goals did McDonald get last night? Did you see Gassoff pound that guy? Who's gonna draft Lysiak?'' After the players graduate their feats are remembered with dewy-eyed sentiment. They pass into the mythology of the city — figures who grow larger than life in the process.

Medicine Hat, from a distance, appears to be a quaint, little Prairie city, nestled along the South Saskatchewan river valley. But there is a tough, pioneer spirit here that belies its gentle appearance. In 1973, the Medicine Hat Tigers won the Western Hockey League championship and came within a game of advancing to the Memorial Cup final. Along the way, the Tigers built an ''affaire de coeur'' with their city. And, in many ways, the character of that team reflected the character of Medicine Hat.

The Tigers have suffered indifferent success in their most recent 14-year incarnation in the WHL. To be sure they've usually been competitive, but rarely have they crossed the line into greatness. The 1973 team broke their monotony of mediocrity. The 1972-73 Tigers had everything: flashy goal scorers in Lanny McDonald and Tom Lysiak, solid two-way players in Eddie Johnstone and Barry Dean and an element of thuggery in the three Gassoff brothers and Jim McCrimmon that really endeared them to the Hat.

MEDICINE HAT TIGERS 1972-73

Top row (l to r): Bob Gassoff, Barry Dean, Dick Jellema, Jim McCrimmon, Brian Maxwell, Paul Granchukoff, Greg Vaydick, Randy Aimoe. Centre row (l to r): Jerry Farwell, Murray Worley, Brad Gassoff, Ed Johnstone, Lou Klashinsky (trainer), Ryan Wecker, Ken Gassoff, Boyd Anderson, Jerry Thomas. Front row (l to r): Lanny McDonald, Joe Fisher (owner), George Maser (owner), Sam Clegg, Rod Carry (owner), Jack Shupe (coach manager), Tom Lysiak.

The WHL was a different league then. There was no underage draft. Players stayed with teams for three and four years. By the end of their junior careers they were men. It was a tough league. This was the era when the big, bad Boston Bruins and the Broad Street Bully Philadephia Flyers were winning Stanley Cups. Their example carried over to juniors. There was an atmosphere of professional wrestling in most arenas of the time. Brawls were commonplace and encouraged by fans...the Tigers went along with the spirit of the times.

That same team wouldn't win anything now, says Bob Ridley who has broadcasted Tigers games on the local radio station since their inception in 1970. They couldn't play that way or they'd spend all their time suspended. Kids were different then. If you told a kid to run through the wall for you he would. Now he'd tell you to get lost.

It was their toughness, as much as their hockey skills, that sold the Tigers to Medicine Hat. The new Arena Convention Centre was jam-packed for every playoff game that year and the fans were bloodthristy. So was the media. A reporter named Al Mainline covered the Tigers for the Medicine Hat News that year and spent more time going over the details of the fights than the hockey game.

Jack Shupe built the Tiger's championship team. He acted as coach and general manager of the team for their first seven years of existence and had dictatorial powers over all hockey decisions. The team was owned by three local businessmen: Rod Carry, Joe Fisher, and George Maser. Maser would eventually take control of the team himself.

The foundation of the 1973 Tigers was laid in 1970-71, the Tiger's first year in the league. To stock the expansion team a draft was held. Existing WHL teams could protect players and the Tigers had their pick of leftovers. It was in this draft that the Tigers nabbed Lysiak and McDonald. There is still some debate whether this was from design or good fortune. The Tigers had originally drafted a player named John Sinkfield from Calgary Centennials. Sinkfield, however, refused to report and in his place the Tigers took a 17-year-old, clean-shaven player from Hanna, Alberta, named Lanny McDonald. The same thing happened with Lysiak. The Tigers picked Henry Van Drunen from the Edmonton Oil Kings. Van Drunen had been one of the Oil King's top scorers and he too, refused to report to the expansion Tigers. In his place, the Tigers picked 17-year-old Tom Lysiak from High Prairie, Alberta.

Initially, there was no reason to think the Tigers had gotten hold of anything special. As is the case with most expansion teams, the Tigers struggled their first year finishing in last place in the WHL's Western Division. Lysiak played in 60 games, picking up 14 goals and 16 assists. McDonald played in just six games and did not score a goal.

The following year was a different story. The Tigers, led by two stars, finished fourth and made playoffs. Lysiak scored 46 goals and added 97 assists and led the league in scoring. McDonald, his right winger, added 50 goals and 64 assists. The two returned in 1972-73 to a tough league. The Tigers main competition was expected to come from an Edmonton Oil King's team that featured future NHLers Darcy Rota and Harold Snepts and a Calgary Centennials team that had John Davidson in goal and were led by Danny Gare and Mike Rogers upfront.

In the Eastern Division, the Saskatoon Blades had built a powerhouse around defencemen, Dave Lewis and Pat Price and forward Bob Bourne. The Oil Kings won the Western pennant, finishing one point ahead of the Tigers. Lysiak and McDonald dominated the leagues' individual statistics. Lysiak again led in scoring, with 58 goals and 96 assists for 154 points. McDonald finished third with 62 goals and 77 assists for 139 points.

The regular season, though, would prove to be just a preliminary to the main event because the real fun for the Tigers started in the playoffs. Their first round opponents were the Scotty Munro coached Centennials. The Tigers beat them four games to two and advanced to the next round against the Oil Kings. The Centennial series was not without incident. Bob Gassoff, who along with his brother Brad and Ken, formed the Gassoff gang, fought with Calgary backup goalie, Doug Sauter, three times in the series. Sauter is now the coach of the Tigers.

The Tigers went on to beat the Oil Kings in six games, after losing the first two at home, and advanced to the league championship series against the Blades. Both cities were ready for the impending war. The Tigers won the series in five games with three wins and two ties (There was no overtime in those days. The first team to get eight points won the series) and won the fight to boot. That is what has endured to Hat fans, not only did the Tigers win, but they did it with style.

Russ Williams, a native of Saskatoon, who is now general manager of the Pioneer Baseball Leagues' Medicine Hat Blue Jays, recalls the turning point of the series occured when Lysiak speared Lewis for 15 stitches, an incident that went without retaliation. "Hell, he might have been the toughest son-of-a-bitch on the team. When he speared Lewis you could just see the Blades die." Later on, Bob Gassoff speared Blade's coach Jackie McLeod. McLeod grabbed Gassoff's stick and was assessed a two minute bench minor. By the time the Tigers left Saskatoon they needed police protection to get on and off the ice and into the team bus.

Back home in the Hat, McDonald scored 3 goals in the fifth and deciding game as the Tigers beat the Blades 6-3, to earn a trip to the Memorial Cup. The following day an editorial appeared in the pages of the Medicine News congratulating the Tigers for their win.

In 1948 a band of fans from Calgary turned the Grey Cup into a national drunk. In 1973, 500 fans from Medicine Hat tried to do the same thing with the Memorial Cup. They failed to win the cup but it wasn't from lack of effort.

There was just one week between the Tigers win over the Blades and the start of the Memorial Cup. With hockey fever now clutching at the vitals of the city, hurried arrangements had to be made to get Hat fans to Montreal with their team. Pat Cooke, who works for a local travel agency, eventually got 389 fans to Montreal on a chartered air flight. A further 100 drove, walked, snowshoed or backpacked to Montreal for the start of the national Junior chamionship. "It was unreal," says Cooke. "Everybody in town wanted to go. Anybody who could go went."

Medicine Hat took on a carnival atmosphere in the week leading up to the Memorial Cup. The Medicine Hat News had a two-page ad that read, simply, 'Go Tigers Go', and was endorsed by a plethora of local business-men. One thousand people attended a civic reception to send the Tigers off from a city of 29,000.

But the real star of the week was Mayor Harry Veiner. Veiner could be best described as equal parts Hughie Long and P.T. Barnum. He was Mayor of the Hat for 22 years between 1952 and 1974. Veiners's exploits could fill this book and four others. He had a penchant for bizzare publicity gimmicks and, with the Hat now gaining some national attention, he saw a big opportunity. This was a man who challenged the Mayor of Edinburgh to see who could kick a soccer ball the furthest. He also raced Brandon Mayor Jim Creighton. Local legend says Veiner was losing the race until he tripped Creighton, breaking his leg. Along somewhat the same lines, Veiner challenged the Mayors of the two other towns competing in the Memorial Cup, Quebec City and Toron-to, to a heel-and-toe race. Hat businessmen even put up $1,000 to back their Mayor. However, the race never came off. As New's managing editor Pete Mossey says, "By that time people were starting to get a little tired of Veiners' antics."

The Tigers, replete with their noisy entourage, arrived in Montreal to face the Toronto Marlboros and the Quebec Ramparts. The teams played each other once in the round-robin portion of the tournament and the two teams with the best records advanced to the championship game. The Tigers were probably considered the un-derdogs of the tournament. The Marlies were an exceptional junior team led by Mike Palmateer in goal, Bob Dailey on defence and Mark Howe upfront. The Ramparts, which had reigned in the Quebec league for years were led by forwards Andre Savard and Guy Chouinard. They were coached by former Chicago Black Hawks boss Orval Tessier.

The Tigers drew a bye in the first round and watched the Marlies dismantle the Ramparts. Their fans took the opportunity to have some good clean fun. "It was four in the morning and I was asleep," says Cooke, who misguidedly booked all the Hat fans into the same hotel.

The hotel security phoned and asked me to come and get a man who was hanging off the chandelier and eating the light bulbs. A couple of nights later they phoned again. Someone had passed out in the hall in front of his door with his key in his hand, but he couldn't make it into his room. He was out cold.

Thankfully, for the fans' livers, the Tigers finally took to the ice for their first game against the Marlies. The WHL representative upset the powerful Toronto team 3-2 and seemed to have a lock on the final. The same summary showed no indication of the Tiger's usual antics but Mainline, with his unerring eye for detail, reported the next day in the News the turning point in the game came when Bob Gassoff punched out Marlies tough guy, John Hughes.

With the win only the Quebec Ramparts stood between the Tigers and a spot in the Memorial Cup champion-ship game. But the Tigers pulled a self-destruct number in the first period of their final game. Victimized by bad goal tending and a whistle-happy referee, they trailed 6-1 after the opening period. They finally lost the game 7-3 and were eliminated because of their goals for, goals against record.

End of Dream.

The next day Mainline reported the Tigers lost because Gassoff didn't beat anybody up, "like in the Marl-boros' game".

"That's what I remember most about the trip to Montreal," says Rod Carry. "The loss to Quebec. We had a great year and should have been in the finals. There was a real sense of disappointment."

The Tigers limped home to the Hat and were greeted by 1,500 fans at a parade held in their honor. The fans left in Montreal didn't go down quietly. On the same day as the Marlies crushed the Ramparts 9-1 to take the

Memorial Cup, they crammed in one final party as a last hurrah. "They put all the leftover bottles in one room and had a big smash," remembers Cooke.

"We were waiting for the busses to take us to the airport and our fans were out on the streets direct-
ing traffic with styrofoam hats on their heads. Then they started eating the hats. We finally got them
out of there. After they all left I poured myself a stiff drink and went and spent a quiet week with
my mother. I've never had a week like that.

Lysiak and McDonald stayed in Montreal for the NHL draft. Rumor had Lysiak or the Rampart's Savard going second to the Montreal Canadiens after New York Islanders took Ottawa 67's defenceman, Denis Potvin, with the first pick of the draft. But the Canadiens traded down and let the Atlanta Flames take the Tigers centre.

LANNY McDONALD — CAPTAIN, CALGARY FLAMES

Photo courtesy of Bob Mummery

McDonald went fourth overall to the Toronto Maple Leafs and the Canadiens surprised everyone by taking little-known Peterborough Pete's forward Bob Gainey as their pick.

Lysiak, McDonald, Bob Gassoff and Jim McCrimmon all signed up with agent Richard Zorken after the draft, hoping to cash in on their junior careers. Bad move. Zorken, a shady character, bilked Lysiak out of $150,000 and McCrimmon and Gassoff out of $40,000 each. He eventually went to jail.

Only McDonald got out unscathed.

There are a few interesting footnotes to the Tiger's season in the sun. Lysiak never realized his superstar potential in a checkered NHL career. McDonald went on to fame and fortune as the NHL's most famous moustache. Eddie Johnstone has turned in a solid career as a workman-like journeyman and Boyd Anderson, the third member of the Lysiak-McDonald line, enjoyed some success in Sweden. Bob Gassoff, who no-less-an-expert than Tiger Williams called the toughest hockey player he's ever seen, died in a motorcycle accident.

The Tigers, for their part, lapsed back into mediocrity after 1973. The next season, still riding the coattails of the Memorial Cup team, they sold over 3,000 season tickets but finished third in their division and were knocked out of the playoffs in the first round. Shupe was let go in 1976-77 and the Tigers struggled the next two years.

They hired Patty Ginnell, four times WHL Coach of the Year, in 1979-80 to turn the team around. But Ginnell, whose approach to hockey was right out of the 'Stone Age' did little to build more good teams. Ginnell himself, was suspended for 36 games for fighting with a linesman. He was let go at the end of the season.

In 1982, with the team in disarray, George Maser, who bought out Carry and Fisher, turned the team over to 26 year old general manager Russ Farwell. Farwell, and his coach, Ray McKay, guided the team to a playoff spot in their first year and a berth in the Eastern Division final in 1983-84 against the Regina Pats. The Tigers were ousted in five games and McKay was fired at the end of the year. Farwell brought his old Calgary Centennial Wrangler buddy, Doug Sauter, in to coach the team this year. Sauter, one of the brightest young minds in hockey, got the team off to a 9-2-1 start, second best in all of Canada.

Medicine Hat hockey fans are staying tuned. They're still waiting for another year like 1973.

* * *

The Western Canada Junior Hockey League had not even started its league play when President Ed Chynoweth suspended eleven players and fined three coaches. This was on September 28, 1973 and the league schedule was not ready to start until October 4th. Chynoweth, then 31, had served the previous year as executive secretary of the league under previous President Tom Fischer. At that time Chynoweth said, "What we're trying to do is to make sure that somebody doesn't get seriously hurt. We can do that if we eliminate stick swinging, spearing and butt ending."

Despite all the rough play, the Western Canada Hockey League did get to finish the 1973-74 season. At the conclusion, Ron Chipperfield of the Brandon Wheat Kings finished with 162 points made up of 90 goals and 72 assists. Dennis Sobchuk of the Regina Pats finished second with 146 points, including 68 goals, while Mike Rogers of Calgary Centennials was third with 140 points, including 67 goals.

The top goalkeeper in the league was Garth Malarchuk who finished with a goals-against average of 3.0557 compared to 3.0587 for Ed Staniowski of the Regina Pats. The league had eight 50 goal scorers with others being Danny Gare of Calgary with 68, D. Johnstone of Medicine Hat with 64 and Jerry Holland of Calgary with 55.

"Terrible" Ted Olsen of the Edmonton Oil Kings set the league record in penalty minutes with 435, shattering the previous record of 388 set by Bob Gassoff of Medicine Hat, in the previous season.

In the 1973-74 playoffs the Edmonton Oil Kings defeated the Calgary Centennials 4-3 in overtime to tie their semi-final series at one game apiece. The victory for the Kings in Calgary was unbelievable as it was their first victory in fourteen games against the Centennials. Mike Will scored at 1:23 of sudden death overtime to give the Kings their victory. Bill Hunter predicted that history would repeat itself and he would again defeat Scotty. Hunter called it the greatest victory in Oil King history.

However, Scotty Munro and the Calgary Centennials came back to shellack the Edmonton Oil Kings 7-0 and win the best-of-seven series in five games. Junior hockey was popular in Calgary as 6,674 fans at the Corral witnessing the match. This was the first time Scotty had beaten Bill with the Centennials in a post season playoff. For the Centennials, Don Ashby scored three, Mike Rogers two, with singles going to Grant Mulvey and Danny Gare.

Attendance for junior hockey in Edmonton was declining with the competition from the World Hockey Association. Only around 2,000 fans per game watched the Oil Kings play their playoff games.

The Centennials advanced further in the playoffs by eliminating the Estevan Bruins. The Regina Pats defeated Bryan Trottier and the Swift Current Broncos 4-1 and earned a final playoff spot in the Western Canada Hockey League final against Calgary. Greg Joly scored two for Regina while Clark Gillies and Rob Laird scored one each for the Pats. Dave "Tiger" Williams got the lone goal for Swift Current.

The highly favored Regina Pats dumped the Centennials 5-2 before an overflow crowd of 7,074 fans at the Calgary Corral to win the Western Canada Hockey League best-of-seven finals, in four straight games. For coach Bob Turner, of the Pats, the game and the series sweep was not a surprise as they went on to win the Memorial Cup.

By November 17, 1974 the Edmonton Oil Kings had played one quarter of their league schedule and were entrenched in fifth place in the West Division. Only the Calgary Centennials were worse. The Centennials had won only one game in their first twenty and were 9 points behind the Oil Kings. Alberta teams all exited early in 1974-75. Teams that reached the quarter-finals were the Regina Pats versus the Saskatoon Blades, and the Victoria Cougars versus the New Westminster Bruins. The Bruins represented the West in the Memorial Cup final. They got their second chance in two years to go to the Memorial Cup as they defeated the Saskatoon Blades in the seventh game of the Western Canada Hockey League final series. In front of 3,049 fans in New Westminster, the Bruins defeated the Blades 3-1.

In June, 1976, it was announced that the Edmonton Oil Kings, once the class act of the Western Canada Hockey league, would move to Portland, Oregon. The Kings had finished next to last in their division in 1975-76, and crowd support had dropped to an average of 1,500 fans per game. Part Owner-General manager Brian Shaw felt that relocation was necessary. The franchise moved to Portland and became known as the "Winter Hawks".

In 1977-78 the Calgary Centennials of the Western Canada Hockey League pulled up stakes and moved to Billings, Montana. This left Calgary in an awkward position. It also had no major hockey team in town, as the Calgary Cowboys of the World Hockey Association were also ready to fold. This move spelled the end of a ten year association in Calgary, which saw the Centennials bring junior hockey respectability back to the city.

The Centennials had replaced the Calgary Buffalos, who had at times played to fewer than a hundred fans in the then spacious Stampede Corral. Under the direction of Scotty Munro, the Centennials became a success story, frequently filling the 6,495 seat Corral and generating over $100,000 in annual rental revenue for the Calgary Exhibition Association.

The owner of the Centennials, Dick Koentages felt that the competition of the Calgary Cowboys for fans as well as playing dates and the high rental fee for the Corral, made the move desirable. Billings boasted an 8,600 seat sports complex with no other hockey team for competition. Bob Strumm, who at the time was assistant to WCHL President Ed Chynoweth, was appointed the new general manager of the Billing's Big Horns. Saskatoon's Dave King was the first coach. This was Dave's first full time job in hockey. For Calgary, the next junior team would be the Wranglers.

CALGARY WRANGLERS

BY DARYL SLADE, sports writer, Calgary Herald

Optimism was high back in 1977 when owner Gerry Brisson packed up his Winnipeg Monarchs and moved them to Calgary, to fill the Western Hockey League vacancy created by the recently-departed Centennials. That spring, the once-beloved Centennials moved not only away from Calgary, but clear out of Alberta to Billings, Montana, to become the Bighorns. About the same time, the Calgary Cowboys had just struck out after two financially-plagued seasons in the dying World Hockey Association.

CALGARY WRANGLERS 1980-81

First row (l to r): C. Sebastian, B. Hobbins, C. Fehr, R. Cote, D. Sauter, D. Keller, B. Bascotto, M. Vernon. Second row: L. Verstraete, D. Anhoft, B. Taylor, C. Chisholm, B. Robertson, G. Stilling, J. Smyth, R. Tutt, B. Brigley. Third row: G. Stamler, B. Vince, D. Mulvenna, G. Dickie, D. Thompson, M. Heidt, D. Bourbonnais, G. Chudiak, S. Mounkes, A. Murray.

There was no other worthy tenant for the old 6,495 seat Stampede Corral, so it appeared Major Junior Hockey just might survive in the cowtown. Competition in the near future did not seem to be a problem since prospects of a National Hockey League team were extremely remote. The NHL frowned upon placing a team in the tiny old Corral, and there was not yet talk of a new facility that would meet league standards. During the next couple of years, the Wranglers thrived as the No. 1 team in town. However, just over the horizon, Calgary was to become a major league sports town.

A group that called itself the Calgary Olympic Development Association was preparing a bid that would eventually lead to the city winning the right, in September 1981, to play host to the 1988 Winter Olymics, and in the spring of 1980, Nelson Skalbania was buying the Atlanta Flames with the intention of moving them here. Both ventures meant imminent financial doom, if not eventual death, for Major Junior Hockey in Calgary.

The coming of the Olympics meant there would be a new, 16,000 seat facility, but, it would be out of the price range of the Wranglers, and fans who had a taste of the new Olympic Saddledome, would no longer cast a glance at the neighboring "Barn". Perhaps the Wranglers still live today only because the Flames had to play three seasons in the Corral as the Saddledome was being built. Demand was much higher than availability for Flame season tickets, so Flame officials worked out a deal with then Wrangler owner, Pat Shimbashi for fans to purchase an option for season tickets when the Flames moved into the new building.

It worked for two years. And just in the nick of time for Shimbashi, who had bought the club from Jim Morley, who had bought the club from Brisson, sold out to Wilf Richard and Jim Kerr. The promotion greatly aided the Wranglers, who were playing winning hockey under General Manager-Coach Doug Sauter. They drew crowds in excess of 6,000 for league games and more than 7,000 in the 1981 WHL final series, when the club took the Victoria Cougars, led by now Edmonton Oiler goalie Grant Fuhr, to a dramatic seventh game before losing.

Season tickets dropped off dramatically once the Flames moved into the Saddledome, creating more than twice as many seats available to hockey fans, and set the stage for a dramatic collapse in junior attendance. Wrangler season ticket sales plummeted from more than 2,000 and 1,700 in the "option years" to 550 in 1983-84, when the Canadian Olympic team, playing out of the Saddledome, also provided competition for the fan's hockey dollar. Kerr, who had assumed control of the Wranglers from Richard during the 83-84 season, sold out to a group headed by businessman Brian Eckstrom in the summer of 1984. Eckstrom vowed to keep the team in Calgary, but had to work out a new ease agreement with the Calgary Exhibition and Stampede in order to make the venture even moderately feasible.

While many ex-Centennials have stepped into starring roles in the NHL and leave a legacy with former line-mates, Danny Gare and Mike Rogers, still enjoying success, an ex-Wrangler has yet to make that big break-through. Entering the 1984-85 season, only one ex-Wrangler, centre Kelly Kisio, now with Detroit Red Wings, was playing regularly in the NHL. Several players, like Glenn Merkosky, Ray Cote, Mike Vernon, Dan Bourbonnais, Warren Skorodenski, Leigh Verstraete and Mike Heidi, are amoung the few others who have had a taste of the big time.

* * *

The Edmonton Oil Kings made a comeback in 1978-79. Don Scott was hired in August 1978 to become general manager of the new Oil Kings. In 1963 he had been public relations director with the Kings and later became assistant general manager, under Bill Hunter. In 1975, he became general manager of the Kings, until the group was sold to Brian Shaw. Vic Mah was president of the Oil Kings for the 1975-76 season. In 1978-79 Mah became the major shareholder in the new team and their first Vice President and Chairman of the Oil King's management. Wayne Tennant became a part owner and coached and developed that team for the first eighteen games. As planned Tennant stepped down and Norm Ferguson took over as coach until the end of the season. Bill Hunter was another part owner and President of the new Oil Kings.

EDMONTON OIL KINGS 1978-79

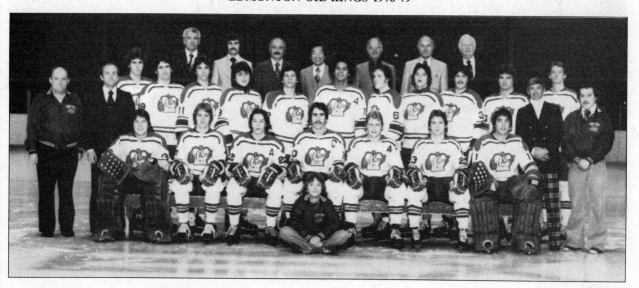

Front row (l to r): Gord Garbutt, Mel Piluk, Terry Davis, Steve Blue, Craig Levie, Bruce Jacobson, Al Wiebe. **Middle row (l to r):** Jerry Blackwall (assistant trainer), Norm Ferguson (coach), Dave Barr, Gerard Jubinville, Ryan Switzer, Franco Disciglio, Ray Karlson, Ray Neufeld, Greg Tennant, Derek Davis, Kevin Shaigec, Mike Moskalyk, Larry McCargar, Donald H. Scott (general manager), Lyle Kulchisky (trainer). **Back row (l to r):** James J. Pelehos (director), Harvey Henkle (scout), Wayne Tennant (director), Vic Mah (first vice-president), George Assaly (director), Ed Assaly (second vice-president), W.D. "Bill" Hunter (president). **Missing:** Edward Hughes (director), Al Cameron (director), Ray Barth (comptroller).

Photo courtesy of Edmonton Archives

This new group of Junior owners were hoping the fans would rather pay $3.00 to $4.00 to watch an Oil King game than put out $9.00 to $10.00 for the professional Oilers. The rejuvenated (formerly Flin Flon Bombers)

Kings lasted until the end of the 1979 season. They made the playoffs in their division and played in a round robin with Saskatoon and Brandon. Brandon won the round by one game to eliminate the Kings.

This "last" Oil King team had players such as Ray Neufeld who ended up playing with the Hartford Whalers, Craig Levie, St. Louis Blues, Dave Barr of the Pittsburg Penquins, Gord Garbutt, a goal tender in the Edmonton Oiler organization, Steve Blue and Derk "Boxer" Davis in the International league. These were the last Oil Kings to turn professional.

The Oil Kings were sold to Bob Cooper from Portland, Oregon. Cooper moved the team to Great Falls, Montana where they became known as the Americans.

Wayne Tennant believed that the Oil Kings failed in a number of areas but basically in fan attendance. He was of the opinion that had the team been purchased a year later, the Kings would still be in Edmonton. Vic Mah, a sportsman and team sponsor at several levels, continues to feel that major junior hockey can be successful in Edmonton and is continuing efforts to have a Tier 1 team operating out of Edmonton Northland's new Agri-Com Sports Complex, which includes a 4,000 seat arena.

LETHBRIDGE BRONCOS

BY DAVE SULZ, sports writer, Lethbridge Herald

When John Chapman became coach of the Lethbridge Broncos prior to the 1980-81 season, he began laying the groundwork for a three-year plan, aimed at taking the team to the Memorial Cup playoffs. The plan culminated on schedule, producing the high point of the Bronco's Western Hockey League history when, in the 1982-83 season, Lethbridge captured the WHL championship and went on to the Memorial Cup championships in Portland, Oregon.

The on-ice leaders of the Broncos were two brash 19-year-olds — twins Ron and Rich Sutter, who had played on Chapman's Red Deer Rustler team that captured the Tier 2 Centennial Cup in 1980. Ron and Rich were the last in a line of six Sutter brothers who wore the Bronco colors before going on to National Hockey League careers. The others were Brian, Duane, Darryl and Brent, and along with "The Twins", they helped write many colorful chapters in the Bronco's history.

LETHBRIDGE BRONCOS 1974-75

Front row (l to r): Rollie Boutin, Ron Delorme, Greg Woods, Earl Ingarfield (coach and assistant manager), Bryan Trottier (captain), Bill Burton (president and general manager), Dean Samis, Bill Jobson, Lorne Molleken. Middle row: Alec Tidey, Brian Sutter, John Lutz, Archie Henderson, Dick Abel (trainer), Don Johnson, Steve Lee, Les Crozier, Jerry Bancks. Back row: Wade Smith, Darcy Regier, Stan Jensen, Garth Morgan, Doug Gillespie. *Photo courtesy of Edmonton Archives*

The story of the Lethbridge Broncos began prior to the 1974-75 season when owner W.A. "Bill" Burton packed up his Swift Current Bronco's franchise and moved the club west to Alberta. The Broncos were coming off the most successful season in their seven years in Swift Current, having finished third in the league's Eastern Division and reaching the playoff semi-finals before losing to the eventual Memorial Cup champions Regina Pats.

Burton brought with him a future NHL star named Bryan Trottier, who had been drafted by New York Islanders after scoring 112 points in the 1973-74 season. Trottier, then 18, didn't stay with the Islanders the first time and returned to the Broncos to finish second in the Western Canada Hockey league scoring race in '74-'75, collecting 46 goals and a league leading 98 assists.

Broncos, playing in the new 5,500 seat Sportsplex, built for the 1975 Canada Winter Games, held in Lethbridge, finished below the east as western teams dominated that season.

Bronco's first coach in Lethbridge was hometown product Earl Ingarfield, who had scored 179 goals in a 12 year NHL career. Trottier, of course, wasn't the only future NHLer on that first Lethbridge club. Brian Sutter, a tough, aggressive winger, scored 34 goals and started the family tradition that would eventually see his five younger brothers follow in his footsteps to Lethbridge and on to the professional ranks.

LETHBRIDGE BRONCOS 1982-83

Front row (l to r): Ken Wregget, Doug Macauley (head scout), Rob Fritz (trainer), Ross McKibben (owner — general manager), Ron Sutter, John Chapman (coach), Harvey Beech (public relations director), Dwayne Murray. **Middle row:** Paul Fellger (bus driver), Bob Rouse, Troy Loney, Todd Stokowski, Marty Ruff, Rich Sutter, Grant Couture, Darcy Kaminski, Dwight Mullins, Rick Gral, J.C. McEwan, Ray Austring (bus driver). **Back row:** Doug Kyle, Kevin Pylypow, Steve Mounkes, Gerald Diduck, Mark Tinordi, Scott Shaw, Darin Sceviour, Ivan Krook. **Missing:** Shawn Green. *Photo courtesy of Edmonton Archives*

Lethbridge dropped to third place in 1975-76. Sutter scored 36 goals in his final junior season while Steve Tabellini, a slick-skating centre from Trail, B.C., paced the club with 97 points, inlcuding 38 goals.

Another member of the Broncos that season was Joel Meli who later became a Canadian champion in Judo. Meli represented Canada at the 1984 Summer Olympics in Los Angeles.

Mike Sauter replaced Ingarfield as coach for the 1976-77 season, but the Broncos still had an Earl Ingarfield on the club in the person of Earl Jr., who ironically had just completed a 36 goal season with Swift Current, of the Saskatchewan Junior Hockey League.

The WCHL was split into three divisions in '76-'77 and Lethbridge finished third in the four-team Central Division, having won 28 games for the third straight year. Rocky Saganiuk, a popular 5'8'' right winger, set a Bronco club record with 60 goals and Tambellini added 42. Two more products from the Sutter hockey player factory — 18 year old Darryl and 17 year old Duane — joined the Broncos for the playoffs.

After the season Burton sold the Broncos to Lethbridge businessman Dennis Kjeldgaard. The new owner didn't have to wait long to see his club become a contender. Under coach Howie Yanosik, another local product, the Broncos set a club record with 36 wins while placing atop the Central Division standings. Tambellini wound up his junior career in fine fashion, setting club marks with 75 goals and 155 points enroute to winning his second consecutive Frank Boucher Memorial Trophy as the league's Most Gentlemanly Player. "Tamby" also broke Trottier's career scoring record with 336 points to Trottier's 301.

By 1978-79, the league had shortened its name to the Western Hockey League and Patty Ginnell had become coach of the Broncos. The club dropped to sixth place in the Eastern Division as the league returned to its two division format. Duane Sutter wrapped up his Bronco career with 50 goals and 125 points while Gord Williams and Doug Morrison chipped in with 117 and 123 points respectively. The next year, Morrison collected 117 points and concluded his three-year Bronco career as the club's all-time leader with a total of 163 goals, 206 assists and 319 points.

Then came 1980-81 and the start of the John Chapman era, an era whose history is still being written.

* * *

ALBERTA JUNIOR HOCKEY LEAGUE

The Alberta Junior Hockey League began in the 1964-65 season. In the beginning AJHL teams competed in Memorial Cup playoffs, but in the 1970-71 season the league was designated Tier Two (as opposed to Tier One, the top level of junior hockey) and teams played off for the Centennial Cup.

The AJHL was usually under the shadow of the mighty Edmonton Oil Kings, a team so powerful it played in intermediate or senior leagues; no AJHL team ever got past the Oil Kings in Memorial Cup playoffs. Few hockey people thought the AJHL would last long or that it would grow to the highly competitive league it is today. The Oil Kings are gone and the AJHL remains as the only junior A hockey league in Alberta. It supplies players for the Western Hockey League (Tier One), for American and Canadian colleges and universities and some former AJHL players go directly on to the professional game.

THREE CANADIAN CHAMPIONSHIPS

BY MARTY KNACK, *Edmonton Journal,* sports writer

The 1970-71 Red Deer Rustlers did much more than win the inaugural Centennial Cup Championship and their first of two in a nine-year span. They also produced three outstanding Alberta hockey officials. Dale Henwood, the goalie with the 1970-71 Alberta Junior Hockey League champions, became the Technical Director of the Alberta Amateur Hockey Association in 1980. Two other Rustlers from the first Canadian Amateur Hockey Association Tier 2 Junior Champions, Wynne Dempster and Perry Pearn, became champions as coaches.

RED DEER RUSTLERS 1970-71

Back row (l to r): Dr. W.A. Carter (team physician), Don Bolkowy, Wayne Savill, Reno Siipola, Perry Pearn, Dennis Resch (trainer), Bill Scott (trainer), Hank Sanderson. Second row: Lorne Bartel, Mickey Girard, Mickey Unger, Tom Lindskog, Dave Andruchiw, John Davidson, Dwayne Bolkowy, Ross Frisken, Brent Going, Leo McDougal, John Laskoski. Front row: Jerome Keller (assistant captain), Ken McLash, Wynne Dempster (general manager — coach), A.W. Cadman (captain), Terry Wedderburn (manager), Lyle Sharp, Doug Stumpf (assistant captain), Brian Ogilvie, Dale Henwood, stick boys, Danny Cadman, Ronald Cadman.

Photo courtesy of Provincial Archives

Dempster took over the Rustlers in 1980-81 after John Chapman had led them to their second Centennial Cup title. Dempster was voted the league's Coach of the Year in 1982-83 and 1983-84, and consistently had Red Deer in contention for the Southern Division championship. Pearn became the head coach of the Northern Alberta Institute of Technology Ooks in 1978-79 and earned national titles in 1982 and 1985. In 1982 he took the Ooks to the Canadian Colleges' Athletic Association Championship after they finished second in the Alberta Colleges' Athletic Conference behind the Southern Alberta Institute of Technology Trojans. In 1985 the Ooks won every ACAC game.

"I think it was likely the best hockey of my career," says Henwood, one of the stars as the Rustlers defeated the Charlottetown Islanders 4-2 in a best-of-seven Centennial Cup Final. "That was two good weeks in my career." Henwood made 41 saves in Red Deer's 6-3 win in the opening game. After the Islanders narrowed the Rustler's series lead to 3-2 with a 7-2 decision in the fifth game, he was outstanding again as the AJHL winners rebounded for a 7-4 win and the title. "We did it all on the road," says Henwood, recalling some details of the march to the championship. "We played the Western Canadian finals in Taber and Winnipeg, because the arena in Red Deer was booked. Then we played all six games of the final in Charlottetown."

"I remember one other thing very clearly. Because of the length of the season, it was the first time I had played hockey without having to go to school during the day." A three-year Rustler's veteran, Henwood was a University student who had finished his studies for the year because the Cup final was in May. "Mount Royal College was in the AJHL then," he says.

We beat them in the AJHL final. That helped us, because they were an older and more experienced team. Then we played Penticton (from British Columbia Junior Hockey League). We beat them, it seems to me, in seven games. We won two out there and came home to finish the series. After that, we played Winnipeg St. James in the Western Final. I believe we swept them.

SPRUCE GROVE METS 1974-75

Front row (l to r): Richard Fuhr (president), Paul Messier, Julian Baretta, Doug Messier (coach), Kelly Bunn, Tim Thomlison, Jim Cross, Jack Reid (general manager). Second row: Charlie Mainhood (equipment manager), Murray Dea, Barry Brown, Eric Christiansen, Brian Granfield, Kim Spencer, Dave Hoyda, Keith Hertz, Ron Lecuyer, W. "Buck" Buckanesky (trainer). Third row: John Blackwell (trainer), Dan Shearer, Gerry Cormack, Vince Magnan, Roy Sommer, Brady Mason, Jeff Elkow, Tony Lecuyer, Brant Sim, Wayne Turner, Mike Cartwright (stick boy). Missing: Dr. J. Westwood, Bill Moores (assistant coach).

Photo courtesy of Provincial Archives

Henwood rated the Islanders "probably better than us." But the Rustlers, an experienced team like Mount Royal, prevailed. "Any time you win the first one, it's nice," says Henwood, who went on to help the University of Alberta Golden Bears to the Canadian Intercollegiate Athletic Union Championship in 1974-75.

Pearn, a centre and left winger, joined the Rustlers after playing for the U. of A. Junior Bears until Christmas. He agreed with Henwood's statement about the initial Cup competition. "That's one of the things I reflect on," says Pearn. "It was the first time and we went on and won it." He also remembers how well the Rustlers played away from home, which was a team trait. "Another thing which was a key to it was that we had played fairly well on the road all season," he says. "Going there (to Prince Edward Island) knit us all together. But it wasn't easy beating the Islanders."

We had a few harrowing moments," says Pearn, recalling how Charlottetown had an outstanding opportunity to tie the series in the fourth game before Red Deer erupted for what might still stand as a Cup record.

In the fourth game, if I remember correctly, we were down 2-1, Al MacAdam (an Islander who went on to play in the NHL) came in on a partial breakaway, Henwood made an excellent skate save and we went right down and scored. Then we got two more quick ones (goals) for three in 43 seconds. We went from what could have been even (in the series) to up 3-1. I thought the whole series keyed on those three goals in 43 seconds.

Like Henwood, Pearn feels that Brian Ogilvie *"was the key to the offence."* Henwood terms Ogilvie — who became top scorer in the Central Hockey League and played briefly in the NHL — as *"the only one who went on to do anything (professionally), in my opinion."* *"I don't think we had a great defence,"* says Pearn. *"But our defencemen were really intense, physical and intimidating. They liked to play it rough and tough."*

RED DEER RUSTLERS 1979-80

Back row (l to r): Chris Mundle (director — promotions manager), Dr. John McLuhan (team doctor), Dr. Bill Carter, Terry Sexsmith (trainer), Cliff Bailey (equipment manager), Dr. Gordon Huff (team dentist). **Third row (l to r):** Kim Marsh (statistician), Bill Blanchard, Ron Pierce, Ron Sutter, Tony Wozny, Rich Sutter, Joe DeMoissac, Ray Houle, Darren McKay. **Second row (l to r):** Garth Hildebrand, Doug Rigler, Darwin Casebeer, Darrell Anholt, Randy Moller, Glen Johanneson, Roger Pierce, Gord Ing, Ivan Krook. **First row (l to r):** Darryl 'Tiger' Pierce, Clarence Koch (director), Bob Bedier, John Chapman (coach), Brent Sutter, Graham Parsons (general manager), Joe Cunningham, Alf Cadman (director — president), Rory Delouise. **Kneeling (l to r):** Trevor Hunter (stick boy).

Photo courtesy of Provincial Archives

That meant plenty of extra work for Pearn, one of the leading penalty killers on the team. "Henwood was a key, too," he says. "He would let in some bad goals. But he always made the key saves at the right time."

Strangely enough, the Rustlers could have missed the Cup Playoffs. "Alf Cadman, the owner and coach, signed the players to Junior 'B' cards, so they'd be eligible to play in the Canada Winter Games that year," says Pearn. "But they lost in the Provincial tournament at Christmas and didn't qualify for the Games." Dempster was the other scoring star besides Ogilvie. In fact, Dempster tied a league playoff record when he scored 5 goals against Mount Royal in a March 7th game.

Garry Unger — who went on to become the NHL's leading ironman during a lengthy pro career — first set the AJHL single-game playoff goal-scoring record in the first season. He had 5 goals in a 1965 game for the Calgary Buffaloes in a playoff series against the Edmonton Movers. Another former Rustler, Corey Martin, shares the goal-scoring record with Unger and Dempster. Martin accomplished the feat March 17, 1968, in a game against the Lethbridge Sugar Kings. Because of Ogilvie's prowess as a scorer, it was fitting that he accounted for the winning goal in the final game of the series with the Islanders. Ogilvie's second goal of the game, on a breakaway at 7:37 of the third period, stood up as the winner.

Although the Rustlers showed others the way, an AJHL team did not win a national title again until 1975, when general manager-coach Doug Messier and super scout Jack Reid assembled a solid team with the Spruce Grove Mets. The Mets — which later became the St. Albert Saints — were led offensively by Paul Messier and Kelly Bunn, two 45 goal scorers during the regular schedule. Messier had 101 points and Bunn totalled 95, but an unlikely hero emerged in the championship final against the Guelph, Ontario, Holody Platers.

"Ron Lecuyer, a 20-year-old, was the hero in the finals," says Ray Turchansky, who covered the series for the *Edmonton Journal*. "He played in only 22 games during the regular schedule and had 14 points. But he led all point-gatherers against Guelph with 13." Spruce Grove beat the Platers in six games in a series played in its entirety at the old Edmonton Gardens on the Exhibition Grounds in Edmonton. A crowd of 2,800 watched the final game.

Julian Baretta was the Met's goalie and later went on to star with the University of Wisconsin Badgers of the Western Collegiate Hockey association. Dave Hoyda and Roy Sommer were two others — besides Messier — who went on to play professional, Hoyda as a tough guy with the Philadelphia Flyers and Sommer as a rugged winger in the Juniors.

"The Platers are a fairly experienced team with the possible exception of 15-year-old defenceman, Craig Hartsburg," Turchansky wrote in the program for the third game. Hartsburg went on to become an outstanding player with the Minnesota North Stars in the NHL but was barely noticeable against the Mets.

Spruce Grove finished first during the regular season, eliminated the Calgary Canucks in five games in the league semi-final and then had to recover from a 3-1 deficit with three straight wins in the final against the Drumheller Falcons. The Mets then defeated the Bellingham, Washington Blazers of the BCJHL before beating the defending Centennial Cup champion Selkirk Steelers of the Manitoba Junior Hockey League to earn the right to play Guelph. Paul Messier — Doug's son and the older brother of Mark, who went on to star for the Edmonton Oilers — shot the winning goal in the Met's 97th game of the season, at 1:59 of overtime in the sixth game against the Platers. Keith Hertz scored three times for Spruce Grove in the 6-4 win.

Five years later, the Rustlers managed to win their second title in a round-robin series against the north York Rangers of the Ontario Junior Hockey League and the Sherwood-Parkdale Metros from PEI. Brent Sutter — who established an AJHL record with 171 points during the regular schedule and helped the New York Islanders to their third and fourth consecutive Stanley Cup Championships in 1982 and 1983 — was voted the Most Valuable Player in the Centennial Cup final.

Sutter had two goals to lead Red Deer to a 3-2 decision over the Rangers in the final game before 1,051 fans at the North York Centennial Centre, and the page one headline in the following day's Red Deer Advocate proclaimed "Rustlers Reign Supreme — Canada's Champions."

"The primary reason nobody showed up was that nobody really cared," John Stewart wrote two days later in the "Advocate," condemning CAHA officials for allowing the final to be played in metropolitan Toronto.

> A Junior 'A' hockey game ranks well down on the potential entertainment list in giant Toronto, just as it undoubtedly would in any other Canadian metropolis, even if the teams involved are the best in the country.

When the Rustlers edged the Rangers earlier, 5-4 in double overtime, just 790 spectators showed up. That alone gave Stewart reason to chastise the CAHA.

Sutter had set up Ivan Krook for a goal during the first 10 minute overtime of the 5-4 game. North York rebounded to force another tie before Ron Pierce scored the winning goal 20 seconds into a sudden death overtime as the Rustlers improved their record to 2-1 in the double round-robin tournament.

Chapman had to sit out the first two games of the final because CAHA President suspended him and Metro's coach Angus Carroll as a result of a pre-game brawl in their first meeting, but Chapman continued to wear the same suit, trench coat and stetson until Red Deer claimed the championship in their 100th game of a long season.

The Rustlers eliminated the Canucks in the AJHL final before having to contend with two perennially powerful teams in their march to the Cup. Red Deer defeated the Penticton Knights of the BCJHL in the Western semi-final and then played the defending Cup champion Prince Albert (Sask.) Raiders in the Western Final. Doug Rigler — a 75 goal scorer as a rookie — scored his 100th goal of the season as the Rustlers opened the Western final with a 6-1 win before 2,274 Red Deer fans. The Sutter twins — Rich and Ron, who became the fifth and sixth brothers to make it to the NHL and linemates with Philadelphia — were also instrumental in helping the Rustlers start with superb defensive performances against the Raider's highest-scoring line. The Rustlers twice led the series by two games but the Raiders kept battling back. Red Deer finally won in the sixth game at the Max Bell Arena in Calgary, with Cadman coaching because Chapman had been suspended for one of numerous occasions in a rambunctious season which would not go down as one of the most positive in league history.

Doug Messier, Reid, Terry Sexsmith and Doug Balough were the principals in a November 21, 1979 brawl which had given the league one of its biggest black eyes. It was fairly typical of the shenanigans between the Rustlers and Saints that season. Sexsmith was suspended for a year and Reid was fined a meagre $150.

The Cup wins by the Rustlers and Mets provided the highlights for the league which was formed in September, 1964 to provide an alternative for players who did not want to play major Junior. But the Rustlers, Mets and Saints also accounted for many of the negatives because of their emphasis on highsticking and fighting over the years. "I don't kid myself that it will be on a par with the Edmonton Oil Kings or the Saskatchewan Junior Hockey League," AAHA President Jimmy Brown of Camrose told *Journal* reporter Dave White after the AJHL was formed with five teams playing a 16-game schedule in 1964-65.

But it's long overdue and could very easily develop into a good thing for hockey in Alberta. At the rate hockey's going in our province, it won't be too long before we won't have any intermediate teams if there isn't a Junior league.

The Buffaloes dropped out of the Central Alberta Hockey League — which gained most of the media attention in those days — and wound up winning the initial title, thanks largely to Unger. The 17-year-old Unger — he celebrated his birthday in December of that season — averaged more than three points per game and edged teammate Marty Desmairais for the scoring title.

The Calgary Cowboys, Edmonton Canadians, Edmonton Maple Leafs and hapless Sugar Kings were the other original AJHL franchises. The Buffaloes won the best-of-five final 3-1 before losing in three straight games when they challenged the Oil Kings in the provincial Junior 'A' final for the right to enter the Memorial Cup playoffs.

Dave Duchak of Edmonton served as the first Commissioner of the AJHL and encountered some of the problems which became prevalent later with the Rustlers, Mets and Saints. Duchak assessed suspensions to Maple Leaf's coach Gordon Buttrey and four players after a stick-swinging incident in a February game between the Leafs and Cowboys. He had to act again in a similar heavy-handed fashion a week later because of a brawl in a game in which the Buffaloes ran roughshod over Lethbridge, 19-0. Buttrey was suspended for five games after swinging a stick at the Cowboy's Sid Carothers after he had attacked the coach following an exchange of remarks. The Cowboy's Bob Richter was also banned for five games and Leaf goalie Jim Coombes, the Cowboy's Brian McNutt and Dwight Dombrowsky were ordered to sit out for three games because of infractions in the same game.

The toughest suspension of that first season was handed down the following week, when Keith (Pinky) McDonald of Lethbridge was thrown out for the remainder of the season after leaving the penalty box to start a fight. "We realize that the quickest way to ruin this league is to start paying salaries and importing players," Duchak told the *Journal*'s Wayne Overland early in that initial season.

The league's secretary-treasurer, Dick White of Edmonton, also had some thoughts for Overland. "We believe that junior hockey can be an exciting spectator sport and good competition for local boys and is thus worth promoting," White told Overland. Those ideals remain today for teams which encourage players to pursue United States University scholarships and professional careers. And that philosophy has made the AJHL a success, for the most part.

Players like Garry Unger, the Sutters, Mark Messier, Troy Murray, Lanny McDonald, Jim Benning, Dale Henwood, Perry Pearn and Wynne Dempster give AJHL executives reason to boast. They help us forget the records like Neil Wagner's 387 penalty minutes with the Pass Red Devils in 1975-75, the numerous suspensions, fines and front office bickering.

* * *

AJHL — THE OTHER YEARS

The Edmonton Oil Kings were the top junior club in Alberta in 1964-65. At this level of junior hockey, only the Calgary Buffaloes and the Kings existed and both played in the Central Alberta Hockey League — junior hockey was obviously at a low point, so prominent hockey people met in Red Deer to form the Alberta Junior Hockey League.

The Chairman for the first AJHL meeting was Stu Peppard of Calgary, President of the AAHA. Others who attended and were instrumental in forming the league included Syd Hall and Carl Trentini of the Lethbridge Sugar Kings, Jimmy Stewart and Ken Kuchinski of the Edmonton Maple Leafs, Jim McAdie and Fred Lupul of the Edmonton Canadians, Jim Cross of the Calgary Buffaloes, and Stan Jaycocks and Tom Lynch of the Calgary Cowboys. The Calgary Junior Hockey League sponsored the Cowboys. Dave Duchak and Dick White of Edmonton became the first Commissioner and Secretary-Treasurer.

By the first meeting the league still had no funds. Budgets, as recalled by Jimmy Stewart, "were approximately $5,000.00 per team plus gate receipts. Most players brought their own skates and a weekend schedule of 16 games was set up." It was a shoestring operation; however, the league would offer a chance for Alberta juveniles to continue their hockey in Alberta.

The Calgary Buffaloes represented the AJHL in its first two post season Alberta playoffs. In 1964-65 the Buffaloes lost to the Oil Kings 6-5, 3-2 and 6-1 in the Alberta final.

As the AJHL prepared for its second season it appeared the Edmonton Oil Kings would join. Bill Hunter had the Kings quietly enter the league for a month and, at the same time, did not give notice to leave the Central Alberta League. The CAHA wanted all junior clubs to play in their own groups but the regulation was withdrawn and the King's paper entry to the AJHL did not materialize on the ice. Hunter described his near entry as simply "protecting our club."

CALGARY BUFFALOES 1964-65

Front row (l to r): "Yunk" (trainer), Dan Houghton, John Kell (coach), Marty Demarais, Mr. Curr, Bob Tuff, Al Johnston (manager), Pat Given, Mike Berridge. Second row (l to r): Garry Unger, Jack McRae, Ron Koury, Fred Batten, Barney Pashak, Al Larratt, Terry Cochlan, Al Brooks, Doug Cruikshanks, Frank Currie (manager), Mike France. Third row (l to r): Gord Karch, Cam Boyer, Randy Murray, Randy Ward. *Photo courtesy of Jack Delorme, Calgary and Glenbow Archives*

The AJHL final of 1965-66 involved the Edmonton CAC Western Movers and Calgary Buffaloes. The Buffaloes were surprised in the series opener when the Movers won 6-5. Some 3,000 fans in Calgary watched the Buffaloes tie the series as they scored an 8-5 win. This final went to seven games. The Movers pulled ahead three games to one when Garry Unger scored five and three goals in two successive games to tie the series at three all.

The Buffaloes won their second AJHL crown and the right to play the Edmonton Oil Kings when they won 5-3. Unger was shut out; however, Brian Teed scored two and Al McLeod, Doug Cruickshank, and Mike Lemieux had singles. Milt Hohol, Ray Melnyk and Jim Brown shared the goals for the Movers.

Due to the unavailability of ice in Edmonton the Oil Kings played two games against the Buffaloes in Fort Saskatchewan. Two easy wins, 9-2 and 7-2, plus a 10-3 score in Calgary gave the Kings the 1965-66 Alberta Championship and the right to continue in the Memorial Cup Playoff. Buffalo manager Frank Currie conceded after the series that "it was one of the best Oil King clubs" he had ever seen.

(Tier 1 junior hockey is described in the previous junior section. The story of the Oil Kings and their march to the Memorial Cup in 1965-66 is featured.)

The 1966-67 AJHL champions were the Edmonton CAC Western Movers. Due to conflicts over the age of junior players with the CAHA and the Western Canada Junior League, the AJHL champion became the sole Alberta representative in Memorial Cup competition. The Movers, coached by Don Hunt and managed by Bud Kerslake, defeated the Lethbridge Sugar Kings in the provincial final. The team then went seven games against the New Westminster Royals before losing 6-5 in overtime. The Movers were ahead when George Watson tied the game 37 seconds from the end. In overtime Watson scored again at 8:10 to eliminate the Movers.

The 1967-68 AJHL representative again was the Edmonton Movers. The Movers lost the fifth game of the best-of-five B.C.-Alberta series to the Penticton Broncos.

Don McLean coached the Lethbridge Sugar Kings to the 1968-69 AJHL championship. The Sugar Kings played off against the Victoria Cougars of the British Columbia Junior Hockey League. Wayne Zuk, a pickup from the Red Deer Rustlers, accounted for team leading seven goals in the series to advance Lethbridge against the Regina Pats.

The Pats eliminated the Sugar Kings 5-4 in the sixth game of the series before 2,700 fans in Lethbridge. Ron Garwasiuk scored with only 22 seconds left in regulation time to give the Pats the win.

In 1969-70 the Red Deer Rustlers represented the AJHL. The Weyburn Red Wings defeated Alf Cadman's Rustlers four games to two. This ended AJHL participation in Memorial Cup playoffs.

(The Red Deer Rustlers represented the province in 1970-71 and won the first Centennial Cup. See Marty Knack's story.)

EDMONTON WESTERN MOVERS 1966-67

Back row (l to r): A.C. Kerslake (manager), B. Kalis (president), H. Willis, D. Moore, M. Hohol, R. Stephens, S. Carlyle, S. Knox, C. Coultman, K. Wozniak, R. Williams, R. Lalacheur, K. Liebel, K. Cadger (J. Lalacheur, spon.), F. Steer (trainer). Front row (l to r): D. Hunt (coach), W. Zuk, T. Dube, W. Kettle, L. Kopp, A. Cameron, R. Melnyk, O. Beissel.

Photo courtesy of Edmonton Archives

In 1971-72 the Red Deer Rustlers tried for a repeat of their 1970-71 Centennial Cup victory. After defeating the Vernon Essos from British Columbia, the Rustlers made short work of the Humboldt Broncos four games to one. The Rustlers won their second straight Western Canada Tier 2 title when Doug Lindskog scored two goals while Dale Lewis and Doug Kinch got singles in a 4-2 victory.

LETHBRIDGE SUGAR KINGS 1968-69

Front (l to r): Don Hall, Craig Simmons (captain), Adrian Vitbeyerse, Syd Hall (manager), Carl Trentini, Don McLean (coach), Jack Kerr (trainer), Darrel Knibbs, Gerry Carmichal. Middle: Karl Sorkoski (assistant coach), Len Chalmers, Jerry Letrander, Roy Fox, Len Frie, Keith Ferrel, Howie Hegepdal, Gerald Zaichkowsky, Fraser Robertson, Mac Kerr (assistant trainer). Back: Dave Shardlow, Gary Paskoski, Ken Lupul, Alex Koeler, Dave Steward. *Photo courtesy of Edmonton Archives*

The Rustlers then played in Guelph, Ontario against the CMC's. Graham Parsons once again proved his value in the Red Deer goal when he stopped 46 shots but Guelph won 2-1 to take a three game lead. In the fourth and final game, Doug Risebrough scored twice and Bruce Harridge one for a 3-0 shutout to give Guelph the 1972 Centennial Cup in straight games.

The Calgary Canucks and Red Deer Rustlers took the AJHL 1972-73 finals to seven games. Under coach Ralph Burgess before 2,800 fans at Foothills Arena in Calgary, the Canucks won 6-2 in the seventh game. The Canucks, who scored 439 goals through the regular season, were led by the line of Dale Eloschuk, Dean Magee and Mark Lomenda. Eloschuk scored three and set up one for Lomenda while Warren Cook got the other two. For Cec Swanson's Rustlers, Irvine Bowles and Dale Bingham had two goals each.

The pennant and playoff champion Canucks journeyed over the mountains to play the Penticton Broncos. A 5-4 win before 1,600 fans got the Canucks off to a good start. Penticton protested, however, that Calgary dressed 18 instead of 17 players. No decision was taken immediately about the protest. The series became deadlocked at two game each.

On April 18, 1973, moments before the fifth game started, game one was declared void and taken away from Calgary. This announcement, plus 3,174 Penticiton fans, helped raise the Bronco's spirits. Two straight wins by 8-5 and 6-2 by the Broncos eliminated the Canucks four games to one.

The Pass Red Devils (played in Blairmore) reached the AJHL finals in 1973-74, however, Red Deer Rustlers became the AJHL champions four games to one. Kelly Bunn scored three goals in the third period to give the Rustlers the final game 5-2. Other tallies for Red Deer were from Cam Coburne and Brian Sutter. Wayne Turner and Lyle Murray scored for the Red Devils.

The same series result occurred in the next round for Red Deer against the Kelowna Bucks. However, it was the Bucks who won four games to one. In the final game Cec Swanson's Rustlers were defeated 8-7 in overtime to advance the Bucks into the western finals.

In 1974-75 the Taber Golden Suns were admitted to the league. It was hoped one of the original entries, the Edmonton Maple Leafs, would rejoin after a two year absence, and discussion was held about Spokane, Washington being an entry. The Maple leafs never reorganized as a junior club and Spokane was considered too distant.

CALGARY CANUCKS 1972-73

Front row (l to r): John Bachysnki (assistant coach), Ian MacPhee, Ron Burgess, Tom Walls (general manager), Mike Priestner, Blaine McLeod, Warren Cook, Ralph Burgess (coach). **Centre row (l to r):** Earl (Cat) Browne (trainer), Joe De Lure, Roger Lamoureux, Dale Eloschuk, Dean Magee, Grad Robson, Mike Bruce, Stu Younger, Lou Saucier (equipment manager). **Back row (l to r):** Jim Patenaude, Jim Setters, Brock Kaluznick, Marke Lomenda, Brian Miller, Greg Smith.

Photo courtesy of Glenbow Archives

Teams in the AJHL had various plans to sell season tickets. The Pass Red Devils sold regular adult seats for $2.00, students and pensioners for $1.75 and children for $.75. The major advantage for the 30 game schedule was only that season ticket purchasers who bought in advance could choose their seats and have an option on playoff games.

It was said at the time by Red Devil President Francis Catonio that the Junior 'A' hockey situation never looked better. An announcement was made on July 10, 1974 that Ron "Toby" Collins of Coleman would coach the club as John Chapman was going to coach the Calgary Centennials. On October 2, 1974, Collins turned in his resignation to team manager Richard Koentages due to pressure of business and Bill Ramsden became coach. The problem here and for all AJHL teams is and was that coaches usually have another job and cannot, without great sacrifice, spend all the time they may wish on the team.

(See Marty Knack's story on the Centennial Cup Champions Spruce Grove Mets for 1974-75.)

The Spruce Grove Mets of 1975-76 became the Western Canadian champions when they defeated the Vancouver Nor-Wes Caps and the Prince Albert Raiders. The Canadian final was played against an Ottawa suburb based team called the Rockland Nationals. The Nationals, coached by Brian Murray, went on to defeat Doug Messier's Mets 7-3 to win the Centennial Cup four games to one.

In the seasons of 1976-77 and 1977-78 the Calgary Canucks, under the watchful eye of Cec Papke, proved to be the powerhouse of the AJHL. Many felt the Canucks should have won the championship three years in a row but in 1975-76 they lost an early round in seven games to the Taber Golden Suns. This upset, apparently, inspired the Canucks to two straight championships.

The Canucks avenged the defeat of 1975-76 as they defeated the Golden Suns 8-6 to win the series four games to one in 1976-77. Next, Calgary eliminated the Richmond Sockeyes but then the Canucks faced the formidable Prince Albert Raiders. Terry Simpson's Saskatchewan pucksters moved two games ahead as they won 7-6 and

CALGARY CANUCKS 1976-77

Front row (l to r): Peter Friestadt, Hal Papke, Cec Papke (coach), Mendel Vysohlid, Ron Brumwell (manager), Terry Johnson, Brad Hall, Murray Papke. Centre row (l to r): Ken Taylor, Chad Rice (equipment), Jack Neumann, Brian Hatton, Brad Neufeld, Robin Laycock, Jeff Neufeld, Cal Roadhouse, Larry Bergum, Dave Paulson. Back row (l to r): Gord Wright, Dave Speer, Bob Kerr, Dennis May, Todd Scott, Garth Morgan, Tony Stiles, Darcy Way, Vince O'Hara, John Krellsted.

Photo courtesy of Glenbow Archives

8-4 at home. The Canucks came closer to elimination when they lost the third game at the Max Bell Arena in Calgary 7-3.

The Canucks, however, did not give up. In the next game, Bruce Hutton scored a shorthanded goal at 6:59 of the second overtime to give Calgary its first win, 7-6. Hutton had three goals, Robin Laycock two, while Mendel Vysohlid and Cal Roadhouse had singles for Calgary. The Canucks used three goalies in the series, Darcy Way, Brad Hall and Pete Friestadt.

Hall was selected to play goal for the Canucks in the fifth game, however, the Raiders won 8-5. Even though the Canucks were now out of the Centennial Cup playoffs, this was their most successful season in their six year history.

In 1977-78, Papke's role shifted to becoming a consultant to new coach Russ Farwell. The Canucks continued to be successful and won the 1977-78 AJHL crown when they defeated Gene Achtymichuk's Fort Saskatchewan Traders 4-3 before 1,800 fans at the Max Bell Arena. Canuck's Robin Laycock who scored 80 goals and had 76 assists and Neil Wagner claimed the "champagne" tasted better than it had the previous year.

For Fort Saskatchewan's Dave Babych, then sixteen, it marked the end of a brilliant season. He was named Rookie of the Year, was on the league All-Star team and was winner of the Bill Scott Memorial Trophy as the league's top defenseman. For the Calgary Canucks the win would mean two new battles — one on the ice against other teams and the other off the ice.

Today, referees and linesmen in all hockey, except the NHL, must wear helmets. After the Calgary Canucks won the 1977-78 AJHL, the issue almost destroyed Alberta's representation in the Centennial Cup. The AAHA had decided three years earlier to have all officials on the ice wear helmets. Doug McKenzie, President of the AAHA, enforced the regulation at the end of the AJHL playoffs as the team was to play another branch of the CAHA. This was a Canada-wide regulation. Jim Scoular, head of the AJHL and former AAHA President, wanted helmets brought in on a gradual basis as was done for players. The helmet issue overshadowed the next series.

Larry Wood of the *Calgary Herald* wrote that:

It has been verbal warfare in the trenches ever since, in fact with a lot of people saying a lot of things they'd probably like to forget. Personalities have clashed, notably those of McKenzie (Doug, President of AAHA) and his predecessor at the AAHA helm, Jim Scoular of Calgary, who regards the issue the last straw in a haystack of problems, he doesn't need.

Wood went on to report that:

The referees, obviously are the "bad guys" in the script. It's more difficult bringing the "good guys" into focus. But it's crystal clear who's getting shafted.

The Canucks were suspended from future playoffs by the AAHA. Doug Eastcott, owner of the Canucks said, "We're just going to have to wait and see about our team's playoff future." Eastcott continued to negotiate and finally Jack Neumann, publicity director for the Canucks announced that Merrit, B.C. would play the Canucks. This also put Merritt in a position of being suspended by the BCAHA for playing a team without officials wearing helmets.

In game one, referee Orie Mandyrk and linesmen Grant Mitchell and Gary Groves of the outlawed Alberta Independent Referees Association wore helmets. Tkatchuk, Canuck goalie faced 40 shots to keep the Canucks in a game lost 6-4. The referees handed out three minors and one major to each club.

Calgary were ahead two games to one when the series switched to Merritt. Keith Sharpe of the "Calgary Herald" referred to Merritt as the "Boot Hill" of the Canucks as the Centennials shellacked Calgary 12-0, 8-1 and 6-0 to win the series four games to two. In the three Merritt games the Canucks were outscored 26-1 and outshot 141-66.

FORT SASKATCHEWAN TRADERS

Top row: D. Shudra, D. Wakal, T. McGillivray, M. Ferris, S. Geary, D. Keller, J. Benning, G. Yaremchuk, P. Elliott, W. Lamb, W. Shudra, K. Thorne. Middle row: J. Bok, R. Rippel, P. Pelensky, I. McLelland, R. Meyers, J. Engert, D. Postlewaite, R. Turnbull, K. Holden. Front row: J. Rodgers, M. Achtymichuk, J. Stannard, G. Achtymichuk, J. Ewasiuk, K. Lamb, G. Hornby, T. Oakes, C. Malarchuk.

Photo courtesy of Edmonton Archives

The Canuck's Doug Eastcott, upset with the helmet issue, sold the ownership of the Canuck franchise at the end of the season and all officials started to wear headgear in AAHA sanctioned games.

The AJHL of 1978-79 played a round-robin to determine the top two clubs for the final. The Calgary Canucks once again played the Fort Saskatchewan Traders. The Traders pulled ahead three to one in games when they defeated Calgary 5-4 in Fort Saskatchewan. Dean Postelwaite scored in the last four minutes for the Fort's win. The Canuck's Todd Scott did the same thing in the next game when he scored near the end of the game to give Calgary a 4-3 win. Calgary won again 7-3 to tie up the series at three games each. In the seventh game, Fort Saskatchewan won its first AJHL championship when Mike Ferris scored five times in Calgary for a 9-2 win. Ferris had scored one goal in the previous six games and was playing his first game on right wing. It made the difference.

The Richmond Sockeyes won the first game of the B.C.-Alberta round. The Traders came back to defeat the Sockeyes four straight including a final 10-3 decision. In this game Ferris scored three times to eliminate Richmond.

The Traders were considered a good road team as their record away from home in the AJHL was 21 wins and 9 losses. Their opposition was the Prince Albert Raiders who had won 14 of 15 playoff game starts that year. As well, Terry Simpson's Raiders had won Western Canada honors in Centennial play for the last two years. The Raiders moved ahead three games to two and were ready to start their 91st game of the year.

The season ended for Fort Saskatchewan when it was edged 8-7. Trader coach Gene Achtymichuk was angry after the game at some tactics used by Prince Albert. He claimed that Jim Benning was speared five times in the warmup. As well, it was claimed Clint Malarchuk was jabbed twice and Don Keller once after scoring. Achtymichuk felt the Raiders deserved credit for their win, but questioned the use of the stick. John Ewasiuk and Jim Benning scored two goals each for Fort Saskatchewan in their final loss while Marty Achtymichuk, Gary Yaremchuk and Don Keller got singles.

(The 1979-1980 Red Deer Rustlers won the Centennial Cup and are featured in Marty Knack's earlier article.)

In 1980-81, the Saint Albert Saints won their first AJHL championship over the Taber Golden Suns. Before 800 fans in St. Albert's Akinsdale Arean, the Suns went down to an 8-2 defeat in game seven of the series. John White equalled his output in 11 previous playoff games when he accumulated four points. Other top scorers for St. Albert were Dave Donnelly and Don Mercier who scored two goals apiece.

ST. ALBERT SAINTS 1980-81

Front row (l to r): John Reid, Scott Webster, Doug Messier (head coach), Dave Donnelly, Bob Russell (president), Don Hyland, Brian Hermanutz. Second row (l to r): Rene Pouliot (bus driver), Doug Schum (assistant coach), Father W. Borden (director of education), Bob Morton (public relations director), Gavin Shuya, Brad Fox, Don Mercier, John White, Jeff Marshall, J.C. McEwan, Mike Taschereau, Steve Bell, Jack Reid (general manager), Charlie Meredith (secretary treasurer), Charlie Lavallee (assistant trainer), Buck Buckanesky (trainer). Third row (l to r): Ron Brodeur, Harvey Smyl, Dean Clark, Brad Hammett, Darrell Turnbull, Brent Weller, Glen Klotz, Rick Serniak. *Photo courtesy of Edmonton Archives*

The Saints under coach Doug Messier were awarded the Clarence Moher Memorial and the Carling O'Keefe Brewery Trophies from the AJHL. Donnelly (the only Albertan to play on the 1984 Canadian Olympic team) the 17-year-old captain led the Saints throughout the year, scored 60 goals and had 71 assists in 71 games. In playoffs to this point he had 19 goals and 15 assists.

Saint Albert then travelled to Penticton to register 8-5 and 5-4 victories over the Penticton Knights. The series ended in the fifth game when the Saint shutout the Knights 3-0 at home. The Prince Albert Raiders would play the Saints for the right to enter the national final.

After the 3-0 shutout, goalkeeper Jeff Lastiwka who had been added from the Sherwood Park Crusaders said,
I played a year in the Saskatchewan Junior Hockey League when I was 17...the Raiders are the thing in Prince Albert. They get crowds of about 4,000...and the fans go nuts.

As expected, the Prince Albert Raiders won the opener. In the second game, the Raiders outshot the Saints 43-8 by the end of the second period. However, the Saints were ahead 1-0. Lastiwka finally stopped 68 shots but the Raiders eventually won 3-1. Four thousand rabid Prince Albert fans "went nuts" and gave their team a standing ovation for their fine performance.

In an effort to start winning after two losses, the Saints moved the next two games to Edmonton's Northlands Coliseum. The attendance was less than overwhelming as only 2,553 watched the Raiders skate to a 5-3 overtime win. The superiority of the Raiders continued in the final game as they defeated the Saints 6-2. Doug Messier praised the Raiders saying, "they have excellent mobility and they've got four lines."

In 1981-82, Saint Albert Saints won their second AJHL championship in a row since their transfer from Spruce Grove. In the final league series, the Calgary Spurs and Saints had each won three games at home. The Saints won the seventh game 6-3 at the Foothills Arena in Calgary. In 38 home games, the Spurs had lost only twice.

CALGARY CANUCKS 1982-83

Back row (l to r): Ronald Siemens, Norm Watson, Ken Taylor (minor officials); Gwen Taylor (secretary), John Dyer, Sonny Sands, Dr. Don Johnston, Brian Strum, Bill Maclure, Glenn Brost (assistant coach), Dave Elston, Ken Fordyce, Ken Maclure. Third row (l to r): Jerry Thorson (trainer), Carey Bracko, Roger Kirchnak, Paul Geddes, Kent Hayes, Bob Griffin, Brian Munroe, Roger Mulvenna, Ken Grant, Tom Geib. Second row (l to r): Wade Michalenko, Carey Coroy, Ross McGowan, Mike Mansfield, Rob Heidt, Terry Knight, Brian Taylor, Todd Williams, Ken Heppner, Paddy Maclure (stick boy). Front row (l to r): Eric Morrison (trainer), Tom Grant, Darrell Mulvenna, Wally Kozak (coach), Dan Mulvenna (general manager), Barry Brigley, Jim Morley (president and owner), Al Confrancisco (assistant coach), Ron Slenders, Jamie Bowman.

Photo courtesy of Glenbow

Mark Messier and the Edmonton Oilers were playing the Los Angeles Kings while Doug Messier was coaching the Saints against the Penticton Broncos. The Oilers lost the series when the Kings won the final game 7-4. Mark's father Doug, however, had some reason to smile as his Saints outscored the Penticton Broncos 4-3 to take the seventh game of the series. John Reid scored the fourth goal for Saint Albert at 18:10 of the third period for the game and series win.

Once again the Saints met the powerful Prince Albert Raiders in the Western final. The Raiders won the first two games and outshot the Saints 98-58 in the process. The Raiders won the next two games 3-0 and 6-1 to win four straight. Doug Messier spoke again in generous terms, "Prince Albert has the best Tier 2 team in Canada...They have good organization and excellent coaching with Terry Simpson and Rick Wilson." (Canada won the World Junior title in 1985. Terry Simpson was the head coach.)

In 1982-83 the Calgary Canucks did not appear to have a chance in the AJHL. The Canuck record was three wins and nineteen losses. Wally Kozak was appointed the coach and the team reached the AJHL final against the Fort McMurray Oil Barons.

Coach Gary Braun's Barons checked aggressively to win the first game 7-2. Calgary was behind 2-0 and finally 7-0 after two periods and outshot 35 to 18. In the second game, Barons' Ron Slatten and Mark Davis had three goals each and a single from Kermit Exkelbarger to win 7-3. Brian Taylor scored two and Roger Mulvenna got one for the Canucks. In the season Fort McMurray had not lost at home since the Olds Grizzlies defeated it on December 19, 1982, while Calgary had not lost at home for the calendar year of 1983. Two games behind and coming home was not a surprise for coach Kozak. The Canucks won three successive games at Calgary's Max Bell Arena to go ahead three games to two. Fort McMurray almost won the first game in Calgary; however, Barry Brigley scored at 3:13 of the second overtime period to give the Canucks a 6-5 win and put them back in the series. The teams then returned to the Thickwood Arena in Fort McMurray and the Canucks ended the Baron's home winning streak when they won 5-4.

Abbottsford Flyers were the next opposition for the Canucks. The series direction was determined before the opening whistle said Mario Toneguzzi of the "Calgary Herald". The hockey stick was used for more than shooting a puck.

> The teams used them (sticks) *more or less as weapons as they hooked, slashed and highsticked their way through a three hour fiasco in the opening game...Inside the MSA Arena the peace was shattered before the opening whistle...The first period produced 112 minutes in penalties.*

The Flyers beat the Canucks 8-4 and 7-6 in Abbottsfield and they could not wait to get back to Calgary. Home ice was not enough as the Flyers made it four straight including a final 4-3 victory at Foothills Arena.

The better players in the Tier two AJHL are sometimes lost to the Tier one WHL, college teams or drafted at 18 to the NHL. This means a coach must work quickly to have a strong team to keep fan support. Coach Doug Schumm of the Fort Saskatchewan Traders ended up in third position in 1982-83. In 1983-84 the Trader's record went from 26-34-0 to 40-19-1 for a 29 point improvement. Fort Saskatchewan had a talented squad as Sid Cranston was the league's Most Valuable Player, Gord Thibodeau was the best defenceman and Kevin Stapleton was selected as the top goal keeper. Schumm was able to coach this nucleus of players to the 1983-84 AJHL championship over Wynne Dempster's Red Deer Rustlers.

The British Columbia-Alberta round between the Traders and Langley Eagles was played in its entirety at the Jubilee Recreation Centre in Fort Saskatchewan.

The Traders knew after the first game that they were in for a tough series as they lost 6-2. Two goals by Sid Cranston in the first period failed to be enough. However, after the third contest the Traders were ahead 2-1 in games.

Langley came back to even the series and in game five took a commanding 3-2 lead in games. A final 4-1 victory gave the Eagles their fourth win and eliminated the Fort Saskatchewan Traders.

The Red Deer Rustlers won the 1984-85 AJHL over the Sherwood Park Crusaders. The club was unsuccessful in interprovincial play. Due to financial reasons the Rustlers announced they would not rejoin the AJHL for the 1985-86 season.

JUNIOR HOCKEY EPILOGUE

Junior hockey is "where the money's at" in amateur hockey. It is the major source of players for professional hockey. Although universities and colleges provide professionals too, most have competed in junior hockey first.

Professional hockey organizations no longer sponsor individual junior clubs directly. Each NHL club recruits players as young as 17 in their universal June draft. The more draftees a club has, the more money it makes. The early draft age prompts junior teams to drop players over age 18 who have not been drafted and to concentrate on grooming players not yet of draft age. There is intense scouting and intense pressure on midget and bantam age hockey players; the trend of lowering the draft age continues to be a highly controversial topic.

Because of the high cost of junior hockey some clubs are community-owned and registered under Alberta's Societies Act. Under this arrangement there is little personal financial risk. But, to ensure a club's future it must make the playoffs on a regular basis; if not, the yearly gate revenue can be reduced by at least one-third.

Top dollars for top players spells success in junior hockey. But, today junior clubs also encourage their players to continue with formal education; in fact, they give players financial assistance to stay in school. This is a far cry from twenty years ago when very few serious junior hockey players hit anything other than members of the opposing team.

FORT McMURRAY OIL BARONS
1982-83 League Finalists

First row (l to r): Randy Workman, Hammi Donnelly (trainer), Kermit Eichelberger, Ches. Dicks (president), Dale Argue, Gary Braun (coach), Mark Davis, Don Hyland. Second row: Rob Semchuk, Kevin Mayner, Mike Reidy, Grant Sedlik, Don Herzog, Rod Slatten, Mike Kellam, Darren Steer. Third row: Jason Thorpe (stick boy), Gerry Lamoreux, Greg Button, Brent Waller, Rick Pankiw, Larry Furkilo, Dennis Villeneuve.

Photo courtesy of Edmonton Archives

Back row (l to r): Ray Werner (director — Club 600), Audrey Craig (secretary), Ken French (president, treasurer), Tracey Zubrecki, Roger Payment, Murray Melynk, Arnold Cullum, Kurt Roebuck, Troy Jacobsen, Butch Thomlinson (vice president), Al MacLeod (director — junior B), Ray Craig (director — program). Middle row (l to r): John Bauer (director — general manager), Alf White (trainer), Judy Voshell (director — season tickets), Blair Davidson, Don Schmidt, Bob Butler, Lubo Dzurillo, Colin Mizier, Brian Spence, Steve Grumley, Bruce Babych, Kelly Dombroski, Paul Phillip (director — equipment), Carole McIntyre (director — fund raising), Dave Wakal (director — arena manager), Dave Cranston (director — manager). Bottom row (l to r): Lyle Mast, Mario Sicolo, Gord Thibodeau, Doug Schum (coach), Sid Cranston, Rob McIntyre, Kent Prins, Kevin Stapleton, David Cranston (stick boy). Trophies: Back row (l to r): Alberta Junior League Supremacy, Top AJHL Defenceman — Gord Thibodeau, AJHL Most Dedicated — Kent Prins. Most Valuable AJHL Player — Sid Cranston, Alberta Amateur Provincial Junior A (Carling O'Keefe Cup). Front row (l to r): Top AJHL Scorer — Sid Cranston, AJHL Northern Division Trophy, Top AJHL Goalkeeper — Kevin Stapleton.

SHERWOOD PARK CRUSADERS 1984-85 LEAGUE FINALISTS

Top (l to r): Howie Draper, Dave Reich, Mike Zimmel, Brad Fenton, Jay Reid, Jason McKinnon, Lonnie Spink, Gord Green, Mike Gilmore. Second row: Harry Zuzak (president), Marty Schmidt (trainer), Gord Batey, Don Talbot, Brett Pearce, Gary Valk, Scott Harlow, Jeff Preece, Jim Ennis, Dave Wadell, Colin Korber, Dave Buist (equipment manager), Billy Warwick (director of hockey operations), Bob Green (statistician). Front row: Darren Turner, Larry Geertsen, Al McDonald (assistant coach), John Walker (captain), Al Hamilton (coach), Al Tarasuk, Jim Crossen (assistant coach), Darrell Heck, Gord Ruzicka.

Photo courtesy of Edmonton Archives

RED DEER RUSTLERS 1984-85 AJHL CHAMPIONS

Back (l to r): Terry Robinson (stick boy), Dr. John McLuhan, Bill Blanchard (assistant coach). Third (l to r): Cliff Bailey (equipment), Mike Swainson, Darryl Shudra, Simon Juckes, Peter Stelmaschuk, Dan Toperosky, Jeff Gosselin, Jason Helfrich. Second (l to r): Troy Soley, Rob Fitzgerald, Steve Mains, Garth Premak, Duane Mofford, Ron Shudra, Glen Barre, Darryl Cust, Al Karpyshyn. Front (l to r): Colin Robinson (stick boy), John Helfrich, Maury Grant, Ben Smith (trainer), Dean Cowling, Wynne Dempster (general manager/coach), Harold Belleross, Glen Raeburn.

Photo courtesy of Sportpix, Red Deer

CHAPTER 6
UNIVERSITY AND COLLEGE HOCKEY

SCHOOL OF HARD KNOCKS

D.P. McDonald was considered one of the premier goalkeepers in Alberta from the mid twenties to the thirties. McDonald says, "Camrose had an open air rink. It was well lit and I knew it would be a classic encounter. It was one of the oddest experiences in hockey that I or anyone else has ever experienced."

This 1924 game featured the University of Alberta and the Camrose Seniors in the Edmonton District Hockey League. Besides the regular goal equipment McDonald wore a tweed hat with a peak. For most games it provided some protection and helped keep him warm. In this game McDonald had good reason for his hat.

In the third period when the puck came close to McDonald, the goal judge started to hit McDonald.

He started to hit me over the head with a carpenter's hammer which happened to be left by attendants who had fixed the goal. I tried to defend myself. Spectators in my end of the rink were amused. Finally, the referee saw the rucus and removed the goal judge from the game. It was a classic encounter.

(McDonald is a Calgary lawyer. He was President of the AAHA in 1937)

U. OF A. TEAM OF 38-39 VISITS L.A.

BY GEORGE STUART

(George Stuart continued to play hockey with the Edmonton Flyers, Edmonton Independent All-Stars, New Method Laundry and the 1949 Edmonton Mercurys. His father, Ira, was coach of the 1932 Edmonton Superiors.)

In November 1938, the hockey "Golden Bears" accepted an invitation to journey to Los Angeles to play two exhibition games with the University of Southern California "Trojans". We were limited to a budget of $1,500.00. Scarcity of funds placed a restriction on the size of the squad, the mode of travel and accommodation.

We boarded a train in Edmonton and travelled by colonist car to the west coast. Although our accommodation improved after we changed trains our finances demanded that we sleep two persons to a bunk, including the uppers.

The Golden Bears squad consisted of no more than nine players, namely: Pat Costigan, Sam Costigan, Vern Drake, Frank Hall, Dave MacKay, Gray McLaren, Don Stanley, Bill Stark and George Stuart. They were accompanied by coach Stan Moher, manager Bill Haddad and faculty member Dean Howes. Howes was Dean of the Faculty of Agriculture and was selected to fill the role of "chaperone".

Upon arrival in Los Angeles we checked in at one of the older hotels called the Lankershin, where the rates fitted our budget.

The Golden Bears were scheduled to leave Edmonton before the natural ice could be made at the University rink. The players' conditioning for this trip consisted of four one-hour practice sessions on artificial ice at the old Edmonton Arena. The well-conditioned Trojans squad consisted of juniors and seniors. In addition to a couple of goalkeepers the Trojans trotted out onto the ice with seven defencemen and three forward lines. They also had several players out of uniform standing by in the event they were needed. It is hardly surprising to report then that the Trojans won both games, but the margin by which they did so in each instance was close.

We played in an arena improvised from a large skating pavilion. This was accommodated by erecting temporary boards around the designated playing surface. The lights were showlights of various colors.

An interesting sidelight involved a man well-known to Edmontonians — particularly in baseball circles. When we arrived at the hockey arena we were welcomed by the arena's manager, who was none other than John Ducey. When we enquired about facilities for sharpening skates; the function was taken over and performed by the same John Ducey. When we skated onto the ice to commence the game the referee we faced was again our friend John.

There are several other highlights worth mentioning. Before embarking on our journey the University was contacted by Bill Reid, who had managed the Golden Bears hockey team during his student days at the University many years earlier. Following our arrival in Los Angeles we were the beneficiaries of his warm hospitality. He made his company's limousines available and conducted us on a tour of the area, including Long Beach, where we dined at his club as guests. He organized a cheering section for both games replete with banners and ribbons of green and gold. Reid our benefactor was the President of Hancock Oil Company of California and I recall seeing his service stations spotted throughout the area.

The games we played were attended by several well-known movie stars, most of whom had come out to see hockey for the first time.

UNIVERSITY OF ALBERTA AT 20th CENTURY FOX 1938-39

Left to right: Frank Hall, Tony Martin (singer), stage director of 20th Century Fox, Benny Nivecki (U. of S.C. from Calgary), Dean Howes, Gloria Stewart (actress), George Stuart, Dave MacKay, Norman Costigan, Vern Drake, Bill Haddad (manager), Pat Costigan, Stan Moher (coach), Don Stanley, Greg McLaren, Bill Stark. *Photo courtesy of Edmonton Archives*

The team made a complete tour of the 20th Century Fox movie lot. We were also taken onto the set of a movie being filmed by the name of "Winner Takes All". The stars of that film, whom we met, were Gloria Stewart and Tony Martin, supported by Henry Armetta. It was directed by Brower.

We dined on one occasion at the celebrated restaurant of the day known as the "Brown Derby", a favorite eating place of the movie industry. Some of our squad took time one evening to attend the renowned nightclub "The Coconut Grove" to listen to the well-known bandleader of the time Rudy Vallee and his orchestra. For most of us it was the first time we had seen or eaten avocados or picked an orange from a tree. We were impressed. It was indeed a memorable experience for students from the University of Alberta in the fall of 38.

THE U. OF A. GOLDEN BEARS HOCKEY TEAM 1947 — 1951

BY P.J. MORAN, Director of Wascana Centre Authority Regina, Saskatchewan and former Bear goalie (known then as "Jumping Joe")

During the period 1947 to 1951, the Intercollegiate hockey competition for the U. of A. was confined to Western Canada because national competition had not come to fruition. Over this four year period the University of Alberta Golden Bears hockey team was the Western Canada Intercollegiate champion and defended this distinction for the 13th, 14th, 15th and 16th consecutive years. The Halpenny Trophy, emblematic of the championship supremacy, was retired permanently to the U. of A. in 1950 on the occasion of the 15th consecutive year of championship teams and the new Hardy Trophy, which replaced it, was captured for the first time.

The hockey teams of the '47 to '51 era were fortunate to have some outstanding coaches in Andy "Shorts" Purcell, Clarence Moher and Art Wiebe. "Swede" Liden, "Firey" George Hughes and John Church were the team managers over this same period. "Swede" is tagged with the distinction of not having the hockey equipment arrive with the bus and team for a game one night in Camrose.

John Church was versatile as the back-up goal tender. Clarence Moher had lost most of the hair on his head and George Hughes always sported a brush cut hairdo. It was probably for this reason that both wore wide, mafia-type fedoras. Both were small but stocky in stature with big hearts and over the years they frequently bantered back and forth, snarling about who was taller. The players wearied of the banter.

Finally, one day after a game in Colorado Springs we had Clarence and George take off their shoes and stand back to back. The laughter of the players was uncontrollable because, after several measurements, it turned out that both were precisely the same height with the only difference being the stubble of George Hughes' brushcut above Clarence Moher's bald head.

It would be most unfair of me to single out individuals who were particularly outstanding players during this four year period other than to mention that Jim Flemming captained the team during most of this period. Jim was a team leader with an excellent physique. a smooth yet powerful skating stride, great speed, who could successfully play any position and had professional experience with the Kansas City Playmors.

In addition to the annual Western Intercollegiate Hockey championship, teams of 1947-51 engaged in a number of invitational collegiate hockey series in Vancouver, Denver and Colorado Springs.

BEARS AND BOB HOPE 1950-51

The Golden Bears Hockey Team received a visit from the Hollywood celebrity Bob Hope while playing Colorado College. Pictured are: Front row (l to r): Joe Moran, Gerry Maier, Keith Lea, Art Weibe (coach), Bob Kirstine, Bob Hope, Keith Kidd, Dr. Maury Van Vliet. Second row: John Church (manager), Don Kirk, Denny Ratcliffe (equipment manager), Ted Kryczka, Harry Mandryk, Jim Meers, Ed Zukiwisky and Leroy Field.

The series of games with the Colorado College are remembered for two reasons.

When the famous five for two trade was made between Chicago Black Hawks and Toronto Maple Leafs in the 1940s, Max Bentley was the best known of the two players Toronto received in the trade. The other player, and almost forgotten, was "Cy" Thomas.

In 1949 "Cy" was attending University. He played for the Golden Bears Hockey team and made the 1951 trip to Colorado Springs. On arrival here, and much to our disappointment, the Colorado College hockey officials refused to permit him to participate. They felt that his former professional career would jeopardize their team's amateur classification. Movie stars Bob Hope and Marilyn Maxwell attended a 1951 game in the Colorado Springs series.

It was a thrilling game in which Colorado College came from behind in the dying minutes of the game and won it in overtime, much to our team's chargin since we had no advance knowledge that Bob Hope would be making a presentation to the winning team and that Marilyn Maxwell would be providing the kisses. However, Bob did come to visit us in our dressing room immediately after the game to crack a few jokes, pose for some team pictures and express several superlatives on the thrilling game which he described as having a "Frank Merriwell" finish. (If you don't know a "Frank Merriwell" finish is, you'll have to look it up in a history book.)

BEAR'S MARATHON
BY JACK CUMMINGS

(Before University hockey, Cummings played for the Edmonton Oil Kings, Columbus Owls of the International League and now is an assistant coach with the Bears.)

It began as a typical road trip to Saskatoon. We departed Thursday after practice and stopped at the Chatelaine Restaurant in Vegreville. These huge feasts always eagerly awaited, were one of the highlights of the year. Players such as Dave Hindmarch, "Terrible" Ted Olson and Stan Swales became famous for the quantities of food they could devour. Perhaps this over-indulgence was a contributing factor in the Bears playing in the longest game in Canada West history against Saskatchewan on January 21, 1977.

Rutherford Rink, home of the Huskies, was not our favorite place to play. Spectators were few and two showers were shared with the opposition. The dressing rooms were cramped and up a long set of stairs. It was so cold the backup goalie often sat in the press box and coach Clare Drake wore his red longjohns plus a green toque.

The original 60-minute game was not a classic. We got off to a poor start and were down 2-0 by 1:13 of the first period. We battled back to a 4-3 lead but Randy Wiebe scored for Saskatchewan to force overtime.

The rules called for a ten minute overtime period. If the game was still tied, a series of 20 minute sudden-death periods would be played. Saskatchewan moved early but its lead didn't last as Brian Sosnowski tied it up.

During the intermission at least half the original 50 fans left. Twenty more minutes were played to no avail. It was up the steps again for a rest. In the dressing room the guys pleaded for someone to score or we would miss the last call at the bar. It was even suggested that I should let one in on purpose. Anything to end this.

We began our third overtime confident we could score. The fans dropped off to about ten. But twenty minutes more saw no final results so it was up the long stairs. By this time it was after midnight. Our dressing room was quiet. A pool was organized for everyone to put in a quarter for the winning goal scorer.

Down the steps again we went only to realize the remaining ten fans had left. Finally at 5:50 of the 4th overtime period, during a powerplay, John Devaney banged in a rebound off a shot by Randy Gregg. Sosnowski also drew an assist.

It wasn't the prettiest goal but it was a thing of beauty to our eyes. For John, it was his third goal of the evening. So at 1:00 a.m., some five hours later it was over. Total playing time was 115 minutes and 50 seconds for the 6-5 win.

(For the win, Cummings stopped a total of 55 shots, while Alberta had 63 on Pat Walsh of Saskatchewan.)

GOLDEN BEAR HOCKEY
BY STEVE KNOWLES, Sports Information Director, University of Alberta

The University of Alberta has been in existence since 1908-09, when the first students began classes on the southern bank of the North Saskatchewan River in Edmonton. During the 77 years of its existence, the University of Alberta has gained an international reputation for excellence in academics and athletics.

In its 73 years, the Golden Bears hockey team has become known throughout North America as one of the most successful intercollegiate teams, winning 34 conference championships and six national championships.

On January 8, 1909, Varsity, in their uniform crested with green wings and a V on a yellow field, took to the ice at the Strathcona Rink. With a lineup of seven players, Varsity met the Alberta College seven for the first game in their history. Max Fife, who played three seasons for Alberta, scored Varsity's first and only goal of the game as Alberta College was victorious 4-1. The remainder of the 1908-09 season saw similar results for Varsity as they lost their remaining five games to finish last in the Edmonton Collegiate League with a 0-6 record.

Their second season, 1909-10, was more successful than their first as Varsity again competed in the E.C.L. Varsity's first ever victory came on December 18, 1909, with a 7-3 victory over Alberta College. Herb Dixon and York Blayney each scored twice in the victory, with Blayney scoring the winning goal. Varsity went on to finish with a 3-3 record and a second place tie in the E.C.L. standings.

During the 1910-11 season, the senior team played in the Alberta Amateur Hockey Association.

At the conclusion of the AAHA schedule Varsity played a series of games against teams in Alberta and Saskatchewan. Varsity travelled to Saskatoon for two games in late February. Their first game, on February 27, was against the University of Saskatchewan. This game marked the first ever that the University of Alberta played against another University. With Roy Goodridge leading the way with an eight goal performance, Varsity easily defeated the Saskatoon scholars 16-0. The next day, Varsity met the Saskatoon senior team, and lost 9-4. The two game series marked the first intercollegiate game played by Varsity as well as the first game played by a University of Alberta team outside the province of Alberta.

The 1911-12 season saw Varsity compete once again in the AAHA's Northern Division. Varsity was unable to repeat their success of 1910-11 and finished fourth in the senior loop. But all was not a loss for Varsity in 1911-12. For the first time ever, a trophy, the Brackman-Kerr Cup, was put up for senior hockey supremacy in the City of Edmonton. The competition for the trophy allowed any senior or intermediate team to challenge for the trophy.

The first year saw Varsity and the Maritimes, another team from the Northern Division of the AAHA, compete for the Brackman-Kerr Cup in a best of five series. After splitting the first two games, Varsity won the next two to take the series three games to one and win their first championship!

For the next several years Varsity played in the AAHA's Northern Division, placing second in 1913-14. The 1912-13 season saw Alberta defeat the University of Saskatchewan twice in a home and home series. Varsity defeated the Saskatoon sextet 7-4 at Edmonton's South Side Rink and 4-2 in Saskatoon. In 1912-13 Varsity lost the Brackman-Kerr Cup to the Dominions, losing the final game of the challenge series in overtime.

In 1913-14, Varsity expanded their intercollegiate play, travelling to Manitoba to play the University of Manitoba and Brandon College. The three game trip also included a stop in Regina to play the Regina Victorias. In their first meeting with the University of Manitoba, Varsity was victorious, winning 6-4. A tie with Brandon College and an 11-0 loss to Regina left Varsity with an even record on their first trip to Manitoba.

In 1915-16 with the First World War in full force, Varsity played in the Edmonton Intermediate League's "B" Division. For the duration of the war, Varsity played intermediate hockey in Edmonton, placing second in 1915-16 and third in 1917-18.

A major event in University of Alberta hockey occurred during the 1917-18 season. For the first time Varsity had a coach. Sandy Caldwell became Varsity's first ever head coach.

From 1917-18 to 1919-20 one of Canada's greatest sportsmen and public figures was a member of the Varsity hockey team. The Right Honorable Roland Michener played three seasons with Varsity, spending equal time with both the senior and intermediate squads.

Upon graduating from the University of Alberta, Michener went to Oxford as a Rhodes Scholar, the only Varsity athlete to be so honored.

As the "Roaring Twenties" approached and the world began to recover from the cataclysm known as the "War to End All Wars," intercollegiate athletics in Western Canada took a monumental step forward. Officials from the three western universities, Alberta, Saskatchewan and Manitoba, met at the MacDonald Hotel in Edmonton in the fall of 1919. Their purpose was to form an athletic conference for the western universities similar to the "Big Four" in Eastern Canada.

In a historical meeting the delegates created the Western Canadian Intercollegiate Athletic Union (WCIAU).

The WCIAU's first scheduled sport was hockey, which began during the 1919-20 season with a four game schedule between Alberta, Saskatchewan and Manitoba.

During the next two decades, the 1920's and 1930's, Varsity split their time playing in the Edmonton City Senior League, Edmonton Intermediate League and the Northern Alberta Intermediate League. In 1920-21, Varsity won the Duggan Cup emblematic of the Edmonton City Championship. Several years earlier the Duggan Cup replaced the Brackman-Kerr Cup as the championship trophy for the Edmonton City Senior League. This resulted when the Brackman-Kerr Cup was put up for the senior championship of Northern Alberta.

The 1923-24 season was one of Varsity's most successful in their early history. After winning the city senior championship for the second time in four years, Varsity then defeated Camrose and the Penn Miners to win the Northern Alberta Senior championship and the Brackman-Kerr Cup. With their northern championship, the Varsity six travelled to Canmore for the provincial semi-finals. Canmore defeated Varsity in straight games 7-3 and 8-5 to advance to the provincial finals. In 1926-27 Varsity won their third city championship of the decade and lost in the finals in 1924-25, 1927-28 and 1930-31.

Several key events took place during this period to the Varsity hockey team. In 1923-24, a professor of Classics at the University of Alberta, Dr. W.G. Hardy, became the head coach of the hockey team. Hardy was instrumental in developing the Alberta hockey program into a serious contender in the provincial senior ranks. He was also a key figure in the move to have an arena built on campus.

With very few ice rinks in Edmonton at the time, and a large increase in the numbers of teams playing hockey, the University of Alberta was finding it hard to find enough ice for its teams. Dr. Hardy organized a fund raising campaign among the students, alumni and businessmen of Edmonton to help raise the necessary monies for construction of an arena. After two years of campaigning, enough money was collected to fund the construction. Due mainly to the efforts of Dr. Hardy, the University's first ice arena, Varsity Arena, was completed and opened for use in time for the 1927-28 season. Located at the corner of 87 Avenue and 114 Street, the Arena would serve the University for 33 years.

In 1922, Dr. J. Halpenny of the University of Saskatchewan donated a trophy to the WCIAU to be presented annually to the W.C.I.A.U. hockey champions. The Helpenny Trophy was competed for every year, until 1950, with the exception of several years during the late 1920's and early 1930's when the Depression curtailed the extent of intercollegiate athletics, and for a five year period during the Second World War.

Alberta's success in intercollegiate hockey began in 1933-34. Under the guidance of head coach Al Wilson, the Albertans captured the Halpenny Trophy for the first time.

The 1933-34 championship was to start a string of championships unparalleled in WCIAU history. After winning the Halpenny Trophy in 1933-34, Alberta was to remain in possession of the championship trophy for another 17 years. During this 17 year span the trophy was competed for a total of eleven times with Alberta winning it each of the eleven years. In the other six years, there was no competition for the Halpenny Trophy due to the Depression and the Second World War; however, the trophy remained in Alberta's possession.

In March of 1950 the Halpenny Trophy was retired in the permanent possession of the University of Alberta upon the occasion of their 17th consecutive year of winning the trophy. A new trophy was instituted in the 1950-51 season for the WCIAU hockey championship. The W.G. Hardy Trophy, named in honor of the former Alberta head coach, was inaugurated in 1950-51.

With the outbreak of the Second World War in September of 1939, intercollegiate athletics were drastically curtailed due to travel restrictions. Hockey was particularly hard hit. After winning the Halpenny Trophy in 1939-40, Alberta saw its intercollegiate program disbanded in 1940-41. Both Varsity Arena and the University of Saskatchewan's Rutherford Rink were used by the military for training purposes and were therefore unavailable for use by the hockey team.

Alberta did ice a team in 1940-41 but played only a very limited schedule against intermediate and junior teams. From 1941-42 to 1944-45, the only hockey played on campus was of the interfaculty or intramural variety. Stan Moher, the Alberta head coach, was retained by the University to organize and administer the interfaculty program during the war years. Moher organized a six team league that competed for four years on an outdoor arena.

With the conclusion of the Second World War the intercollegiate hockey program returned to the University of Alberta. Playing in both the intercollegiate and intermediate leagues the Golden Bears (as they became known in the late 1930's) continued their success. The Golden Bears won six consecutive WCIAU championships immediately following the war to bring their total to eleven by 1949-50.

The coaching chores in the immediate post war years were held by men not associated with the University of Alberta in a working capacity. From 1945-48 Andy "Shorts" Purcell led the Golden Bears. In 1948-50, Clarence Moher was at the helm. He too was a local man with his business unrelated to that of the University's. In the 1950-51 season the coaching position was given to another local man named Art Wiebe, a former NHL defenceman. However, it was during this time that the Athletic Council, headed by Dr. Maury Van Vliet, felt it would be in the University's best interest to have a coach who was from the Faculty of Physical Education. Therefore, Don Smith, a professor of Physical Education at the time, was appointed as assistant Coach to Art Wiebe during the 1951-52 season. The following year Smith became the full time coach of the Golden Bear Hockey Team.

The 1950's brought Alberta continued success as they won seven more WCIAU championships. Led by players such as Vern Pachal, Cy Ing, Don Kirk, Adam Kryčzka, Les Zimmel and Ted Mitenko, they won conference titles in 1953-54 to 1957-58 and 1959-60.

At the end of the 1957-58 season Don Smith stepped down as the Golden Bears head coach. Taking his place was a young man who would have a monumental effect on intercollegiate hockey at Alberta and throughout Canada. His name — Clare Drake.

Drake came to Alberta in 1953-54 from the University of British Columbia. He played one season for the Golden Bears in 1953-54. As an assistant captain he led the Golden Bears to a WCIAU championship and was the team's leading scorer in conference play.

In his 24 years as Alberta's head coach he has compiled an outstanding record. Among his victories are 16 conference championships and five Canadian Interuniversity Athletic Union national championships. On October 8, 1985 Drake became the winningest coach in North American intercollegiate hockey history. The leader was Michigan Tech's John MacInnes who compiled a record of 555-295-39 in 26 seasons behind the Huskie's bench. Drake is now 556-240-34.

Named the CIAU's Coach-of-the-Year in 1974-75, Drake has also compiled a very outstanding coaching record at the international level. He coached the Canadian Student National Team, composed mainly of Golden Bears, to the gold medal at the 1981 World Student Games in Jaca, Spain and to a silver medal in 1972 at Lake Placid, New York. Along with Bill Moores, he coached the Golden Bears to two championships at the Pacific Rim Tournament (1977-78 and 1978-79).

In 1980, Drake, along with Tom Watt and Lorne Davis, was appointed as one of three coaches to guide the Canadian Olympic Team. The team finished sixth at the Winter Games in Lake Placid, and overall had a 29-20-4 record. During the 1975-76 season he was the head coach of the Edmonton Oilers World Hockey Association.

The Golden Bears continued their success during the 1960's winning nine more conference titles from 1959-60 to 1968-69, including a string of five from 1965-66 to 1969-70. The 1960-61 season saw the Golden Bears move to a new arena. Built as part of the new Physical Education Building, the second Varsity Arena opened in 1960-61. A 3,000 seat arena located on campus, Varsity Arena has served as the home of Golden Bear hockey for the last 25 years and has been host to many thrilling moments in Golden Bear hockey history.

After having won the WCIAU championship in 1963-64, the Golden Bears advanced to the CIAU championship held at Kingston, Ontario. Under the direction of Clare Drake the Golden Bears defeated the University of New Brunswick 5-3 in the semi-finals. In the final, the Golden Bears met Sir George Williams from Montreal and in a rather lopsided game Alberta won the University Cup for the first time in its history with a 9-1 victory. The Golden Bears would make four more appearances in the CIAU tournament during the 1960's including another championship in 1967-68 when Ron Cebryk scored the winning goal with only 17 seconds remaining in the game as Alberta defeated Loyola University 5-4 before 12,000 fans at the Montreal Forum.

Other highlights of the 1960's for the Golden Bears included winning the gold medal at the First Canadian Winter Games held in Quebec City during the 1966-67 season.

Alberta's success continued in the 1970's. From 1969-70 to 1979-80 the Golden Bears were one of the dominant teams in CIAU hockey. Seven times they won conference championships and four times they were crowned national champions.

In 1974-75 the Golden Bears won their 29th conference title and hosted the C.I.A.U. championships at Varsity Arena.

Led by defenceman Ross Barros and goaltender Dale Henwood, who recorded three shutouts during the playoffs to establish a CIAU record, the Golden Bears hosted their eastern rivals, the Toronto Varsity Blues in the best of three final. Organist Rick LeBlanc came up with a theme song for the 1974-75 Golden Bears. Every time that the Golden Bears would score a goal during the playoffs, LeBlanc would play his version of "Barros and the Bears" (adapted from Elton John's *Benny and the Jets*) sending the Varsity Arena faithful into a frenzy.

In the finals, Henwood recorded his third shutout as the Bears defeated Toronto 5-0 in the first game. The Blues rebounded in the second game with a close 3-2 victory to set up the final. The final was a classic as Toronto opened the scoring only 52 seconds into the game. Alberta rallied to tie the game 2-2 after one period, and Oliver Stewards' goal only seven seconds into the second period proved to be the winner as Henwood shut out Toronto the rest of the way. Barros led the Alberta attack with two powerplay goals and sent organist Rick LeBlanc and the 4,000 fans crazy as Alberta claimed their third national championship. Henwood was named the MVP of the tournament, while Barros and coach Drake were named to the CIAU All-Canadian team.

In 1970-71, the CIAU introduced the All-Canadian team, a selection of all-stars from across the country. That year Steve Carlyle, a defenceman, was selected to the team, becoming the first Golden Bear to be so honored. In the 15 years since the selection of the first team, a total of 13 Golden Bears have been honored as All-Canadians: the most by any school in the CIAU. Four players have been named All-Canadians twice. They are goaltenders Ted Poplawski (1978-79, 1979-80), Ken Hodge (1983-84, 1984-85), and defencemen Randy Gregg (1976-77, 1978-79) and Carlyle (1970-71, 1971-72).

For four seasons, from 1976-77 to 1979-80, the Golden Bears were the dominant team in the CIAU as they appeared in four national championship games, winning three consecutively. In 1976-77 Drake, who returned from a one year stint as the head coach of the WHA Edmonton Oilers, took a team with 17 freshmen to the national finals. They won the Canada West conference title with a conference leading 21-3 record and advanced to the final against Toronto. Before a home crowd of 4,000 at Varsity Arena, the Golden Bears were unable to match Toronto as they lost 4-1.

The result would be different the next time these two teams would meet. In 1977-78 the Golden Bears again won the CWUAA title and advanced to the CIAU finals, this time played in Moncton, New Brunswick. Winning their two preliminary round games, Alberta met Toronto once again in the final. This time, with the 17 freshmen of a year ago now seasoned veterans, the Golden Bears defeated Toronto 6-5 as Kevin Primeau, who would later play with the WHA's Edmonton Oilers, was named the tournaments MVP. The championship, their first since 1974-75, would be the first of three that the Golden Bears would win in the next three seasons.

Alberta's second consecutive national title came in 1978-79. The Golden Bears won 20 of their 24 Canada West games and in a best of three final against the second place Calgary Dinosaurs, the Golden Bears prevailed two games to one, to claim their 32nd conference championship. Advancing to their third CIAU national tournament in three seasons, the Golden Bears were the favorites to retain the University Cup.

UNIVERSITY OF ALBERTA GOLDEN BEARS 1963-64
C.I.A.U. National Champions
WCIAA Champions

First row (l to r): Clare Drake (coach), Jim Fleming, Terry Bicknell, Dick Wintermute, Ian Baker, Leigh McMillan, Eugene Gushaty (manager). Second row (l to r): Dale Harder, Howie Green, Jim Reaman, Ralph Jorstad, Butch Hyde, Dave Jenkins. Third row (l to r): Brian Harper, John Aubin, Ed Wahl, Dave McDermid, Les Payne, Dale Rippel. Missing: Earl Gray.

In the preliminary round Alberta defeated the Concordia Stingers, the host school for the tournament, 7-1, and the Regina Cougars 3-1 to advance to the championship game. In their third championship game in four years, the Golden Bears met the Dalhousie Tigers. With Dave Hindmarch scoring two first period powerplay goals, the Golden Bears showed their dominance and skated to a 5-1 victory and their second straight CIAU championship. Hindmarch was named the tournament's MVP and was also named to the all-tournament team along with defenceman Stan Swales and John Devaney. Devaney led all scorers in the tournament with eight points on four goals and four assists. As well as tournament honors, three Golden Bears were named to the CIAU All-Canadian team. Defenceman Randy Gregg was named to the team for the second time in his career and forward Chris Helland and goaltender Ted Poplawski were both selected to their first All-Canadian team. Gregg also became the only Golden Bear to be awarded the Senator Joseph A. Sullivan Trophy as the most outstanding player in the CIAU.

Alberta's third consecutive CIAU championship came in 1979-80, but it was different than any other.

The 1979-80 season was a rebuilding year for Alberta as the Golden Bears lost Coach Drake and four players to the 1980 Canadian Olympic Team as well as seven other players to graduation. With eleven regulars gone from the team that had won the previous two CIAU National Championships, the Golden Bears faced a difficult job in rebuilding.

Bill Moores was named the new head coach of the Golden Bears for the 1979-80 season. Moores, a former Golden Bear, put together a mixture of veterans and freshmen that once again were highly competitive. On the season the Golden Bears were 29-13 overall and finished first in the Canada West conference with a 20-9 record. In the conference playoffs, the Bears were upset by the Calgary Dinosaurs in two games 3-1 and 2-0, and found their season at a finish. So everyone thought.

Two weeks later the Golden Bears were awarded a wild-card berth in the CIAU tournament.

The Golden Bears won their third consecutive and sixth national crown overall defeating Regina 7-3 in the final. The Bears were led by team captain Larry Riggin who anchored the defence that had four freshmen as regulars.

By winning their third national championship the Golden Bears became only the second team in the CIAU to win three titles in a row. Seven players were members of each of the University Cup teams, becoming the only Golden Bears to win three national titles in their careers. The seven were Ted Poplawski, Larry Riggin, Bruce Rolin, Mike Broadfoot, Jim Lomas, Barrie Stafford, and Chris Helland.

The 1980 Winter Olympic Games in Lake Placid, New York, had a distinct Golden Bear flavor as Clare Drake and five Golden Bears were members of the Canadian Hockey team. Drake, one of the three co-coaches of the National team, was joined by defencemen Randy Gregg and Don Spring, and forwards John Devaney, Dave Hindmarch and Kevin Primeau. The Canadians finished sixth at the Olympics and completed their season with a 29-20-4 record. Gregg was named the team's captain and Devaney, Hindmarch, and Primeau formed the team's number one line during the Olympics, with Devaney finishing as the second leading scorer on the team.

UNIVERSITY OF ALBERTA GOLDEN BEARS 1967-68

Bottom row (l to r): W. Kettle, R. Cebryk, G. Braunberger, S. Belcourt, D. Halterman. Second row (l to r): C. Drake (coach), G. Tucker, J. Stambaugh (manager). Third row (l to r): D. Zarowny, B. Suter, B. Robinson, D. Falkenberg, M. Stelmaschuk, M. Hohol, L. Zalapski, J. Seutter. Fourth row (l to r): W. Wiste, R. Reinhart, J. Gibson, D. Manning, D. Couves, T. Devaney, D. McIntyre.

The Golden Bears have enjoyed a successful record in international play. Besides their Olympic contribution in 1980, the Golden Bears have won two Pacific Rim tournament championships, 1977-78 and 1978-79, and one World Student Games gold medal.

In the 1972 World Student Games held at Lake Placid, Golden Bears Barry Richardson, Steve Carlyle, Dave Couves, and Jack Gibson joined Drake to win the silver medal, losing to the Soviet Union in the championship game. In 1981 the Golden Bears represented Canada at the World Student Games in Jaca, Spain. Going undefeated in four games, including a 31-0 romp over the South Korean student national team, the Golden Bears won the gold medal, Canada's first in any international tournament since 1961, with a 6-1 victory over Finland.

The 73 year history of Golden Bear hockey is one of success. From city championships in their early years to national and international recognition in the 1960's, 1970's and 1980's, the Golden Bears have been at the forefront of intercollegiate sport in Canada.

UNIVERSITY OF CALGARY DINOSAURS

BY JACK NEUMANN, Sports Information Director, University of Calgary

The University of Calgary made its competitive debut in varsity hockey in the 1965-66 season in the Western Intercollegiate Athletic Association (which was the forerunner of what is now the Canada West University Athletic Association). The Dinosaurs suffered a somewhat demoralizing introduction to WCIAA hockey circles — it took them three years to win a league game under Coach Al Rollins. Rollins, a former NHL netminder and goalie for the Calgary Senior Stampeders suffered through a string of forty-four straight losses as the Dinosaurs set a record for futility in the Canadian College hockey circles.

UNIVERSITY OF ALBERTA GOLDEN BEARS 1977-78
C.I.A.U. National Champions
CWUAA Champions

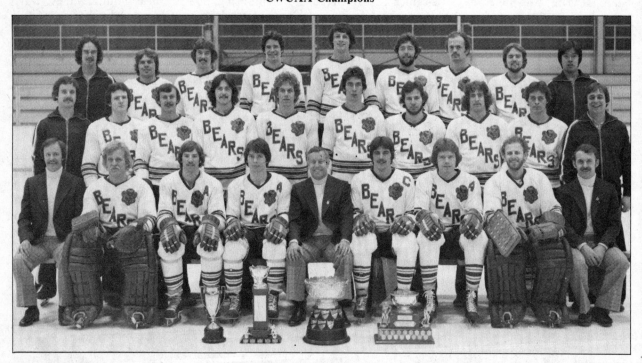

First row (l to r): Peter Esdale (assistant coach), Jack Cummings, John Devaney, Jim Carr, Clare Drake (head coach), Kevin Primeau, Ted Poplawski, Bill Moores (assistant coach). Second row (l to r): Dan Smith (assistant coach), Barrie Stafford, Jim Lomas, Stan Swales, Mike Bachynski, Bruce Rolin, Jim Causgrove, Dave Hindmarch, Don Spring, Derek Drager (manager). Third row (l to r): Brian Heck (manager), Chris Helland, Darrell Zapernick, Mike Broadfoot, Kevin Bolton, Larry Riggin, Ted Olson, Dave Breakwell, Danny Nakamura (manager).

In 1968, Athletic Director Dennis Kadatz hired George Kingston, and the team had a winning season in his first term as Dinosaur Hockey Coach. In 1970 Calgary captured their first WCIAA pennant only to lose in the playoffs to the U. of A. Most notable on the 1970 team were Daryl Maggs who went on to play professionally for the Chicago Cougars of the World Hockey Association, and the Richardson brothers (Frank and Steve) from Olds, Alberta. Steve later played professionally with the Indianapolis Racers of the WHA and with the Cincinnati Swords of the American Hockey League. Gordon Jones, Colin Petterson, Rob Wright, Dave Margach and John Kinsmen all went on to major contributions to minor hockey development after graduation.

The Dinosaurs won their first Canada West University Athletic Association title in 1974 and advanced to the Canadian Interuniversity Athletic Union semi-finals that year. Anchorman on that team was all-Canadian defenceman John Jenkins. Kingston coached the Dinosaurs to their second CWUAA title in thre years in 1976 as the Dinos won the CWUAA title. The Dinos were led to the title by a trio of high socring forward — Ron Gerlitz, Rick Hindmarch and Bob Laycock. The Dinos won the CIAU Western Regional Tournament but had to settle for being semi-finalists at the CIAU National Tournament in Waterloo.

From 1976 to 1979 Calgary had to settle for being runners-up to the University of Alberta. The 1979 Dinosaur hockey team was perhaps the second best club in Canada as they forced the power packed Golden Bears to a third and deciding game in the CWUAA final in Edmonton. The 1979 Dinosaur Hockey Team had Jim Nill up front. He joined the Canadian Olympic Team the following year and later went on to play professionally in the NHL with St. Louis, Vancouver and Boston. The blueline was anchored by Terry Johnson who played for the St. Louis Blues in 1983-84. In 1980 the U. of C. got revenge as they swept the Bears in Varsity Arena to claim the CWUAA title. Blairmore's Terry Kryczka and Red Deer's Jerry Farwell put on an incredible netminding display in Edmonton as the number one ranked Bears were swept in two straight games scoring just one goal. Offensively Jerry Bancks led the Dinos while defenceman Rick Williams was named to the CIAU all-Canadian team. The Bears broke the Dinos' hearts two weeks later as they gained a "wild card" spot in the CIAU tournament at Regina and edged the Dinos 2-0 and eventually gained the CIAU National Championship which still leaves a bitter feeling at the U. of C.

Calgary hosted the Men's CIAU Hockey Championship in 1981 at Max Bell Arena. The Dinosaurs were ranked in the top three most of the year and won the CWUAA pennant. They hosted Saskatchewan in the playoffs losing to the Huskies in the final of the best-of-three playoff. The Dinos lost their opening round game in the national Tournament in overtime to the eventual champion Moncton Blue Eagles and had to settle for third place. The 1981 squad was a solid unit led by all-Canadian goalie Farwell and defenceman Ron Fischer who was an all-Canadian and top rearguard in the conference. The following couple of seasons the CWUAA was dominated by the Saskatchewan Huskies as the Dinos suffered through a rebuilding period.

George Kingston has been associated with the Varsity hockey program at Calgary since his hiring by Athletic Director Dennis Kadatz in 1968 and has twice been named CIAU Coach of the Year in 1974 and 1981. He was away from the hockey program attending other duties or on leave in 1974-75 and 1976-77. Kingston assisted Canadian Olympic Team Coach Dave King in 1984 and returned to his post as Hockey Coach at the University of Calgary in 1985.

1978 UNIVERSITY OF CALGARY EUROPEAN TOUR
BY JERRY FARWELL

(Farwell played goal for the University of Calgary from 1977 to 1981. He was voted to the CIAU All Canadian team in 1981, and the First All-Star team in 1980 and 1981 in the CWUAA. In 1980 he played with the Canadian Olympic team in a Post Olympic Tournament in Sweden. He led the Red Deer College Kings to the Canadian College Hockey Championship in 1977 and played for the Medicine Hat Tigers in the Western Canada Hockey League from 1972 to 1975.)

Of all the fond memories I have of my days at the University of Calgary, our European Tour in the summer of 1978 rates as one of the highlights.

Our home away from home was a large house in Fussen, West Germany in the beautiful mountains of Bavaria. Our first few days were quite an experience for most of us who had never experienced jet lag combined with extensive training. One of our coaches, Gord Cowan, who became known as Commandant Cowan for his continual marching around the house to ensure no one was grabbing an afternoon snooze. Within a few days adjustments were made on our part. We would prop up a book to make it look as though we were reading when the Commandant made his inspection and this seemed to do the trick. The irony of the whole thing was one aftenoon a couple of us went looking for Gordy and low and behold we found him with a book propped up and eyelids closed.

After a very rough start to our tour, a meeting was called one evening. During the meeting coach George Kingston paused for a moment to give us the opportunity to reflect on what had been started so far. The silence was abruptly broken by the sounds of "Brama" (Paul Blaney) snoring. George had been known to put at least one player (Rick Williams) to sleep in one of his classes at the University, but this was the first time at a team

UNIVERSITY OF ALBERTA GOLDEN BEARS 1978-79
C.I.A.U. National Champions
CWUAA Champions

First row (l to r): Nick Sanza, Darrell Zapernick, John Devaney, Clare Drake (head coach), Randy Gregg, Don Spring, Ted Poplawski. Second row (l to r): Peter Esdale (assistant coach), Ron Urness (arena supervisor), Steve Knowles (manager), Larry Riggin, Mike Broadfoot, Mike Bachynski, Bruce Rolin, Jim Causgrove, Dale Ross, Stan Swales, Ron Mattison (manager), Bill Moores (assistant coach). Third row (l to r): Dave Breakwell, Barrie Stafford, Jim Lomas, Ted Olson, Dave Hindmarch, Greg Skoreyko, Chris Helland.

UNIVERSITY OF ALBERTA GOLDEN BEARS 1979-80
C.I.A.U. National Champions

First row (l to r): Brad Hall, Chris Helland, Larry Riggin, Mike Broadfoot, Jim Lomas, Ted Poplawski. Second row (l to r): Peter Esdale (assistant coach), Steve Knowles (manager), Danny Arndt, Duncan Babchuk, Garnet Brimacombe, Bruce Rolin, Terry Sydoryk, Dale Ross, Rob Daum, Bill Moores (head coach). Third row (l to r): Dan Peacocke, Rod Tordoff, Joel Elliott, Barrie Stafford, Lee Arthur, Terry Lescisin, Brad Schneider, Greg Tennant, Greg Skoreyko.

UNIVERSITY OF CALGARY DINOSAURS 1975-76

Front row (l to r): Russ Hall, Shane Bassen, Bob Galloway, Jim Setters, Ron Gerlitz, Craig Stewart, Terry Kryczka, Joe Miller, Phil Jensen. Middle row (l to r): Peter Howe (general manager), Dr. Jack Bullard (team physician), Phil Irwin, Rick Alexander, Bob Laycock, Shane Tarves, Paul Ciemny, Bob Murray, Craig LeMere (manager). Rear row (l to r): Gord Cowan (coach), Tom Yates, Robin Laycock, Frank Raddatz, Rick Hindmarch, Doug Colville, George Quinn, George Kingston (coach).

UNIVERSITY OF CALGARY DINOSAURS 1979-80

Front row (l to r): Drew Tumbach, Bob Irvine, Randy Joevenazzo (captain), Jerry Bancks, Jerry Farwell, Terry Kryczka, Rick Williams, Paul Blayney, Jim Bertram, Derek Spring, Craig Lemere (equipment manager). Back row (l to r): Dexter Nelson (trainer), George Kingston (coach), Steve Blyth, Cal Halasz, Paul Murray, Tom Gould, Roger Mitchell, Cary Cummins, Rob Labelle, George Gonis, Jerry Orban, Craig Bentley, Ron Fischer, Gord Cowan (coach), Deak Cassidy (general manager). Missing: Frank Harbich.

meeting. George was quick to put the incident into perspective by explaining that Brama had gone on a long bicycle trip that afternoon. I still wonder if it was only the bicycle trip.

That same afternoon the local people had a treat of their own as Jerry "Evil Knevil" Bancks put on a show at the lake. With rescuers ready in the water, he pedaled hard down the hill, along the dock and plunged bicycle and all into the lake to the cheering of his fellow teammates and local tourists.

George Kingston has always been known to call instructions to his players on the ice using descriptive adjectives. By the time we arrived home George had used one so often he will always be known to us as "Heavy" Kingston.

The trip was a smashing success as our goal was Class, Sportsmanship and Excellence in ice hockey, all of which were achieved as well as an experience of a lifetime for a fine group of athletes and coaches.

ALBERTA COLLEGE ATHLETIC CONFERENCE (ACAC)

BY AL BUTTLE, Executive Director ACAC

The predecessor of the Alberta Colleges' Athletic Conference — the Western Inter-College Conference — was formed in 1964. Hockey was introduced as a major team sport in 1965 and involved Camrose Luthern College, Calgary's Mount Royal College, the Northern Alberta Institute of Technology, and the Southern Alberta Insititue of Technology. Since that time, participation has ranged from these original four to as many as seven entires, and the calibre of the college game has improved to the point where ACAC clubs are competing openly with Tier One and Tier Two junior teams and other senior University squads for player personnel.

CAMROSE LUTHERAN COLLEGE VIKINGS 1974-75

Front (l to r): Rodney Lee, reporter, Tom Gould, Larry Stewart, Russ Shandro, Lee Cumberland, Bill Andreassen, Phil Irwin, LeRoy Johnson (general manager), Joe Voytechek (coach). Second (l to r): Jim Voytechek, stick boy, Joe Miller, Darrel Runka, Peter Hanson, Bob Large, Harley Johnson, Dennis Becker (manager), Lynn Getz, Karl Falten (trainer), Dennis Dunn. Back (l to r): Morley Dunlop, John Danko, Svend Green, Elston Solberg, Don Boyce, Gary Fortier.

In 1984, six ACAC member institutions were involved in the race for College Hockey supremacy and the right to represent the Conference at the national college championships. Gold medals have been brought to Alberta

RED DEER COLLEGE KINGS
Canadian College Hockey Champions 1977

Back row (l to r): Curtis Crough, Bob Haldane, Ron Joel, Ron Mykyta, Ken Hilsenteger, Brent Westley, Eric Kassian, Blaine Hanson. Middle row (l to r): Larry Green, John Rycroft, Bruce Schmidt, Ken Klinkhammer, Bob Graham, Dale Horsley, Al Jacobson, Jim Causgrove, Randy Lewis (assistant manager). Front row (l to r): Rich Riedel, Rollie Gerwing, Terry Fuga, Bob Bennett (manager), Al Ferchuk (coach), Bob Stevenson (coach), Ray Hall, Gerry Farwell.

RED DEER COLLEGE KINGS
Canadian College Champions 1979

Back row (l to r): Larry Jones, Mark VonHagen, Ron Kulych, Rick Odegard, Andy Clark-Marlow, Scott Hucul, Ron Pierce, Todd McAuley. Middle row (l to r): Shirley McEwan (physio), Les Cust, Rob Dyck, Mark Wakey, Dave Tietzen, Bruce Small, Cam McNaughton, Stew Mitchell (trainer). Front row (l to r): Peter Friestadt, Carl Graham, Rod Gillespie, Bob Bennett (manager), Allan Ferchuk (coach), Dan McDonald (coach), Bill Wilkins, John Kulych.

and the ACAC on seven occasions; by the Camrose Lutheran College Vikings in 1975, by Red Deer College Kings in 1977, 1979 and 1980, by the SAIT Trojans in 1981 and by the NAIT Ooks in 1982 and 1985.

In addition, silver medals were won by the Red Deer College Kings in 1978 and 1983, and by the SAIT Trojans in 1979 and 1980. Red Deer College's Allan Ferchuk and NAIT's Perry Pearn received Canadian Colleges' "Coach of the Year" awards in 1983 and 1984 respectively.

CCAA CHAMPIONS 1980
Red Deer College Kings

Back row (l to r): Ray Keith, Ron Kulych, Gord Dodd, Brad Helfrich, Brian Lees, Ron Rogers, Bruce Young, George Wright, Rick Odegard. **Middle row (l to r):** Randy Lewis (therapist), Ron Parent, Mark Von Hagen, Warren Bell, Bernie McNeil, Bruce Small, Scott Hucal, Alvin Szott, Dave Tietzen. **Front row (l to r):** Jim Gerwing, Rob Dyck, Cam MacNaughton, Dan MacDonald (assistant coach), Bob Bennett (manager), Allan Ferchuk (coach), Bill Wilkins, John Kulych.

SOUTHERN ALBERTA INSTITUTE OF TECHNOLOGY TROJANS 1981
Canadian College Champions

Back row (l to r): Al McLeod (manager), Kim Hilkewich, Darren Woitas, Scott Parkinson, Wayne Merkel, Rodger Pierce, Jim Snodgrass, Brad Carlson, Myron Romaniuk, Greg Luhr, Dennis Connelly, Bob Moore (coach). **Front row (l to r):** Blair Pomahac, Ron Pierce, Ron Elder, Brent Lock, Bobby Deschamps, Doug Panchuk, Jamie Hodgins, Mike Sears, Steve Hanna, Mark Hollenbeck (stick boy).

Most Valuable Player Awards from the ACAC won at National Championships commencing in 1975, include Dennis Dunn, Camrose Luthern College 1975, Gerry Farwell, 1977 Red Deer College, Bill Wilkins, Red Deer College 1979, Alvin Scott, Red Deer College 1980, Ron Pierce, SAIT 1981, and Ken Hodge NAIT 1982.

CCAA NATIONAL CHAMPIONS 1982
NAIT Ooks

Back row (l to r): Bruce Watson (manager), Ken Ludwig, Tom Tookey, Kent Wilmot, Greg Tennant, Pat Kernaghan. Middle row (l to r): Paul St. Cyr (assistant coach), Patti Dahl (trainer), Terry Bakken, Rod Arychuk, Warren Sanregret, Dale Kolada, Mike Moskalyk, Gary Hoekstra, Marg Stack (trainer), Perry Pearn (coach). Front row (l to r): Ken Hodge, Brian Hermanutz, Ron Chorney, Ray Anderson, Wayne Perkins, Darrell Slupek, Dave Souch, Daryl Holmquist, Brad Breakell.

NAIT HOCKEY TEAM 1984-85

Front row (l to r): Cleo Rowein, Murray Melnyk, Mark Schultz, Kevin Imrie, Tom Tookey, Jamie Bartman, Gary Haddon, Mike Tookey, Randy Repchuk, Jeff Lastiwka. Middle row: Patti Dahl (trainer), Perry Pearn (head coach), Rick Yaschyshyn (trainer), Don Simpson, Ron Amyotte, Hugh McCaskill, Garth Hayes, Sid Cranston, Kevin Stapleton, John Phelan (assistant coach), Paul St. Cyr (assistant coach), Wayne Perkins (assistant coach), Cindy Schultheiss (trainer). Back row: Bruce Watson (manager), Brenn Leach, Ken Goodwin, Mike Spencer, Darrell Bokenfohr (assistant coach), Ross Kenny, David Simmons, Gary Leach, Scott Melnyk, Brian Stein (media relations). *Photo courtesy of NAIT Photography*

THE VIKING CUP

BY LeRoy Johnson

(While serving as Director of Athletics at Camrose Lutheran College (1977-1982), Johnson originated and developed the Viking Cup. The tournament was made possible and continues as part of an exchange program developed by Johnson between the Camrose Lutheran College Vikings and the European hockey fraternity. Johnson has arranged and directed four highly successful European hockey tours of the CLC Vikings to countries including Sweden, Finland, Denmark, Russia, Czechoslovakia, Austria and West Germany. Johnson continues as an instructor at Camrose Lutheran College.)

VIKING CUP PROGRAM

Photo courtesy of Edmonton Archives

Like so many people of the Camrose area, the Viking Cup has its roots in northern Europe.

It was during the CLC Vikings second European hockey tour (Sweden, Finland, USSR) that the idea for a Viking Cup gained necessary momentum. In fact, it was on a wobbly train from Leningrad to Helsinki that the manager, coach and other officials of the CLC Vikings began to make plans in earnest.

International Tournaments, it was observed, have their common place in European countries, particularly during the mid-season break. Such tournaments at the Junior or College level have been less common in Canada, perhaps due to intense schedules of Canadian junior hockey teams and costly travel exchange. Also because the NHL draft of European players, the time was right for an international tournament of top level Junior clubs.

The invitation to two of Sweden and Finland's top clubs, both of which played the CLC Vikings in Europe, was accepted and the Viking Cup with International status was off to a good start. The tournament immediately attracted a host of NHL scouts and the keen interest of the media and hockey fans in Central Alberta. Seven players of Viking Cup '81 were drafted by NHL teams in June, 1982, including the tournament's Most Valuable Player, Hannu Virta of the champion TPS Finland team, now with the Buffalo Sabres, and James Patrick of the Prince Albert Raiders who in 1984-85 was with the New York Rangers.

The major attraction of Viking Cup '82 was undoubtably the Czechoslovakia Junior Selects — a national All-Star team of 17 and 18-year-olds, including such greats as forward Peter Klima and goal tender Dominik Hasek, now both outstanding players with the Czech National Team.

Once again the Centennial Cup Canadian champion Prince Albert Raiders provided the strongest opposition for the poised Czechs. Viking Cup '82 also marked an important milestone in friendship relations as the young Czech boys were permitted for the first time to be billeted in Western homes. This proved to be highly successful and was repeated at Viking Cup '84.

After Viking Cup '82, the tournament was officially established as a biannual New Year's event sponsored and operated by Camrose Lutheran College.

Viking Cup '84 for the first time produced a Canadian champion in the NAIT Ookpiks of Edmonton who defeated the defending champion Czech Junior Selects in the final game.

The Hockey fraternity can continue to look forward to world class hockey in Camrose every two years as six of the worlds' outstanding Junior/College hockey teams compete for the prestigious "Viking Cup".

1984 — 85 COLLEGE CHAMPIONS — NAIT OOKS

BY Brian Stein, Director Sports Public Relations, NAIT

The 1984-85 NAIT Hockey Ooks will be remembered as one of the finest college hockey teams in Canadian history. Perry Pearn's team consisted of a perfect blend of veterans and rookies with depth at every position.

FORMER EDMONTON FLYER ROGER DeJORDY WITH HOCKEY PUCK COLLECTION

Roger's collection is at NAIT where he is the rink manager.

Photo courtesy of Rosina Ritson-Bennett, NAIT Photographer

The NAIT Ooks began the 1984-85 pre-season in a different way. For the first time in history, the Ooks won the ACAC Pre-season Hockey Tournament with a 9-1 triumph over the MRC Cougars in the tourney final at Red Deer. The Ooks were then known as contenders for the ACAC title.

Following 11 wins and no losses at the end of the first half of the regular season, the Ooks turned their sights toward a 12 day exhibition tour of Switzerland. NAIT's record on the December 1984 series was four wins, no losses, and one tie. The highlight of the tour occurred on December 29th, when the Ooks nipped the future 1985 CIAU champion York Yeomen 5-3 to bring home the Altjahres Cup from Adelboden.

When the ACAC regular season drew to a close on February 24th, NAIT finished with an unprecedented perfect record of 25 wins. The Ooks led the league with the most goals for (221) and fewest goals against (57).

The Ooks repeated as ACAC hockey champions on March 14th completing a three game sweep over Red Deer. The Ooks had advanced to the final with a pair of overtime wins over Camrose.

One of the most memorable nights in Edmonton college hockey history occurred on March 19th when 13,354 fans turned up for "Faceoff 85" at Northlands Coliseum between the Ooks and the U of A Golden Bears. The Ooks played valiantly but dropped a 5-4 decision to the Bears.

NAIT capped off the 1984-85 hockey season when they became CCAA (National) hockey champions on March 30th in Moose Jaw, Saskatchewan with a 9-2 win over the Victoriaville Vulkins. As a result, the NAIT Ooks ended the campaign with a mark of 33 wins and no losses in regular season and playoffs. It's a record to remember.

CHAPTER 7
NATIVE HOCKEY

NATIVE HOCKEY CHAMPIONSHIP 1954

Chief Big Snake of Black Foot Tribe and Chief Dan Minde of the Cree were clad in magnificent tribal costumes complete with feathered eagle bonnets. They shared a peace pipe.

On March 18, 1954, in Ponoka, the two chiefs were at centre ice prior to the opening face-off of the first "Indian Hockey Championship of Alberta and the North West Territories".

Dr. W.B. Murray helped make this championship possible. He had spent twenty years with Indian Affairs at Morby and Sarcee. He then began a private medical practice in Calgary. But he could not forget an important part of his life. In order to help create closer relationships Dr. Murray developed the idea of a native hockey championship.

Accepting the trophy for the Blackfoot Braves from Gleichen was captain Francis Big Tobacco. Charlie McMaster and Mark Wolfe Leg scored twice and single goals came from George Many Shots, Ernie Yellow Fly and Irvin Brass. For the Hobbema Ermineskins, Joe Lightning tallied two goals, while Ross Littlechild, George Louis and Percy Wolfe had singles. The first encounter in Calgary ended 5-5. By virtue of the 7-5 win the Blackfoot Braves from Gleichen became the first champions. Dr. W.B. Murray was on hand to present the trophy and see the idea on ice.

The Blackfoot Braves were coached by Syd Moore and Peter Many Guns. Their manager was Rev. A. Charoon. The Hobbema team was coached by Fred Hodgson and Frank Kresanoski. Team manager was Jim Ermineskin.

The following year two games were played in one day in Ponoka. In the afternoon the Hobbema Eagles and the Gleichen Braves tied 3-3; however, at night the Eagles easily won 13-1 for a 16-4 total-goal victory. David Littlechild was impressive as he scored four goals in the second game. Hobbema took the Dr. Murray Trophy.

This tournament sparked interest in native hockey and was the forerunner in the AAHA and the formation of the Hobbema Hawks in the AJHL.

INSPOL (INDIAN SPORTS OLYMPICS) THUNDERBIRDS TO HOBBEMA HAWKS

BY J. WILTON LITTLECHILD

(J. Wilton Littlechild was born in Hobbema on April 1, 1944. His sports achievements include the Tom Longboat Trophy, Canadian Indian Athlete of the Year in 1967 and 1974 and the Alberta Achievement Award for Excellence in Sports, 1975.

From the University of Alberta, Littlechild received a Bachelor of Science Degree in Physical Education (1967) and a Master of Science Degree in Physical Education (1975). In 1976 Littlechild earned a Bachelor of Law Degree.

He coached the INSPOL Junior Thunderbirds for three years and organized clinics in a variety of sports, including hockey, basketball, fastball, track and field, golf and rodeo.

Besides his sports involvement, Littlechild is a leader in the business community. He was awarded the Canadian Indian Businessman of the Year Award in 1983.)

For many years prior to 1970, natives have been playing hockey throughout the province, either as all-native teams or as individuals on various clubs. Hockey was becoming popular all over Alberta. However, on the reserves there was only limited success. Jim Gladstone initiated the idea of taking the best native talent and putting them together on one team.

The Ermineskin Indian School, under head coach Nick Kohlman, had midget and juvenile teams, with players from the four bands of Hobbema and other reserves which were rated among the best in Alberta in the late 50s. But the real impetus for an all-native junior team was the Canada Winter Games.

On December 1, 1970, the first Junior 'B' All-Star team from the Southern Reserves was formed and entered into the Alberta Winter Games Trials. With only two weeks to prepare the "Thunderbirds" did not qualify, however, a program idea materialized. The Indian Association of Alberta and Health Minister John Munro, recognizing the need and importance for sport and recreation development of Indian Reserves, agreed to continue a pilot project as part of the national Fitness and Amateur Sports Branch. Thus began the Indian Sports Olympics (INSPOL) Association and the INSPOL Thunderbirds; Canada's first All-Star native junior hockey team.

In developing the team there was considerable emphasis on the purpose and objectives of the hockey club. Many people had opposed the concept as "separatist", "without merit", or simply "one that would never work." On the other hand, there were the comments: "he was such a natural athlete, but he drank so much" or "he would show up for some games" or "one day he just quit."

Consequently, the underlying philosophy was to develop discipline and leadership through the sport of hockey and show that native athletes could succeed. Furthermore, since there had been some who tried junior hockey, only to return home, having left both hockey and school, there was special stress on education.

The first club assembled under this program in January of 1971, was therefore housed at St. Anthony's College where trials were held and classes arranged for the student athletes. The Reserves were asked to nominate players with junior calibre and a desire to complete their education. With very capable assistance from George Calliou, Floyd Buffalo, Ron Davis, Art Gingras and Louie Halfe, the club stayed together for three years. Although the aim was to form a Junior 'A' team, the INSPOL Thunderbirds made an application to join the Central Alberta Junior 'B' Hockey League. At a league meeting in Camrose on September 12, 1971, the Thunderbirds were voted into the CAJHL. The Enoch Reserve contributed tremendously to the Thunderbirds as they allowed the program to use their arena as a home base. The exposure the team and players received was to serve as a great encouragement ot Indian hockey, as teams began to develop all over the province, thus meeting an initial objective of developing amateur hockey on Indian Reserves.

With this minimal achievement of placing an all-Indian junior team in the CAHJL with players from various Reserves who would otherwise never have had a chance to play junior hockey, it was on to the Alberta Junior 'A' Hockey League. Jim Gladstone and the writer then approached the executive of the AJHL with a similar proposal. Because of the initial encouragement received from Jim Scoular, Cec Swanson and Ian McKenzie, presentations were made to the League Executive on March 12 and 13th, 1971 at Lethbridge, and to the Board of Directors on May 16th at Red Deer. Thus, Junior 'A' hockey for more Indian players was now a possibility. However, it was to take years of additional development.

HOBBEMA HAWKS 1981-82

Back row (l to r): Jerry Duff (trainer), Curtis Ermineskin (director), John Bull (director), Ben Wildcat (director), Gord Currie (director), Brace Klein (assistant trainer). **Third row (l to r):** Gord Cheechoo, Tim Long John, Dennis Villeneuve, Ray Houle, Brent Steblyk, Allan Conroy, Garth Hildebrand. **Second row (l to r):** Randy Ermineskin, Adrien Daigneault, Joey Potts, Shane Bly, Dan Anderson, Gary Daniels, Mazen Debaji, Des Lowe, Bill Greenway. **Front row (l to r):** Daryl Kuntz, Vern Spence (vice president — secretary), Kevin Hildebrand, Don Brennan (coach), Darcy Dixon, Graham Parsons (general manager), Dave Noyes, Jim Minda (president), Frank Close.

Photo courtesy of Edmonton Archives

Given a chance to select from an untapped player pool available at all Indian Reserves, it was a dream that a team of Native players could be assembled and exposed to hockey scouts so that the players could continue as far as each desired. To actualize this further, an all-native hockey school was organized at Valleyview. It was to serve both as a school and a scouting camp. Two former junior players who went on to professional hockey, Reg Leach and Ted Hodgson, were brought in with the assistance of Hockey Canada to serve as instructors.

Through these years there was a parallel development of all levels of hockey on the reserves such that it came to the forefront as the most popular sport.

However, there was to be a major setback. The INSPOL Association was to be disbanded due to the withdrawl of financial support from the Ministry of Sport in Ottawa.

After a dormant period, Hobbema came to the forefront with assistance in continuing what proved to be a very worthwhile program. In the intervening years Hobbema built an arena and was very supportive of the development of sports for Indian reserves.

Another hockey proposal was presented on October 2, 1980, this time to four Chiefs: Maurice Wolfe, Victor Buffalo, Peter Bull and Leo Cattleman. This proposal was to finally bring Junior 'A' hockey to a reserve. The four chiefs considered it for various aspects, but once again the key was education. The AJHL stressed an educational component for all players to maximize scholarship opportunities. The Chiefs on this basis approved the team as a program of the four bands. It was a program which could be offered to natives and other players who wanted to take advantage of their hockey and scholastic abilities. Thus, the program which had been restructured on August 26, 1980, received four Band Council approval on October 10, 1980.

In the meantime, the Alberta Junior Hockey League application was presented on October 4th, 1980 and the League approved the franchise on November 22, 1980.

A concern of the initial management — President Jim Minde, General Manager Graham Parsons, and Coach Don Brennan — was to be competitive in the AJHL and to involve the surrounding communities. As a result, several local players played on the Hobbema Hawks.

The objective of an all-native Junior 'A' hockey team has not been reached, maybe it never will. But certainly many have received an opportunity to play on a Junior 'A' team. One of the evident, positive and beneficial results is that many of the players, who through the years decided hockey would not be a career, are now leaders on many reserves in Alberta.

NATIVE HOCKEY COUNCIL

BY J. WILTON LITTLECHILD

While the concept of an all-native junior team was a positive approach to the sport development, it also exposed a great need for many communities to assess their minor hockey programs. An evident weakness of the INSPOL Thunderbird program was the lack of feeder teams from the reserves. Consequently, another program was organized to stress leadership development at all levels of hockey.

Fortunately there was an existing group of people who could provide the necessary expertise. Each person was approached and requested to become involved in a series of leadership clinics. Larry Hodgson undertook to qualify as many coaches as possible in the native communities, under the CAHA certification program. Jim Goodstriker assisted with the General Manager's and Trainer's aspects of the program while Chuck Stevenson presented a series of referee's clinics. To coordinate many of the clinics, was a sports consultant for INSPOL, Mr. Ray Arcand. With the invaluable assistance of Dave Simpson of the AAHA there was a tremendous increase in the number of qualified coaches, managers and referees at many of the Indian reserves and Metis communities.

The result of these leadership clinics was a sudden increase in the number of players at all levels of hockey, including tournaments. Meetings were then held with Doug McKenzie, the President of the Alberta Amateur Hockey Association, to discuss possible ways of joint involvement in the common objective of amateur hockey development. Prior to this time there was indication from many areas that the AAHA had never been on the reserves. Understandably, they were very busy with city and rural programs in the rest of the province. A Native Hockey League was organized which developed a forum for competition throughout the year and with the Treaty 7 Hockey League of Southern Alberta, a natural playoff format to determine an Alberta Native Championship team.

Following the Murray Trophy which was awarded to the best Indian senior team, there was great interest in tournament hockey. It was not long before every major Reserve in Alberta, with the facilities, hosted tournaments at the various categories of minor hockey.

With this series of events, the INSPOL Association sought approval of Native Hockey Council from the AAHA as the official sanctioning body of native hockey tournaments. With the assistance of Doug McKenzie and others of the AAHA, the Native Hockey Council authorized many tournaments each year. This led to some positive results: players could not jump from team to team as team registration became mandatory and referees were protected through the sanction permit system.

Annual reports to the AAHA annual meeting became regular with the first being filed at Grande Prairie on June 19, 1976. The 1975-76 report indicated 25 sanctioned tournaments in Pee Wee, Bantam, Midget and Intermediate zone playoffs. As well, coaches were certified to Level 2 throughout the province. Two senior mens' leagues were in operation, involving eleven reserves. Recognition was granted to the Indian Hockey Council, the first members being: Larry Hodgson, Jim Goodstricker, Chuck Stevenson, Richard Arcand, Ray Arcand and Bill Sewepagaham. Using the AAHA and other formats, the Council sanctioned Alberta Native Championship tournaments in all the minor and senior categories. thus, we now have official recognition of Alberta Native Hockey Champions in all categories of hockey.

To strengthen the work of the Native Hockey Council, a resolution was tabled at the June 18, 1977 (Red Deer) meeting of the AAHA to amend the constitution to include a representative of native hockey on the Board of Governors. This amendment was ratified in Red Deer on June 9, 1979. Thus, Alberta became the first and only province in Canada to recognize native hockey to such a degree. At first the writer attended jointly with Chuck Stevenson. However, the representative is now elected to the AAHA Board at the annual meetings and it has continued to be Stevenson.

The positive results from these joint affiliations has been increased participation and skill development, increased cultural exchange with many communities, increased calibre of play on reserves with regulations, and hockey programs have continued on many reserves as self-sufficient and non-government funded.

Many thanks are owed in all parts of Alberta to the local coaches, managers and volunteers who have supported the idea of hockey development on Indian Reserves. Directors Phil Mistaken Chief, John Fletcher, Marvin Fox, and Joyce Goodstriker, all contributed significantly in the initial stages of organized native hockey.

CHAPTER 8
LADIES HOCKEY HERITAGE

The exact origin of ladies hockey is unknown. Alberta had an 1893 start for men. An early report was recorded in the "Medicine Hat Times" on March 11, 1897. It said that ladies played but spectators were not allowed to watch. The women were wearing dresses. The "Edmonton Bulletin" in 1899 described ladies playing. The players apparently wore a variety of borrowed equipment for their games.

EDMONTON LADIES' TEAM 1899

Photo courtesy of Provincial Archives, Ernest Brown Collection

The peak period in ladies hockey in Alberta was in the 1920's and 30's. At that time the Edmonton Rustlers were credited with two Canadian championships. Some fifty years later the Edmonton Chimos won two straight Canadian titles.

Ladies' matches can provide exciting moments and many of them were low scoring. In Banff on Saturday, February 17, 1908, a noisy crowd cheered their home town ladies to a 2-0 win over the Calgary Barracks. W.A. Brewster was referee and Dr. Callum the judge of play. They called four penalties which were one minute each. After the game Howard Douglas presented the Rocky Mountain Park Trophy to Banff.

Banff became a focal point for ladies hockey championships. The Banff Winter Carnival played host for championships for over thirty years to the end of the 1930's.

A remarkable number of ladies teams were operating in 1927 in Calgary. Some teams did not play in leagues but high interest was evident. Teams in Calgary at this time included the North East Community Club, Technical and Normal Schools (six teams), P. Burns Company, Grand Trunk Community, Robin Hood Mills, Great West Saddlery, Imperial Oil (Service Department and office), Shelly's Bakery, Precision Machine Company, Maclan

Top (l to r): Lydia Fulsher, Mary Crick, Margaret Slaalien, Paige Houston, Evelyn La Marche, Gladys McLean, Evelyn Munroe. Third row: Nettie Taylor, "Babs" Hodgkinson, Margaret Pruden, Aleen Malm, Helen Wilder, Pearl Edmanson, Adilina Fulsher. Second row: Jessie Creighton, Edna Bishor (goalie), Mrs. S. Savage (president), Velma Trimble, Mrs. A. Van Buren (chaperone), Flo Martin, Margaret Smith. First row: Jessie Forsey. Bottom circle (l to r): Nelli McLellen, John Hazza (honorary vice-president), H.P. Van Buren (manager), W.E.W. Lent (honorary president), George Lynch (coach). Second circle from bottom: Audrey Savage. Bottom right circle: Hazel Cameron.   *Photo courtesy of Courtlaw Studio, Calgary*

Motors, Universal Motors, Canadian General Electric, Ashdowns church teams (Hillhurst, Hillcrest, Westley, Central United.)

The top team from Calgary in 1926-27 was the Calgary Hollies. They captured the Banff Winter Carnival when they defeated the Edmonton Monarchs 3-0. Later in the year the Hollies defeated the Monarchs 1-0 in overtime to win the Alberta Ladies championship.

The Hollie lineup included Mrs. Hannay, defence, Mrs. Robertson, Mrs. Morton, forwards Luci Lee, Daisy Blight, Isabelle Duncan, Aileen Malm and Gertie Bowman. For the Monarchs the goalie was Sewell, defence Myrt Strong, K. Ross, forwards Madelaine Case, Helen Wolfe, Marg Pruden, Isabell Nairin and Vi Davis.

In 1927-28 Edmonton Monarchs and Calgary Hollies played again for the championship. This time Margaret "Prudie" Pruden scored on a solo rush with four minutes left in the game to give the Monarchs the title.

The 1930's continued as a prominent era for ladies hockey. The Jasper Place Rustlers (now Crestwood on 149 St area of Edmonton) were the most dominant club. The Rustlers defeated the Edmonton Ross Flats Capitals 2-1 in overtime to win the northern Alberta title. In the provincial Ladies Intermediate championship the Rustlers defeated the Drumheller Colleens 2-1 and 5-0.

Back (l to r): Elaine Ross, Helen Wolfe, Isabel Coffey, Potts Newman, Sparky Wolfe, Margaret Stevenson. Front: Vi Davis, Prudie Harris, Dot Howie, Madeline McKenzie, Myrtle Strong. *Photo courtesy of Edmonton Archives*

The lineup for Drumheller included goalie A. Gammie, E. Whitmore, M. Gibson, I. Brown, Miss Nichol, M. Clifton, R. Hatfield, A. Davis, Page and Jeffries. The Rustlers had Effie Dalamore, Elenore and Rosemary Tufford, Muriel Duncan, Marion Walker, Pat Myatt, Hazel Case, Olive Reid and Olive Porter.

In 1932 Shorty Howlett's Drumheller Colleens did win the intermediate crown when they defeated Don Pettits Red Deer Amazons 3-0 before 400 fans at the Drumheller Arena. The Amazons came back in 1933-34 to win their category.

The Jasper Place team continued their climb to the top of ladies hockey. It started with the following 1932 series.

RUSTLERS CAPTURE MARATHON SERIES

The Edmonton and District Women's Hockey Assocation conducted one of the most unusual series ever recorded. Jasper Place Rustlers and Edmonton Monarchs started their hockey series in early February 1932 and concluded the series on March 9th.

On February 10th, the Association announced a replay of the February 4th game was required. On February 26th two clubs played on a soft, slushy ice surface at Edmonton's Varsity Rink. The girls played to a scoreless draw. It was decided to wait for colder weather to settle the issue.

On March 9th, it was announced that the two clubs would play the next day. To date the two clubs had 4 ties, 1 default and 1 victory each. This was now the eighth match in the proposed best-of-three series. Hazel Case (now Hazel Jamison, who became a reputable curler and golfer) brought victory to her team seven minutes into the second period by converting Rosemary Tufford's pass from centre and drove a hard shot for the corner. Goalie Dot Howie made a great effort to ward off the puck, but was a fraction too slow. The "Edmonton Bulletin" reported this last game to be "bristling with fast skating on both sides and exceptionally good goalkeeping". The Rustlers drew two penalties while the Monarchs took three. Gordon Williamson and Art Davis were the officials.

The Jasper Place Rustlers were victorious by 1-0. It was indeed a memorial moment for both teams and Ladies' hockey in Alberta as on this date March 9, 1932, at Edmonton's Varsity Rink the W.A. Thomson Trophy for the Edmonton Open City Women's Championship was finally won.

EDMONTON MONARCHS 1930-31

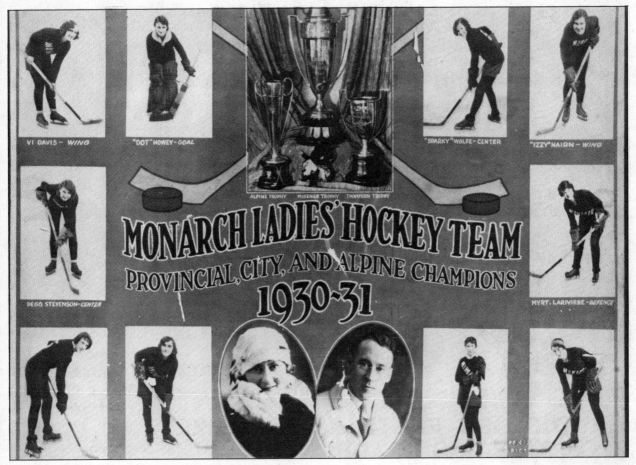

Top row (l to r): Vi Davis, Dot Howey, Sparky Wolfe, Issy Nairn. Centre row: Pegg Stevenson, Myrt Lariviere. Bottom: Helen Wolfe, Prudie Harris, Isabelle (Coffey) Coleman (manager), Potts Newman (coach), "Doc" Ross, "Cal" Ross.

Photo courtesy of McDermid Studios, Edmonton

On March 14, 1932, the Jasper Place Rustlers went on to win the Alberta Ladies' Hockey Championship over the Canmore Fliers, 11-0 and were awarded the Dr. Misener Cup as the Ladies' Champions of Alberta. They only needed one game to decide this one.

RUSTLERS CORRAL DOMINION CROWN

In 1933, the Edmonton Rustlers defeated the Preston Rivulets 3-2 before 2,000 fans in Edmonton to win the first Dominion Women's Hockey Championship. As a result they won the Lady Bessborough Trophy.

Rosemary Tufford scored two goals for Edmonton while Hazel Case scored the other on a solo effort. The Edmonton defence of Elenore Tufford and Muriel Duncan, along with Rosemary Tufford at centre were the mainstays of the Edmonton team, in game one.

The lineup for Edmonton included Goldsworthy in goal, Elenore Tufford, Duncan, R. Tufford, Case, Walker, Porter, Reid, Little, and Myett.

In the second encounter Elenore Tufford scored for Edmonton when they defeated Preston 1-0. A total of 11 penalties were handed out by referee Gordon Williamson.

In 1933-34 the Rustlers were again awarded the Western Canadian championship when they won the first game of a two-game-total-goal series against the Winnipeg Eatons by a score of 4-0. The Rustlers took the second game 4-1 and the round 8-1.

Top (l to r): Dorothy Blodgett, Eleanore Tufford, C.R. Tufford, Patty Myatt, Olive Reid, Muriel Duncan. Bottom: Olive Porter, Marion Walker, Effie Dalamore, Hazel Case, Rosemary Tufford.

Photo courtesy of Provincial Archives

C.R. TUFFORD, RUSTLERS ORGANIZER, PROMOTER AND COACH

Ladies' hockey in the late 20s and in the 30s required an organizer and promoter and C.R. Tufford was the man to do the job. Tufford's squad, the Jasper Place Rustlers, were most prominent in the 1930s, as the top woman's hockey team in Alberta. It was no accident.

Just like Percy Page's Edmonton Grads, C.R.'s Rustlers were the most promising and successful team in Alberta.

Competition for funds, promotion and publicity was tough, with male hockey teams such as the EAC Juniors, the NADP Poolers, the Superiors and the professional Edmonton Eskimos receiving major media coverage and fan support. Tufford managed, however, to keep the Rustler's profile very high.

He was an innovative person. Besides the coaching format of putting his players through drills on the ice, Tufford held blackboard sessions where he diagrammed how the plays should be undertaken and exercised.

Hazel Case (Jamison), who played for his team, has many fond memories of Tufford. She recalls that the team was always on the go trying to raise money to keep them in existence.

On one occasion, when all the girls were crammed into Tufford's Desota, the police stopped him on the road for a traffic violation. Tufford being the persuasive person he was, visioned that he was going to get a ticket for at least $5. The policeman looked into the automobile and saw all the girls in their hockey outfits and inquired about the team.

That was his mistake. Tufford gave a brief summation of their plight and was let off with a slight warning. In addition, the policeman made a $5 donation to the Jasper Place Rustlers.

Rosemary and Elenore were C.R.'s daughters. They were super hockey players. One cold winter, Tufford parked his car outside on the street rather than in his garage in order to provide practice sessions for his girls. He cleaned the garage of all obstructions and flooded it. The team was able to practise their shooting inside Tufford's garage instead of the frigid outdoors.

Top (l to r): Evelyn Hewson, Lois Botterill, Irene Dell, Dorothy Kitching, Helen Hayhoe. Centre row: Evelyn Bond, Evie Nicholls, Audrey Stephenson, Adelyne Stephenson, "Babe" Thompson. Bottom: Scotty Lee (coach), Ernie Wells (manager).

Photo courtesy of Fleming Studio

The Jasper Place Rustlers became the Canadian Senior Ladies Champions of 1933 and 1934, largely due to the managing and coaching of Corwin (Coordination to Win) Ray Tufford. It took extra effort and desire to produce a championship team, and Tufford certainly exemplified that.

Another ladies' hockey coach of prominence at the time was George Hustler, Principal of Bennett School. The efforts of people like him allowed women's hockey to florish in the 30s.

With the outbreak of World War II, women's hockey lost much of its interest and prominence.

EDMONTON CHIMOS — CANADIAN LADIES' CHAMPIONS 1984 AND 1985

Women's hockey returned to Edmonton after many quiet years in 1972. A group of women wishing to play hockey got together and two teams were formed. Several of the women could not even skate and most knew very little about the game itself. Practices and a few exhibition games were all that the first year consisted of.

The following year one of the teams decided to call itself the Edmonton Chimos (an Eskimo word meaning hello). Hockey began to grow a little more and a league of four teams (two Edmonton, Namao and Bon Accord) was formed. The Chimos won the first league and have continued to dominate hockey in Edmonton and Alberta

Top (l to r): **Marion Walker, Hazel Case, Rosemary Tufford, C.R. Tufford, Patty Myatt, Olive Reid, Oliver Porter. Bottom row: Muriel Boyd, Eleanore Tufford, Mildred Little, Isobel Nairn, Marion Goldworthy.**

since. Because of this domination they were soon classified as an 'A' team, the rest of the league 'B' and therefore there were no women's teams to play.

The team had to look for competition elsewhere. For several years they played Bantam and Midget boys' teams. They also began travelling around the province playing Oldtimer mens' teams. For the first couple of years many of the small towns were sold out as everyone wanted a "laugh" and came out to watch women "figure skate" with the men. They soon began to realize these women were serious as they won more than they lost and they were not figure skating.

The Chimos also travelled to Eastern Canada to play in tournaments in Ontario. Women's hockey in Ontario was well established for several years so the women on the team wanted a chance to find out just how good they were.

The Chimos rejoined the Northern Alberta Ladies' Hockey League in 1981-82. A Canadian National Championship was also formed where the best team of each province would be represented. The Chimos won the provincials and were off to Brantford, Ontario for the Abbey Hoffman Cup Championships. The team played excellent hockey only to lose to Ontario in overtime in the final. Dawn McGuire, a defenceman for the Chimos was selected the Most Valuable Player.

In 1982-83 the Championships were again held in Brantford with the same results, a loss to Ontario in the finals. Barb Nugent a winger from the team was voted Most Valuable Player, Dawn McGuire — top defenceman and Jane Legace, top scorer.

This set the stage of Spruce Grove in March, 1984. The Chimos playing in their home province hoped to get revenge for the two previous years. After losing their first game to Quebec in overtime and falling behind they started to click winning their next three round-robin games. This put them in the quarter final against Manitoba which they won quite easily. The next game, the semi-final was to be against their archrival, Ontario.

:: EDMONTON'S RUSTLERS ::

DOMINION LADIES' SENIOR HOCKEY CHAMPIONS

HALLOWE'EN DANCE

Rosemary Tufford   Muriel Ramsay   Hazel Case   Marion Goldsworthy   Eleanore Tufford   Pattie Myatt   Marion Walker   Mildred Little

TO BE HELD IN THE
CLUB ACADEMY
ON

Olive Reid

Olive Porter

FRIDAY, OCTOBER 27th

9 to 12 p.m.   Admission, 35c.

Top (l to r): Rosemary Tufford, Muriel Ramsay, Hazel Case, Marion Goldsworthy, Eleanore Tufford, Patty Myatt, Marion Walker, Mildred Little. Lower row: Olive Reid, Olive Porter.

EDMONTON'S RUSTLERS

PERSONNEL

ROSEMARY TUFFORD
MURIEL RAMSAY
HAZEL CASE
MARION GOLDSWORTHY
ELEANORE TUFFORD
PATTIE MYATT
MARION WALKER
MILDRED LITTLE
OLIVE REID
OLIVE PORTER

C. R. TUFFORD,
   Manager and Coach

THE WAY WE WIN
IS MORE IMPORTANT THAN WINNING

RECORD

1928-29—Junior Provincial Champions.
1929-30—Junior Provincial Champions.
1930-31—Intermediate Provincial Champions.
1931-32—Senior Provincial Champions.
1932-33—Open City Champions.
   Senior Provincial Champions.
   Banff Carnival Champions.
   Alberta - B.C. Champions.
   Western Canada Champions.
   Dominion Champions.

EDMONTON, ALBERTA,

Not wanting to lose three years in a row to Ontario and with the boisterous cheering of their fans, the Chimos played their finest game, defeating the Ontario champs 4-1. This put them into the final for the third year in a row. Their opponents would be Quebec who had beaten them earlier in the tournament.

With the arena filled to capacity the Chimos took an early lead and held this going into the third period. Quebec got a quick goal which seemed to spark them on. Another goal quickly after and the game was tied. With the Chimos on the powerplay the puck was stolen by a Quebec forward who scored giving them the lead for

RED DEER NOVAS — WESTERN CANADIAN CHAMPS 1982-83
(Western Canadian Shield)

Back row (l to r): Kern Von Hagen (coach), Marilyn Shand, Jan Brown, Rose Coates, Pam Fagan, Mary Jane Postma, Shelley Paulsen, Cheryl Barrett, Sandy Foster. Front row (l to r): Anita Nelson, Lori MacGillvary, Melody Davidson, Heather Stark, Tracy James, Wendy Wittchen, Ann Fisher, Wanda Martens. Missing: Deanna Miyauchi, Roxanne Cameron.

CANADIAN CHAMPION EDMONTON CHIMOS 1983-84

Top (l to r): Jane Legace, Barb Nugent, Kathy Berg, Alison Ramsley. Second row: Brenda Smith (manager), Belinda Tymko, Leah Lilley, Anne Landry, Rose McEachern, Lil Brault, Roxanne McKean, Dennis Wolfe (coach). Bottom: Shell Hyland, Dawn McGuire, Shirley Cameron (captain), Laurina Ranger, Maureen Dupre. Missing: Deanna Miyauchi and Pauline Leger.

the first time in the game. The Chimos came back quickly to tie the game, only to have the French women go ahead again. With time running out it looked like the Chimos would be runnerups for the third year in a row.

Back row (l to r): Dennis Wolfe (coach), Hank Renzenbrink (trainer), Dawn McGuire, Joanne Brander, Cheryl Nielson, Barb Nugent, Donna Gorda, Ann Landry. Second row: Sue LaFrance, Deanna Miyauchi, Lorina Ranger, Roxanne McKean, Rose McEachern, Alison Ramsley, Brenda Smith (manager), Kathy Berg. Front row: Maureen Dupre, Shirley Cameron, Lisa Adolphe, Shelene Hyland. Missing: Brenda Tymko.

But, a penalty to Quebec and a powerplay goal tied the game. Overtime. After only 41 seconds, Kathy Berg scored for the Chimos giving them the Canadian Championship in the Shopper's Drug Mart Women's National.

In the Canadian final of 1983-84, centre Shirley Cameron, the only original Chimo player was chosen the Most Valuable Player. In 1984-85 the Chimos repeated as Canadian Champions.

Since 1978 an Alberta Women's Council of the AAHA has existed. Chairpersons since have been Doug McKenzie, Don Dillon, John Kosolowski, and now Suzanne Triance.

In 1982 the Female Council of the CAHA was founded with all ten zones represented. Today 42, girls-ladies teams are affiliated. This compares to 23 in 1978. The future of women's hockey is promising.

CHAPTER 9
MINOR HOCKEY HIGHLIGHTS

PEE WEE HOCKEY IN CALGARY

On December 17, 1935, Pee Wee National League Hockey was introduced to Calgary at the Victoria Arena under the direction of Harold "Spud" Murphy. The league featured boys 12 and 13 carrying the name of an NHL star on the back of their sweaters.

"Gail Eagan's" Toronto Maple Leafs tied Murphys' "New York Americans" 3-3. It was called a "brilliant" match as "Nick Metz" Grant scored on an assist from "Red Horner" Smith to open the league for the Leafs. Other goal scorers for "Toronto" were "Harvey Jackson" Brackenbury and "Charlie Conacher" Crowley. The three goals for the Americans came from "Dave Schriner" Brandeth, Harry "Wiseman" Lewis and "Harold Cotton" Shira. Norm "Dutch" Gainor, centre iceman of the Calgary Tigers was the referee for the inaugural match. No penalties were called.

The lineup for Toronto included "Hainsworth" Murtha, "Blair" Tarves, "Horner" Smith, "Clancy" Cable, "Primeau" Morrison, "Jackson" Brackenbury, "Conacher" Crowley, "Day" Quigley, "Kelly" Duncan, "Metz" Grant and trainer Joe Hill. For "New York" it was "Worters" Lawrence, "Dutton" Maryland, "Brydge" Brooks, "Murray" Grey, "Chapman" Harrigan, "Schriner" Brandeth, "Carr" Snider, "Stewart" Perry, "Cotton" Shirra, "Wiseman" Lewis and trainer Jimmy Bruce.

ALBERTA AMATEUR HOCKEY ASSOCIATION ANNUAL MEETING 1951

Back row (l to r): Ken McCauley (Edmonton), Sid McLeod, Jack Kelly (AAHA, Ponoka), Dr. A.J. Elliot (Lacombe), Earl Samis (Edmonton), C.A. Taylor (AAHA, Medicine Hat), J.T. North (AAHA, Calgary), Joe Milne (Edmonton), B. Garnett (Calgary), J.S. Pepard (Calgary), Norm Christie, Bill Ruff (AAHA, Edmonton), Jim Kerr (AAHA, Calgary). **Second row:** Ken Jennings (Edmonton), V.C. Stanley (AAHA, High River), Dr. W.G. Hardy (AAHA, Edmonton), R.M. Mackenzie (AAHA, Lacombe), J.A. Christiansen (Edmonton), Harold Brandreth (AAHA, Calgary), Art Potter (AAHA, Edmonton), G. Habkirk (Olds), J. Watson (Calgary), Ed Bruchet (Lethbridge), Dr. W. Broadfoot (AAHA, Lethbridge). **Front row:** A. Mann (Alix), Harper Parry (Keeler, Sask.), Reg Houghton (Calgary), Bert Shaw (Edmonton), W. Walters (Calgary), D. Duchak (Calgary), Art Jackson (Edmonton), Jim McAdie (Edmonton).

Back row (l to r): Paul Cote (Edmonton), Henry Caldwell (Edmonton), Dave McGee (Edmonton), Leo LeClerc (Edmonton), Ed Bruchet (Lethbridge), A.B. King (Life Member A.A.H.A., Edmonton), Arlie Keller (Calgary), Cec Swanson (Calgary), Fred Lupul (Edmonton), Ken Manning (Calgary). Centre row (l to r): Jerry Trudel (Calgary), Harry Maubert (Calgary), Jim McAdie (A.A.H.A., Edmonton), Stu Pepard (A.A.H.A., Calgary), Art Potter (Past President A.A.H.A., Edmonton), Dr. W.G. Hardy (Life Member A.A.H.A., Edmonton), Ralph Alford (A.A.H.A., Calgary), Earl Samis (Asst. Reg. A.A.H.A., Edmonton), C.H. Taylor (A.A.H.A., Medicine Hat), Bill Douglas (A.A.H.A., Lacombe). Front row (l to r): Reg Houghton (Registrar-Treasurer A.A.H.A., Calgary), John Watson (President A.A.H.A., Calgary), Jim Brown (Vice-President A.A.H.A., Camrose), Mrs. Jerry Trudel (Calgary), Mrs. J.R. Kohn (Calgary), Tom Lynch (Calgary), Ernie Smalian (A.A.H.A., Edmonton), Bob Lister (Edmonton).

CALGARY BUFFALO ATHLETIC ASSOCIATION

BY JAMES KERR

(Calgary's Jim Kerr was a leader in the Calgary Buffalo organization, chairman of the hockey committee for the Calgary Exhibition and Stampede. In 1942 Kerr was the team manger for Ottawa RCAF when it won the Allan Cup.)

In the mid 1930's Harold "Spud" Murphy, created a "Pee Wee" hockey program of six teams, who wore the uniforms and carried the names of teams of the NHL; Maple Leafs, Canadiens, Americans, Bruins, Red Wings and Black Hawks.

It turned out to be a very large commitment for one individual, and when it appeared possible that it might no survive, J.B. Cross undertook to broaden the program.

Dave Duchak (Moose Jaw, North Battleford Beavers, Trail Smokeaters, Calgary Stampeders) now a resident of Edmonton then employed by Calgary Brewing and Malting Co. Ltd., became the "organizer" of the program.

Other ex-hockey players, employees of the company (Art Rice-Jones, Sam Timmins, Joe Shannon) along with many other ex-players, residents of Calgary — Joe McGoldrick, Irvine Frew, Gordon McFarlane became coaches and managers.

Some property on the bank of the Bow River, adjacent to the downtown area of the city, was acquired and developed into Buffalo Stadium, where summertime baseball catered to large crowds in twilight games and where the outfield became three outside natural ice rinks for the Association's winter hockey program.

The early format consisted of six pee wee, four midget, and four juvenile teams. It became the prime hockey organization in Calgary. As players "graduated" from juvenile their next team (as talent might so warrant) was in the Junior 'A' category.

A significant number of "over age" juveniles were sufficiently talented to attract the attention of teams in the Junior 'A' class and departed the local scene, which was the cause of some local concern. When there was no local sponsor forthcoming, the Buffalo Association finally undertook such sponsorship in an expanded league which ultimately reached across Alberta, Saskatchewan and into Manitoba.

At that time the NHL consisted of six teams, carrying sixteen players per team on their rosters. The prospects of a player from amateur ranks "crashing" the "Big Time" were pretty overwhelming and the Buffalo Association was not overly concerned about developing players for the pro market — rather it endeavored to provide an outlet for the younsters from its minor program.

BUFFALOES PEE WEE CHAMPIONS 1943-44

Top row (l to r): Jack Arbour (coach), Bob Hebenton, Bob Hunt, Ted Valentine, Bob Heathcott, John Galloway, Pete Simon, Trevor Walters, Bob Rutter, Walter Bruce (manager). Bottom: Bruce MacDonald, Dave Laven, Sherrold Moore, Bob Bartlett, Louis Fyffe, Dirk Douglas, Art Wells, Graham Bruce (mascot).   *Photo courtesy of Calgary Exhibition and Stampede*

However, some of these graduates did distinguish themselves in major pro circles: Henry "Hank" Bassen, Sid Finney, Johnny McKenzie, Ron Stewart, Garry Unger, Randy Murray with numerous others in the then "minor" pro category, while others went on to successful and honorable careers in the business world.

As Calgary expanded in size, community associations displayed interest in accepting some of the responsibilities for the sponsorship of teams. The Buffalo Association maintained its format and aided the communities with financial grants for the purchase of equipment, etc.

In 1962, the Cross family sold Calgary Brewing and Malting Co. Ltd. J.B. Cross remained as President until 1963 when he retired. The new owners of the company, having national rather than regional concerns, did not see fit to continue sponsorship of the Association.

CALGARY MINOR HOCKEY

BY J.S. "STU" PEPPARD AND MURRAY COPOT

(Stu Pepard's involvement in Alberta hockey extends over six full decades. He was President of the Calgary Community Recreation Association and the Alberta Amateur Hockey Association. The present day Alberta Junior Hockey League resulted from his inspirational and organizational talents. In 1985, an arena in Calgary was named for Stu Peppard. As a life member of the AAHA, he still acts as an advisor.

Murray Copot was President of the MHA of Calgary and has been Vice-president of the AAHA for six years.)

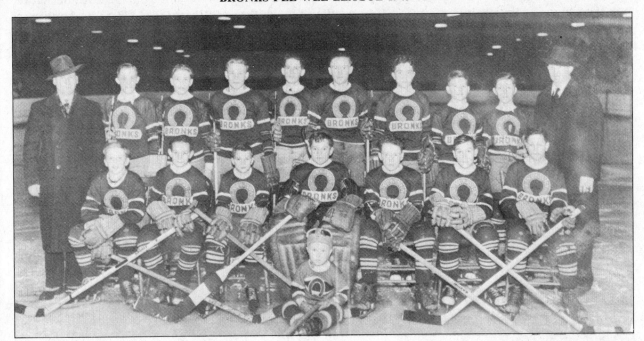

Back row (l to r): Guy Hamilton (manager), Rod McConnell, Clif Larsen, Al Purvis, Lyle Livingstone, Jim Cameron, Don Trivett, Ken Lang, Jerald Jury, Joe McGoldrick (coach). Front row: Fred Jarrett, Alex Alexander, Don McRae, Bob Phillips, Alvin Stuart, Bob Carlson, Orvil Martini. Front: Joe McGoldrick (mascot). *Photo courtesy of Calgary Exhibition and Stampede*

CALGARY MAROON MIDGET CHAMPIONS 1935-36

Back (l to r): Bobby Steedman, Jim Powell, Bob Harrison, Doug Smith, Paul Radunsky, Bob Wise, Don Menzies, Bill Speck, Walter Corry, Ken Arkley, Len Chisholm. Front row (l to r): Bill Powell (manager and owner), Peter Scott (mascot), Bob Arkley (coach and owner). *Photo courtesy of Glenbow*

The Calgary Community Recreation Association was organized in the late 1930's. It became active after World War II under the leadership of President Art Larsen, (1945-47). For the next 22 years the CCRA was the reigning body for community hockey, fastball and soccer. In 1945, the CCRA was proud to have an active membership of 18 communities. Each community sent a representative to meetings to assist or lead anyone of the three sports committees.

Stu Peppard the 1950-51 President, had the good fortune to have Mrs. Julia Rose Kohn as Secretary. Mrs. Kohn had been a leading executive of the Victoria Community Association, one of the earliest and most active communities in Calgary. She spent the next decade as Secretary, Registrar and Vice-president. Her enthusiasm acted as a strong base for all CCRA activities. She remained "on the job" during many changes in delegates and presidents which saw community membership grow from 20 to 68. Mrs. Kohn was also active in the AAHA as the organization's first lady executive member. Here, she also planned and promoted a renewal of ladies' hockey. The naming of the Rose Kohn Arena in Calgary reminds all of us of her dedication to sports in Calgary.

CALGARY BANTAM 'A' EAGLES 1961-62

Back row (l to r): George Boothman, Bill Miller, Roger Smith, Bruce Ritchie, Stewart Gledhill, Angus Gent, Dave Watson, Doug Edwards, Barry Bennett, Rob Sanders, Tom O'Rourke, Fred Brechtel, Mr. Derral. **Front row (l to r):** Don Derral, Garry Unger, Mike Hart, Les Masey, Gordie Anderson.

Photo courtesy of Glenbow

In the late 1960's the population growth in Calgary, was too much for the CCRA to handle under the old system. By mutual consent, the association split to form three separate bodies. The Minor Hockey Association of Calgary, the Calgary Fastball Association and the Calgary Minor Soccer Association formed their own governing bodies. In hockey, the Calgary Minor Hockey Association of Calgary began.

The MHAC had an outstanding record of achievement during Calgary's population explosion from 130,000 to over half a million. This population "flood" could easily have caused a complete breakdown for this volunteer organization, but a combination of a great administration at City Hall and a sequence of interested, capable and hardworking hockey leaders became Presidents of the MHAC and molded a fine program.

During this expansion period from 1960 to 1975, Harry Boothman, the Parks Superintendent, proved not only to be a top agriculturist, but a super booster for all kinds of sports. From 1964 to 1975 the City of Calgary built twelve hockey arenas. Due to Mr. Boothman's belief in hockey for young people, the arenas were made available at a minimum cost. His death in 1976 meant that Calgary youngsters lost a great friend and citizen. However, the successors Boothman trained have continued to actively promote sport in Calagary.

Leading the MHAC during the expansion and into the 1980's have been a succession of Presidents who have had a genuine interest in minor hockey and a willingness "to put out" the time and effort. Presidents Jack Setters, George Cooke, Ken Craig, Murray Copot, Vance Peters, Grant Richards, Bob Landry, Ken McIntosh, Martin Blake and Ray Hospland have led the MHAC through the growth period to now. Almost all of them have acted as Directors of the AAHA. As of 1985, Ken Craig has been Executive Director of the AAHA for

11 years, Vance Peters the Southern Minor Vice-chairman for four years, Murray Copot, Vice-President for six years, and Bob Landry Executive member for three years.

The MHAC has an outstanding record of leadership. Alongside the Edmonton Metropolitan Hockey Association and the hundreds of other Alberta communities, it is no accident that our province more than holds its own in national and international hockey.

CALGARY TRIWOOD JUVENILE BB 1969-70
Provincial Champions

Back row (l to r): Lexie Murray, Dave Creurer, Darrell Cooke, Rick Boser, Jan Kristensen, Garry McEahern. Centre row (l to r): Monty Durand (trainer), Terry Copot, Wayne Whittaker, Doug Berry, Bob Connolly, Paul Bendzik (assistant trainer). Front row (l to r): Brian Glubrecht, Paul Hepher, Peter Hepher (manager), Phil Jarvis, Murray Copot (coach), Bill Chalmers, Brock Jacobs.

Photo courtesy of Glenbow

EARLY MINOR HOCKEY NIGHT IN ALBERTA

BY EARL R. CHADWICK

(Earl is a former Red Deer Sportsman of the Year. He recently went on a Facility and Tournament Location Tour to Finland, Latvia and Russia. There is now an International Bantam Hockey tourament in Europe named in his honour.)

One of the earliest Minor Hockey nights in Alberta, as we know it today, was held in Red Deer in the spring of 1957. The most surprising aspects of the project were the wonderful response the organizational committee of the Red Deer Minor Hockey Association had from the merchants of the city and the former professional players throughout the province who volunteered their services.

It was covered by all the news media in Alberta including Ed Whalen of Calgary getting play by play descriptions for television coverage. One of the main personalities who appeared was Fred "Cyclone" Taylor. Mr. Taylor travelled from Vancouver to be a part of this program and salute Minor Hockey. (Taylor played for hockey's first professional team in 1905 in Houghton, Michigan. Later he played for the Renfrew Millionaires, Ottawa Senators and Vancouver Millionaires.)

Back row (l to r): **Bill Kennes (coach), Bruce Hatton, Ricky Travis, Kevin Pilikowski, Neil Ouellette, Hal Gordon, Brian Lenzen, Steve Rogers (manager). Front row (l to r): Bill Parker, Brian Hatton, Jerry Bancks, Roy Howerton, Mike Rogers, Dale Kennes.**

Photo courtesy of Glenbow

No individual junior player or official was especially honoured that night, but each group was given their own time during the program. Now, Minor Hockey Night and Minor Hockey Week is a National affair in Canada honouring the players, the game and the volunteers.

ROAD HOCKEY IN ALBERTA

BY LARRY LEACH

(Leach played professional hockey for over 17 years with the Victoria Cougars, Providence Reds, Portland Buckeroos and the Boston Bruins, before returning to Lloydminster. In 1973-74 Leach was the first coach for the Lloydminster Junior Blazers. Most hockey players have played road hockey including Larry Leach.

The following is part of Leach's account from ''75 Years of Sport and Culture In Lloydminster 1903-1978''. George K. Ross Editor, and James A. Hill — compiler of the Ice Sports section.)

My first recollections of hockey were on our farm in Westdene. We always had an outdoor rink in the front yard where all the neighbours used to gather on Sundays for hockey games and skating. I know that at age three, I was skating.

We moved to Lloydminster during World War II and I can remember being in an indoor rink for the first time, skating around the boards and they seemed so high, it was quite a thrill.

We lived on a block directly west of the hospital and there was a good sized outdoor rink at the end of our block. There was a power pole on the corner with probably a 200 watt bulb on it. It supplied the lights for our night-time hockey. Between there and playing road hockey on our block, I'm sure most parents knew where we were.

We lived on a block directly west of the hospital and there was a good sized outdoor rink at the end of our block. There was a power pole on the corner with probably a 200 watt bulb on it. It supplied the lights for our night-time hockey. Between there and playing road hockey on our block, I'm sure most parents knew where we were.

Most of the men on our block were away at the war. It seemed that in Lloydminster, at that time, you very seldom ventured into other parts of town. We had our own ''gang''that played on our block. Some of my friends were Bill Browne, Ray Hamlin, Allan Dean, a Rowbottom boy, Gerry Mills, Bob Bellward and Henry Seibel.

Road hockey was quite a popular pastime and I can remember Bill Browne was the envy of all, because he had made a pair of goal pads out of 25 lb. Robin Hood flour bags filled with hay. Next door to Browne's was Mr. Clarkson, a drayman, and he had horses. We relieved him of four sets of hame staps which were put through the flour sacks. Whoever got in goal could wear these pads. Bill also had a good pair of hockey gloves, so as I say, he was the envy of our block.

I think curved hockey sticks started with tennis balls. Hockey sticks would get worn down so thin at the toe, they were easy to curve in hot water. These sticks and a tennis ball were just about perfect to play road hockey with. Our goal posts were usually small piles of snow puched up. With so many boys playing on the street and cars passing all the time, it became quite a conflict between us and the people driving cars. They used to run over our goal posts.

Once we were playing right in front of our house and we saw the police car coming. Everyone immediately disappeared, and there I was, the one that was caught and given a stiff warning. The police car left and everyone appeared back on the road and the game continued. The police car just drove around the block. We saw it coming again and everyone disappeared. It was a worse warning for me then, with a real threat.

Again, the game continued and around the block he came and caught me for the third time — my name went down in the dreaded ''Black Book'' and I was immediately judged one of Lloydminster's villains.

AAHA EXECUTIVE 1983-84

Back (l to r): Dale Henwood (technical director), Ernie Boruk (referee in chief), Perry Pearn, Bob Strachan, Ken Matthews, Don Dingwall, Dick Hollen, Vern Paul, Don Gannon, Eardley Braton, Ken Craig (executive director), Gordon Knebel. Front row: Wendy Rasmussen, Doug McKenzie, John Bauer, Murray Copot (vice-president), Orest Korbutt (president), John Kelly, Bob Landry, Suzanne Triance. Absent: Chuck Stevenson.

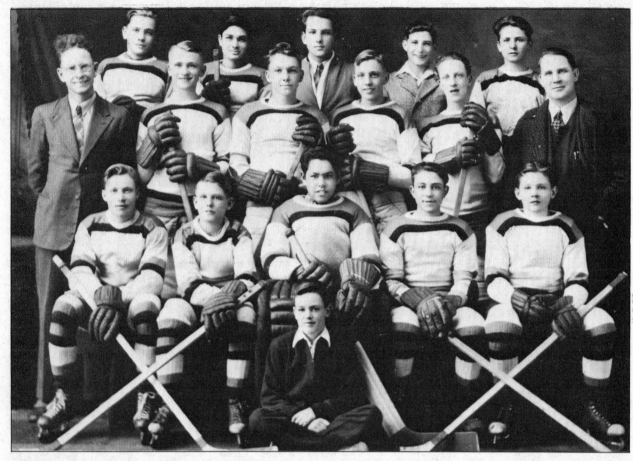

Back row (l to r): Richard Antonenko, Ernie Lant, Mike Hudz (coach), Randy Kulig (trainer), Jack McIntyre. Middle row (l to r): Ray Spillers (secretary), Alex Kovacik, Ted Kryczka, Norman Ford, Bill Anderson, Sonny Richards (manager). Front row (l to r): Louis Sikora, Sid Jackson, Reg Aldoff, Joe Gattman, Neil McNeil. In front: Ken Jackson (mascot). Missing: Ronald Jones.

PEE WEE HOCKEY IN EDMONTON (1937)

BY HARRY ALLEN

(Harry Allen was a player for the Montreal Canadiens on opening night in the Pee Wee Hockey League. Harry later went on to play for the Waterloo Mercury Hockey team, the World Champions of 1950 and later coached the Edmonton Oil Kings.)

One very cold Saturday morning in late December, 1936, over 500 very young hockey hopefuls showed up at the Edmonton Old Arena for a try out in the hope of catching a spot one one of the teams that would make up the soon to be formed Edmonton Lions Club Pee Wee Hockey League.

All 500 of these kids dressed and undressed in one large waiting room in the south east corner of the Arena building. The room was heated by one large pot bellied stove. The teams were to be called the Boston Bruins, Chicago Black Hawks, Montreal Canadiens and New York Rangers. The uniforms were the exact duplicates of those worn by the NHL players.

The opening games in Edmonton's first Pee Wee Hockey League were played on January 12, 1937 at the Edmonton Arena. It was a large ice surface for such small competitors.

In the first match the Bruins and the Black Hawks played to a 3-3 draw, while in the second game the Rangers were defeated 4-1 by the Montreal Canadiens. The referee for these opening games was none other than Reginald Percival "Pep" Moon.

Members of the Edmonton Lions Club organized the whole league. Those playing major roles in this organization were Gordon Smeltzer, Bert Knowles and Phil Davis. Coaches and organizers in the league included: Henry White, Jim Crockett, Clarence Moher and Bert Crockett. Cecil "Tiger" Goldstick was also one of the organizers for this league which started many hockey players down the hockey trail. Some later played pro hockey and others who went on to represent Canada at the World Championships.

On March 21, 1937, the first season of the Lion's Pee Wee Hockey League ended with the New York Rangers winning the final game in Edmonton. The Rangers defeated the Montreal Canadiens 5-1 to capture the championship.

Playing for the New York Rangers were: Ken Torrence, Norm Heller, Arn Ferris, Harvey Arnold, Roy Nikiforik, Albert Superstein, Allan Ward, Bill Wilson, Ray Lemieux, Roy Curry, Burt Pringle, and Bill Letain. For the Canadiens it was: Doug Stevenson, Wally Emberg, Fred Guest, Will Hall, Harry Allen, Art Rougan, Jim Flett, Howard Niblett, Bill Phillips, Chuck Hall, Terry Flaherty, John Lee, and Harvey Young.

THE EDMONTON FEDERATION OF COMMUNITY LEAGUES

BY JOE CASWELL

(Caswell was a volunteer in the Federation hockey program. From 1955 to 1973, he could be found at hockey practices or games all over Edmonton. In 1937 he was a member of the provincial Junior 'A' champion, Edmonton Gas Rangers.)

The Federation of Community Leagues has played a leading role in the organization and promotion of hockey in Edmonton. In fact it was the first major organization in Edmonton to have a hockey program.

The founding meeting of the Federation was held at the office of E.A. Ottewell, at the Extension Department of the University of Alberta. T.P. Malone was elected the first president; he was a southside businessman who became a city alderman (The T.P. Malone Block still stands at 104 Street and Whyte Avenue.)

Community leagues existed before the Federation. In 1917 the 142nd Street Community League was formed (now called Crestwood). Bonnie Doon started in 1918 and was followed by Riverdale in 1919. Thereafter, Westmount and West Edmonton in 1920 became community leagues. Bennett School (Cloverdale) Forest Heights, Highland and Calgary Trail followed. In 1921 the Federation was formed.

Originally there were 16 hockey teams. The Federation's objective was to link communities together and create city wide programs to compliment the local programs.

To give community level hockey more creditability, the Federation became affiliated with the AAHA in 1923. For this purpose a meeting was held at Joe "Bullet" Simpson's Sporting Goods Store. Affiliation was important. They could now use certified referees in their Junior 'B' League. They realized then that hockey without referees is "shinny".

Through time more organization evolved. Hockey was only one of the Federation's programs, but it became the largest. Most minor sports were under the supervision of the Federation. This included baseball, fastball, basketball, lacrosse and hockey. In 1956 it became apparent that hockey was a full time job and the Federation formed a separate group called the Federation Hockey Council.

Charles Simmonds became the first chairman of the 1956 Federation Hockey Council. He was the community league chairman of hockey from 1951 to 1961, so he knew the problems. Simmonds had a special knack of recruiting volunteers and actually challenged them to come to the next meeting to express themselves and do something for all the programs in the Federation.

Other major figures over the years who offered outstanding volunteer service were Earl Samis, Steve Wyker, James McFall, George Harvie, Ron Joslin, Bob Bothwell and Clark Powers. Thousands of volunteers and players have supported and played in Federation programs. To mention all of them is impossible; however, one series in 1960-61 comes to mind. That season the Federation started a Bantam AA program.

The Bantam final featured Pleasantview Essos and Bellevue Community League. The first three games ended in ties. The fourth game looked like it would never end. After three more periods overtime was required. David Spiviak scored in the third overtime period to give Angus Murray's Pleasantview team the city championship. Lethbridge defeated them in the provincial final.

Another program I remember in the 50's was one done by the Federation in cooperation with Edmonton Parks and Recreation. The "Gold Dust Twins", Doug Anderson and Colin Kilburn plus "Tiger" Goldstick provided their volunteer services to organize hockey at the Edmonton Gardens. It provided the opportunity for boys not on organized teams to play every Saturday morning. Kilburn enjoyed the program. "I really looked forward to playing with those boys and helping them develop. For most of them it was the only hockey."

The Edmonton Federation of Community Leagues has and still is considered one of the most successful recreational programs in Canada. J.P. (Jack) Reilly and A. (Bert) Pettigrew of Edmonton Parks and Recreation were most instrumental in assisting the Federation to grow and it still keeps its identity and objectives. The Federation has kept pace with Edmonton's rapid growth and now has 136 communities as members. The community program in Edmonton compliments the Edmonton Minor Hockey Association.

(This brief history of Federation hockey was done with the assistance of Edith Sparks, Federation Secretary, and Vern Davis, Hockey Council Secretary.)

EDMONTON'S MAPLE LEAF GARDENS

BY JAMES "BUD" AND SOMETIMES "BOOMER" MACPHERSON

(MacPherson later turned pro with Le Club de Hockey Canadiens (Montreal Canadiens) for six years. The Canadiens won the Stanley Cup in 1952-53. The club was coached by Dick Irvin with players like Maurice "The Rocket" Richard, Bert Olmstad, Elmer Lach, Jean Bellevue, Bernie Geoffrion, Paul Meger, Doug Harvey, Tom Johnson, Butch Bouchard, Gerry McNeil, Ken Mosdell and Baldy McKay, and of course "Boomer" MacPherson.)

I can remember my dad Jim taking me to hockey games in 1932 in the old Edmonton Arena. Individual wooden chairs and boxes that were about the same height as the rink boards surrounded the ice. Big coal and wood heaters provided heat under the stands. One of the referees was Clarence Campbell who used a small bell rather than a whistle.

I watched my father play at Jimmy Smith's rink near 103rd Street and 83rd Avenue. It was commercial league hockey and seemed to be made up of equal part of fighting.

About this time Foster Hewitt was the greatest broadcaster in the world, speaking from exotic places such as Toronto, Chicago, Boston, New York and Montreal. Many times I thought of playing for one of these teams.

Sometime during the 1930s, the city of Edmonton in their wisdom decided to erect and maintain an outdoor skating rink at 96th Street and 118th Avenue. This rather plain structure was known by us as "Maple Leaf Gardens", partially because of Hewitt, but mainly because it was the home of the Maple Leaf Athletic Club.

M.L.A.C. 1943-44

Back (l to r): F. LeTain, O. Sollanych (coach), J. King, P. Samis, J. Klesko, A. Jackson (manager), J. Patterson. **Front:** J. Heron, M. Thomas, J. Finlay, Bud MacPhereson, D. Carver, C. Wallace, R. Harvie, W. Thomas (in jacket).

Photo courtesy of Edmonton Archives

Our backyard at 11831-97th Steet (now an apartment) entered the alley at the north end of the rink so it became natural for my brother Bill and I to spend a great deal of time at or around the 96th Street rink. Early on Sunday mornings we would get on the rink and skate, pass the puck, and shoot. It became an obsession with me to be able to skate as fast as my father. When I was finally able to achieve this step I found I was pretty well qualified to compete with kids my own age and was able to enjoy some success in minor hockey.

Power skating was in vogue in the 30s and 40s. But the only time we really worked at it was after a snowfall. The scrapers required a lot of power to push the snow to the boards where a variation of body building was practised. This consisted of shovelling snow up and over the rink boards.

During the war years the RCAF had the Edmonton Arena as a training centre so there was no artifical ice available. For a few years the finals were played in Red Deer where the Maple Leafs won their share of championships except in Junior Hockey.

Junior 'A' teams in Edmonton finally got to play in the Arena. It was a big thrill; the ice surface was immense. However, the Maple Leafs usually finished second to the Edmonton Canadians who were sponsored by the Chicago Black Hawks. Bill Gadsby and Cy Thomas were a couple of their better players.

Also, during the war, Terry Cavanagh, Don Murray and I were invited to the New York Ranger training camp in Winnipeg. However, after a short stay Don Murray went to the New York Rovers, while Terry and I and a fellow named Gordie Howe, were sent home.

After one season with the Oshawa Generals (OHA) I became a rookie with the Edmonton Senior Flyers. It became apparent that I was too big (6'4" — 210 lbs.) and awkward to claim a regular job as a leftwinger which I had played. Fortunately for me about halfway through the season we ran into a number of injuries to our defensive core and I had a chance to play regularly as a defenceman. During the extended playoffs which would culminate with the Flyers defeating the Ottawa Senators for the Allan Cup, one Edmontonian was cheering against our home team. My fiancee, Marjorie Majeau had to keep postponing our wedding date as we continued to win the playoff games. We finally managed to meet at the church on May 26, 1948, two weeks after the Flyers won the Allan Cup.

Looking back, I find myself thinking of the people I have met and who have assisted me. It makes me realize just how lucky I have been.

(Finally, Bud did get to play in Maple Leaf Gardens in Toronto. "It was like a second home to me as I had already played at our Maple Leaf Gardens on 96th Street and 118th Avenue outdoors in Edmonton. Those were the days"...recalls "Boomer.")

EDMONTON METROPOLITAN HOCKEY ASSOCIATION

BY R.E. (BOB) BOTHWELL

(Bob Bothwell remained active in hockey for many years after the initial EMHA start and was elected president in 1972-73. In his 1972-73 President's address he reported that some 15,000 Edmonton boys and probably 25,000 adults were involved in this minor hockey program. "This has to be one of the largest, if not the largest, minor hockey program in all of Canada.")

Following the war years of 1939 to 1945, the City of Edmonton, like many western cities, entered a period of rapid growth spurred on by the discovery of oil in the Leduc area and the general economic resurgence after six years of restraint.

Business was good, the Edmonton Flyers and the Oil Kings reigned supreme, and minor hockey was enjoying a modest comeback under the guidance of the Canadian Athletic Club, the Maple Leaf Club, the Knights of Columbus, and for a short period the Southside Athletic Club. These Athletic Clubs sponsored teams from Bantam 'A' through Juvenile 'A' and operated under the wing of the Edmonton District Hockey Association.

The Edmonton and District Hockey Association was subsidized by the Edmonton Exhibition Association who in turn through the Edmonton Flyers and the Oil Kings were affiliated with the Detroit Red Wings of the NHL. Edmonton was a "Detroit" city and many players were considered Detroit "property" as a result of signing contracts. Generally speaking it was an adequate minor hockey setup at that time. However, times were changing.

By the mid-50s the post-war baby boom was beginning to catch up. New community leagues were operating throughout the city, and the Federation of Community Leagues was operating a rapidly expanding minor hockey program under the guidance of Mr. Charles Simmonds and the Federation Sports Council with Earl Samis as registrar.

These community leagues were operating a 'B' hockey program across the city and playing their games on community league or city owned and operated rinks. Unlike the Athletic Clubs, the community league hockey teams for the most part were made up of boys from within their own community while the Athletic teams were drawn from anywhere in the city of immediate district. ('B' hockey was more "recreational" in nature while the 'A' programs were for the top calibre players.)

MAPLE LEAF ATHLETIC CLUB 1931-32

Back row (l to r): W. Gardner, F. Hall, H. White (coach), T. Cole, T. Allard, A. MacPhee (manager), S. Reidford, M. Colville. Front row: L. Schafer, H. Young, W. Orr, L. Haswell, W. Smith. *Photo courtesy of Alfred Blyth Studios*

Competiton for city owned rinks was intense. Rivalry between the 'A' and 'B' leagues became serious. Parents became involved and many complaints were directed towards City Hall and the Parks and Recreation Department. It was obvious that we were embarked on a collision course.

In the winter of 1960-61 the Federation Sports Council began operating a Bantam 'A' program in the City of Edmonton and this continued successfully through the winter of 1962-63.

In the meantime, the Canadian Athletic Club, the Maple Leaf Athletic Club, the Southside Athletic Club, and the Knights of Columbus, were operating 'AA' clubs in the Midget and Juvenile categories, and the Federation of Community Leagues and the Knights of Columbus parochial leagues were operating 'B' teams at all levels. It was obvious that minor hockey in the City of Edmonton was out of control.

In the spring of 1962, Mr. George Harvie, president of the Edmonton District Hockey Association was asked by the City of Edmonton Recreation Department to call representatives of all city minor hockey clubs together with a view to solving the existing turmoil and to come up with a solution and a compatible and efficient minor hockey program for the City of Edmonton.

The meetings that followed were long and at times rather tedious and bitter. The attendance, however, was excellent and included such hockey buffs as Tom Devaney, Frank Bischoff, Dick White, Ted Burger, Father L.J. Bonner, from the Knights of Columbus, Jim McAdie, Ben Kalies, Ernie Love and Fred Lupul from the CACs, Don Brown, Jim Stewart, Jim McPherson, Al Green from the Maple Leaf Athletic Club, Ron Joslin, Alex Pringle, Graham Barker, Gordon Robbins, and Bob Bothwell from the Southside Athletic Club, Joe Caswell, Ken Carson and Earl Samis from the Federation of Cummunity Leagues, Jack Reilly and Ed Demchuk from Parks and Recreation, and Gil Bellevance from the Alberta Amateur Hockey Association.

Under the chairmanship of George Harvie the city was divided into four and one athletic club was assigned a zone.

Players would be required to play within the zone they lived thus eliminating raids. The Federation would operate 'BB' hockey within these zones and the Knights of Columbus would continue their 'BB' program through the parochial leagues.

In all fairness, the Athletic Clubs had the most to lose and they fought hard to maintain their status quo. Members stormed out of meetings, some would not make a decision without supposedly contacting Detroit, while

MAPLE LEAF JUVENILES 1936-37

Top row: W. Whitehouse (trainer), T. Allard (coach), H. White (manager), F. Drayton (president). Second row: F. Ashbaugh, J. Wegren, G. Harvie, J. Davis, C. Patry, J. Cook, A. Newsome. Bottom row: D. Campbell, H. Black, K. McAuley, J. Shamper, J. Barbeau.

Photo courtesy of McDermid Studios

others threatened to resign from minor hockey. Throughout it all, George Harvie chaired the meetings like the leader he was. He recognized he had a job to do and at a meeting on April 30, 1963, at City Hall, a steering committee was formed to gather up the pieces and bring in the recommended constitution as soon as possible for the formation of the Edmonton Metropolitan Hockey Association.

A steering committee made up of George Harvey, Ted Burger, Fred Lupul, Don Brown, Bob Bothwell, Ken Carson, Ed Demchuk, Earl Samis and Gil Bellevance was formed. It operated throughout the summer of 1963 under the guidance of chairman Harvey and the legal expertise of Ted Burger.

The EDHA held its last meeting on October 7, 1963. Forty five respresentatives of various hockey organizations were in attendance. The EDHA annual report was adopted as presented and the new constitution of the Edmonton Metropolitan Hockey Association (EMHA) was reviewed clause by clause. It was moved by ''Babe'' McAvoy and seconded by Don Brown that the proposed constitution of the EMHA be accepted in principle. The EMHA was finally in place.

George Harvie was elected to carry on as the first president of the EMHA, with other officers were Ben Kalis vice-president, Bob Bothwell treasurer, and Edmonton Parks and Recreation's Hank Kernan as secretary. The only problem was that the EMHA was long on enthusiasm and short on money.

Our records indicated that on November 23, 1963, we (EMHA) started out with $111.19 in our bank account. Our only source of revenue was the silver collection at the indoor rinks, possible grants from the City of Edmonton and possible help from Edmonton's corporate citizens.

Edmonton Parks and Recreation had turned all the city owned minor hockey rinks over to our Association and it was our responsibility to pay rental to the city for this ice time. In addition, we were responsible for the payment of all referees and timekeepers working in the 'AA' leagues. This was a sizeable undertaking.

Probably the most interesting portion of our fund raising took place each spring, when we would apply for a grant from City Council. Our applications for grants were sent. It almost seemed mostly they were approved because they didn't want the hockey program back in their hands.

I recall an old Scot, who was a city comptroller at the time. He would phone me at my office and in his best Scottish brogue would say, "Mr. Bothwell, I have been instructed to issue a cheque to the EMHA for $5000

EDMONTON MAPLE LEAFS 1949-50
Western Canada Juvenile Champions

Back row (l to r): Jim Christensen (sponsor), Mike Melnyk (manager), Bob Jubb, Eddie McDonald, Bob Cowan, Bill Bucyk (captain), Bob McGee (assistant manager), Ken McAuley (coach). Middle: Roger La Plante, Bill Grocnolski, Jerry Karpinka, Jack Lyndon, Bill McNeill, Jerry Melnyk, Don Jones, Ron Donnelly. Front: Orville Burchby, George Townsend, Dave Laurie (stick boy), Wally Serediak (equipment manager), Dave Magee, Ed Zemrau.   *Photo courtesy of Edmonton Archives*

grant money'', and then he would pause and add, "But only if you bring me a cheque for $3500 for ice rental money''. We would then meet and exchange cheques. Needless to say, the program survived.

Silver collections on Sunday were slow, however, as time went on the spectators became more used to giving. Sunday became the big day. The rinks were full and our family spent many Sunday nights rolling nickels, dimes and quarters for bank deposit Monday morning.

George Harvie was an extremely capable hockey executive and upon completion of the 1964-65 hockey season he was able to pass the chair to the new incoming president, Don Brown of the Maple Leaf Athletic Club.

The EMHA has expanded rapidly and operated efficiently under the guidance of such capable hands at Phil Clarke, Henry White, Bill Wintermute, Frank Newbert, Larry Clark, Rod Mathews, Jack Laurie, Vern Davis, Joe Fridel, Al Dawson, Doug McKenzie, Russ Barnes, Archie Heather, Eric Reilly, Harry Lewis, Orest Korbutt, Gordon Knebel, Paul Cote, Don Dingwall, Helmar Holstron, Ross Olive, Harold Neate, Ray Tenney, Al Olson, Bob Wood, Ernie Reid, Jack Reilly, Ron Ferguson, John Shires, George Hughes, Jim McFall, Alf Savage, Les Hernstedt, Gordon McLean, Henry Keiser and Bill Fehr, and a host of other dedicated hockey people.

The record of the Edmonton Metropolitan Hockey Association is second to none in all of Canada and at various times, other cities have asked for a copy of our constitiution as the pattern for their minor hockey programs.

After over twenty years the EMHA is still going strong. Looking back over those years to our founding meeting on October 7, 1963, it is obvious that whatever success the Association may have attained, it can be attributed to a great degree to those minor hockey "buffs" that came out of the late 40s and 50s.

CANADIAN ATHLETIC CLUB 1953-54
Lupuls Bantam Breakers

Top (l to r): Fred Lupul (coach), Dave Collier, Doug Hepburn, Jerry Krayco, Ken Rhodes (manager). Bottom: Freddie Lupul, Ken Sobkovich, Eddie Lupul (goal), Richard Pitfield, John Givens, Jimmy Lupul (stick boy in front).

Photo courtesy of Garneau Studios, Edmonton

* * *

TOE TO TOE

BY STAN BALL, Coach of the 1984-85 Riverbend Rats

Saturday, January 12, 1985, at the Southside Arena, the Riverbend Rats played the Millwood Raiders in a Mite 'BB' league game as part of the EMHA program.

It was a normal game. As is often the case this year, we were behind. The puck came out of the Riverbend end to centre. For some reason I looked back and saw three players where there should have only been the goalie.

Darrell Berg of Riverbend and Mike Vanderwater of Millwoods were toe to toe and looking like they were jawing each other, wanting to fight. They were pulling away from each other and not moving. The referee finally saw something was wrong and stopped the play. As he went closer all of us could see what the problem was.

Approximately 10 seconds after the referee reached the boys he solved the problem. Darrell's SK600 Cooper and Mike's CCM helmet were totally locked. For me and most of the parents watching it was a strange happening. It made at least half of us forget the 5-1 score.

BILL BOUCHARD MEMORIAL PEE WEE TOURNAMENT

Many hockey tournaments for minor hockey teams exist in Alberta. Teams participate for fun and the chance to win a few awards. Tournaments and trophies have meanings for the donators and receivers. In the case of the Bill Bouchard Memorial Tournament at Edmonton's Rosslyn Community Outdoor Rink, the competition represents the goals of minor hockey players and coaches who love the game. The main trophy is named after Bill Bouchard and the goal keeper trophy after Rick Shevolup.

CFRN SUNWAPTAS JUNIOR B's 1957-58

Back row (l to r): Don Rosiechuk, Butch Thomlinson, Ron Fenton, Ernie Takacs, Borden Lypowy (trainer), Joe Kay (manager, coach), Art Hanasyk (equipment manager), Ron Rooke, Norm Rooke, Lynn Sereda, Jim Shologan. Front row (l to r): Del Roberge, Dave Clelland, Rick Mullen, Ted Shavchook, Neil Tucker, Ray Morton, Dennis Kassian, Roy Turner, Bob Mac-Pherson, Paddy MacCrimmon (stick boy).

BILL BOUCHARD

RICK SHEVOLUP

Bill Bouchard was a member of Local 488 Pipefitters and Plumbers Union. As a volunteer sports director of Rosslyn Community League he had an interest in all sports in his community. In 1975 he organized a pee wee tournament for teams who did not make the playoffs. Enthusiasm and effort were trade marks of Bouchard.

In 1977 Bouchard's Rosslyn Pee Wee "A"'s were sponsored by G.W. Ming. The team decided to play beyond the boundaries of Edmonton. Bouchard and the team proceeded to raise $10,000 to go to a tournament in West Covina, California. It was a phenomenal enterprise. Raffle tickets were sold door to door and in shopping centres by the boys and parents. The team responded to Bouchard's philosophy of team effort and cooperation. Discipline was also stressed; however, the objective was to play for the sake of the game. The team ended fourth in the 28 team tournament.

On November 2, 1981, Bill Bouchard was attending a community hockey meeting at the Rosslyn Community league. He had a heart attack and died at age 49. His wife Marjorie felt the tournament should continue and has been the key organizer ever since.

Another trophy was given to the top goalie in the tournament. This one is named after Rick Shevolup. Rick never became a professional hockey player; however, his hockey life was noted for enthusiasm and sportsmanship.

Hal Pawson of the Edmonton Journal attended a sports banquet held by the Northeast Zone of the EMHA. Total attendance at the banquet was 1600 and Clare Drake of the U of A and Al McCann of CFRN TV had 348 awards to give out. The award to Rick Shevolup was noted by Pawson on April 14, 1966.

Another startling award was made to Ricky Shevolup of the Rosslyn Mites. Ricky, you see, could barely skate when last season started. So, what did this kid do? Between periods at each and every game, while the Rosslyn Mites rested in the dressing room, Ricky stayed out and skated around the rink. But that isn't why he is named the player showing the most gentlemanly conduct. It was because this pint-sized character, after each and every game, made a point of shaking hands with each member of the opposition. In fact, he shook hands with his own guys.

EDMONTON ST. JOSEPH'S BANTAMS 1961-62

Back row (l to r): Terry Kowalchuck, John Foy, Brian Teed, Rick Wooley, Ray Purches, Pat Wilson. Middle row: Tom Devaney Jr., Ed Senchyna, Adrian Lambert, Tom Devaney Sr., Bob Devaney. Front row: Phil Ingram, Rich Hebner, Mike Clermont, Terry Nowicki, Mike Conroy. *Photo courtesy of Edmonton Archives*

Rick continued his playing interest in hockey and played goalie in his community. Sportsmanship and the ability to keep his teammates' spirits high were qualities remembered.

Dave and Virginia Garth, Mike and Adeline Berezuik, Bill and Germaine Marshall, Mike Kowalyk, Marjorie and her sons Paul and Bill Bouchard and other Rosslyn community members are now making plans for the 1986 tournament, Carmen Lori Shevolup will again present the top goalie award.

It is not always the big stars who make things happen in minor hockey. On the contrary, determined coaches and organizers like Bill Bouchard and enthusiastic players like Rick Shevolup are key ingredients. Trophies and tournaments have history, tradition and reasons beyond the game for their existence.

UNIVERSAL CONCRETE JUVENILES 1959-60

Back row (l to r): Brian Gillard, Derek Truswell, Bob Howse, Gary Sangster, Ron Sarnowsky, Ron Marteniuk, Ben Kalis (chief hockey director), Bill Lupul (trainer), Dale Conrad, Dave Foster, Dave Vaughan, Doug Duncan, Ken Bacon (manager). Front row (l to r): Buster Brayshaw (coach), Doug McAvoy, Pete Badowsky (captain), Roy Turner (goal), Bob Otto, Jack Potts, Artie (stick boy).

Photo courtesy of Garneau Studios

BUTCHERS & PACKERS 1974-75

Front row (l to r): Bill Hobbins, Dan Peacocke, Bart Hunter, Kevin Mitchell, Rod Peacocke, John Good. Middle row (l to r): Bob Wood (C.A.C. midget director), Marvin Benson (trainer), Tim Doyle, Doug Smith, Marc Gagne, Mark Tonack, Terry Oakes (captain), Don Benson (coach), Bernie O'Connor (sponsor). Top row (l to r): Randy Rimstad, Pat Elliot, Joel Elliot, George McKenzie (manager), Gerry Towns, Joe Kapitzke, Larry LeBlanc.

Photo courtesy of Edmonton Archives

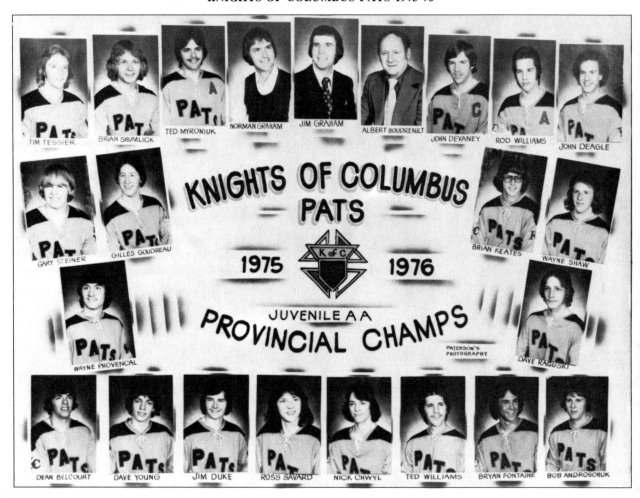

Photo courtesy of Paterson's Photography

RIVERBEND JAWS 1981-82

Back row (l to r): Jim Bondy (coach), Spencer Zeman, Travis Guthrie, Craig Dockrill, Jason Greig, Steven Berg, Gary Zeman (manager). Front row: Jason Peters, Jay Bondy, Brady O'Hara, Derek Brown, Trevor West. Inserts: Tim Lown, Christopher Norman.

BARRHEAD — PROVINCIAL PEE WEE CHAMPIONS 1976-77

Back row (l to r): Maury Grant, Shane McNiven, Parie Proft, Randy Kuhn, Laurie Dent, Don Rossman, Greg Jackson, Lyle Treleaven. Adults: Fred Proft (coach), Don Rossman Sr. (equipment manager), Harry Proft (assistant coach), Bill Dent (manager). Front row (l to r): Kim Schultz, Phillip Henke, Allan Measures, Brian Moore, Pat Mohrmann, Wes Proft, Mark Proft.

BARRHEAD JUNIOR ELKS — PROVINCIAL CHAMPIONS 1979-80

Back row (l to r): Sid Schooler (executive), Richard Rau (executive), Bob Ryder (executive), Dan Edinga (executive), Mat Hayduk, Nat Fenton, Murray Butler, Colin Grant, Maury Benson (executive), Alan Suchow (executive), Harvey Shaw (executive). Second row (l to r): Cal Visser (executive), Ron Schmidt, Brad Schmidt, Pete Bokenfore, Reiny Koberstein (coach), Mike McKeever, Brad Tetz, Bruce Pusch, Mike Wareheim, Marion Dowd (trainer). Front row (l to r): Dwayne Baird, Yvon deChamplain, Don Koberstein, Denny Potvin, Jim Gottschalk, Dwayne Moore, Ken Manz.

VIMY BANTAMS 1954-55

Top row (l to r): Wilfred Provencal (coach), Wilf Provencal, Morris Provencal, Richard Seguin, Leo Provencal, Clem Fagnan, Joseph La Plante, Louis Burns, Emil St. Arnaud, Paul Regimbald. Bottom row: Robert Burns, Jimmy DeLorme, Albert Sabourin (goal), Morris St. Arnaud (captain), Robert Beart, Richard La Plante.

Photo courtesy of Westlock Studios

LACOMBE JUVENILES 1947-48

Top (l to r): Allan Chiswell, Alvin Johnson, Bob Gilmour, Al Calkins, Fred Rusk, Don Blades, Walter Baines. Middle: Don Frizzell, Andy Whyte, Norm Lund, Bill Parks (mascot), Bob Holmes, Bob Marshall, Ron Kasha. Bottom: Jack Mac-Donald (stick boy), Don Haworth, Ernie Tredget (secretary), Bob Parks (manager), Al Myers (coach), Don Hay, Jerry Danner (trainer).

Photo courtesy of Cameron Studios

CHAPTER 10
THE HOT STOVE LEAGUE

This section contains stories on individuals, teams or events. These are some of the stories that help add the extra dimension to hockey. Hockey is played on the ice by the players, while the fans play in the HOT STOVE LEAGUE. Welcome to the biggest league in hockey!

'THE TRUTH'

A Fiction by W.P. KINSELLA

(W.P. (Bill) Kinsella is the author of ten books including *Dance Me Outside* and *The Moccasin Telegraph*. Several of his books are narrated by Silas Ermineskin and feature Frank Fencepost and Mad Etta. Those stories are mostly set in Hobbema, Alberta. Kinsella cracked the American market with *Shoeless Joe*, a fictional account of baseball's Joe Jackson of the 1919 Chicago White Socks scandal. Although Kinsella is most often associated with the sport of baseball, he was born in Darwell, Alberta and saw ''Pug'' Young and the Edmonton Flyers win the Allan Cup in 1948. This is his first story about hockey. It was written expressly for *Alberta On Ice*.)

It wasn't us who started the riot at the St. Eduord Hockey Arena. The story made quite a few newspapers and even got on the Edmonton television, the camera showing how chairs had been ripped out of the stands and thrown around the ice. According to the TV the hamlet of St. Eduord was going to sue the Town of Hobbema for damages, but nothing ever came of that.

For a long time the rumor went around that it was because my friend, Frank Fencepost, had a dog named Guy La Fleur that the riot got started. Not true either. Frank does have a dog named Guy La Fleur, and he did have him in the St. Eduord Arena, and Guy La Fleur was sitting on a seat right behind our team's player's box. The dog would bark whenever our team, the Hobbema Wagonburners, got the puck, and Frank would say "Shut up the barking, Guy La Fleur, you son of a bitch." A lot of heads turned every time he said it, because as you may of guessed St. Eduord was a French-Canadian town. But it was something else that started the riot.

We never should have been there anyway, but Frank, he read in the newspaper about a small town hockey tournament with a $1,000 first prize. He did the entering, then started rounding up a team. I don't skate and neither does Frank. But we located a couple of guys who used to be pretty good ten years ago, a few others who can stand up on skates, and a goalie who just got new glasses last week.

Indian Affairs paid for the uniforms, shirts white as bathroom tiles with a bright red burning wagon on the front. Indian Affairs is a soft touch for anything to do with sports; they figure playing games keeps you sober and out of jail.

Frank is manager; I am his assistant, and Mad Etta our 400 lb. medicine lady, is doctor and trainer; Guy La Fleur is the mascot.

Soon as we start to warm-up we can see we is outclassed. This team from St. Eduord is young and fast and tough. Someone tell us they ain't lost a game in two seasons.

Soon as the puck is dropped St. Eduord carry it in on our goal. They shoot, hit our goalie on the chest; he fall forward on the puck. A St. Eduord player come down with a knee on the back of the goalie's head, smash his mask, his face, and his glasses into the ice. That was a really unlucky thing for them to do. I'm sure they would of scored ten goals each period if they'd just been patient. We carry the goalie to the bench, strip off his pads and look for somebody to fill the net.

It is then Frank gets his idea. We hold up the game for about fifteen minutes until we can find skates big enough to fit Mad Etta. Frank have to promise her $900 of the $1,000 for her to agree.

Three of us have to walk on each side to guide her to the net. Once there she just kick at the ice until she get down to the floor. Then she stand with one arm on each goal post, look fierce from behind the goalie mask what painted like a punk rock album cover.

Whenever the puck come over our blue line, which is almost all the time, Etta just turn her back on the game. Doesn't matter where they shoot or how often there is some part of Etta blocking every part of the net. Trouble is Etta figure the game is only one period long.

"That little black biscuit hurts like hell", she say. Then when the second period start she take from a pocket in her five-flour-sack dress some greenish looking sandy stuff, sprinkle it across the goal line. Then she waddle over to the faceoff circle, sit down crosslegged, light up an Export "A". The St. Eduord team sweep in and blast a shot at the empty goal, but it just zap off to the corner as if there was a real good goalie there. After about 10 shots like that they get pretty mad. It is like Etta covered the front of the net with clear plexiglass. But when the referee test it with his hand there is nothing there. He throw the puck in the net. Then he get a stick and shoot in it. "Stop bitchin' and play hockey," he say to the St. Eduord players.

No matter how bad your team you bound to score a goal sometime. Rufus Firstrider, who skate mainly on his ankles, carry in the puck, try to pass to Gorman Carry-the-Kettle. The goalie see the pass coming and move across the net, but Rufus miss the pass and poke it at the net by accident and score. That is all the score there is Hobbema Wagonburners 1, St. Eduord 0.

It was them and their fans that started the riot. We is a lot better fighters than we are hockey players. We win the fight by more than 1-0. They pay us off and send us home after that, finish the tournament with teams they understand. And that's 'The Truth'.

PRO HOCKEY IN THE TWENTIES

An interview with Lloyd McIntyre

(Lloyd McIntyre played for the 1926 Edmonton Eskimos in the Western Canada Professional Hockey League. He was born July 15, 1901 in Strathcona, Alberta. His father George played hockey just before the turn of the century for the Strathcona Seniors. The McIntyres moved to Fort Saskatchewan where Lloyd started playing shinny and pickup games. One of the best hockey players at the Fort was Harold "Dude" or "Duke" Kimball, father of Norman Kimball, who is General Manager of the Edmonton Eskimo Football club.

In 1927 Lloyd married Connie Smith, the captain of Percy Page's world famous Edmonton Grad Basketball team. Lloyd also played football for the Edmonton Eskimos in 1924 and was a member of the Cliff Manahan Rink which won the Canadian Brier in 1937.

Lloyd McIntyre was interviewed at his home in Viking in the summer of 1984. The following are a few of his memories of the WCPHL.)

I played my first professional game on January 9, 1926, for the Edmonton Eskimos against the Saskatoon Sheiks. Ken MacKenzie was manager of the Eskimos and paid me $100 a game for sixteen games. I also worked at Edmonton Motors for $40 a week.

The Eskimos were a great team. The lineup proves it. We should have won but the lack of artificial ice in Edmonton really hurt us. We had to play the final playoff game on the coast.

We had some fantastic players on our team — Ernie Anderson of Calgary, George Boucher of Ottawa (Frank's brother), Bob Benson, Emery "Spunk" Sparrow from Moose Jaw and Russell "Barney" Stanley.

Calgary had Mervyn "Red" Dutton. In Edmonton they called him "Dirty" Dutton but in Calgary he was the "greatest". Duke Keats and Merv tangled all the time whether it was on the puck, for the puck or without the stick. Fans came to see Dutton and Keats scrap it out. I remember as many as 5,500 fans a game. Dutton later went on to the Montreal Maroons and New York Americans in the NHL. After that he became part owner of the New York Americans with Bill Duyer. He was also President of the NHL from 1943-46.

Newsy Lalonde was the playing coach of the Saskatoon Sheiks. He was near the end of his playing career when I was playing pro hockey. He was a great puck handler and must take some credit for the development of Bun and Bill Cook of the Saskatoon Sheiks. George Hainsworth, later a famous NHL goalie, was a Saskatoon player.

Eddie Shore was the best man at my wedding in 1927. Shore was around 5'10", 190 pounds, a very solid guy. I recall after practice a whole carload of us always dropped Shore at 101st Street and Jasper Avenue at Morris' Physical and Cultural School where Shore took some boxing lessons. Many players in the WCPHL and later in the NHL regretted those lessons. Charlie Sutter, who was the grandfather of the Sutter boys, was a trainer of the Eskimos and he used to assist Shore in these martial arts. Russell "Barney" Stanley played defence with Shore. He was clever and hardly ever got a penalty — a real contrast with Shore. When he played with Shore he changed his pattern and became a more defensive player. Of course, Barney could rush in any time he wanted to. I played at 176 lbs. and Barney was 175 lbs. and around 6'. Everybody liked Barney. He was our experienced player, a real star. Art "Cyclone" Gagne was a slender player, probably 165 lbs. and 5'11". He had been a brakeman on the railway out of Kamloops. His appearance was deceiving; he reminded me of a banker or a scholar; he could use a butt end and get away with it. In practice or games he played just as hard. He was the smoothest forward we had on our team. (Gagne is approaching 90 in Kelowna)

Gordon "Duke" Keats was the best player of all time. He almost had a nail on the end of his stick to carry the puck around, he was that good. He was close to 6' and 190 lbs. No one could knock him around and he could score.

In the spring of 1926 the pro league folded. Most of the players were sold to NHL clubs. I can't think of a WCPHL player who wasn't offered a NHL contract. I had an offer to go to the Detroit Cougars, in the days before the Red Wings, but I decided to stay home and work at Edmonton Motors. 1926 was the end of my pro career but I got to play with some of the best players in hockey.

Lloyd McIntyre passed away on November 29, 1984. Art "Cyclone" Gagne is the only living member of that Edmonton Eskimo team.

RENAISSANCE MAN — DR. W. GEORGE HARDY 1895-1979

In October, 1939, Bill Tobin, General Manager of the Chicago Black Hawks, wired Edmonton's Dr. William George Hardy for permission to sign Bill Mosienko, a player for the Winnipeg Monarch Hockey Club, to a pro contract. The first question is, naturally, why did Tobin need permission (see following story about Hockey's "New Deal") and the second question should be: why would Tobin ask permission from a man who was Professor of Classics at the University of Alberta?

DR. W. GEORGE HARDY

Photo courtesy of Victoria Daily Times

The real explanation lies in the philosophy of George Hardy. He believed passionately in the Greek ideal of the unity of body and soul. And he lived his life by it. That is why George Hardy, Renaissance Man "moonlighted" as President of the Alberta and Canadian Hockey Associations and International Ice Hockey Federation.

Although Hardy had played and coached some hockey. he was not divinely inspired about the game until he visited Athens in 1928 (from an unpublished letter c. 1940):

(In Athens)...I saw Athens carved in a bas relief on one side of a square block of stone and dating back to the fourth century B.C....a sculpture of two Greek boys with sticks carved at one end "puck-ying" off while a referee stands behind ready to drop the puck.

There were no war planes over Athens then and standing there and looking at the picture of those long dead Greek athletes, I could, for a moment, see myself in an Ontario schoolyard chasing a small wooden block with a "shinney-stick" cut from a tree and wondering how I'd explain to my mother the black eye I'd just got.

Any child who could read by the age of three, be qualified for high school by age 10 (after having only attended elementary school part time) and who taught himself Greek in between farming could very likely come up with a good explanation for his mother.

It was during his youth on the farm that Hardy first demonstrated his passion for the Greek ideal. He directed the Hardy team of horses around the field six times. Then while the horses rested, young Hardy brushed up on his Greek grammar. In this way he learned to make use of every spare moment, a habit that he continued throughout life.

After high school he attended the University of Toronto with the help of academic scholarships. He won a Gold Medal in Classics. Mathematics and Latin were his strongest subjects because of his love of structural logic. He earned his Doctor of Philosophy in Classics in the fall of 1919 and was hired By Dr. William Hardy Alexander to teach in the Classics Department at the University of Alberta.

Professor Hardy's boyhood interests led him into creative writing (historical novels with classical themes), historical writing, drama, debating and boxing as well as hockey. Some of his most well-read historical works include *From Sea Unto Sea* (1960) and *The Greek and Roman World* (1960). Hardy was editor in chief of *Alberta — A Natural History* (1967). By 1975 63,000 copies had been printed. He wrote plays performed on the CBC Radio and was an original committee member when the Banff School of Fine Arts was established. He excelled in debating at the University of Toronto and it was Hardy — not his friend Lester B. Pearson — who was the University Liberal opposition leader. He boxed at the U. of T. as a 142 pounder and could read up to 300 pages an hour.

Sometimes Dr. Hardy's academic and athletic worlds overlapped. In 1984 Dr. Walter Johns, former President of the University of Alberta, recalled his first introduction to Dr. Hardy. Johns went with his wife to see Hardy for a job interview at the Royal York Hotel in 1938. When they went to Hardy's hotel room at 7 p.m. they found:

...the dresser and table covered with liquor bottles and glasses and the room filled with smoke. Dr. Hardy apologized and explained he had had a meeting with officials from the CAHA and others and that the room had not been tidied up.

Amidst this was a copy of the proposed jacket cover for his novel Turn Back The River *(1938) which was due to be published by McMillan.*

This was a type of Professor of Classics which was strange to me and my wife, but Dr. Hardy was such a pleasant host that we had a fine dinner and evening of conversation before heading back to Waterloo in the wee small hours. (Dr. Johns got the job in Alberta!)

Hardy's keen mind served him well in his life as a hockey administrator. In 1933, when the CAHA adopted the forward pass in amateur hockey it was Hardy, Clarence Campbell of Edmonton, George Dudley of Midland, Ontario and Cecil Duncan of Ottawa who were successful in the debate.

Hardy was also politically astute enough to note that sport and politics were becoming inavoidably linked. In an October 25, 1935 letter to W.A. Hewitt, CAHA Registrar and Treasurer (and father of broadcaster Foster Hewitt) Hardy wrote:

I have noted, in addition, that the Nazis appear to be employing all important meetings in their country (prior to the 1936 Olympics in Berlin) for propaganda in favour of the Hitler regime. Thus, they are dragging sports into the realm of politics and this in turn, makes it necessary for us not to divorce sports from politics but to consider them in conjunction.

Hardy became President of the AAHA from 1931 to 1933 and the CAHA for 1938 and 1939.

Hardy became President of the International Ice Hockey Federation and "pulled the strings" to get the Edmonton Mercurys and the Lethbridge Maple Leafs to the World Hockey Championships in the early '50s.

Dr. Hardy was showered with honours — the University of Alberta National Award in Letters in 1962, the Centennial Medal in 1967, an Honorary Degree of Laws from the University of Alberta in 1973, the Order of Canada in 1973 and Excellence in Literature award in 1976 to name a few — but one of the very special tributes to this Renaissance Man comes from his barber George Baros of Lansdowne Barber Shop:

I cut his hair at the Garneau Barber Shop on 109th Street and Whyte Avenue from 1957 to 1969. He was President of Alberta, Canadian and World Hockey before I knew him . If you're going to do a hockey history of Alberta, Dr. Hardy has to have a very special place in your book.

DR. GEORGE HARDY ENGINEERS HOCKEY'S "NEW DEAL"

During the Depression the President of the United States, Franklin D. Roosevelt, inititated a program of relief, recovery and reform in his country called the "New Deal". It was based on the idea that the government should assume more responsibility for the welfare of its people. Seizing on the same idea, Dr. George Hardy of Alberta, President of the CAHA thought it only right that his organization would take more responsiblity for amateur hockey in Canada. In 1939 he negotiated amateur hockey's "New Deal" with NHL owners.

Before 1939 NHL teams had not been required to make official payments to amateur teams providing them with professional hockey players. At that June's Annual CAHA meeting at the Fort Garry Hotel in Winnipeg, Dr. Hardy and other CAHA officials met with Mervyn "Red" Dutton, representative for the NHL Board of Governors. It was agreed that Dr. Hardy would meet with NHL representatives and present the CAHA proposal.

The proposal had been drafted by Angus McClasky, a lawyer and member of the Saskatchewan Amateur Hockey Association and Saskatoon lawyer Donald C. Disbery (see footnote) at the request of Dr. Hardy. Disbery had found an early case in England. A minor signed what amounted to a personal services contract to box. The minor's father objected and the contract was declared void.

That fall Dr. Hardy met the NHL Board of Governors in New York. He met them in his capacity as Chairman of the CAHA committee to negotiate with the professionals and as President of the International Ice Hockey Association. The following is Dr. Hardy's account (an unpublished letter printed with permission of his daughter, Mrs. Margaret Simpson of Edmonton) of the September 12, 1939 meeting and his impression of the NHL men sitting at the table with him:

...with the exception of Jim Norris, the hard-headed practical magnet of the Detroit Red Wings, they are an energetic and highly capable group...Bill Tobin of the Chicago Black Hawks, Lester Patrick, the clever and handsome President of the New York Rangers, Red Dutton of the New York Americans, Connie Smythe, the blunt straight-thinking man who runs the Toronto Maple Leafs and next to me was Art Ross and there is no one in hockey shrewder or more reasonable than Art Ross. At the further end of the table was Lester's brother Frank Patrick and the resourceful Tommy Gorman both of the Montreal Canadiens. Next to them was the bluff Jack Adams of Detroit. Two chairs from me sat Colonel Kilpatrick, the polished yet direct President of Madison Square Garden Corporation. At the end of the table was Frank Calder, the tactful and forceful hockey genius who was President of the NHL.

Sitting there and listening to these men discuss hockey schedules and reserve lists and whether or not it would be good business to fly their clubs to games, and, if so, to what extent, a good many reflections occurred to me. Among them was the thought that partically all these men were or had been Canadians.

This is important. It meant that most of these men had actually played hockey. It also meant that they knew what conditions are like in villages and towns of the East or out on the snow-swept prairies from which the raw recruits of hockey come down to the bright lights. Likewise, these men understood the CAHA set-up...

...on September 12th within an hour we reached an agreement whereby the NHL and its affiliated minor pro leagues pay to the IIHA $250 for each player signed by a minor pro club and $500 for each player signed to an NHL contract.

You will note that this payment is to the IIHA and not to the CAHA. This is because an occasional American born hockey player turns pro and also because of those Candians playing on American Hockey Association (AHA) clubs in the U.S. who are turned pro. This in my opinion is one of the most progressive steps taken under the title of "New Deal in Hockey"...

...(to illustrate how the system worked Hardy used the case of Winnipeg's Billy Mosienko who had just signed with the Chicago Black Hawks)...if Mosienko had played on both CAHA and AHA clubs in the U.S. I would have to decide in consultation with George Dudley (CAHA) and Tommy Lockhart (AHA) just how the money should be divided between the AHA and the CAHA. Since, however, Mosienko was a CAHA player only, I'll send the money on to George Dudley. In his turn Dudley

will distribute it among those clubs of the CAHA, Bantam, Midget, Juvenile and Junior who gave Mosienko his chance to develop into a player of pro calibre...

One of the reasons the NHL had little choice but to agree to the new terms was that it relied almost entirely on junior clubs for its recruits. Only a very few NHL players had been recruited from American or Canadian colleges and universities at that time. (It would be two decades until more NHL players would be recruited from post secondary educational institutions.)

The agreement sealed the interdependence between NHL and junior hockey in Canada and led to direct NHL sponsorship of selected junior clubs.

There was great money to be made in the number one winter entertainment in North America; Dr. Hardy and his CAHA colleagues had just ensured that minor hockey should also benefit from the new era of prosperity.

*Author's note: I grew up one block away from Donald and Marion Disbery in Saskatoon, and became a friend of their son Ian. Donald Disbery became Judge Disbery. In 1980 I saw him again after a long absence. It was just after Wayne Gretzky had signed his NHL contract with the Edmonton Oilers. The Judge commented, "I know a little about hockey contracts and it sounds like Gretzky made a good deal." The Judge passed away in 1981. I did not find out until doing the research for this book that a man I had known all my life really did know "a little about hockey contracts!"

J. LLOYD TURNER (AUGUST 9,1884-APRIL 7, 1976) ALBERTA HOCKEY BUILDER

BY TOMMY GRAHAM, Associate Editor, Alberta on Ice

The legacy of J. Lloyd Turner will go down in the annals of Alberta sport as one of the major hockey builders and organizers of all time. Turner was a leader, a master of finese and a go getter. Once his mind was made up he left no stone unturned to reach his objective.

Turner got involved. He was a player, coach. manager, promoter and executive in sports. He was associated with every minor sports activity in Calgary and district and was know throughout Canada for his participation and overall knowledge.

Some Calgarians remember Turner as Manager of the Calgary Corral; a few the Victoria Arena; but he was even Manager of the Sherman Rink.

PAINTING OF LLOYD TURNER

Photo courtesy of Calgary Exhibition and Stampede

He was born in Elmvale, Ontario, lived in Sault Ste. Marie and came west in 1907 to seek a career as a baseball player. He played the game with creditibility; but his main forte became hockey and he dedicated his life to it.

In 1910, Turner could be seen scraping ice for hockey encounters. He became associated with teams like the Calgary Shermans, Calgary Tigers and Calgary Stampeders. The Tigers reached the Stanley Cup finals in 1924 and the Stampeders won the Allan Cup in 1946.

One of Lloyd's favorite sayings was, "there's a little good in everyone and everyone deserves a break". At a testimonial dinner on September 26, 1964 almost everyone in hockey paid tribute to Turner.

For the souvenir program, Gorde Hunter wrote that Turner benefited many minor hockey groups. "I can't tell you how many minor hockey groups played at the Corral in the old Victoria Arena, I guess, even in the old Sherman Rink, at something less than the going rate."

His wife Hazel was a solid supporter of his activities and took an active interest in all his endeavors prior to her death on October 25, 1924. Turner never remarried.

Lloyd Turner died on April 7, 1976; however one just has to walk around the concourse in the Calgary Corral to view the history of sport in Calgary. His work actually started at the Sherman Rink. A fire destroyed all the photos except one of Norval Babtie, then a world champion speed skating champion. All the mounting, framing and collecting was done by Turner. The collection was not restricted to professional and senior hockey. Many pee wee, midget, juvenile and other catagories and leagues were displayed. Lloyd Turner was a sportsman. His collection also made him a sports historian.

Calgary Sportsman of the Year (1984), Jim "Deak" Cassidy remembers, "I started out as rink rat around 1936. Lloyd really only needed eight rink rats but must have had eighty just to keep the boys off the streets. He was a guiding force behind my life and many others." Besides the teams, rinks and players, the legacy of Lloyd Turner lives in his photos, but also in the people he influenced.

(In 1958, J. Lloyd Turner was inducted into the Hockey Hall of Fame.)

LLOYD TURNER'S ICE BOX

BY ART EVANS, Edmonton Journal

(This story was written by Evans for the Lloyd Turner Testimonial Dinner held on September 26, 1964.)

Few people outside the refridgeration field know that Lloyd Turner was instrumental in developing the first walk-in freezer. The largest deep freeze of its kind (with the exception of the Artic and Antartic regions) was known as Calgary's Victoria Arena...

How well I remember that advertisment popular in Calgary newspapers thirty years ago, "Lloyd Turner's Heated Arena". Even now the thought of that advertisement is enough to send old-timers scurrying to the basement to turn on the furnace on a hot July day. (Pardon me while I put on a sweater. There is a sudden chill in the air. There, that's better.)

The patrons of Lloyd's "heated arena" in those days were rugged hockey fans in this era. They had to be. If the temperature outside the arena was -30 degrees (Farenheit) the temperature inside could be relied on to dip even lower. Compared to the Victoria Arena the rink at Nome Alaska, was in the Gulf Stream.

Despite frigid evidence to the contrary the belief persisted in some circles that Victoria Arena actually did have a heating plant. This rumor was fostered by the appearance in the rink of ducts mistakenly called hot-air vents. The first fans to arrive at the rink always sealed off these vents with their bodies so it was impossible to tell if they did supply hot air or were merely decorative. If the arena did have a furnace, Mr. Turner's cigar generated more heat.

...Father (Art Evan's father) was a great hockey fan and frequently I accompanied him to Mr. Turner's "Ice Palace" (I use the term in its literal sense). We were there the night it was so cold inside the arena that the game between the Calgary Tigers and the Portland Buckaroos (or was it the Seattle Seahawks?) was cancelled...

...I think I caught a glimpse that night of Mr. Turner wearing a straw hat and eating an ice cream cone to dispel any suspicion that he thought it was too cold to play hockey. I think Mr. Turner could play hockey leaping from ice floe to ice floe in the Artic ocean.

LLOYD'S HOT STOVE LEAGUE

BY GORDE HUNTER

There was nothing really imposing about the place, it was just a big comfortable room filled with some old, overstuffed furniture. It was the Inner Sanctum at Calgary's famed Corral, the best hockey arena of its time.

It was the office of Lloyd Turner, Manager of the Corral, and indeed, the place had become known as "Lloyd's Place". And what a magnificent spot that inner office was before any pro or junior hockey game. For that was where they held the Hot Stove League, an assembly of writers, broadcasters. players, ex-players, managers and owners. For any star-struck young reporter, it was heaven, it was the finest ambrosia.

It was also informal. Lloyd presided over the sessions as a benevolent uncle, only interceding if the arguments became overly loud or threatening. But that was rarely the case because who would want to argue with hockey immortals like Eddie Shore, Jack Adams, Tiny Thompson and his brother Paul?

We listened because we were listening to the history of hockey. On any given night you could find two-thirds of the greatest line the Toronto Maple Leafs ever had — Sweeney Schriner and Lorne Carr. Big Bob Davidson was another ex-Leaf who reported in regularly in his capacity as chief scout for that team and yes, the legendary Punch Imlach made his presence felt on more than one occasion. Emile Francis is another Hockey Hall of Famer who shot the breeze with us as was Scotty Morrison, who went on to become the chief official of the NHL.

Joe Primeau and Charlie Conacher dropped around and so did Black Jack Stewart and Gordie Howe of the Red Wings. The Rocket came in and yes, even the Golden Jet. Hey!, "Red" Dutton was there damned near every game and Dutton, remember, had done it all. He was a star defenceman in the NHL. He owned the New York American franchise, coached them, managed them too. And he was President of the NHL for a couple of years before he decided to make a few million in the construction industry.

And some of the guys with the questions were legends in their own rights. Broadcasters like Gordie Williamson, Henry Viney, Eric Bishop, Bryan Hall, Wes Montgomery, Ed Whalen, Ken Newans and Stan Foss. Writers like Dick Beddoes, Hal Pawson, George Macintosh, Stan Moher, Tom Moore, George Bilych and Don Fleming.

And Frank McCool qualified as both writer and player for everyone knew that Frank had that one superb NHL season in goal for Toronto Leafs, when he led them to a Stanly Cup.

It was a trip down hockey's memory lane and hockey night at the Corral. It was maybe one of the best Hot Stove Leagues anywhere and those privileged to attend "Lloyd's Place" will never forget them.

No, such sessions aren't around anymore. Hockey unfortunately, has become too sophisticated for such cornball niceties.

CLARENCE SUTHERLAND CAMPBELL
BY DICK BEDDOES, now of CHCH T.V., Hamilton, Ontario

CLARENCE CAMPBELL IN 1929

Photo courtesy of Provincial Archives

(Beddoes is originally from Daysland, Alberta. He is one of Canada's top sports journalists, having worked in Edmonton, Vancouver, and Toronto for major newspapers.)

Clarence Sutherland Campbell always answered his telephone with the salutation, "Campbell here". Mr. Campbell was here, in Alberta, involved with several sports many years before his eminence as President of the National Hockey League from 1946-1977.

He was born to farm parents near the Saskatchewan Hamlet of Fleming in 1905. In 1920 he moved to Edmonton and went to Strathcona High for one term, preparatory to attending the University of Alberta.

Campbell whizzed through an Arts course in three years, at 18, one of the youngest to earn a degree from the Univeristy of Alberta. He won a scroll with honors in two more years and, in 1925, was chosen a Rhodes Scholar, the only one ever picked from Fleming, Saskatchewan.

In 1926, with Rhodes contemporaries from other countries in the British Commonwealth, Campbell enrolled in Lincoln College under the old grey spires of Oxford, the best known of Britains' academic towns. He won, among other prizes, an Oxford Blue for playing a robust brand of field lacrosse.

He returned in 1929 to Edmonton, there to join the legal firm of Wood, Buchanan and MacDonald. He also picked up the loose threads of his sporting scarf.

Before his Oxford tenure, Campbell played for Alberta's champion rugby team in 1925. He was prominent in organizing the Independent Baseball League, formed of teams named Centrals, Elks, Red Socks, YMCA and CNR.

Earlier in 1924, he and A.S. Matheson established the Edmonton and District Hockey Association. Campbell was a longtime secretary of the EDHA, as such, a deledge to annual conclaves of the Canadian Amateur Hockey Association.

In 1933, at the CAHA meeting in Vancouver, Campbell, vice-president of the AAHA, joined Dr. W.G. Hardy,President of the AAHA, from the U. of A., and George Dudley of Midland, Ontario and Ottawa's Cecil Duncan, in promoting the forward pass as a swift method of opening up sluggish hockey. The forward pass previously was a professional tactic devised by the inventive Frank Patrick of Vancouver.

Campbell became a referee in the 20s, tough and competent, squeaky clean as the arbiter of games up to the Allan Cup level. His first pro appearance, on January 25, 1933, featured the Edmonton Eskimos beating the Vancouver Maroons 4-2 in Edmonton. The Eskimo roster included goal tender Earl Robertson, defenceman

Cam Smith and Red Redpath, forwards Art Gagne, Ching Johnson and the slightly immortal Gordon Blanchard (Duke) Keats. Subsitutes were Buster Huffman, Hot Gibson, Laurie Scott and Wilf Kenny.

Campbell's ability to control boisterous games carried him to the refereeing ranks of the NHL, prior to the second great war. Then he enlisted in the Canadian Army as a private, rose to lieutenant-colonel in the tank corps and was mentioned in dispatches for certain valor. He subsequently served with the Canadian prosecutors of Nazi war criminals before being demobilized in 1946 to begin his prolonged presidency of the NHL.

Those are the essential facts on Clarence Sutherland Campbell in Alberta, with scant space for the necessary flavor. Some of that was provided in 1937, in a paragraph of praise written by Tommy Graham in the long-gone "Edmonton Bulletin".

Graham wrote:

> *No man connected with amateur sport in Edmonton has done more toward its promotion and development than Clarence Campbell. The young Edmonton Barrister is the Czar of local sport circles, known by every enthusiast from the smallest lad to the oldest dad.*

Campbell died in the early summer of 1984, old and worn but still administering a NHL fund for impoverished ex-pros. Upon his final admission to the Great Hot Stove League, he may have said merely "Campbell here."

ED BRUCHET — 1911 TO 1979

BY DON H. PILLING, former sports editor, Lethbridge Herald

Edmund George Bruchet was one of a kind.

One of the founding fathers of the minor hockey movement in Lethbridge, he later became a key figure in Canadian junior hockey circles — a man known, respected and admired from coast to coast. Sport, and a desire to assist the youth of our land to become involved in the field of athletic endeavor, was Ed Bruchet's life. And certainly his happiest and most rewarding moments were those times when he was directing the fortunes of his many hockey clubs through the years. Although hockey was number one on his sporting hit parade, he was interested and took an active part in other phases of the athletic scene in Lethbridge and area.

ED BRUCHET

Photo courtesy of Edmonton Archives

Even though he was a young man at the time, he managed Lethbridge Supinas to an Alberta senior men's soccer championship in the early 1930s. And in the early 1940s, it was Ed Bruchet who established the Lethbridge Arcades as one of the real powers in Alberta junior baseball circles. Hockey, however, was where Ed Bruchet made his mark and where his dedication and determination led to the gounding of the Lethbridge Native Son organization. One juvenile and two midget teams put the wheels in motion, followed by the junior Native Sons who became one of the premier organizations in Canadian amateur hockey.

Using his Native Sons as the base, he was the driving force behind the formation of the Alberta Junior Hockey League, eventually teaming up with such junior hockey pioneers as Moose Jaw's Harper Parry and George Vogan to establish the Western Canada Junior League. This was the league that produced an endless stream of talent for the NHL, with dozens of graduates reaching star status in professional ranks and teams which year in and year out, provided formidable opposition for Eastern Canada in the annual chase for the Memorial Cup.

Ed Bruchet's hockey accomplishments were plentiful. He was a coach, manager, scout, executive and a founder who will and should always be fondly remembered as "Mr. Hockey". His chief accomplishment, however, was the pinnacle he attained as a human being. Hockey and sport in general, were, in reality only a part of the major role he played in developing and preparing hundreds of young men for the challenges they would face in their lives ahead. He was their mentor and he was their friend, and the ones who earned his friendship and respect were, indeed, the fortunate ones. You could pay him no higher compliment than to say he was a man's man — genuine, absolutely genuine, in every sense of the word.

To know him was to love him. He was that kind of a rare human being. In fact, when the end was near in November, 1979, before he fell victim to cancer, dozens and dozens of the young men who had carried the Native Son banner proudly returned to see him, to talk to him, to be with him one last time. They came from as far east as Toronto and as far west as Victoria.

And when Ed Bruchet died there wasn't a church in Lethbridge large enough to accommodate the people from all walks of life who wished to pay their final respects. Hockey in Alberta is richer because of Ed Bruchet and that holds true for anybody who knew this man of spirit, substance and integrity.

BILL HUNTER — SELLER OF DREAMS

BY BRENDA ZEMAN, Chief Associate Editor, *Alberta On Ice*

(My sister Brenda and my father Joe co-authored Hockey Heritage: 88 Years of Puck Chasing in Saskatchewan (1983). Brenda is a cultural anthropologist who has made radio and television documentaries for the CBC and has written for newspapers and magazines including Sports Illustrated. She rushed home from the 1985 World Hockey Championships in Prague, Czechoslovakia to help edit this book and make sure she made it in her first Hot Stove League.)

"There's no sin in making money." That's what Bill Hunter told me the first time we met in the fall of '83. If that's the case, Hunter — seller of sporting goods, cards, oil stocks, hockey franchises and dreams — can rest assured there's a spot for him in hockey heaven. Add to that the fact he believes in miracles and he may wind up next to his mentor, the late Pere Athol Murray of Notre Dame College.

BILL HUNTER

Photo courtesy of Provincial Archives

In 1982, Hunter left Edmonton, his adopted city, and came home to Saskatoon. His mission? To work a miracle and bring NHL hockey to the people of Saskatchewan. In no time at all, Alberta's "Wild" Bill Hunter, the man who had masterminded the World Hockey Association, became Saskatchewan's Bill "Messiah" Hunter. He was going to feed the starving multitudes with their first big-time hockey since the 20s.

There was one problem. John Ziegler and the NHL Board of Governors don't believe in miracles or in messiahs in three-piece suits. But as far as Hunter is concerned he has every intention of rising again. Bill Hunter still believes.

Hunter comes from a long line of believers. He says of his father, J.H. "Jack" Hunter, "he never should have been in the civil service. He was entrepreneurial. He believed people should do more than just work...you should put a bit of yourself back into your community."

Bill Hunter was only five years old when the Saskatoon Sheiks; Regina Capitals, Edmonton Eskimos and Calgary Tigers, were the hottest thing going in the coldest rink he can remember. It was 1925 and the Western Canada Professional Hockey League provided Hunter with all the thrills of professional hockey. Little Bill used to go up to the music box in the rafters of Saskatoon's old tin arena and watch players like Bill and Bun Cook, Newsy Lalonde and Red McCusker.

Hunter was passionate about sports. He played every sport going and then he became Saskatchewan's only high school student to coach his school's football team to a city title. From the beginning Hunter had chutzpah.

When Hunter was 18 he ran away from home to go to Notre Dame at Wilcox, Saskatchewan. Hunter says:
I'd seen them play hockey and I wanted to be a Notre Dame Hound. It was the greatest thing that ever happened to me in my life (pause) other than having my family. Father Murray sold people on being individuals, on being an entrepreneur and on not being afraid of failure.

With those thoughts in mind, Hunter became a pilot in World War II, opened a sporting good store in North Battleford after the war, became a broadcaster with CFQC radio and jumped into hockey as part-owner of the senior Regina Capitals. It wasn't long until he saw "the death knell of senior hockey after the demise of the semi-pro league" and turned his attention to junior hockey. It was the start of a long-time rivalry with his best friend, Scotty Munro.

Hunter became a major junior league entrepreneur in the early 50s, first in Saskatchewan and then in Alberta. When the league folded Hunter says he knew it would come back. He was right and by the mid 60s he was a co-owner of the Edmonton Oil Kings. In answer to minor league hockey supporters who opposed the formation of major junior leagues (saying it killed off junior hockey in small centres and hurt minor hockey), Hunter counters:

> *The critics were small empire builders who were envious of major junior league entrepreneurs. We were the best friend minor hockey ever had. The Edmonton Oil Kings gave over $15,000 to minor hockey every year.*

Hunter claims top executives of the CAHA envied the Oil Kings too. According to Hunter in the 1966-67 season the Oil Kings were suspended for not accepting the allotted travel expenses and couldn't compete for the Memorial Cup. (See junior hockey section for complete story.)

St. Catharines played Quebec Ramparts but when the Ontario team was suspended before the end of the series, Hunter called up Leo LaBelle, President of the Quebec Amateur Hockey Association.

> *'Leo, what has the CAHA ever done for you?' I wanted the Oil Kings to play the Ramparts. I told Leo, 'We'll go to the Prime Minister with it.' We arrived in Quebec City to an 800 car parade to signs 'Vive Les Oil Kings!' and 'Vive Le Hunter!' We were the people's choice.*

In 1971 American promoters Dennis Murphy and Gary Davidson contacted Hunter. Their mission? To form the WHA. Hunter's imagination was piqued. "I thought these fellows didn't know anything about hockey but they had a great idea. There was unrest among players in the NHL and owners were arrogant. The climate was right."

Thus began a bitter struggle with the NHL. Hunter says he respected NHL President Clarence Campbell as "a totally dedicated hockey man" but he fought him all the way. Even though the WHA got off the ground and signed seventy eight NHL players in its first season, Hunter always hoped for an amalgamation with the NHL. He says, "The amalgamation (1979) should have happened three years sooner but we couldn't control American owners. They kept breaking commitments. We didn't have a Clarence Campbell." Hunter believes Edmonton would not have a NHL team today if the WHA hadn't paved the way. He believes his obstinancy paid off.

Hunter's every red hair has turned to white and he says he's mellowed; but don't count on it. He may have learned to control his temper but one of his favorite stories is still about Thomas Edison, "One day Edison's assistant said to him,

> *We've tried over 2,000 ways to find light. And we've failed! Edison said, What do you mean, son? We know 2,000 ways that don't work. We haven't failed.*

After 10,000 or more attempts Edison discovered light.

Do you hear that John Ziegler?

SCOTTY MUNRO

BY DUNC SCOTT, former sports writer, Calgary Herald

Under coach Scotty Munro, the Calgary Centennials won three division championships in eight seasons, 1969-1970, 1971-72, and 1973-74. The finished second twice and third once. The only time the rotund Scotsman missed the playoffs was in the 1975-76 season.

SCOTTY MUNRO

The most memorable sports series in junior hockey as far as Calgary fans are concerned was the playoffs against Regina Pats in the 1973-74 season, when the two "power-houses" of the Western Hockey League met in a best-of-seven final. Pats won the series in four straight but each game could have gone either way. The teams were that close.

When Scotty's health started to fail him, junior hockey in Calgary started its decline and it was only through Doug Sauter, a player who came up through the ranks under the tutelege of Scotty and Ernie McLean, did Calgary start its assent again.

When Bob Brownridge owned the Calgary franchise, after the first year and there were severe financial losses at the gate, Brownridge stated, "I wanted the smartest hockey man in Canada to pull the Centennials out of the doldurms and that is why I wanted Scotty".

The first coach Scotty hired in Calgary was Cec Papke, a successful businessman in the oil business and a smart hockey man.

Papke stated:

The only reason Scotty didn't win a Canadian championship was because he let his heart rule in many instances. I had my disagreements with him, as did everyone he came to know, but there wasn't a thing I wouldn't have done for him. He was just that great a guy.

In a bull session with Scotty when the Centennials were playing the Tigers in Medicine Hat in the playoffs, he was asked about the chances that Sauter, a back-up goal tender to John Davidson at the time, would have as coach. "I predict that some day, Dougie will be the best junior coach in Canada," said Munro.

When cancer claimed his life on Friday, September 19, 1975 at just 57 years of age, the sport of hockey lost one of the great men in the game. That was one game that you knew Scotty couldn't beat.

But he was smart enough to get another wise man to guide the destinies of the Western Hockey League in Ed Chynoweth, a man he knew would never let the league die.

The one thing that Scotty wanted to do before leaving this world, was to write a book on coaching junior hockey. But Father Time didn't permit his dream.

Oldtimers in Western Canada will never forget the formation of the Western Canada Junior Hockey League or the World Hockey Association. Three men who were responsible for the formation of these two leagues were often referred to as the "Big Three" — Scotty Munro, Bill Hunter and Ben Hatskin. The new Western Canada League is still the major junior league in Western Canada. The World Hockey Association amalgamated with the National Hocey League. Hunter operated out of Edmonton and is now the chief organizer in trying to obtain a NHL franchise for Saskatoon. He was the promoter for both leagues. Hatskin of Winnipeg was the financial benefactor and Munro the idea man.

Wherever Scotty Munro went, hockey blossomed, and the proof of that was in Calgary, particularly at the junior level. In the Foothills city, attendance at junior hockey games averaged between 200-300 and when Munro came to the city the attendance improved immediately. It was not uncommon to read about and see crowds of between 5,000 and 6,000 at the Stampede Corral for league games and they pushed high into the 7,000 for playoffs.

Born in Cabri, Saskatchewan, November 10, 1917, Roderick Neil "Scotty" Munro started his career in hockey as a goal tender in Shackelton, just 8 miles west of his birth place. Later in life he moved to Melville where he spent his recreation time playing hockey in the winter and baseball in the summer.

On February 5, 1937, Scotty married Rose Bashnick in Melville. Rose was not only his wife but partner in all his endeavors. During Scotty's long coaching career he was suspended several times and sometimes Rose filled in for him behind the bench. (One might have guessed in their courting days they were bound to be united in wedlock as Scotty was a catcher in baseball and Rose a catcher in women's fastball.)

In 1939, Scotty and Rose moved to Yorkton where he made his coaching debut with a midget team and two years later, while employed with British American Oil Company, Scotty and Rose were on the move again, this time to Moose Jaw.

Still connected with hockey as a coach and manager, Scotty took over the reins of the Juvenile team in the 1945-46 season. One of his players on that team was Emile "The Cat" Francis, now general manager of the NHL Hartford Whalers. The two of them kept close contact with one another and they always talked hockey in their many meetings. In the 1945-46 season, Scotty and the late Father Athol Murray of Notre Dame College in Wilcox, Saskatchewan became associated.

He then moved to Lethbridge, Alberta and coached the Native Sons in the 1947-48 season. With general manager and long time close friend, Ed Bruchet, they made hockey history as the first hockey team in the world to charter a plane for a game. They chartered a flight to Vancouver that year.

In 1948-49, Bellevue enticed Scotty to come to the mining town in southern Alberta where he coached the Bellevue Lions until they folded in 1950. While in Bellevue, he and Bruchet helped form the original Western Canada Junior Hockey League in the 1948-49 season involving teams from Alberta and Saskatchewan. After the Lions folded, Scotty and Rose pulled up stakes and moved to Humboldt, Saskatchewan, where they operated a bowling alley as well as the Humboldt Indians Junior hockey club. In 1955, Scotty and his Indians fought their way to the Western final but lost to the strong Regina Pats.

Two years later, Scotty moved his team to Estevan and the Bruins were born. While in Estevan, Scotty spearheaded the construction of a new arena. Scotty had Moe George, brother of Jeep George, present scout for NHL Scouting Services, as his first coach and one of his former players, Ernie McLean, as an assistant coach. When Scotty was suspended for hitting a referee, he brought in Howie Milford, who played for him as a juvenile in Moose Jaw and as a junior in Lethbridge as his second coach.

In the summer of 1968, he left the Estevan Bruins to Ernie McLean and Bill Shinsky and answered the call of the late Bob Brownridge in Calgary, to come and coach the Centennials. When Scotty came to Calgary, the Centennials had won only 13 games in 116 tries and were playing before a handful of fans. But it must be remembered that the Centennials had a lot of 14 and 15-year-olds competing with the other clubs.

Scotty brought three Estevan Bruins with him when he moved to Calgary — goal tender Ed Dyck, defenceman Gary Braun and Jimmy Watson. Watson, a tough, 15-year-old youngster was a star with the Centennials and later was instrumental in helping Philadelphia Flyers win two Stanley Cups. There are literally thousands of successful businessmen, hockey players, fans and other people who are proud to be able to say, "I knew Scotty Munro."

LEO "THE LIP" LECLERC

BY J. LORNE BRAITHWAITE

(J. Lorne Braithwaite was a defenceman with the Oil Kings from 1957-61, and later with the U. of A. Golden Bears and Lacombe Rockets. He has followed in Leo's footsteps. In December of 1985, when the Thornhill, Ontario Midget Thunderbirds went to Finland, Sweden and Russia, his son Troy was a forward with the club. Presently, Braithwaite is President of Cambridge Leaseholds Limited, Toronto.)

Jim Christenson, owner of the old Edmonton Waterloo Mercury Hockey team, in the early 50s wanted a Junior Hockey team also. Thus, in 1951 Leo LeClerc started out as Manager of the Edmonton Oil Kings Junior Hockey Club.

Leo "The Lip", "The Skulker", "The Pipe-Cleaner", and "The Hockey Stick" are all handles that junior hockey players put on Leo LeClerc during the flamboyant era that he was General Manager of the Edmonton Oil Kings. Leo was famous for lurking in the shadows of the Old Edmonton Gardens (since demolished), watching what was going on both on and off the ice. The Oil Kings, in the 50s and 60s were, for the most part, sponsored by the Detroit Red Wings and were considered one of the premier Junior 'A' franchises in Canada. Leo, as General Manager, in my opinion, did an excellent job working for and with young hockey players from all across Canada, for those days the franchise had that kind of draw.

LEO LE CLERC

All Leo wanted was media recognition and an expense account In Bryson Stone's opinion; perhaps the club should go first class, and certainly little or no pay for the players was his success formula. Fred Windwick and Leo, both working at Edmonton Telephones (Yellow Pages), teamed up in 1951 and designed a crest with a local artist and the Oil Kings were born. All of the initial equipment for the Kings was bought at Woodward's old downtown store at 101st Street and 102 Avenue.

LeClerc's record in hockey speaks for itself. The Oil Kings under LeClerc ended up with six Abbott Cup championships, several Memorial Cup finals, and a Memorial Cup winner. LeClerc's energy and drive can be said to be responsible for the super record of the Kings. As manager Leo LeClerc was and is one of Canada's most unique characters. There are hundreds of LeClerc stories.

There was one time that Leo caught the ire of Hal Pawson, Sport Editor of the "Edmonton Journal". Leo and Mike Lashuk concocted a plan where Leo was going to announce that Lashuk could no longer play football if he played hockey. Pawson wrote about this terrible situation.

Mothers phoned, hockey fans phoned to register their displeasure. Lashuk still played football and hockey; however, Hal Pawson did write-up the story and was not very pleased with Leo. He would have liked to have been in on the charade. All Leo wanted was a bit of publicity for the Kings.

One of the better stories that I recollect was in the spring of 1961, in the Memorial Cup Final in Toronto where the Oil Kings were playing against St. Catharine Tee Pees (Chico Maki, Pat Stapleton, Roger Crozier). We were staying at the Westbury Hotel, on Yonge St., and every morning Leo would roust us out of bed and send us on a two mile stroll around the adjacent park. Leo, of course, would stay in the hotel lobby and have coffee, waiting for the team to return with Coach Harry Allen. One morning, when it was particularly brisk, Phil Dutton noted that Leo was standing in the lobby with a wolf fur coat on, waiting the return of the team.

Phil, at that point, proceeded to tell Leo that he really should not wear a fur coat because he's so skinny that people will think that he's a pipe-cleaner. The team roared with laughter at that comment for it was rare that a player could get the last word on Leo.

Another incident that I recollect from those great years in my life, was the occasion of the 1972 Russia/Canada series. Roger Bourbonnais and I, along with Waldo Serediak and some of the Oil Kings alumnae, decided to hold a ten-year Oil King reunion. We held it at Roger's house in St. Albert. Eatons, who was my employer at that time, provided three or four colour televisions so that we could all watch the particular game of the series that was on that evening. We also had large photographs of Leo blown up and posted around Roger's home. As the evening progressed and people became more relaxed, the truth on Leo's management style eventually came to the forefront.

Bruce MacGregor and Don Chiz got into a big argument over Leo paying Bruce more than the so called standard pay scale. I was trying to convince Leo that the team should have been payed holiday pay! Wayne Mulloin (Gert), at one stage of the evening, proceeded to hurl a lawn dart at a head and shoulders photograph of Leo with the statement, "I hope I get his bad eye". All in good fun, of course, for it was again a rare occasion on which the hockey players could poke fun at Leo with no threat of repercussions.

Leo was tough with the kids who played on the Edmonton Oil King's team. In the early years of the team he had his so-called standard salary rates for the players. They were as follows: first year was $100 a month, second year $125 and the fourth year $175. However, you could always count on a free cup of coffee in the old King Edward Hotel downtown.

Leo was famous for building up the already inflated egos of the young hockey players if only to "poke a big hole in the balloon" at the appropriate time to further the cause of the team. I can vividly recall Leo telling me on several occasions on the deadline date for signing a contract that "he liked the way farm boys acted and cut their hair (brush cut)". At the time I was cynical. But today I look back with fond memories and on behalf of all the players that had the Leo LeClerc experience I say — "Leo, thank you for the memories and the part you played in our Hockey Lives".

The history of the development of the game of Hockey in Western Canada would not be complete without many words and acolades about Mr. Leo LeClerc for the great contribution he made over the years as General Manager of the Edmonton Oil Kings from 1951 to 1965.

ED CHYNOWETH — WHL PRESIDENT

BY RICHARD DOERKSON, Executive Assistant, WHL

Ed Chynoweth has been President of the WHL for the past thirteen years with only one year out of the chair during that span.

His first tenure started in December of 1972, when a committee of Del Wilson, Bill Burton and the late Scotty Munro, hired him as the first full time President in the league's history. His first title was as an assistant to executive secretary Tom Fisher, who resigned his position effective June, 1973. The League office was moved from New Westminster to Saskatoon in early January and Chynoweth was to assume presidential duties in June.

But an incident in the playoffs that spring almost robbed the WHL of his services. Munro felt that his Calgary Centennials were mistreated by the Medicine Hat Tigers in the opening West Division playoff round and wanted some disciplinary action from Chynoweth, who, in his position as assistant, could not rule on the issue. At this point Munro vowed to run the newly hired executive out of the League. It was at the annual meeting in Saskatoon that the whole affair was finally straightened out, and Chynoweth was in the chair to stay.

ED CHYNOWETH

Through the early heat the Board of Governors realized that they had acquired a top notch executive, one who could handle adversity and yet assert leadership. Through several following achievements Chynoweth proved his value to both the WHL and Major Junior Hockey in Canada.

In 1974, he persuaded the WHL, OHA and QMJHL that the West could host the Memorial Cup and make money. Although there were many skeptics, Chynoweth's foresight was proven correct when Calgary, as host, did a tremendous job in staging the affair. The tournament was a financial success, and in terms of the competitions Regina Pats won the Cup. In 1977, the Memorial Cup was held in Vancouver, and in 1983 in Portland, Oregon, and both were successes.

Chynoweth was also responsible for originating the Labatt Cup, the first International Junior Hockey Tournament to be held in Canada, which took place in four Alberta centres (Calgary, Edmonton, Medicine Hat and Lethbridge) over Christmas of 1977.

Another formation which Chynoweth helped to initiate was the Canadian Major Junior Hockey League. The original groundwork had been done by Regina's Del Wilson and Jim Piggott from Saskatoon, Howard Darwin from Ottawa and John Horman from Montreal. With Chynoweth's driving force providing the impetus, the CMJHL became a reality uniting the three Tier 1 Leagues into one association. Under this umbrella organization, he engineered an agreement with the NHL for the payment of players drafted from the CMJHL. (See Hot Stove League for the First NHL agreement in 1939.)

After a one year leave of absence in 1979-80, when he took a job as General Manager and part owner of the Calgary Wranglers, he returned to the President's chair.

Ed and his wife Linda have two sons, 18 year old Jeff and 16 year old Dean. Jeff is currently taking journalism at SAIT in Calgary, while handling assistant trainer duties for visiting clubs at NHL games in the Saddledome. Dean is playing midget hockey for the Calgary Buffalos and is on the protected list of the Medicine Hat Tigers. Dean recently accompanied the Alberta Midget All-Star Team on a two week tour of China , and was also on the Under 17 B.C-Alberta All-Star Team (Team Pacific) which defeated the Russian National Midget Team in January of 1985.

ALBERTA AND HEILONGJIANG HOCKEY EXCHANGE — 1984

BY PHIL CLARKE

(An Alberta All-Star squad of under 17 age players toured China for part of November and December, 1984. The arrangements for the trip were handled by the AAHA and the Alberta Government.

Coach Wally Kozak, assistant Dennis Zukiwsky and Phil Clarke as manager handled the team. Representing the AAHA were President Orest Korbutt and executive member Vern Paul. Mission head was Julian Nowicki along with Al Zimmerman from the provincial government.

Clarke compiled a diary of the trip dealing mainly with the sights and sounds of China as it affected the players and personnel with the club. The following is a portion of the trip rewritten for "Alberta on Ice", which highlights a 22 hour plus train trip from Beijing to Harbin. To put it in gentle terms, coach Kozak referred to it as "22 hours without facilities".)

The team arrived in Beijing on a dull, drab, gray day. We were to stay in the airport for an hour or so and then switch to Air China for a one hour and twenty minute flight to Harbin. It dind't seem like a big deal as we were in the Capital of China and going to a provincial capital, but the next flight was in four days.

Orest Korbutt and Al Zimmerman checked out taking the train. It seemed like a good idea except it was to take 22 hours. The next day, on November 17, 1984 the day began at 5:45 a.m. A day I will always remember.

At the train station there were literally thousands of people. Two players, Daryn McBride and Kevin Hoffman handed out a few Canadian pins and a mob scene developed. It took a guard to clear away the crowd. We found out that our luggage finally got on the train. Apparently a truck from the Canadian Embassy was brought into the train station without a permit. We were charged $500 to move about 64 pieces plus we had to buy plastic locks for each bag. Finally everyone was aboard.

Car #9 was a coach with hard seats, small tables and not much else. There were at least 250 people trying for 75 seats. Our team had no idea of the type of seats they had but found themselves sitting beside non English speaking Chinese who carried little pieces of paper in their hands.

It was thought these people had tickets for specific seats so the boys got out of their seats. A stampede of three or four racing to each seat resulted. After hearing calls for help, the best we could think of was to do nothing. In other words, don't move under any circumstances. Finally, we were able to get a sleeper car with bench bunks which looked like heaven compared to #9.

Brian Shavchook told me later that he pannicked trying to get out of Car #9 and that his life "flashed before his eyes."

Coach Wally Kozak, in an effort to keep the team loose had them doing isometrics in the sleeper car compartment at 3 p.m. and again at 7 p.m.

On the train we had our first true Chinese meal. It consisted of items most of us had never seen before. The team finally slept where they could and I ended up reading a book in the train corridor from 11:30 p.m. to 4:30 a.m.

The washrooms on the train were also an experience. As it turned out, anyone using the facilities wondered if they could hang on for the duration without going back.

On this trip Zimmerman had the task of negotiating for seats and if possible, to get better locations on the train. Without an interpreter the best he and the rest of us could do was sign language.

It was hard to tell when day four ended and five began but at 7:15 a.m. on November 18, 1984...we arrived in Harbin...on time. Some 700 miles were covered in the train experience of our lives.

* * *

The new experience of those on the trip could not be documented in total so one aspect was highlighted. Clarke reported:

> *The Chinese people tried very hard to give us the best they had and to make our stay as comfortable and enjoyable as possible.*
>
> *The traffic in China is unbelievable...In China it is the responsibilty of the pedestrian to miss the vehicle...I don't think we saw more than two accidents. At least in China it works.''*

ALBERTA UNDER 17 HOCKEY TEAM

Top row (l to r): Dennis Zukiwsky (assistant coach), Rob DiMaio, Don Schmidt, Barry Chyzowski, Jeff Gawlicki, Roby Goodwin, Mike Van Slooten, Wally Kozak (coach), Phil Clarke (manager). Middle row: Kevin Hoffman, Ron Lebsak, Daryn McBride, Bryan Bosch, Braden Shavchook, Mark Kuntz, Brian Gerrits, Garth Premak, Dean Chynoweth, Vernon Paul (Alberta Amateur Hockey Association representative). Front row: Darryl Davis, Brad Werenka, Dan Logan, Orest Korbutt (president, Alberta Amateur Hockey Association), Julian Nowicki (assistant deputy minister, Alberta Recreation and Parks), Alan Zimmerman (consultant, Alberta Recreation and Parks), Shaun Clouston, Tracy Katelnikoff, Randy Kwong, Paul Krake.

On the ice Alberta won five games and lost one during the 14 days in China. A game is a game but to play and travel in China was an experience Clarke and the rest will never forget.

Phil Clarke is a lawyer and a past President of the EMHA.

ALBERTA COACHES TO CHINA — 1983

Hockey coaches clinics are now an integral part of the AAHA program. Acceptance of the program by coaches in Alberta is no longer questioned. Alberta coaches have gone to other provinces to do clinics, but two went one step further. They went to China.

In the fall of 1983 as part of a sports exchange between the governments of Canada, China, the provinces of Alberta and Heilongjiang and the hockey associations of each country, two Albertans, Dennis Zukiwsky of St. Paul and R. Bruce Hutton of Grimshaw, travelled to China to teach hockey. Accompanying the Albertans was Dr. Cecil (Cec) Eaves of the University of Windsor who had made previous trips in 1973 and 1978.

The threesome spent three months coaching the national Youth (under 17), one Provincial team, and also did a number of coaching clinics for various levels of Chinese hockey.

The exchange saw Alberta receive Chinese expertise in Table Tennis and Gymnastics. This type of sports exchange will continue between the oil producing provinces of Heilongjiang and Alberta. In the fall of 1984, Wally Kozak took a team of midgets to China.

One of the forerunners of hockey coaching clinics in Alberta was operated by Labatts. On November 27, 1974, 133 directors or coaches attended a clinic in Edmonton.

In Alberta, Wally Bentley and Bob Kabel, who were the representatives of Labatts did many of the on ice and classroom sessions. Since then the AAHA, under Technical Directors Dave Simpson and now Dale Henwood, has developed a strong program where almost every coach in Alberta receives training. Labatts has continued to assist financially throughout Canada.

For the 1984-85 season the AAHA conducted 145 clinics. 1255 coaches took Level I, 1203 at Level II, 245 at Level III and 82 at Level IV were certified. Indeed, coaching clinics for hockey coaches are a major part of the AAHA program.

MARK MESSIER — FROM A FAMILY OF CHAMPIONS

BY TOMMY GRAHAM

Mark Messier, the fast skating, rugged centre sometimes winger for the two time Stanley Cup champion Edmonton Oilers, comes from a family of champions. Many of Mark's relatives have acquired hockey fame as far back as 1923. The Messiers, Deas and Rimstads probably make the most prominent hockey clan in Alberta.

Howard Dea, Mark's great uncle was a member of the 1923 Edmonton Eskimos, champions of Western Canada and Stanley Cup finalists. Howard received a paltry $116 as his share of the Stanley Cup pool, while Mark, in 1985, received over $20,000. Three of Howard's sons; Gerry, Billy and Murray carried on the family tradition.

Gerry's club, the HMCS Nonsuch won the Alberta junior hockey championship in 1943. The team was unable to progress any further because of military restrictions. Billy made his mark playing for the Lethbridge Native Sons in 1948-49, and later with the Edmonton Flyers and Detroit Red Wings. Murray, the youngest of the Dea trio, played midget and juvenile hockey and earned a hockey scholarship to the university of Colorado. He then helped the Lacombe Rockets to the 1961 Western Canada Intermediate championship.

The Rimstad brothers, Louis, Morey and Walter, grew up in Edmonton's McCauley community. This trio of pucksters also knew their way around the rink.

MARK MESSIER

Photo courtesy of Bob Mummery

Louis, the oldest, did not fare as well as Morey and Walter, but "Big Lou" made his presence known in both hockey and football. Morey and Walter both played for the Edmonton Athletic Club juniors. Their play in 1934 helped the EAC's to Edmonton's first western junior title, the Abbott Cup.

Walter "Fats" Rimstad was a member of the 1950 Lethbridge Maple Leafs who won the Western Intermediate championship. In 1951 Walter, and the Leafs, won the World Amateur championship.

Walter acquired a new nickname in Lethbridge. His teamates pinned the name "Whitey" on him because he had a good head of light blonde hair. "Whitey" was also a member of the Currie Barracks Army team during World War II.

Morey was undoubtedly the best of the Rimstads. This determined talented centre was a gifted sharp shooter and an unselfish playmaker. He played professional hockey for four years at St. Louis and then four more with the Buffalo Bisons.

After Morey's professional days in the American Hockey League, he joined the Edmonton Flyers in the Western Canada Senior League. He helped the Flyers to Edmonton's one and only Allan Cup in 1947-48. He retired as a player and became the first coach of the Edmonton Oil Kings.

Morey's son Dave followed in his father's footsteps. He played for the 1955-56 Edmonton Oil Kings, Toron-

MARK MESSIER

Photo courtesy of Bob Mummery

to St. Mike's juniors and then professional with Seattle and Victoria before his hockey retirement.

Mark Messier's father, Doug, while maybe not as proficient as his son, did earn respect as a player. He gained recognition as a player on the Edmonton Oil Kings, Lacombe Rockets and Edmonton Flyers. The Rockets won the Western Intermediate Championship in 1960-61 and the professional Flyers won the 1961-62 Western hockey League title.

Doug became a coach and took the Spruce Grove Mets to the 1974-75 Centennial Cup for tier 2 junior hockey in Canada.

Mark's older brother Paul was an accomplished player for the 1974-75 Spruce Grove Mets. Paul was one of his dad's better hockey players throughout that year.

The Messier hockey relations are not restricted to the province of Alberta. Mark's mother. Mary Jean Dea Messier, is the aunt of Don Murdock who has played several seasons with the New York Rangers and Detroit Red Wings.

The Messier trophy room boosts a large collection of trophies, silverware and pennants. If one adds up all the major trophies available to Alberta teams; the only one missing is the Memorial Cup.

Angie Dea, the wife of Howard, 88 years old is still an avid hockey fan. She married Howard on New Years Day, 1921, and has watched the families participation in hockey ever since. She is always ready to discuss the entire family at reunions or get togethers.

Mark Messier won the Conn Symthe Trophy as the Most Valuable Player in the 1984 playoffs and helped the Oilers to the Stanley Cup. In 1985 the Oilers won the crown again and it looks like they can do it a few more times.

They are indeed a family of champions.

THE BROTHER ACTS

BY TOMMY GRAHAM, Associate Editor, Alberta On Ice

(Tommy has seen every one of these brothers play.)

Over the years in Alberta hockey a number of brothers have gained recognition and gone on to fame and glory as a result of their play. Many did not make it to the "Big Time" to perform in the NHL — the ultimate goal, but in the majority of cases they did achieve success in their respective leagues.

More famous among the brother acts were the Rimstads (See Mark Messier — From a Family of Champions), Colvilles, Carses, Babychs, Kilburns and Sutters (See The Sutter Story).

THE COLVILLES (NEIL AND MAC)

Neil and Mac Colville, who hailed from the northeast section in the Alberta Avenue District, of Edmonton were regarded in their young playing days as two of the finest and most promising hockey players in the city. As midget and juvenile players, the Colvilles led their respective leagues as top scorers and playmakers and paced their teams to championships.

The Colville brothers gained major attention when they moved into the junior ranks and played for the EAC's. It was their performance with this organization's teams that attracted the interest of National Hockey League scouts and they made it to the "Big Apple" playing for New York Rovers before turning pro with the New York Rangers. Both gaining further stardom.

Neil was considered, in his prime, as one of the headiest hockey players that ever laced on hockey skates. He was a talented, abundantly gifted puckster, the type that separates the merely great from the super star.

Neil had the uncanny skill of deaking the opposition out of position and heading in to score or passing to allow a teammate to tally. He was a heads up hockey player that seemed to always be in the right spot at the right time and he made his prowess on the ice recognized.

During the second war Neil played for the Ottawa Commandoes and helped win the Allan Cup. When his playing days were over he made his name in the business world on the west coast and is a successful business personality in Vancouver.

Mac, while maybe not quite as talented overall, was nonetheless a brilliant hockeyist. He starred in many encounters with his scoring ability and did not take a backseat to any one.

Mac played for the Calgary Currie Army team during the war years and made his home in the southern city after he retired from hockey. He was employed as an electrician in Calgary and still makes Calgary his home.

THE CARSES (BILL AND BOB)

Bill and Bob Carse, who South Edmonton sport enthusiasts used to brag about, along with Joe and Buster Brown and Jimmy and Bob Graham, both made a name for themselves in the professional ranks.

Bill and Bob were better than average puck-chasers while playing at the midget and juvenile level and were in demand when they graduated to junior status.

Sons of a well-known and prominent plumbing contractor, the Carse brothers shone as juniors before turning professional. Bill played for the professional Edmonton Eskimos, along with Morey Rimstad before they both went to Vancouver. Bill played one year for Chicago Black Hawks. After his junior stint in Edmonton, Bob played for Cleveland in the AHL and makes his home there. Bill lives in Penticton, B.C.

THE BABYCH BOYS (DAVE AND WAYNE)

The Babych brothers, Dave and Wayne, are Edmonton raised players who made it to the NHL as a result of their stellar performance in the minor circuits.

Their sporadic rise to recognition gained momentum as they advanced in age. They excelled at the midget and juvenile level and hit the spotlight with their performance as juniors.

Sturdy Dave and his agile brother Wayne, bewitched, bothered and bewildered their opponets throughout their youthful days. It was enough to attract the attention of NHL scouts.

Dave plays for the Winnipeg Jets while Wayne is presently performing for the Pittsburgh Penguins.

THE BENNING BROTHERS (JIM, MARK AND CRAIG)

Another combination of brothers who have managed to acquire attention and recognition in the puck chasing domain are the Bennings.

Elmer Benning, the boy's father, an admitted hockey enthusiast, is largely responsible for the success that his youngsters have and are achieving. He encouraged them to participate in the game and assisted them in every way possible with the assistance and blessing of his wife.

The boys did the rest.

The older of the trio, Jim is presently on the Toronto Maple Leafs roster and is one of their top performers.

Mark, who was considered potential NHL material with a promising future, decided to forego the urge to play pro and opted for a University eduction, with the view to looking at future hockey heights later. He is presently playing for Harvard University Crimson of the Ivy League.

Craig is only a youngster, but at 13 years of age, he has gained recognition for his style of play. A defenceman like big brother Jim, Craig is presently playing for Scott Pump in the Edmonton Metropolitan Hockey Association.

He has attracted the attention of three teams in the Western Hockey League, the Portland Winter Hawks, the Moose Jaw Warriors and the Kamloops Blazers.

Standing 5'7'' and weighting 150 pounds, Craig feels he has to fill out a bit before thinking of his hockey future, despite the fact that he is playing quite well in the bantam major 'AA' league this season. He admits he might, like brother Craig, opt to seek a college education rather than a pro hockey career. But adds, "It's a little too early to think about it."

THE KILBURNS (CLIFF, JIMMY, COLIN, DOUG)

The Kilburns grew up on Edmonton's soutside, moving from the Bonnie Doon area to 9864-82 Avenue to the Tipton Block at 10359-82 Avenue during their youth. They were spunky, hard rock performers. Short in stature but solid, they were continually kidded about their height which averaged 5'7'' to 5'8''.

Cliff ("two foot"), Jimmy ("one and one half foot") and Colin ("Tonto" or "Rock") all started as goalies. When the oldest (Cliff) started in the net, the rest wanted to follow suit. Doug was a defenceman.

Cliff was one of the goalies who "took on" Billy "The Kid" Taylor in the Memorial Cup final of 1939 for the Edmonton EAC's. Jimmy continued the tradition and played goal on the winning Waterloo Mercurys of 1950 in the World Hockey championship.

Colin switched from goal to become a rugged and durable forward and later defenceman on many nights for 15 years of pro hockey in the American and Western Hockey Leagues. He scored over 350 goals in pro hockey in the 50s and early 60s. He played Intermediate hockey with the New Method Laundry pucksters winning an Alberta Championship before becoming a junior hockey player with the Wetaskiwin Canadians.

Doug, "Sonny," the kid brother, made his mark playing for the world famous Grant: Billy, and Dick Warwick led Penticton Vs of 1955.

The B.C. club's victory over the Russian "Bear" squad is still regarded as one of Canada's greatest moments in hockey history ranking with the 1972 Canada-Russia Series. Doug made them keep their heads up in the 5-0 win.

Jimmy's son Randy, carries on the sport's tradition broadcasting on K-97 Radio in Edmonton, while Colin's son Barry, coaches Spokane Flames in the East Kootney Junior Hockey League.

The seven Miller brothers (See Intermediate Hockey 1920) from Calgary all played on the same team in the southern city back in 1920. Another brother act that achieved media and fan attention was the Hansens of Camrose.

Twin brothers, Carey and Geoff Wilson, who while born in Winnipeg and played there in their younger days, made their debut to the hockey limelight at the age of 16 while playing for the Calgary Chinooks in the Alberta Junior Hockey League. Both were drafted — Centre Carey by the Chicago Black Hawks in 1980, and Geoff, a right winger, by the Pittsburg Penguins in 1981.

Carey is presently with the Calgary Flames, while Geoff, who felt he was destined to the minor leagues after not being able to cut it to the satisfaction of his coaches in the NHL, opted to attend college rather than remain in the farm circuit. He is attending Mount Royal College in Calgary.

OTHER BROTHER COMBOS

Over the years playing together or for other teams in the various leagues surfaced in the hockey picture.

There was Jimmy Graham, the shifty play-making star and sharpshooter with the Gainer Superiors who stole the spotlight from younger brother Bob.

Bunny Dame gained more fame than brother George.

Danny McLeod topped big brother Tommy.

Tom Devaney Sr. slightly shaded brothers Charlie and Eddie.

Louis Trudel made the NHL and the Chicago Black Hawks while brother Eddie had to be content with his role in the amateurs.

Andy "Shorts" Purcell was a starry player in the Edmonton amateur ranks but big brother Eddie managed to make it to the professional level for several years.

The McCallum brothers, Jack, Mackie, Kitchen and Norm, who grew up in Edmonton's west end community of Glenora, were better than average performers in their heyday in the minor amateur leagues.

Sports fans will recall a lot of other brothers who played the game in the province such as the Graham brothers, who played, managed and coached, the Gooders from Olds, the Dorohoys from Medicine Hat, the Jerwas from the Crowsnest Pass loop, the Hucals and Michaluks of Calgary, the Wrights from Drumheller, the Blacks, the MacKays, the Haleys, the Beauchamps, the Mohers, the MacPhersons, the Mahers, the Dawes, the Zapernicks, Bob, Tom Jr. and John Devaney of the U. of A., just to mention some that come to mind and now to the famed present day Sutter clan who have six brothers playing in the NHL.

FOOTNOTE:

When George Hughes suggested we contact Tommy Graham to edit and write in this publication, we secured the services of a man with over sixty years of newspaper experience. We realized he was well versed in sports activities at all levels. We discovered that his first interest in hockey developed as a newsboy selling the *Edmonton Bulletin* and *Journal* on the corner of Johnsons Cafe on 101 St. and Jasper Ave. His customers included Duke Keats, Eddie Shore, Joe Simpson and Art Gagne.

Tommy was a young friend of Deacon White and Bill Tobin. He was persuaded by these hockey people to apply for a job as a copy boy for the Journal. He then developed into a full-fledged newspaper writer.

Some of Tommy's relations have also made their mark in hockey. The Graham boys, Frank, Jim, Hal, Norm and John, sons of his brother Frank and his wife Kitty, all played and later coached. Frank, the oldest, played in the Edmonton Knights of Columbus leagues and went on to play for the Combines, Nuggets, Monarchs and now with the oldtimer Prime Evils. Jim played for the Oil Kings and the Moose Jaw Canucks and turned professional with Kansas City, Denver, San Diego and Dallas Black Hawks. Hal played for the Drumheller Falcons, Medicine Hat Tigers, Cape Cod Cubs, Johnston Jets and NAIT. Norm and John played in the K. of C. program and later joined Jim as assistant coaches in the program.

Tommy's sister Mary and late husband Fred were strong sports enthusiasts. Their second son Bill La Forge became coach of the Vancouver Canucks. (Bill is featured in Alberta Senior Hockey in the late 1970's.)

Another brother Jack has a son Marty who played junior hockey in Edmonton and was an All Star.

SUTTER COUNTRY — SECTION 1-49-12 COUNTY OF BEAVER

BY BRENDA ZEMAN

1-49-12 could well represent three choices in Loto 649. But in Viking, Alberta, 120 kilometres east of Edmonton, it represents the farm of Grace and Louis Sutter, parents of the most famous brother act in the National Hockey League. There have been other NHL brother acts — the Bentleys (Reg, Doug and Max), the Bouchers (Frank, Buck, Billy and Bob) and the Conachers (Lionel, Roy and Charlie) to name a few — but none to match the "Sutter Six." The odds of having seven sons in one family or six brothers playing in the NHL, in fact, are far less likely than someone winning the Loto 649 jackpot (see footnote).

Main Street Viking is lined with the likes of Rudy's Restaurant, Viking Pool Hall and Barber Shop, the Weekly Review newspaper office. The Viking Meat Market proclaims itself "Home of the Viking Sausage," but in this town of 1,227 people hockey pucks sometimes sell faster than sausage.

Take, for example, May of 1984 when Ray Labreche's Viking Texaco was selling gasoline along with pucks with NHL crests. The Edmonton Oiler crested pucks sold out quickly. But, in Viking, St. Louis Blues, Chicago Black Hawks, New York Islanders and Philadelphia Flyers crested pucks were hot items too. Not surprising since Brian Sutter is captain of the Blues, Darryl Sutter is captain of the Black Hawks, Duane and Brent Sutter play with the Islanders and the twins Richard and Ronald Sutter wear the Flyer jersey.

The oldest brother Gary is the only one who did not make the jump to professional hockey. His forte is coaching and he has worked for clubs in Red Deer (Rustlers), Vegreville, Calgary (Canucks) and in Lethbridge (Broncos). Gary was always there to guide his younger brothers in minor hockey.

But then so were Grace and Louis. Viking's Gary Wolosinka who coached four Sutter boys says:

THE SUTTER BROTHERS

Brent, Darryl, Ron, Rich (now with Philadelphia), Duane, Brian.   *Photo courtesy of Paul Woodhouse, Edmonton Sun*

Grace spent more time at the arena than the caretaker and Louis was always there to raise hell with referees whenever one of his boys got a close call on a penalty! Grace and Louis drove the boys all over and if ever there was a tournament in Viking, Grace would help organize and serve breakfast for all the teams.

Grace does not think her devotion was extraordinary; nor does she have any explanation why six of her boys are in the NHL. "Once the first seemed to make it the rest just wanted to carry on," she says simply. She adds, "all my boys are aggressive."

Percy Wilkie, former owner of the IGA where Grace now works, knows exactly what Grace is talking about:

I coached the twins for two years. They were dedicated kids and they hated to lose. I remember Grace used to deal in the IGA. I used to josh back and forth with her and call her "Coach" when the twins were six or seven years old. One day one of the twins — I don't remember which one — didn't like me teasing his mother. He grabbed my leg and bit it in the IGA aisle!

Gary Wolosinka remembers that one of the twins (he does not remember which one because he could not always tell them apart) also astounded him in the middle of a tiny mite game:

I was getting ready to drop the puck between one of the Sutter twins and a kid from a Bruce, Alberta team. The kid from Bruce looked over at the twin and asked, "Are you one of the Sutters?" I almost dropped the puck early when the twin answered, "What the hell does that matter to you? Let's play!"

The kid from Bruce had every reason to be intimidated. While the Sutters were finishing their minor hockey in Viking they played in an approximate 130 kilometre radius of the town — east as far as Lloydminster, north to Cold Lake, south to Forestberg and as far west as Tofield — and the Sutter name carried weight in minor hockey circles.

But it was not all hockey for the Sutter boys. They were also farm boys with chores to do. Garry Wolosinka recalls that it was not always easy to combine the two but Darryl triumphed even under the most adverse conditions:

The Sutters lived three miles off highway 14 and we had to pick Darryl up for a game in Wainwright. There was such a bad blizzard that we couldn't get into the farmyard. Darryl was so keen to play that he walked three miles with his gear and waited for us on the highway. After the game we let him off at the same point and he walked home instead of spending the night in town. He had chores to do the next morning. Louis is a damn good farmer and he instilled that in his boys.

That kind of determination has carried the Sutters from Viking's Carena Rink (with a two door fire hall attached to its front and livestock pens at its rear) to the top of the hockey world.

Duane has four Stanley Cup rings and Brent two, but the real story of the journey lies in the basement of the Sutter's second home in Viking. It is filled with trophies and assorted hockey memorabilla and remains under the loving care of Grace and Louis Sutter.

Footnote:

The chance of winning Loto 649 (July, 1985) was 13,986.816 to 1, or $.714 \times (10)^7$ (.0000000714)

Professor J.S. Devitt of the Mathematics Department at the University of Saskatchewan has done the following quick calculations on the Sutters based upon estimated numbers.

Devitt explains that "independent probabilities" can change the outcome. For example, once the first Sutter made the NHL the other brothers desire or family influence to do the same cannot be mathematically calculated. Regardless, the odds are astronomical.

(1) If one took 10,000 families who each had seven children the odds of having seven boys or seven girls is $.78 \times (10)^2$ (.0078)

(2) The estimated odds of having six brothers in the 21 team NHL with 25 players based on a 600,000 player minor hockey system in Canada is:

(a) for one player $.875 \times (10)^3$ (.000875)

(b) for six players $.448 \times (10)^{18}$ (.000000000000000000448)

VIKING'S "CARENA"

The Sutters played their minor hockey in the Carena before moving on to juniors. Odds also played a part in the construction of this 1951 building.

Station agent and Mayor of Viking, Lauritz "Raz" Rasmussen spearheaded Viking's first covered rink. It was the first in the area for towns this size. (1951 population was around 700). Along with other members of the community "Raz" designed a plan to sell raffle tickets on automobiles. At first one car a month was drawn for, but this method proved too slow. Then it was decided to raffle off ten cars in one night. Five thousand tickets were sold at $10.00 each. It was easily the largest draw of its kind in Canada.

Problems did occur with the provincial and federal governments, who termed it a lottery. (Lotteries were illegal in 1951.) Somehow, Viking managed to have a second car night where twelve more cares were given away. Thus, the name of the rink is the Carena.

At the official opening the following summer, an estimated 5,000 people were in Viking. Foster Hewitt cut the ribbon.

Viking's "gambles" have paid off.

WAINWRIGHT'S GLEN SATHER

(interviews with Gord Mills, former sports editor of the Wainwright Star Chronicle and Dale Bevans, former Commando teammate)

Most people think that Glen Sather has only recently reached the top of the hockey world as coach of the Edmonton Oilers. But his old friends in Wainwright, Alberta know that Sather has been to the top before — as a 15 year old left winger for the Wainwright Commando seniors of the Battle River Hockey League.

GLEN SATHER

Photo courtesy of Bob Mummery

In 1960 Sather joined the Commandos fresh from success as a Wainwright Midget Elk. He had worked hard as a midget player; he often practised at 6 a.m. at the arena and when he could not get indoor ice, at a slough on the outskirts of town. Sather was never without a towel around his neck to keep warm and a bottle of cough syrup to stave off colds.

As a new Commando, Sather was not content to merely make his name on left wing. That Halloween he scaled 90' up an AGT microwave tower and left a hanging dummy.

The next morning his father looked out and saw the dummy. He called it to Glen's attention but, of course, Glen did not know anything about it. The police chief did, however, and for the second time in two days young Sather scaled the tower and brought down the dummy.

Sather, Ken Kile, Doug Sheffield and Dale Bevans alternated on a forward line. "Glen was so young," recalls Bevans, "that we called him "Chick". He was a good skater but where he really excelled was in checking and getting the puck out of the corner."

One night Sather got left in the corner in Killam. The Commandos had played the Killam Indians and Sather missed his ride. No one knows where Sather spent the night but after it was discovered he was missing, one of the Commandos picked him up the following night. There was a game in Stettler and he was needed on left wing.

Sather was not the only one from Wainwright to ever be stranded. A few years later he was playing for the Edmonton Oil Kings. The team was on its way to the Memorial Cup final in Toronto. Sather had been visiting in Wainwright and he asked his friends Bevans, Rick Walker and Bill Cebuliak to drive him to Edmonton for the King's final practice and to drive his car back to Wainwright.

Sather got to his practice alright and his three friends even enjoyed watching him. After the practice Sather headed for the dressing room and then to Toronto. The only problem was he took the car keys with him. Bevans says, "The three of us were unfamiliar with Edmonton. But, eventually, we found a hotel room and got a ride back to Wainwright. (A pause and a smile.) Glen still owes us one!"

Sather later moved on to professional hockey as a player. When he started a hockey school in Banff he did not forget Wainwright. Gord Mills recalls that "Sather would pay us a visit in the spring and sponsor at least two players from the Wainwright Minor Hockey Association to his hockey school."

Glen's many friends in the Wainwright-Viking area are proud of his accomplishments. But then they are used to seeing Sather at the top!

LONGEVITY

BY R. "DICK" WHITE, Vice President, Killam Indians

Killam, Alberta, population 1000, is located 68 kilometers east of Camrose. For continuous hockey history Killam has few peers in Alberta. Since Killam's beginnings in 1905 hockey has been a major part of winter life. Players from here have moved from road hockey under local streetlights to our local arena and on to senior or professional clubs.

Back row (l to r): Tony Empter, Jack Halls, Dewi Kilpatrick, Lew Johnson, Glen Sather, Dale Bevans, Ralph Bell, Vern White. Front row (l to r): Ed Bozak, Ken Kile, Dave Prior, Gerry Harden, Wayne Boles.

Ron Anderson, Dale Guame, Allen "Bearcat" Murray Sr., Moe Sorken, Russell Grant, Ralph Smith, Ross York and Archie MacEachern are some of the players who advanced. The Killam Indian hockey team was organized in the 1930's and at that time played in the Highway 13 Hockey League. The team is still in operation today as part of the Alberta Major Intermediate Hockey League.

This longevity was almost curtailed when a fire on January 8, 1960, destroyed the Killam Arena. The community regrouped and today a modern arena with artifical ice is home for approximately 20 teams.

Probably the longest regular hockey tournament did not happen in 1985. Archie Black in 1921 organized a New Years tournament that ran until 1984. Killam is proud of this continuity and plans are now underway to restart the tournament in 1986. The town anticipates a long and bright hockey future.

CLOSE SHAVES WITH LLOYD TURNER AND "NEWT"

Edmonton was in a panic. On March 2, 1923 Duke Keats, Eddie Shore and the rest of the professional Edmonton Eskimos Hockey Club were scheduled to play Newsy Lalonde and his Saskatoon Sheiks. But the natural ice was a mess — covered with water and uneven.

Not to worry. A call was put into Lloyd Turner, Manager of Calgary's Victoria Arena, and he showed up with — no, not his own private Zamboni — but with "Newt."

Turner was no ordinary ice barber and Newt was no ordinary ice machine. Actually, Newt pulled the machine. All it took to keep Newt running efficiently was a daily ration of oats and water and maybe a lump of sugar for good measure.

Eskimo Manager Kenny McKenzie had made the final arrangements. It was such an important event that Edmonton's Mayor Duggan met Turner and his prized horse Newt at the train station. Other city dignitaries were there including City Commissioner Yorath.

Turner claimed that he alone could work with Newt. He said that Newt was the best horse for the job; in fact, he believed Newt was the best horse for the job in western Canada and no horse in Edmonton could match him. Newt's only bad habit, according to Turner, was "that of rearin'" and that was impossible to correct "because of the high altitude".

Newt also pulled a flawless machine. It was made of steel and Turner claimed it was designed for Calgary's arena by Henry Ford himself. It could shave off ice as thin as tissue paper or as thick as half a foot.

Newt was scheduled to make a personal appearance at the March 2nd game but as the "Edmonton Bulletin" reported the following day:

The Ice Barber (Turner) had worked on it all day with his shaver and it was flooded during the afternoon with excellent results.

Unfortunately, Mr. Turner was unable to exhibit his faithful assistant Newt and it was a diappointment to the multitude...Newt was indisposed and declined to make an appearance.

Edmonton Eskimos defeated the Saskatoon Sheiks 8-1. (Later in the season the Eskimos lost to the Ottawa Senators in the Stanley Cup final.)

Turner, Shore, Keats and Lalonde all ended up in Canada's Hockey Hall of Fame, perhaps, as the story shows, with a little help from Newt.

SINGERS ON ICE

Interviews with Brian "Baritone" Boytang and Norman "Tenor" Gee of the Alberta Mixed Chorus Hockey Team

"It is true that I play on a team where most of the players can carry a tune better than a hockey stick," says Brian "Baritone" Boytang of the Alberta Mixed Chorus Hockey Team. The team plays in the intramural hockey program under the direction of Hugh Hoyles at the University of Alberta.

Actually, the name is inaccurate. The team does not truly represent Dr. Ron Stephen's Mixed Chorus. It only has male representatives and, since everyone is at least over the age of 12 there are no sopranos — only tenors, basses and baritones.

In the 1984-85 season the team only had one player with any hockey experience. Therefore, it was not surprising that "Baritone" Davis Graham had three goals and one assist in the first two games. It was no surprise that Boytang scored only one goal. He is at the other end of the hockey scale; he only learned to skate two years ago.

The rest of the players' skills varied. Some had played bantam and fewer yet midget level hockey. Will "Baritone" Bauer, Richard "Baritone" Smith, Dwayne "Baritone" Garneau and John "Tenor" Zabiuk all played wing while Allan "Tenor" Coldwells, Cameron "Bass" Sterling and Ralph "Baritone" Henze centred. Jeff "Bass" Goldie, Norman "Tenor" Gee and Bill "Tenor" Sellers played defence. Percy "Baritone" Janke stood in the net.

Although some competitors think the closest this team should get to a hockey game is singing the national anthem, the last game illustrates the team's competitive spirit. It was the last game of a four-game schedule. (The team had lost the first three.) The "Chorus" was pitted against a team from the Geology Department called "P.S. Warren Society." For two periods the "Chorus" was up two goals but with three minutes left in the game P.S. Warren tied it at 6-6.

"Then we got heroic," says Norman "Tenor" Gee. "We pulled our goalie. Things got tense. Especially when the P.S. squad won the draw in the last face-off. But we hung on, saved the tie and made believers of the cynics."

FRIENDSHIP HOCKEY — CANADA VS. USSR 1984

BY WALTER BABIY

(Walter Babiy is Past President of the Edmonton Old Timers Association. This story is based on his diary transcripts throughout the journey.)

It all began at the beautiful Lodge in 1982, while attending their Annual Old Timer Hockey Tournament. Amid the laughter and the stream that traverses the Lodge, a group of Edmonton Old Timers were sitting, sharing a drink and wondering about the ultimate hockey trip...Russia.

Around the table were the likes of Gene and Ray Kinasewich, Roger Gelinas, Bob Solinger and myself. It was Gene who suggested the Soviet Union and how it was possible to make arrangements. Previously he had taken a group of Boston high school players to Russia.

On December 9, 1984 we found overselves in the depths of Russia in Leningrad, the cradle of many revolutions. What seems to many as their golden hockey days, occurred for many of the Edmonton and Calgary Old Timers on this adventure into the Unknown Land of "Kievan Ris." For the likes of Ray Kinasewich, Boris Pausch and myself, the trip was easier due to our personal command of Slavic languages.

Much has been written and told about the feats of the Soviet's hockey machine. Their hockey philosophy techniques, skills and obsessions for perfection were revealed. For whatever the reason, one must truly admire their ability to fashion excellence in the face of the many adversities in their system.

Yes! The hockey team we faced in Leningrad, Minsk, Kiev and Moscow was assembled by the "Old Master of Sport," Coach Tarasov. He was present at our final match in Lenin's Central Stadium, Palace of Sports.

Some of the players we played against are cast in granite (or so it seemed) even though they are the vestiges of that team our Canadians beat in Moscow in 1972. Through older and all but forgotten stars like Petrov, Vasiliev, Kuzkin, Starshinov and the like, still skate amiably with the style and grace of yesteryear.

Though efforts had been made to obtain valuable information with regard to the Soviet player roster, no names were forthcoming until we met — Viktor Polyakov — the straightlaced, sober manager-coach of our opposition.

There we sat, (Ray Kinasewich, Tony Mokry, Roger Gelinas, our guide Switlana, Vicktor and myself). We were all eating borsch and discussing the upcoming series of games.

Viktor was quick to point out that we had some "underage players," that there was to be no body contact, and motioning high with his arms — no slapshots and above all no masks or antics. We all looked at each other and thought it looks like the Canada Cup all over again — it dampened our spirits — yet no line up from Viktor — very secretive indeed.

Roger Gelinas produced his album of photos from Soviet and Canadian players of bygone days and soon the meeting thawed. Ray winked and said, "We'll give them something to remember," and thus we left the table. Tony continued and a minute later, raced frantically upstairs saying, "he's got the line up," and said, "this is a top notch club."

Sure enough, besides the players mentioned earlier add Tsygankov, Golikov and Polupanov. It set us back, but upon coming to our senses, we said, "what the hell, let's get on with it."

Through the next nine extraordinary days, we played, toured, ate, toasted with wine and vodka, again and again, from Leningrad through Minsk, Kiev, and Moscow, all in a flurry of the Russian winter. The pace was so hectic, someone remarked we had omitted sleep on our itinerary.

Our games ended in scores of 11-7, 9-5, 10-8 and 15-6, all in their favor, but in the end we were all winners, with friendship and kindness extended to all of us by so many.

This was truly a marvelous experience to catch a glimpse of, to view how hockey is fashioned Soviet style, and yet there remained this inner, overriding feeling of new found pride and admiration for our many great Canadian hockey players, who played the game with intensity in the arenas of the world. Enough can not be

CANADIAN AND RUSSIAN PLAYERS — 1984

Back row (l to r): Yuri Pepnyov, Don Graves, Alexandr Martynyuk, Rick Sentes, Vladimir Luchenko, Bob Duncan, Anatoly Motovilov, Viktor Polupanov, Ivan Tregubov, Gennadi Tsygankov, Vladimir Migunko, Vladimir Petrov, Wayne Stephenson, Yuri Shatalov, Bob Tuff, Bob Henderson, Gord Vejprava, Boris Paush, Gord Cowan, Yuri Blinov, V.M. Polyakov (manager), V.I. Kozin (trainer). Front row: Gene Achtymachuk, Gary Kokolski, Yuri Lyapkin, Walter Babiy, Viktor Tsyplakov, Roger DeJordy, Evgeni Poleev, Ray Kinasewich, Gary Desaulnier, Murray Dodd, Jamie Walton, Viktor Kuzkin, Roger Gelinas, George Hill. Missing: Roger Otteson, Terry Proskurniak, Ron Merkel, Bob Pofenroth, Pete Milne, Bill Daniel, Anatoly Motovilov, Vyatcheslav Starshinov.

said about the timeless work of coaches, strategists and players who make our Canadian game the envy of other nations. We too, smouldered in all crucibles of Canadian Hockey and were a part of it all.

BLINK BLINK BLINK

BY DANIEL JOHNS, editor, Bonnyville Nouvelle

Three goals in 12 seconds won the battle but not the war for the Bonnyville Pontiacs during an Alberta Intermediate 'C' Provincial final against the Innisfail Eagles on Easter Friday, 1977. The home town Pontiacs were playing for their most prestigous title in several years and the Fire Marshall was turning a blind eye to the number of people packed into the arena.

Innisfail had already won the first contest of the two-game-total-point series, 5-3 and at 18:35 of the third period, in the second game, victory appeared certain as they led 10-8. However, at that moment, Mitch Sylvestre scored on a wrist shot, from the side of the net. The big winger had a little more room than normal to operate in as both teams were short handed.

As play resumed, centre Grant Ferbey carried the puck over the blue line and fired a hard shot that was tipped by winger, Randy Yavis, behind the Eagle goalie. On the ensuing faceoff, due to the coincidental penalties, no one lined up against Sylvestre. Ferbey won the draw and Sylvestre flipped a high shot into the Eagle zone. It took a crazy hop and bounced past the startled net minder. The 3rd goal won the game for the Pontiacs, 11-10 but with 1 minute and 13 seconds to go they still needed one more goal to tie the series. Innisfail tightened up and held off the late charge.

The goals came so quickly that Sylvestre's father, Gerry, a former Pontiac, remembers the ocassion with some chargin. He deserted the game as a lost cause just before the final goal was scored and was just leaving the parking lot outside the arena. When the radio announced the first goal, he decided he should return. But by the time he parked the car the other two goals were already made.

(Bonnyville locals claim that these three goals in 12 seconds is a world record. Johns reports that an article appeared in Sports Illustrated, that a high school team in the United States had apparently scored three goals in 11 seconds. Alberta's adult standard of three goals in 12 seconds stands as an incredible accomplishment and record.)

FANS

This scene from the stage play "FANS" which was performed by the Small Change Theatre group in Edmonton, December, 1984. "Fans" was written by Jan Henderson, Jan Miller and Wendell Smith. Music by Marsha Coffey, design by Barbara Devonshire and directed by Robert Astle.

The following is a telephone call from Annis, the father of minor hockey player Marty, to coach Clipper Williams. Annis has talked to Clipper before; however, this time the coach is out. Annis takes the identity of sports reporter Barry North and ends up speaking to Mrs. Williams.

Phone Call

PHONE RINGS AND DOT HEADS FOR THE PHONE

ANNIS TAKE A SWIG OF BEER, THEN PLACES A FILTY OLD RAG OVER THE PHONE TO MUFFLE HIS VOICE

DOT   Hello?

ANNIS   Hello Mrs. Williams...This is Barry North. I'm a sports reporter, you've probably heard of me...

DOT   Oh yes...Mr. North...What can I do for you Mr. North?

ANNIS   Well...it's a curious thing...I've been watching this kid who plays for the team that your husband coaches. His name is...RUFFLES SOME PAPERS...let me see...uh...Marty...number 5. This kid is good. He's NHL material, and I was going to write about him in my column. But I thought by now he'd be playing double 'A'...but he isn't. And I find out that your husband is holding him back. So where is my story? And what's the story on this kid being stopped in his rise to stardom?...Well, I just want you to know that your husband is breaking the heart of that kid's father. I know that family, and his father always wanted to be a hockey great...but he had a weak right ankle...and well...he just couldn't skate...so all his hopes are with that kid...and your husband is killing those hopes and dreams for that kid...it's a cruel thing to do.

DOT   HANGS UP PHONE QUIETLY

ANNIS   All your husband would have to do is push that kid as far and as fast as he can go...and inside a year he'd be there...and I'd be right there with him...But no...

            HANGS UP PHONE

            MUSIC "IT COULD'VE BEEN ME"

THE HANSONS OF CAMROSE

BY TOMMY GRAHAM

The city of Camrose, 58 miles southeast of Edmonton has maintained its share of recognition in sports. One family that brought early fame to Camrose was the Hansons. The family numbered ten including seven boys. Brothers, Emile, Oscar and Emery went on to play professional hockey on clubs such as the Minneapolis Millers and Saint Paul Saints. This story relates two unusual times for the Hansons. In 1927-28, five of them almost made the American Olympic team and how a fight was stopped.

After graduation from the town of Camrose school system all seven sons attended Minnesota's Augsburg College. Coach Si Melby coached five of the brothers (Oscar, Emil, Louis, Julius and Joe) in 1927-28. The College team defeated everyone and impressed the American Olympic Committee. It was recommended the college represent the U.S.A. at the 1928 Olympics.

Governments did not give much financial aid for Olympics in 1928 in comparison to today. Augsburg College could help but the individuals on the team would have to raise the majority of money. It was reported that the Hansons were ready as Julius had 10,000 bushels of grain stored in Camrose valued at $1500.00. It was only after the players made applications for passports that the team was informed they could not represent the U.S.A. as the Hansons were Canadians.

One of the major competitors for Augsburg College was the army team stationed at Fort Snelling, Minnesota. The Fort were talented but were invariably defeated by the college, thanks to the Hanson brothers.

Reporter Rolf Felstad of the Minneapolis Times-Tribune reported that a fight in a game between the two clubs was stopped in a sudden manner. A melee ignited when Oscar Hanson was crushed into the boards on a heavy check by one of the army players. Brother Emil observed his family member lying in a heap and rushed to his rescue. He fought the army player and both the benches cleared. It was a fight to the finish. An army commander did not feel the fights would stop so he came on to the ice, pulled his revolver. Emil and the rest of the pugilists immediately ceased fighting.

Younger brother Emery was in Camrose playing for the junior Camrose Flyers. He went later to Augsburg and then turned professional. Julius became a minister after college, Joe became a teacher and Louis obtained his PHD. in Chemistry. The Hansons made their mark on hockey.

HOCKEY HAS BEEN GOOD TO ME

Interview with Garry Unger

(Garry Unger achieved a remarkable record in the National Hockey League. He is still today's "Iron Man" as he played 914 consecutive games. He was selected to seven all-star teams while he scored 413 goals and 381 assists for 804 points. He received 1075 penalty minutes. When the Alberta Junior Hockey League started, Unger played for the Calgary Buffaloes in a 16 game schedule. To set a continuous streak of games equal to his NHL record he would have had to play over 57 seasons in the first AJHL format. The following story describes a few fond moments from his junior days in Alberta.)

As a youngster I acquired an early interest in hockey due in part to the enthusiasm and encouragement from my parents. My parents were believers in the age-old adage and saying "What ever you do, do well."

We lived at Currie Barracks in Calgary where hockey took a lot of my time. Boxing was another activity I pursued. My parents, Olive and Jack, did not mind my interest in boxing. They encouraged it. I won't dwell on fisties but while engaged in the sport, I learned to hold my own.

It seems a long time ago now but in 1964, I played for the Calgary Rangers in the Midget 'A' League. Having enjoyed success as a pee wee, bantam and midget, I was fortunate enough to receive a chance to play for the Calgary Buffaloes in the "new" 1964-65 Alberta Junior Hockey League. I thought I had reached the pinnacle of my hockey career. Every young hockey player dreams of making the NHL. At 15, I never dreamt I would be playing junior.

The Calgary Buffaloes played their 16 game schedule mainly on weekends so my school life was not interrupted. The teachers at Calgary's Viscount Bennett High School did not make any big deal about players on the Buffaloes. As a result few, if any, compensations were made.

I recall my first "road" trip as a junior was to Edmonton. Then it was the greatest thrill of my life. We stopped at Highway 2's Juniper Inn. Here at 15, I was sitting down with "older" players (Marty Demmarais, Don Phelps, Mike Lemeux) having a steak. Including everything it cost around $4.50. When we went to Lethbridge to play the Sugar Kings it was hamburgers and shakes after the game. The three stars after the game in Lethbridge received free hamburgers. We played hard and felt very good to win the award.

During part of my Calgary junior career, I continued to deliver the "Calgary Herald." It was tough to do this six days a week, so I got up enough nerve to ask Buffalo coach John Kell for $5.00 a week... which needless to say, was denied. Kell told me that the club only paid for the players' expenses and that if I wanted compensation, I could deliver gas bills. The offer was accepted but I only continued for two weeks as the route was too extended and it was just too windy and frigid.

Even with my retirement in 1983 from the Edmonton Oilers, and all the teams before, the game has been good to me. I have been happy to still stay in touch as a color commentator on television. Over the years from the beginning of my hockey career it has been a positive learning experience.

(For 1985-86 Unger has moved to Scotland to coach and play.)

I REMEMBER GARRY UNGER

Interview with Frank Currie

(Frank Currie coached the 1953-54 Edinburgh Cup Calgary Stampeders and was manager of the first AJHL Calgary Buffaloes. Currie signed Unger for the Toronto Maple Leafs and followed Garry's career. Some junior players from Western Canada went east for "seasoning." Unger was one of these. Currie is still involved in hockey as a scout for the Toronto Maple Leafs.)

In hockey, I have been associated with a number of personalities as a player, coach, manager and scout. My thoughts on Garry Unger have always been near the top. He was a natural hockey player who didn't have to labor to make things happen. When he moved up to the Calgary Buffaloes at 15, I became more interested in his progress. In Calgary, I was able to place and sign him to the Toronto Maple Leafs if he ever turned pro.

While still in junior, Garry was moved to Toronto to continue the same level. For reasons best known to Garry, he did not like Toronto. A transfer to the London Nationals of the OHA was arranged by Leaf's scout Bob Davidson. Playing under the guidance of coach Turk Broada, Unger's career took a turn for the better. As a rookie on the Nationals, part of the introduction was to have his hair cut by his teammates. The "hair cut" was so bad, he had to see a barber.

In London, Ontario, a junior hockey player was known by many. The barber immediately said, "you're Garry Unger, aren't you?" This friendly approach started to make Garry feel like he did in Calgary. I watched Garry move through the hockey pro ranks from Toronto, to St. Louis and Edmonton. It is sometimes the little things that count. In this case a friendly barber who made Unger feel at home helped to motivate one of the game's stars.

J.B. "JIM" CROSS

BY JIM KERR

President and Chief Operating Officer of Calgary Brewing and Malting Co. Ltd., grandson of the man who gave Calgary its name, Jim Cross established his principal community activities in the 1930s and 1940s as a volunteer with the Calgary Exhibition and Stampede. The Stampede, as owners operators of the Victoria Arena had successfully hosted some Allan Cup playoffs.

The Stampede Hockey Committee, under the chairmanship of Cross, recognized that a purely local team would not be competitive against teams the calibre of the Trail Smokeaters, Kimberley Dynamiters, North Battleford Beavers, Cornwall Flyers and others. Good, local, senior players left Calgary to join such teams, leaving Cross and his committee to go out and build a team which could be competitive — the result, the Calgary Stampeders. The Stampeders won the Allan Cup in 1946 and were runners-up in 1949.

During his term as President of the Calgary Exhibition and Stampede, the Stampede Corral was built — costing $1,300,000 — a quite substantial sum in the 1950s. His interest in the "kids" never diminished as he continued to lend financial and moral support to the activities of the Calgary Buffalo Athletic Association.

TIMES HAVE CHANGED FOR REFEREES

Rules of hockey in the early days were very simple and referees were granted or allowed to take considerable latitude in their interpretation of regulations when making or assessing infraction calls. Uniforms generally consisted of street clothes and sometimes a derby hat was worn as a signal of authority.

One referee was in charge, without linesmen for many years in Alberta. Some of them used a bell rather than a whistle as rinks were not heated and most games were played ouside. (Lips could freeze with whistles.)

In 1906 Mike Grant, a referee in Ottawa created quite a stir when he appeared on the ice with a hard hat. He claimed it was for his own protection. Little did he realize that 70 years later "hard hats" or helmets would be worn by all amateur officials.

The referee's method of determining goals is done in cooperation with goal judges who are behind the nets. Previously, two "umpires" stood on the ice behind the goal and usually signalled a goal by waving a small flag.

The elimination of the rover position has reduced the number of players on the ice from seven per team to six. However, the referee who was once by himself now has two linesmen.

The game used to be divided into 30 minute halves. Substitiution regulations were much stricter in earlier days and teams had few if any extra players in their lineup.

Notable changes have occurred for officials. From street clothes to the black and white striped jersey (even red and white in the WHA during the 1970s) and the introduction and widespread use of hockey helmets. There are still many people who claim helmets take something away from the game's tradition, nevertheless they are here to stay for the safety of the officals.

Today, referees are trained in all provinces under senior officials who supervise their progress through six levels. This is the National Referees Certification Program.

Present day Alberta has 3,600 ice tooters registered with the Referee's Committee of the AAHA. Eight years ago the number was 1,600. Clinics were held through the province, 120 times in 1984 to help ensure proper conduct of games and continually upgrade the calibre of officiality.

Alberta referee in Chief, Ernie Boruk of Edmonton praises the present system:

> It is the best we have ever had and we continually strive to assist each official. Whether the players, coaches or fans realize it or not, the outcome of the vast majority of matches are determined by the players and we hope to keep it that way.

While many referees hope to progress to the pro hockey ranks Boruk emphatically states, "we intend to produce a few for the NHL, but our purpose in the AAHA is hockey, right here in Alberta."

Alberta has produced some excellent referees in Pep Moon, Clarence Campbell, Harry Scott, Joe Cassidy, Bill Bucyk, Daryl Havrelock, Billy "Dutchy" Van Deelan, "Swede" Knox, Barry Fraser, Ray and Gordon Thompson, and Bernie Haley — just to mention a few.

JOHNNY MACDONALD

Excerpts from an article by Kathy Murrie, writer, Grande Prairie Daily Herald-Tribune May 1, 1984

The Rec Plex Arena is now officially known as the Johnny Macdonald Arena.

The decision to rename the ice surface in honour of a man who became recognized to Grande Prairie and area as Mr. Hockey was announced Monday, April 30, 1984 at the Volunteer Awards Banquet.

Mr. Macdonald who died in March at the age of 84, had been active for decades as a hockey player, coach. manager, and organizer and had been instrumental in the bulding of the City's Old Memorial Arena in the late 1940s.

Mayor Oscar Blais had been on the Athletics hockey teams of the mid 1950s and read a tribute to his former coach. He told how Mr. Macdonald had come to Grande Prairie in 1913 with his parents from the Merritt, B.C. area and played his first hockey game with adult teams in December of that year. It was between Lake Saskatoon and Grande Prairie at Lake Saskatoon. The game was described in the Grande Prairie Herald later that month as "one of the fastest and classiest... that ever took place on northern Alberta ice." And the lone Grande Prairie supporter, Bill Innes, rode out on horseback to see his team.

Throughout the years he continued to organize hockey. He managed the Wapiti Rink (built in 1919) the Town's first rink, and in 1946 Town Council decided to replace it with a fitting memorial to those who served in the two World wars. Johnny spent five years planning and helping to build the Memorial Arena.

Mr. Macdonald was well remembered for the many teams he coached, of all ages, but probably best for his involvement with Johnny's Red Devils. They were a Senior team like the Dawson Creek Canucks and Hythe Mustangs and in 1955 became the Athletics. Some of the players he has coached included: Charlie Turner, Pete Eagar, Roy Wright, Brian McCurdy, Bob Neufeld and Max Henning. Mr. Macdonald coached for over thirty years and by the mid 1960s retired from the lumber business but still never missed a game as long as his health allowed.

CANADA'S OLYMPIC PROGRAM FOR 1988

BY DAVE KING, Coach/General Manger, Team Canada '84

Canada returned from the 1984 Winter Olympics in Sarajevo, Yugoslavia with a respectable fourth place finish. Many valuable lessons were learned in 1984 and therefore with great optimism Hockey Canada is vigorously planning the programming from 1984-1988.

Forming a National Team in Canada is a very difficult process as it takes a great deal of co-operation from many levels of hockey. University, Major-Junior and National Hockey League's co-operation will all be needed if the 1988 team is to be competitive. Gaining this co-operation will therefore be Hockey Canada's first priority. Meetings with all levels of the game will take place at which Hockey Canada will lay out the blueprint for the program in hopes of receiving support for the program.

One of the first priorities for the program is the identification of talent. This means that a comprehensive identification process will be set up to work in conjunction with the CAHA's Program of Excellence. This Program of Excellence involves summer camps for Canada's elite young prospects.

Talent identification also must be combined with an evaluation process. Therefore, Hockey Canada will hold summer camps as well as tours with teams in Canada and Europe. For these tours, players will be brought in for a short ten to fourteen day period from the various club teams to be part of the evaluation. Once the tours are over the players will immediately return to their club.

It is hoped that Canada's Olympic Team may be together on a full-time basis for more than the 1987-88 season. If the talent identification process is successful and enough serious players are willing to commit to an ongoing team, Canada's full-time National Team may become a reality before the 1987-88 season. This would be a great advantage to the program but obviously once again the co-operation needed will be very great.

One can therefore expect the Olympic Program in Canada to be an active and operational program over the next four years leading into the '88 Olympics in Calgary. It is hoped that the profile of the Olympic team can be maintained so that young Canadian players will look upon the Olympic team as being a goal in their development process.

Canada's Olympic Team now has permanent administrative offices in the new Olympic Saddledome in Calgary. This excellent facility will allow for co-operation of the program to occur on an ongoing basis. Along with the administrative office, Hockey Canada is embarking on a research area within the Saddledome. It is hoped that through leadership from Hockey Canada, the game can be examined and studied from many aspects so that improvements in the game will be a direct result. If Canada is to regain prominence at the international level the research into hockey will have to be upgraded.

One of the real bright spots on the horizon for Canadian hockey is that now the CAHA and Hockey Canada have combined their efforts into development of the Olympic Program. This coordinated effort will produce a consistent program that should have an improved chance of success.

Provincial Midget Camps lead onto a series of Regional Under 17 camps. These under 17 camps will assist in identification of talent for future National Junior teams, which will in the end assist in the development of future Olympians. This type of progressive identification and evaluation will be a great asset in developing competitive international teams at all levels.

THE JUDGE HAS HIS SAY

BY DON COLLINS, Calgary Herald staff writer

Behind the impressive wooden door at the Calgary Court House lies the judicial domain of Joseph Julius Kryczka — hockey fan par excellence.

The casual visitor might mistake it for something else other than a judges' chambers. Along one wall of the comfortable eigth floor office are photographs and other mementoes of the game of hockey and the part this man has played in it. "This was my younger brother, Adam," he says, producing a time-worn photograph from his desk. Side by side in the pcture are Adam the goal tender and Joe Kryczka the defenceman.

It is at this same desk that the 49-year-old Justice Kryczka buries himself in the details of cases that come before him in the Court of Queen's Bench. But on this day he is off duty and in an open-necked shirt. This place of dispassionate jurisprudence has been magically transformed into Joe Kryczka's world of hockey. It is a world in which he has played an important role, something of which the Canadian public is largely unaware.

With the Canada Cup series under way once again, as a model of international hockey at its best, the man in the spotlight, as usual, is tournament chairman, Alan Eagleson. But, in his own way, Kryczka had as much to do as anyone in setting the stage for what is happening today. As president of the CAHA in 1972, and before, president of AAHA, he was this country's chief negotiator during the talks in Prague that led to the Canada-

Soviet Union Summit series, a long-awaited matchup between the best teams the two nations could produce. Won by Canada, in a final game in Moscow, it was an event that captured the imagination and attention of the world. Eagleson got much of the credit of making the series possible. Kryczka is quick to point out that the Eagle had been pushing for just such a confrontation for three years. His efforts had begun with the departure of the Canadians from the world hockey stage in 1969, following a disagreement over the type of players eligible.

But it was Kryczka and his team that hammered out the 1972 agreement with their tough but fair counterparts from Russia. That team included men like Gordon Juckes, Charles Hay and Lou Lefaive. "Eagleson wasn't even in Prague until after everything was signed, sealed and delivered," says Kryczka. There are no gold medals handed out to international negotiators. And if there were, Kryczka probably wouldn't be able to say whether his side or the Soviets deserved it after the 1972 session.

Of the Soviets, he says: "They were certainly going to get everything they were looking for. But they were prepared to give when the time came to give." They weren't, however, ready to agree to Canada's proposal that NHL referees and linesmen be used. But time has a way of changing minds. "They have come to realize that if you are going to play against top-calibre teams you need top-calibre officials," Kryczka says. If there was a game of onemanship to be won in negotiations, the Soviets won it — at Kryczka's expense.

Photo courtesy of Glenbow Archives

Born to Polish parents, he understood what the Soviets were saying among themselves. but didn't tip his hand. He spoke through an interpreter, thinking his special knowledge might give his side the advantage. At the beginning of the third day, the Soviets poured vodka into tumblers and proposed toasts to the respective countries. When they caught him sipping instead of gulping, they told him they knew his background was Polish and suggested that he "get drinking." They had also known right along that he could understand their language. "Somewhere I had tipped my hand," he says, smiling at the recollection. "In Czechoslovakia, things don't stay secret very long."

In Kryczka's books, it was all worth the effort. He likes what he has seen on the international hockey front.

I think international hockey has made a lot of positive strides. There has been an international spinoff. You just have to look at what Edmonton (NHL) has done in adopting the European type of hockey. There is a lot more finesse.

Appointed to the bench in 1980, Kryczka hasn't been as heavily involved in hockey as he once was. He would, however, like to somehow get involved with hockey at the 1988 Winter Olympics.

EARLY EDMONTON HOCKEY RADIO

BY FRANK MAKEPEACE

I was a home ham operator when radio first started. I read a book on the wireless during World War I and then got a radio licence in 1922.

DR. RICE ON CJCA IN MID 1920's

Photo courtesy of Sunwapta Broadcasting

I remember Dick Rice on CJCA in 1923 broadcasting the Edmonton Eskimos versus Ottawa Senators in the Stanley Cup finals. King Clancy played for Ottawa while Duke Keats, Ty Arbor and Eddie Shore were Eskimo players. I heard Dick talk about them on my crystal set with earphones. The earphones in our house were placed in a punch bowl in order to magnify the sound so up to six people could listen even though the equipment was only set up for one. The radio range on the crystal was probably only about 25 miles around the City of Edmonton at that time.

In order to do this broadcast a reporter at rink side in Vancouver would have to send the plays by telegram. Rice would read the story. He would "hold" several plays in order to get a full minute or two of "live" broadcast. Interest in hockey was aided by radio but more sophistication and technology was developed.

By 1928 I was an engineer and announcer at CJCA. The station transmitter was on the roof of the Journal Building across from the present Chateau Lacombe. The station did remotes from the Edmonton Arena in the days before the rink was heated. I arrived at the rink with one box 2' x 1' x 1' with a microphone, cable and amplifier, 'B' batteries to supply power and a storage battery to add power for remotes. Broadcasts were done from the centre of the rink at ice level with Jack Horler doing the broadcast.

I remember it being very cold at times at the rink and quite often Jack and I would have to keep warm with the odd bit of liquid refreshment. I had to watch and adjust the equipment for Jack quite frequently because the sound level at hockey games changes.

Clarence Campbell in the late 1920s and early 1930s did most of the refereeing. On a couple of occasions he ended up doing the radio broadcast — the actual play by play. He was an excellent referee, but his radio broadcasting was sometimes behind the play.

Gordon Williamson's career in hockey broadcasting started on December 12, 1931, on CJCA, when Jack Horler had to stay back at the Journal and do some extra work (the Journal owned CJCA). Gordon had a wide range in his voice and was fair to both teams, giving real life to the broadcasts.

Robert "Pussey" Prioux was a big stocky player and a good skater who could really rough it up. On at least one occasion Prioux had a mix up in front of the equipment which caused the radio equipment to move around and us to sprawl all over the area.

Tom Campbell from Campbell's Furniture sponsored parts of the broadcast. Commercials were read from the studio. Edmonton Journal and Edmonton Bulletin sports writers were sometimes interviewed between periods.

CFRN started in 1934. I moved over to CFRN with Williamson to work for Dick Rice and Hans Neilson. Radio hockey broadcasts were done from the arena from a gondala approximately 30' high in the rafters. Our amplifier equipment increased in size but was still only one box. This box (2 1/2' x 2' x 1') now had to be carried up a ladder without any railing on the side to the platform above the ice. In thinking back the most dangerous time for me was carrying this large 60 to 75 pound case up and down the ladder.

I really enjoyed working in the early days of hockey broadcasting. In those days there was the broadcaster, an engineer at the rink, and an announcer at the studio. I marvel at the present day radio and television accounts, however, so many more times the number of people are involved.

CALGARY NEWSPAPER AND RADIO REPORTING IN 1924

The Calgary Tigers verses the Vancouver Maroons. The third game of the 1923-24 Stanley Cup semi-finals was "Live from Winnipeg" on CFAC, the Herald Broadcasting station. The two clubs were battling to reach the 1924 Stanley Cup finals against the Montreal Canadians. (In 1924 the Calgary Tigers defeated Vancouver Maroons in Winnipeg to win the series. All they won was a bye to the Stanley Cup final. See Senior and Professional Section.)

Telephone, newspaper and telephone service complimented each other. The Herald put in an extra ten telephone lines for additional service to the editorial room. Ten operators repeated the score for an estimated 5,500 calls. A megaphone service on 1st Street West from the office of Hornibrook, Whittemore and Allan, was provided by the herald. Another 2,500 Calgarians received a special telegraph service from Winnipeg. "Play by play" accounts were written and telegraphed by the Herald's sports' editor, Howard Kelly.

At 9:30 p.m. the Herald put out an extra issue which contained Kelly's account of the game, plus the Union-Miner strike in Alberta and the Bellevue-Melville Millionaire Allan Cup series as feature stories. Others could read the Herald bulletin board.

However, despite all the other services to let Calgarians know the results; it was the radio service that caused the majority of the calls after the game. Fans were excited and told CFAC's Fred Carleton said they were impressed with "the efficiency of the service maintained throughout the game".

The next day, March 17, 1924, the Herald told readers they could expect the same service "when Vancouver and Calgary meet the Canadiens of Montreal". All the services would be provided again.

For the Stanley Cup final the phone number once again would be M7981 for the Herald. The Herald's competitor, the Albertan, provided megaphone service from one of their windows, newspaper accounts and a special hockey line — M9537.

(CFAC also broadcasted professional hockey when the Calgary Cowboys were in the WHA. Eric Bishop and George Bilych provided the action. When the Calgary Flames entered the NHL, Bart Dailey was the first play-by-play broadcaster on CHQR. Today, Peter Maher is the "Voice of the Flames." Doug Barkley has been the color man since the start of the Flames. John Henderson handles the post game show on CHQR.)

SUPPORTERS MAKE THE GAME
BY JIM FISHER

In sport you always need characters. Fans can make the game more interesting. Drumheller was noted for great fan support.

True, Drumheller has had some almost unbelievable hockey stories. In the 1930's former NHL President Clarence Campbell had occasion to referee in Drumheller. As he came down the ice a "little old lady" knocked him unconscious. She had put old irons that grandmother used to heat on the stove and wrapped them in a pillow case.

In the 1960's Joyce Walker became the number one fan for the Drumheller Miners. Her enthusiasm is still remembered around the Big Country as a fan every club would want to have. She worked hard for the team and cheered just as hard. At times Joyce did not stop there.

One night she decided to get into the Edmonton Oil King box and have it out with Buster Brayshaw, Al Hamilton and Co. Then there was the night the CAHA brought a referee into Drumheller from Vancouver. Even though the Miners were in the lead, Joyce gave the referee a stinging upper cut.

Joe Kryczka, now a judge, and Stu Peppard, were so dismayed they decided that Joyce not be permitted to watch anymore of the series. That view quickly changed when the Miners decided they were not coming out for the next period. Matters were straightened out and Joyce was back in her usual spot — leading the cheering.

* * *

Terry Jones is a sports columnist at the *Edmonton Sun*. His journalistic road to the *Sun* began in Grade 7 when he wrote amateur sports for the Lacombe Globe. By high school he was also writing for the Red Deer Advocate. From 1967-82 Jones wrote for the *Edmonton Journal*. In 1982 he joined the *Sun*. He has authored five books on Canadian professional football, co-authored *Decade of Excellence* and does "Just a Minute" on CHQT Edmonton.

Jones has closely followed Wayne Gretzky in his regular column and in his book *The Great Gretzky*.

WAYNE GRETZKY
BY TERRY JONES

Okay. You've just finished reading about the 1,001 teams and the 100,001 players who have made Alberta's hockey history.

Now that you've met them...forget them.

One player has done more to put Edmonton and Alberta on the map than all of the rest combined.

If you're from Edmonton and you travel, you know it's like a word association test with just about anybody from anywhere.

Edmonton?

Gretzky!

Before Gretzky the National Hockey League was a million miles away to an Albertan. The Stanley Cup was something you saw on TV.

The Edmonton Oilers and Gretzky survived the World Hockey Association together in super shape and were so successful out of the gate in the NHL that in next to no time at all the Atlanta Flames were moved to Calgary.

Today the Edmonton Oilers have won back-to-back Stanley Cups and are being compared with the greatest teams in hockey history. And The Great Gretzky is The Greatest.

Only in the league for six seasons, Gretzky and the Oilers have done what some NHL franchises have never done and what some of the original six teams haven't done in a long time. The New York Rangers haven't won a Stanley Cup since 1940, the Chicago Black Hawks since 1961, the Detroit Red Wings since 1955 and the Toronto Maple Leafs since 1967. The Oilers have won two in a row.

There is little doubt that Gretzy has become the Babe Ruth of hockey.

"I sometimes wonder where the National Hockey League would be without him," says NHL president John Ziegler.

"Wayne has done more for hockey than any person who has ever played or likely ever will," says Bobby Hull.

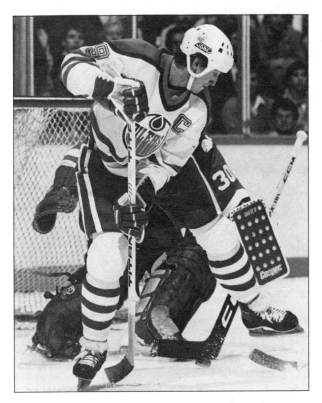

Photo courtesy of Bob Mummery

Photo courtesy of Bob Mummery

"He's made the record book obsolete," says Minnesota North Stars general manager Lou Nanne. "From now on his only point of reference is himself."

"He's the best," says Gordie Howe.

Through six seasons, Gretzy has won the Hart Trophy as the most valuable player in the NHL six times. He has five Art Ross Trophies as the top scorer in the league and missed the sixth on a technicality when he finished tied with Marcel Dionne in his first season but had fewer goals. He's won the Lady Byng.

And now he has two Stanley Cups, a Canada Cup and a Conn Smythe Trophy.

The Stanley Cup has never really had such an affair with a town and a team. Never have so many fans been asked to drink from the Cup. And smack-dab in the middle was Gretzky.

"The best part of it all was sharing it with everybody in Edmonton. Every night the first time we won it we'd take the Cup out to different restaurants and nightclubs. People in Edmonton had seen the Stanley Cup from a distance on television all those years when it was something the Montreal Canadiens or the Boston Bruins used to win. So to take it around, sort of unannounced, every night for a couple of weeks and to let hundreds of people drink from it...that was the biggest kick of all."

The record book? After only six seasons his name is on almost every page.

He holds 29 league and playoff records and shares 10 more. He has the single season record for most goals (92), most assists (135), most points (212) and eight other categories. He scored 50 goals in 39 games to make them forget about Rocket Richard's 50 in 50. It goes on and on.

After six seasons he has 1,123 points. That put him 14th on the all-time scoring list. At his current pace, Gretzky will move past Gordie Howe (1,850 points) and a record which was supposed to never be broken in the spring of 1989. Gordie Howe was 52 when he retired. Wayne Gretzky will be 29 in 1989.

Fame?

In one two month span Gretzky was on the covers of Sports Illustrated, The Sporting News, Time and was the No. 1 featured story in the Saturday Evening Post and was the Playboy interview.

Making a reported $800,000 a year from the Oilers, he more than doubled it with endorsements which include Canon cameras with the biggest billboard on Times Square in New York.

Wayne Gretzky is more than a hockey player. He's hockey!

* * * * * *

UNIVERSITY OF ALBERTA 1916-17

Back row (l to r): C.P. Ottewell (cover point), A.L. Caldwell (left wing), E. East (rover), H.T. Emery (spare), J.T. Lehmann (goal). **Front row:** W.F. Seyer (manager, right wing), W.F. Clark (rover), A. Talbot (president), S.B. Smith (point), J.K. Fife (captain, centre).

Photo courtesy of Edmonton Archives

MEDICINE HAT TIGERS 1949-50

BOB HOLMES (L. WING)

LEN HALEY (R. WING)

BRUCE DICKSON (CENTER)

DOUG HAGE (CENTER)

GERRY BARRE (CENTER)

BILL INNES (R. WING)

ELDOR THOMAS (R. WING)

MEDICINE HAT TIGERS
1949   1950

DAL DIE BOLD (L. WING)

BOB LEEK (DEFENCE)

EDDIE SCHMIDT (DEFENCE)

ERNIE RUCKS (L. WING)

DON HAY (DEFENCE)

JACK SHUPE (DEFENCE)

JAY JENKINS (L. WING)

LORNE BAUMBACH (GOAL)

JOE FISHER (COACH)

BUDDIE NOON (GOAL)

Photo courtesy of Gainsboro Studios, Medicine Hat

STRATHCONA HOCKEY TEAM 1908-09

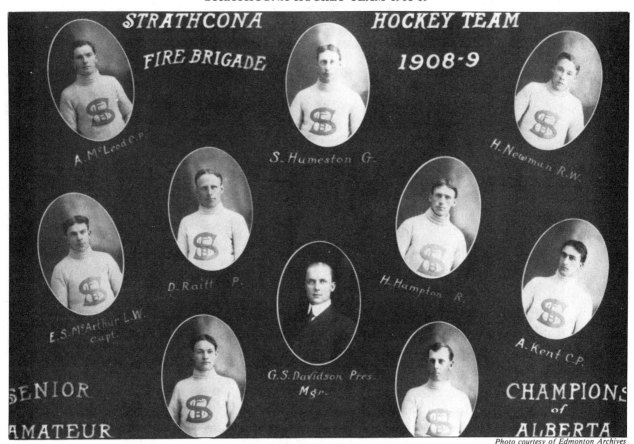

Photo courtesy of Edmonton Archives

WETASKIWIN COLONIALS 1945-46

Back row (l to r): Rene Beguin, Fred Kirstein, Bill Gostick, Bert Brown, H. Kelly, Bill Gauf, James Paton. Front row (l to r): Dunc Grant, Tom McCready, Jack Ingram, Earl Baker, Jack Steadman, Len Roberts, Tony Hauck, Jim Malin. Stick boy: Buddy Stansberry.

Photo courtesy of Provincial Archives

COLEMAN COMETS PROVINCIAL COUNTRY MIDGET CHAMPIONS 1949-50

Front row (l to r): Barry, Stanley Halluk, Stanley Saloff, Peter Chaluk, Adam Kryczka, Frankie Oliva, Andy Siska. Centre row (l to r): Ray Spillers (secretary), Noel Levasseur, Joe Kryczka, George Jenkins, John Nowasad, Walter Doubinin, Ken Fry (treasurer). Back row (l to r): Hector DeCecco, George Kolibas, David Vasek, A. Fry (president), George Jenkins (coach).   *Photo courtesy of Glenbow and Gushul Studios*

VEGREVILLE RANGERS PROVINCIAL INTERMEDIATE "B" CHAMPIONS 1955-56

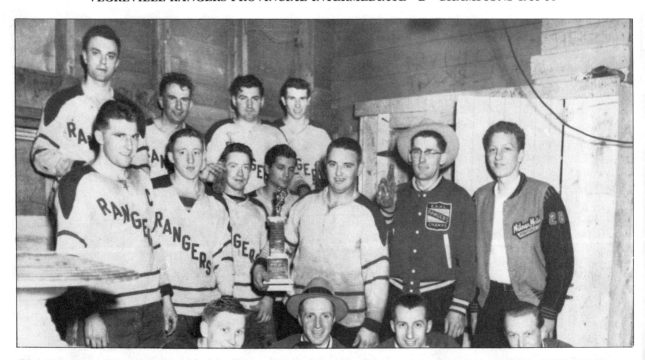

Back row (l to r): Don Kirk, Bing Merluk, George Dowhaniuk, Mike Vegera. Second row (l to r): Wilfred "Wuff" Horton, Ken Dancocks, Eugene "Chops" Makowichuk, Otto Letourneau, Marv Lesnick, Ted Umphrey (manager), Ron Chyzowski (equipment manager). Front row (l to r): Ihor "Buzz" Charuk, George Hughes (coach), Jerry Uhryn, Lloyd Bauer (trainer). Front: Brent Hughes (mascot).   *Photo courtesy of Edmonton Archives*

SOUTH CALGARY PEE WEES
Provincial and City Champions 1967-68

Back row (l to r): Randy Weisbrot, Jim Law, Keith Yamauchi, Paul Carson, Bill Anderson, Ron Elliott. Centre row (l to r): Martin Vernon, Colin Schille, Terry Quinn, Todd Schille, Daryle Moriyama, Dwight Hearn, Bob Sinclair (manager). Front row (l to r): Duane Godfrey, Michael Bruce, Dan Shearer, Robbie Morrison, Ron Reid, Michael Vernon, stick boy.

OUTDOOR HOCKEY IN 1975